GATEWAYS TO UNDERSTANDING MUSIC

Gateways to Understanding Music explores music in all the categories that constitute contemporary musical experience: European classical music, popular music, jazz, and world music. Covering the oldest forms of human music making to the newest, the chronological narrative considers music from a global rather than a Eurocentric perspective. Each of sixty modular "gateways" covers a particular genre, style, or period of music. Every gateway opens with a guided listening example that unlocks a world of music through careful study of its structural elements. Based on their listening experience, students are asked to consider how the piece came to be composed or performed, how the piece or performance responded to the social and cultural issues at the time and place of its creation, and what that music means today. Students learn to listen to, explain, understand, and ultimately value all the music they may encounter in their world.

Features

- **Global scope**—Presents all music as worthy of study, including classical, world, popular, and jazz.
- **Historical narrative**—Begins with small-scale forager societies up to the present, with a shifting focus from global to European to American influences.
- **Modular framework**—60 gateways in 14 chapters allow flexibility to organize chronologically or by the seven recurring themes: aesthetics, emotion, social life, links to culture, politics, economics, and technology.
- **Listening-guided learning**—Leads to understanding the emotion, meaning, significance, and history of music.
- **Introduction of musical concepts**—Defined as needed and compiled into a Glossary for reference.
- **Consistent structure**—With the same step-by-step format, students learn through repeated practice how to listen and how to think about music.

In addition to streamed audio examples, the companion website hosts essential instructors' resources.

Timothy Rice is Distinguished Professor, Emeritus, and founding director of the University of California, Los Angeles (UCLA) Herb Alpert School of Music.

Dave Wilson is Lecturer in Music at Victoria University of Wellington, New Zealand.

For all of the young people on the journey of understanding music and its power in human lives and in the world, especially the ones in our families, with love, Camryn and Connor; J.R. and Lainie; and Liv, Lij, and Luke.

GATEWAYS TO UNDERSTANDING MUSIC

Timothy Rice
University of California, Los Angeles

Dave Wilson
Victoria University of Wellington
Te Whare Wānanga o te Ūpoko o te Ika a Māui

Routledge
Taylor & Francis Group

NEW YORK AND LONDON

First published 2019
by Routledge
52 Vanderbilt Avenue, New York, NY 10017

and by Routledge
2 Park Square, Milton Park, Abingdon, Oxon, OX14 4RN

Routledge is an imprint of the Taylor & Francis Group, an informa business

Library of Congress Cataloging-in-Publication Data
Names: Rice, Timothy, 1945– author. | Wilson, Dave (David R.) 1980– author.
Title: Gateways to understanding music / Timothy Rice, Dave Wilson.
Description: New York : Routledge, 2019. | Includes index.
Identifiers: LCCN 2018030380 (print) | LCCN 2018033226 (ebook) |
ISBN 9781315176130 (ebook) | ISBN 9781138039056 (hardback) |
ISBN 9781138039063 (pbk.)
Subjects: LCSH: Music appreciation.
Classification: LCC MT90 (ebook) | LCC MT90 .R53 2019 (print) | DDC 780.9—dc23
LC record available at https://lccn.loc.gov/2018030380

ISBN: 9781138039056 (hbk)
ISBN: 9781138039063 (pbk)
ISBN: 9781315176130 (ebk)

Typeset in Univers and Optima
by Florence Production Ltd, Stoodleigh, Devon, UK

Visit the companion website: www.routledge.com/cw/gateways

BRIEF CONTENTS

Preface   xvii
Acknowledgments   xxii
Author Profiles   xxiv

INTRODUCTION   1

PART I: MUSIC HISTORY TO 1500 CE   19

1   Music of Small-Scale Societies   21

2   Ancient and Medieval Religious Music   39

3   Ancient and Medieval Secular Music   67

PART II: MUSIC HISTORY FROM 1500 TO 1900   93

4   Music from the European Age of Discovery (1500–1600)   95

5   Music from the Age of Global Commerce (1600–1750)   129

6   Music from the Age of Enlightenment and Revolution
    (1750–1800)   169

7   Music from the Early Nineteenth Century (1800–1850)   203

8   Music from the Late Nineteenth Century (1850–1900)   231

PART III: MUSIC HISTORY DURING THE LONG
TWENTIETH CENTURY   261

9   Music from the Turn of the Twentieth Century (1890–1918)   263

10 Music from the Interwar Period (1918–1939)   299

11 Music during World War II and its Aftermath (1939–1950)   339

12   Music from an Age of Disenchantment and Protest
     (1950–1975)   371

13   Music and Community (1975–1994)   407

14   Music Today   439

WHERE DO WE GO FROM HERE?   **467**

Glossary   473
Sources   485
Index   489

DETAILED CONTENTS

Preface	xvii
Acknowledgments	xxii
Author Profiles	xxiv

INTRODUCTION 1

Music 1
Understanding 3
Gateways 4

PART I: MUSIC HISTORY TO 1500 CE 19

1   Music of Small-scale Societies 21

Gateway 1   Music of Foragers 22
"Bisengo Bwa Bolé"

BaAka people of Central Africa
Music and social structure
Music and subsistence
Herbie Hancock

Gateway 2   Music of Nomadic Pastoralists 28
"Borbangnadyr with Stream Water,"
performed by Anatoli Kuular

Tuvan people of Siberia
Music and the environment
Musical acoustics
Traditional music goes global

Gateway 3   Music of Horticultural Societies 33
"Pisi Ni Tootora"

'Are'are people of the Solomon Islands
Indigenous music theory
Appropriation of "world music"

2   Ancient and Medieval Religious Music   **39**

Gateway 4   **Buddhist Music**   40
"Invoking the Spirit of Kindness through Sound,"
performed by Eight Lamas from Drepung

   Tibetan monks from the Drepung Monastic University
   Music and worldview

Gateway 5   **Christian Chant**   46
"Quia ergo femina," by Hildegard von Bingen

   Music and gender
   Music and religion
   Music and politics
   Music theory

Gateway 6   **Qur'anic Chant**   54
Verses from Book 3, The Family of 'Imran,
performed by the Al-Kindi Ensemble

   Hamza Shakkur
   Verses from Book 3, The Family of 'Imran
   Music and religion
   Aesthetics

Gateway 7   **Early European Polyphonic Music**   59
"Gloria," from *Messe de Nostre Dame*, by Guillaume de Machaut

   Theory of harmony
   Organum

3   Ancient and Medieval Secular Music   **67**

Gateway 8   **Music of China**   68
"Three Variations on Yang Pass," performed by Lin Youren

   Music and Confucianism
   Music and class

Gateway 9   **Music of the Middle East**   73
"Taqasim and Sama'i Bayyati Al-Arayan," performed by A. J. Racy

   Melodic and rhythmic modality
   Music and emotion

Gateway 10   **African Music**   80
"Nyamaropa," by Hakurotwi Mude from Zimbabwe

   Music and trance
   Thomas Mapfumo
   Music and colonialism

Gateway 11   **European Village Music**   85
"Kopanitsa," performed by The Group from Strandzha, Bulgaria

   Music and identity
   Music and dance
   Musical folklore

PART II: MUSIC HISTORY FROM 1500 TO 1900   **93**

4   Music from the European Age of Discovery (1500–1600)   **95**

> **Gateway 12   Renaissance Sacred Vocal Music**   **97**
> "Sicut Cervus," by Giovanni Pierluigi da Palestrina
>> Music and the Reformation
>> Guillaume Dufay
>> Josquin des Prez
>> Music and art

> **Gateway 13   Renaissance Secular Vocal Music**   **103**
> "Fair Phyllis I saw sitting all alone," by John Farmer
>> Madrigals
>> Music and text painting
>> Claudio Monteverdi
>> Thomas Morley

> **Gateway 14   Renaissance Dance Music**   **107**
> Suite of *Volte*, by Michael Praetorius
>> Music and dance
>> Instrument making

> **Gateway 15   Renaissance Lute Music**   **113**
> "Quatro diferencias sobre Guárdame las vacas,"
> by Luys de Narváez
>> Sources of Latin American Music

> **Gateway 16   North Indian Classical Music**   **118**
> "Raga Bhairvi – Dadra Taal," performed by Sharmistha Sen
>> Melodic and rhythmic modality
>> Musical professionalism
>> Music and patronage

5   Music from the Age of Global Commerce (1600–1750)   **129**

> **Gateway 17   Baroque Opera**   **131**
> "Speranza, tu mi vai," from *L'incoronazione di Poppea*,
> by Claudio Monteverdi
>> Music and theater

> **Gateway 18   Baroque Orchestral Music**   **139**
> Violin Concerto in E Major, RV 269, "Spring," Mvt. I,
> by Antonio Vivaldi
>> Music and reference
>> Music and tonality
>> Music and patronage

> **Gateway 19   Baroque Sacred Music**   **145**
> "Hallelujah," from *Messiah*, by George Frideric Handel
>> Oratorio and opera

Music and patronage
Johann Sebastian Bach

Gateway 20 Baroque Keyboard Music   **151**
"Prelude and Fugue in C major," *The Well-tempered Clavier*,
Book I, by Johann Sebastian Bach

  The system of keys
  Keyboard instruments
  Music and patronage

Gateway 21 Javanese Court Music   **159**
"Ketawang Puspawarna Laras Slendro Patet Manyura"

  Gamelan
  Music and theater: *wayang kulit*
  Music and patronage

6 Music from the Age of Enlightenment and Revolution (1750–1800)   169

Gateway 22 Classical-period Chamber Music   **172**
String Quartet Op. 76, No. 3, "Emperor," Mvt. III, Minuet and Trio,
by Franz Joseph Haydn

  Sonata form
  Elegant style
  Music and patronage

Gateway 23 Classical-period Symphonies   **179**
Symphony No. 40 in G Minor, Mvt. I,
by Wolfgang Amadeus Mozart

  Music and art
  Music and patronage

Gateway 24 Classical-period Opera   **186**
"Cinque . . . dieci," from *Le nozze di Figaro*,
by Wolfgang Amadeus Mozart

  Music and politics
  Music and gender
  Music and text painting

Gateway 25 Classical-period Piano Music   **192**
Piano Sonata in C Minor No. 8, Op. 13 (Pathétique), Mvt. I,
by Ludwig van Beethoven

  Music and emotion
  Music and art

Gateway 26 Music of the Atlantic Slave Trade   **197**
Candomblé: "Ijexá for Oxum," performed by Jorge Alabê

  Music and religion
  Music and trance
  Music and slavery
  Brazilian popular music

7 Music from the Early Nineteenth Century (1800–1850)   **203**

Gateway 27 Beethoven's Symphonies   **204**
Symphony No. 5 in C Minor, Op. 67, Mvt. I,
by Ludwig van Beethoven

    Musical Romanticism
    Music and art

Gateway 28 Programmatic Orchestra Works   **211**
Symphonie Fantastique, Mvt. I and Mvt. IV, by Hector Berlioz

    Musical Romanticism
    Music and patronage
    Programmatic music

Gateway 29 Romantic-period Piano Music   **217**
Waltz in C-sharp Minor, Op. 64, No. 2, by Frédéric Chopin

    Music and emotion
    Franz Liszt
    Felix Mendelssohn
    Fanny Mendelssohn
    Robert Schumann
    Clara Schumann

Gateway 30 Early American Popular Music   **223**
"Julie," by Rhiannon Giddens

    Music and identity
    Music and minstrelsy
    Elizabeth Cotten
    Bluegrass
    Stephen Foster
    Louis Moreau Gottschalk

8 Music from the Late Nineteenth Century (1850–1900)   **231**

Gateway 31 Nineteenth-century Opera   **234**
Prelude and *Liebestod*, from *Tristan und Isolde*,
by Richard Wagner

    Music drama
    Music and nationalism
    Italian opera (Rossini, Donizetti, Bellini, Verdi, Puccini)

Gateway 32 European Musical Nationalism   **242**
The Moldau, by Bedřich Smetana

    Music and national sentiment
    Programmatic music
    Antonín Dvořák

Gateway 33 Classical Music at Century's End   **248**
Prélude à l'après-midi d'un faune, by Claude Debussy

    Impressionism
    Symbolism
    Stéphane Mallarmé

Gateway 34   African American Religious Music   253
"Swing Low, Sweet Chariot," by the Fisk Jubilee Singers

Spirituals
Music and religion
Music and race
Gospel music
Henry T. Burleigh
Soul music

PART III: MUSIC HISTORY DURING THE LONG TWENTIETH CENTURY   261

9   Music from the Turn of the Twentieth Century (1890–1918)   263

Gateway 35   The Blues   265
"Backwater Blues," by Bessie Smith

Gertrude "Ma" Rainey
Robert Johnson
Music, injustice, and solidarity

Gateway 36   American Band Music   273
"The Stars and Stripes Forever," by John Philip Sousa

Music, patriotism, and social cohesion
Charles Ives
James Reese Europe
Drum and bugle corps

Gateway 37   Ragtime   279
"Maple Leaf Rag," by Scott Joplin

The "Latin tinge"
Stride piano
James P. Johnson

Gateway 38   Music of Early European Modernists   283
The Rite of Spring, by Igor Stravinsky

Music and ballet
Arnold Schoenberg

Gateway 39   Balinese Gamelan   289
"Tabuh Sekar Jepun"

Gamelan *gong kebyar*
Music and colonialism
Music and community
Music and theater: *wayang kulit*

10   Music from the Interwar Period (1918–1939)   299

Gateway 40   Early Jazz   301
"Struttin' with Some Barbecue," by Lil Hardin Armstrong,
performed by Louis Armstrong and His Hot Five

Jelly Roll Morton

Joe "King" Oliver
New Orleans jazz

Gateway 41 Swing   **309**
"Black and Tan Fantasy," by Duke Ellington and Bubber Miley

    The Cotton Club
    Music, entertainment, racism, and segregation
    Ella Fitzgerald
    Billie Holiday
    Benny Goodman
    Billy Strayhorn
    Count Basie

Gateway 42 American Popular Song   **316**
"I Got Rhythm," by George and Ira Gershwin

    Sheet music
    Tin Pan Alley
    Broadway musicals
    Jerome Kern and Oscar Hammerstein II

Gateway 43 American Symphonic Nationalism   **324**
Rhapsody in Blue, by George Gershwin

    Aaron Copland
    Music and immigration
    Max Steiner and film music
    Paul Whiteman

Gateway 44 Mexican and Mexican American Mariachi Music   **329**
"La Negra," by Mariachi Vargas de Tecalitlán

    Music and identity
    Mariachi Los Camperos de Nati Cano
    Music and gender

11 Music during World War II and its Aftermath (1939–1950)   **339**

Gateway 45 Country Music   **341**
"I'm So Lonesome I Could Cry," by Hank Williams

    Music and community
    Authenticity
    Music and tradition
    Hillbilly music
    The Carter Family
    Jimmie Rodgers
    The Nashville Sound and the Bakersfield Sound
    Classic country
    Pop and country

Gateway 46 Bebop   **348**
"Ko Ko," by Charlie Parker

    Dizzy Gillespie
    Music and racial injustice
    Thelonious Monk

Gateway 47   Classical Music and World War II   357

Symphony No. 7 ("Leningrad"), Mvt. I ("War"), by Dmitri Shostakovich

Music and politics
Olivier Messiaen
Viktor Ullmann
Arnold Schoenberg

Gateway 48   Trinidadian Steel Pan Music   363

"Mystery Band," by Renegades Steel Orchestra

Calypso
Music and carnival
Lord Kitchener
Music and class
Music and patronage

12   Music from an Age of Disenchantment and Protest (1950–1975)   371

Gateway 49   Rock   373

"All Along the Watchtower," by Jimi Hendrix

Rock 'n' roll
Rhythm and blues
Chuck Berry
Bob Dylan
The British Invasion

Gateway 50   New Directions in Jazz   382

"Acknowledgement," from A Love Supreme, by John Coltrane

Modal jazz
Miles Davis
Hard bop, Art Blakey, and Horace Silver
Cool jazz
Jazz fusion, Herbie Hancock, Wayne Shorter
Free jazz
Ornette Coleman
Charles Mingus
Jazz as protest

Gateway 51   The Classical Avant-garde   390

In C, by Terry Riley

Total serialism, Milton Babbitt
Indeterminacy, John Cage
Electronic music
Musique concrète
World music influences
Minimalism, Steve Reich, Philip Glass

Gateway 52   Salsa   397

"Oye Como Va," by Tito Puente

Latin jazz
Fania Records
Willie Colon
Celia Cruz

13 Music and Community (1975–1994)   **407**

    Gateway 53 Rap and Hip-Hop   **409**
        "Fight the Power," by Public Enemy

            Music and politics
            "The Message"
            The golden era of hip-hop
            Hardcore rap
            Gangsta rap, N.W.A, Tupac Shakur

    Gateway 54 Neo-traditional Jazz   **419**
        "Caravan," by Wynton Marsalis

            Music and patronage

    Gateway 55 Postmodern Classical Music   **425**
        Symphony No. 1, "Chaconne: Giulio's Song," by John Corigliano

            John Adams
            Ellen Taaffe Zwilich
            Neo-Romanticism, George Rochberg, David del Tredici

    Gateway 56 Reggae   **430**
        "Buffalo Soldier," by Bob Marley

            Rastafari Movement
            Music and politics

14 Music Today   **439**

    Gateway 57 American Popular Music Today   **439**
        "Til It Happens To You," by Lady Gaga

            Music and social media
            Synthpop, electronic dance music

    Gateway 58 Jazz Today   **445**
        "Black Gold," from *Radio Music Society*, by Esperanza Spalding

            Music and gender
             Music and racial injustice

    Gateway 59 Classical Music Today   **453**
        Anthracite Fields, "Speech," by Julia Wolfe

            Music and gender
             Bang on a Can

    Gateway 60 World Music Today   **458**
        "La Bala," by Los Tigres del Norte

            Music and identity
            Music and oral history

WHERE DO WE GO FROM HERE?   **467**

Glossary   473
Sources   485
Index   489

PREFACE

Gateways to Understanding Music invites students to listen to and understand music of all kinds. The book is designed for readers to explore deeply the music they already love and to gain knowledge and appreciation for music that they don't yet understand. It is also designed for instructors who believe that all music has human, aesthetic, and social value and who are dissatisfied with the typical college curricula that divide music and the people who make it among different courses. The book brings together all the big categories of music that surround us every day: popular music, classical music, jazz, and world music. Doing so brings together the people who make all those kinds of music into a conversation already going on among today's musicians, many of whom are listening and collaborating across the boundaries constructed by these categories. In dialogue with one another and with their audiences, they are making new music that expresses their musical and ethical values, their desires for a better future, and their need to support themselves.

GOALS FOR READERS

We have written this book so that readers will:

- learn about a broad selection of the world's music;
- learn how to describe and analyze music;
- learn how to interpret the psychological, aesthetic, social, and cultural meaning of music;
- learn how to ask and answer questions about any music;
- learn about world history and music history; and
- learn about the importance of music in human life.

To achieve these goals, we have integrated music from the European classical tradition, jazz, popular music, and various "world music" traditions into a chronological narrative. This approach yields many exciting and unexpected pairings and juxtapositions of musical styles and genres. These juxtapositions illustrate fascinating similarities and differences in the way musicians have responded to the cultural, social, political, and economic conditions in which they live. It allows us to make the case that all forms of human music making are worthy of careful listening and study. And it provides timely and relevant choices for today's students.

Breaking out the different genres of music presented, we include:

- Classical music   44%, 26 gateways
- World music   30%, 18 gateways
- Popular music   13%, 8 gateways
- Jazz   13%, 8 gateways

WHAT IS DISTINCTIVE ABOUT THE APPROACH IN THIS BOOK?

Teaching this vast range of music may seem like a daunting task, and it probably is. And so we have designed this book to help instructors who are not expert in all this music (and doesn't that include most of us?) take on the task successfully. We do this in a few ways.

The book is modular, our modules are called "gateways," and three to five gateways make up each chapter. Every gateway has the same structure and takes the reader on a path toward understanding the music of a particular time or people or place.

Each gateway is unlocked by a single recording of music. By beginning with listening, we mimic and formalize the informal and direct way all of us encounter and learn about music in our everyday lives: hearing it on the radio, attending a concert, or having a friend play it for us on YouTube. Sometimes our curiosity leads us to ask and answer questions about this new experience, and that is what each gateway of this book does. Listening to and analyzing this recording opens up a world of music and all of its rich meanings, histories, and legacies, whether that world is the European Baroque period, Chinese music, country music, or the music of John Coltrane.

Each gateway is consistently organized with the same step-by-step format, starting with listening and moving to cultural and historical explanations. As the content changes, the similarity of structure creates a welcome sense of familiarity and reinforces the basic analytical and descriptive methods the book conveys.

Each gateway asks—and answers—the same five questions:

- What is it?
- How does it work?
- What does it mean?
- What is its history?
- Where do I go from here (to explore this world of music)?

The answers to the first two questions, What is it? and How does it work?, don't demand that the instructor have deep historical and cultural knowledge of the world of a particular genre or style or recording. Instructors with musical training in any area can help students answer these questions. That training is the only necessary prerequisite for teaching effectively with the assistance of this book. These first two questions guide students through deep and detailed listening as they learn to describe and explain musical sound using the elements of music (timbre, texture, rhythm, and so on). Instructors can help their students understand the book's explanations of the elements of music and help connect these elements and related terms to the students' listening experience.

Equipped with that understanding, students can read on their own the answers to the next two questions in the gateway: What does it mean? and What is its history? This design allows instructors with widely varying expertise in the musics we introduce in the book to be successful teachers with this book as their aid.

The fifth question is Where do I go from here? In other words, what else can I listen to in this vein and how can I learn more about it? These questions are ideal prompts for students to journey farther down the path into a musical world in class discussions and writing assignments.

This model allows us to achieve one of the book's goals: to teach students how to ask and answer questions about music. We hope to stimulate curiosity about music by, first of all, asking questions about it. Asking questions is, after all, the first act of a curious mind. The five questions that organize each gateway are questions that we imagine students may already be asking about new music that they encounter, whether accidentally, through friends, or through surfing YouTube or listening to Spotify or iTunes playlists. These questions follow a model that mirrors the ways that students encounter and discover music in their lives today. Each gateway, instead of starting with pages of historical context or explanation, begins with listening. Instead of prompting students to ask questions that might be typical in their everyday listening practice (for example, do I like it or not?), we guide them through questions that move beyond taste and aesthetic preference. These questions unlock understanding, help students acquire knowledge, and cultivate in them an attitude of openness to new ways of making and listening to music.

TO THE INSTRUCTOR

The Teaching Method

The fundamental activity that we encourage in each gateway is listening. At the beginning of each gateway we ask students to listen to the opening thirty seconds or so of the recording to acquaint themselves with the sound before explaining how it works. Then, after describing the recording using seven elements of music (timbre, texture, rhythm, melody, harmony, form, and performance techniques), we ask the students to listen again. Finally, we ask them to listen a third time while following a timed listening guide. Then, as the text explores the meanings connected to the musical sound, we may ask them to listen again for how the sounds and meanings are interrelated. So one of our goals is to encourage students to learn by listening, and listening again, with the conceptual tools we provide them. If they follow this procedure, with the help of the instructor from time to time, their understanding of the music they listen to will be transformed as new music becomes familiar through repeated listening and explanations. In other words, we don't aim merely to teach them stuff about music. We aim to teach them how to teach themselves about music and transform their relationships to the wide world of music.

After students have explored the world of the recorded example, we ask the fifth question, Where do I go from here?, and answer it by providing three or more suggestions for other recordings to listen to, videos to watch, and books to read. When we have used these suggestions as writing prompts, students have told us that they enjoy having a range of choices and that assignments built on this mandate to explore a world of music on their own is one of their favorite parts of the course. It gives them a feeling of freedom and some control over their education within an otherwise tightly organized framework.

Term

The book's Introduction and 14 chapters are designed to fit into a standard fifteen-week semester. But the modular structure makes the book useable in shorter courses. The course website contains suggested schedules of reading assignments for ten-, twelve-, and fourteen-week terms.

Modular Organization

The modular structure of gateways gives instructors enormous flexibility in how they organize their courses. The chapters of the book are organized in chronological order, and each chapter contains four or five gateways. But because they are modular, each gateway could be ripped from its chapter and reordered in any number of ways:

- Reverse chronological order.
- A few weeks on each category (e.g., classical, world, jazz, and popular).
- By themes. Seven themes recur with different emphases in each gateway: aesthetics, emotion, social life, culture, politics, economics, and technology. These will be marked with signposts in

the margins. An instructor could organize the course based on a selection of these themes and choose gateways that illustrate these themes particularly well. Suggestions along these lines are provided on the book's website.

There are several ways that instructors may want to use this textbook. Because of its clear, repeating structure and thoughtful pedagogy, the book gives instructors many choices concerning how they use the book. Here are a few of them:

- Use the book and its gateways as the basis for lectures and classes.
- Introduce the gateway recording, have students listen multiple times as directed in the text, have them note their changing responses with each hearing, and help them understand our explanations of how the music works. Students seem to appreciate instructors who do this.
- Have the students read the sections on meaning and history as homework and discuss a theme that comes up in the reading (gender, politics, aesthetic debates).
- Assign the students to "go somewhere" (Where do I go from here?), write a brief one-page essay about what they learned, and present it in class for discussion.
- Use the book as background for your lectures and classes.
- Assign students to read, for example, the gateway on one movement from Haydn's Op. 76, No. 3 String Quartet and lecture on:

  - The other movements of the quartet
  - Another quartet by Haydn
  - A quartet by Mozart or Beethoven
  - A symphony by Haydn.

- Assign the students to read the gateway on European village music that features men playing a Bulgarian instrumental dance tune and lecture on a related tradition:

  - Bulgarian women's singing
  - Gender and music
  - Irish traditional music
  - Spanish flamenco.

- Assign students to read the gateway on neo-traditional jazz and go more deeply into the way soloists improvise melodies over the chord progression of the head.
- Assign students to read the gateway on rap and hip-hop and lead a class discussion on issues of gender and race that have arisen in this genre.
- Use the gateways of the book selectively.
- Lecture on the genres and styles you are most familiar with and assign the students to read about styles you know less well, for example, lecture on classical music and jazz and have students read about world music and popular music.
- Leave out some of the gateways but keep the chronological narrative flow (this works because of the modular structure). For example, lecture about the classical gateways in Chapters 4–8 but leave out the world music gateways, or have students read only two of the three or four classical gateways in each chapter, or have them read only about popular music and world music during the long twentieth century and skip the gateways on classical music and jazz.

SUPPORTING MATERIALS

The book's website at www.routledge.com/cw/gateways includes the following material:

- The gateway musical examples are delivered on Spotify (and other sources), or on the book's website.
- Multiple-choice and short-answer quiz and exam questions.
- Suggestions for essay questions and in-class discussions.
- Listening guides for related examples, e.g. Mvt. II and III of Vivaldi's "Spring" Concerto, another example of the classic blues, a rap recording by Kendrick Lamar, and another mariachi example.
- PowerPoint slides for each gateway with an outline of the main points, photos, and links to the recording, related recordings.

Timothy Rice
Dave Wilson
June 2018

ACKNOWLEDGMENTS

Thank you to the reviewers who read, discussed, advised, and commented on various sections of this book.

Ric Alviso, California State University, Northridge
Paul Berliner, Duke University
Elizabeth Clendinning, Wake Forest University
Larry Crook, University of Florida
Jeffrey Cupchik, Independent Scholar
Noe Dinnerstein, John Jay College of Criminal Justice, CUNY
Kevin Delgado, San Diego State University
Jacqueline Dje Dje, University of California, Los Angeles
Stephanie Doktor, University of Utah
Shannon Dudley, University of Washington
Sam Girling, University of Auckland
Deonte Harris, University of California, Los Angeles
Michael Iyanaga, College of William and Mary
Michele Kisliuk, University of Virginia
Kelsey Klotz, University of North Carolina at Charlotte
Stephen Jones, Independent Scholar
Mark Lamson, Musician
Theodore Levin, Dartmouth College
Scott V. Linford, University of Cincinnati
Olivia Lucas, Victoria University of Wellington
Maureen Mahon, New York University
Peter Manuel, The Graduate Center, CUNY
Alyssa Mathias, University of California, Los Angeles
Timothy J. McGee, University of Toronto
Eddie Meadows, San Diego State University
Anna Morcom, University of California, Los Angeles
Jocelyn Neal, University of North Carolina at Chapel Hill
Daniel Neuman, University of California, Los Angeles
Rahul Neuman, University of California, Los Angeles
Nancy November, University of Auckland
Samantha Owens, Victoria University of Wellington
Eftychia Papanikolau, Bowling Green State University
Jann Passler, University of California, San Diego

Leonor Xóchitl Pérez, Independent Scholar
Marianne Pfau, University of San Diego
Howard Pollock, University of Houston
A. J. Racy, University of California, Los Angeles
Anne K. Rasmussen, College of William and Mary
Helen Rees, University of California, Los Angeles
Alex W. Rodriguez, University of California, Los Angeles
Lauryn Salazar, Texas Tech University
George Sawa, Independent Scholar
Anthony Seeger, University of California, Los Angeles
R. Anderson Sutton, University of Hawaii at Manoa
Inge van Rij, Victoria University of Wellington
Richard Valitutto, Cornell University
Patrick Warfield, University of Maryland
Louise Wrazen, York University, Toronto
Tyler Yamin, University of California, Los Angeles
Hugo Zemp, Centre National de Recherche scientifiques, Paris

We are also grateful to our many interlocutors, colleagues, and friends who have helped us understand so much music and served as ever-patient sounding boards for our thoughts and ideas. We thank Callum Allardice, Michael Appleton, Nayantara Appleton, Jonny Avery, Caroline Bennett, Ashley Elinoff, Eli Elinoff, Lauren Ellis, Leslie Hall, Liam Harker, Ben Hunt, Rose Jago, Raymond Knapp, Carol B. Muller, Jeremy Owen, Alex Sawicka-Ritchie, Catherine Trundle, Aleisha Ward, Eilish Wilson, and Mo Zareei.

   We also thank the instructors and teaching assistants of M10 at UCLA who helped us develop many of the perspectives and pedagogical strategies at the heart of this book: Julius Reder Carlson, Lindsay Johnson, Hojoon Kim, Eric Schmidt, Luke Storm, and Ty-Juana Taylor. From UCLA we also thank Donna Armstrong from the Department of Ethnomusicology and Aaron Bittel from the Ethnomusicology Archive. And Ann Rice acted as our ever-faithful and indefatigable editorial assistant, researching figures, managing our files, checking for consistency, and innumerable other tasks, all with unlimited patience and good spirits. Finally, we thank Constance Ditzel, our Routledge editor, whose faith in the worthiness of this project has meant the world to us.

AUTHOR PROFILES

Timothy Rice has taught undergraduate courses based on the content and principles of this book since 1981. A Distinguished Professor, Emeritus, at the University of California, Los Angeles (UCLA), he is the author of *Ethnomusicology: A Very Short Introduction* (Oxford University Press, 2014). In addition to many books and articles on Bulgarian traditional music, he was founding co-editor of the *Garland Encyclopedia of World Music*. He served as President of the Society for Ethnomusicology (2003–2005) and as founding director of The UCLA Herb Alpert School of Music (2007 to 2013).

Dave Wilson is a Lecturer in Music at Victoria University of Wellington's New Zealand School of Music, Te Kōkī. A specialist in jazz and popular music, he has been consistently teaching courses for undergraduate music and non-music majors based on the approaches of this book since 2014. He conducts research in southeastern Europe supported by the American Council of Learned Societies and the American Councils of International Education and published by *Yearbook for Traditional Music* and *Commoning Ethnography*.

INTRODUCTION

OUR GOAL IN WRITING THIS BOOK is to introduce readers to the vast range of human music making today. We believe that music is a fundamental aspect of our humanity. It is a form of human expression every bit as central to our social and personal well-being as language and speech. So rather than focusing on a particular type of music, like classical music or jazz or popular music or world music, we believe there is much to be learned by thinking about all the ways human beings have chosen to make and listen to music no matter when or where they have lived or what kinds of music they love. Specifically, we hope that our readers will:

- learn about a broad selection of the world's music;
- learn how to describe and analyze music;
- learn how to interpret the psychological, musical, social, and cultural meaning of music;
- learn how to ask and answer questions about any music;
- learn about world history and music history; and
- learn about the importance of music in human life.

Our basic approach to the study of music in this book is summarized in the book's title, *Gateways to Understanding Music*. This introductory chapter explains the words in the title—music, understanding, and gateway—and the distinctions, concepts, and questions that guide the organization of the text. Grasping these distinctions, concepts, and questions will help launch our exploration of some of the fascinating music people are making in the world today.

MUSIC

The book focuses on 60 recordings of music in four large and commonly used categories: classical music, jazz, popular music, and world music. All the recordings are from the last one hundred years. The earliest was released in 1927 and the most recent in 2017. For the book's narrative, the recordings are introduced in a kind of chronological order based not on when they were recorded but on when the musical tradition represented by the recording may have entered human musical experience. In taking this approach, we acknowledge that each tradition we introduce has surely undergone many changes between then (its position in our chronology) and now.

The chronological narrative of the book is organized into three eras:

- Part I: the premodern era up to 1500 CE;
- Part II: the modern era from 1500 to 1900; and
- Part III: the long twentieth century from 1890 to the present.

During the premodern era no single country or empire dominated the world. Music developed in different ways in different places depending on geography, modes of economic production, political control of land, and unique cultures and religions. The book divides this era into three periods:

1. the period of small-scale societies from about 10,000 BCE to 3000 BCE;
2. the Ancient period of kingdoms and empires from about 3000 BCE to 700 CE; and
3. the Medieval period from about 700 to 1500.

Representing small-scale societies are recordings of music by contemporary foragers (people who hunt for and gather their food) from Central Africa, nomadic pastoralists from Siberia, and horticulturalists from the Solomon Islands in the Western Pacific. The Ancient period begins with the invention of writing, large-scale agriculture, and the formation of the earliest cities and empires. One chapter in Part I is devoted to the music of three religions that emerged in the Ancient and Medieval periods: Christianity, Islam, and Buddhism. Another chapter is devoted to secular music with roots in the Ancient and Medieval periods (the period between the Ancient and modern periods): the court musics of China and the Middle East and rural traditions from Zimbabwe in Africa and Bulgaria in Europe.

Part II covers what historians call the modern era in world history from 1500 to 1900. It is defined by European domination in global affairs through colonization and trade. As a consequence, the five chapters in Part II focus on European music, with excursions to other parts of the world where new traditions were being created simultaneously:

1. the age of European discovery (1500 to 1600);
2. the age of global commerce (1600 to 1750);
3. the age of Enlightenment and revolution (1750 to 1800);
4. the early nineteenth century (1800 to 1850); and
5. the late nineteenth century (1850 to 1900).

During the age of European discovery, Christian religious music reached an apex at the same time that the roots of the court music traditions of India were being planted. During the age of global commerce, famous composers like Johann Sebastian Bach and Antonio Vivaldi were composing the first important works for symphony orchestra at the same time that wealthy sultans on the island of Java in present-day Indonesia were patronizing the formation of large orchestras of gongs and other metallic instruments. The age of Enlightenment and revolution witnessed the height of aristocratic patronage of composers Franz Joseph Haydn, Wolfgang Amadeus Mozart, and Ludwig van Beethoven at the same time as enslaved Africans in the Americas and Caribbean were recreating their musical traditions under the harshest imaginable conditions. During the nineteenth century, as the power of the European aristocracy crumbled in the wake of the French Revolution, composers like Frédéric Chopin and Richard Wagner performed and composed for the newly wealthy beneficiaries of the Industrial Revolution, while people in the United States created music that responded to slavery, the Civil War, and post-war Reconstruction.

Part III, the long twentieth century, examines the era of mechanical, electrical, and digital reproduction of music. It began around 1890 with the sale of the first phonograph recordings. During this era, the United States replaced Europe as the center of global geopolitical power and cultural influence, and so American music becomes the focus of the narrative. Part III is divided into six chapters:

1. the turn of the twentieth century (1890 to 1918);
2. the interwar period (1918 to 1939);

3. World War II and its aftermath (1939 to 1950);
4. an age of disenchantment and protest (1950 to 1975);
5. music and community (1975 to 1994); and
6. music today (1994 to the present).

The invention of recording technology has preserved the history of music transmitted in both aural and written traditions for the past century and a quarter. Each chapter in Part III discusses recordings of European or American classical music, American popular music, jazz, and world music. European composers Igor Stravinsky and Dmitri Shostakovich, American composers John Cage and Julia Wolfe, jazz pioneers Duke Ellington and John Coltrane, and popular music stars Jimi Hendrix, Public Enemy, and Lady Gaga share the stage with innovators in mariachi, salsa, and reggae.

UNDERSTANDING

People without musical training sometimes say, especially when they talk to musicians, "I don't understand anything about music." But in fact they understand a lot about music, especially the music they love. Nearly everyone has their favorite songs and pieces of instrumental music. They listen to them all the time, watch videos of them online, and, if they can, they go to live performances of their favorite musical artists. If they really didn't understand music, they wouldn't spend so much time listening to it, enjoying it, and being moved emotionally by it. **Understanding music** simply means that we find some of it orderly rather than chaotic, pleasant rather than unpleasant, predictable rather than unpredictable, meaningful rather than meaningless; and familiar rather than unfamiliar.

We gain these understandings of music through repeated listening over a lifetime. Each of us has a different collection of music we understand. What kinds of music do you understand? Rock or rap? Classical music or jazz? EDM or K-pop? Chinese traditional music or Irish dance music? Soul or Tex-Mex music? Music for guitar or *sitar*? Your answers to these questions depend on your already having spent many years of your life listening to some of these kinds of music. During your lifetime of listening, the music you have listened to has become orderly, pleasant, predictable, meaningful, and familiar to you. Unless you have been living in a cave, isolated from the world of human-made sound, you already understand some significant part of the world's music. One of our goals is to transform and expand your understanding of music. This book will help you to understand the music you already love even more deeply. It will also help you to understand music that hasn't yet become part of your experience, but that is just as important to other people as the music you understand and love is to you.

Our method for deepening and expanding your understanding of music involves explanation. **Explaining music** refers to the creation of statements, descriptions, classifications, labels, analyses, interpretations, and theories of causes and effects that account in words (or in diagrams, formulas, graphs, and musical notation) for particular musical phenomena. Musical explanations will provide the path along which you will move from your current understandings to new, deeper, and expanded understandings of music, both the music you already understand and music that you may understand hardly at all. Probably the most satisfying result of explaining new and unfamiliar music will be that, through repeated hearings, you will come to understand it and find it orderly, pleasant, predictable, meaningful, and familiar.

While music will always remain a source of personal enjoyment, this book suggests that there are real intellectual, aesthetic, and ethical rewards in broadening the horizons of our listening experience and our current understandings of music. That process involves asking fundamental questions about the nature and meaning of music for all human beings, not just for ourselves. Why is music so important that virtually everyone in the world loves it in some form or other? What do differences in musical taste tell us about other individuals and about other groups of people? How does music function in our personal and social lives and in the lives of others? This book challenges the reader to understand the full range of music today, including the music you already know, love, listen to, and perform and the music that you don't know much about or have never heard.

GATEWAYS

Our explanations of each of the sixty recordings featured in the book are contained in short sections called gateways. A **gateway** is a portal to a **world of music**. Such a world might be the music of a composer like Ludwig van Beethoven, a songwriter like Bob Marley, or a performer like Louis Armstrong; a genre or type of music such as Italian opera, salsa, or the blues; or the music of Mexican Americans, Arabs, or the Shona people of Zimbabwe. All the gateways ask the same five questions. Answering them in each gateway takes the reader on a path from initial understandings of the recording through explanations of it to new understandings of the recording and the world of music it opens up. The five questions are: What is it? How does it work? What does it mean? What is its history? and Where do I go from here?

In each gateway, the path from an initial understanding through explanation to a new understanding takes time. That is because, like all listening, listening to music takes time. Music, after all, unfolds in time. Understanding music takes even more time because, in addition to the attention it requires, it requires repeated listening. In that way music is very different from looking at a painting and trying to understand it. When we visit an art gallery, we choose how much time we spend viewing a painting, and how much attention we give it, before we move on to the next one. In contrast, music takes not only our attention, but our time, at least if we wish to understand it. We can't simply walk away in the middle of a recording, not if we want to understand it. Furthermore, understanding depends on repeated hearings of a recording of music. We understand and like music that is familiar to us, that is, music we have heard many times. In each gateway we ask you to follow a path from initial understanding through explanation to a new understanding. The journey begins by listening to the first thirty seconds or so of the recording to gain your first impression, your first understanding. Then you will read about how the music works in a general way, and we ask you to listen again for up to a minute to hear the features of the music that you have just read about. Then we ask you to listen a third time to the entire recording while following a timed listening guide with detailed explanations of important sections and moments in the recording. At the end of that third hearing of the recording you will be familiar with the recording and have a new and significantly richer understanding of the recording and the world of music it represents than after your initial hearing. Don't miss this journey. You can't get this kind of understanding of music by reading about music. You can only get it by listening a few times to a recording and thinking a bit about it. Following this path as you read the book is a shortcut to understanding better the music that is already familiar to you and to becoming familiar with and understanding unfamiliar music. You will get the most out of this book if you follow the path (the listening instructions) we give you in each gateway. We invite you to join us on the exciting journeys to new worlds of music that we have prepared for you.

Listening to music is the key that unlocks each gateway and begins the path to new understanding. Part of walking that path is engaging with musical explanation. That requires some new concepts and vocabulary. Here is an introduction of the basic concepts and terms necessary to answer the five questions in each gateway.

What Is It?

One of the first things humans do when they encounter something in the world is identify, label, or name it. What is it? What is this thing in front of me? Does it resemble anything I've encountered before? Do I have a category I can place it in? In the case of music, we typically name particular pieces and recordings, identify the composer and performers, and place the piece or performance within groups of pieces and performances, for example:

- Symphony No. 40 by W. A. Mozart;
- "Summertime" by George Gershwin;
- "Rokudan" for Japanese *koto*;
- "Formation," from *Lemonade* by Beyoncé;
- a video recording of us singing "Happy Birthday" at my sister's party last Tuesday.

Every recording is a member of a category of music making, and answering the question "what is it" requires identifying and labeling the category to which it belongs. Musicians, listeners, producers, radio DJs, and scholars of music create categories when it is useful to them in some way. A young musician in training might have two categories: the easy pieces and the hard ones. A listener might distinguish among music for contemplating life, music for dancing, and music she likes or doesn't like. A music producer might worry about music that sells and music that doesn't. Someone who lives in a city might distinguish between urban music and rural music. Music can be categorized in endless ways and for a variety of different reasons.

We use four categories as one way to tell our story about all the world's music:

1. American popular music;
2. classical music;
3. jazz;
4. world music.

Two of these categories, jazz and classical music, are musical genres. A **musical genre** is a way of labeling and categorizing music that is associated with a community of musicians and listeners. A musical genre has a social life, and it has a name given to it by its performers, fans, or the people who want to sell it. Both jazz and classical music have many named subgenres as well: in the case of jazz, bebop, hard bop, free jazz and so forth; in the case of classical music, symphonies, chamber music, operas and so on. American popular music and world music are categories created by writers, scholars, and the music industry. They are not genres, but they contain many named genres: in the case of popular music, for example, rock, oldies, metal, punk, EDM, hip-hop, country, and on and on. Similarly, the category world music includes many named genres: flamenco, reggae, and salsa, to name a few.

Musical style is another way to label and categorize music. **Musical style** refers to the manner in which musical elements like melody and rhythm are deployed and combined in a large number of pieces or performances. We can speak, for example, of a composer's style, a performer's style, a national style, the style of a particular period in music history, or the style of a musical genre. Analyzing musical elements helps us characterize the common features of many related pieces and performances. A particular electric guitarist may have a unique way of setting the sound quality on her amplifier in order to create an identifiable, individual style that we recognize as hers. Melodies with a certain rhythm might characterize the national style of a country. In Scotland, for example, many melodies use a device called a "Scotch snap," a sharp, short-long rhythm that helps to define Scottish musical style. The subgenres of jazz can be distinguished by their differing harmonic and rhythmic styles, which allows listeners to distinguish, say, bebop style from the style of free jazz.

Distinguishing among category, genre, and style can be tricky. For example, jazz is a named genre with its circle of players and fans, but its elements may serve as a style in another genre. A classical composer or an American popular songwriter or a Turkish performer might employ some elements of jazz style to create a certain effect in the genre they are working in. With that caution in mind, the terms category, style, and genre appear frequently throughout this book.

American popular music is the most heard music in the U.S. for obvious reasons. First, by definition the term "popular" is an adjective for anything that is widespread among the people (the populous). Second, its primary mode of transmission is through recordings, so it can be heard

FIGURE 0.1
The popular singer Madonna in 1987
Source: Olavtenbroek, Wikimedia Commons.

everywhere, not only in formal concerts. Third, young people use popular music as a resource for courting, for socializing, and for establishing new and emerging identities. Fourth, the United States, throughout most of the long twentieth century, has held the greatest proportion of the symbolic, economic, and military power in the world, and its popular music has spread around the world in the wake of that power. The principal form of popular music is the **song**, a piece of music with poetic lyrics. Since teenagers and young adults are the primary audience for popular music, the main themes of its song lyrics concern newfound and hoped-for love and romance set in danceable rhythms. Beyond romantic love, popular songs have also registered the values of youth, and the populace, in every period of history and in every society.

The term **classical music** commonly refers today to music that was composed for churches, courts, and concerts in Europe from about 900 CE to the present. Classical music is commonly heard today played by large ensembles like symphony orchestras, opera companies, concert bands, and choruses in large concert halls. Small ensembles and soloists play **recitals**, often in smaller halls. The central figure in European classical music is the composer, whose compositions have been preserved in musical notation. Its fans are typically middle- and upper-class patrons wealthy enough to buy expensive concert tickets, contribute to non-commercial, listener-supported classical radio stations, and pay for their children's private music lessons. The genre also gains support from national governments in some countries and from high schools and universities with elaborate music training programs.

Jazz originated at the beginning of the twentieth century among the descendants of enslaved Africans in the United States. Throughout its

FIGURE 0.2
The Chicago Symphony Orchestra
Source: Jordan Fischer, Wikimedia Commons.

history jazz has been played all over the world by musicians of all racial and ethnic backgrounds. It occupies a space between American popular music and classical music, and it overlaps with both. Like popular music, it is transmitted in recordings, and, like classical music, in written form as well. Like popular music, its principal form historically has been the song or other relatively short composed structure. But like classical music it sometimes features intricate long-form compositions, especially those written for large jazz bands. It is carried on in both instrumental and sung traditions. While recordings are important in jazz, it lives in live performances, where musicians show off their improvisatory and technical skills. Like popular music, jazz flourishes in small bars, restaurants, and nightclubs, but, like classical and popular music, the most famous jazz artists fill large concert halls and outdoor music festivals.

The term **world music** refers to music rooted in particular communities that is often, but not always, outside the international mainstream of popular music, classical music, and jazz. "World music" was coined in the 1960s by ethnomusicologists to capture the variety of music they were studying in Asia, Africa, Latin America, the Pacific, and other areas of the world. Today it includes popular music from all over the world as well as the music of ethnic communities within multicultural societies such as the United States, the United Kingdom, Canada, and Australia. In some cases world music traditions flourish locally, largely unknown to the outside world. In other cases these local musical traditions have entered popular culture, as is the case with much African American and Latin music. In late 1980s music industry executives began using the term world music to refer to fusions of traditional music with popular music.

FIGURE 0.3
A jazz combo: Art Tatum (piano), Sid Catlett (drums), Oscar Pettiford (bass), and Billie Holiday (vocals)
Source: Pictorial Press Ltd / Alamy Stock Photo.

FIGURE 0.4
Japanese court orchestra performing in Ukraine in 2010
Source: Antanana, Wikimedia Commons.

How Does it Work?

Asking how a recording of music works is the second step in explaining music and moving from old to new understandings of it. Music, like every field of study, has a vocabulary specific to it, and to explain how music works will require some specialized terms. We will introduce many of these terms as we go along, but for now, we'll lay out some of the basics used to answer the question, "how does it [this recording of music] work."

The most basic concept in music is the musical tone. Metaphorically, musical tones might be called the atoms of music. A **tone** is perceived when an event in the world causes air to vibrate, that vibration hits the eardrum, and those vibrations are processed by the brain as sound. **Musical tones** are those sounds that human beings make and interpret as music. A musical tone has five components: overtone structure, pitch, duration, envelope, and loudness.

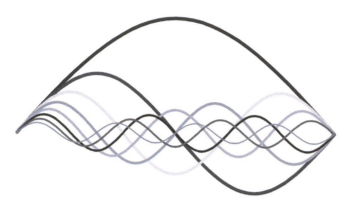

FIGURE 0.5
The fundamental and multiple overtones of a vibrating string producing a musical tone
Source: Alex Sawicka-Ritchie.

Overtone Structure

Every tone consists of a **waveform**, a complex set of waves vibrating in air. The slowest vibrating wave in a tone, the one with the longest wave form, is called the **fundamental**. It is perceived as the pitch of the tone. The set of faster vibrating waves of the tone are called **overtones**. They are typically not heard as pitches but unite in our perception as an impression of tone color or tone quality or timbre. Different timbres allow us to distinguish one musical instrument or voice from others: to tell the difference, for example, between a clarinet, a flute, and a trumpet.

Pitch

Our perception of the slowest vibrating wave in a tone, the one with the longest wavelength, is called the **pitch** of the tone. We call slow-vibrating waves **low pitches** and fast-vibrating waves **high pitches**. These labels are so conventional that we do not recognize that "high" and "low" are actually metaphors. We derive these metaphors from the singing voice, in which fast vibrating tones feel high in our throats and slow vibrating pitches feel low in our throats. This experience is registered in European musical notation, in which slow-vibrating pitches appear lower on the page than fast-vibrating pitches. If we based our terminology on playing the piano, high pitches would be called right pitches and low pitches would be called left pitches.

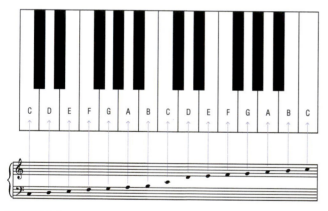

FIGURE 0.6
Pitches of tones indicated on the piano keyboard (with low pitches to the left and high pitches to the right) and in notation (with low pitches low on the music staff and high pitches high on the musical staff)
Source: Alex Sawicka-Ritchie.

Duration

Each musical tone also exists for a period of time, called its **duration**. Durations can be long or short.

Envelope

Tones vary over their duration, forming the tone's **envelope**. Key moments in the envelope are its onset, called the **attack**, and its **decay** into silence. Plucked string instruments like the acoustic guitar have a sharp attack and a rapid decay. Bowed string instruments like the violin and wind instruments like the oboe can produce sustained tones over a long period of time.

Loudness

The **loudness** of a tone depends on the amplitude of the waveform. Musicians use Italian terms to describe loudness: soft is **piano** and loud is **forte**. The difference between the loudest and softest tones in a piece of music is called its **dynamic range** and changes in loudness are called **dynamics**.

One final comment: Some musicians, especially those who read musical notation, commonly refer to tones as notes. Technically, however, **notes** are visual representations of tones in musical notation. Musicians also refer to tones as pitches when the pitch of the tone is the topic of conversation. In this book we tend to use tone when discussing music transmitted aurally without the use of notation and note when discussing notated music.

Musicians combine musical tones in a nearly infinite variety of ways. To understand how they do this, to explain "how the music works," requires the use of a somewhat specialized vocabulary. These terms break music down into its composite "elements." Viewing music as made of "elements" derives from the many philosophical and religious traditions that believe that the world consists of fundamental and irreducible elements, essences, powers, or atomic particles that underlie everything in the universe. Such a view was expressed in the Ancient Greek classification of the world into four elements: earth, air, fire, and water. Modern physics, with its theories of atoms made up of tiny subatomic particles, and modern chemistry, with its notion of chemical elements consisting of pure forms with one type of atom, are legacies of these traditions, as are explanations of music as consisting of musical elements.

In this book we propose that music consists of seven elements:

1. Timbre
2. Texture
3. Rhythm
4. Melody
5. Harmony
6. Form
7. Performance techniques.

Each gateway describes how the musical recording works in terms of these seven elements.

Timbre

The timbre or sound quality of a musical tone is a function of its overtone structure and its envelope. Studies of music perception and cognition show that one of the first things we recognize when we listen to music is its sound quality, which we often associate with the source of the sound. Is it a man or a woman singing? An adult or a child? What instrument is playing? From long listening experience, most people can identify such instruments as the guitar, piano, and violin when they hear them. Naming the musical instruments and vocal sounds in a musical example is one way to describe its timbre.

 Listen to example 1, "A Case of You" by Joni Mitchell. There are just two timbres during the first minute of this recording. What are they?

Other than naming the instruments we hear, we have no systematic way of describing timbre, tone quality, or tone color. Instead, we use metaphors that link our listening experience of sound to other sensory experiences: sight, touch, taste, and, rarely, smell. So, for example, linking tone quality to taste, we might describe a sound as sweet or rich. Linking timbre to touch, we might say a sound is smooth or rough. Linking tone color to sight, we might call a sound bright or dull. Linking timbre to smell, we might call a sound fragrant or fresh. Sometimes we link the timbre of musical instruments

FIGURE 0.7
Joni Mitchell playing guitar in 1974
Source: Whoknoze, Wikimedia Commons.

to other aural experiences, saying, for example, that the sound is noisy or buzzing. We also sometimes link tone quality metaphorically to other experiences, calling the sound clean or dirty, pure or distorted, warm or cold. Beyond the naming of the source of the sound (the instrument creating it), descriptions of the element of timbre are notably subjective.

🔊 **Listen to example 2, Jimi Hendrix performing "The Star Spangled Banner," and example 3, Kenny Burrell playing "But Not for Me." What adjectives would you use to describe and compare the tone quality of these two examples of electric guitar? (Hint: there is no correct answer!)**

Texture

The word **texture** is a metaphor that connects the sound of music to the feel of woven cloth. Just as threads in a cloth interweave to create different sensory impressions when touched (smooth or rough) or looked at (shiny or dull), so also the number of parts or musical threads in a performance of music, and the way they are woven together, create different aural sensory perceptions and effects in music. There are two fundamental types of musical textures: those with a single musical line or part and those with many interweaving musical lines or parts. A performance with a single musical line or part has a **monophonic texture**, and one with many lines or parts has a **polyphonic texture**. **Monophony** derives from Greek words meaning "one sound" and **polyphony** from Greek words meaning "many sounds." We introduce the many different types of monophony and polyphony as needed in each chapter.

🔊 **Listen to the difference between the monophony of the solo male singer and the polyphony of a choir of male voices in example 4, a recording by the South African vocal group Ladysmith Black Mambazo called "Unomathemba."**

FIGURE 0.8
Soloist with choir (Ladysmith Black Mambazo) in 2017
Source: Joe Mabel, Wikimedia Commons.

Rhythm

Music is an art that unfolds in time, and the word **rhythm** refers to the temporal dimension of music in the broadest sense. Rhythm has two features: rhythm and meter. **Rhythm** in this more specific sense refers to the duration of tones and their organization. The rhythm of some performances might consist principally of long tones, another of short tones, and another of a combination of short and long tones. **Meter** refers to the organization of the pulsation or the beat of tones. There are two types of metrical organization in music: **nonmetrical** music lacks a beat or pulse; **metrical** music has a beat or pulse. Some metrical music has a constant, undifferentiated beat, but most metrical music organizes its beats into groups of two or three or more pulses. If the music is organized into groups of two beats, the music is said to be in **duple meter** or **in two**. If the beats are organized into groups of three, then the music is said to be in **triple meter** or **in three**. (In European musical notation such groupings of beats or pulses are called **measures** or **bars**, for example, a four-beat measure; measure and bar are sometimes used even when referring to music transmitted without the use of notation.) Figuring out the meter of a musical performance is one of the most important steps in explaining the music.

 Listen to example 5, "Let's Go Crazy" by Prince. He begins by speaking nonmetrically over a sustained instrumental background until, around 0:38 seconds, the drums introduce a beat organized in a meter of four (or four-beat measures).

Melody

Melody is the term used for the most important line in a musical texture. It consists of a series of pitches performed over time. We hear these pitches strung together in time as a coherent **melody**, **melodic part** or **melodic line** in the musical texture. If we think in spatial terms of pitches moving through time in the horizontal direction and from low to high in the vertical dimension, then we can describe the shape of the melodic line, the **melodic shape**, as ascending, descending, undulating, and flat.

 Listen to example 6, the Duke Ellington Orchestra playing "The Mooche." The opening melody at 0:08 has a descending shape.

Harmony

Harmony refers to the systematic combination of simultaneously sounding tones over the course of a section or piece of music. Usually these systems produce pleasant, harmonious, consonant sounds, but not always. This musical term has been borrowed to describe people, objects, and ideas that go well together as being "in harmony." On instruments like the piano and guitar, a musician can easily produce simultaneous pitches, that is, harmony. On instruments that produce one pitch at a time, like the voice, trumpet, and violin, musicians have to play together in ensembles to produce harmonies. Two or more simultaneously sounding pitches is called a **chord**.

FIGURE 0.9
Five saxophones playing jazz in harmony
Source: René Clement, Wikimedia Commons.

Listen to example 7, a 2013 composition by Caroline Shaw titled Partita for 8 Singers (No. 4: "Passacaglia"). For the first minute and a half, the ensemble of male and female voices sings a progression of different chords, where all of the parts sing different lines simultaneously.

Form

Form refers to the "shape" of a musical performance as it unfolds through time from beginning to end. Form is an important aspect, in addition to rhythm, of the temporal dimension of music. Listening for the form of a piece or a performance means keeping track of how the elements of music change or stay the same from the start to the finish of the performance. Listening for the form of a performance means understanding whether what you are hearing now is a repeat of something you heard before, a variation of something you heard before, or something different from what you heard before. The "something" in this formulation is usually the melody or a melodic phrase, and descriptions of form are often descriptions of melodic form. In principle, however, a performance of music may have timbral form, textural form, rhythmic form, and harmonic form.

One way to notate and describe form involves the application of upper- and lower-case letters to the "somethings," let's say melodies. So the letter A applies to the first melody in the performance, and it is applied to any repetition or return of A. The notation A' (read A prime) is applied to a varied repetition of A. The letter B is applied to a new melody, and after that successive letters of the alphabet are given to yet new melodies. Here are a few possibilities.

A A: a single melody is repeated exactly.

A A': a melody followed by a varied repeat of it.

A B: a melody is followed by a second, different melody.

Forms can also be analyzed at two or more temporal levels. So, for example, the A melody may consist of, say, four melodic phrases indicated with lower-case letters, for example, A = a b a c.

 Listen to example 8, a recording by Irish accordionist Sharon Shannon and her group of the song "Norwegian Wood" by John Lennon and Paul McCartney of the Beatles. How many different melodies do you hear in the course of the song? How many times is each of them repeated? Can you describe the form of the song at two different levels?

Performance Techniques

Performance techniques are a mixed bag of performance practices that musicians use. Here are just a few of them.

- Musicians can manipulate the timbre of their voice or instrument.
- **Dynamics** refers to changes in the loudness of the tones, sometimes abruptly and sometimes getting gradually louder (**crescendo**) or gradually softer (**decrescendo**).
- A melody may be performed with or without **ornamentation**, which are short tones between the main melody pitches.
- **Articulation** refers to the ways musicians connect the tones of the melody: smoothly (**legato**) or with spaces between them (**staccato**).
- Musicians can vary the **tempo**, that is, the speed of performance, from fast to slow.

Listen to example 9, Whitney Houston's recording of "I Will Always Love You," a song by Dolly Parton. Notice how Houston ornaments the melody and progresses from soft to loud over the course of the performance.

What Does It Mean?

Music is a type of art and entertainment made up of musical tones and the seven musical elements outlined above. But music also is a human behavior with deep psychological, cultural, social, economic, and political significance. In this book we interpret the meaning of music in seven categories: (1) aesthetics; (2) emotional resonance; (3) cultural linkages; (4) social behaviors; (5) political action; (6) economic activity; and (7) use of technology. In this section of each gateway, we discuss the meaning and significance of music in a few of these terms.

Aesthetics

Part of the meaning of the music is revealed when we describe and explain the way composers and performers put the seven elements of music together and the way listeners hear them. These descriptions are at the root of understanding people's musical tastes, that is, what they find beautiful and appealing in music. This type of musical meaning belongs to an area of philosophy known as **aesthetics**. And so when, in a particular gateway, we speak of a composer's aesthetic or a cultural aesthetic, our understanding of that aesthetic depends on our descriptions of music in the "how does it work" section.

> **AESTHETICS**

Emotional Resonance

Humans also sing and play music to express and communicate emotions in a controlled way. Many listeners enjoy music for the emotional response it can generate in them. Music functions in this way because it is, like language, a system of signs that signals our thoughts to others. A **sign** or **signal** is an object or an action that has meaning to a person or a group of people. Musical performances are signs with meaning, just as stop signs, national flags, a smile, or a tattoo are. Every aspect of our life in society, our social life, is suffused with signals and signs. Without them we could not live together in social groups. Music is one type of human behavior and thus a sign that we interpret for its meanings. Music is a particularly effective sign system for conveying and generating emotion.

FIGURE 0.10
Singer Janis Joplin (1943–1970)
Source: Keystone Pictures USA / Alamy Stock Photo.

Music conveys its meanings and emotions in a different way from language and speech. **Language signs** convey their meanings in precise, detailed, and clearly understood ways that everyone who speaks a particular language can understand. All speakers of, say, English will agree on the meaning of the word "tree," for example. Language signs are useful because they allow us to communicate our thoughts and feelings rather exactly to those around us who speak the same language. The gateways in this book are written in words, that is, in language signs. (Of course the ostensibly precise meanings of language signs can be undermined and played with in jokes, double entendres, nods and winks, speech intonation, and poetry. And just because you say something as clearly as you can does not ensure that everyone will understand it in exactly the way you intended.)

> **EMOTIONAL RESONANCE**

Music does not communicate or act as a sign or convey meaning in the same way that language does. The meaning of music is not conveyed by language signs but by two other types of signs: indexes and icons.[1]

An **index** or **indexical sign** is named for the index finger that points to things. For example, the national anthem is a tune that indexes or is associated with or is linked to patriotic events, lyrics, and feelings. Whenever the tune is played, even at a sporting event with no patriotic significance,

FIGURE 0.11

Fans and football players with different responses to the indexical meaning of the U.S. national anthem

Source: Keith Allison, Wikimedia Commons.

it may generate pride in one's nation. However, not everyone may feel the same way. Those disaffected and alienated by the gap between a nation's ideals and its realities may have more complex feelings. Whether our response is a feeling of patriotism or something else, national anthems and the emotions they generate are a part of a shared national culture. Nearly everyone in a nation will understand its anthem's emotional resonance.

Some musical indexes are very personal and even unique to a single person or a few people. One example is the "our song" phenomenon. Two people in love may decide that a particular song they heard on their first date is "our song." From then on that song will be associated with the lovers' relationship and will generate, beyond any rational control, their current feelings about one another. While they are together, they will like the song. If they break up, however, they may come to hate the song because of its negative associations with a failed relationship.

Musical compositions and performances also contain elements that point to or are linked to other parts in the music, in the process creating meaning and emotion. For example, many kinds of music depend on the repetition of melodies. If a melody is performed and then repeated, the repeated melody points to or indexes the first playing of the melody and may create a feeling of familiarity and comfort in the listener.

Musical indexes are very powerful signs and are the bearers of many of the strong feelings we experience when we listen to music. Indexical musical signs generate strong emotions without our thinking about them in words. Because not all of us share the same associations between a musical sign and its references, a given piece or performance of music may generate rather different emotions in different listeners. If we can't link a musical performance to something in our previous experience, then it will probably have no emotional effect on us at all. A musical index is thus a very different type of sign from a language sign, in which agreement as to its meaning is basic to the communicative function of language. On the other hand, every indexical musical sign can be explained in terms of a connection between it and a person's previous experience. Throughout this book certain phrases are synonyms for stating that something is an indexical sign of something else. We might say that it "is an index of," "indexes," "points to," "is associated with," or "is linked to" something else. All these phrases are driving at the same idea: one way music has meaning and generates emotion is through its association with previous experience, whether outside music or within the music itself.

The other type of musical sign conveys meaning through similarity. Musical signs based on similarity are called **iconic signs** or **icons** by analogy with religious icons, paintings in a church that portray in two dimensions the features of a three-dimensional person, typically a saint. Like indexical signs, iconic similarity can take two forms: a musical icon can be similar to something outside of music or it can be similar to music we have heard before. In symphonic music, for example, a fast, low-pitched drum beat and a cymbal crash can be icons of thunder and lightning, which the composer may hope will generate a corresponding feeling of dread in the listener. In heavy metal rock music, loud, distorted guitar chords are called power chords, a name that suggests their loudness. But it is also quite likely that they generate a feeling of social power among fans of this music, many of them male teenagers who might feel otherwise powerless. Musical performances are also iconic of social relationships, both real and imagined. When, in the 1930s, the white jazz bandleader Benny Goodman included black musicians in his small combos, the ensembles became icons of an imagined racial equality and integration in a segregated society and may have generated a feeling of hope in some audience members.

Another kind of musical icon resembles something we have heard before in our previous musical experience. When we hear a new song by a singer we love, for example, it will (we hope) be full of similarities to songs that we have heard before by that singer. Such musical icons create feelings of familiarity, which are often comforting and pleasing. When we hear music with no, or only a few, iconic references to music we have heard before, we may feel uncomfortable, anxious, annoyed, or disoriented, and we may not like it very much. The repetition of a melody in a performance of music has the properties of both an iconic and an indexical sign.

Iconic musical signs are sometimes shared by a culture or subculture and sometimes are individual in their meaning. Some listeners may perceive the similarities of one musical performance to a previous one and some may not. In that way, musical icons differ significantly from language signs, which depend on shared understandings of their meaning to be effective. Certain phrases appear in this book that are synonyms for saying something is an iconic sign of something else. We might say that it "is an icon of," "is a metaphor for," "is similar to," "resembles," "imitates," or "paints" something else. All these phrases are driving at the same idea: one way music has meaning and generates emotion is through its similarity to things outside music and to previous musical experience.

The emotions created by musical indexes and icons do not require language for their effects. These two types of musical signs generate emotions and feelings beyond our control, before we can think about them in language. As we pass through the many musical gateways in this book and answer the question "what does it (the recording) mean," we will speak of elements of musical performance as icons or indexes capable of conveying meaning and emotion in a very direct and powerful way.

Cultural Linkages

Music is also a cultural expression. As such, its elements are nearly always coherent with (icons of) other modes of cultural expression such as cosmology, religion, poetry, painting, sculpture, and theater. Musical elements may amplify the meanings of these other expressive forms. A high-pitched descending melodic phrase can add emotional power to a sad song lyric. Music's formal properties may mirror a culture's philosophical ideas about the nature of time. Musical performances tell us stories about ourselves and others in ways different from language. They are metaphorical texts that we can read to understand our fellow human beings, whether they are sitting next to us in the classroom, come from another part of the country or the world, belong to a different ethnic or social group, or live in a faraway city we someday hope to visit or a rainforest that we may never visit.

> **CULTURAL LINKAGES**

Social Behavior

Music is also a social behavior. As such, it participates in the production of social difference along lines of class, race, ethnicity, and gender. These issues will frequently appear in the book's gateways. Of them, gender and relations between the sexes are fundamental. Love songs are central to nearly all cultures. And music enables dancing, the archetypal arena for displaying gendered selfhood and sexual attraction. But just as important, gender in many societies limits who makes what kinds of music. Men and women may each have their own specialized repertoires and styles. Men may be accorded more freedom to move about in the public square and thus to make music there, while women may be encouraged to make music only in domestic circles.

> **SOCIAL BEHAVIOR**

FIGURE 0.12
Siebenbürgen, a goth metal band from Sweden, in 2008
Source: Levidark, Wikimedia Commons.

This ideological division of labor has had profound effects on the histories of classical music and jazz. Classical composers have mainly been men, as have jazz instrumentalists. The Vienna Philharmonic did not accept women as permanent members until 1997, long after other orchestras had. Women in both traditions have been prominent vocal performers, but their choices of musical instruments have been limited, even until relatively recently, by the perception that certain instruments are gendered: the harp and flute for women; the electric guitar, percussion, and brass instruments for men.

But just because these traditions have typically minimized or ignored music making by women, and just because many societies have marginalized women in music (and in countless other ways), does not mean that women have not been involved as musicians and composers. On the contrary, women composers and musicians have consistently participated in musical traditions of all times and places, from the Medieval European composer Hildegard von Bingen to the nineteenth-century composer-pianist Clara Schumann to the contemporary classical composer Julia Wolfe; and from the early twentieth-century jazz composer and pianist Lil Hardin Armstrong to the internationally known trombonist Melba Liston and the multifaceted jazz composer, bassist, and vocalist Esperanza Spalding. Male musicians throughout the history of classical music and jazz have had profound social advantages over women, and so gateways on J. S. Bach, W. A. Mozart, Ludwig van Beethoven, Louis Armstrong, Charlie Parker, John Coltrane, and others are unavoidable when telling the stories of those traditions. But we intervene in various ways to illuminate this mostly male history of music by focusing on women musicians and composers whenever we can. Today we understand that composing, singing, arranging, playing instruments, producing recordings, and more are legitimate pursuits for people of any gender.

Political Action

For many people music is an escape from the trials of the real world. But precisely because of music's emotional resonance, musicians have also assertively entered the political arena to support nascent feelings of national sentiment, rage against the powers that be, champion a political movement, or amplify the sound of mass demonstrations. Music's significance as a form of political action will appear in quite a few gateways.

Economic Activity

In some cultures music is a pastime or something that nearly everyone does for the fun of it and to contribute to successful social interactions. But in stratified societies with divisions of labor, musicians may be specialists or professionals who are paid for their labor. Patronage, that is, the question of who provides musicians with the means to support themselves, is an important

FIGURE 0.13
Brittney Howard playing guitar with her blues rock band Alabama Shakes
Source: Fred Rockwood, Wikimedia Commons.

factor in the creation of music. The significance of music as an economic activity suffuses many of the gateways in this book.

Technology

We tend to think of technology as the latest electronic gadgets in our world (smartphones, computers, medical devices, synthesizers), the software that runs on them (apps, programs), and the computer networks they use (the internet, Wi-Fi). But in a broader sense technology refers to the tools humans have always used for tasks in their lives: hunting, farming, cooking, building, healing, communicating, thinking, and making music. Musicians from time immemorial have used materials found in their environment to make tools called musical instruments to make the sounds they turn into music. For most of time those instruments exploited the acoustic properties of natural and made objects. They are acoustic instruments. In 1877 the invention of the phonograph opened a new age of musical production using electricity and electronics. Nearly every gateway contains a discussion of the musical instruments and the electronic technology that musicians have invented or used to make the music they want to make.

FIGURE 0.14

Drummers march with indigenous activists in Seattle, Washington, in solidarity with the Standing Rock Sioux in their fight against the Dakota Access Pipeline, 2016

Source: John Duffy, Wikimedia Commons.

> TECHNOLOGY

Watch out for these seven explanations of the meaning of music as you read the sections of each gateway that answers the question "what does it mean."

What Is Its History?

Each gateway recording is also explained by its history. That history includes the origins of the genre or style it represents, the social and cultural conditions that produced the particular work in the past, and the history of that music since it was first created. This section also discusses the way this type of music resonates in our culture and our listening experience today, no matter the place or historical time period that originally produced it. In other words, although our narrative is broadly historical, we are not consigning any of the musical worlds we introduce to the past. Each one has its own history and is alive in the present. If they weren't, we wouldn't include them in the book.

Where Do I Go from Here?

The book answers this question by providing a few suggestions for listening to audio recordings,

FIGURE 0.15

Country singer Dierks Bentley performs at the White House in 2011

Source: The White House, Wikimedia Commons.

watching videos, or doing some additional reading to expand your understanding of the world of music opened up by the gateway example.

Answering the five questions asked about each gateway recording explains how each particular performance of music in the book works, what it means, and how it came into the world. In the future, you should be able to apply this explanatory apparatus to all the music you encounter. You should able to understand and explain what music means to you and to those who make it and love it no matter where in the world they live. Let's get started.

THINGS TO THINK ABOUT

- Think of a recording of music that you react to emotionally and, using the concepts of index and icon, explain why you think it has that effect on you.
- Explain why you like a particular song or genre of music either in terms of the way it expresses your social identity (class, race, ethnicity, gender) or in terms of the way it reflects your political values or worldview (culture).

NEW TERMS

articulation	index/indexical sign	pitch (low, high)
chord	legato	polyphony/polyphonic
crescendo	loudness	rhythm
decay	measure/bar	solo
decrescendo	melodic line/part	staccato
duple meter	melody	style
dynamics	meter	tempo
envelope	metrical	texture
explaining	monophony/monophonic	timbre
form	nonmetrical	tone, musical
forte	note	triple meter
fundamental	onset/attack	understanding
genre	ornamentation	waveform
harmony	overtone	world of music
icon/iconic sign	piano	world music

Music History to 1500 CE

UNTIL 1492, WHEN EUROPEANS set out to explore the world by sea, dominate trade in Africa and Asia, and colonize the Americas, no single cultural, economic, or political center dominated world affairs. Patterns of economic and political life were distributed across the globe. Political power was limited and local. Part I examines some of the musical traditions in the world today with roots in this period of history before 1500. Chapter 1 looks at music of the oldest social formations still in existence today. These are small-scale societies that sustain themselves by foraging (hunting and gathering plants), caring for domesticated herd animals (nomadic pastoralists), and planting small gardens (horticulturalists).

Chapters 2 and 3 examine music with roots in the Ancient and Medieval periods of human history. The Ancient period begins around 3000 BCE with the invention of writing, the advent of large-scale agriculture based on growing wheat, rice, and other grains, and the formation of the first cities and empires. Ancient Egyptian, Chinese, Indian, Greek, and Roman empires began to leave a written and artistic record of their lives and music. And four major religions (Hinduism, Buddhism, Judaism, and Christianity) appeared.

European histories name the time after the fall of the Roman Empire in 476 CE the Medieval period. Formed from the roots "medi" meaning between and "eval" meaning time, it was the time, the "Middle Ages," between the Ancient period and the beginning of European dominance in world affairs. Islam and many secular musical traditions today have their roots in this period between 476 and 1500. Since Buddhist, Christian, and Muslim chanting practices today can be traced only as far back as the Medieval period, Chapters 2 and 3 cover both the Ancient and Medieval periods: Chapter 2 on Ancient and Medieval religious music and Chapter 3 on Ancient and Medieval secular music.

PART I

MUSIC OF SMALL-SCALE SOCIETIES

EVERYONE IN THE WORLD TODAY lives in a complex web of national, regional, and local governments, economies, and media information. About half live in cities and half in rural areas. In the United States about 80 percent live in cities. In rural areas around the world there are a very few small-scale societies that continue to sustain themselves with the oldest still-extant modes of human food production on the planet: foraging, nomadic pastoralism, and horticulture. The gateways in this chapter provide a portal to the musical worlds of these types of societies.

Foraging societies hunt wild game and gather plants, nuts, and seeds to sustain themselves. Human forager societies date to the late Paleolithic Period (Old Stone Age), which began around 2.5 million years ago. Around 10,000 BCE humans began a transition from food gathering to food producing. At that time humans learned how to domesticate plants and animals, a set of practices known collectively as agriculture. Horticulture refers to the domestication of plants for food, but in small quantities that support only small groups of people. This "Agricultural Revolution" or "Neolithic Revolution" first took place in four regions of the world: grain farming in the fertile crescent, the area along the Tigris and Euphrates Rivers in present-day Iraq and along the Nile River in Egypt; rice growing in the Yangtze and Yellow River Basins of China; maize growing in Central America; and root crops in Papua New Guinea. From these regions it took until about 2000 BCE for agriculture to spread to most regions of the world.

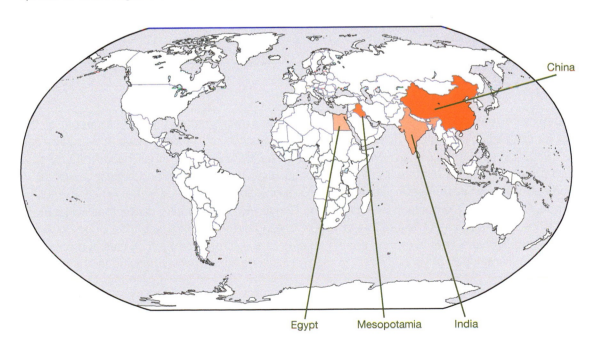

FIGURE 1.1
Map of Ancient Civilizations

The music of these still-extant social formations is mainly known today through recordings made by ethnomusicologists who have lived in these isolated places for a year or more to study their music. In a few cases musicians from these cultures have toured around the world and played with musicians from the classical and jazz scenes. Sometimes these musicians, seeking new sources of inspiration, have used or referenced ethnomusicologists' recordings in their own creations. This chapter contains three gateways, one example from each of these three types of societies: Central African foragers; nomadic pastoralists from Inner Asia (Siberia); and horticulturalists from the Solomon Islands in the Western Pacific. In all these cases the music making of these foragers, nomadic pastoralists, and horticulturalists is intimately linked to the natural environment in which they live. Their music contributes in important ways to the social organization, psychological well-being, and work patterns of these societies.

Because the histories of these musical traditions were not written down before their contact with explorers, missionaries, ethnomusicologists, and tourists, we do not claim that the actual music in these recordings is thousands of years old. But we place them first in our chronology because the social formations that these musical practices contribute to and draw from are the oldest on earth today. And some of the general elements of the musical cultures we observe today may, indeed, be very old:

- the understanding of the resonant potential of found and made objects for making music, for example, from a hollow log, a piece of bamboo, a cooking pot, or a hunting bow;
- the prominent use of the human voice to create social harmony and communicate across social barriers;
- the iconic and therefore expressive, emotional link between singing and crying;
- the intimate relationship between the sound of music and the sound of the environment; and
- the belief that singing can be more effective than speech for contacting the supernatural world of ancestors, spirits, and gods.

These very old understandings of the nature of music form the bedrock of all human musical cultures today.

GATEWAY 1
MUSIC OF FORAGERS

What Is It?

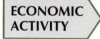

ECONOMIC
ACTIVITY

Our gateway to the music of extant forager societies is a recording of the BaAka people of the Central African Republic singing "Bisengo Bwa Bolé" in a dance form called *mabo*. It was recorded in the 1980s by ethnomusicologist Michelle Kisliuk. The BaAka live in small bands of fifty to a hundred people in a huge rainforest along the Congo River basin, the second largest rainforest in the world after the Amazon River basin, near the borders of four countries: Central African Republic, Cameroon, Congo, and Democratic Republic of the Congo. *Mabo*, a hunting dance that was current during Kisliuk's visits there in the 1980s and 1990s, is sung before, during, and after hunts in which the community spreads nets in a circle around an area of the forest and then chases and ensnares animals, mostly antelopes of various sizes, in them. This song accompanies dancing led by men but including women.

 **Listen to the first thirty seconds of the recording.**

FIGURE 1.2
**Map of Africa
(BaAka people)**

Home of the BaAka people

How Does It Work?

Timbre

This performance includes men's and women's singing with yodeling, along with low- and high-pitched drum sounds, and a stick beating time.

Texture

The texture is polyphonic, consisting of many people singing different rhythmically independent melodic lines.

Rhythm

The drums play a pattern of four strong beats each subdivided into three pulses by a pattern of low- and high-pitched sounds (L-H-H-L-H-H) to create a meter of six beats. Notice that the pulses are not absolutely even, but have a slightly lilting character. The melodic lines interlock with the drum rhythms but in a way difficult to hear.

FIGURE 1.3
BaAka women dancing *mabo*
Source:
Michelle Kisliuk.

Melody

A prominent feature of some BaAka songs is yodeling. **Yodeling** is an alternation between chest-resonated tones and high-pitched, head-resonated tones, which produces melodies with disjunct or leapwise melodic motion

Harmony

The harmony is not systematic but the result of the simultaneous singing of many melodic lines.

Form

The basic form consists of fixed melodies, some of which are repeated and treated to improvised melodic variations. As a new song gets older and becomes familiar, singers stop singing the main theme. With the main themes silent but in their ears, they sing variations on them. The singers listen carefully to each other and echo, repeat, and vary what they sing in response to what they hear. Careful listening is a skill necessary for survival in the forest and interpersonal and social well-being. The loudest melodic line in the texture is not the melody but the voice of the person, named Mokpake, who was sitting closest to the ethnomusicologist's microphone. The text is a single line of text plus a variety of **vocables**, nonlexical syllables like "i yay i oh."

Performance Techniques

The most striking performance techniques are the yodeling by some of the singers and melodic variations in their singing.

Listen to this recording with these elements in mind and while following this timed listening guide.

LISTENING GUIDE 1.1

TIME	DESCRIPTION
0:00	The recording fades in.
0:04	A woman close to the mic starts a yodeling melody; other melodies are heard in the background.
0:30	The yodeling line is no longer heard but a melody line without yodeling is prominent.
1:12	A yodeling melody returns.
1:45	The yodeling line again disappears.
1:58	The yodeling line returns.
2:18	And so on to the end.
5:27	End

What Does It Mean?

SOCIAL BEHAVIOR

A performance of *mabo* during a BaAka music-and-dance event mirrors the social organization of BaAka society and the physical activity of the hunt. BaAka and other forager societies are often described as egalitarian, meaning that they value and maintain a social order that makes few if any of the distinctions that most large-scale societies have between leaders and followers, high and low classes, and occupational categories. They own very few things except hunting nets, spears, machetes, cooking pots, and some clothing, and these are routinely shared, traded, and even swiped when the swiper claims it is common property. When they want drums for a *mabo* dance, they quickly make a temporary drum from a rotting log and an animal skin or, if circumstances allow, they borrow more substantial drums from village horticulturalists who live on the edges of the forest and where the BaAka live during some parts of the year.

Every able-bodied man and woman participates in food-gathering activities, although men usually take the lead in net hunting while women gather roots and seeds on the way to help with the hunt. To ensure the success of the hunt, men start and lead the *mabo* dancers just as they start and lead the hunt, but women soon join in both activities, helping with the hunt and singing and dancing enthusiastically for the success of the hunt. Women also have dances that they control entirely, some of which mock men as a way of restoring the balance of power.

Circular forms permeate their lifeways. The nets are spread in a semicircle in the forest just as, in their forest camps, people's small, one-room, dome-shaped houses, made by women out of forest materials, are arranged in a circle. *Mabo* dancers dance counterclockwise in a circle within a circle of spectators within the circle of houses constructed in circular form. The iconicity of these circular architectural, social, and musical structures creates a feeling of familiarity, comfort, and coherence for the BaAka.

Although BaAka society is closer to an egalitarian ideal than most societies in the world, they distinguish four important social categories: (1) eldest sibling, (2) lead hunter, (3) healer, and (4) expert teacher of songs and dances. The lead hunter and healer are usually men, an indication of some inequality between men and women. Both men and women may be eldest sibling and act as expert teachers of songs and dances. Children learn the songs and dances by watching adults, but adults sometimes invite master teachers from other camps to teach them new songs and dances. Some of these songs and dances are attributed to particular individuals, who have some heightened status on that account.

Although they are taught new songs and learn old songs by watching, they are not taught fixed parts to sing in the polyphonic texture. Instead, they develop the ability to create numerous variations, which they are free to sing at will, on the melody of each *mabo* song. Sometimes, as in the recording, they drop out for a while, only to enter again when they feel like it. Consistent with their egalitarian social structure, no one leads the performance and tells others what to do. If they try, they are usually ignored. All the lines in the polyphony are equally important. Their ability to create polyphony spontaneously stands in striking contrast to spontaneous group singing in American culture, where singing, say at a birthday party, is typically monophonic. The inability to sing polyphonically in relatively egalitarian social settings is consistent with our stratified social structure, which includes a specialized category of trained musicians who have the ability to sing and play polyphonically, but often only under the direction of a leader who organizes them. The specialization of labor characteristic of our society results in a distinction between the few people who perform polyphonic music very well and most people, who perform monophonically and not always very well.

Polyphonic singing also sounds literally natural to the BaAka, not least because it is iconic of the polyphony of forest sounds (birds singing and calling, leaves rustling, cicadas buzzing, insects chirping) that they hear all around them. Unison singing probably would sound rather unnatural to them and not in harmony with nature. When they are alone, walking or gathering food in the forest, they sing monophonically the solo yodeling melodic lines that make up the texture of *mabo* singing. Each person's particular way of singing these lines is their personal signature and an index of their presence in the forest. During the hunt they use their personal yodeling melodies to signal their position to the other hunters, creating a rich polyphonic texture of yodels and calls that help with the hunting.

For the dancers, the drumming provides the rhythm for their dance movements. They hold their bent arms close to their bodies, while their feet move in a step-touch-step-touch pattern on the main

ECONOMIC ACTIVITY

AESTHETICS

SOCIAL BEHAVIOR

CULTURAL LINKAGES

low-pitched drum beats as they move around the circle. Their hips articulate the subdivisions of the beat, which they may hear in groups of two and in groups of three. Hearing these groups of two is aided by the way the players of the small drum play the triple-sounding L-H-H pattern. They do not use their hands to mirror the sound pattern, they do not use the hand pattern R-L-L-R-L-L to create the sound pattern L-H-H-L-H-H. Instead, they play the sound pattern by alternating their two hands like this:

| Pitches | L-H-H-L-H-H |
| Hands | R-L-R-L-R-L |

AESTHETICS

This difference between the sound and the motion that produces them creates a **polymeter**, the simultaneous presence of two meters, in this case duple meter in the hand motion against triple meter in the sound that results from the hand motion. The dancers hear the two meters and, bent at the waist, move their feet, knees, and buttocks in response to what they experience as a rich polymetric texture. These two parts yield what seems to be a single monophonic drum part, but the polymeter of the duple hand movements against the triple pattern of the drum sounds creates an **inherent polyphony**, an experience of polyphony from a monophonic line or part played by the drummers.

CULTURAL LINKAGES

The genre *mabo* and solo singing in the forest are but two of a number of BaAka genres. Others include music for spear hunting, women's dances, solo lullabies, and songs included in stories that tell of the BaAka's relationship to the animals and the natural and supernatural worlds. They believe, for example, in a benevolent forest god that brings them good fortune. Both men and women sing net-hunting and spear-hunting songs, and the women have their own dance-and-song forms that exclude men to serve their emotional and social needs.

EMOTIONAL RESONANCE

Melodic yodeling lines, as signatures or indexes of particular individuals, may touch those who hear them as they recognize friends. The texts also may be touching, as they express incidents in ordinary life. Memories of people who have died and accusations of bad behavior are just two other examples of what these texts may register.

What Is Its History?

ECONOMIC ACTIVITY

Foraging, which refers to both the hunting of game and the gathering of edible plants, and forager societies arose toward the end of a long era called the Paleolithic (Old Stone Age). It began about 2.5 million years ago when protohuman hominids began using stone tools, and it ended around 10,000 BCE, when modern humans invented agriculture. Forager societies typically operate in small bands, some perhaps no larger than the nuclear family. Such bands need to be just the right size, not too small or too large, to hunt and gather food efficiently enough to feed the group.

Today, only a few forager societies, like the BaAka, still exist. They can be found among some American Indian groups, especially in California and the Great Basin between the Rockies and the Sierra Nevada; the Arctic people known as Inuit or Eskimos; Australian Aborigines; the San people of the Kalahari Desert in Namibia (southern Africa); the Amazon Basin; and societies of forest dwellers in Central Africa like the BaAka. The small stature of these Central African foragers led writers in the past to refer to them collectively as Pygmies. Because this label comes from outside the culture and has developed pejorative connotations, scholars today prefer to call them by the names they give themselves: BaAka, BaBenzele, BaMbuti, and so forth.

TECHNOLOGY

They typically live in small bands that can move quickly in search of game and that can support themselves with the meat from a successful hunt, which is then shared among the relatively small group. Some modern-day forager societies are egalitarian and others are hierarchical. In nearly all cases their music is primarily vocal. Foragers rarely have dedicated or permanently constructed musical instruments. Rather, they transform hunting and cooking tools or objects found in the environment into musical instruments. They do not mind discarding these found instruments and rebuilding them when they need them.

It is possible to imagine, but not prove, that some of the principles behind their music making today are among the oldest on earth. Probably the specific melodies and musical elements heard today in their music are not the same as they were thousands of years ago. And yet some elements of their music may be thousands of years old, including the emphasis on vocal rather than instrumental music and their performance of both solo and polyphonic singing. Other Central African foragers use flutes made from small sections of bamboo and trumpets made from hollow logs, and it is possible that they discovered long ago the music-making capacity of these objects from their environment. Foragers, including the BaAka, turn hunting bows into musical instruments by placing the string in their mouths and resonating overtones of the vibrating bow string, which they pluck. Making a link between present-day and millennia-old musical elements depends on the hypothesis that musical elements are always embedded in social, cultural, political, and economic structures, some of which, like hunting and gathering, have been with us for millennia. So perhaps some elements of foragers' music making today have their roots in millennia-old ways of making music.

The BaAka and other contemporary foragers do not live in the past, however. They live in the modern present and are connected to nearby local groups and Christian missionaries from far away. Possibly for as long as there have been village agriculturalists living near them, foragers may have been exchanging musical styles and musical instruments with them, as the BaAka now borrow drums from nearby agriculturalists for their *mabo* dance. The BaAka live part of year in isolation in the forest and part of the year in or near a village of nearby cultivators, where they may cultivate a small garden for food. They are happiest in the forest, and living in the stratified village society, where they are low in social status, can make the men somewhat anxious. They like exchanging the meat they hunt for some of the products, like drums, the villagers can offer. Their performances of songs and dances can express the pleasure or anxiety they experience in these two different living spaces. They also have to deal with intrusions from the modern world such as the poaching of elephants in the forest and challenges to their worldview from Christian missionaries. In response, they invent new genres of music and dance and learn new songs all the time. The *mabo* net-hunting songs became prominent when the diminishing number of elephants made spear hunting, and spear-hunting songs, less efficient than net hunting for small game. When ethnomusicologist Michelle Kisliuk returned to visit the BaAka a decade after her original research, they were singing another new song-and-dance style. BaAka music today is thoroughly modern, but we include it at the beginning of our music history because we believe it has some iconic links to very old ways of living and making music.

BaAka music could only enter into the global musical soundscape with the invention of sound recording technology and its use by anthropologists and ethnomusicologists. As a result, part of the history of the music of the BaAka and other Central African foragers has been its use by musicians from other cultures who have heard those recordings. In one striking example, the jazz keyboardist Herbie Hancock recorded his composition "Watermelon Man" in 1973 with references to a recording of forager music from a subgroup of the BaAka, the BaBenzele. Instead of yodeling, this recording documents a young woman alternating a low-pitched sung tone with a high-pitched tone produced by blowing over the edge of a hollow twig to create a flute. (A **flute** is an instrument type on which a sound wave in a vibrating column of air is initiated by blowing over an edge, either on the end or the side, of a hollow tube.) "Watermelon Man" begins with one member of Hancock's band, The Headhunters, mimicking this sound on a beer bottle to produce a syncopated **ostinato** (short, repeating) pattern. Eventually a second beer bottle-and-voice part enters after which a bass and jazz drum set enter, increasing the number of parts in a polyphonic texture, which in this case is similar to African ways of making music.

Herbie Hancock's "Watermelon Man" was created in the context of a cultural movement during the 1960s and 1970s among African Americans who sought their historical roots in West Africa and

TECHNOLOGY

FIGURE 1.4
***Djembe* drums for sale in Ghana**
Source: ZSM, Wikimedia Commons.

CULTURAL
LINKAGES

the Congo, the most active regions of the African slave trade. Slavery had denied African Americans the ability to trace their genealogy further back in history than the slave markets of the New World. During the 1960s and 1970s (and since then), many have asserted their African roots through the creation of artistic and cultural forms that recover those origins, particularly using the *djembe* drum and Mande dance styles of West Africa. In 1966 a professor of Black Studies, Maulana Karenga, invented a new holiday called Kwanzaa, a Swahili (East African language) word for harvest. Celebrated at the end of each year, it honors African Americans' African heritage and enacts their hope for a better world. Among the popular manifestations of this cultural movement was a 1976 novel by Alex Haley called *Roots: The Saga of an American Family*. Made into a television miniseries, it was one of the most watched TV shows in history (and remade in 2016). It tells the fictional story of the descendants of Kunta Kinte, a warrior of the Mandinka tribe of West Africa, who was brought to America as a slave in the late eighteenth century and whose story, passed down from generation to generation to the present day, could be traced back to Mandinka oral historians. Herbie Hancock's imitation of this BaBenzele recording was yet another creative act, at about the same time, aimed at making a link to the African roots of jazz and of much American popular music.

WHERE DO I GO FROM HERE?

- Find the recording of the BaBenzele young woman playing her voice-and-flute music and compare it to Herbie Hancock and The Headhunters' 1973 recording of "Watermelon Man." (There is an earlier 1962 recording of "Watermelon Man" that does not include the reference to BaBenzele music making.)

- Find and listen to other recordings of the BaAka and other Central African foragers such as the BaBenzele and the BaMbuti.

- Find and read all or part of the book on which this gateway is based: *Seize the Dance!: BaAka Musical Life and the Ethnography of Performance* (New York: Oxford University Press, 1998/2001) by Michelle Kisliuk.[2]

GATEWAY 2
MUSIC OF NOMADIC PASTORALISTS

What Is It?

Our gateway to the music of nomadic pastoralists is a performance titled "Borbangnadyr with Stream Water" by Tuvan throat-singer Anatoli Kuular. Tuva is a republic in south-central Russia on the northern border of Mongolia. Tuvans speak a Turkic language and herd goats, sheep, yaks, and reindeer across the southern steppes (grasslands) of Siberia, part of a large area known as Inner Asia. Tuvan **throat-singers** produce a drone pitch and, at the same time, use their mouths to amplify the set of overtones in the drone and produce high-pitched melodies. *Borbangnadyr*, one of many genres of Tuvan throat-singing, is associated with the sound of water. Anatoli Kuular sang along the banks of a river for the recording.

 Listen to the first fifteen seconds of the recording.

The Republic of Tuva in Russia

FIGURE 1.5
Map showing the Tuvan region in Russia

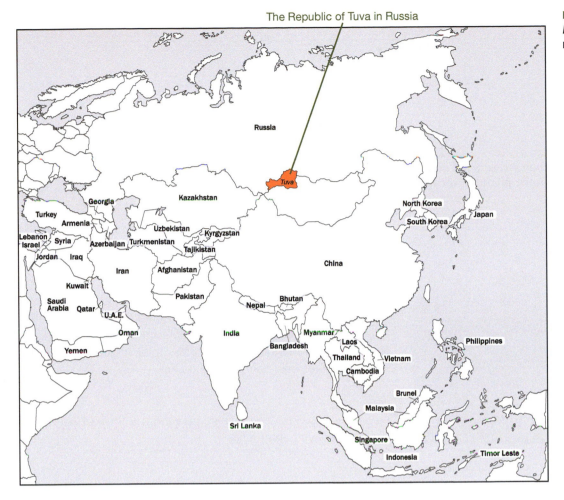

How Does It Work?

Timbre

One male singer produces a wide variety of vocal timbres from low-pitched raspy sounds to high pitches that are clear and flute-like. He sings in duet with the variety of timbres of a shallow river.

Texture

The singer sings both monophonically and polyphonically by producing a vocal drone with overtones. He varies the pitch of the overtones to produce a melody. He is able to do this because the drone tone, like every tone, consists of a fundamental pitch and a set of overtones. He and other Tuvan throat-singers have found a way to amplify those overtones by shifting the position of their tongues, raising and lowering their soft palates, moving their lips, and singing different vowel sounds. The changing vowels are clearly audible in this recording.

Rhythm

The rhythm lacks a clear beat or meter.

Melody

The melody uses just two pitches until the drone begins and four different overtone pitches are heard. If the fundamental pitch is C, then the overtone series looks approximately like that shown in Figure 1.6.

FIGURE 1.6

The overtone series. Solid notes are approximations, as these overtones sound noticeably higher or lower than the pitches indicated.

The singer produces his four-pitch melody by amplifying overtones 6, 8, 9, 10, and 12 of the overtone series.

Harmony

The simultaneous sounding of the drone and overtone melody does not constitute harmony in a systematic way. Rather the harmony Tuvans hear is a timbral harmony consisting of a changing "spray" of overtones. In other words, they engage in "timbral listening" rather than harmonic listening.

Form

The singer sings four sections suggesting the form of a strophic song with nonverbal refrains.

FIGURE 1.7

Anatoli Kuular on the bank of the "Singing River"
Source:
Theodore Levin.

Performance Techniques

Although the timbre of the melody may suggest whistling, the singer is not whistling. Rather this performance features throat-singing or **overtone singing**: two sounds from one voice, one produced by the vocal cords and the other by resonating the overtones of the throat-produced drone tone in such a way as to create simultaneous high-pitched sounds.

Listen to this performance with these elements in mind, following this timed listening guide.

LISTENING GUIDE 1.2

TIME	SECTION	DESCRIPTION
0:00	Prelude	The sound of running river water.
0:09	A (first phrase)	The singer sings words on one pitch.
0:19	second phrase	The singer imitates the gurgling sound of rushing water.
0:32	third phrase	The singer sings words on one pitch and then imitates the sound of gurgling water.
0:43	fourth phrase	The singer sings a drone underneath a changing high-pitched overtone melody.
1:05	A'	The singer sings a two-phrase variant of the first strophe.
1:47	A''	The singer sings another two-phrase variant.
2:26	A'''	The singer performs just one phrase, ending after the gurgling.
2:43	End	

What Does It Mean?

This performance is part of a rich sound world connecting Tuvan pastoralists to the natural environment in which they live. That environment is filled with the sounds of animals, rivers, wind, and echoing caves and cliffs. Their sound culture is devoted to responding in at least five ways to those sounds. First, they employ a rich set of vocal and instrumental sounds to mimic animal calls to aid in the hunt, much as duck hunters do. Second, they make sounds to soothe their domesticated animals and encourage them to suckle their offspring. Third, they believe that animals, rivers, mountain cliffs, and certain locales have spirits, a belief system called **animism**, and they engage in throat-singing to honor and appease those spirits. Fourth, they throat-sing for fun and to entertain the spirits, as in this recording. Fifth, they sing songs about their experiences in the natural world.

Their throat-singing is a creative imitation, an icon but not a perfect copy, of the sounds they hear in that spot or that they hear a particular animal make. When they want to sing near a river, they seek out a place where the water babbles over rocks and makes a nice sound, perhaps with an echo off a nearby cliff, and where they can produce a lovely harmony with the river. They prefer such places to wide, slow-moving spots without an interesting sound or to rushing rapids that drown out their singing. They believe that the river has a voice and sings and that they are singing in duet with the sound of the river.

The genre of throat-singing called *borbangnadyr* means "rolling." The subtle inflexions of the drone and the overtones roll and flow in ways similar to water rolling over river rocks. The Tuvans have other throat-singing genres with names and sounds that respond to the sound of a particular bird, of boots clacking in stirrups, and of places where steep mountain peaks rise out of the steppes. They distinguish genres based on the sound quality, for example between one that uses a drone lower than *borbangnadyr* and another that features higher-pitched harmonics than *borbangnadyr*. Some of these styles avoid manipulating the overtones to create melodic structures, as Anatoli Kuular does in this *borbangnadyr*. Rather, they luxuriate in the timbre of the overtones combined with the timbre of the drone, inviting the listener to listen timbrally to human sounds that are creative mirrors of the timbre of sounds they hear in the natural world.

Tuvan throat-singers are able to imitate not just the general sound of a river, or a cave, or a mountain cliff. They can evoke with great specificity the sound of a particular place, distinguishing in the sound of their singing between high and low mountains, one cave and another, or one river and another. When others hear their singing, they are able to recognize these different locales because they have been there too, and they may weep or laugh or respond emotionally in some way to the singing depending on their associations with that place.

Tuvans are not taught throat-singing by their elders; they learn it on their own. Some claim that they learned while riding a horse or that the river was their teacher. As a Tuvan singer said, "The river is alive. The rivers sing."[3] The fact they select five overtones from the range of seven overtones from six through twelve indicates that, while their throat-singing depends on the physical properties of sound waves, the Tuvans carefully select from all that is available to them in the natural world to create their music culture. In other words, for Tuvans, and indeed all humans, music making is a fact of culture as much or more than it is a fact of nature.

The Tuvans also have quite a variety of musical instruments, all of which are played to emphasize the overtones inherent in their sound. They include a hunting horn to attract wild animals, a two-stringed bowed fiddle that accompanies songs about life on the steppes, and an end-blown, rim-blown flute whose sound mediates between the human and spirit world, bringing healing, success in hunting, and advice from the spirits about what to do in human affairs.

Since we do not share the kinds of associations between sound and place that Tuvans do, it is unlikely that we would find throat-singing as emotionally touching as the Tuvans do—unless you come from rural areas of Texas, where some cowboys sing in a similar style.

> CULTURAL LINKAGES

> EMOTIONAL RESONANCE

> TECHNOLOGY

What Is Its History?

ECONOMIC
ACTIVITY

As with BaAka music, it is impossible to recover the ancient history of music that only existed in face-to-face aural tradition until the advent of sound recordings. We place this example near the beginning of our music history because nomadic pastoralism is one of the earliest forms of human subsistence and social organization. Nomadic pastoralism depends on the ability of humans to domesticate animals, that is, bring them under human control. Humans first domesticated dogs about 10,000 BCE and somewhat later wild sheep and goats, which added important and reliable sources of protein to hunters' diets. The domestication of the horse allowed herders to move large herds over vast distances, creating the possibility of nomadic pastoralism on the steppes of Inner Asia sometime around 3000 BCE. This region does not support agriculture, and so the pastoralists have it to themselves, moving from place to place with the seasons in search of better pastures. They listen for the sounds of insects and birds in their environment as signals of the changing seasons: crows indicate the coming of winter, cuckoos the end of spring, mating calls of bull yaks the beginning of summer, and crickets the start of autumn. The largest and most famous group of nomadic pastoralists in Inner Asia are the Mongolians, who share many aspects of culture and music with their neighbors, the Tuvans, but who speak a different language. Although there is a long history of the movement of peoples across the steppes of Inner Asia that surely influenced some aspects of Tuvan music making today, it does not seem unreasonable to conclude that Tuvans for many millennia have engaged in musical interactions with natural and animal sounds similar in some respects to what ethnomusicologists have recorded in the last few decades.

The Tuvans began to live in cities only after the Russians built one in their territory just before World War I. As part of the Soviet Union in the second half of the twentieth century, professional folklore ensembles and schools were formed to train musicians in Tuvan traditional musical styles. It is possible that these schools and ensembles encouraged some of the extravagantly virtuosic throat-singing we hear today. With the fall of the Soviet Union in 1991, the metaphorical iron curtain between communist eastern Europe and the capitalist world disappeared, easing contact between musicians from that formerly closed-off part of the world and the rest of the world. Musicians in Russia were free to form small folklore ensembles, and entrepreneurs from western Europe and the United States started organizing concert tours for them. On January 1, 1993, Tuvan musicians Anatoli Kuular, Kaigal-ool Xovalyg, and Kongar-ool Ondar were known well enough in the U.S. to ride in the Rose Parade in Pasadena, California.

FIGURE 1.8
Left to right, **Kaigal-ool Xovalyg, Anatoli Kuular, and Kongar-ool Ondar holding a long-necked plucked string instrument with a carving of a horse head on top of the neck**
Source: Theodore Levin.

Later in 1993 Kaigal-ool Xovalyg joined three other musicians in an ensemble called Huun-Huur-Tu and recorded their first album, a CD called *Sixty Horses in my Herd.* Huun-Huur-Tu literally means sunpropeller or sunbeam and refers to the spray of light sometimes seen through clouds at sunrise and sunset. In giving their group this name, the Tuvans were making a metaphorical connection between their visual and aural experiences, a spray of light and a spray of overtones, on the steppes of Inner Asia.

Huun-Huur-Tu and other Tuvan musicians in the 1990s became the darlings of the popular and classical music worlds, admired by and performing and recording with eclectic composer-performer Frank Zappa, traditional Irish band the Chieftains, Mickey Hart of the Grateful Dead, and the Kronos String Quartet. Among them Kongar-ool Ondar (1962–2013) became so well known that, like many pop stars, he was known by one name, Ondar. In 1999 he appeared in the Oscar-nominated documentary film *Genghis Blues* and on the TV show *Late Night with David Letterman,* who promoted his CD *Back Tuva Future,* which includes a duet with country singer Willie Nelson. More recently, the Tuvan throat-singing band Alash has continued Ondar's cross-genre approach by collaborating with musicians from jazz and bluegrass styles, and even with a beatboxer. Some might criticize Alash, Ondar, and other Tuvan musicians for selling out to commercialism and debasing the supposed purity of an ancient tradition. Although they certainly make money from their performances and recordings, they, like so many traditionally trained artists today, have sought to find a meaningful connection between musical styles that are icons and indexes of very old ways of making music and the life experiences of cosmopolitan listeners in Tuva and around the world.

CULTURAL LINKAGES

WHERE DO I GO FROM HERE?

- This gateway is based on a book by ethnomusicologist Theodore Levin, together with Tuvan researcher Valentina Süzükei, called *Where Rivers and Mountains Sing: Sound, Music, and Nomadism in Tuva and Beyond* (Bloomington: Indiana University Press, 2006).[4] Read Chapter 2, "The World is Alive with the Music of Sound," and listen to the CD/DVD that comes with the book.

- Find and listen to recordings and videos of Huun-Huur-Tu, Kongar-ool Ondar, and other Tuvan throat-singers, both with and without collaborators from other musical styles. In what ways do the musical and other elements of their performances change when they collaborate? It what ways do they remain the same?

GATEWAY 3
MUSIC OF HORTICULTURAL SOCIETIES

What Is It?

Our gateway to the music of horticultural societies is a recording made in the 1970s of a panpipe ensemble of the 'Are'are people from the island of Malaita in the Solomon Islands off the northeast coast of Australia. The Solomon Islands, where about 10,000 'Are'are (the primes indicate glottal stops) live in small villages in the interior mountains and near the coast, gained their independence from Britain in 1978. One of the islands, Guadalcanal, was the site of a famous World War II battle between the U.S. and Japan. A **panpipe** is a type of flute that consists of a set of tubes of different lengths, each of which plays one pitch. The panpipes in this 'Are'are ensemble are organized in a straight line, side by side in a wing formation, from low-pitched to high-pitched. The players blow across the top edge of the tubes as we might blow over the edge of a bottle. This ensemble, called *'au tahana*, consists of four panpipes, two small ones playing high pitches and two large ones playing an octave lower. The piece is titled "Pisi Ni Tootora." *Pisi* is the name of a sacred bush used to attract an abundance of people, food, and shell-money. When this piece was played at an important ritual feast called *tootora*, the musicians hoped it would have the same effect.

 Listen to the first fifteen seconds or so of the recording.

How Does It Work?

Timbre

These panpipes, open at one end and closed at the other, have a breathy flute sound.

Texture

"Pisi ni Tootora" has a polyphonic texture consisting of two rhythmically independent melodic lines. Each line is played in octaves. An **octave** is the interval between two pitches whose frequency of vibration has a ratio of 2:1. Pitches an octave apart are perceived as higher and lower versions of the same pitch.

FIGURE 1.9
Map of the Western Pacific (Solomon Islands, 'Are'are people)

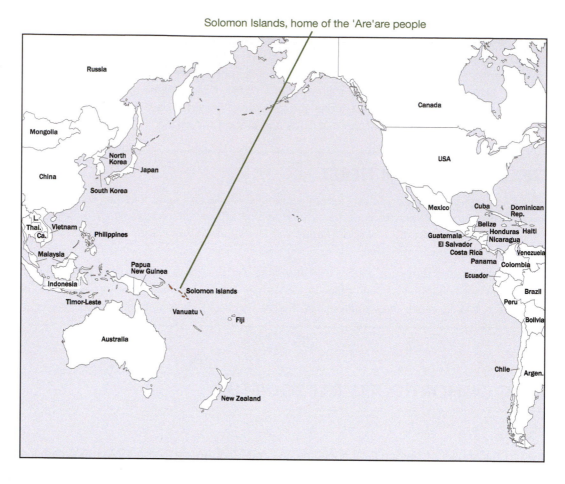

Solomon Islands, home of the 'Are'are people

FIGURE 1.10
Four 'Are'are men play panpipes in an 'au tahana ensemble
Source: Hugo Zemp.

Rhythm

The rhythms of each of the two parts are different from one another in a four-beat meter.

Melody

The polyphonic lines use a seven-pitch (**heptatonic**) scale. A **scale** is the set of pitches in a melody arranged from low to high. The intervals between the adjacent pitches of the scale in this recording are approximately equal.

Harmony

The contrapuntal lines create a variety of harmonic intervals.

Form

The performance is in A A form. Each A section consists of three subsections: a b c.

Performance Techniques

The end of each subsection is marked by slowing down, called **ritardando** or simply **ritard**. Occasionally a player plays a harmonic second by blowing across two adjacent pipes simultaneously.

Listen to this performance with these elements in mind following this timed listening guide.

TIME	FORM		DESCRIPTION
0:02	A	a	After a very soft chord, the panpipes play a series of chords with the pitches sounding simultaneously, a texture referred to as block chord.
0:09		b	The players split into two rhythmically independent parts, each part consisting of a four-beat melody of just three pitches repeated many times before a ritard and the playing of the chords in the a subsection.
0:39		c	The players continue, each part consisting of an eight-beat melody with more pitches than the b subsection. The melody is repeated several times before a ritard and the playing of the chords in the a subsection.
1:18	A	a	The A section is repeated almost exactly.
		b	
		c	
2:33	End		

What Does It Mean?

Unlike foragers, sedentary horticulturalists like the 'Are'are live in permanent houses and subsist on domesticated pigs, taro, and other crops. They do not need to hunt every day as the BaAka do when they live in their forest camps. As a result, the 'Are'are have the time to construct permanent musical instruments that serve only one function, making music, a luxury not available to foragers. The 'Are'are have a more hierarchical social system than the BaAka do. The political hierarchy of leaders known as "big men" is mirrored by a hierarchy of music specialists. Among them is a man named 'Irisipau, one of the best musicians and a specialist in making panpipes and explaining the elements of 'Are'are music. The 'Are'are have developed an astonishing array of panpipes and panpipe ensembles, made from bamboo tubes, on which they play their polyphonic music. Bamboo (called *'au*) is a ubiquitous material in their environment, and they use it to make both their houses and their musical instruments, which they call by the generic name *'au*.

⬦ ECONOMIC ACTIVITY

The 'Are'are play and sing in twenty different genres of music, including four types of panpipes ensembles, four kinds of solo flute music, and panpipe ensembles that are struck rather than blown. The *'au tahana* ensemble heard in this gateway plays in two-part polyphony. In the accompanying photo one part, called "to braid" (*aaritai'i*), is played by 'Irisipau with closed eyes. On his right Warahane plays the same part on a small panpipe an octave higher. The other part, called "head of music" (*pau ni 'au*), is played by the two musicians at right, Kinipa'a and Ooreana. They always play the two polyphonic parts face to face. Another ensemble of six players plays in three-part polyphony an octave apart and another one of ten players plays in four-part polyphony over three octaves. Since the higher-pitched ones are easier to play than the large ones playing an octave lower, beginners play the higher-pitched panpipes and learn their part by standing next to a senior player, who plays the part on the larger panpipe an octave lower.

The 'Are'are panpipe ensembles play during death and funeral rituals and major feasts. Some ensembles, like those played at funerals, have a great deal of spiritual power. Other ensembles with lesser power are used to attract gifts of sea-shell money and a large audience, especially of young girls, and to ward off illness and death. Women occasionally play struck panpipes, not the blown ones, for entertainment. Men use solo panpipe playing as indexes of their presence in a village and their melodies as secret signs to a lover. The ensembles play compositions. Because of their spiritual

⬦ CULTURAL LINKAGES

EMOTIONAL
RESONANCE

power, they take great care to play them exactly correctly. They regard some of the compositions as especially beautiful, and these are able to generate the greatest emotional response including sadness when they remind people of a deceased loved one and feelings of love toward someone they are flirting with. Some ensembles have vast numbers of pieces in the repertoire. Some titles refer abstractly to the content of the piece, whereas some have names that indicate their origin or what they express such as the sound of birds, the sound of human speaking, and so on.

AESTHETICS

The 'Are'are have the most elaborate music theory yet discovered in a nonliterate culture. Ethnomusicologists used to believe that elaborate music theory existed only in the literate cultures of Europe, the Middle East, and Asia, but the music of the 'Are'are disproves that assumption completely. Their melodies are based on a heptatonic (seven-pitch) scale, and they distinguish between two sizes of seconds. They also employ quite a few different kinds of polyphonic textures in their ensemble panpipe music, and they have names for each one. While literate cultures can use writing and musical notation to illustrate their understanding of scales, 'Irisipau does so by turning the panpipes he constructs upside down. There for all to see is the scale of 'Are'are panpipe music in the relative sizes of the tubes.

CULTURAL
LINKAGES

In addition to panpipe music, the 'Are'are play music on large hollow logs into which they cut a narrow slit. One edge of the slit is thin and one thick to produce two different pitches. The edges are then struck with beaters. Ensembles of slit logs play fixed compositions, as the panpipe ensembles do. A single small slit-log can produce coded messages distinguishing, for example, between a death from illness and one from an accident or war. Men sing songs to aid in finding cures for the sick and protecting ocean voyagers in canoes. Women sing funeral laments, lullabies, and love songs. Surprisingly perhaps, love songs are the least important songs and are rarely sung because of the damage they can do to the reputation of those who sing them. Groups of women also play a sound game by standing in waist-deep water beating their hands on and under the water to produce different timbres and pitches in interlocking rhythms.

What Is Its History?

The Solomon Islands and Papua New Guinea are part of a large archipelago in the Western Pacific, known as Melanesia after the dark skin of the people who live there. In the Western Pacific, where the Solomon Islands are located, agriculture developed in Papua New Guinea around 7000 BCE. Pig raising may have been introduced around 500 BCE.

TECHNOLOGY

Whereas the musical instruments of foragers are either disposable or made from hunting and cooking implements, the sedentary nature of horticulturalists' village life allows for the development of more elaborate musical instruments, including specialized ones like the 'Are'are panpipes, which have no direct relationship to food production. We cannot know when the 'Are'are invented these panpipes. They believe that their first flutes were made to imitate bird sounds, and they think that the 'au tahana ensemble is the oldest of their panpipe ensembles.

ECONOMIC
ACTIVITY

There are many such small-scale agricultural societies in the world today. Among them, the 'Are'are people of the Solomon Islands stand out for the complexity of their musical culture. Today nearly 10,000 'Are'are live in small villages, where they subsist on taro, yams, sweet potatoes, domesticated pigs, and fishing. In forested areas of the world, such as the Solomon Islands, the agricultural potential of the land is limited and can only support small-scale societies, some no larger than a few hundred people living in a single village. An early form of this agricultural practice, slash-and-burn horticulture (gardening), involves clearing, with fire, spaces in dense forests where edible root crops such as taro and yams can be planted. This type of farming provided a family or a community's subsistence, but did not allow the accumulation of wealth or power. Sometimes villages could be interwoven into larger social groups united by trade and the exchange of marriage partners, and hierarchical social structures such as 'Are'are big men developed to manage these relationships.

In recent years the 'Are'are have been exposed to Christian and international popular music. They and other Solomon Islanders have created their own popular music for "bamboo bands," some of blown panpipes and some of struck panpipes. Some these bands have toured internationally. In turn, their music has entered global culture through the media of recorded sound and the internet.

The recordings made by ethnomusicologists who travel to such isolated cultures have made it possible for cosmopolitan popular musicians to include these recordings in their mixes of contemporary dance music such as house, techno, and electronica. Two French musicians, calling themselves Deep Forest, used a lullaby of the Baegu people from Malaita recorded by French ethnomusicologist Hugo Zemp, who recorded this gateway example, for a piece they called "Sweet Lullaby" on their first album published in 1992.[5] The producers portrayed the project as a benefit for various environmental projects designed to preserve rainforests. "Sweet Lullaby" enjoyed enormous commercial success. It reached the Top 10 in the United Kingdom and was even used in a number of commercials for famous products. Unfortunately, the producers did not receive permission from Zemp or from the 'Are'are people to use this recording in this way, and their profits on the song were not returned to the community whose music they appropriated. Clearly European and American music producers and their audiences find some music from distant parts of the world a meaningful and attractive addition to their own musical creativity and enjoyment. Very often they fit into romantic notions of a lost natural world and ways of life untainted by industrialization and urbanization. But in failing to cooperate in ethical ways with the people whose music they are sampling, they treat the modern 'Are'are as if they have no rights to their own deeply traditional music. Oddly, and perhaps consistent with the producers' insensitivity to the traditions they were exploiting, the scenes in a video made of "Sweet Lullaby" are of Africa and African people, not of the 'Are'are.

> **TECHNOLOGY**

WHERE DO I GO FROM HERE?

- This gateway is based on Hugo Zemp's ethnographic research, including academic articles, two books, and many LP and CD recordings and films. Watch a six-minute preview of a 141-minute documentary film of all twenty genres of 'Are'are music, available from the film's distributor, Documentary Educational Resources (DER).

- Read about and listen to the music of another horticulturalist society. Two excellent examples are Steven Feld's study of the Kaluli people of Papua New Guinea, *Sound and Sentiment: Birds, Weeping, Poetics and Song in Kaluli Expression*, 3rd Ed., (Philadelphia, PA: University of Pennsylvania Press, 2012) and Anthony Seeger's study of the Suyá Indians of the Amazonian basin, *Why Suyá Sing: A Musical Anthropology of an Amazonian People* (Urbana-Champagne, IL: University of Illinois Press, 2004).

- Listen to and read about another panpipe tradition, that of Indians in the Andes Mountains of Peru. A modernizing tradition, it can be heard on the streets of virtually every major city in the world, played by Indians from the Andes Mountains of South America. Thomas Turino's *Moving Away from Silence: Music of the Peruvian Altiplano and the Experience of Urban Migration* (Chicago, IL: University of Chicago Press, 1993) documents this tradition.

CLOSING

The three gateways in this chapter illustrate the close connection between music and the environment typical of many cultures, but especially of those where people live and work outdoors all the time. The BaAka match their polyphonic singing to the sounds of the forest in which they live. The 'Are'are make their panpipes from the vegetation in the forest around them and take the very idea of flute sounds from the sounds of birds. The Tuvans model an entire sound culture on the sounds of animals, rivers, and mountains.

> **CULTURAL LINKAGES**

All three cultures make music polyphonically but in different ways. The BaAka improvise variations that signal each person's uniqueness within a social setting. The 'Are'are play fixed compositions collectively in two-, three-, and four-part polyphony. Tuvans have found a way for a single, isolated herder, alone with his flocks, to entertain himself with his own polyphonic singing. All these cultures believe that music is a fundamentally important way to connect to the supernatural world. In one form or another these three basic principles—music in harmony with environmental sounds, polyphonic music making in social settings, and music as a pathway to the supernatural world—are important components of music making in nearly all the cultures of the world today.

THINGS TO THINK ABOUT

- Compare the ways that BaAka, 'Are'are, and Tuvan people respond musically to their natural environments and their patterns of work.

- What are some of the ways that musicians living in urban environments today make music in response to the sound environments in which they live?

NEW TERMS

flute	panpipe	throat-singing
inherent polyphony	polymeter	vocables
octave	polyphony, imitative	yodel, yodeling
ostinato	ritardando, ritard	
overtone singing	scale	

ANCIENT AND MEDIEVAL RELIGIOUS MUSIC

THE ANCIENT PERIOD (also called Antiquity or the Classical period) covers nearly four thousand years, from about 3200 BCE to 500 CE, when the Roman Empire fell. The thousand-year period from about 500 CE to 1500 is called the Medieval period, from the Latin roots *medi* ("between" or "middle") and *eval* ("time" or "age") Thus, another name for this period is the Middle Ages. It is a term developed in Europe to label the period between the end of the Ancient period of Greece and Rome and the modern period, when European ideas, economic power, and people spread around the world. For the purposes of this chapter, and the next, we treat the Ancient and Medieval periods as a single unit. That is because, although many of the musical traditions we introduce can trace their roots to the Ancient period, most of what we know about them comes from the Medieval period.

Around 3200 BCE, having domesticated plants and animals millennia earlier, communities living along the world's major rivers learned to smelt metal for tools and irrigate their crops. These inventions facilitated large-scale farming and the production of surpluses of grain, rice, and maize beyond the needs of day-to-day subsistence. An excess of foodstuffs supported greater population densities than ever before, including large cities. Through war, trading, and thievery, some individuals and families acquired and controlled vast areas of land, establishing themselves as rulers over large numbers of people. They traded their agricultural products with new specialized occupational classes that arose to serve their needs. Master builders constructed huge temples and palaces. Craftsmen made tools and decorative objects from metal (bronze, iron, copper, and gold). Priests controlled religious life, their prayers assuring the welfare and success of the ruler. Scribes invented writing to record trades of goods and services and the proclamations and history of their rulers. Traders invented money. Artists memorialized religious and courtly life. And professional musicians provided the rulers' entertainment and sung of their heroic deeds in epic ballads.

The four oldest city cultures, called **civilizations**, depended on the fertility of river valleys: the Nile River in Egypt; the Tigris and Euphrates River basin in present-day Iraq, an area known as Mesopotamia ("between the rivers" in Greek); the Indus River basin in South Asia where present-day India, Pakistan, and Afghanistan meet; and the Yellow and Yangtze River basins in China (see the map of ancient civilizations in Chapter 1). In addition to these four riverine cultures, the Greeks developed an urban culture supported by trading along the shores of the Mediterranean Sea. These societies were at the forefront of the technological, cultural, and social advances that, millennia later, spawned the modern societies we know today.

FIGURE 2.1

Entrance to the temple at Luxor along the banks of the Nile River, built around 1400 BCE

Source: MusikAnimal, Wikimedia Commons.

In addition to agriculture, the Ancient period witnessed three other important developments: (1) the invention of writing; (2) the spread of five religions (Hinduism, Buddhism, Judaism, Christianity, and Islam) to many corners of the world; and (3) the formation of the first large empires. The three principal musical legacies of these ancient empires and religions were: (1) the invention of stringed instruments still played today; (2) the development of written theories about the nature of music; and (3) religious rituals with chanting. This chapter contains gateways to three Ancient and Medieval religious traditions: Buddhism, Christianity, and Islam.

GATEWAY 4
BUDDHIST MUSIC

What Is It?

Our gateway to Buddhist music is a recording of a short excerpt of ritual practice by eight Tibetan Buddhist monks from Drepung, which was once the largest Buddhist monastic university in Tibet. To convey the underlying meaning of this section of ritual practice, the recording is titled "Invoking the Spirit of Kindness through Sound." Opening and closing instrumental sections bracket a middle section with chanting. It is one of thousands of chants performed during daily rituals and ceremonial occasions at this institution of higher learning.

CULTURAL
LINKAGES

The recording is the opening section of a much longer ritual. The instrumental ensemble performs an offering of sound, an invocation of a Buddha deity to come to the site of the ritual. Simultaneously practitioners and ritual music performers visualize the universe resounding with pleasant sound offerings vastly more extensive that what is audibly experienced. Other offerings, described in the written and chanted liturgical texts, accompany the sound offerings: water to wash (the body) with,

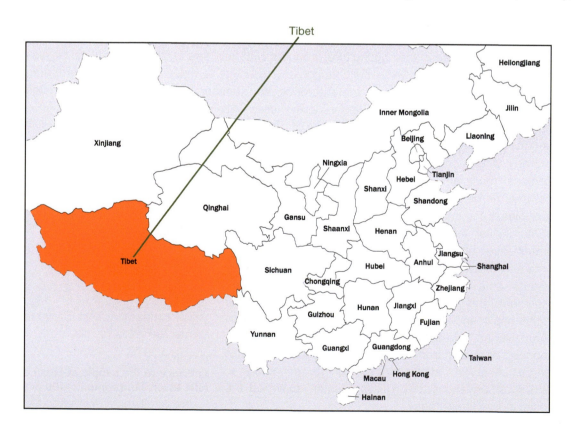

FIGURE 2.2
Map of Tibet, today part of China

water to drink, incense to please the olfactory sense, and delicious foods and other offerings to please the other senses.

 Listen to the first fifteen seconds or so.

How Does It Work?

Timbre

The instrumental ensemble consists of four pairs of instruments: two very long horns that rest on the ground, two double-reed wind instruments, two cymbals, and two double-headed frame drums. We also hear a male **chorus** of specialist ritual performers who are expert instrumentalists and trained vocalists. The vocalists create tones extraordinarily rich in overtones, an aural sheet of rippling sound.

Texture

The instrumental texture consists of a very low-pitched drone played on the two long horns, a few middle and high pitches played by the double-reed aerophones, a nearly continuous shimmering sound on the cymbals, and a rhythmic pattern on the drums. (**Aerophones** are instruments whose sound is produced by a vibrating column of air. In this case the vibration is started by two thin reeds striking one another.) The vocal texture consists of a very low-pitched drone sound with a few high-pitched overtones.

Rhythm

The rhythm varies from nonmetrical to beats that speed up and slow down. There is little sense of meter.

Melody

Discrete pitches are nearly absent in favor of sliding from pitch to pitch.

Harmony

Many pitches sound simultaneously. Each set of two instruments is tuned to play slightly different pitches to create a highly valued resonant beating or oscillation between them.

Form

The recording has an ABA' form, where A refers to the instrumental sections and B to the vocal chant. Each of these sections features very small changes in pitch, timbre, and loudness.

Performance Techniques

The ability of the singers to create sounding overtones from a fundamental requires extensive training.

FIGURE 2.3
Tibetan Buddhist monastery in India near the border with Tibet and Bhutan; it has links to the Drepung Monastic University built in Lhasa, Tibet (est. 1416) and rebuilt in South India during the 1960s
Source: Vikramjit Kakati, Wikimedia Commons.

FIGURE 2.4
Instrumental ensemble of Buddhist monks from another sect, playing instruments similar to those in this recording
Source: Getty Images.

Listen to the entire recording with these elements in mind, following the timed listening guide.

LISTENING GUIDE 2.1

TIME	SECTION	DESCRIPTION
0:00	A (Instrumental ensemble)	A pair of long horns play a very low pitch with slight variations in pitch, loudness, and timbre.
0:38		Cymbals enter with shimmering sounds.
1:10		The cymbals begin playing beats that speed up until they become a continuous shimmering sound.
1:20		Drums enter and the ensemble begins to play a very slow beat.
1:40		A pair of double-reed aerophones enter playing distinct pitches but with a lot of ornamental variation that colors the sound. The beats get faster and then slower, diminishing to just the cymbals and then silence.
3:02	B (Vocal chant)	The monks begin singing a very low pitch with variations in timbre from a relatively pure tone to one rich in overtones that sounds a bit like a growl. The monks produce a pitch high in their range, an overtone of the fundamental tone they are singing. The pitches and the vowel change slightly, and phrases end when the singers take a breath from time to time. There is a marked descent in pitch at the end of the singing.
6:04	A' (Instrumental ensemble	All the instruments of the ensemble enter nearly at the same time. The beats they play speed up throughout this section and the pitch rises.
6:44		The beats nearly disappear and then enter slowly becoming slower and softer until the music dies out.
7:20	End	

What Does It Mean?

This recording challenges many of our basic understandings of the way music works. This music appears to be extraordinarily slow moving with little in the way of a beat or a melody, two fundamental elements in the way we typically understand music. The basic pitch is extraordinarily low, one almost impossible for most men to sing. That suggests that these monks have had extensive training to learn to produce these low-pitched sounds. The sounds of cymbals and drums are familiar but the trumpet and double-reed sound may be rather unfamiliar. Knowing that this is religious music may help us to understand it. We might guess that the sound, as part of a religious ritual, has deep spiritual significance and that would be correct. But we might not guess that it is intended for entertainment and pleasure.

Our initial understandings of this tradition are, of course, based on our previous musical experience. Tibetan Buddhists trained in monastic universities have a completely different understanding of the music. For example, they would know that the apparently slow tempo of this chant is part of a huge corpus of chants with many different styles, including some that are quite fast with singable melodies. Some instrumental music has a strong, rapid beat and accompanies masked ritual dancing in sections that contrast with slow, graceful, and subtle movements of arms, hands, legs, and feet. And these trained experts would be able to read thousands of volumes of notated chant melodies using a line-based graphic notation that conveys the subtle and meaningful nuances of melodic movements. Explaining and understanding Tibetan music at something like this level of detail requires many years of study.

Buddhism consists of a highly varied set of principles and practices based on the teachings of Siddhartha Gautama (*c.* 563–483 BCE), who was born and grew up in the foothills of the Himalayas near the border between present-day India and Nepal. He grew up in a religious culture based on the idea of reincarnation, endless cycles of life that could only end with enlightenment or *nirvana*, a state of release from the troubles of the world and the cycles of life. Gautama achieved this state at the age of thirty-five and spent the rest of his life, until he died at age eighty, as an itinerant beggar, teaching the wisdom he had gained as Buddha, the Enlightened One. His teachings in the form of sermons called *sutras* were preserved by his disciples, who chanted them communally until they were written down as scripture in the first century BCE. To this day, monks preserve the Buddha's teaching and learn his path to wisdom and enlightenment, called *Dharma* ("Law" or "the teaching of Buddha"), by chanting his *sutras*. In Tibetan

CULTURAL LINKAGES

FIGURE 2.5
Tibetan statue of the Buddha
Source: Daderot, Wikimedia Commons.

Buddhism, the chanting of later texts called *tantras* and *mantras*, magical formulas representing deities, is also important. With the goal of achieving wisdom and ultimately *nirvana*, some monks spend as much as twenty to thirty years memorizing all these texts, which contain an encyclopedic body of knowledge.

When the Buddha was enlightened, he achieved vast knowledge and understanding that included the ability to see all his previous lives in cycles going back billions of years; a clairvoyant power to see the death and rebirth of all living beings "according to their good and bad deeds";[6] and the capacity to eliminate or transcend all his human cravings and desires. In the wake of his Enlightenment, his teachings focused on Four Noble Truths:[7] (1) the diagnosis that life is suffering; (2) the explanation that suffering is caused by craving; (3) the insight that suffering can end; and (4) treatment as a path leading to the end of suffering. Thus, as one scholar put it, "the ultimate goal of Buddhism is to put an end to suffering and rebirth . . . by fulfilling the human potential for goodness and happiness."[8]

The surest path to Enlightenment is through a lifetime of monastic devotion to the study of, and meditation on, the teachings of the Buddha. In Tibetan Buddhism, study and meditation are brought together in the chanting of a vast repertoire consisting of the *sutras* of Buddha, *tantras*, and *mantras* and instrumental music. Through meditation and extensive philosophical study under the guidance of qualified teachers, they explore their bodily experiences and mental life (feelings, moods, perceptions) with the help of *mudra*, *mantra*, and *mandala*, ritual practices representing the Body, Speech, and Mind of the the buddhas and the practitioners. *Mudra* is bodily gesture, stance, hand gestures, and imagery representing it. *Mantra* can be anything from repetition of a short formula to a lengthy descriptive liturgy or recitation of a sutra. The descriptive liturgy is connected to visualization practices that generate mental changes through meditation. The descriptions are materialized in *mandala*, which can be either individual deity images or an array of them in circular or tree-shaped or three-dimensional images. The richness of visual and aural practices and sacred dances in Tibetan music may be the result of a fusion of Buddhism from India with local animist practices called *Bon*, which recall in some ways Inner Asian nomadic pastoralists' beliefs in spirits.

AESTHETICS

Early Buddhists worried that instrumental music, singing, and dancing could create the very desires they sought to eliminate through study and meditation. However, the Buddha sanctioned chanting as a desirable and pleasurable middle ground between the dry asceticism of merely reciting his teachings and the distracting pleasures of secular music. The chanting and instrumental music we heard in this example are considered a "sensually pleasing offering" to the Buddha and to other deities, for the monks and nuns who recite them, and the lay people who hear them.[9] Thus, the music in this recording, perhaps rather unconventionally beautiful in terms of the musical elements familiar to us, is in fact a serious and demanding practice developed, through years of training, into music even more beautiful and entertaining than any secular music. "This music," one Tibetan monk said, "is more beneficial than a hundred years of meditation."[10]

CULTURAL LINKAGES

Ritual performances of chants and instrumental music take up an enormous amount of time in monastery life. The largest Tibetan monasteries may have as many as 10,000 residents, with 2000 of them being music specialists. They recite some texts, chant others in a melodic style, and perform still others in the long drawn-out manner emphasizing subtle pitch and timbral changes heard in this example. Many Tibetans are semi-nomadic pastoralists (yak, sheep, goats, horses, cows), and the earliest descriptions of these sounds suggest a link to animal sounds of the sort imitated by Tuvan pastoralists. The Buddha was said to be able to imitate the voices of birds and wild animals, and the Bon religion acknowledged "nine vocal modulations," including "the dog's voice, barking and growling, . . . the beautiful-voiced parrot, . . . [and] the fluctuating voice of the lark."[11] Monks learn to meditate on the sounds actually heard in their chanting and instrumental music and those that exist only in the imagination. They distinguish between four types of vocal production: a throat voice, a mouth voice, a nose voice, and in this recording a "body-cavity voice."[12] Produced by tensing muscles in the throat and diaphragm and applying great breath pressure, it is considered the most beautiful and ritually significant of all the voices. They distinguish two styles of "tone-color chants":[13] the "voice of the hybrid yak-bull"[14] and the "roaring voice of the [slayer of the] Lord of Death." These are considered particularly fierce chants.

The monks also learn to play musical instruments, which in addition to the ones heard in this recording, famously include trumpets made of conch shells and human thigh bones and small drums made from human skulls. The instrumental music represents iconically a combination of the melodic style of chant, which is played on the double-reed instruments, and the tone-color, deep-toned chant of the body-cavity voice, which is played on the long trumpets. Even absent the words of the chant, they form an aural field that aids meditation and pleases the perfect hearing of the Buddha and other deities and those monks initiated into the beauty of this style of musical performance. They recognize the music as sounding fierce, the sort of sound necessary to destroy the evil forces arrayed around them.

What Is Its History?

Buddhism adopted ideas of the cycle of rebirths and the law of causation through deeds (karma) prevalent in ancient India. After the Buddha's death, his disciples and later monks have preserved his teachings in ritual chanting to the present day. Between 100 BCE and 100 CE a schism developed between adherents of older forms of Buddhist teaching, now known as Theraveda Buddhism, and a newer form, Mahayana (Great Vehicle) Buddhism, which teaches that some beings on their way to Enlightenment, called *bodhisattvas*, can transcend their own personal concern for Enlightenment to help others achieve it. In India such teachers are known as *gurus*; in Tibet they are called *lamas*.

Theravada Buddhism is the type found today in Southeast Asia (Burma, Thailand, and the Indonesian island of Bali). It spread south throughout India until it reached Sri Lanka in about 250 BCE. There, in about 80 BCE, the Buddha's sutras were written down for the first time. From the fifth to the fifteenth century CE, Theravada Buddhism spread to Burma and Thailand, where it coexisted for a time with Hinduism, which today is the principal religion of the Indonesian island of Bali. Mahayana Buddhism spread north into Inner Asia and to China during the Han Dynasty (206 BCE to 220 CE). It arrived in Japan from Korea in the sixth century and entered Tibet between 700 and 900 CE. Wherever Buddhism took root in Asia, it had a slightly different character and different ideas about how to combine the study of scripture with meditation to traverse the path to Enlightenment.

Although we introduce Buddhism at this point in our music history because of its beginnings in the life of Buddha, Buddhism and Buddhist music in Tibet and elsewhere have their own histories of development since then. Buddhism was introduced to Tibet in the seventh century. After the fall of the Tibetan Empire in the ninth century, new sects arose in the eleventh and fourteenth centuries. The drawn out "body-cavity" chant style in this recording has been traced to the eighth century. The cymbals and drums are the oldest of the instruments in the ensemble. The long horns were introduced in the eleventh century, written musical notation in the thirteenth century, and the double-reed instruments in the fifteenth or sixteenth century. Monasteries became an important institution in the sixteenth century, in some ways rivaling and threatening secular governmental structures.

With few exceptions, the leader of one school of Tibetan Buddhism, the Gelugpa sect, a Dalai Lama ("Ocean of Wisdom") believed to be a reincarnation of the *bodhisattva* of compassion, was also the political ruler of Tibet. From 1642 to 1912 Tibet was a protectorate of the Qing emperors of the last imperial dynasty of China. After the fall of the Qing Empire in 1912, Tibet maintained its independence until 1951, when a military invasion forced it to incorporate into the newly created People's Republic of China, ruled by the Communist Party of China. The Chinese communist government, officially atheistic, took a malign view of this religion. The 1950s until the later 1970s saw the destruction of temples, monasteries, and sacred art. The Fourteenth Dalai Lama (b. 1936) decided to leave Tibet for his own safety in 1959. Since then, Tibetan Buddhist monasteries have been re-established in neighboring Nepal, India, Sikkim, and Bhutan, and monks and have established learning centers in many countries around the world. In Tibet in the late 1980s many monasteries and temples were rebuilt atop old ruins. In recent years there has been official but measured tolerance of Buddhism in some regions, but repression continues in many ways.

Recordings of Tibetan Buddhist music were part of the world music scene in the 1960s and found a following among musicians who championed their music and sponsored concert tours, notably Mickey Hart, drummer for the Grateful Dead, who said of these monks' chanting, "They will rattle your bones."[15]

WHERE DO I GO FROM HERE?[16]

- Listen to other recordings of Tibetan Buddhist chant.
- Watch some videos of Tibetan Buddhist rituals and ritual dancing.
- Read about and view Tibetan Buddhist art and architecture on the internet, in online galleries, or books you find in the library.
- Listen to Japanese *shomyo* Buddhist chant. It is different from Tibetan Buddhist chant but shares a similar characteristic of sliding between pitches.

GATEWAY 5
CHRISTIAN CHANT[17]

What Is It?

Our gateway to Christian chant is a composition in the Roman Catholic tradition called "Quia ergo femina" (Since therefore a woman) by Hildegard von Bingen (1098–1179).[18] A nun and founder of a convent near the small town of Bingen on the Rhine River in Germany, she wrote the music and text, which praises the Virgin Mary as the greatest example of the female form or idea since God made Man. In "Quia ergo femina," Mary is depicted as greater than Eve herself, who could not conquer death, as the Virgin did, through her son. Although the piece was composed for nuns to sing during religious services, this modern performance, by a small ensemble of women singers called the Mediatrix Ensemble, is intended for secular concerts.

 Listen to the first thirty seconds of the recording.

How Does It Work?

Timbre

Women's voices sing with a relative clear, pure, relaxed tone quality.

FIGURE 2.6
Hildegard von Bingen receives divine inspiration and passes it on to her scribe
Source: Rupertsburger Codex, Wikimedia Commons.

Texture

The texture is monophonic, sung in **unison**, that is at the same pitch, by a choir.

Rhythm

The rhythm is nonmetrical and relatively free, with some mix of short and long tones.

Melody

The melody moves mainly in **stepwise**, **conjunct motion**. This phrase is used to describe melodies that mainly move through adjacent pitches of a scale. The melody occasionally employs **disjunct melodic motion**, that is, leaps from one pitch to nonadjacent pitches in the scale. The melody employs a seven-tone, heptatonic scale.

Harmony

Since the texture is monophonic, there is no harmony in this example.

Form

The form consists of a series of melodic phrases each with new musical material (a b c d, and so on). However, the stepwise motion using a scale of seven pitches creates a sense of unity. Against that unity, each melodic phrase has a unique character, some rising, some falling, some arc-shaped, some undulating, some with a few leaps, some with mainly stepwise motion. The form is also shaped by the way the music is matched to the text. Some syllables are set on just one or two pitches (called **syllabic singing**); other syllables have many pitches (called **melismatic singing**). A **melisma** is a single syllable set to many pitches.

Performance Techniques

The singers perform straight tones without vibrato, ornamentation, or changes in dynamics.

Listen to the first thirty seconds of the recording and pay attention to the unison monophonic texture and the stepwise melodic motion.

Listen to the entire recording following this timed listening guide.

LISTENING GUIDE 2.2

TIME	LATIN	ENGLISH	DESCRIPTION
0:00	*Quia ergo femina*	Because therefore a woman [Eve]	The melody ascends with two leaps.
0:10	*mortem instruxit,*	battled death,	The melody descends mainly stepwise, but with some leaps.
0:24	*clara virgo illam interemit,*	a bright virgin defeated it.	The melody descends before leaping through two large intervals to a pitch an octave above where it started.
0:45	*et ideo est summa benedictio*	And so the greatest blessing	The melody undulates in stepwise motion
0:57	*in feminea forma*	in the female form,	The melody descends in stepwise motion and then continues with an undulating motion.
1:10	*pre omni creatura,*	before every creature	The melody stays in a narrow range. Range is the distance between the highest and lowest pitches in a section or piece of music.
1:18	*quia Deus factus est homo*	since God made man,	The melody rises and falls in stepwise motion through an octave range.
1:31	*in dulcissima et beata virgine*	is the sweet and blessed Virgin	The melody moves in stepwise motion through a narrow range.
1:52	End		

What Does It Mean?

The calm, relaxed sound of monophonic Christian chanting echoing through a large church or cathedral creates a sonic icon of other-worldliness. For believers, it suggests that the chanting of the monks or nuns is resonating in heaven and that God is listening to the praises in the sacred Latin texts, many of them taken from the Bible. Its pure vocal quality, moderate tempo, nearly equal-length tones, and relatively smooth, stepwise motion lend dignity to the ceremonial events of the **liturgies** (the ritual rules and practices for sacred services) of the Catholic Church. The sound of chanting is as important as the meaning of the text for the spiritual efficacy of the liturgy.

Hildegard's artistry and her expression of emotion and meaning are carried in the variety of melodic motions she creates and her use of melismas on certain syllables of the text. Before Hildegard, traditional Christian chant emphasized stepwise motion, so her use of leaps, especially an upward leap on the first syllable of *virgo* (Virgin) is, in this context, an ecstatic expression of joy and admiration. In each line, one syllable of an important word is singled out for expressive treatment with a long melisma: *femina* (woman); *mortem* (death); *virgo* (Virgin); two syllables of *feminea*

CULTURAL LINKAGES

EMOTIONAL RESONANCE

(female) in the line *"in feminea forma"*; Deus (God); and, in the last line, all three syllables of *virgine* (Virgin). Hildegard, using the monophonic texture of her time, creates music with deep emotional resonance from what may seem to us like the tiniest of melodic gestures. It is tempting to interpret the ascending melodies of the first and third phrases, which mention women and the Virgin, and the descending melody of the second phrase, "battling death," as musical representations of celebration and struggle, respectively. Such text painting was common in later centuries, and it seems to be a characteristic feature of her musical style.

SOCIAL BEHAVIOR ▷

Meaning in this example comes from the simple fact that a woman composed it, and women are singing it, in what was and remains a strongly patriarchal tradition. Hildegard herself disclaimed authorship of the text and music and believed that she was a mere conduit for Divine creativity. The text juxtaposes and exalts the two most important women in Christianity, Eve and Mary, praising Mary in terms analogous to the way the Church praises Jesus. In the context of a religion that only allows male priests, Hildegard's person and compositions argue for the perfection of women as well as men.

The tenth child of a noble, land-owning family, Hildegard was given to a Benedictine monastery as a tithe at the age of eight. There she came under the influence of an anchoress, a woman who lived in contemplative isolation in a cell in the monastery and who taught her the biblical psalms. At fifteen she became a nun, and soon her and her mentor's teaching attracted a growing number of women to the monastery. At thirty-eight, after the death of her teacher, she was elected the head of the assembled nuns. At the age of forty-two, she experienced her first mystical vision, in which "the heavens were opened to me and a blinding light of exceptional brilliance flowed through my entire brain. And so it kindled my whole heart and breast like a flame, not burning but warming . . . Suddenly I understood the expositions of the books . . . of the Old and New Testaments."[19] Although she also received a command from God to write down her vision, she was at first reluctant, due to "a low opinion (of myself)." Eventually, she began to write them down with the aid of a male secretary. When the pope read them, he interpreted them as authentic "secrets of God" and commanded her to transcribe what she, and he, believed to be the word of God. In other words, they both considered her to be, like Jesus and other Biblical figures, a prophet.

As her fame grew, the number of nuns at the monastery increased until, at fifty-two, she took them, over the objections of the abbot, to a spot on the Rhine River near the town of Bingen, where she founded a convent. At sixty-seven she founded a second convent across the river from the first. She composed much of her religious poetry and music for services at those nunneries. She also wrote extensive volumes on a wide range of matters including natural history, medical practices of the period, theology, and music. She was one of the most prolific writers and composers of the period, at a time when most women could not even write a letter. In a patriarchal church, her success as a writer was possible because her knowledge and insights were "Divine secrets," not her own insights. For this reason, she refused the sort of agency and authorship that men claimed for their writing. She preached publicly in several cities, where she helped with exorcisms and cured the blind using water from the Rhine. After her death, she was proposed for sainthood, which the Church refused. She was beatified instead. Although she was called St. Hildegard for centuries, she was canonized a saint only in 2012.

CULTURAL LINKAGES ▷

Her musical compositions were intended for the liturgies of her convents and were probably not known beyond them. Two main types of services developed in the Church governed from Rome. One was for the Mass, the celebration of Christ's Last Supper with his disciples before his death and resurrection. Performed for lay people in church and by monks and nuns in monasteries and convents, the Mass liturgy includes a prescribed succession of chants, prayers, sermons or homilies, and lessons (readings from the Bible). The chants, like ceremonial processions, the priests' elaborate vestments, the smell of incense, the chiming of bells, and the opulence of church architecture, were designed to amplify the meaning and impact of the prayers and lessons on those in attendance. The chants for the Mass are of two types: those **proper** to the particular day in the church calendar and **ordinary** ones sung during every Mass. The texts of the proper and ordinary chants were taken from passages in the Bible and from the teachings of early religious leaders such as St. Augustine, St. Benedict, St. Ambrose, and St. Gregory, called the Four Doctors of the Church. In 2012 Pope Benedict XVI declared Hildegard a Doctor of the Church for her contributions to theology and doctrine.

The second type of liturgy was developed for the ceremonial life of monasteries and convents, where monks and nuns spend many hours each day, from before dawn into the night, in a set of eight prayer services called Divine Offices (Duties) or "hours." Hildegard's "Quia ergo femina" is for these services. The chants for these services were based on the Old Testament Book of Psalms. During one week of offices the monks and nuns perform all 150 **psalms** (Biblical poems in praise of God). The Old Testament psalms were introduced by newly composed chanted texts, called **antiphons**. Antiphons in general, and Hildegard's in particular, were more musically elaborate than the psalms, each line of which was often recited mainly on a single tone with a short opening and closing melodic gesture. Some antiphons asked for God's mercy and help with such practical matters as the weather and the fertility of animals and crops. Others related the message of the Old Testament psalm to ideas in the New Testament, especially veneration of Jesus and the Virgin Mary. Hildegard's "Quia ergo femina" is just such a composition, linking New Testament Mary to Old Testament Eve.

What Is Its History?

Christian chanting has roots deep in human history not least because Catholic liturgies use texts from the Jewish Torah, the first five books of the Bible, dated to around the seventh century BCE, and other books of the Old Testament. The Old Testament Book of Psalms, the basic text of the Divine Offices, contains songs composed over many centuries after about 500 BCE. Some attributed apocryphally to King David, who reigned about 1000 BCE and was a singer and poet (psalmist) and player of the lyre. (The **lyre** is a stringed instrument with a resonating body and a frame holding five or six strings, which are plucked.) The Christian liturgy, including the chanting of psalms, may have been shaped in some way by Jewish liturgy and chants, but making any precise link is virtually impossible. This early Christian chant tradition is also historically important because some music terminology and musical notation were developed to serve it.

Christian liturgical practices developed slowly following Christ's crucifixion. They grew in complexity after Emperor Constantine adopted Christianity as the official religion of the Roman Empire in 324 CE. Sometime around 500 CE these liturgies began to take the shape they have today, aided by the foundation of monastic orders. St. Benedict (480–543) developed the first one in central Italy and wrote the first rules for monastic behavior around 530. Huge numbers of chants developed to serve the Divine Offices and Masses, which were performed daily as well as special ones on Sunday and important events in the Christian calendar such as Christmas, Easter, and saints' days. The chants were created and transmitted in oral tradition, and monks and priests had to learn and memorize hundreds of chants. Large churches supported schools where young boys were trained for a decade or more before they took up the priesthood or became monks. It helped that many chants were formulaic, that is, they were based on melodic formulas, relatively short melodic passages used over and over in many chants and, as a result, easily remembered. Still, some traditional chants were elaborate and unique and had to be memorized, as did new compositions such as Hildegard's antiphons.

FIGURE 2.7
Achilles playing a lyre, c. 480 BCE
Source: Marie-Lan Nguyen, Wikimedia Commons.

FIGURE 2.8

Map of the Holy Roman Empire around 1000

Source: OwenBlacker, Wikimedia Commons.

CULTURAL LINKAGES

Today we know this repertoire of music, developed in these early years of Christianity, because it began to be written down in a form of musical notation in the ninth century at the court of the Emperor Charlemagne in northern Europe. After the fall of the Roman Empire in 476, Charlemagne's family of Germanic language-speaking people known as Franks established in 751 the first large-scale political entity in western Europe, known as the Holy Roman Empire. Today both Germany and France trace their roots to this empire. The French call Charlemagne Charles the Great, the Germans Karl der Grosse.

Charlemagne (c. 747–814), the third ruler in his family's dynasty, became king in 768. On Christmas Day of 800, he crowned himself Emperor of the Holy Roman Empire, which covered much of western Europe, including the city of Rome. In a ceremony at St. Peter's Basilica in Rome, the pope conveyed to him the status of the Christian emperors of Rome. Charlemagne was an able administrator, directing reforms in virtually all domains of life from governmental, economic, and military matters to culture, literacy, and religion. Anxious to establish his empire as the legitimate successor to Rome and its Christian heritage, he supported monastic life, schools, and *scriptoria* (manuscript-copying rooms). Musical notations, copied in *scriptoria*, were a way to regulate and preserve the liturgical practices of his empire. Hildegard's writings and compositions are a legacy of Charlemagne's support of Latin literacy and the Roman Church in a rebirth of learning after the fall of the Roman Empire. Eager to invest the religious practices of his dynasty with the prestige of Rome, his reforms of chant singing and their preservation in notation were given the name **Gregorian chant** in honor of Pope St. Gregory I, who had reigned two centuries earlier from 590 to 604. Enormously successful in theology and church politics, Pope Gregory was apocryphally credited with writing these chants. More likely, they were traditional chants with no known authors.

During the ninth century the first musical notation in this tradition helped to regularize and discipline the singing of monks and priests. It used a combination of dots or points and curved lines, a collection of symbols called **neumes**, to indicate the shape and character of the melody, a kind of graphic representation of the shape of chant melody. Neumes written above the text were used as an aid in learning and remembering the chants, but they failed to register the intervallic relationships between pitches, as modern notation does. The desire to do so was stimulated when monks studying Ancient Greek manuscripts learned of Ancient Greeks' music theory and philosophy.

The first of these Ancient Greek music theorists, and the first to call himself a philosopher, was Pythagoras (c. 570–c. 495 BCE). A mathematician (remember the Pythagorean Theorem), he discovered that many basic musical intervals could be explained by ratios of small whole numbers. The two pitches of an octave vibrate in a ratio of 2:1. Each pitch in a scale is called a **scale degree**. The final pitch of a chant melody is called the **final**, and it is assigned the first scale degree. The first scale degree is also indicated with the Arabic numeral one (1). Other pitches in the scale are assigned numbers in ascending order: second degree (2), third degree (3), and so forth. The interval between the first degree and the fifth degree of a heptatonic scale has a ratio of 3:2. The interval between the first and the fourth degree has a ratio of 4:3. And the interval between the first and the second degrees has a ratio of 9:8. Pythagoras believed that these ratios also governed astronomical relationships among stars and planets and created what he called "the harmony of the spheres."

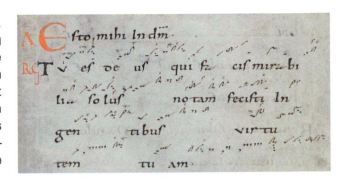

FIGURE 2.9
Christian chant notation using neumes

Medieval Christian theologians applied these Ancient Greek explanations of the workings of the cosmos to Christian theology about heaven and earth, God and humankind, and body and soul. The most famous of them, Boethius, a Roman senator who lived from *c.* 480 to *c.* 524, reconstructed Ancient Greek music theory, which had been lost for many centuries. The Greeks gave letters to pitches, used them as a musical notation, and constructed an elaborate classification of melodic scales. They named the scales after various Greek ethnic groups such as the Dorians, Ionians, and Phrygians and assigned ethical qualities to each **mode** based on stereotypes about the behavior of these groups. The philosopher Plato (*c.* 428–348 BCE) famously argued that some scales should be avoided because they caused the bad behaviors associated with particular ethnic groups while other scales could be used fruitfully for the education of philosopher-kings.

Christian scholars adapted these Ancient Greek ideas about scales to a set of four scales to which they gave the Greek names Dorian, Phrygian, Lydian, and Mixolydian but without assigning ethical qualities to them, as the Greeks had. These four scales are called **modes** because they are, in a sense, different manners of making melodies. Each mode has a **final**, that is, the pitch on which a chant ends. And Boethius gave each step in a heptatonic scale a letter name: A B C D E F G. Each of the four modes has a final on a different step of the collection of seven pitches:

Dorian mode	=	D	E	F	G	A	B	C	(D)
Phrygian mode	=	E	F	G	A	B	C	D	(E)
Lydian mode	=	F	G	A	B	C	D	E	(F)
Mixolydian mode	=	G	A	B	C	D	E	F	(G)

These modes based on scales with whole steps and half steps are called **diatonic scales**. The distances between these scale degrees are not equal, as they are in 'Are'are music. These heptatonic scales have two sizes of intervals, whole steps and half steps. If the number 1 equals a whole step and 1/2 equals a half step, then here are intervals in a heptatonic scale, starting on A:

```
 1   1/2   1   1   1/2   1   1
 A    B    C   D    E    F   G   (A)
```

Hildegard's "Quia ergo femina" has a final on E, so it is in the Phrygian mode. Its intervallic pattern is:

```
 1/2   1   1   1   1/2   1   1
  E    F   G   A    B    C   D   (E)
```

Much later, during the sixteenth century, modes on A, C, and B were added to complete this system. Later still, the mode on A came to be known as the minor mode and the mode on C as the major mode. Those two modes, rather than the original four, became the basis for European music after 1500 and popular music and jazz in the twentieth century. Around 1960 jazz musicians developed a style that became known as "modal jazz." It explored the melodic and harmonic possibilities of these Medieval Christian modes.

The composers of early Gregorian chant are not known. They were transmitted in oral tradition until they were written down in the ninth century. Beginning in the tenth century, the names of composers of new chants, such as for local saints, began to be notated. Not technically Gregorian chant (because they cannot be attributed to Gregory), they were somewhat more elaborate in musical style than the older traditional chants. Hildegard's compositions from the twelfth century fall into this category. Today the term Gregorian chant is commonly used to encompass all monophonic Christian chanting, including the chants of Hildegard.

As the size of the chant repertoire grew with new compositions, problems of transmission and memorization grew with them. The theory of modes led teachers to emphasize intervallic relationships in a given mode, something not indicated in musical notation with neumes. Guido of Arezzo (*c.* 991–*c.* 1033), a Benedictine monk from central Italy, solved these problems in two ways. First, to aid the teaching of chant, he invented a system of note names based on the first syllables of a six-line poem (*ut-re-mi-fa-sol-la*). Singers could sing these syllables more conveniently than the letter names for pitches. Called **solmization** or **solfege**, the system later changed *ut* to *do* and added a seventh pitch name, *ti*. This modified eleventh-century pedagogical technique is still used today to train musicians. It was famously the basis for the song "Do-Re-Mi" from the Rodgers and Hammerstein 1959 Broadway musical, *The Sound of Music*. Second, to specify the intervals of chant more precisely, Guido placed the neumes on a four-line **staff**, a set of four equally spaced lines. He placed one of two clefs (keys) at the beginning of the staff to indicate which pitches were assigned to which lines: the letter C, the C clef, was placed on the line for the pitch C; the letter F, the F clef, was placed on the line for the pitch F. Guido claimed that his pedagogical techniques would eliminate

FIGURE 2.10
Guido of Arezzo's four-line staff notation (1335–1345)
Source: Codex Sangallensis 359, Wikimedia Commons.

the poor performances he observed during services and the variations he heard from church to church and monastery to monastery. He wrote, "Who does not bewail . . . that when we celebrate the Divine Office we are often seen rather to strive among ourselves than to praise God? One scarcely agrees with another, neither the pupil with his master, nor the pupil with his colleague."[20] And he claimed that, whereas teaching the entire repertoire of a monastery's chants in oral tradition could take ten years, he and his "helpers . . . can produce a perfect singer in the space of one year, or at the most two." In 1028 the pope invited him to Rome to demonstrate his new techniques.

FIGURE 2.11
The Modern Grand Staff

In the thirteenth century, as the range of music expanded, a fifth line was added to form the five-line staff used today. A G clef was added to the C and F clefs, and today the G and F clefs are combined in the **Grand Staff**, two parallel five-line staves linked together. The top staff uses the G clef, called the **treble clef**; the lower staff uses the F clef, called the **bass clef**. The C clef, called the **alto** or **tenor** clef, can be placed on any line of the staff and is used for instrumental parts in the middle range.

In the sixteenth century the Catholic Church thought it necessary to revise chanting to bring it into line with new developments in polyphonic music. Reacting to what seemed like permission to revise and even replace old chant melodies with new ones, the French in the seventeenth and eighteenth centuries massively changed their chant repertoire. Composer-priests in other countries followed suit. Perhaps in response to the French Revolution of 1789, a conservative reaction during the nineteenth century led to the restoration of old Gregorian chant, first in France and then elsewhere. Spearheaded by monks at the Benedictine Abbey of Solesmes in northwest France, this revival stimulated a tremendous amount of scholarship on Gregorian chant and is the source of the sound of the Gregorian chanting we hear today.

The central role of Gregorian chant in the Roman Catholic liturgy ended with the Second Vatican Council (1962–1965), which allowed vernacular (that is, local) languages to replace Latin in the Mass and popular and local traditional music styles to replace Gregorian chanting. Reformers hoped to make the Mass more attractive to modern congregations. After a hiatus, the Latin Mass has been revived in some locales, and Divine Offices in Latin continue in monasteries and convents. Recordings of Gregorian chant occasionally make their way to the top of the *Billboard Magazine* classical music charts, including one in 2015 called *Benedicta: Marian Chants from Norcia* by the monks of St. Benedict's Monastery in Norcia, Italy. One chant, "Dies irae" (Day of Wrath), performed as part of the Proper of every funeral Mass and during three days set aside for honoring the dead—in the United States Halloween, All Saints' Day, and All Souls' Day and in Mexico the Day of the Dead or *Día de los Muertos* (October 31 to November 2)—has lived a long life as an index of death in many secular classical compositions and in popular music and film, including *The Exorcist* (1973) and *The Shining* (1980).

WHERE DO I GO FROM HERE?

- Listen to examples of monastery choirs such as *Benedicta: Marian Chants from Norcia* singing traditional Gregorian chant. Compare their style of Gregorian chant to Hildegard's newer "Quia ergo femina."

- While Roman Gregorian chant has been the most influential in the history European music, other early Christian chant traditions are well worth listening to. Listen to some of these and compare them to each other and to Gregorian chant: Ambrosian chant, from Northern Italy, and named for St. Ambrose, the fourth-century Bishop of Milan; or Byzantine chant of the Greek Orthodox Church; note their use of ornamentation and drone; or Armenian chant; or Syriac (Syrian) chant, sung in a dialect of Aramaic, Jesus' language; or Ethiopian Orthodox chant.

- Listen to Jewish chant of the Ashkenazic (European) and Sephardic (North African and Spanish) traditions.

- Find sources for the life and work of Hildegard von Bingen and read them.

GATEWAY 6
QUR'ANIC CHANT[21]

What Is It?

Our gateway to Qur'anic chant is a passage from the Qur'an recited by Sheikh Hamza Shakkur (1947–2008) from the Great Mosque in Damascus, Syria.

 Listen to the first thirty seconds of the recording.

How Does It Work?

Timbre

The reciter chants in a relaxed, resonant low-pitched voice in the beginning and then moves slightly higher in his range.

FIGURE 2.12
Qur'anic reciter Sheikh Hamza Shakkur
Source: Al-Kindi Ensemble.

Texture

The texture is monophonic, a solo male voice without accompaniment.

Rhythm

The meter is nonmetrical, without a beat. The rhythm varies from one tone for each syllable of text (syllabic singing) to a few tones for each syllable (melismatic singing).

Melody

The melody is based on a seven-tone scale with a few additional pitches. The melody moves principally in a smooth stepwise motion.

Harmony

This is monophonic chanting, so there is no harmony.

Form

The form consists of many improvised phrases. The performance begins with just two pitches and very gradually and continuously adds higher and higher pitches until it reaches its highest pitch two octaves above the final about two thirds of the way through the recitation.

Performance Techniques

The reciter starts by chanting rather plainly but then begins to add subtle ornaments as he proceeds through the text. At the ends of phrases the reciter clearly pronounces the consonant and guttural vowels of the Arabic language in the Qur'an.

 Listen to the first sixty seconds for the increasing phrase lengths and the gradual addition of pitches.

All Qur'anic recitations begin with the same line of text (in Arabic): "In the name of God the compassionate, the merciful." This particular recitation is an excerpt from Book 3 of the Qur'an: "The Family of 'Imran." After the formulaic opening, it begins, "God chose Adam and Noah and the family of Abraham and the family of 'Imran above all his creatures." It goes on to tell the story of the wife of 'Imran, who dedicated her child, Mary, to God's service. An angel tells Mary that, although "no man has touched" her, she will give birth to a child whose "name is the Messiah, Jesus." Qur'anic portions always end with these words: "In the name of God the most merciful, the most compassionate. God, the Great, has spoken the truth."

CULTURAL LINKAGES

Listen to the first three minutes or so of the recording following this timed listening guide.

TIME	PHRASE	DESCRIPTION
0:00		**Section A with low-pitched tonal center.**
	1	A short phrase on two pitches a whole step apart. A whole step is also called a **major second**. He ends on the higher pitch, establishing it as the final, also called the **tonal center** or **tonic**.
0:12	2	Another short phrase, this one with two new pitches (the second and third degrees of the scale) above the tonal center.
0:23	3	A longer phrase with four pitches and with some slight melodic ornaments toward the end.
0:45	4	A slightly longer phrase that begins with a leap to the fourth degree of the scale, later adds the fifth degree, and ends on the fourth degree.
1:04	5	Begins on the seventh degree of the scale and descends in a rapid stepwise run to the third degree and continues with mostly stepwise motion to a cadence on the tonal center. A **cadence** is a musical marker of the end of a section or piece of music.
1:15	6	Repeats familiar pitches in a short phrase emphasizing the fourth degree of the scale.
1:30	7	A long phrase on the middle pitches of the scale, again emphasizing the fourth degree of the scale.
1:52	8	Begins on the fifth degree of the scale, adds a new pitch, the sixth degree of the scale and then sings a new descending interval before descending to the tonal center.
2:11	9	A short phrase on familiar pitches.
2:23		**Section B with higher-pitched tonal center on the fourth degree.**
	10	Adds the higher octave seventh degree of the scale and engages in extensive melodic runs (melismas) on a single syllable, ending on the fourth degree. From here on the fourth degree of the scale is the new tonal center.
2:41	11 and beyond	Sings in the high part of the range, on the fourth, fifth, sixth, and seventh degrees of the original scale.
4:04		Rises to a new high pitch, the octave above the original tonal center, and for the rest of the passage sings predominantly on five pitches between the fourth degree and the octave with the fourth degree continuing as the tonal center.
5:52	End	

LISTENING GUIDE 2.3

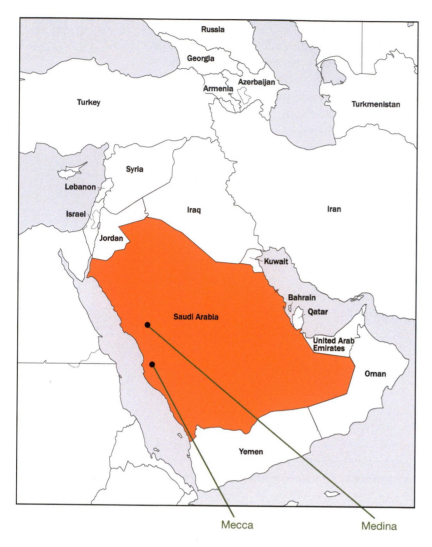

FIGURE 2.13
Map of the Arabian Peninsula with the cities of Mecca and Medina

What Does It Mean?

The Qur'an is the holy text of Islam. Muslims believe it is the final revelation of God's will for humankind, succeeding and perfecting earlier ones to Adam, Abraham, Moses, Jesus, and some others not known to the Jewish and Christian traditions. The angel Gabriel recited its verses to the Prophet Muhammad (c. 570–632 CE), who lived in the cities of Mecca and Medina on the Arabian Peninsula, in a series of revelations between 609 and 632. Muhammad preached the lessons of the Qur'an during his lifetime, starting with family and friends and then to a widening circle of pagans and Jews on the Arabian Peninsula. In the late seventh century, after Muhammad's death, the recited revelations were compiled into a book of 114 chapters containing three to 286 verses each, plus an opening prayer of seven verses. Muslims around the world study Qur'an translated into their local language. But it is always recited in Arabic, and its recitation fills the soundscape of the Islamic world: in mosques, on the radio, and on the streets.

The word Qur'an comes from a root word meaning to recite, and it is in this recited form, more than through study of the written text, that it has its most powerful effects on the faithful. Children are taught to memorize parts of the Qur'an as a pathway to understanding. Someone who memorizes the entire Qur'an is called a *hafiz*, and some of these become professional reciters like Hamza Shakkur. The Qur'an proclaims monotheism and opposes paganism; tells stories of earlier prophets like Abraham and Jesus; prescribes righteous behavior, including submission to God's will and obligatory acts (the pillars) of worship (recitation of its creed, daily prayers, giving alms to the poor, fasting during the holy month of Ramadan, and a pilgrimage to Mecca); and warns of the fate of believers and nonbelievers on Judgment Day. The simplest statement of its creed is "There is no God but God, and Muhammad is his prophet." The text of the Qur'an is considered the standard for the vocabulary and grammar of classical literary Arabic. The way reciters pronounce the words is the model for speaking classical Arabic.

To believers, both the words of the Qur'an and sound of its recitation are profoundly moving because together they recreate the moment of God's revelation to Muhammad. In other words, the Qur'an is meant to be recited. The words and their recitation represent "divine and inimitable beauty," and they must be performed with absolute accuracy.[22] Since the very sound of the words comes from God, many rules, called *tajwid*, govern pronunciation and require lengthy study. Reciters also spend years studying the meaning of the words. Even the pauses in the recitation, so prominent in this recording, are crucially important and subject to the rules of *tajwid*. They signal the reciter's understanding of the text and give the listeners time to absorb and reflect on its meaning. Because of the prestige of the Qur'an's language, some secular singers practice Qur'anic recitation to improve their pronunciation of Arabic song texts.

Muslims have taken two contrasting positions on the musical qualities of the recitation, which include its melody, ornamentation, rhythm, and the voice quality of the reciter. Some Muslims associate music with evil in the form of distractions from proper religious observance, captured in the English expressions as "wine, women, and song." Conservative Muslims censor excessive displays of musical skill on the part of a reciter and insist on a clear distinction between singing a song and reciting or chanting the Qur'an. Other less conservative but also devout Muslims acknowledge the power of music to affect the human spirit (it "calms the child and refreshes the camel on the long journey")[23] and value highly the musicality of reciters' performances. They argue that "the beautiful melody is a spirit from God which revives burning hearts"[24] and makes people kinder and gentler. Both camps agree that music is powerful, but one takes a negative and the other a conditionally positive view, the condition depending on intent: the musical qualities of the recitation must serve devotion to God in both the reciter and listener. Reciters must manage this tension in their performances. If they try to please the first group with a spare, barely musical performance, others may find it boring and unmoving. But if it is too beautiful, it may distract listeners from the meaning of the text. Navigating this divide is a source of excitement for discerning listeners.

AESTHETICS

To enhance the musical qualities of their recitations, many professional reciters study, in addition to the meaning and rules of the text, the Arab secular classical music system, which forms the musical foundation of their recitations. This system was codified in the tenth century and includes an extensive set of melodic modes, called *maqamat* (sg. *maqam*). A **maqam** is a melodic mode that specifies intervals between pitches, characteristic melodic gestures, the addition of chromatic pitches, and typical modulations to other *maqamat*. (**Modulation** refers to changes in one or another element of music: a modal modulation, a key modulation, a metric modulation, and so forth.) Unlike early Christian chant, with its heptatonic modes with intervals of whole steps and half steps, the *maqam* system has more than fifty heptatonic modes, each with its own name, employing "microtonal" intervals. A **microtone** or **microtonal interval** may be smaller than a half step, the smallest interval in the European musical system, or between a half step and a whole step.

Arab musical theorists of the tenth century associated emotions with particular *maqam*s in the tradition of Ancient Greek music theorists, who had assigned the ethical qualities of ethnic groups to the melodic modes they used. Qur'anic reciters have some leeway in the *maqam*s they use for particular verses. Given the association of emotion and meaning of a *maqam*, their choices signal to listeners their understanding of the text. Proper choices are said to "extract" the meaning of a verse and "bring the listener closer to the Qur'an."[25] On the other hand, a poor choice may be criticized by knowledgeable listeners. One reciter sang a text about hell and damnation so beautifully that a critic commented, "If hell is so lovely and pleasant, take me to it."[26]

EMOTIONAL RESONANCE

The link between the meaning of a properly chosen *maqam* and the meaning of a verse is called "picturing the meaning," a statement that transforms the indexical link between the emotion and *maqam* into a musical icon of textual meaning. For example, one verse of the Qur'an has a person reflecting on their fate on the Day of Judgment: "Ah, would that I had sent forth [good deeds] for [this] my [future] life."[27] To express the meaning, one singer might choose a *maqam* associated with "grief and pain." Another might chose a *maqam* associated with "self-reproach and repentance."

CULTURAL LINKAGES

The *maqam* system allows both secular singers and Qur'anic reciters to improvise during their performance. So, for example, a reciter may change between lower and higher pitch ranges within the *maqam*, as Hamza Shakkur does in this recording, to signal the voices of different figures in dialogue and recite on higher pitches to signal particularly exciting moments in the text. These formal principles guide Qur'anic reciters, respected singers, and talented instrumentalists.

The sound of Qur'anic chanting is ubiquitous in Muslim societies. It is recited in Friday prayer services throughout the year, at daily prayers during Ramadan, for secular events to celebrate family rituals such as weddings and funerals, to celebrate the opening of a shop or restaurant, and in gatherings of aficionados to listen to a skilled reciter. Always performed in Arabic, it is chanted wherever Muslims gather regardless of their native language.

CULTURAL LINKAGES

What Is Its History?

During his lifetime Muhammad managed, despite significant opposition from pagan tribesmen, to unify politically the Arabian Peninsula based on Islamic principles. By 750, little more than a century after his death, a succession of leaders of the faithful, called caliphs, had succeeded in spreading Islam west across North Africa to Spain, north to much of the present-day Middle East, and east to southern Pakistan. Ruled from Damascus in present-day Syria, this caliphate, the area ruled by a caliph, was the largest empire in the world to that date. Between 750 and 1258, the capital of the caliphate moved to the city of Baghdad in present-day Iraq, where science, art, music, and literature flourished in a golden age of Islamic culture. Qur'anic recitations based on secular Arab classical music may date to this period. The capital of the caliphate shifted to Cairo from 1261 to 1517 and to Istanbul in the Ottoman Empire from 1517 to 1924, when the president of the new Republic of Turkey abolished the caliphate.

As early as the ninth century Islam spread into sub-Saharan Africa, including present-day Mali and Sudan. Today nearly half of Africa's population is Muslim. In the tenth century it had spread to Central Asia. Between the thirteenth and the seventeenth centuries Islam also traveled east to parts of southeast Asia including Malaysia on the mainland and some islands of Indonesia and the Philippines. Today Indonesia has the largest Muslim population in the world, more than 200 million out of an estimated total of 1.7 billion Muslims. It is the second largest religion in the world after an estimated 2.4 billion Christians.

Qur'anic chant has only been transmitted orally for centuries. Since the early twentieth century recordings and radio and television broadcasts have transmitted the Arab style heard in this recording to many parts of the world. International recitation competitions contribute to the standardization of oral practices. Nevertheless, it is difficult to know how Qur'anic recitation has changed through the centuries since it was revealed to the Prophet Muhammad. The chanting style seems to have molded itself to the *maqam* practices of secular classical music (introduced in Chapter 3, Gateway 9), which has historically documented roots going back at least to the tenth century, but whose practices have changed in details over time. Also in each of the many societies where Islam has taken root, Islam has accommodated local social and cultural views particularly with respect to the position of women in society and in Islam. In Indonesia, for example, women may become skilled reciters and work alongside men.

WHERE DO I GO FROM HERE?

- This gateway is based on Kristina Nelson, *The Art of Reciting the Qur'an* (Austin: University of Texas Press, 1985). Read Chapter 4, "The Ideal Recitation of the Qur'an," pp. 52–100.

- Listen to, and compare, the Qur'anic chanting of reciters from Egypt, Saudi Arabia, Turkey, and female reciter Maria Ulfah from Indonesia with the recitation of Hamza Shakkur in this gateway.

- For an account of gender in Qur'anic chanting, read Ch. 6, "Rethinking Women, Music, and Islam," in Anne K. Rasmussen, *Women, the Recited Qur'an, and Islamic Music in Indonesia* (Berkeley: University of California Press, 2010), pp. 211–243.

- To understand more about recitation in the scale (*maqam*) Hamza Shakkur uses in this gateway recording, read Ch. 3, "Learning Recitation: The Institutionalization of the Recited Qur'an," in Rasmussen, pp. 74–124.

GATEWAY 7
EARLY EUROPEAN POLYPHONIC MUSIC

What Is It?

The written record of polyphony in European religious music begins in the ninth century, about the same time as the earliest notations of monophonic Gregorian chant. While these early notations do not record polyphonic music, a few ninth-century manuscripts give rules for the way a soloist could add a second voice beginning on the fourth or fifth degree of the scale above or below the final of the chant melody. For the next five hundred years priests, monks, and nuns developed a number of styles of polyphonic singing to enhance the religious and aesthetic effect of their liturgies. During the fourteenth century the French poet and musician Guillaume de Machaut (1300–1377)[28] composed the first polyphonic setting of five sections of the ordinary of the Mass: Kyrie, Gloria, Credo, Sanctus, and Agnus Dei. Machaut's multi-movement [Mass] (a **movement** is a section of a larger work) has inspired many classical composers ever since to write in a genre he created.

Our gateway to polyphonic Christian Church music of the Medieval period is the Gloria from this Mass. Machaut composed it for performance at the Notre Dame de Reims Cathedral in Reims, France. Known as *La Messe de Nostre Dame* (The Mass of Our Lady), he composed it around 1360. The Mass in this recording is not sung by priests or monks, but by an early music group called the Oxford Camerata. **Early music** refers to European church, court, and concert music composed before 1750 (or by some reckoning before 1650). *Camerata* means room or dormitory in Italian. Today musicians use the term to refer to small music ensembles that might once have played in small rooms.

FIGURE 2.14
Guillaume de Machaut
Source: Alamy Stock Photo.

 Listen to the first thirty seconds of the recording.

How Does It Work?

Timbre

The timbre is created by four male voices singing in a range of about two octaves.

Texture

The texture consists of four different vocal lines, also called four-part polyphony. The four parts move in the same rhythm, that is, the singers pronounce each syllable of the text at the same time. However, on the concluding word, "Amen," each of the four parts moves with its own set of rhythmic durations.

Rhythm

For most of the Gloria, there is a steady beat created by relatively short tones on each syllable of text. From time to time, tones are held for a long time on important syllables: "Jesu Christe," "Deus" (God), and "Amen."

FIGURE 2.15
**Map of Reims,
northeast of Paris**

Reims

Melody

The texture consists of four polyphonic vocal lines of more or less equal importance. Each line moves mainly in stepwise, conjunct motion with a few leaps. The parts are based on a diatonic scale (DEFGABC), but nondiatonic, chromatic pitches are added from time to time. **Nondiatonic pitches** are pitches other than the seven pitches separated by whole steps and half steps in a heptatonic, diatonic scale. They are also called **chromatic pitches** since they are said metaphorically to add color to the music produced by the basic seven diatonic pitches.

Harmony

The four parts move together in the same rhythm, creating four-pitch chords heard throughout the piece. The most common type of chord is an open fifth, doubled at the octave: D-A-d-a, which we call a **perfect fifth chord**. (By analogy with the distance between the first and the fifth degree of a scale, a **fifth** is an interval between any two scale degrees five pitches apart; the interval between D and A is called a perfect fifth because the D and A vibrate in a "perfect" ratio of 3:2.) But other chords are heard as well. Especially striking is a chord with two nondiatonic, chromatic pitches at the end of phrases and before the D-A-d-a chord. This chord can be written as C♯-E-G♯-C♯. The C♯ is a half-step below D and is said to lead to D. The G♯ is a half-step below A and is said to lead to A. Thus, C♯ and G♯ are called **leading tones**. Leading tones create a sense of tension in music until they resolve to a pitch a half step higher. The chord is called a **double leading tone chord**.

Form

The form is a through-composed treatment of the text of the Gloria. It has two main parts: the main text with each part performing the same rhythm and the melismatic, rhythmically independent texture of the "Amen."

Performance Techniques

The singers sing relatively pure tones in a relaxed manner with no **vibrato**, a slight change of pitch on a held tone. Their dynamic changes between loud and soft are not marked in the notation, but are their own interpretations of how to sing the composition effectively. In another interpretation on their part, they sing the Latin text not as Latin is pronounced today, but rather using the pronunciation of French singers in the fourteenth century. So, for example, they drop the final *s* on many words, pronounce *qui* as "kee" rather than "kwee," and change "mundi" to "mondi," as these words are pronounced in French.

Listen to the first thirty seconds of the recording for the chordal polyphony and the harmonic cadence.

Listen to the entire recording following this timed listening guide.

TIME	FORM	DESCRIPTION	LATIN TEXT	TRANSLATION
0:00	A	The first line is sung monophonically by a soloist, as in Gregorian chant.	*Gloria in excelsis Deo.*	Glory be to God on high,
0:11	B	This short section begins with a long-held tone to emphasize this important thought: "peace on earth."	*Et in terra pax*	and on earth peace,
0:30	C	The text and polyphony now move faster until the pause on the double leading tone chord on the "te" of "Laudamus te."	*hominibus bonae voluntatis.* *Laudamus te.*	good will towards men. We praise thee,
0:42	D	The first chord resolves the preceding double leading tone chord. Three equal-length treatments of these parallel thoughts end with a long-held tone on the perfect fifth chord at the end.	*Benedicamus te* *Adoramus te.* *Glorificamus te.*	we bless thee we worship thee, we glorify thee,

LISTENING GUIDE 2.4

continued

TIME	FORM	DESCRIPTION	LATIN TEXT	TRANSLATION
0:56	E	This line ends with a clear cadence from the double leading tone chord to the perfect fifth chord.	*Gratias agimus tibi propter magnam gloriam tuam.*	we give thanks to thee for thy great glory,
1:13	F	The first phrase ends on the double leading tone chord and the second one ends on four long held tones on "Iesu Christe."	*Domine Deus, Rex caelestis, Deus Pater omnipotens.*	O Lord God, heavenly King, God the Father Almighty.
			Domine Fili unigenite, Iesu Christe.	O Lord, the only-begotten Son, Jesus Christ;
1:52	G	These three phrases, one for each line of text, each end in a slightly different way. Notice the emphasized cadence at the very end of the section.	*Domine Deus, Agnus Dei, Filius Patris.*	O Lord God, Lamb of God, Son of the Father,
			Qui tollis peccata mundi, miserere nobis.	that takest away the sins of the world, have mercy upon us.
			Qui tollis peccata mundi, suscipe deprecationem nostram.	Thou that takest away the sins of the world, receive our prayer.
2:37	H	The first line ends on the perfect fifth chord, the second on the double leading tone chord, and the third on long-held tones on "Iesu Christe."	*Qui sedes ad dexteram Patris, miserere nobis.*	Thou that sittest at the right hand of the Father, have mercy upon us.
			Quoniam tu solus Sanctus. Tu solus Dominus.	For thou only art holy; thou only art the Lord;
			Tu solus Altissimus, Iesu Christe.	thou only the most high, O Jesus Christ,
3:32	I	The text concludes with a short phrase ending on the perfect fifth chord.	*Cum Sancto Spiritu, in gloria Dei Patris.*	With the Holy Spirit in the glory of God the Father.
3:45	J	The polyphony changes dramatically on the concluding "Amen." Instead of the mainly syllabic treatment of the long text, the first syllable is set as an elaborate melisma before the now familiar cadence from the double leading tone chord to a perfect fifth chord on "-men."	*Amen.*	Amen.
4:39	End			

What Does It Mean?

Machaut's Mass was composed for one the most glorious cathedrals in Europe, the Cathedral at Reims. Its polyphonic style was almost surely heard as a musical metaphor for the majesty of the architecture, which was a symbol of God's glory. This cathedral was the site of the coronation of French kings. Built between the eleventh and fourteenth centuries in a style today called Gothic, this and other enormous cathedrals in France featured extraordinarily tall interior spaces, which echoed with the sound of this polyphony.

Mathematics in the form of ratios of small whole numbers governed both the architecture (ratios of length to width, length to height) of the churches and the emphasis on fifths (a 3:2 ratio of the frequencies of the two pitches) in the polyphony. Those ratios were regarded as perfect representations of heavenly perfection. Such fifths (3:2) and fourths (4:3) were called **perfect fifth** and **perfect fourths**. Composers during the Medieval period were expected to employ perfect fifths in their harmonies at emphasized moments in the rhythm and text. (The other scale degrees are of two types as well. If they are a whole step apart, they are called **major seconds**. If they are a half step apart they are called **minor seconds**.) They could employ other harmonies in passing between those perfect moments, and Machaut's consistent use of the same chord, the double leading tone chord, which contains a perfect fifth between C♯ and G♯, shapes the music at the ends of text phrases. Machaut also matches his music to the text to some extent, for example, holding the words "Iesu Christe" and "Deus" on long tones to emphasize them. And the importance of the word "amen," which signals that what precedes it is true and should be believed, is treated to a long melismatic passage.

FIGURE 2.16
The Notre-Dame de Reims Cathedral in Reims, France
Source: Johan Bakker, Wikimedia Commons.

What Is Its History?

Machaut's fourteenth-century polyphonic Mass and Hildegard von Bingen's twelfth-century monophonic chant melody and text "Quia ergo femina" belong to the same European tradition of Christian religious music. So the obvious historical question is: How did this change from one-voice monophony to four-voice polyphony occur?

From the ninth to the beginning of the fourteenth century, the practice of singing chants in parallel motion between the voices on the interval of a perfect fourth or perfect fifth above or below the chant pitch expanded in scope. For example, **contrary motion** (one voice goes up while the other goes down) and **oblique motion** (one voice stays on a given pitch while the other voice goes up or down) between the voices were added to **parallel motion** between the voices. A third and a fourth voice were added to the texture. Around 1200, at the same time as the famous Notre Dame Cathedral in Paris was being built, notations of two- and four-voice polyphony, called **organum**, were written down in staff notation for the first time and attributed to composers. These ambitious new polyphonic performance practices seemed to mirror the planned grandeur of the cathedral under construction. In yet another innovation, the tones of the chant melody were held for an extended period of time while a soloist created a melismatic melody above it. The held tone, called the *tenor* (from Latin meaning "hold") functioned like a drone, which was common at the time in secular instrumental dance music and is a feature of Greek Orthodox Christian chanting.

It is likely that these styles of *organum* were created in oral tradition by the best singers and music teachers in cathedral and monastery choirs. Through practice and a knowledge of rules about how to create perfect fourths and fifths, they could sing together the two, three, or four parts without the aid of notation. Some music theorists and composers experimented with adding new instructions or signs to the neumes and staffs of chant notation to indicate the rhythm of the voice parts. In the late thirteenth century, theorists developed a notational system using the shape of notes and added stems and dots to indicate the duration of each tone, a system that is the basis for the musical notation used today.

With the ability to notate duration accurately came the possibility of more complicated rhythmic relationships among the parts. In response, a new category of musician developed in the fourteenth century: the contrapuntalist, that is, a composer in the sense we understand the term today, capable of writing complex harmonies in notation. Since the notation recorded different polyphonic lines in notes or "points" on the page, the writing of polyphony was called **counterpoint** and the textures were called **contrapuntal**. These terms are often used today as synonyms for polyphony and polyphonic. Writers at the time called compositions in this new complex rhythmic style the *Ars Nova* (New Art). A controversy ensued between advocates for it and those for the older *Ars Antiqua* (Ancient Art), one of the earliest examples in the European tradition of a clear break between what might be called traditional and modern styles of music. Machaut was arguably the most important of these early European contrapuntalists up to that point in the history of European music. And he seems to have known it. Near the end of his life, to ensure the preservation of his compositions, he prepared six manuscripts of his works, totaling more than 2000 leaves.

The notation he used was one of the earliest to record rather exactly both the pitches and the durations that he intended for every note in his compositions. Still, today's musicians and scholars intent on performing this music in something resembling its original style have had to reconstruct its performance style from other manuscripts giving rules and instructions for how to perform them. These manuscripts suggest that the C and G must be raised to C♯ and G♯, before cadencing on the D-A perfect fifth chord. They also suggest that the polyphonic portions of the Mass ordinary were performed by well-trained soloists in alternation with a choir of priests singing the Proper of the Mass in the monophonic style of Gregorian chant. The Oxford Camerata follows this suggestion and performs this Gloria with four soloists on each part rather than with a choir with many singers on each part. Also, all of the Camerata's voices are male voices, because it would have been sung in Reims by priests and monks, not by nuns, creating a sonic image of a male-dominated church order.

During the two centuries between Hildegard's life and Machaut's, the shape of political power in Europe changed dramatically. Charlemagne's dynasty was not able to control the vast lands of western Europe. Conflicts arose between local landlords and those who proclaimed themselves kings of large territories. By Machaut's lifetime, something like today's political map of Europe had taken shape, and the rulers of England, France, Spain, and the Holy Roman Empire (by then a German-speaking region) were battling one another for control of land. The most important of these conflicts during Machaut's lifetime was the Hundred Years War (1337–1453) between England and France for control of northern France. In addition to deaths caused by war, Europe was ravaged during Machaut's lifetime by a bacterial plague, the Black Death (1346–1353), which killed roughly one third of Europe's population. During the two centuries between the lives of Hildegard and Machaut, Paris had emerged as by far the largest city in Europe and France as the most powerful kingdom. So it is no surprise that the most important developments in European polyphonic music, including those of Machaut, took place there.

We know little about Guillaume de Machaut's birth, death, or musical training. He probably belonged to a landowning family near the town of Reims, France, with the financial resources to secure a good education for him at a church school. He was ordained and took vows of celibacy, but at a rank below that of priest. As a well-educated cleric, he was closely associated with the community of priests, deacons, and canons at the Cathedral of Reims, but he lived his life outside the church. Early in his adult life he was employed as a clerk and advisor to King John of Bohemia (a region in today's Czech Republic), who also held the title King of Poland. King John, educated in France and loyal to the French king, traveled widely in Europe, providing his secretary Guillaume de Machaut the opportunity to mix with royalty throughout his life.

Machaut was a gifted poet as well as composer. He created a large body of love poems for his royal acquaintances, who rewarded him with gifts in exchange for his musical compositions and poems. He was famous throughout Europe for his poetry and his monophonic and polyphonic song settings of them. These poems and songs may have served as a form of consolation for nobles and royalty during the troubles of the fourteenth century. After King John died in a battle against the English during the Hundred Years War, Machaut continued to travel in royal circles until he settled down in a house near the Cathedral at Reims around 1360, an occasion he marked with the composition of his Mass. In his honor his wealthy friends contributed money, which supported soloists to perform his Mass each Saturday during his later life and possibly for fifty years or so after his death. Visitors to the cathedral from all over Europe would have heard it and absorbed its musical lessons, including the idea of composing a polyphonic setting of the Mass ordinary. Since then, many composers in the European tradition, including some Protestant and Jewish ones, have composed at least one and sometimes many polyphonic settings of the Mass. Machaut's vocal polyphonic Mass may also have served as a precursor of later multi-movement instrumental compositions such as sonatas and symphonies.

Machaut's *Messe de Nostre Dame* was performed every Saturday at the Cathedral in Reims well into the fifteenth century. But after that, new styles of music supplanted it, and it fell into disuse. It has only re-entered the repertoire of European classical music due to music historians' interest in its historical significance. Today it is mainly performed, as in this recording, by early music groups interested in the revival of this old music.

> **CULTURAL LINKAGES**

Not only was Machaut an important composer, he was the most prolific and respected French poet of the fourteenth century. Although he is less famous today than some of his contemporaries, at the time his writings were as well known as Dante Alighieri's (*c.* 1265–1321) *Divine Comedy*, Giovanni Boccaccio's (1313–1375) *Decameron*, and Geoffrey Chaucer's (*c.* 1343–1400), *The Canterbury Tales*, the last of which Machaut is said to have influenced. Of course none of them wrote music as well as poetry. We can understand something of his stature in the fourteenth century if we think of him in mid-twentieth-century terms as someone who combined the poetic skills of songwriter Bob Dylan, the musical skills of composer Leonard Bernstein, was paid to advise Presidents Eisenhower and Kennedy, and occasionally popped over to the National Cathedral in Washington, D.C. to officiate at services.

WHERE DO I GO FROM HERE?

- We focused in this gateway on Machaut's only composition for the Roman Catholic liturgy, his polyphonic Mass setting, rather than on his much more numerous secular and non-liturgical vocal compositions. Find and listen to one or more of these compositions by Machaut.

- Listen to an example of a four-part *organum* composed for the Notre Dame Cathedral in Paris around 1200 and compare it to Machaut's Gloria. A famous example is "Viderunt Omnes" by Pérotin, a master musician at the cathedral in the late twelfth and early thirteenth centuries.

- Philippe de Vitry (1291–1361) was a French contemporary of Machaut's and has been credited with inventing the new notation system of the *Ars Nova*. He had a career in service to royalty similar to Machaut's, but few of his compositions survive and none of them has been as influential as Machaut's Mass. Find and listen to one of his compositions and compare it to Machaut's Gloria.

CLOSING

The religious chanting of the major world religions enhances religious experience and the meanings of liturgical texts by adding elements associated with music: melody, rhythmic recitation, special timbres and performance techniques, and in the case of Tibetan Buddhism, musical instruments. Since religious music often supports the recitation of a great deal of text, they all employ syllabic singing on a very few pitches, as Christian and Qur'anic chant and Machaut's Gloria of the Mass exemplify. When worshipers want to express the mystical and emotional nature of religious belief, they amplify the aesthetic quality of the sound in special ways: Tibetan Buddhists with their two-tone vocal production and raucous instrumental music; Christians and Muslims with their melismatic singing.

AESTHETICS

Buddhists, Muslims, and Christians share a concern that too much emphasis on the musical elements of religious chant will lead believers away from true devotion to the serious obligations of their faith toward distracting and lascivious thoughts associated with secular music. In all cases, believers in these Ancient and Medieval religions share with small-scale societies a belief that music has special powers that humans can use to communicate effectively with the supernatural world.

Buddhism, Christianity, and Islam have all spread over wide areas of the world with the support of secular political power, sometimes via crusades and holy wars (*jihad*) and sometimes as the adopted state religion of kings, emperors, and sultans. Under the umbrella of state protection, all have developed strong institutions to teach and support religious devotion and music: Buddhist and Christian monasteries; Christian churches and Muslim mosques; and full-time ritual specialists (*lamas*, priests, and imams), some of whom are chanting and music specialists.

THINGS TO THINK ABOUT

- How do modern religious believers amplify the meanings of religious texts with musical elements? How is what they do similar to, and different from, the Medieval practices described in this chapter?

- Historically many religions have spread with the support of secular political regimes. To what extent are the political and the musical interconnected in religious settings today?

NEW TERMS

accidental
aerophone
alto clef (or tenor clef), C clef
antiphons
Ars Nova
bass clef, F clef
camerata
chorus
civilization
conjunct melodic motion
counterpoint, four-part
counterpoint, contrapuntal texture
disjunct melodic motion
double leading tone chord
early music
final
grand staff

Gregorian chant
leading tone
leapwise melodic motion
liturgies
lyre
major intervals
maqam
melisma, melismatic singing
microtone, microtonal interval
minor intervals
mode
modes, diatonic
modulation
movement
neumes
nondiatonic pitches
oblique melodic motion

ordinary of the Mass
organum
parallel melodic motion
perfect fifth chord
perfect fifths, perfect fourths
polyphony, four-part
Proper of the Mass
psalms
scale degree
solmization, solfege
staff
stepwise melodic motio
syllabic singing
through-composed vocal music
treble clef, G clef
vibrato

ANCIENT AND MEDIEVAL SECULAR MUSIC

THE FIRST CITIES WERE LOCATED along important rivers in Mesopotamia, Egypt, India, and China. The rich soils along these rivers produced unprecedented wealth for the rulers who controlled these terrains. Their wealth and power grew in tandem with the vastness of the land they controlled. Those with domains large enough to contain diverse populations not united by language or ethnicity were called emperors and their territory was called an empire. On the peripheries of empires, some city-states, notably those of the Ancient Greeks, thrived culturally and politically. But none of these empires was at the center of the then-known world. Though each controlled a large area, none of them dominated the globe militarily, economically, intellectually, or artistically.

During the Medieval period, the empires of the Middle East, East Asia, and Africa shone especially brightly. Court music, some still performed today, was brilliant and impressive. Europe, by contrast, was a relative backwater. After the fall of the Roman Empire in 476 CE, Europe was a wasteland of small-scale agriculturalists, a few warlords claiming control of extended territories here and there, and a growing number of isolated Christian monasteries. Around 1350 the largest city in Europe was Paris (200,000). Rome (15,000) and London (25–50,000) had much smaller populations. At the same time the four largest cities in the world were Baghdad (1,000,000), Beijing (400,000), Cairo (300,000), and Kyoto, Japan (300,000).[29] Delhi in India and Timbuktu in West Africa had populations of about 100,000. Given those population numbers, it is no coincidence that most of the creative musical energy in Europe during the late Medieval Period was concentrated in and around Paris, where Guillaume de Machaut and his contemporary Philippe de Vitry were developing polyphonic music. Beyond Paris, religious chanting in monasteries and churches and singing, playing, and dancing in rural villages and small aristocratic courts were the most important forms of musical expression during the Medieval period.

Some secular musical traditions thriving today can trace their beginnings to the Ancient and Medieval periods, and this chapter contains gateways to four of them: (1) the music of Chinese literati; (2) the court music of the Middle East; (3) an African tradition with roots in the Medieval city of Zimbabwe; and (4) the rural music of Bulgaria.

GATEWAY 8
MUSIC OF CHINA

What Is It?

Our gateway to Ancient and Medieval Chinese music is a recording of a composition entitled "Three Variations on Yang Pass" played on a plucked zither called *qin* (pronounced "cheen").[30] **Zithers** are stringed instruments with a resonator but no neck. The **qin** has seven silk strings stretched along the top of a long (about one meter) wooden box with an arched top and a flat bottom with two "sound holes." Along the top of the resonator are thirteen inlaid circles indicating where the player is to stop the strings (to press them down with a finger against the wooden resonator). "Yang Pass" refers to a melody associated with a poem about a passage through the mountains in western China. The phrase "three variations" indicates that the piece consists of three versions of a melody. The performer on this recording, released in 2000, was a highly respected scholar and teacher at the Shanghai Conservatory of Music named Lin Youren (1938–2013).

 Listen to the first thirty seconds of the recording.

How Does It Work?[31]

Timbre

The player produces a variety of timbres, including plucked open strings, harmonics, tinny, thin sounds, full, rich tones, and scraping sounds on the strings.

Texture

The texture is mainly monophonic with occasional octaves and perfect fifths.

Rhythm

The rhythm has an elastic beat with an irregular meter.

Melody

FIGURE 3.1

Lin Youren plays the *qin* at gathering of qin aficionados, Suzhou 1987. With beard, the great *qin* master Wu Zhaoji

Source: Stephen Jones.

Five of the *qin*'s seven strings are tuned to a pentatonic scale. A **pentatonic scale** has five pitches in an octave. The other two strings double two of the five pitches at the octave. The melody employs a pentatonic scale and moves mainly in stepwise motion among the five scale degrees.

Harmony

Except for the occasional perfect fifth, harmony does not play a role in this performance.

Form

The piece has three main sections, each a variant of others: A A' A''. Each section contains a through-composed set of melodic phrases. The piece ends with a short **coda** (ending) that repeats one characteristic melody from the main part of the piece.

Performance Techniques

The player's manipulation of timbre is a striking performance technique in this piece.

Listen to the first thirty seconds of this recording for its pentatonic scale and the timbre of the instrument.

CULTURAL LINKAGES

Listen to the entire recording following this timed listening guide.

LISTENING GUIDE 3.1

TIME	SECTION	DESCRIPTION
0:00	Intro	Five low pitches are plucked.
0:09	A	The player plays the melody with different timbres on repeated pitches, various attacks and slides into pitches, and the sliding sound of the hand stopping the strings as it moves.
		The player repeats the melodic phrase played near the beginning and continues with some short melodic phrases until he ends by repeating one pitch a number of times.
1:38	A′	The melodic phrase played twice in the previous section starts the second variation, this time played as harmonics. A **harmonic** is produced when the sound of an overtone, rather than the fundamental, is heard. In this case the harmonic produced is the overtone an octave higher than the fundamental for each of the pitches played. The short melodic phrases of the previous variation return. The section ends in the same manner as the previous section.
3:10	A″	The third variation begins with the now-familiar melody in harmonics, as the previous section did. The short melodies return as well. Sometimes only the sliding of the finger on the string is heard after the tone decays. The sections ends as the previous two did.
5:09	Coda	This section begins a bit differently before the familiar opening melody is played. But it doesn't continue with the other melodies and ends rather quickly with a single sounding of a pitch, rather than with repetitions of a pitch as in the previous sections.
5:41	End	

What Does It Mean?

The poem "Yang Pass" was written in the eighth century CE by one of China's most famous poets. It is about travelers leaving China for unknown and dangerous lands in Central Asia beyond the Great Wall of China. Knowledgeable players and listeners associate this instrumental melody with the poem's wistful sentiment of parting with loved ones, because "going west through Yang Pass there will be no acquaintances." They also listen for how carefully the performer brings to life the timbral richness of a composition that first appeared in notation in 1491. This latter interpretation flows from the position of the *qin* in Chinese culture, where it has long been associated with the ancient Chinese sage, Confucius (c. 551–479 BCE).[32] In that tradition, careful performance on the *qin* is a sign of the musician's great learning and discipline.

CULTURAL LINKAGES

SOCIAL BEHAVIOR

Qin players have historically been scholars who devoted their lives to learning across a wide variety of disciplines, including not only the reading of classic texts but the arts of music, painting, calligraphy, and archery. They used this learning to serve the state as well-educated rational, knowledgeable administrators, as Confucius said they should. Thus a performance on the *qin* can be read as a metaphor for the player's education and refinement. The player uses performance on the *qin*, and other artistic practices, for training the mind and disciplining the body. As a consequence, the performance is meant most of all for the performer, not for an audience. Practicing, not performing for others, is what is crucial. Occasionally the performer might play for another scholar or a few friends and students who are equally dedicated to the scholarly life Confucius modeled. Two elements of the sound are essential to this intimate performance context. First, the silk strings produce a very faint sound. Second, the timbre of this quiet sound, including sliding on the strings, requires the complete attention of the players and listeners.

"Three Variations on Yang Pass" is one of nearly 3000 pieces in the *qin* repertoire. Collected in books of notation for more than a millennium, they are, along with neumatic notations of Gregorian chant, among the world's earliest examples of written music still performed today. *Qin* notation is a type of **tablature**, a notation method that indicates how an instrument is to be played (guitar tablatures are a well-known example). European music notation, in contrast, indicates the pitches and rhythms that are to be played but not how each instrument will play those pitches. In *qin* tablature, each tone is indicated by a complex written figure that is a composite of four Chinese characters: (1) the number of the string to be plucked (1 through 7); (2) the number of the marker to be stopped (1 through 13); (3) the manner of holding down the string (for example, to produce a harmonic or not); and (4) the finger and the direction (in or out) of the pluck. Notating the way each tone is to be played clearly places a great deal of emphasis on the timbre of the resulting tone.

Directions for each tone are written, and, like Chinese writing, proceed down the page in columns beginning on the right side of the page and proceeding to the left. The tablature does not specify the rhythm of the tones, and players either create their own rhythmic interpretation after careful study or learn one from their teachers in aural tradition.

In addition to musical notation, the Chinese also have a long history of music theory. They were probably the first to (1) classify musical instruments; (2) invent a system of fixed pitch; and (3) create the theory of an equal-tempered scale. Already around the time of Confucius, Chinese music theorists recognized five-tone (pentatonic), seven-tone (heptatonic), and twelve-tone (dodecaphonic) scales and had names for each of the pitches in them. A few centuries later they understood that the interval of a fifth created by the ratio 3:2 would result in a closed circle of pitches, the **circle of fifths**. The first five notes of the circle of fifths result in a pentatonic pitch set: starting on F the circle of fifths yields F C G D A and, when rearranged into a scale, the pitches F G A C D. The next two pitches in the circle of fifths, E and B, create a diatonic, heptatonic scale: F G A **B** C D **E**. The next five pitches in the circle of fifths, F♯ C♯ G♯ D♯ A♯, close the circle to create a **dodecaphonic** or chromatic scale: F F♯ G G♯ A A♯ B C C♯ D D♯ E. On a piano keyboard the white keys play diatonic scales, the black keys play pentatonic scales, and black and white keys play a dodecaphonic scale.

The Chinese were also the first to create the idea of fixed pitch, that is, the setting of a pitch to a particular number of vibrations per second (in European music, for example, the idea that the pitch A equals 440 cycles per second). In keeping with Confucian ideas about the importance of music for the stable functioning of society and the state, the measurement of the exact pitch of notes was a matter of importance to the state, and each dynasty maintained a bureau of weights and measures where

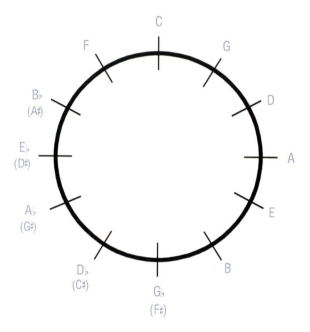

FIGURE 3.2
The circle of fifths
Source: Alex Sawicka-Ritchie.

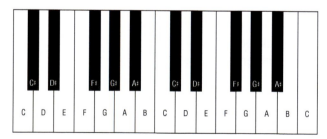

FIGURE 3.3
The piano keyboard with pitch names
Source: Alex Sawicka-Ritchie.

standards for pitch were kept alongside exact measurements of weight, length, and volume (in American terms, the exact weight of a pound, the length of an inch, the volume of a gallon, and so forth). These measurements were believed to be so fundamental to political and social functioning and stability that when a dynasty was overthrown and replaced by a new one, the new dynasty would reset the standards of weights and measures, including the fixed pitches of their music, to new levels.

The Chinese also have a long history of giving pitches meaning. For example, the five pitches of the pentatonic scale were associated with five bodily organs, five directions (north, east, south, west, and center), five elements (earth, fire, water, wood, and metal), five flavors (sweet, spicy, bitter, sour, and salty), five known planets, five colors, and five odors. The twelve pitches were associated with the twelve hours of the day, the twelve months of the year, and the twelve signs of the zodiac. Similarly, the Chinese often give compositions names that suggest a mood, an image from a painting or from nature, or the text of a poem or story. These symbolic associations of Chinese music with other elements of human experience are one indicator of the central importance the Ancient Chinese placed on music in human life. It may also be part of a heritage, from earlier agricultural and pastoralist ways of life, that connects music to the natural environment.

> **CULTURAL LINKAGES**

The Chinese are among the earliest people to classify musical instruments according to the primary material producing the sound: metal, stone, silk, bamboo, gourd, earth (pottery), hide, and wood. The *qin* and all stringed instruments are members of the silk class of musical instruments.

What Is Its History?

Historical records suggest zithers resembling the *qin* existed in China as early as 1000 BCE. One of the earliest representations in art of a similar instrument is a terracotta figurine made between 100 BCE and 100 CE. The *qin*, its repertoire, and its players constitute a 2000-year tradition of Chinese education and political organization associated with the teachings of Confucius. And legend has it that Confucius played the *qin*.

Confucius lived before China was first unified into an empire during the Qin Dynasty (220 BCE–207 CE). He devoted his early life to reading and studying the growing body of Chinese literature. In middle age, after failing at government service, he traveled to many kingdoms searching for the keys to a well-lived life. As an older man he taught students what he had learned from his studies and travels. They transmitted his lessons in oral tradition until they were written down as his *Analects* (edited conversations) during the Han Dynasty (206 BCE–220 CE). From that time to the present his philosophy has formed the foundation of much of Chinese culture. His principal insights are ethical and moral rather than metaphysical or theological, as religious beliefs are. Raised in a time of conflict among small states, he believed that social organization at the family and political levels could be peaceful and successful if individuals, from ordinary peasants to the ruler, followed three ethical principles: (1) benevolence and kindness to others; (2) the righteous and just treatment of the ruled by rulers; and (3) filial piety and brotherly love within the family. The paths to achieving these qualities were learning and ritual, both of which trained the mind and body to overcome base instincts such as greed, cruelty, and selfishness. Learning to play the *qin* and performing music during state rituals helped achieve these ethical goals, which Confucianists call the Way of Heaven. Rulers who followed the Way would not act despotically but in the interest of their subjects, who would flourish as a consequence of wisdom and benevolence of the ruler. All would seek a balance between Heaven and Earth through ritual and its music. Once China was unified into a vast empire by the Han Dynasty and successor dynasties, emperors claimed they were Sons of Heaven and so detached from those they ruled. To rule

FIGURE 3.4

Terracotta figurine of a musician playing a *qin* or *qin*-like instrument (100 BCE–100 CE)

Source: De Agostini Picture Library / Getty Images.

FIGURE 3.5
The Imperial Vault of Heaven at the Temple of Heaven, Beijing, constructed in the fifteenth century
Source: Philip Larson, Wikimedia Commons.

benevolently their vast land, they created a bureaucracy administered by scholars who studied the classics of Chinese literature, music, and art.

CULTURAL LINKAGES

Confucius is said to have believed that training in proper or good music, like that for the *qin* and that played during state rituals, could cultivate good qualities in the ruling class and in the state itself. Confucianist ideas about the importance of music, in the context of their influential views on state management and ethical behavior, meant that music appeared at the center of political and social processes as one of the contributors to political and social stability. For 2000 years, during a time when a large meritocracy of highly educated Confucianist scholars (called mandarins by the Portuguese) ruled China on behalf of its emperor, music was central to the life of Chinese society.

TECHNOLOGY

The *qin*, as one of the important symbols of this educated elite's learning and political power, enjoys tremendous prestige in Chinese culture. That prestige continued even after the fall of the last Chinese emperor in 1911 and the formation of the Republic of China. The People's Republic of China, founded in 1949, has supported the *qin* tradition not as a symbol of imperial class hierarchy but as a valued historical achievement of Chinese culture. However, they mandated that it should enter the musical life of all classes through public concerts, commercial recordings, instruction at music conservatories, and the composition of new works for *qin* in ensembles with other instruments. To produce a louder, more audible sound in these new settings, some players, like Lin Youren in this recording, have substituted metal strings for silk strings, which change the timbre and some of the playing techniques on the instrument. By the 1980s some *qin* players were professional musicians, a status at odds with their traditional position as highly educated amateurs who made their living in service to the emperor and the state.

WHERE DO I GO FROM HERE?

- Listen to Lin Youren's other recordings of compositions for the *qin*.

- Find and view recordings of Chinese musical instruments representing the eight classes of Chinese musical instruments: silk—*erhu*, a two-stringed bowed lute; bamboo—*xiao*, end-blown, notched flute; earth (pottery)—*xun*, globular flute; gourd—*sheng*, a set of reed pipes in a resonator once made of gourd; hide—a large variety of Chinese drums; wood—clappers; metal—bells and bell chimes; stone—chimes made of slabs of jade.

- Read more about Chinese music in the *Garland Encyclopedia of World Music: Volume 7: East Asia: China, Japan, and Korea* (New York: Routledge, 2002).

GATEWAY 9
MUSIC OF THE MIDDLE EAST

What Is It?

Our gateway to secular musical traditions of the Middle East, which have their roots in the Medieval period, is a performance titled "Taqasim and Sama'i Bayyati Al-Arayan," on the *'ud* by A.J. Racy, with the accompaniment of a *riqq* (a small frame drum with jingles). The *'ud* is a fretless, short-necked, pear-shaped, plucked lute with a vaulted (that is, rounded) back and a pegbox bent away from the neck. It has five double courses and one single course (the lowest-pitched string), and the player plucks the strings with a plectrum. (A **course** is one string or a set of close-together strings tuned to the same pitch and stopped or pressed onto the fingerboard by one finger.) The title of the piece refers to two important musical forms in Arab and Turkish music. A **taqsim** (pl. *taqasim*) is a nonmetrical improvisation in a particular melodic mode (*maqam* in Arabic).

A **sama'i** is a composed instrumental form in a meter of ten beats. *Bayyati* in the title is the name of a *maqam*. The combination of an opening nonmetrical improvisation followed by a metrical composed piece, both in the same melodic mode, is a common formal principle in Arab and other Middle Eastern musical traditions. Al-Arayan in the title is the family name of the composer of the *sama'i*, Ibrahim Al-'Arayan (1892–1953) from Cairo, Egypt.

 Listen to the first thirty seconds of the performance.

How Does It Work?

Timbre

The sound of the *'ud*'s plucked strings, with their characteristic rapid decay, and the thump of a drumhead and jingles on the *riqq* create the timbres of this performance.

Texture

The texture combines a single ornamented melodic line with occasional drone effects and drum accompaniment.

Rhythm

The opening section is nonmetrical followed by a metrical section that features a meter of ten beats. The meter is marked by a repeating pattern of drum strokes played on the *riqq*. Toward the end of the metrical section the meter shifts from a ten-beat meter to triple meter or a meter of six beats before returning to the ten-beat meter at the very end. The rhythm varies from rather slow to quite fast.

Melody

The melody moves mainly in stepwise motion through a seven-pitch melodic mode. The mode resembles the European minor mode, but some of the pitches are microtones between the whole- and half-steps of European music.

Harmony

Aside from the occasional sounding of octaves and drones, harmony is not an element in this performance.

Form

The form consists of two parts defined by rhythmic treatment: the first part is nonmetrical and the second part is metrical. Within the metrical section new melodies alternate with a repeating melody called a **refrain**: A R B R C R D R. In European music this form is quite common and is called **rondo form**.

Performance Techniques

The performance features rapid strumming, rapid melodic runs from time to time, and ornamentation.

Listen to the performance from 2:30 to 3:30 and pay attention to the shift from a nonmetrical to a metrical approach to rhythm.

Listen to the entire performance following this timed listening guide.

LISTENING GUIDE 3.2

TIME	SECTION	DESCRIPTION
0:00	*taqsim*	**nonmetrical melodic improvisation**
	first section	The melody, consisting of a series of short phrases marked by pauses, begins near the middle of the scale before descending to a cadence on the tonal center.
0:34	second section	The melody moves to higher pitches in the scale.
1:04	third section	The melody is played in the lower octave with a drone above the melody. The drone then ceases and the melody works its way through a series of short phrases and fast scale passages to cadence again on the tonal center.
1:48	fourth section	The melody, based on melodic sequences, is played in the middle and high registers with punctuating low pitches. A melodic **sequence** is a melodic phrase repeated at different pitch levels
2:51	*sama'i*	**composed metrical section**
	first section (A)	The melody consists of five measures of ten beats each.
3:22	refrain	A five-measure melody in a meter of ten beats is based on a descending sequence.
3:51	second section (B)	A new five-measure melody in a meter of ten beats.
4:20	refrain	A repeat of the refrain.
4:47	third section (C)	A new five-measure melody in a meter of ten beats.
5:15	refrain	A repeat of the refrain.
5:42	fourth section (D)	The meter shifts to six beats per measure and two melodies are played in the form AABBA'A'.
6:39	refrain	The refrain melody returns in its original ten-beat meter.
7:09	End	

What Does It Mean?

AESTHETICS

Musical performances in all traditions gain aesthetic meaning from the musical system of which they are a part. This performance exists within Middle Eastern systems of musical theory dealing with melodic and rhythmic modes. It also has meaning in relation to other musical instruments common in this style of performance and in relation to a variety of social settings and their associated genres of music.

The gateway on Qu'ranic chanting introduced the Arab *maqam* system of fifty or so heptatonic modes. Although fifty or more modes exist in theory, in practice there are nine common *maqamat* (plural of *maqam*).[33] The theoretical system has so many modes because they are constructed from a theoretical system of twenty-four equally spaced pitches, twice as many as in the European system of twelve pitches. The twelve additional pitches are, in theory, a quarter-tone above or below those in the European pitch system. They are said to be half-flat or half-sharp. The result is that Arab musical modes have half-steps and whole-steps and also microtones of three-quarter steps. In fact, Arab musicians play some smaller microtones than this theory explains. *Maqam bayyati*, heard in this recording, is written with the tonal center on D: D E-half-flat F G A B-flat C D. It has four whole steps (F to G, G to A, B-flat to C, C to D), one half-step (A to B-flat), and two three-quarter-steps (D to E-half-flat, E-half-flat to F). To further complicated matters, in *maqam bayyati* the B-flat sometimes shifts to B-half-flat. Although the intervals of *maqam bayyati* are fixed in music theory, skilled musicians on the *'ud*, which lacks frets, have an even more refined sense of the exact pitches they should play depending on the direction of a melody or the location of a pitch in a phrase. Sophisticated listeners hear these tiny differences in pitch, and they judge musicians on their ability or inability to bring them out in performance.

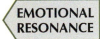 **Listen one more time to the first minute or so of this recording and try to identify the second degree of the scale as an E-half-flat between E-flat and E-natural.**

These slight differences in pitch, plus the different scale structures of each *maqam*, are associated with different emotions. For example, some listeners associate *maqam rast* with masculinity and pride and *maqam bayyati* with femininity and joy. Other *maqamat* are linked to love, sadness, and the "distant desert." The *maqam* associated with the distant desert is called *maqam hijaz*, named after the region of the Arabian Peninsula where Islam was born in the cities of Mecca and Medina (see the map of the Arabian peninsula in Chapter 2). Its scale is written as follows:

> **EMOTIONAL RESONANCE**

D E-flat F-sharp G A B-flat (also half-flat) C D.

The interval, a second, between E-flat and F-sharp, is called an **augmented second** because it is bigger than a whole step. In *maqam hijaz*, musicians reduce its size by slightly raising the E-flat and slightly lowering the F-sharp, creating a microtonal interval not explained by Arab musical theory. In European and American music the *hijaz* scale has become an index of the "exotic" Middle East, which, from a Euro-American perspective, might be considered a "distant desert."

> **AESTHETICS**

Sophisticated listeners also gain pleasure from hearing this performance as a manifestation of a well-known musical form. So, for example, they expect a musician improvising in *maqam bayyati* to begin his (and they are traditionally men) *taqsim* near the middle of the scale before descending to the tonic, as A. J. Racy does in this recording. They also expect a performer to improvise melodies and explore the *maqam* using a full octave range and, for an instrument like the *'ud*, a variety of plucking techniques just as Racy does. In a concert setting or an intimate performance in someone's home, the musician's goal is to tell an emotional story, to take listeners on a musical journey they are already somewhat familiar with. As they pass along a familiar yet unique route, listeners seek to enter an ecstatic emotional state known as *tarab*. Rather than sitting quietly, as audiences for European classical music do, they signal their pleasure at particularly delightful moments during the improvisation (a clever modulation to a new *maqam*, an interesting cadence, a subtle variation in intonation) with short cries and subtle body motions. The performer, in front of a knowledgeable and engaged audience, also enters a state of inspired ecstasy, called *saltanah*, and plays with even more emotion. In this tradition, becoming a master musician and a masterful listener requires practice and experience.

> **EMOTIONAL RESONANCE**

A composed *sama'i* has a relatively fixed form with four sections, each ending in a refrain, and a change of meter in the fourth section. The *sama'i* in this performance provides a degree of aesthetic pleasure just by meeting audience expectations and providing a particular instance of an ideal form that listeners are expecting to hear in such a performance. While the *sama'i* and its characteristic rhythm are meant for listening, other types of short composed pieces, especially in duple and quadruple meter, can accompany dancing, including so-called belly dancing meant for the entertainment of the audience.

The meter of ten beats is heard not only in the melody but in a repeating rhythmic cycle played on the *riqq* in a succession of low strokes (called *dumm*) and high strokes (called *takk* and *takka*) on the drum head. Arab music employs many of these rhythmic cycles, which are called *iqa'at* (s. *iqa'*) in Arabic. The ten-beat cycle in this recording is called *sama'i*. It features this repeating pattern of *dumms* and *takks* (||: :|| are **repeat signs** indicating that the musical material between them should be repeated):

||: 1 2 3 4 5 6 7 8 9 10 :||

    D - - T - D D T - -

The drummer fills in the pauses (-) in the skeleton rhythmic structure with improvised drum strokes. The cycle of six beats in the fourth section is called *sankin sama'i* and has this set of *dumms*, *takks*, and *takkas*:

||: 1 2 3 4 5 6 :||

   D TK T D T -

The performance on the *'ud* also gains meaning within a set of familiar Arab instruments. The *'ud* has been, since the Medieval period, a favorite instrument of singers to accompany their performances. Since singers in this tradition have long enjoyed more prestige than instrumentalists, probably because of their ability to express the sentiments in song lyrics, the *'ud* shares in the vocalists' high regard. The *nay*, an end-blown, rim-blown reed flute, is held in high regard because its sustained tones mimic the sound of the human voice. The *qanun*, a plucked zither, and the *buzuq*, a long-necked plucked lute, are other important Arab melodic instruments.

This performance is part of a classical musical tradition going back to the ninth and tenth centuries. Like European classical music, Middle Eastern classical music requires close listening and appreciation in courtly and concert settings. Today the *'ud* is probably the most highly regarded instrument in the Arab world. Sometimes called the prince (*sultan* or *emir*) of instruments, it is seen as an index of high Arab culture and a sign of musical pleasure as well as intellectual and scientific sophistication.[34] Today a performance like this one sounds dignified in contrast to Arab popular music heard in nightclubs and recordings and performed on amplified instruments like synthesizers.

What Is Its History?

Arab music belongs to a world of related musical traditions spreading from the present-day Middle East west across North Africa to Morocco and east across Central Asia. All these traditions have roots in the Medieval period, when Islam spread rapidly out of the Arabian peninsula after the Prophet Muhammad's death in 632. Arabic is the main language in North Africa, the eastern shore of the Mediterranean, Mesopotamia (present-day Iraq), and the Arabian Peninsula. Turkish and other Turkic languages are spoken in Turkey and the Central Asian countries of Kazakhstan, Uzbekistan, Turkmenistan, Kyrgyzstan, and northern Afghanistan. Farsi (Persian) is the language of Iran, the Central Asian country of

FIGURE 3.7
A. J. Racy playing the *nay*
Source: Daniel Neuman.

Tajikistan, and western Afghanistan. Besides Islam, another unifying cultural feature of this vast and varied region is the presence of musical traditions of classical music based on elaborate systems of melodic and rhythmic modes performed monophonically or with a drone and featuring melodic improvisation with many local variations. As Islam spread, Middle Eastern musical instruments followed in its wake. The long-necked plucked instrument spread around the Islamic world, including into Europe. The 'ud became the European lute and the Chinese *pipa*. The qanun provides a suggestive model for European keyboard instruments like the harpsichord and piano. And the *riqq* is the inspiration for the tambourine.

FIGURE 3.8
George Sawa, originally from Alexandria, Egypt, playing the qanun
Source: Pedro Bonatto de Castro.

This unity of culture in religion and music encompassed much of the present-day Middle East from the late seventh century to the fall of the Ottoman Empire in 1922 in a vast Islamic caliphate. The caliphate's first capital was in present-day Damascus, Syria. In 750 CE a new caliph established its capital in Baghdad in present-day Iraq. A fabulous musical, artistic, and intellectual life flourished in the courts of the caliphs, and during the Medieval period the cultural and musical life of this city easily outshone that of Paris and Rome in Europe. Baghdad was, in some sense, the capital of the Silk Road: goods and ideas flowed into and out of it from the west and the east.

Muslims were, like the Jews and Christians before them, people of the book, and they placed a great deal of value on the written word, not only the written Qur'an, which was the sacred word of God, but also collections of deeds and sayings of the Prophet Muhammad and the early days of Islam (*hadith*) and records of Islamic laws (*shari'a*). They created libraries, not only to save their own written records, but the written record of humankind from ancient Mesopotamia and Persia and the manuscripts of the Ancient Greeks. Much of what we know today about Ancient Greek philosophy, history, and music would have been lost had it not been translated into Arabic by Medieval scholars and preserved in the enormous libraries of the caliphs. During the Medieval Period one library in Egypt had more than 1.5 million volumes, at a time when a library in Europe might have had a few hundred. The Arabs

FIGURE 3.9
A. J. Racy playing the buzuq
Source: Daniel Neuman.

learned, from Silk Road traders, about the Indian idea of zero and of numbers in groups of ten, which then entered European thinking. They replaced Roman numerals with the Arabic numerals used today, and they worked out the fundamental principles of arithmetic, geometry, and algebra, a word derived from the Arabic word *al-jabr*.

Medieval musical style and practice in the Middle East is known today because the caliphs commissioned scholars and philosophers to write in detail about all branches of knowledge, including musical theory. These scholars, writing in Arabic, had access to Greek manuscripts about music and they borrowed many ideas about musical scales and modes and rhythm and meter from Greek writings, especially those of Aristotle's student Aristoxenus, who lived in the mid-fourth century BCE. The music the Middle Eastern scholars describe consisted of monophonic, ornamented melodies with rhythmic accompaniment on drums. It was passed down in aural tradition rather than written tradition. It featured improvisation as an art equal to and even more valued than composition. Scholarly writings on music from the Medieval period document both the rich musical life of professional court musicians and an elaborate system of melodic and rhythmic modes. The descriptions of this life in the past are consistent in many ways with the musical life and musical structures heard today in the Middle East.

AESTHETICS

In the later Medieval Period from around 1100 to 1500, groups of nomadic pastoralist warriors from Central Asia and Siberia moved east, west, and south. They challenged virtually the whole known world at that time: the Caliphate, China, India, and Europe. The first were the Mongols, led by

FIGURE 3.10
Map of the Middle Eastern Musical World

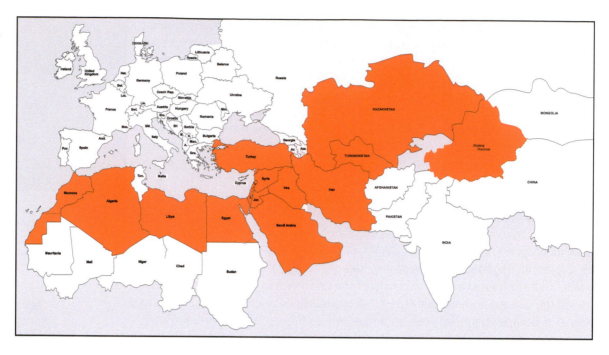

Genghis Khan (*c.* 1155–1227), a ruthless conqueror who showed his victims no mercy but who may have been able to perform throat-singing akin to the examples in Chapter 1, Gateway 2. Of course no one knows for sure. Seeking world domination, the Mongols imposed their rule on China and its urbanite Han people. They moved into India and in 1526 established a Muslim Mughal (Mongolian) court there. They attacked the Caliphate in Baghdad in 1258, slaughtering hundreds of thousands of people and breaking up the unitary power of the Caliphate.

In the early 1300s the Mongols were conquered in turn by another group of nomadic horsemen, the Ottomans. The Ottomans were a Turkic-language-speaking group like the Tuvans. In 1453 they succeeded in establishing a stable Ottoman Empire that endured to 1922, after which the country of Turkey was established. Like its many predecessors in the region, the Ottoman Empire ruled over vast lands from southeastern Europe, through the Anatolian (Asia Minor) peninsula, and across the Middle East and North Africa. They took control of the Greek Orthodox capital city of Constantinople and renamed it Istanbul. They fought their way to the gates of Vienna, where the Europeans finally stopped their westward advance in 1529.

FIGURE 3.11
Whirling dervishes accompanied by two Turkish *neys* (end-blown, rim-blown flute) and violin in 1890
Source: Pascal Sébah, Wikimedia Commons.

The Ottomans adopted Islam as their state religion, claimed the mantle of a Caliphate, and built grand mosques as symbols of state and religious power. Particularly influential on the musical life of Turkey was a mystical Islamic practice known as Sufism. Sufis seek purification of the self and the direct experience of God through ritual practices in which singing and music play a central role. In Turkey musicians and composers of the Mevlevi Order, named for the Persian mystical poet Mevlana Çelaleddin Rumi (1207–1273), developed the modal and rhythmic systems of Middle Eastern music to accompany ceremonies for devotees called "whirling dervishes" because they spin as they receive, and are energized by, God's spirit. The Ottoman sultans (rulers) established a rich courtly musical life at Topkapı, their palace in Istanbul, and sponsored elaborate concerts and musical entertainments for their courtiers. Some Turkish music today has its roots as art and entertainment music for the Ottoman sultan and his court and as religious music for the Sufi order of Islam. Today the Turkish National Radio and Television and university-based conservatories of music are the principal patrons of this classical musical tradition because of its importance as a symbol of national identity.

Ottoman musical life and its musical system seem to be continuations of what was written about and described in Arabic treatises and encyclopedias during the ninth and tenth centuries. The same sorts of instruments, a similar music theory, and the patronage of professional musicians were typical of both the older Arabic-language and the newer Turkish-language imperial cultures. Many features of this Medieval musical culture reverberate in Middle Eastern music today.

FIGURE 3.12
Ancient Egyptian long-necked lute and harp on papyrus from _c._ 1400 BCE (a reconstruction)

Source: De Agostini Picture Library, Wikimedia Commons.

Among the earliest lutes in the historical record are long-necked ones shown in Egyptian paintings of the second millennium BCE. Played by women, the body has a skin covering a gourd resonator. Short-necked lutes like the _'ud_, with bodies covered by a wooden face, may have developed from these ancient long-necked lutes. (The word _'ud_ means twig or wood in Arabic.) They traveled east to China, where similar short-necked lutes are called _pipa_, and west into Europe, where they are called lute, from the Arabic _al-'ud_ meaning "the ud."

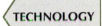

TECHNOLOGY

In Middle Eastern musical traditions, the history of music is not recorded in musical notation as it was in Europe. Rather, it is carried in theoretical treatises, paintings, and musical relics dating from the Medieval period. It has also been passed on for centuries in an aural tradition that included improvisatory practices and that has changed in many difficult-to-document ways through time. Notated compositions appear rather late in the history of this tradition. What we know of Arab composers comes mainly from the twentieth century.

A.J. Racy[35] was born into a well-educated family in Lebanon in 1943. His father was a famous poet and folklorist. His mother, who played violin, and her brothers, who played _'ud_ and violin, introduced him to music. As a child he made musical toys including flutes out of reeds cut from his family's garden. After learning to play violin and _'ud_, he began to play _nay_ and _buzuq_ during his early teens. After graduating from the American University of Beirut in 1968, he came to the United States, received a Ph.D. in ethnomusicology from the University of Illinois at Urbana-Champaign, and became a professor at the University of California, Los Angeles (UCLA). Respected as both a performer and scholar, he has composed pieces in the Arab tradition and for symphony orchestra and string quartet. He has performed with many popular singers and for film composers.

WHERE DO I GO FROM HERE?

- Watch video recordings of A. J. Racy playing _'ud_, _buzuq_, and _nay_.
- Listen to a recording of A. J. Racy's composition "Ecstasy" commissioned by the Kronos Quartet for string quartet, _nay_, and Arab hand drum.
- Listen to recordings of the most famous Arab singer Umm Kulthum (_c._ 1904–1975). Trained by her father to recite the Qur'an, she moved vast audiences to emotional heights with her perfect pronunciation of classical Arabic, the delicacy of her melodic embellishments, and orchestral accompaniments that eventually combined European and Arab instruments to create the iconic sound of a modernizing Arab, and specifically, Egyptian tradition.
- Listen to a recording of the Turkish _ney_, a flute deeply important in the Sufi tradition of Islam. Ripped from a bed of reeds as humans are separated from God, _ney_s are believed to yearn for their origins just as humans yearn for connection to God's love.

GATEWAY 10
AFRICAN MUSIC

What Is It?

Our gateway to African music is a recording from Zimbabwe in southeastern Africa, where about ten million Shona people live. The musician plays an *mbira*, an instrument found in many parts of Africa in a multitude of forms. The *mbira* in this recording has twenty-two metal keys and is called *mbira dzavadzimu* (also *mbira huru*). It is one of several types of *mbira* played in Zimbabwe. The composition's title, called "Nyamaropa" ("Meat and Blood"), references a hunt. The instrument is often placed inside a gourd resonator to amplify its sound. The singer on this recording, originally released in 1973, is respected elder Hakurotwi Mude.

 Listen to the first thirty seconds of the recording.

How Does It Work?

Timbre

The plucked metal keys of the *mbira* produce a sound rich in overtones. The rattles on the *mbira* and the *hosho* (rattle) add a buzzing sound. The singer commands a variety of vocal timbres, including a raspy quality at times.

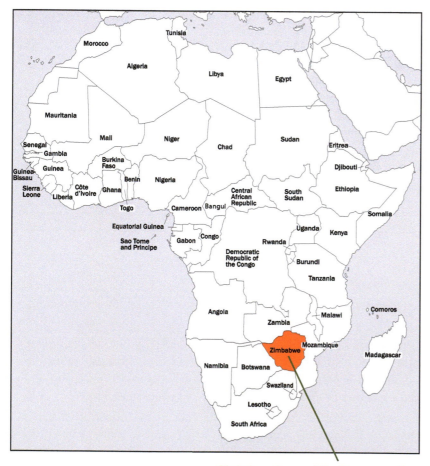

Zimbabwe, home of the Shona people

Texture

The *mbira*s play different polyphonic patterns in an interlocking style: high-pitched melodic lines produced by the thumb and forefinger of the right hand; mid-pitched melodic lines produced by the left thumb on high row of keys on the left side of the *mbira*; and low-pitched melodic lines produced by the left thumb on the low row of keys on the left side of the instrument. The *hosho* adds another strand to the texture, as does the singer with his melodic lines.

Rhythm

The piece is based on a rhythmic cycle of sixteen beats divided into four four-beat sections. Each beat is subdivided into three pulses or forty-eight pulses in total. The *hosho* articulates the three-pulse divisions of the beats.

Melody

There are many melodies inherent in the *mbira*s' polyphonic texture, which the musician brings out in his singing. Melodies fall into high, middle, and low ranges.

FIGURE 3.13
Map of Africa (Shona people)

Harmony

The harmonic structure is created by interlocking melodies, which sound a variety of intervals.

Form

The form consists of a forty-eight-beat pattern on the *mbira*. One complete cycle consists of four progressively altered four-beat phrases, which suggest a harmonic sequence. The four-phrase forty-eight-pulse pattern is repeated over and over with improvised variations on the *mbira* and improvised vocal lines.

Performance Techniques

The singer employs three different styles of singing, which the performer inserts at will in an improvised fashion.

FIGURE 3.14
Cosmas Magaya, a member of Hakurotwi Mude's ensemble, models the *mbira*'s playing technique
Source: Paul Berliner.

FIGURE 3.15
Hakurotwi Mude playing the *mbira* inside a gourd resonator
Source: Paul Berliner.

1. Vocal style #1, called *huro*, consists of high-pitched, descending melodic lines sung with yodeling on syllables like "wo-i-ye, i-ye, i-ye."
2. Vocal style #2, called *mahon'era*, is sung softly on "yah" in the lower part of the vocal range. It is usually a series of ascending phrases using somewhat disjunct melodic motion.
3. Vocal style #3, called *kudeketera*, carries improvised lines of poetry sung syllabically. The singer reflects on the context of the performance, the people listening, and his personal life.

Listen to the first forty-five seconds of this recording for the triple feel of the pulses of each beat and the shift from *huro* vocal style to *mahon'era* style around 0:30.

Listen to this recording following this timed listening guide.

TIME	DESCRIPTION
0:00	Fade in on the sound of the *mbira* and the *hosho*.
0:06	*Mbiras* play the repeating pattern, and the singer enters in an ornate, descending exclamatory style that includes yodels (*huro*).
0:30	The singer changes to a low, bass style with ascending phrases (*mahon'era*).
0:54	The singer changes to *huro* style.
1:20	The singer changes to *mahon'era* style.
1:36	Melodic variation in the *mbira* part.
1:44	The singer alternates between *huro* and *mahon'era* styles.
3:18	Melodic variation in the accompaniment part. The singer changes to *kudeketera* vocal style (improvised poetry in Shona).
4:07	The singer alternates between *mahon'era* and *huro* styles.
5:28	The singer drops out and the *mbiras* play melodic variations.
5:43	The singer re-enters in *huro* style.
6:01	The singer changes to *mahon'era* style and the recording fades out.
6:20	End

LISTENING GUIDE 3.3

What Does It Mean?

Today the Shona constitute the majority ethnic group of the country of Zimbabwe in southeastern Africa. In addition to gifted, specialist performers, like Hakurotwi Mude, Shona music making is distributed among the population, which mainly consisted of farmers before modernization transformed the urban population into educated cosmopolitans. The Shona possess a wide variety of musical instruments, including drums, flutes, and stringed instruments. They are most famous for the many types of *mbira* they play, including a number, like the *mbira dzavadzimu* (*mbira huru*) that are played of the ancestral spirits.

The *mbira dzavadzimu* has twenty-two metal keys organized in three manuals with a three-octave range. The keys in the lower left manual are an octave lower than those in the upper left manual. The left thumb (LT) plays both these manuals. The right manual plays an octave above the upper left manual. On the right manual, the right thumb (RT) plucks down and the right forefinger (RF) plucks up.

Fixed patterns and improvised variations are played by alternating the right and left hand in this pattern: LT on the lower left manual—RT on the right manual—LT on the upper left manual—RF on the right manual. This sequence of finger movements is repeated throughout the performance. Improvisations on the basic pattern involve more complicated fingering patterns. Since the pitches of the piece are spread over three octaves, the brain chunks the resulting pitches into at least three mentally constructed melodic lines in counterpoint. Complicating the inherent polyphonic texture even further, the brain can chunk pitches at the top of one octave with pitches at the bottom of the next higher octave to create even more mentally constructed melodic lines. The musician playing the instrument listens intently to the instrument to pull out these inherent lines. Some players affectionately personify the role of their instruments in the process, as if the instrument itself is suggesting musical ideas to the player.

> **AESTHETICS**

The form of a performance consists of the repetition of a cyclical pattern, which is then the basis for instrumental and vocal improvisations. As a result, in this tradition, when we hear singing, we are not dealing with a song accompanied by instrumental music, as in most traditions around the world. Rather, the voice accompanies an instrumental tune in various ways. Musicians say that the *huro* and *mahon'era* styles are "molded to the voice of the *mbira*," that is, they articulate some of the inherent polyphonic lines the musician is hearing on the instrument. All three styles establish the reflective mood of most Shona *mbira* music.

> **CULTURAL LINKAGES**

The third style, *kudeketera*, carries elusive text in a highly coded form of the Shona language known as "deep Shona," meaning that it is subject to interpretation in a way that captures profound truths. Such singing was very important to the Shona people at the time of this recording during the 1960s and 1970s when the Shona fought a war to liberate the country, then known as Rhodesia, from the control of British colonists. The three vocal styles alternate in a fashion that is completely up to the musician. In this recording of "Nyamaropa," the singer sings a series of improvised single lines of poetry in *kudeketera* style about a wide variety of topics, which include flirting with a woman in the audience, complaining about his troubles with women, praising his mother, lauding his own performance, reporting a bit of local news, worrying that he is getting too old to play well, and voicing concern about an ancestor's interference in his life.

> **TECHNOLOGY**
>
> **AESTHETICS**

Another important characteristic of the *mbira*'s sound is its buzzing tone quality. This is created by the *hosho* and also by a set of bottle caps (in the old days snail shells and imported sea shells) attached to the soundboard or to the gourd resonator in such a way as to rattle in sympathy with the plucked metal keys. This rattling sound is a highly desired quality of musical sound in much of sub-Saharan Africa and may well help musicians and listeners hear the many potential, inherent polyphonic lines in the musical texture. It contrasts strikingly with the European notion of "pure tones" favored in classical music. Enslaved Africans transported this buzzing sound aesthetic from Africa to the New World, where, arguably, it found its place in the vocal effects of jazz singer Louis

Armstrong's voice, James "Bubber" Miley's trumpet solos for the Duke Ellington Orchestra in the 1920s, and the gritty guitar aesthetic of early rhythm and blues (R&B) recordings, among many other examples in African American music.

The *mbira*'s keys are tuned to a seven-tone, heptatonic scale. Instead of a fixed scale and set of intervals, however, musicians employ a variety of tunings from those that tend to equidistant models to diatonic models. By sliding the metal keys forward and back over the instrument's bridge, they can change intervallic relationships of the *mbira*'s tones to "tune" them to a tuning model or to change slightly the character of the tuning. When two *mbira*s play together, they take great pains to tune them very precisely to each other, so they "sound as one," but the precise intervallic relationships within an octave are not measured against an external standard. Musicians sometimes delight in changing the tuning system they use from time to time, and they say that such retuning has the effect of refreshing their entire repertoire.

Mbira music and its accompanying vocal styles are sung for entertainment, including self-entertainment, for dances, and for spirit-possession ceremonies. It seems to have been mainly a male instrument, though today fine female players are well known. The most spectacular occasions for performance of the *mbira dzavadzimu* are spirit possession ceremonies, called *bira*s, for the ancestral spirits who act as intermediaries between the living and the Creator. *Bira*s are held when a person becomes sick and traditional healers believe that a social problem rather than a medical one has caused the illness. In these cases the healer suggests that a *bira* be held so that an ancestor spirit can appear and identify the cause of the mysterious illness. At the *bira* a group of *mbira* players is hired to play for a large gathering of family members and neighbors of the patient. They lead the assembled group in skillful and energetic singing, dancing, and hand-clapping in the hope that an ancestor will like what he or she hears and be tempted to appear at the *bira* by taking possession of the ancestor's human medium or, occasionally, an unsuspecting attendee. Two factors seem to determine success. One is that the musicians and attendees have to play, sing, and dance well and with enormous energy, and they have to find a piece that the ancestor really likes. Sometimes the ancestors never appear, and other times it can take nearly all night. "Nyamaropa" is part of a repertory of traditional pieces believed to be old and thus especially popular with the ancestors and effective in bringing them to the *bira*. Once the ancestor appears by taking possession of a person, the performance ends. The ancestor is consulted and provides a solution that will cure the illness.

What Is Its History?

Traders and scholars from the Medieval Caliphate, with its capital in Baghdad, very quickly spread across the Sahara Desert of Africa to the southwestern coast of sub-Saharan Africa and along the East Coast of Africa as far south as present-day Kenya (see Figure 3.11). During the Medieval Period the Mande people of West Africa formed the Mali Empire around 1000 CE. The Shona people of East Africa formed the kingdom of Great Zimbabwe at about the same time. Both the Shona and Mande developed great wealth from the mining of gold, which they exchanged with Arab traders from the north. Many cities developed in the Shona lands, the greatest of which was known as Great Zimbabwe. It was famous for its massive walls made of stone.

FIGURE 3.16
Thomas Mapfumo
Source : Jeremy Hogan/Alamy Stock Photo.

Though we have no way of knowing the age of Shona *mbira*s, it is likely that zithers and *mbira*-type instruments with idiophonic keys made of wood and bamboo and other natural materials have existed in sub-Saharan Africa since the formation of village agricultural life there many millennia ago. The Shona developed iron smelting and thus the potential to make iron *mbira* keys before 1000 CE. In 1589 a European missionary provided the first written reference to a *mbira* with nine iron keys.

During the nineteenth century the British, French, Germans, and Dutch colonized Africa. Cecil Rhodes (1853–1902) and British businessman invaded Shona lands in the 1890s and the territory was named Rhodesia. In 1965 a white rebel coup, anxious to head off progressive changes in the country involving greater parity for Africans, declared independence from Great Britain. That act ignited a fifteen-year guerrilla war that ended with black majority rule in 1980 and the renaming of the country as Zimbabwe. During the war traditional *mbira* music became an important symbol of resistance to white rule, as did popular music based on the *mbira*'s sound and repertoire.

POLITICAL ACTION ▷

For decades Zimbabweans, like Africans across the continent, have been listening to recordings of American popular music and creating popular music that either imitates it or alters it in ways to suit local musical taste. The most famous Shona musician in this regard is Thomas Mapfumo (b. 1945), "the lion of Zimbabwe," and his band, The Blacks Unlimited. Mapfumo began his musical life playing covers of rock and soul music, but in the 1970s, during the war for independence from white rule, he turned away from this foreign music and toward traditional Shona music to create a new style of popular music he dubbed *chimurenga* ("struggle"). His guitarist performed the patterns of *mbira* music, and after independence he added *mbiras* to his bands. The effect is an aural icon of Shona traditional and modern identity. A decade after Zimbabwe's independence in 1980 he released an album called *Corruption*, which criticized the government of Zimbabwe's former president Robert Mugabe, the person Mapfumo had supported during the war against the British colonists. The album engendered Mugabe's wrath, and ten years later, in the face of increasing pressure, Mapfumo left Zimbabwe for the United States.

The musical traditions of the Shona people have also found new life in the United States. Shona music thrives throughout the Pacific Northwest, with many active ensembles and eager students from Berkeley to Seattle. This is due largely to the influence of Dumisani Maraire (1944–1999), a Zimbabwean *marimba* (xylophone) and *mbira* teacher who settled in the region in the late 1960s. Maraire taught at the University of Washington from 1968 to 1972 and again from 1986 to 1990, and a number of his American students have carried on his legacy in the region, including Seattle *marimba* groups Kutamba and Musango and the Mahonyera Mbira Ensemble, among others.

ECONOMIC ACTIVITY ▷

Often finding greater opportunities abroad than at home, Shona musicians today have extended their horizons and recast traditional models of patronage, performance, and transmission with a global audience in mind. No longer limiting their opportunities for patronage to ceremonial *biras*, these artists have forged productive relationships with everyone from government officials and academics to cosmopolitan musicians and world music promoters across the globe. Shona *mbira* players have offset the grinding poverty they face in Zimbabwe and resistance by the country's charismatic churches by turning to their many enthusiastic students and sponsors abroad. The expansive growth of the world music recording industry and "world music" concert promotion in the U.S. and U.K. during the 1980s saw ever-increasing opportunities for Shona and other African musicians to perform for large audiences outside of academic and community contexts. With their extended patronage networks, new lines of transmission, and successful popular hybrids, the Shona *mbira* tradition has been strengthened at home. Over the last forty years, it has begun taking new shape as Shona music entered into the global, cosmopolitan, mediated world of recordings and concerts.

WHERE DO I GO FROM HERE?

- Listen to some of the many recordings of "Nyamaropa" available on streaming services to experience how differently the same piece can be performed.
- Find and watch a video of the *mbira* being played.

- Listen to a recording by Thomas Mapfumo that references traditional Shona music and singing styles. "Ngoma Yarira" or "Bukatiende" are two of the many examples.
- Read about traditional Shona *mbira* music in Paul Berliner,[36] "African Mbira and the Music of the Shona," in *The Soul of Mbira: Music and Traditions of the Shona People of Zimbabwe* (Chicago: University of Chicago Press, 1993), pp. 8–27.
- Read about Thomas Mapfumo in Thomas Turino, "Stars of the Seventies: The Rise of Indigenous-Based Guitar Bands," in *Nationalists, Cosmopolitans, and Popular Music in Zimbabwe* (Chicago: University of Chicago Press, 2000), pp. 262–310.

GATEWAY 11
EUROPEAN VILLAGE MUSIC

What Is It?

Until the twentieth century most Europeans lived an agrarian life. They lived in small villages and sustained themselves with small-scale agriculture on small plots of land. These rural cultures, while poor and fragile in economic terms, enjoyed a rich musical life full of of singing, dancing, and playing on homemade instruments. Starting in the nineteenth century, many of these old traditions began to fade as villagers in western Europe moved to cities to work in the new factories of the Industrial Revolution. But some of these traditions, many with roots in the Medieval period, have continued into the present. The countries of southeastern Europe have been among the last to modernize because, from the fifteenth to the nineteenth centuries, they were part of the Ottoman Empire and cut off from modern developments in western Europe. One such country is Bulgaria, a land of Slavic-

FIGURE 3.17
Map of Bulgaria

FIGURE 3.18

The small ensemble of Bulgarian traditional instruments in the recording, left to right: *kaval* (Stoyan Velichkov), *gaida* (Kostadin Varimezov), *gadulka* (Neno Ivanov), *tambura* (Yordan Tsvetkov), **and** *tapan* (Ognyan "Jimmy" Vasilev)

Source: Ivan Varimezov.

language-speaking people on the Balkan Peninsula. Our gateway to European village music with roots in the Medieval period is a performance of Bulgarian dance music titled "Kopanitsa." *Kopanitsa* is a dance genre in a meter of eleven (2+2+3+2+2)." It was recorded in the 1950s by a small ensemble of five traditional instruments: **gaida** (bagpipe), *kaval* (end-blown, rim-blown flute); *gadulka* (short-necked, fretless bowed lute), *tambura* (long-necked, fretted plucked lute), and *tapan* (double-headed bass drum).

🔊 **Listen to the first thirty seconds of the recording.**

How Does It Work?

Timbre

The timbre of this recording is created by the four instruments sometimes playing solos and sometimes in combination. The *gaida*, like all bagpipes, is a reed instrument, so describing the timbre as reedy is both accurate and redundant. A **reed instrument** has a vibrating column air started either by two thin pieces of cane or wood beating against one another (a double reed) or one piece of cane beating against a fixed stock (a single reed). The *gaida* is a single-reed instrument. The *kaval* is an end-blown, rim-blown flute with a flute's characteristic brilliant, pure tone quality. The *gadulka* has a rich but somewhat dull or muted timbre. The *tambura* has high-pitched, somewhat thin, metallic sound. The *tapan* plays both low-pitched and high-pitched sounds.

Texture

The texture consists of the *gaida*, *kaval*, and *gadulka* playing melody accompanied by rhythmic strumming on the *tambura*, a drone on the *gaida*, and a drum part. The melody instruments play together with very slight differences mainly in ornamentation, a monophonic texture called **heterophony** or **heterophonic texture**.

Rhythm

A *kopanitsa* is a fast-tempo dance piece in an additive meter of eleven pulses grouped into measures of five beats counted 1-2-3-4-5 or short-short-long-short-short. The short beats are divided into two pulses and the long beat has three pulses for a total of eleven pulses counted 1-2-1-2-1-2-3-1-2-1-2 or 2+2+3+2+2. The beginning of each measure may be difficult to distinguish in the first sections of the recording, but it is frequently marked by a low accented tone on the drum, the first one appearing at about 0:05. **Additive meters** combine beats of two and three pulses that add up to meters of 5 (2+3), 7 (2+2+3), 9 (2+2+2+3), 11 (2+2+3+2+2), and so forth. The rhythm consists of almost constant pulses with only a few long tones here and there.

Melody

The melodies in this piece cover a range of about an octave in a number of different modes on different pitch levels. They move mainly in stepwise, conjunct motion.

Harmony

The harmony is based on the sound of a drone.

Form

The form consists of opening and closing sections in which all the instruments play together. Between these sections, each melody instrument plays a solo.

Performance Techniques

The principal performance technique is the ornamentation. Between the main tones of the melody the players add all sorts of short ornamental tones.

Listen to the first thirty seconds of the recording and count the five main unequal beats: short-short-LONG-short-short.

Listen to the entire recording following this timed listening guide.

LISTENING GUIDE 3.4

TIME	FORM	DESCRIPTION
0:00	A	The full ensemble plays a narrow-range melody that consists of four eleven-pulse measures.
0:07	A	The A melody repeats.
0:11	B	A new melody similar to the first, also four measures long.
0:18	B	The new melody repeats.
0:23	CC	A new melody based on just three pitches.
0:35	DD	A new melody with a wider range of nearly an octave.
0:46	EE	A new three-pitch melody, similar to C.
0:56	FF	A new melody with an ascending leap is introduced.
1:07	G	The *gaida* changes mode and plays six different short four-measure repeating melodies.
1:37	H	The *kaval* changes mode, signaled by two held pitches, and plays three eight-measure repeating melodies.
2:10	I	The *gadulka* changes mode and plays three eight-measure repeating melodies.
2:37	AA, BB, CC, DD, EE, FF	The entire ensemble enters and repeats the opening section.
3:41	End	

What Does It Mean?

This performance gains some of its meaning as an expression and symbol of an ethnic group. Bulgaria is a small country of eight million people in southeastern Europe. Bulgarians speak a Slavic language, written in the Cyrillic alphabet. They are ethnic cousins of Russians, Czechs, Poles, Serbs, and other Slavic-speaking ethnic groups. They get their name from a group of Turkic-language speakers, the Bulgars, from Central Asia (themselves linguistic cousins of the Tuvans), who moved into southeastern Europe in the seventh century CE and were absorbed culturally by the Slavs who already lived in the region. Among the most distinctive features of Bulgarian musical style are the

CULTURAL LINKAGES

homemade musical instruments heard in this recording, dances and songs in a variety of additive meters, and women's singing with a sharp, loud vocal timbre.

Until the second half of the twentieth century most Bulgarians were subsistence farmers living in rural villages. This recording represents an instrumental musical practice deeply embedded in that rural, agricultural, and pastoral lifestyle. The *gaida* and *kaval* have long been the instruments of shepherds, who entertain themselves, and their herds, during many hours spent in pastures outside the village. The *gadulka* and *tambura*, on the other hand, are often used to accompany singing at weddings and other family celebrations and gatherings.

SOCIAL BEHAVIOR

Within Bulgarian culture, instrumental music, especially the playing of the *gaida* and *kaval*, carries a strong gendered association. All traditional Bulgarian musical instruments are played almost exclusively by men, while women are the best singers. In traditional village culture, women spent all their time raising children, cooking, spinning wool into yarn, weaving yarn into cloth, sewing cloth into clothing, and embroidering the clothing to make it beautiful. Their hands were never free to practice and play a musical instrument. Men on the other hand built and maintained homes, plowed and planted fields, and shepherded animals. During long hours in pastures, they had time to develop the virtuosic instrumental skills demonstrated in this recording.

EMOTIONAL RESONANCE

This recording of a *kopanitsa* also gains meaning from the types of performance contexts it references. Bulgarian listeners would immediately understand it as dance music, especially wedding dance music. Weddings in Bulgarian villages involve long hours of feasting before and after the marriage ceremony at midday on a Sunday. During wedding feasts, while guests eat and drink often at one long table, a bagpiper plays nonmetrical melodies that evoke the sadness the bride's family feels at losing their daughter, who will move to the home of the family of the groom. As an important moment in the ongoing history of a family, a village, and a people, a wedding recalls past weddings and family members, living and dead, going back as far as memory allows. The *gaida*'s nonmetrical melodies amplify feelings of nostalgia on such occasions. On the other hand, weddings are joyful occasions celebrating a promising future of children and grandchildren and continued family prosperity. These feelings are expressed in energetic music and dancing.

Bulgarian dancing is done mainly in long lines of people holding the hands of those on either side of them. Called *horo* from the Greek word for chorus, meaning a group of people (not a group of singers), the dancers often arrange themselves socially. A man leads the line, reflecting the patriarchal nature of village society, and men dance as a group near the front of the line. Women dance together farther down the line with children at the end. Sometimes young men dance in one part of the line, their energetic, large movements an icon of their youthful masculinity. Women dance with smaller, more careful movements to signal their modesty. Traditionally, everyone watched others dancing in the line, young people checking out potential marriage partners, and older people noting any flirting for future reference in a society where arranged marriages were once the norm.

AESTHETICS

The musical form of dance performances is not fixed, but neither are they completely improvised. The performers begin by playing melodies from a stock of familiar tunes they all know. At an actual dance this pattern would repeat many times for as much as an hour of continuous dancing. The musicians change the character of their tunes either at a signal from the lead dancer or by observing and sensing what they think the leader might enjoy at that moment. This performance is constrained by the conventions of recordings and lasts only a few minutes.

Bulgarian dance pieces are given genre names according to the meter of the dance. *Kopanitsas* are all in a meter of 11 = 2+2+3+2+2. The dance in a meter of 5 = 2+3 has its name, *paidushka*, and so forth. Each dance genre has a huge number of melodies, and some of them are named for the village or region where they are popular or for a person who loves the particular opening melodies.

What Is Its History?

The instruments in this recording have their roots in the Medieval period. The bagpipe is an instrument that has existed among shepherds in Europe for probably 2000 years. There are suggestive references to them in the plays of the Ancient Greek dramatist Aristophanes. The bag of the *gaida* is made from a goatskin turned inside out, and the word *gaida* probably has a Germanic-language root meaning goat (*gaid*). The instrument and its name may survive from a time in the fifth century CE when the paths of migrating Germanic and Slavic people crossed in central Europe. Over the past two millennia European bagpipes flourished or disappeared depending on particular cultural histories. In the industrialized countries of western and central Europe, bagpipes have largely disappeared, replaced by two other reed instruments, the clarinet and the accordion. They have flourished mainly in a few peripheral areas of Europe. Scottish bagpipers at some point added two additional drone pipes to the older single drone, which the Bulgarian *gaida* preserves. Irish bagpipers entertained the upper classes in their salons, adding keys to the melody pipe and a set of pipes that could play chords in addition to a drone. Irish pipers play it sitting down rather than standing. They call it the Uilleann (elbow) pipes, because they pump air into the bag from a bellows under the elbow of one arm, rather than blowing into the bagpipe as most bagpipers do. At some unknown time in the past, Bulgarian bagpipers reduced the size of the top hole on the melody pipe, making it possible for them to play a fully chromatic scale on the instrument without using keys.

The Scottish bagpipes are the best-known bagpipes. They suffuse our culture: pipe bands play in holiday parades, and solo pipers play at funerals for soldiers, firefighters, and the police. They were brought to North America by Scottish and Irish immigrants, for whom bagpipes are a symbol of national identity and resistance to English domination. As a consequence they have a long association with the military. But for an even longer time bagpipes have been part of European pastoral culture, where they have none of the links to the military that Scottish bagpipes do.

Bulgaria's history helps explain why the Bulgarian bagpipe and the instruments in this recording continue to flourish today. During the ninth and tenth centuries the Kingdom of Bulgaria was one of the largest countries in Europe. Its rulers had adopted Eastern Orthodox Christianity as their national religion. By the fifteenth century the Turkish Ottoman Empire had conquered Bulgarian lands and occupied most of southeastern Europe. Although the Slavic population remained Christian, Bulgaria was part of the Islamic Caliphate ruled from Istanbul until Bulgaria re-emerged as an independent kingdom in 1878. During the Ottoman period a number of Middle Eastern musical instruments joined the *gaida* in the performance of Bulgarian rural, village music. The double-headed cylindrical bass drum, called *tapan* is one of them. The *tambura* is related to the Arab *buzuq*, and the *kaval* is similar to the Arab *nay* (see Gateway 9 in this chapter). The *gadulka* is related to a Middle Eastern instrument called *rebab* and its European descendent, the Medieval rebec. For five hundred years under the Ottoman Empire and until the 1950s, most Bulgarians missed out on the industrialization, modernization, and religious and philosophical changes going on in central and western Europe. Bulgaria's agrarian society preserved features of European rural, peasant culture, including bagpipe playing and traditional singing and dancing until the late twentieth century.

Widespread education and urbanization, which are threats to traditional village culture, only began in Bulgaria after 1944, near the end of World War II, when a communist regime under the influence of the Soviet Union came to power. Although the communists fostered dramatic changes in traditional ways of life that undermined the foundations of Bulgarian traditional music and dancing, to their credit they adopted those same threatened Bulgarian traditions as symbols of the Bulgarian nation. To keep these rural traditions from dying out completely in the face of mass urbanization and universal education, they established schools and conservatories where young people could study these traditions. Graduates of the schools were hired to play in professional folklore ensembles, which presented these waning traditions to the nation's people and to audiences abroad. And they directed and coached village amateur groups, which performed in government-sponsored local,

CULTURAL LINKAGES

ECONOMIC ACTIVITY

regional, and national festivals. The continuing strength of the Bulgarian instrumental music tradition heard in this recording is the product of this history of preservation, first by a rural society largely untouched by modernity for the past five hundred years, and second by a totalitarian government that institutionalized its performance as a symbol of the nation.

Small ensembles like the one heard in this recording first began to appear and record in the 1930s. From the 1950s on, classically trained composers began to arrange village instrumental music using European harmony and counterpoint for an orchestra of Bulgarian village instruments, including *gaida*s, *gadulka*s, *kaval*s, *tambura*s, and the *tapan*. These orchestral arrangements of traditional village music were heard every day on the radio, transforming what Bulgaria's urban, educated elite interpreted as a backward, muddy village tradition into a clean, modern sound suitable for a modernizing society.

These composers made similar changes to village songs, which were sung mainly by women. They transcribed them into musical notation and arranged them in three-part harmony and counterpoint for professionally trained village singers to perform. That choral sound also became an important symbol of Bulgaria's modern national identity. In the late 1980s a Swiss music producer happened on these recordings and released three LP/CD albums of them under the title *Le mystère des voix bulgares* (The Mystery of the Bulgarian Voices). The striking village vocal timbres and the interesting harmonies captured the attention of the burgeoning audience for world music in western Europe, North America, and Japan. Bulgarian music rose to the top of the world music charts.

TECHNOLOGY ›

When Bulgaria entered the European cultural orbit after becoming an independent country, musicians, including village musicians, began to play European musical instruments like violin, clarinet, and accordion. They competed with players of Bulgarian traditional instruments for jobs at weddings and other celebrations. Virtuoso players of these instruments plus saxophone, synthesizer, and drum set developed among a minority group in Bulgaria called Roma (also known disparagingly as Gypsies). In the 1990s their recordings also started appearing abroad, and a few of them, notably those of clarinetist Ivo Papazov and saxophonist Yuri Yunakov, became quite well known. Today the tradition of Bulgarian rural village music is still taught in Bulgarian schools and music conservatories, and musicians showcase their virtuosity in competitions, festivals, and on the radio and television.

WHERE DO I GO FROM HERE?

- Listen to Bulgarian traditional instruments playing solo or in communist-era orchestral arrangements on an album entitled "Great Masters of Bulgarian Instrumental Folklore—vol. 1," especially Kostadin Varimezov, *gaida*; Nicola Ganchev, *kaval*; Atanas Vulchev, *gadulka*; and Rumen Sirakov, *tambura*. You can also hear another kind of Bulgarian bagpipe, a low-pitched *gaida*, played by Dafo Trendafilov and Stefan Zachmanov.

- Listen to recordings of modern arrangements of Bulgarian village songs sung by women's choirs on albums entitled "*Le mystère des voix bulgares*," especially "Polegnala e Todora," "Kalimankou Denkou," "Pilentze Pee," and "Erghen Diado."

- Find videos of "Bulgarian folk dance" and "Bulgarian weddings" and watch professional folklore ensembles as well as videos of modern weddings.

- Listen to Bulgarian virtuosos: clarinetist Ivo Papazov, saxophonist Yuri Yunakov, and accordionist Petar Ralchev.

- Read more about Bulgarian music in Timothy Rice, *Music in Bulgaria: Experiencing Music, Expressing Culture* (New York: Oxford University Press, 2004).

- Listen to the Irish Uilleann pipes and the Scottish bagpipes.

CLOSING

The gateways to Ancient and Medieval secular music in this chapter include two examples of music supported by elegant and wealthy courts, those of China and the Middle East, and two with origins in preindustrial, subsistence farming societies, those of Bulgaria and the Shona people of Zimbabwe. In fact, some historical sources describe Shona *mbira* players who were retained in courts of "kings" and "spirit mediums." Taken together, these gateways make the point that wonderful music can be created when musicians can devote themselves to music because they are paid handsomely for their labor and when they must labor on the land to feed themselves, making music in their spare time in exchange for little more than the gratitude and admiration of their friends and family.

These gateways all focus on one or a small group of specialized musicians: a Chinese *qin* player; an Arab *'ud* virtuoso and composer; a quintet of Bulgarian traditional instrumentalists; and a trio of two *mbiras* and rattle. While solo and small-ensemble playing were important during this period, courts patronized large ensembles. In small-scale societies sometimes the whole village would gather to sing and play together. The imperial courts of Ancient and Medieval China, Korea, and Japan had large court orchestras. *Gagaku*, the music of the Japanese court orchestra, survives from this period. In agrarian cultures, most people could play and sing to some extent because these were socially necessary skills. Large groups of people often sang together on special occasions and during social gatherings. The Bulgarian instrumentalists and Shona *mbira* players featured in these gateways represent a small fraction of the wealth of musicality in these societies.

Finally, the music and the ideas about music in the gateways of this chapter are known to historians in different ways. Compositions for the Chinese *qin* are preserved in musical notations, some of which date to the Medieval period. Ideas about the meaning of music, its aesthetic and social value, come from Ancient Chinese philosophical treatises. Arab music, dependent as it is on improvisation rather than composition, was not recorded in notation. Instead, Medieval Arab philosophers wrote extensively about music theory and musical life, some features of which are preserved in modern compositions and performances. In contrast, Bulgarian and Shona musical traditions possess little or no written record from the Ancient or Medieval period. What we know of the history of these traditions is based largely on historical inferences and analogy with modern musical practices. Frescoes and paintings from the Medieval period suggest that bagpipes have long been part of the European pastoral tradition. The Bulgarian word for bagpipe, *gaida*, probably dates from a time more than a thousand years ago when Slavic and Germanic tribesmen came in contact. But the actual music in the gateway example is a modern manifestation of Ancient and Medieval ways of making music in Europe. The metal keys of the Shona *mbira* may date from the Medieval period, and we can assume from the similarity of this instrument to African instruments with cane and reed keys that it derives from Ancient instrumental technologies. But the actual age of the tune, which the Shona regard as very old because of its links to the ancestors, is unknown. Even though all four gateways in this chapter tell us much about Ancient and Medieval ways of thinking about and making music, they are all modern manifestations of those ways of thinking, and show us some of the ways that people today are making music with Ancient and Medieval roots meaningful in the worlds they inhabit.

THINGS TO THINK ABOUT

- Compare the ways musicians in each of the musical traditions in this chapter have used new technologies to change something about their tradition.
- How are the societies described in this chapter organized with regard to social categories like class, gender, race, ethnicity, or age? How do those social divisions affect music making in each one?

NEW TERMS

additive meters

coda

course

gaida

harmonic

heterophony, heterophonic
   texture

mbira, Shona

pentatonic scale

qin

reed instrument

sama'i

tablatures

taqsim

'ud

zither

Music History from 1500 to 1900

THE WORLD'S HISTORY CHANGED DRAMATICALLY after 1492, when the Italian navigator Christopher Columbus set sail with three ships and a crew of Spanish sailors from Andalusia (southern Spain) in search of fabled India. Throughout the sixteenth century dozens of other Spanish, Portuguese, English, and French explorers inaugurated a new era of European influence in world affairs. Between 1500 and 1900 Europeans, their culture, their Christian religion, and their economic and political power came to dominate large areas of the world.

As a consequence, Part II places European music at the center of the narrative without losing sight of other musical traditions around the world. Chapter 4 deals with music from 1500 to 1600. It is the height of the European age of discovery, a period called the Renaissance in Europe and a time when the North Indian classical music was taking shape. Chapter 5 examines music from 1600 to 1750, a period of global commerce when a style of music and art called Baroque flourished in Europe and large gong orchestras called gamelans appeared in present-day Indonesia. Chapter 6 explores music from 1750 to 1800, the age of Enlightenment and Revolution in Europe and the Americas but also the height of the transatlantic slave trade. In Europe art and music were under the sway of neoclassicism while enslaved Africans were reimagining their religious traditions in strange and horrible conditions. Chapters 7 and 8 look at European music during the nineteenth century and introduce, for the first time, the music of the United States.

PART II

MUSIC FROM THE EUROPEAN AGE OF DISCOVERY (1500–1600)

THE FIRST PERIOD OF THE MODERN ERA, from about 1500 to 1600, was a European age of discovery. During this century, Europeans expanded their maritime exploration of the world around the Horn of Africa to the shores of Asia and across the Atlantic Ocean to North and South America. But Europeans were not only discovering what they called the New World. They were also intensely engaged for the first time in scientific investigation. Astronomers demonstrated that the earth must revolve around the sun, not the other way around as they had thought for centuries. This conceptual reorganization of the cosmos dislodged humans from the center of God's creation and challenged a millennium of teaching by the Catholic Church.

These discoveries in geography and astronomy followed a century of rediscovery of the art and philosophy of Ancient Greece and Rome, which had been lost to Europeans after the fall of the Roman Empire in 476 CE. A pre-Christian heritage of humanism, that is, the notion that humans, not God, are the source of meaning and value in the world, began to animate European intellectual and artistic life. In the nineteenth century a French scholar labeled this phenomenon a *renaissance*, a rebirth of Ancient Greek and Roman philosophy and art. Since then this period in art, literature, and music has commonly been known as the **Renaissance**. But this artistic renaissance was but one of many kinds of discoveries during this period.

Historians of literature find in this period a renaissance of Ancient Greek and Roman stories, myths, and characters. Historians of art see a rebirth of Greek and Roman realistic representations of the nude human body and individual faces after centuries of Medieval Christian art that covered the body and abstracted the face to represent ideal religious sentiments. In striking contrast to the Gothic Cathedrals of Medieval France, with their jumble of gargoyles and spiky towers and buttresses, St. Peter's Basilica in Rome, begun in 1506 and completed in 1590, exhibits the collonaded regularity and simplicity of the Parthenon in Ancient Greece.

The ferment in science, literature, and the arts undermined the Catholic Church's previously unquestioned authority and prepared the ground for a critical assessment of its activities and teachings. In 1517 one of its priests, Martin Luther (1483–1546), nailed to a church door in Germany a document with ninety-five indictments of the Catholic Church's doctrines and practices, thus igniting the Protestant Reformation and a new chapter in Christian history, one in which priestly authority gave way to interpretations by individual literate readers of the Bible.

Reconfiguring the world from a human-centered point of view led to important innovations in literature and art. Miguel de Cervantes (c. 1547–1616) wrote what some consider the first modern European novel, *Don Quixote*, to narrate the adventures of an individual. William Shakespeare (1564–1616) told stories of the full range of human emotion and experience in his plays. Artists learned to paint scenes as humans see them, in three dimensions. Previously, Medieval painters had represented the world as God might see it, from a great distance through a metaphorical telephoto lens that flattened humans and their world into a single plane. Renaissance painters discovered a way to

FIGURE 4.1
The Parthenon in Greece
Source: Steve Swayne, Wikimedia Commons.

FIGURE 4.2
St. Peter's Basilica in Rome
Source: Jean-Pol Grandmont, Wikimedia Commons.

represent the world with close objects larger than distant objects to create the illusion, on the two dimensions of a canvas, of three-dimensional human experience. Called **perspective**, the technique allowed painters to paint the world from a human point of view—or perspective.

<table>
<tr><td>

CULTURAL
LINKAGES

</td></tr>
</table>

Music of this period is less notable for its renaissance of Ancient Greek musical ideas than for its stylistic innovations based on the humanistic spirit of the times. Composers turned away from the abstract definition of perfection based on ratios of small whole numbers thought to represent the perfection of God's creation, the sort of harmony heard in Machaut's Mass. Instead, they invented new harmonies and counterpoints that the human ear judged pleasant, and they found ways to express human emotion. In other words, they created music based on the same humanistic principles that painters, novelists, and playwrights were using.

In this chapter we examine gateways to four important European musical genres of this period:

- sacred vocal music, a continuation of the Gregorian chant and Medieval polyphonic mass traditions introduced in Chapter 2;
- polyphonic secular songs still sung today by school and amateur choirs and professional early music ensembles;
- some of the earliest polyphonic ensemble music; and
- music for the precursors of the modern guitar.

We also provide a gateway to one of the most well-known styles of world music: the classical music tradition of North India, also called Hindustani music. Although the instruments in this gateway recording acquired their present form only recently, we introduce them in this chapter for two reasons: first, the most "serious" forms of today's Hindustani instrumental music appeared during the sixteenth century; and, second, nearly all modern North Indian classical instrumentalists trace their musical lineage to a single sixteenth-century musician and his son and daughter.

GATEWAY 12
RENAISSANCE SACRED VOCAL MUSIC

What Is It?

Our gateway to sixteenth-century European sacred vocal music is a motet called "Sicut cervus" (As a deer) composed by Giovanni Pierluigi da Palestrina (c. 1525–1594) and published in 1584. For Renaissance composers, many of whom were from France and Belgium, a **motet** (from the French *mot* meaning word) was a sacred work composed on a Latin text, either newly created or taken from the Bible, and sung during the Catholic liturgy. The poem "Sicut cervus" is an excerpt from the text of the Book of Psalms in the Bible's Old Testament. It expresses the passionate nature of faith:

Sicut cervus desiderat ad fontes aquarum	As a deer thirsts for spring water,
ita desiderat anima mea ad te Deus.	so thirsts my soul for you, God.

The performance is by the Cambridge Singers, directed by the renowned English choral conductor John Rutter (b. 1945). His choral compositions and arrangements are frequently performed by school choirs.

 Listen to the first thirty seconds of the recording.

How Does It Work?

Timbre

Male and female voices across a wide range from low pitches to high pitches sing with a relaxed vocal quality.

Texture

The texture is based on imitative polyphony or imitative counterpoint. **Imitative polyphony** involves each part in the choir singing the same melodic phrase in succession, entering one after the other. When all the parts have entered, the result is four-part harmony created by four rhythmically independent voices. Each such succession of entrances is called a **point of imitation**. The pitch range of Renaissance music included four parts from low to high called **bass**, **tenor**, **alto**, and **soprano**.

Rhythm

The rhythm of each part combines long and short tones in a slow-tempo four-beat meter.

Melody

The melodic lines feature mostly conjunct, stepwise motion.

FIGURE 4.3
Giovanni Pierluigi da Palestrina. Lithograph (1828) by Henri-Joseph Hesse (1781–1849)
Source: Wikimedia Commons.

Harmony

The harmony features chords called triads. **Triads** contain three pitches separated from each other by the interval of a third, for example, C E G. The resulting harmony is called **triadic harmony**.

Form

The form is through composed with two main sections (A B) corresponding to the two lines of the poem.

Performance Techniques

The singers sing long tones without vibrato or ornamentation.

Listen to the first twenty-five seconds of the recording for the first point of imitation, that is, the entrance of each voice (tenor, alto, soprano, bass) in succession in imitative counterpoint.

Listen to the entire recording following this timed listening guide.

TIME	SECTION	TEXT	ENGLISH TRANSLATION
0:00	First point of imitation: the melodic line enters first in the tenor, then the alto, then the soprano and finally the bass. The melody has a graceful, singable, slightly ascending melodic contour. Each part's melodic line is a variant of the tenor's melody, altered slightly to create pleasing triadic harmonies.	*Sicut cervus desiderat ad fontes aquarum*	As a deer thirsts for spring waters
0:25	Second point of imitation: just after the bass enters, the tenor repeats the text on a variant of the first melody before the other parts have finished their first version of the melody. When they finish their first line, they follow the tenor for a second time in another point of imitation. This point of imitation is rather buried in the texture until the bass part enters on this repeated text at 0:38.	*Sicut cervus desiderat ad fontes aquarum*	As a deer thirsts for spring waters
1:09	The music on the first line of text cadences on a long-held tone, and the basses begin a third point of imitation on a descending melody, followed in order by the tenors, sopranos, and altos.	*ita desiderat*	so thirsts
1:34	The basses initiate a fourth point of imitation, repeating the words. The tenors, sopranos, and altos follow.	*ita desiderat*	so thirsts
1:54	The tenors initiate a fifth point of imitation, repeating the words. The basses follow.	*ita desiderat*	so thirsts
2:03	Almost immediately the sopranos initiate a sixth point of imitation with a descending melody on new words overlapping with "ita desiderat." The alto, tenor, and bass parts each follow in turn.	*anima mea ad te Deus*	my soul for you, God

LISTENING GUIDE 4.1

TIME	SECTION	TEXT	ENGLISH TRANSLATION
2:30	The sopranos initiate a seventh point of imitation, repeating the words. The bass and the tenors follow while the alto completes the first time through the words. The section and the motet end on a cadence formed of two long-held chords, the last a perfect fifth recalling the perfection of Medieval harmony.	*anima mea ad te Deus*	my soul for you, God
3:07	End		

What Does It Mean?

A number of elements combine to create a dignified, reverential effect appropriate for a religious service:

AESTHETICS

- the relaxed, pure voice quality and slow tempo;
- the slow declamation of the words, repeated during each point of imitation, focuses attention on the words;
- the harmonies based on triads create a soothing, pleasant effect;
- the stepwise, ascending and descending melodies consisting of long-held tones create a calm effect;
- for sixteenth-century listeners, the text in Latin linked this performance to more than a thousand years of *a cappella* singing, that is, **choral singing** without instrumental accompaniment, enhancing the sense of the continuity and authority of the church's teaching;
- the text evokes religious belief in a poetic and emotional way that inspired both Palestrina and worshippers;
- a choir singing in four-part harmony in this manner would echo rather grandly through the large churches of western Europe, creating an aural image of the Catholic Church's rich traditions, which were also expressed in its extravagant buildings, paintings, and sculptures by the best Renaissance painters, and the elaborately embroidered vestments of the clergy.

Listen to the recording one more time with these effects and sentiments in mind.

Palestrina carefully combined these features during a period called the Catholic **Counter-Reformation**. The pope, church leaders, and musicians sought to restore the dignity and sanctity of the church in the wake of the Protestants' attacks on both. Popes, accused of corruption and licentiousness, adopted modest, ascetic habits as a sign of their renewed dedication to the Christian value of humility. A nearly twenty-year-long (1545–1563) conclave of cardinals and archbishops convened in the northern Italian town of Trento. At this gathering, known as the Council of Trent, delegates reconsidered every aspect of church doctrine, including the liturgy and its music. They rejected the Protestant practice of singing in local languages to educate their congregations in Biblical lessons and Christian theology. Instead, they reaffirmed the use of Latin in the liturgy. They considered rejecting polyphonic music and returning to monophonic Gregorian chant to focus worshippers' attention on the text and not distract them with the pleasures of music, a concern echoing those of Buddhists and Muslims about music's seductive powers. They abandoned this proposal, not least because Palestrina and his contemporaries adopted the contemplative, slow-moving style, with appropriate attention to textual clarity, exemplified by "Sicut cervus."

CULTURAL LINKAGES

What Is Its History?

Palestrina lived his whole life in service to the Church, most of it in Rome as a singer, choirmaster, and composer for various papal chapels, including for a time at the Sistine Chapel, the pope's chapel famous today for its frescoes painted by Michelangelo (1475–1564). Palestrina could not stay there long, however, because he was not a priest. He married twice and had a number of children. "Sicut cervus" is one of 375 motets he wrote during his lifetime. Some critics consider these motets his greatest works, perhaps because of the marriage of his sensitive music with religiously enthused texts. Even more important historically are the 104 polyphonic masses he wrote, following in the footsteps of Guillaume de Machaut and composers of the fifteenth century. Machaut wrote the first polyphonic mass around 1360, his *Messe de Nostre Dame*, whose "Gloria" (Chapter 2, Gateway 7) was very well known. It inspired composers during the fifteenth century to write suites of compositions for the ordinary of the mass (Kyrie, Credo, Gloria, Sanctus, Agnus Dei). Their polyphonic masses are the earliest examples in European music of multi-movement works. Compositions for these texts for the Catholic mass have continued to attract composers from Palestrina's time to the present, including Protestant and Jewish composers.

If we compare the counterpoint and harmonies of Machaut's "Gloria" from 1360 to Palestrina's "Sicut cervus" of 1584, we can hear that much had changed in European music during the intervening 200 years. Imitative polyphony, unknown to Machaut, had become a common practice. Harmonies based on thirds replaced Medieval harmonies based on perfect fourths and fifths. One of the most important reasons for these changes was the influence of English music on the music of northern France and Belgium. During the Medieval period musicians in England favored the interval of a third over fourths and fifths. They also sang in a particular kind of imitative polyphony called a round. In a **round** a single melody is sung with staggered entrances to create a polyphonic texture. "Frère Jacques" and "Row, Row, Row Your Boat" are well-known examples. The earliest notated round was sung by monks at a church in England during the thirteenth century. It has a religious text, but they sang the same melody to a secular text for their own entertainment: "Sumer is icumen in, lhude sing cuccu" ("Summer has arrived, loudly sing cuckoo!"). This round generates harmonies based on thirds.

CULTURAL LINKAGES

The English practice of imitative polyphony and harmonies based on thirds attracted the interest of composers in northern France, Belgium, and the Netherlands when the English occupied northwestern Europe during the Hundred Years War (1337–1453) between England and France. English nobility established courts in northern Europe, and French composers began to write in a manner designed to suit their tastes. The most important composer of this transition from fifth-based Medieval harmonies to Renaissance triadic harmonies was Guillaume Dufay (c. 1397–1474), who lived through most of the fifteenth century. Born in northern Europe near Brussels, he was educated in the church and may have been paid as a church composer as early as age sixteen. Throughout his life he traveled between the French-speaking area of northern Europe and the Italian cities of Rome, Florence, and Bologna, where he taught Italians these new French polyphonic techniques. Among his many compositions was a set of lamentations on the fall of the Eastern Orthodox Christian city of Constantinople to the Ottoman Turks in 1453. He wrote in many genres including motets, secular French *chansons*, and settings for seven complete mass ordinaries.

He is perhaps most famous for his masses based on a *cantus firmus* (fixed song) taken from popular, secular music to make church music more engaging for worshippers. Sometimes the chosen song melody appears in all the movements of the ordinary of the mass, providing it with a unifying musical element and creating what is called a **cyclical mass.** Using a secular song as a *cantus firmus* connected religious worship to everyday secular experience, the same impulse that has led the Catholic faithful since the mid-twentieth century to compose folk masses, mariachi masses, and African masses. One of Dufay's most famous works is his *Missa L'homme armé* (Mass [based on the song] "The Armed Man"). The song "L'homme armé" may have been composed in

1453 at the fall of Constantinople to the Ottoman Empire. A call for a crusade against the Ottoman Empire in 1460 may have inspired Dufay to write this *cantus firmus* mass based on it.

Fifty years after Dufay's birth, a second important precursor of Palestrina was born in northern France or Belgium: Josquin des Prez (*c.* 1450/1455–1521), often called simply Josquin. During his lifetime he worked at the courts of a number of French dukes, but also traveled to Italy, where he worked for a time at the papal chapel. Twenty of his complete masses survive, including one using "L'homme armé" as the *cantus firmus*. He is also well known for his polyphonic secular *chansons*. His works were among the first to be published in musical notation on the new printing presses invented in Germany by Johannes Gutenberg in 1453. Printed music allowed musical scores to be reproduced in greater quantities than ever before. Printed versions of Josquin's music circulated widely around Europe, making him famous and amplifying the influence of his innovative compositional style.

Giovanni Pierluigi da Palestrina was born near Rome seventy-five years after Josquin. He was the first Italian composer to match the fame and skill at polyphony of Dufay and Josquin, both of whom had lived for a time in Italy. Palestrina worked at St. Peter's Basilica in Rome after 1551 as its *maestro di cappella* (conductor of the chapel choir), where he was a prolific composer of religious compositions. In them Palestrina followed Dufay and Josquin and firmly established thirds and sixths as consonant intervals. He also developed imitative counterpoint to a very high level. A great deal of Palestrina's music survives largely due to his long-lasting employment at St. Peter's in the Vatican. A century or so later, eighteenth-century Austrian composer Johann Joseph Fux (1660–1741) codified Palestrina's style in his highly influential treatise *Gradus ad Parnassum* (figuratively, "steps to the loftiest peaks of art"). The book introduced the concept of "species counterpoint" (types of counterpoint, that is, ways of writing polyphony), a pedagogical tool still used today in some university music theory classes.

IOSQVINVS PRATENSIS.

FIGURE 4.4
Josquin des Prez (ca. 1450–1521)
Engraving after a portrait in the Cathedral of Brussels
Source: Prisma Archivo/Alamy Stock Photo.

The harmony of "Sicut cervus" sounds rather familiar, especially compared to Machaut's harmonies of 200 years earlier. That is because the harmony is based on triads, the sort of harmony we hear commonly today in much classical and popular music. Music of this period also used different types of cadences than did Machaut, cadences still heard today in classical and popular music. Machaut's double leading tone cadence (C♯-E-G♯ moving in parallel fifths to D-A) in the "Gloria" was, over the course of two hundred years, replaced by two new types of cadence. One moved from a triad based on the fifth degree of the scale, a chord called the **dominant** (V), to the triad based on the tonic (I). Music theorists label chords with Roman numerals based on the number of the scale degree a chord begins on, so the triad based on the tonic would be called "I" and the triad based on the fifth scale degree, the dominant, would be called "V." The V–I movement between two triads is called an **authentic cadence** and can be represented as G-B-D to C-E-G. In this cadence there is only one leading tone (B leads to C), and movement by parallel fifths, as in the double leading tone cadence, is avoided. This half-step motion from the seventh degree of the scale to the first is today the only motion that is known as a **leading tone**, because it leads to the tonic (I). The other cadence moved from the pitch a fifth below the tonic, actually the fourth degree of the scale (IV), to the tonic (I). Called a **plagal cadence**, this IV–I cadence can be represented as F-A-C to C-E-G. Again, parallel fifths are avoided, and there is only one instance of motion by a half-step (F falls a half-step to E). The plagal cadence came to be associated with the singing of "amen" at the end of a hymn, and is sometimes called an **amen cadence**.

For much of "Sicut cervus" the moving contrapuntal parts create the harmonic impression of rocking between the tonic triad (I) and the triad on the fourth degree of the scale, called the

subdominant (IV). The first section ends with a V–I authentic cadence (at 1:09), and the second ends with a IV–I plagal cadence (at the end). Using these two cadences to end sections of a composition is harbinger of a new style of harmony, which after 1600 became the new method for organizing musical forms and remains in use today, especially in popular music.

 Listen one more time to "Sicut cervus" with attention to the V–I cadence at 1:09 and the IV–I cadence at the end.

> **CULTURAL LINKAGES**

This historical change from harmony based on fourths and fifths to harmony based on thirds can be interpreted as one aspect of the larger humanist impulse of the fifteenth and sixteenth centuries. Harmonies based on perfect fourths and fifths were linked metaphorically to God's creation and Pythagoras's harmony of the spheres. They were God's harmonies or nature's harmonies. Harmonies based on thirds seemed to be based on what humans preferred to listen to, at least humans in England and western Europe. In that sense third-based harmonies proceeded from the same aesthetic framework that led painters to create three-dimensional perspective.

Before the Renaissance, Medieval paintings of scenes on earth were treated as if seen by God using a telephoto lens. Painters squashed everything into a single, flat plane just as a telephoto lens would do. The principal Renaissance achievement in painting was the invention of perspective, credited to the early-fifteenth-century Florentine artist Filippo Brunelleschi (1377–1450). He provided a geometrical solution to the problem of how to represent the three dimensions of space on a two-dimensional canvas, creating paintings with objects in the foreground larger than objects in the background and with the ratio of their sizes carefully calibrated so they were apprehended as natural to the human eye. In an early example of perspective in painting from the late 1400s, the artist Pietro Perugino (c. 1450–1523), who worked in Florence and Rome, drew lines on the city square, all receding to a single point in the distance, to make the new technique explicit. In later Renaissance paintings by Titian (c. 1490–1576) from Venice, Pieter Bruegel (1525–1569) from Antwerp, and many others the lines disappear but the principle remains. The application of perspective to painting creates a view of the world from a human, rather than a heavenly, point of view just as harmonies in thirds did for human listeners.

Today choral singing like that of "Sicut cervus" occupies a somewhat peripheral place in American musical life, which is centered on the instrumental music of jazz combos and ensembles, the symphony orchestra, the string quartet and solo sonatas, popular music groups, and popular and

FIGURE 4.5
Pietro Perugino (c. 1450–1523), "The Delivery of the Keys" (1481)
Source: Sistine Chapel, Wikimedia Commons.

classical solo singers. Today European-derived choral singing finds its home principally in school and university music programs, churches, and synagogues, and a few professional ensembles devoted to its performance. These institutions have in turn incubated the current interest in *a cappella* singing on college campuses and on TV shows like *The Sing-Off*, films like *Pitch Perfect*, and, a century earlier, barbershop quartet singing, college glee clubs, and African American spirituals.

WHERE DO I GO FROM HERE?

- Listen to the "Gloria" from Palestrina's *Missa Pater Noster* (Our Father). Notice the way each of the first three voices enters in imitation after just two syllables of the previous voice. The bass voice enters with the same melody just a bit later. Listen also for the harmonies in thirds.

- Listen to the "Kyrie" from Guillaume Dufay's *Missa L'Homme armé*, written in the 1400s. It is separated by about a century from both the "Gloria" of Machaut's *Messe de Nostre Dame* and Palestrina's "Sicut cervus." Which does it more closely resemble in musical style, and what are those similarities?

- Listen to the "Kyrie" from Josquin's "*Missa L'Homme armé super voces musicales*," composed about 1502. It is closer in time to Dufay's mass than to Palestrina's "Sicut cervus" of 1584. How is it similar to and different from those two other works?

- "Sumer Is Icumen In, Lhude Sing Cuccu" has been recorded in many iterations from versions by popular singers to those played by various Medieval musical instruments or sung by classical choirs. It seems to have become Europe's earliest pop song. Listen to a few of these versions, and find one that you imagine might be closest to the sound of English monks in the thirteenth century. Which of these many versions do you like the best, and what in its musical elements leads you to like it the best?

GATEWAY 13
RENAISSANCE SECULAR VOCAL MUSIC

What Is It?

Medieval secular love songs like those of Guillaume de Machaut are rarely performed today. But the same is not true for Renaissance secular vocal music. It is quite commonly performed by high school and college choirs as well as professional early music groups. Our gateway to Renaissance secular vocal music is a madrigal called "Fair Phyllis I saw sitting all alone." John Farmer (c. 1570–c. 1601), an Englishman, published it in 1599. **Madrigals** first appeared in Italy around 1530 as a genre of polyphonic love songs in Italian, the secular counterpart of the sacred motet. The term may derive from the Latin *matri (lo)quela*, meaning mother tongue, that is, Italian rather than Latin. When the English began composing and singing them in English later in the sixteenth century, they kept the Italian name madrigal. "Fair Phyllis" is a cheeky song about a shepherd boy named Amyntas in search of his lost lover, Phyllis, a shepherdess. Well-educated sixteenth-century singers of madrigals knew Phyllis and Amyntas as the names of a shepherdess and shepherd from their study of Latin literature from Ancient Rome. The Roman poet Virgil, famous for his epic *Aeneid*, wrote that Amyntas played a reed pipe, perhaps a bagpipe like those that shepherds all over Europe have played since antiquity. The performance is by four members of The King's Singers, a group of six male vocalists formed at King's College, Cambridge, founded in the 1960s.

 Listen to the first fifteen seconds of the recording.

> CULTURAL
> LINKAGES

FIGURE 4.6
The King's Singers in 1970
Source: United Archives/Alamy Stock Photo.

How Does It Work?

Timbre

Four male singers sing relatively pure tones over a wide range from bass to soprano.

Texture

The texture changes from monophonic to polyphonic, including imitative counterpoint.

Rhythm

The meter changes back and forth between duple and triple.

Melody

The melodic motion is conjunct.

Harmony

The harmony is based on triads, with authentic cadences (V–I) at the end of each line of text.

Form

The form can be described, using letters, as AABCC.

Performance Techniques

To reach the high pitches in the soprano voice, the male singer sings in **falsetto**, a "false" voice that allows men, and women, to sing in a register above their normal, speaking vocal range. The singers of the two highest parts sing in this manner and are called **countertenors** rather than sopranos or altos, as female singers are. They sing without vibrato in a very fast tempo.

Listen to the recording for the monophonic and polyphonic textures.

Listen to the entire recording following this timed listening guide.

LISTENING GUIDE 4.2

TIME	FORM	TEXT	DESCRIPTION
0:00	A	Fair Phyllis I saw sitting all alone	It is sung monophonically by a single voice in duple meter.
0:04		Feeding her flock near to the mountainside	All voices sing four-part polyphony in the same rhythm mixing triple and duple meter.
0:06	A (repeat)		
0:12	B	The shepherds knew not whither she was gone	The first point of imitation in duple meter enters.
0:16		But after her lover Amyntas hied	The second point of imitation.
0:21	C	Up and down he wandered	A third point of imitation tosses a short melodic phrase "up and down" from soprano to bass among the four voices.

TIME	FORM	TEXT	DESCRIPTION
0:31		While she was missing	In a brief contrapuntal passage the basses and tenors enter together in contrary motion followed by the sopranos and altos also in contrary motion.
0:33		When he found her	The soprano part, called countertenor when sung by a man, and bass sing in parallel tenths (an octave plus a third) while the middle voices sing two different melodic lines with contrasting rhythmic durations.
0:36		O, then they fell a-kissing	Three- and four-part polyphony sung in the same rhythm in triple meter
0:44	C (repeat)		
1:12	End		

What Does It Mean?

While you were listening to the text and the musical elements of this performance, you may have already noticed the way the music mirrored the text. Composers during the Renaissance, like their counterparts in art and literature, sought to express individual human emotions in their work. In their secular vocal compositions, they created musical icons for the ideas and sentiments in the text, a technique known as **text painting**. In "Fair Phyllis," Farmer and the performers combine fast tempo and suggestive lyrics to create a jolly mood.

CULTURAL LINKAGES

 Listen again to the recording following the chart below and paying attention to the way Farmer paints the text in musical gestures.

Fair Phyllis I saw sitting alone	A single voice evokes her solitude.
Feeding her flock near to the mountainside	The polyphony of voices singing in the same rhythm suggests a unified "flock."
The shepherds knew not whither she was gone But after her lover Amyntas hied	The introduction of imitative polyphonic suggests shepherds, and Phyllis's lover Amyntas, scurrying around.
Up and down he wandered	The short melodic phrase jumps rapidly up and down in pitch, the first time referencing the search and the second time, after "O, then they fell a-kissing," a more intimate form of wandering up and down.
While she was missing	
When he found her	From the Renaissance on, singing in parallel thirds (in this case the sopranos and basses sing in an octave plus a third) became an icon of togetherness, love, and shared views.
O, then they fell a-kissing	Here the unified rhythm of all the voices suggests a kind of musical embrace.

What Is Its History?

John Farmer served as organist and choirmaster at the Anglican St. Patrick's Cathedral in Dublin, Ireland. He dedicated his one book of madrigals to Edward de Vere, Earl of Oxford, an important poet and patron of the arts. Farmer was a contemporary of William Shakespeare, most of whose highly regarded plays were published between 1589 and 1613. Although Farmer was not an especially prolific composer—he lived only thirty years after all—"Fair Phyllis" is a classic of the English madrigal genre. High school and college choirs regularly perform it today.

FIGURE 4.7
Portrait of Edward de Vere, 17th Earl of Oxford
Source: Wikimedia Commons.

The Italian madrigal caught on in England after 1560, when publications of Italian madrigals with texts translated into English began to appear there. Italian culture enthralled the English at the time. Shakespeare set a number of his plays in Italy, including *Two Gentlemen of Verona*, *Romeo and Juliet*, *The Merchant of Venice*, and *Othello, the Moor of Venice*. Singing madrigals after dinner was one of the principal forms of entertainment at courts of the nobility and in the homes of the growing class of merchants and traders enriched by Atlantic trade. Groups of all women, all men, and mixed groups sang them (Figure 4.8). Learning to sight-read from books of madrigals in musical notation was an important social grace for courtiers and wealthy, educated amateurs. King Henry VIII (reigned 1509–1547) composed songs and played musical instruments. His daughter with Anne Boleyn, Queen Elizabeth I (reigned 1558–1603), learned to play musical instruments and enjoyed dancing. In the *Merchant of Venice* (Act V, Scene 1), written about the same time as "Fair Phyllis," Shakespeare writes in a way reminiscent of Confucius and Plato about the positive effect of musical performance on the character of kings and those who serve them:

But music for the time doth change his nature.
The man that hath no music in himself,
Nor is not moved with concord of sweet sounds,
Is fit for treasons, stratagems, and spoils.
The motions of his spirit are dull as night,
And his affections dark as Erebus.
Let no such man be trusted. Mark the music.

ECONOMIC ACTIVITY

Although widely sung by educated amateurs, there is some record of professional entertainers singing madrigals. During the late sixteenth century northern Italian courts supported groups of professional female singers called *Concerti delle donne* (Ensembles of Women). They competed for attention with the beauty of their voices, hand gestures and meaningful looks, and the addition of all sorts of added musical devices not in the notation (ornaments, virtuoso melodic runs, sighs), all the more obviously to express the meaning of the text and charm their patrons.

FIGURE 4.8
Sixteenth-century Venetian painting of a group of madrigal singers with lute
Source: Music-Images/Alamy Stock Photo.

All over Europe courtly secular songs like the Italian and English madrigal were known by local names: in French *chansons*, in German *Lieder*. The earliest such songs surviving in the written history of European music are love songs in manuscripts after 1100. Medieval court entertainers, courtiers, and nobility from southwestern Europe known as **troubadours** (in French *trouvères*), including a few women, composed their lyrics and melodies and sang them solo with or without instrumental musical accompaniment. Guillaume de Machaut, the composer of the *Messe de Nostre Dame*, was better known in the fourteenth century for his secular love songs than for his Mass. And during the fifteenth century Guillaume Dufay and Josquin composed secular *chansons* as well as motets and masses. Madrigals stand out at this moment in history, the sixteenth century, because they were written in a new harmonic style based on triads, which became the harmonic foundation for later European classical music, American popular music, and jazz. As a consequence they are the oldest style of European secular vocal music widely performed today. Madrigals are also foundational for an important feature of European instrumental music: its ability to express emotions. Madrigals associated certain musical elements so tightly with textual ideas that when, in later instrumental music, the words were omitted, the idea or emotion in the musical gesture (say, a descending melodic line) retained its meaning for composers and listeners (a fall from grace, a descent into hell, or sadness, for example).

EMOTIONAL RESONANCE

WHERE DO I GO FROM HERE?

- Listen to a few performances of "Fair Phyllis" and describe the way each one differs in performance technique from each other and from the one in this gateway by The King's Singers.

- Claudio Monteverdi (1567–1643), a master of the Italian madrigal, wrote eight books of them. The first four employ Renaissance multipart vocal polyphony. Listen to a performance of one of his most famous madrigals, "Si ch'io vorrei morire" (Yes, I want to die), published in 1601 and notice the way he paints the text in his music, including his use of chords based on the dissonant interval of a second to express a lover's yearning.

- Listen to a recording of "Now is the Month of Maying," a madrigal by Thomas Morley (c. 1557–1602), perhaps England's most famous madrigal composer of the Elizabethan era.

- Listen to a recording of a Renaissance *chanson* (song, the French equivalent of madrigal) by Clément Janequin (c. 1485–1558) called "Le chant des oyseaux" (The Song of the Birds), quite remarkable for its iconic text painting.

GATEWAY 14
RENAISSANCE DANCE MUSIC

What Is It?

Renaissance instrumental dance music employed the new triadic harmony of religious and secular vocal music. As such, they are important precursors of later forms of instrumental music including those of the present day. Our gateway to European dance music of the sixteenth century is a performance by the Early Music Consort of London of a suite of four compositions for a type of dance called *volta* (plural *volte*). **Volta** means turn; it refers to a movement in which the male dancer lifts his partner off the ground and rotates her through a ninety-degree turn. In music **suite** commonly refers to a set of dance tunes. **Tune** can be a synonym for melody, but musicians most frequently use it as a label for relatively short, easy-to-remember, repeating melodies, especially song melodies (song tunes) and melodies that accompany dancing (dance tunes). The *volte* in this suite come from a collection of 312 dance compositions called *Terpsichore* published in 1612 by Michael Praetorius, a German composer, organist, and scholar of music who lived from 1571 to 1621. In Greek mythology, Terpsichore was the Greek goddess of the dance and one of the nine muses. Her name means "delight in dancing."

FIGURE 4.9
Michael Praetorius
Source: Granger Historical Picture Archive/Alamy Stock Photo.

 Listen to the first thirty seconds of the recording.

How Does It Work?

Timbre

This performance features four isolated and contrasting timbres in each *volta*, in order: (1) the sound of whistle flutes called recorders; (2) the sound of bowed stringed instruments called violin and viol; (3) the sound of buzzed-lip instruments called cornetts and sackbuts; and (4) the sound of the full ensemble. In addition, a drum called tabor accompanies the musicians throughout.

Texture

These dance pieces have four parts (also called voices) from soprano to bass.

Rhythm

A six-beat triple meter (3+3) matches a six-beat repeating dance movement.

Melody

The tunes are constructed mainly in eight measures of six beats and move mostly in stepwise motion.

Harmony

The harmonies are triadic in the new style of the sixteenth century with V–I authentic cadences at the end of each phrase.

Form

Each of the four *volte* in the suite employs AABB form, with the exception of the fourth *volta*, which has an AAB form. In the abstract, AABB can be labeled **binary form**, but, because of its association with dance tunes, we call it and similar forms, such as the Bulgarian *kopanitsa* in Chapter 3, Gateway 11, **European dance form.** Since new melodies are introduced in each *volta*, the form of the whole performance could be rendered as ABCD, where A = aabb, B = ccdd, and so forth.

Performance Techniques

The most striking performance technique is heard in the first *volta* for recorders, in which the player of the highest-pitched soprano part adds ornamental variations to the melody on the repeat.

Listen to the first thirty seconds of the recording for the ornamentation in the high-pitched part and the AABB form.

Listen to the entire recording following this timed listening guide.

LISTENING GUIDE 4.3

TIME	SECTIONS	DESCRIPTION
	Volta #1	Recorders playing in four-part harmony
0:00	A	8 measures of six pulses
0:18	A'	Repeats with added ornaments
0:35	B	8 measures
0:51	B'	Repeats with added ornaments
	Volta #2	Viols and violins (bowed strings) play in four-part harmony
1:09	A	4 measures of six pulses
1:18	A	Repeat of A with a slightly varied accompaniment
1:26	B	4 measures of six pulses

TIME	SECTIONS	DESCRIPTION
1:35	B	Repeat of B with a slightly varied accompaniment
1:44	C	2 measures of six pulses
1:49	C	Repeat of C with a slightly varied accompaniment
1:53	D	2 measures of six pulses
1:58	D	Repeat of D with a slightly varied accompaniment
	Volta #3	Cornetts and sackbuts playing in four-part harmony
2:01	A	4 measures of six pulses
2:10	A	
2:19	B	5 measures of six pulses
2:31	B	
	Volta #4	Full ensemble
2:42	A	2 measures of 9
2:50	A	
2:57	B	7 measures of 3
3:06	Repeat of ABB	
3:29	Repeat of ABB	
4:03	End	

What Does It Mean?

These dance tunes and suites accompanied dancing at the courts of the nobility. Like the ability to sing madrigals in four-part harmony by reading from books of musical notation, skill at dancing was

> **CULTURAL LINKAGES**

an important social grace expected of lords and ladies at court as well as of princes, kings, and queens. Courts employed professional dance instructors to teach the steps of a large repertoire of courtly dance types. In most courtly dances of the period, the partners either danced facing one another without touching or they held hands as they processed in a circle around the dance floor. The *volta* was the only court dance of the period in which the bodies of the dancers touched, so the erotic implications were clear. Queen Elizabeth I of England was an avid dancer. A sixteenth-century painting purports to show a famous incident at court, when she danced a *volta* with her favorite male friend and a former suitor, Robert Dudley, Earl of Leicester. (She never married and was known as the virgin queen.) She is able to rise so far off the floor because her partner grabbed her bone corset at the waist and lifted her off the floor with the help of his leg. She is sitting on her partner's raised thigh as he turns her in a *volta*. A stylized version of the incident can be seen

FIGURE 4.10
Queen Elizabeth I and Robert Dudley, Earl of Leicester, dancing a *volta* accompanied by two violins and bass viol
Source: Wikimedia Commons.

in the 1998 film *Elizabeth* starring Cate Blanchett and Joseph Fiennes, in which Elizabeth orders the musicians to "play a *volta*." While the filmed dance bears little resemblance to the *volte* of the sixteenth century (Fiennes raises her with two hands around her waist, not with her corset and his leg), the scene does capture the sexual undertone of the dance.

Dance music shares many of the elements (harmony, rhythm, scales, and polyphonic style) of madrigals, Catholic motets, and Lutheran hymns. But given the absence of a text, emotional expression was not at stake in this kind of dance music. The dancers and others in attendance mainly judged the performance in terms of the skill of the musicians, that is, their ability to play in tune and with a strong, steady beat suitable for dancing. The composers of instrumental dance tunes in this period did not specify which instruments were to play them, so the sound of each performance depended on which instrumentalists were present at that particular court. In this recording, the Early Music Ensemble of London selected four *volte* from Praetorius's *Terpsichore*, arranged them into a suite, and assigned the instrumental groups to them. Praetorius did not specify the suite form, the instruments to use, any sort drum accompaniment, or the tempo. As a result early music groups today have quite a bit of freedom in how they perform these sixteenth-century dance compositions. Changing the instruments in this recording helps provide some welcome variety for a modern audience.

What Is Its History?

The roots of this kind of European instrumental dance music can be found in the village dances of Europe, the sort of music in the gateway to European village music in Chapter 3, Gateway 11. During the Medieval period one or a few instrumentalists played dance tunes monophonically, and everyone joined in dancing a relatively short pattern of repeated steps in a circle holding hands. Court dances like the *volta* had more elaborate choreographies than the circular country dances. As polyphonic vocal music developed in the churches and courts of Europe, composers began to write polyphonic dance music as well. The AABB dance form (with its extensions CC, DD, and so on as heard in the Bulgarian *kopanitsa*) became quite common. The first large collection of polyphonic dance tunes, printed in movable type, appeared in 1551 in Antwerp, an important Atlantic trading city on the coast of Belgium, and spread rapidly around Europe. The six-beat meter of the *volta* is shared by another dance, the *galliarde*, which omits the turn. The most common rhythm of the *galliarde*, also heard in these *volte*, can be notated this way, where each number is a pulse and each x indicates when the rhythm of the tune occurs:

```
1   2   3   4   5   6

x   x   x   x       x x
```

This *galliarde* and *volta* rhythm is retained today in the tune of the patriotic American song "My Country 'Tis of Thee," borrowed from the English anthem, "God Save the Queen."

Michael Praetorius was born into a family of Lutheran pastors in what is today central Germany. Educated in a Latin school, his Latin name is a translation of the common German name Schultz, meaning mayor or sheriff of a village (like Constable in English). After finishing school he worked as a church organist and as the *Kapellmeister* (conductor) of a local duke's court musicians and singers and as director of a town band. He saved enough money to establish a foundation for the poor after his death. He was a prolific composer of Lutheran hymns in the harmonic style of the day. His harmonization of the Christmas carol *Es ist ein Ros entsprungen* (a rose has sprung up, sung in English as "Lo How a Rose E'er Blooming") is widely performed today. The dance tunes from *Terpsichore* are his only surviving secular compositions. Perhaps befitting a member of a well-educated family (both his father and grandfather were Lutheran pastors and his older brother was a university professor of theology), Praetorius wrote three volumes of a planned four-volume encyclopedic treatise on music. They are an important source of information about Renaissance musical practices and instruments.

Renaissance dance pieces were played by a growing number of musical instruments, some of which were native to Europe and some of which came into Europe either from the Byzantine and Ottoman Empires to the southeast of Europe or through Spain and Italy from Arab lands in North Africa. Here is a brief history and description of the ones heard in this gateway recording of four *volte* from Praetorius's *Terpsichore*.

The recorders heard in Volte #1 and the sackbuts and cornetts heard in Volte #3 belong with a large family of instruments called **aerophones**: instruments whose sound is created by air vibrating in a column or tube. The recorder is an end-blown whistle flute in which air from the player's breath passes through a tube (with a "beak" that goes into the player's mouth) and over the edge of the tube. It has seven finger holes and a thumbhole. Whistle flutes have a wide distribution around the world. In Europe they originated as a shepherd's instrument before they entered the world of courtly music. In most of Europe during the Renaissance they were known by a local variant of the word flute. In France, for example, they were called *flûte à bec* (beaked flute). In England the word "recorder" was used, as the verb to record means, among other things, to sing like a bird. A recorder is, in that sense, something that warbles like a songbird. From the sixteenth century to the present this metaphorical connection between the sound of a flute and the sound of a bird singing has continued to be used whenever a composer of instrumental music has wanted to suggest an outdoor scene with the sound of birds singing.

The recorder was already part of courtly music making during the Medieval period. During the Renaissance musical instrument makers constructed recorders and many other types of musical instruments in sets of different sizes, so they could play over the wide range of voices or parts in the new harmonic style of the period: soprano, alto, tenor, and bass. Such an ensemble of instruments was called a **consort**. A consort consisting of the same type of instruments, such as the consort of recorders that plays Volta #1, is called a closed consort. Consorts that mixed different types of instruments were called "broken consorts."

The cornetts and sackbuts in Volta #3 are also aerophones, but the sound is started by buzzed lips rather than the edge of the tube. The oldest forms of buzzed-lipped aerophones in Europe had no finger holes. Their pitches were those of the overtone series of an open tube. A common generic word for them is **trumpet**, which comes from a French word which links their shape to a nose or an elephant's trunk. They are also very loud, so trumpet has come to mean any sort of loud proclamation, as in to trumpet one's success. Shepherds made them from wood, cutting a tree branch in half lengthwise, hollowing out each half, and tying the halves back together with birch-bark strips. The most famous instance is the Swiss alphorn, but similar instruments exist in many parts of Europe. Shepherds used them to signal from one hillside pasture to another. Militaries around the world use a brass bugle to signal

FIGURE 4.11
The Fontanella Quintet, a recorder consort from the U.K., playing, from left to right, great bass, tenor, alto, basset (little bass), tenor
Source: Fontanella Quintet.

CULTURAL LINKAGES

FIGURE 4.12
Swiss alphorn
Source: Hans Hillewaert, Wikimedia Commons.

function various events during the day such as reveille, mess call, and taps. Similar rural instruments were also made from animal horns, and so the name **horn** is also used as a generic term for buzzed-lip aerophones. Some trumpets and horns have been made of metal since at least Roman times, where they were associated with outdoor ceremonies and processions, a connection that European composers have used for hundreds of years to suggest the solemnity and power of the state.

Renaissance cornetts and sackbuts are names for particular trumpets or horns. The **cornett** is made of a piece of wood, often slightly curved and cut in half lengthwise, hollowed out, held together with a leather covering, with six finger holes and a thumbhole. The holes allow players to play diatonic scales mainly in the highest parts in the texture of instrumental music. The cornett flourished in instrumental music from about 1500 to 1700, and was revived in the twentieth century as part of the early music movement. The **sackbut** was the old English name for what the Italians were calling a *trombone* and the French a *trompette saicqueboute*. Made of brass, sackbuts and trombones had a slide so the player could change the length of the tube and thus the pitch of the instrument. *Saicqueboute* is a combination of French words for pushing and pulling, a description of the instrument's playing technique. Like the recorder, the sackbut or trombone was made in a family or consort of instruments of different pitches to mimic the range of vocal polyphony. Sackbuts were used in court and town bands. In some churches they played the parts of religious vocal polyphony (motets and masses) along with the singers, a practice called doubling the parts. Their association during the Renaissance with the solemn rituals of the church, especially funerals, has meant that, ever since then, composers have used trombones in their instrumental music to evoke a dignified and serious mood.

Volta #2 employs viols and violins, bowed string instruments that belong to a large family of **chordophones**: instruments with vibrating strings. Both viols and violins have a "waisted" shape. They seem to have developed from pear-shaped bowed instruments, like the Bulgarian *gadulka*, that entered Europe during the Medieval period. Some, called lyra, came into western Europe from the Byzantine Empire, with its capital in Constantinople (present-day Istanbul). Others, called *rebab*, came north into Europe from Arab North Africa. During the Medieval period their European descendents were commonly called rebec.

Viols and violins with a waisted shape became common during the late fifteenth century. **Viols** have frets on the neck, are held vertically between the knees (*da gamba*), have five or six strings, and a relatively muted, quiet sound. They were a favored instrument of courtly amateurs. The **violin** has no frets, is held horizontally against the chest or shoulder (*a braccio*), has four strings, and a relatively bright, loud sound. It was favored by professional musicians because they could play it loudly enough to be heard during outdoor festivities. They also substituted it in broken consorts for the cornett and other loud instruments. Both viols and violins were made in sets with different sizes from soprano to bass. By the eighteenth century the viol had disappeared from the scene, and the violin family was ascendant in four sizes from treble to bass, but with names harkening back to the sixteenth century: violin, viola, violoncello (or simply cello), and bass (or bass viol), the first two played *a braccio* and the second two played *da gamba*.

FIGURE 4.13
Painting of a consort of sackbut and cornetts, *c.* 1545 by Giorgio Vasari (1511–1578)
Source: Isabella Stewart Gardner Museum, Wikimedia Commons.

FIGURE 4.14
A Medieval, thirteenth-century manuscript illustration of two players of the bowed lute called rebec or *rebab*
Source: *Cantigas de Santa Maria*, Wikimedia Commons.

FIGURE 4.15
The Smithsonian Consort of Viols,
performing in 2009
Source: Badagnani, Wikimedia
Commons.

The drum used in these recordings is called tabor and belongs to a large family of instruments called **membranophones**, instruments whose sound comes from a vibrating skin held to a frame, cylinder, or bowl under extreme tension. Drums of four main types came into Europe during the Medieval period from today's Middle East: (1) large double-headed cylindrical bass drums; (2) the mid-size, double-headed, cylindrical tabor, today called a **snare drum** (a snare is a string that rests against the nonstruck drumhead and that rattles or buzzes when the other drumhead is struck); (3) **kettledrums** consisting of one skin stretched over a bowl; and (4) **tambourines** with one drumhead stretched over a shallow circular frame. The first three are played with one or two sticks. The tambourine is played with fingers and hands.

WHERE DO I GO FROM HERE?

- Find a video of the Renaissance dance *volta* to see how it was danced and how the steps fit the six-beat rhythm of the music.

- Find videos for performances of common Renaissance dances: *volta, galliarde, branle, courante, basse danse, ronde, passamezzo,* and *pavane*. Describe the differences in meter, rhythm, and tempo among these dance types.

- Find modern-day audio and video examples of the predecessors of the courtly instruments heard in this gateway: the Swiss alphorn, the Greek *lyra,* and the Serbian *frula* (a whistle flute with six finger holes, no thumbhole, and no "beak").

- Listen to a recording of Michael Praetorius' arrangement in four-part harmony of the Lutheran hymn, *Es ist ein Ros entsprungen.*

 GATEWAY 15
RENAISSANCE LUTE MUSIC

What Is It?

The guitar, so ubiquitous in popular music today, took shape during the Renaissance. European luthiers (lute makers) reshaped the long-necked fretted *buzuq* and the short-necked, fretless *'ud* from the Arab world into a "waisted" plucked lute with a relatively long fretted neck and gave

FIGURE 4.16
Musician playing a *vihuela* in the Borgia Apartments (Vatican)
Source: Painting by Bernardino di Betto di Biago (c. 1454–1513). Musicarticon, Wikimedia Commons.

instruments of this type the names guitar and *vihuela*. The word **lute** is a generic name for a family of chordophones with a resonator and neck. Violins, viols, guitars, and *vihuela* all belong to the lute category of instruments.

Our gateway to music for Renaissance lutes is a composition called *Quatro diferencias sobre Guárdame las vacas* (Four variations on [the song tune] "Take care of my cattle"). In this recording the four variations are played on a plucked lute called **vihuela**, a flat-backed waisted lute with gut frets tied around the neck and six double courses of gutstrings plucked by the fingers. A **course** is a set of close-together strings tuned in unison or octaves and played together as if they were a single string. This composition appeared in 1538 in a collection of compositions by Spanish composer Luys de Narváez, whose birth and death dates are not known but who was active from 1526 to 1549.

🔊 Listen to the first fifteen seconds of the recording.

How Does It Work?

Timbre

The timbre is bright. The double courses of strings improve the resonance of the instrument and provide a characteristic timbre slightly different from single-string courses on the guitar.

Texture

The texture consists of two polyphonic lines, one high-pitched moving rapidly and the other a low-pitched line moving slowly

Rhythm

The meter is a slow meter of six beats similar to the *volte* in the previous gateway. The rhythm of the high-pitched line features short tones of equal length for the most part.

Melody

The melody, carried in the high-pitched line, mainly moves stepwise over a two-octave range. The melody of each section is organized into two phrases of four measures each.

Harmony

The harmony is based on triads. The first phrase of each melody ends on a chord on the fifth degree (V); the second phrase ends with an authentic cadence.

Form

The composition is a set of four variations on the melody of a traditional song, followed by a brief coda. It is the earliest precursor of a form commonly used in the eighteenth century called **theme and variations,** the word "theme" referring to the opening melody. Each variation uses the same chord progression in the low part.

Performance Techniques

Plucking the strings with the fingers, rather than with a plectrum as the *'ud* player did in Chapter 3, Gateway 9 on Middle Eastern music, is the most notable performance technique.

Listen to the recording for the six-beat meter and the two-part polyphony.

Listen to the entire performance following this timed listening guide.

TIME	SECTION	DESCRIPTION
0:00	Variation #1	
0:00	A	The melody descends in thirds ending on V.
0:09	A′	The melody repeats ending with an authentic cadence on the first degree.
0:18	Variation #2	A new melody moves twice as fast as the first melody, in an undulating shape.
0:34	Variation #3	Another new melody consists of a short three-tone motive played in sequence.
0:51	Variation #4	This melody is a series of stepwise ascending melodic lines.
1:09	Coda	A descending line played in parallel thirds half as fast as the previous three variations.
1:20	End	

LISTENING GUIDE 4.4

What Does It Mean?

Well-educated male and female courtiers played the *vihuela* alone for their own amusement rather than in consorts with other instrumentalists. Narváez's compositions were meant to be aesthetically pleasing rather than to express emotion. The pleasure for players and listeners derives both from the technical skill and variety of playing techniques required to play the piece and from the shifts in melodic direction and rhythm of each variation in the set of four variations. The performance may please modern listeners because of its similarity to the familiar plucked sound of the modern guitar.

AESTHETICS

 Listen one more time to the performance for pleasure, paying attention to the melodic and rhythmic changes from variation to variation.

Amateur courtly musicians in Spain and all across Europe were taught to play lutes by outstanding professional court musicians and composers like Luys de Narváez. His six books of polyphonic compositions for *vihuela* contain thirty-three pieces: *diferencias*; a form called *fantasia* featuring imitative polyphony; and arrangements, with extensive ornaments and melodic embellishments, of well-known polyphonic secular songs, motets, and masses. Narváez added another skill to those of his amateur students: he was able to improvise additional melodic lines while his students played the parts he had composed for them.

In addition to the *vihuela*, two other plucked lutes were common in Europe during the sixteenth century. The others were the guitar and the lute. The sixteenth-century guitar was a waisted, flat-backed plucked lute with tied-on gut frets. Smaller than the modern guitar, it had five strings in single courses. It seems to have been a favored instrument in the countryside and may have been played by strumming across the strings with a plectrum or fingers.

TECHNOLOGY

The most popular Renaissance plucked lute in most of Europe was one named **lute**. The instrument with the name "lute," as opposed to generic lutes, was a plucked pear-shaped lute with a vaulted body (that is, a rounded back rather than a flat back) made from a set of thin wooden ribs glued together. It had six courses of strings, some single and some double, and a much shorter

FIGURE 4.17
The Lute Player by Caravaggio, *c.* 1600
Source: Hermitage Museum, Wikimedia Commons.

fretted neck than the guitar and *vihuela*. At the end of the neck the pegbox was bent back at an angle to the neck, just like the Arab *'ud*. All these instruments had a wide range suitable for playing the wide-ranging soprano-to-bass polyphonic music of the period. Arab *'ud* players like A. J. Racy in the gateway to Arab music in Chapter 3, Gateway 9, perform mainly monophonic melodies, while European lute, guitar, and *vihuela* players perform polyphonic music.

What Is Its History?

Luys de Narváez was born in Granada but his birth and death dates are unknown. Between 1526 and 1549 he served at the court of the Spanish King Charles V (1500–1558) and his son, crown prince Felipe, who would become King Philip II (1527–1598). Philip ruled at the same time and for nearly as long as Elizabeth I of England. Charles V and Philip II, both devout Catholics, were the most powerful European monarchs of the sixteenth century. Although understood today as kings of Spain, they controlled vastly more land than that. They also ruled territories in the present-day Netherlands, the German-speaking Catholic territories of southern Germany and Austria, a part of Italy, and most of South America. Desiring to unite Europe and defend the Catholic faith, Charles V battled a host of enemies: the King of France, whose territories he coveted; German Protestants in the name of the Catholic faith; the Muslim Ottomans, whose advance into Europe he helped to stop in a decisive battle for Vienna in 1529; and the Incas and Aztecs, whose empires in Mexico and Peru his conquistadors crushed. Apparently exhausted from the bloodshed, he abdicated his many thrones in his late fifties, retreated to a monastery, and died a few years later in 1558. Philip II continued his father's imperial ambitions, sending the Spanish Armada to humiliating defeat against Protestant England in 1588 and colonizing an archipelago in the western Pacific named after him: the Philippines.

AESTHETICS

Narváez's *diferencias* are the earliest European compositions in theme and variation form, which became one of the common forms in later European music. Its AABBCCDD form suggests that it may have been a concert version of European dance form. The eighteenth-century composers Franz Joseph Haydn (1732–1809) and Wolfgang Amadeus Mozart (1756–1791) routinely used theme and variations form in their symphonies, string quartets, and solo piano pieces. One of the most frequently performed examples in this form is Maurice Ravel's (1875–1937) symphonic work *Boléro*, first performed in 1928. Named for a Spanish dance type and composed for a ballet, the variations in *Boléro* are based on changing orchestral timbres rather than on melodic variations of the sort associated with Narváez, Haydn, and Mozart. A typical jazz performance, with its melodic head and a series of choruses on the chord progression of the head is another example of theme and variations form pioneered by Narváez.

The history of lutes, whether bowed like the viol and violin or plucked like the *vihuela*, guitar, and lute, can be traced to the Middle East. The first plucked lutes entered Europe when Arabs from North Africa conquered Spanish lands in 711. Called Moors by Christians during this period, they ruled Andalucia, the southern region of Spain, until Christians defeated them in 1492. During the ninth century a fabulous Arab *'ud* virtuoso named Ziryab appeared at the court of the Andalucian *emir*. Born and trained in music in Baghdad, Ziryab moved to Syria, Tunisia, and then Córdoba in Spain. By the thirteenth century Christians in northern Spain were playing its European descendant, the lute. By the sixteenth century its name had changed from *al'ud* (the *'ud*) in Arabic to *la ud* (the *ud*) in Spanish and to lute in English. The waisted, plucked guitar and *vihuela* seem to have developed from the bowed viol and violin. *Vihuela* may be a Spanish language variant of viol.

During the sixteenth century the *vihuela* and guitar were more popular in Spain than was the lute. The lute seems to have passed through Spain to the rest of Europe, where amateurs and professionals used it to accompany singing and to play instrumental compositions. It appears in many sixteenth-century paintings, often accompanying singing. Queen Elizabeth I of England enjoyed playing the lute. John Dowland (1563–1626), the most prominent English lutenist of the period, composed many instrumental pieces and **lute songs** (songs with lute accompaniment), including a *galliarde* titled "The most sacred Queen Elizabeth, her Galliard."

Even after 1492 Moorish culture continued to flourish in Andalucia until the Moors were finally expelled in 1603. Since the nineteenth century, *flamenco*, a music with Moorish roots featuring the guitar, developed among Spanish Gitanos (Gypsies), an itinerant people with roots in India. Today a new genre called *flamenco arabe*, a hybrid of *flamenco* and North African Arab music, links Spanish musical culture with the culture of new immigrants to Spain from North Africa.

FIGURE 4.18
Miniature painting of Queen Elizabeth I playing the lute
Source: Painting by Nicholas Hilliard (1571–1610). David Van Edwards, Wikimedia Commons.

Spanish colonists took the *vihuela* and guitar to South America, Cuba, Puerto Rico, and the Dominican Republic, where today they exist in a tremendous number of variant forms and names. The Mexican *vihuela* (different from the Renaissance instrument), *bajo sexto*, *guitarrón*, and *requinto jarocho* and the Puerto Rican *tres* (with three triple courses), *cuatro* (with not four but five double courses), and *tiple* (with five single courses) are just a few of many examples.

The modern guitar is an outgrowth of its Renaissance predecessors. Today it has metal frets inlaid in the neck rather than tied-on gut frets, and nylon or steel strings rather than gut strings. Its current size is attributed to Spanish guitar maker Antonio de Torres Jurado (1817–1892). The electric guitar, so important in popular music and jazz, emerged in the 1920s and 1930s.

WHERE DO I GO FROM HERE?

- Listen to recordings of John Dowland's "Queen Elizabeth's Galliard" and two of his most popular lute songs, "Flow My Tears" and "Come Again, Sweet Love Doth Now Invite." Compare the performances of these songs by, for example, the male countertenor Gérard Lesne, the opera and recital singer Dame Janet Baker, and the popular singer Sting.

- Listen to or watch performances of *flamenco* guitar and *flamenco arabe*.

- Listen to or watch performances of Puerto Rican *tres*, *cuatro*, and *tiple*.

- Listen to recordings of one of these famous compositions in theme and variations form: Mozart's Twelve Variations on "Ah vous dirai-je, Maman" (the tune of "Twinkle, Twinkle, Little Star") for solo piano and Ravel's *Boléro*.

GATEWAY 16
NORTH INDIAN CLASSICAL MUSIC

What Is It?

Had Columbus landed in India, his intended destination, instead of the islands of the Caribbean Sea (the West Indies) on his voyage of discovery westward across the Atlantic Ocean in 1492, he would have found an area of the world with astonishing musical variety; a tradition of writing about music dating back to antiquity; and the Hindu and Muslim religions with their Ancient and Medieval traditions of monophonic chanting. In addition to a flourishing classical music tradition at the courts of its rulers, the Indian subcontinent was awash in a spectacular mosaic of diverse religious, popular, folk, and tribal music. During the 1500s, the same century as the European Renaissance, some of the basic principles of North Indian classical music were taking shape. Many North Indian classical musicians today trace their musical ancestry to a seminal musician of the sixteenth century, a lute player, singer, composer, and contemporary of Palestrina named Tansen (c. 1506–1589).

Our gateway to North Indian classical music is a recording titled "Raga Bhairvi—Dadra Taal" performed by Sharmistha Sen on the *sitar*. A **raga** (also spelled **rag**) is an Indian melodic mode, analogous to an Arab *maqam*. *Bhairvi* (usually spelled *Bhairavi*) is the name of one of the melodic modes in the Indian system of *ragas*. A **taal** (also spelled **tal** or **tala**) is an Indian rhythmic mode, analogous to an Arab *iqa'*. *Dadra* is the name of one of the modes in the Indian system of *talas*. What the title indicates is that this is a performance in a specific melodic mode (*raga bharavi*) in a specific rhythmic mode (*dadra tal*). What the title does not say is that this performance will consist almost entirely of improvisations within these two modal systems.

Sharmistha Sen performs the melody in *rag bhairavi* on the *sitar*. The **sitar** is a long-necked, fretted plucked lute with more than twenty strings. Six or seven of them run on top of the frets and are plucked. The remainder run under the frets and are **sympathetic strings**, that is, strings that vibrate in response to the plucked pitch. They help to amplify the loudness and improve the resonance of the sound. Faiyaz Khan plays the drum accompaniment in *dadra tal* on the *tabla*. The **tabla** is a pair of kettle drums played with the hands. An unacknowledged player, likely a student of the melodic soloist, provides a drone accompaniment on the *tambura*. The **tambura** is a four-stringed, fretless plucked lute. The player plucks each open string in turn as though playing a harp.

FIGURE 4.19
Sharmistha Sen playing the *sitar*
Source: Daniel Neuman.

FIGURE 4.20
Abhiman Kaushal plays the *tabla* while accompanying *sitar*ist Sharmistha Sen
Source: Daniel Neuman.

 Listen to the first thirty seconds of the recording.

How Does It Work?

Timbre

The timbre of the *sitar*'s plucked strings is relatively thin and metallic. The timbre of the *tabla* includes ringing pitched sounds and dull, unpitched sounds across a range from low to high.

Texture

The texture consists of melody with drone and drum accompaniment.

Rhythm

The performance begins nonmetrically and then, after about two minutes, the *tabla* enters to create a steady beat and meter.

Melody

The melody moves mainly in stepwise motion using a heptatonic scale with a few added pitches from time to time. The melodic range is about two octaves.

Harmony

The harmony consists of the intervals between the pitches of the melody and the drone. The drone has two pitches: the tonic and the perfect fifth above it.

Form

The form has two parts, a nonmetrical opening section followed by a metrical second part, very similar to the performance of Arab music in Chapter 3, Gateway 9.

Performance Techniques

The *sitar* player sometimes pulls the string to slide from pitch to pitch and sometimes directly plucks the string.

 Listen to the first thirty seconds of the recording for the melody-and-drone texture and the sliding from pitch to pitch.

Timed Listening Guide

Before listening in more detail to this example, some concepts specific to North Indian music need to be introduced. The nonmetrical opening section is called **alap**. During this section the player introduces each pitch of the *raga* very carefully, one after the other, as well as melodic phrases using those pitches. The scale in *rag bhairavi* has seven basic pitches in a mode called the Phrygian mode in European music theory: E F G A B C D E. *Rag Bhairavi* also includes some additional pitches: the raised 7th degree (D♯ in the scale above) is heard a few times in this performance. At the beginning Sharmistha Sen plays just three pitches, but by the end of the *alap* she is playing over a range of nearly two octaves. The timed listening guide indicates when she performs each new pitch in the *raga*.

   The metrical section, when the *tabla* plays, is called **gat**. The meter is based on a **tal**, that is, a repeating cycle of strokes on the *tabla*. The basic pattern of strokes for a given *tal* is called the **theka.** Associated with each stroke is a mnemonic syllable, which allows *tabla* players to speak the rhythmic pattern during lessons and even during concerts. The basic stroke names are:

Dha = low-pitched drum stroke on the low-pitched drum played together with a bright, pitched stroke on the rim of the high-pitched drum;

Dhin = low-pitched drum stroke on the low-pitched drum played together with a dull, damped stroke on the high-pitched drum;

AESTHETICS

ta   =   bright pitched stroke on the rim of the the high-pitched drum;

na   =   ringing stroke in the center of the high-pitched drum.

In *dadra tal*, the *theka* of six beats produced by these strokes can be heard as a pattern of low and high strokes and spoken as a series of syllable names for the player's strokes:

1	2	3	4	5	6
Dha	Dhin	na	Dha	tin	na
low	low	high	low	high	high

In addition to these basic sounds on the *tabla*, the player improvises additional filler strokes and occasionally omits the low tone on beat 4.

The *sitar* alternates between playing a fixed melody, also called *gat*, and improvised solos. The *gat* melody is one way of expressing the *tala*: while the *sitar* plays it, the *tabla* player can add improvise elaborate solos. In this performance the *gat* melody is twelve beats long and covers two cycles of *dadra tala*. Like *tabla* players, melodic soloists can sing melodies, while teaching or in performance, using mnemonic syllables similar to the ones used by European musicians. Instead of do-re-mi-fa-sol-la-ti-do, Indian musicians name the pitches sa-re-ga-ma-pa-dha-ni-sa. The pattern of intervals (half steps and whole steps) in the standard Indian scale can be written as a mode with a final on C: C D E F G A B (C). Using European pitch names and scale degree numbers (first degree = 1, second degree = 2, and so forth), the standard Indian scale and its intervallic structure can be written like this:

1	1	1/2	1	1	1	1/2	
C	D	E	F	G	A	B	C
1	2	3	4	5	6	7	8

In the Indian scale system the first degree (1) and the fifth degree (5) are fixed. Degrees 2, 3, 6, and 7 can be either "natural" as in the C scale or "flatted" by a half step. These flatted scale degrees are indicated with a "flat sign" (♭). The fourth degree also has two forms, either natural or "sharped," indicated with a "sharp sign" (♯). Natural scale degrees are normally taken for granted, but if necessary they are written with a "natural sign" (♮).

Four of the pitches in the scale of *raga bhairavi* are flatted by a half step. Its pattern of intervals is written, starting on C, this way:

1/2	1	1	1	1/2	1	1	
C	D♭	E♭	F	G	A♭	B♭	C
1	♭2	♭3	4	5	♭6	♭7	8

The scale *raga bhairavi* is read "C D-flat E-flat F G A-flat B-flat C."

The *gat* melody begins on beat 11 of two cycles of *dadra tal* and can be rendered like this using Indian pitch names and the numbers of the scale degrees:

11	12	1	2	3	4	5	6	7	8	9	10	11	12	(1)
♭3	4	5	–	5	5	5	5	♭7	♭6	5	–	♭3	4	5
ga	ma	pa	–	pa	pa	pa	pa	ni	dha	pa	–	ga	ma	pa

The *sitar* soloist ends two of her solos with a cadential gesture called a *tihai*. A **tihai** is a highly syncopated rhythmic pattern played three times at the end of a *sitar* or *tabla* solo that ends, in this case, on the first beat of *dadra tal*.

Listen to the entire performance following this timed listening guide.

LISTENING GUIDE 4.5

TIME	SECTION	DESCRIPTION
0:00	*Alap*	Nonmetrical treatment of the *raga* in which each pitch of the scale is introduced in succession.
0:00		The opening phrase moves through characteristic phrases of *rag bhairavi* starting with a descending slide to ♭3 before introducing 4 and sliding upwards to 5.
0:14		This phrase adds two more pitches ascending with a characteristic melodic phrase of *rag bhairavi*: 1 ♭3 4 5 ♭6 5.
0:28		The *sitarist* introduces the ♮7th degree of the scale below 1 as a kind of leading tone.
0:49		The *sitar*ist introduces the ♭7 degree of the scale near the upper octave.
1:10		The *sitar*ist introduces the ♮7th degree of the scale on the way to the upper octave.
1:22		The *sitar*ist descends to the lower tonic (1) adding ♭2 to the scale.
1:26		The *sitar*ist expands the range of the melody below the tonic, introducing ♭6 before arriving on low 5 and returning to end the *alap* on 1.
2:03	*Gat*	The *tabla* enters in a meter of 6 beats in a *tala* called *dadra tal*.
2:03		The *sitar*ist plays the 12-pulse gat melody three times while the *tabla* improvises.
2:21		The *sitar*ist improvises a solo over the 6-pulse *tabla theka* played two times.
2:26		The *sitar*ist plays the 12-pulse *gat* melody one time while the *tabla* improvises.
2:32		The *sitar*ist improvises a solo over the 6-pulse *tabla theka* played seven times.
2:53		The *sitar*ist plays the 12-pulse *gat* melody one time.
3:00		The *sitar*ist improvises a solo over the 6-pulse *tabla theka* played seven times.
3:20		The *sitar* plays the 12-pulse *gat* melody one time.
3:26		An elaborate *sitar* solo introduces chromatic pitches in addition to the basic seven pitches of *rag bhairav* over a 6-pulse *tabla theka* played fifteen times.
4:10		An elaborate *tabla* solo over the 12-pulse *gat* melody played five times by the *sitar*ist.
4:32		The *sitar*ist improvises a solo ending in a *tihai* over a 6-pulse *tabla theka* played four times.
4:42		The *sitar*ist plays the 12-pulse *gat* one time.
4:49		The *sitar*ist improvises a solo with rapid runs ending in a *tihai* over a 6-pulse *tabla theka* played six times.
5:06		The *sitar*ist plays the 12-pulse *gat* melody one last time.
5:11		Nonmetrical close
5:19	End	

What Does It Mean?

CULTURAL
LINKAGES >

This performance might be heard against the background of the relatively long history of North Indian classical music in American culture. During the 1960s many young Americans sought relief from the value system and political structures that led the United States into war in Vietnam. Alienated from the mainstream, they took refuge not only in sex, drugs, and rock 'n' roll, but in world religions and world music. They studied Buddhism and Hinduism as alternatives to Christianity and Judaism and flocked to concerts by Ravi Shankar, a Hindu *sitar* player who became a spiritual and musical *guru* to a generation of young people hungering for alternative styles of life and music. Listeners today, like those in the 1960s, may find the sliding pitches, drones, and nonmetrical melodies of North Indian music an icon of a dreamy, perhaps intoxicated, world unbounded by social conventions. And the rapid melodic runs and fast *tabla* solos may have an attractive similarity to the virtuosity of classical, popular, and jazz musicians.

Beyond the way some Americans might interpret this performance, it opens a door to an extraordinarily rich musical culture. Its meanings derive from its social position within Indian culture, its position within an elaborate system of *raga*s and *tala*s, audience expectations about how a performance will evolve through time, and ideas about the emotional meaning of music.

EMOTIONAL
RESONANCE >

In terms of audience expectations during the *gat* section, for example, audience members count the beats of the *tal* as they listen, noticing each time the cycle returns to beat 1. Sometimes beat 1 occurs in the middle of a *sitar* or *tabla* solo, creating a sense of tension in listeners. The solo then ends dramatically on beat 1, sometimes after a *tihai*, creating a sense of pleasurable release in listeners who are closely monitoring the cycle of beats, in this case the six beats of *dadra tal*. They monitor the *tal* by clapping, waving their right hand, and touching their fingers against the thumb of their right hand in succession from little to third finger. In effect, they perform the *tala* along with the musicians. In the case of *dadra tal* the audience claps the *tal* like this:

1	2	3	4	5	6
low	low	high	low	high	high
clap	touch	touch	wave	touch	touch
	little finger	third finger		little finger	third finger

🔊 **Listen another time to the *gat* section of this recording, clapping the *tala* and paying special attention to moments at which the *theka* or *gat* melody arrives on beat 1 of the *tal*.**

The length of a performance of North Indian classical music varies with the context. In informal settings or for recordings, performers can demonstrate the basic form of a *raga* and *tala* performance in just five or six minutes, as Sharmistha Sen does in this recording. In a formal concert, however, it has become customary for the first *raga* performance to be quite "serious," as Indian musicians and fans say. It can take an hour or longer, a half hour or so for each section (*alap* and *gat*). This is about the length of a nineteenth-century European symphony. After such a serious performance, performers may either launch into a second serious performance or play a few shorter, more easily accessible "light" pieces requiring less concentration from the audience.

AESTHETICS >

The length of a serious performance varies considerably as performers sense how engaged the audience is. If the audience seems tightly focused on the details of what the performer is doing, the performance can stretch out well beyond an hour. If the audience is not made up of connoisseurs, performers may hurry things along so the audience does not become bored. *Rag bhairavi* is considered a light *raga*, a favorite of audiences, and *dadra tal* is a light *tal*, shorter than the standard "serious" *tala* of sixteen beats. They are typically played at the ends of concerts. Sharmistha Sen placed this recording at the end of an album that contained two longer, more serious performances, one of nearly twenty-five minutes and the other of nearly thirty minutes.

A performance like this also gains meaning through its position in two theoretical systems: the system of *rag*s or *raga*s and the system of *tal*s or *tala*s. Both of these systems have evolved over time from similar systems of melodic modes and rhythmic cycles borrowed from Middle Eastern music like the example in Chapter 3, Gateway 9. There are, however, five important differences between modern Middle Eastern practice and modern North Indian practice. First, North Indian music is based on twelve pitches to the octave and does not use the microtones of the Arab and Turkish traditions. Second, whereas Arab and Turkish music balances the opening, improvised section (the *taqsim*) and the composed piece that follows, in North Indian music the pre-composed elements are drastically reduced in favor of virtually constant improvisation. Third, the rhythmic aspect of North Indian music is more highly developed as a compositional and improvisational domain than in Middle Eastern music, where it serves mainly an accompanying role. Fourth, in the Indian tradition a drone tone is played throughout, which helps make clear the position of each note in the scale. Such drones are either absent or much less prominent in Middle Eastern music. Fifth, the virtuosity of North Indian musicians is notable, a consequence of an ethic of lengthy practice linked to devotion and the monetary rewards of the virtuosity that results from extended practice.

AESTHETICS

Even though performances of this tradition have long been held in strictly secular contexts, whether at the courts of sultans and emperors in the past or modern-day concert halls in the great Indian cities of Delhi, Mumbai, and Kolkata, the notion persists in India that musical practice and training are acts of devotion. Modern players, whether Hindu or Muslim, believe that music is a spiritual gift and that playing music is a kind of prayer spoken in heavenly language. Musical training and practice are understood as a kind of *yoga* (pathway) to a higher, purer, more refined plane of spiritual existence. Enjoying a performance of music is only one goal. Its higher purpose, for performers and listeners, is as a path to nirvana through total concentration on the details of musical sound. Many amateurs, both men and women, take music lessons with no thought of becoming professionals, but as an act of spiritual and educational refinement, a process similar in some respects to upper-class or upwardly mobile families in Europe, America, and Asia providing their children, especially their daughters, with piano lessons.

CULTURAL LINKAGES

While amateur musicians may be male or female and Hindu, Muslim, or Christian, historically the most important and prestigious professional musicians, and the teachers of amateurs, were Muslim hereditary musicians. A hereditary musician has an **ascribed status**, one limited to certain musical families who were not anxious to share their trade secrets with potential competitors outside their family. The status of professional musicians in India was, in the past, not something that just anyone, by dint of hard work and talent, could achieve. The role of musician was not an **achieved status**, as it is in parts of the world. Since the music existed only in aural tradition and was passed on only in music lessons, not in musical notations, it was easy to keep intimate knowledge of the tradition within families of hereditary musicians. Each family and its students is called a **gharana** ("house") and is recognized for having a unique style and repertoire that distinguishes it from other *gharanas*. A figure known as a **guru** (guide, teacher) teaches the tradition, passing on not only lessons about music but about the practical and spiritual aspects of life as well. As a consequence, the person who receives this musical and life training is given the religious designation "disciple," not simply student. The disciple, historically a relative of the *guru*, did not pay for lessons, but lived for long periods in the house of the *guru*, absorbing the music whenever the *guru* practiced or performed with colleagues and performing daily chores to assist the household as recompense for the lessons. Assisting the *guru* in concerts by playing the *tambura* was one such task, and an honor for the disciple. Nowadays North Indian classical music is also taught in musical conservatories and is available to a much wider circle of people than in the past.

ECONOMIC ACTIVITY

Traditional Muslim hereditary players of the *sitar*, other melodic instruments, and vocalists traditionally came from a higher social class or caste than *tabla* players. The musical result is exemplified in this gateway recording. Melodic soloists with higher social status than the drum

SOCIAL BEHAVIOR

accompanist command performances. They make the contract with the recording company, the concert promoter, or the host of a concert in someone's home. They give the *tabla* player a relatively small percentage of the concert fee. They take the leading role throughout the performance, relegating the *tabla* player to an accompanying role most of the time and giving him little time in the performance to show off his considerable skills.

What Is Its History?

At the end of the fifteenth century, present-day India was divided among a number of sultanates competing for power with each other. In 1526 a great warrior named Babur united the Indian sultanates into an empire that covered a great part of India and parts of present-day Pakistan and Afghanistan. Babur claimed descent from Genghis Khan, the Mongol warrior whose hordes had conquered much of Asia in the 1200s and from Timur (Tamerlane), a Central Asian Turkic warrior who controlled much of the same area in the 1300s. Babur founded the Mughal Empire, a name based on the Arabic word for Mongol. It lasted from 1526 to 1857, when it fell to the British Empire. The third Mughal emperor, Akbar the Great, extended the reach of the empire and presided over a golden age of Indian culture and art from 1556 to 1605, a period that coincides almost exactly with the long reigns of Queen Elizabeth I of England (1558–1603) and King Philip II of Spain (1556–1598). Akbar and his successors supported a fabulous court life including painting, architecture (one of Babur's successors built the Taj Mahal in the mid-seventeenth century), and music. They were also noted for their religious tolerance. Both Muslims and Hindus enjoyed considerable sway at court and in the arts.

CULTURAL LINKAGES

Sharmistha Sen, along with virtually all the instrumentalists in the North Indian classical music tradition today, traces her artistic lineage to the most famous musician at Akbar the Great's Mughal court of the sixteenth century. Named Tansen, he was a contemporary of Palestrina, Farmer, Praetorius, and Narváez. Tansen's teacher was Swami Haridas (*c.* 1535–1595), a fine singer and the founder of a Hindu sect that emphasized devotional singing. Worshippers sang songs in different *raga*s throughout the day, and today Indian musicians and music theorists associate each *raga* with a time of day. *Raga bhairavi* is said to be an early morning *raga*, performed at the end of a long night

FIGURE 4.21
Map of the Mughal Empire
Source: Santosh.mbahrm, Wikimedia Commons.

of music. Associating *raga*s with times of day may have its source in these sixteenth-century Hindu services. Tansen spent most of his life at the court of a Hindu king, where he gained fame as a singer, composer, and player of the *rabab*, a long-necked plucked lute and ancestor of the modern Indian long-necked plucked lute called *sarod*. He composed in a new vocal genre in the Hindi language called *dhrupad*, which became the model for the most serious performances of North Indian instrumental music. The texts of his *dhrupads*, one scholar has written, "could address a god or goddess, laud a king, express feelings of intimate romantic love, describe a season, transmit musicological knowledge, or deal with a metaphysical or religious concept."[37] He is also credited with composing instrumental music, including new *raga*s.

Late in life, word of his genius reached the court of Akbar the Great, and in 1562 Tansen, apparently hoping to retire, reluctantly accepted an invitation to become one of the nine "jewels" of the Mughal court. By tracing their artistic lineage to Tansen, modern North Indian classical instrumentalists like Sharmistha Sen seek to enhance their credibility and prestige with audiences and students, just as some pianists today trace their artistic heritage to famous nineteenth-century virtuosos like Franz Liszt. For these Indian musicians Tansen is the father of present-day Hindustani or North Indian classical music. *Sarod*ists trace their roots to his son, who played *rabab*, and *sitar*ists trace their roots to his daughter, who played an ancestor of the *sitar*.

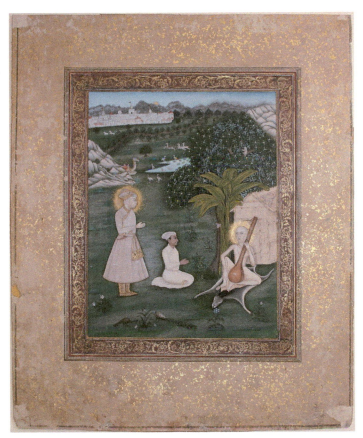

FIGURE 4.22
An eighteenth-century painting of Emperor Akbar, on the left, and Tansen, in the middle, both enthralled by the playing of Haridas, on the right
Source: Wazir Khan Khandara, Wikimedia Commons.

FIGURE 4.23
Sharmistha Sen taking a lesson from her *guru*, Ustad Mushtaq Ali Khan
Source: Daniel Neuman.

SOCIAL
BEHAVIOR

Sharmistha Sen is one of the few female instrumentalists to have attained prominence in North Indian classical music. She is a woman, a Hindu, and a musician by achieved status. She is not a male, hereditary Muslim musician, the type of musician at the center of this tradition for hundreds of years. Her main teachers were Ustad Mushtaq Ali Khan (1911–1989) and Professor D. T. Joshi (1912–1993). Mustaq Ali Khan was a prominent *sitar*ist of the early twentieth century and the scion of the *Seniya gharana*, named after Tansen and noted for its adherence to older traditions of playing. Sen is one of a few accomplished musicians in this tradition to have been trained in both the traditional master–disciple tradition and the newer university system, where she earned a doctoral degree. After making her public debut at age thirteen, she performed regularly for All-India Radio and major music festivals. During 1983 and 1984 she was an artist-in-residence at the University of Washington and recently retired as professor of music at Delhi University.

During the second half of the twentieth century two other *gharanas* besides the *Seniya gharana* emerged as homes for the primary musical styles of *sitar* and *sarod* performance. Named for musical ancestors more recent than Tansen, they still trace their lineage to him. The *Imdadkhani gharana*, named for famed *sitar*ist Imdad Khan (1848–1920), includes many prominent *sitar*ists of the second half of the twentieth and early twenty-first centuries, including his grandson Vilayat Khan (1928–2004) and his great-grandson Shujaat Khan (b. 1960). This *gharana* is noted for a style that features singing along with *sitar* playing. Sharmistha Sen's style, including her treatment of *raga*s, is a cross between the Imdadkhani and Seniya styles, but her touch, glides, and tone quality reflect her own personal style.

Another *gharana* traces its lineage to *sarod*ist Allauddin Khan (c. 1862–1972). He was the *guru* of a host of prominent musicians, including his son, famed *sarod*ist Ali Akbar Khan (1922–2009), and *sitar*ist Ravi Shankar (1920–2012), both of whom gained prominence in the United States. When Ravi Shankar and Ali Akbar Khan gave concerts in America in the 1960s, they and their drummers quickly realized how impressed American audiences were with the virtuosity of the *tabla* playing. In response to their foreign audiences, this *gharana* evolved a style in which they shared much more of the creative, improvisatory role with the drummer than the older practice of Sharmistha Sen's *Seniya gharana* allowed.

ECONOMIC
ACTIVITY

Today professional performers in this tradition make a living by working for the radio, giving concerts, giving lessons to private students, often Hindu and female, for pay, and moving abroad to western Europe and the United States, where their artistry is highly appreciated. As a consequence of these changes in patronage, this music is heard much more widely in India today than in the past, and the *gharanas* of particular Muslim hereditary musicians now include professionals and amateurs from far beyond their narrow circle of kin.

CULTURAL
LINKAGES

Unlike many other world musical traditions, North Indian classical music has never absorbed much in the way of foreign influence. On the other hand, European and American jazz, popular, and classical artists have incorporated Indian musical instruments in their music since the 1960s. George Harrison, guitarist with the Beatles, studied *sitar* with Ravi Shankar and played it on a number of recordings. In his song titled "Within You, Without You" for the Beatles' 1967 album *Sgt. Pepper's Lonely Hearts Club Band*, the instrumental prelude begins with Harrison strumming across all of the *sitar*'s sympathetic strings, a characteristic gesture at the beginning of a *sitar* performance. He plays a short, nonmetrical *alap* before the Indian bowed fiddle called *sarangi* enters and continues the *alap*. After a minute of this introduction the *tabla* enters playing a familiar *tala*. The long durations of many of the song's tones and the sliding between the pitches, relatively rare qualities for European and American melodies, are striking elements of the song linking it to North Indian classical music. While George Harrison may be the most famous foreign champion of North Indian classical music, the important classical violinist Yehudi Menuhin also devoted many years of study to it and recorded an album of improvised duets with Ravi Shankar.

Of all the Indian instruments, however, it is the *tabla* that has become a fixture in the contemporary world music scene. Its jittery, dry sound has become a cliché of fusion and hybrid musical forms all over the world. Zakir Hussain (b. 1951), the son of one of Ravi Shankar's favorite accompanists and a teacher at Ali Akbar Khan's school of Indian music in the San Francisco Bay Area, is perhaps the most highly regarded *tabla* player of his generation. He lives in California, accompanies the greatest Indian melodic soloists, and participates in concerts with some of the great artists of jazz and popular music. Many of these fusions seem to be searching for some middle ground between Indian music, jazz, and popular music with a lot of attention to rhythm. Such searches are sometimes commercially driven, but they also come about when musicians seek new musical inspiration or when they want to communicate through music a new sense of social identity and connection to others in a multicultural society.

CULTURAL LINKAGES

WHERE DO I GO FROM HERE?

- Listen to Sharmistha Sen's more extended recording called "Raga Bihag—Vilambit Roopak Taal – Drut Teental." On the internet, find and learn the definitions of these terms: *raga bihag*, *vilambit* and *drut*, and *roopak tal* and *teental*. Try to hear them and follow them along in the recording.

- Watch a video of one or more of the artists mentioned in this chapter: Ravi Shankar, Ali Akbar Khan, Vilayat Khan, and Shujaat Khan.

- Watch a video of Zakir Hussain showing off his *tabla* technique in a solo performance.

- Watch or listen to a performance of Zakir Hussain playing with such musicians as guitarist John McLaughlin, banjo player Béla Fleck, bassist Edgar Meyer, and saxophonist Jan Garbarek.

CLOSING

Many of the basic features of European and American music today can trace their roots to the sixteenth century, the European age of discovery, including:

- harmony based on triads with phrases ending in V–I cadences;
- families of instruments with ranges from low bass parts to high soprano parts;
- imitative polyphony as a way to organize sections of pieces;
- theme and variations form;
- the expression of emotion in instrumental and vocal music through its association with texts and its similarity to sounds in nature; and
- the invention of the violin and guitar.

These innovations reflect the humanistic and scientific spirit of the time. Similar things can be said of Indian classical music: important *ragas* and vocal and instrumental forms appear in this century.

In both Europe and India the powerful courts of Queen Elizabeth I of England, King Philip II of Spain, and Akbar the Great of the Mughal Empire, and the chapels and cathedrals of the Catholic Church, made unimaginably rich from trade and conquest of new territories, energized and supported musicians and their art in ways that have continued to reverberate through history to the present.

THINGS TO THINK ABOUT

- Consider the six features of European and American music listed above and think of some examples of music you already know that exhibit one or more of those features. Does your conception of the music you already know shift when you realize that these features are products of the Age of European Discovery? Why, or why not?

- The sixteenth-century imperial courts of England, Spain, and India are no longer important patrons of music, even if the music they patronized lives on in various forms. What institutions or people are the most important patrons of music today?

NEW TERMS

a cappella	guru	subdominant
achieved status	horn	suite
alap	imitative polyphony	tabla
alto	kettledrum	tal, taal, tala
ascribed status	leading tone	tambourine
authentic cadence	lute	tambura
bass	madrigal	tenor
binary form	membranophone	text painting
cantus firmus	motet	theka
choral singing	perspective	theme and variations
chordophones	plagal cadence, amen cadence	tihai
consort	point of imitation	triads
cornett	rag, raag, raga	trombone
Counter-Reformation	recorder	troubador
countertenor	Renaissance	trumpet
cyclical mass	round	tune
dominant	sackbut	vihuela
European dance form	sitar	viol
falsetto	snare drum	violin
gat	soprano	volte, sg. volta
gharana		

MUSIC FROM THE AGE OF GLOBAL COMMERCE (1600–1750)

DURING THE SIXTEENTH CENTURY the European seagoing expeditions of Christopher Columbus, John Cabot, Vasco da Gama, Ferdinand Magellan, Jacques Cartier, and many others set in motion dynamic new patterns of trade and forged new connections between continents and cultures. Between 1600 and 1750 European colonists, enslaved Africans, valuable commodities, culture, and musical styles began to circulate within a global economy, not just within small regions or along overland trade routes like the Silk Road. Globalization shaped new understandings not only of cultural differences but also of the place of one's own culture in the world. Europeans' command of the sea extended their power and influence around the world. For the first time in human history, one region of the world began to seem at the center, and everyone else had to react to it in some way.

Trade played a major role in making connections between cultures and shaping new habits of everyday life. Cotton from India and silk from China changed European styles of dress. Coffee from the Ottoman Empire and the Arabian Peninsula, tea from China, and cocoa and tobacco from the Americas were consumed in new public coffee houses as well as at home. The Dutch gradually conquered the islands that today constitute Indonesia and grew rich from control of trade in cardamom and cloves from what was called the Dutch East Indies. The Russians expanded east and south to control Siberia and the Caucasus, and Russia became the largest country in the world, as it is today. The Ottomans attempted to extend the reach of their empire beyond the Balkans and farther into Europe, even besieging Vienna before they were finally defeated in 1683.

Trade enabled rulers around the world to expand their powers. The French king Louis XIV, who reigned from 1643 to 1715, proclaimed the "divine right of kings" to rule over their subjects.

> **ECONOMIC ACTIVITY**

FIGURE 5.1
The Palace at Versailles built by French king Louis XIV
Source: Wandernder Weltreisender, Wikimedia Commons.

He established the most lavish court in Europe, and his palace outside of Paris, Versailles, became famous for its elaborate ballets and plays accompanied by music. Louis himself was an avid dancer, and often participated in these productions. Other aristocratic courts around Europe envied and copied the Parisian court as best they could, and the aristocracy competed with both Catholic and Protestant Churches for the services of the best composers and musicians and the largest orchestras.

Because European composers in this period could make a good living answering the demands for new music from the plethora of wealthy kings, princes, and religious congregations in Europe at the time, there were a lot of them. Craftsmen working on demand, they produced vast amounts of music, which audiences for classical music today enjoy because of their clear triadic harmonies and engaging, pulsating rhythms. This chapter focuses on the music of just four of them as stand-ins for the music of many other prolific composers in this period:

- the operas of Claudio Monteverdi;
- the orchestral music of Antonio Vivaldi;
- the Protestant religious music of George Frideric Handel; and
- the keyboard music of Johann Sebastian Bach.

The Dutch engaged in negotiation and diplomacy with the rulers of Java, an island in present-day Indonesia. At that time Javanese court musicians were playing on a large orchestra of gongs and metallophones called gamelan. Music for the Javanese gamelan, the largest orchestra in the world outside Europe, is also presented in this chapter.

Many of the foundational elements of European classical music today have their roots in the period from 1600 to 1750.

FIGURE 5.2
Southeast Asia and the Dutch East Indies (Indonesia)

- The string orchestra, with a few wind instruments and timpani, became a common instrumental ensemble.
- The genre called opera was invented.
- Compositions for keyboard instruments (organ and harpsichord) reached their first apex.
- The very idea of instrumental music (the sonata) as an equal to vocal music (the cantata) is rooted in this period.
- The modal scales and harmonic system of the Renaissance period gave way to a new tonal system of keys.

This period in European music history is often called the Baroque period. The word **Baroque** is believed to come from a Portuguese expression for a misshapen pearl. Music critics in the nineteenth century used it to label what they considered, in retrospect, the exaggeratedly "misshapen" music of this period, especially the long, florid, twisting, ornamented melodic lines of music in this period. Today, in domains beyond music and art, the term "baroque" is applied to anything that seems "elaborate" and "exaggerated."

Baroque is also a term used in art history to describe the art of this period. Perhaps the most important representatives of Baroque (elaborate) style in art are the works of Italian sculptor and architect Gian Lorenzo Bernini (1598–1680). He created fountains and the interiors of many churches still visible today all over Rome. His Baroque style influenced the interiors and exteriors of Catholic Churches in Latin America and throughout the world. The church may have fostered his Baroque artistic style for its ability to express religious emotions in an impassioned way. In turn, the aristocracy adopted it as a symbol of secular wealth and opulence.

FIGURE 5.3
Gian Lorenzo Bernini's *Ecstasy of St. Teresa* **(1647–1652) in a Roman church**
Source: Joawim Alves Gaspar, Wikimedia Commons.

GATEWAY 17
BAROQUE OPERA

What Is It?

Our gateway to Baroque opera is Act I, Scene 4, *L'incoronazione di Poppea* (The Coronation of Poppea) by Claudio Monteverdi (1547–1643). It was first performed in December of 1642 at the beginning of the Venice carnival season, just months before Monteverdi's death in November of 1643. **Opera** is a theatrical musical genre that tells stories through a form of sung or heightened speech called **recitative** (melodic and rhythmic text recitation), songs with clear melodies (called **arias** in opera), choral singing (choruses), instrumental music, acting, and dancing. Invented at the end of the sixteenth century in Florence in Northern Italy, the new genre of opera marks the beginning of a new period in European music history, the Baroque. Monteverdi was the first great exponent of opera and the Baroque style. Concerto Vocale, a vocal and instrumental ensemble from Belgium conducted by René Jacobs, perform.

L'incoronazione di Poppea tells the story of Roman emperor Nero and his mistress Poppea, who has replaced Empress Octavia in his affections. It begins with a prologue in which the Ancient Roman and Greek gods Fortune, Virtue, and Love argue about which one has more influence in

FIGURE 5.4
Claudio Monteverdi
Source: Painting by Bernardo Strozzi (1581–1644). Tiroler Landesmuseum Ferdinandeum, Wikimedia Commons.

human life, a reflection of the renaissance of Greek and Roman myths and characters in the intellectual and artistic life of the sixteenth and seventeenth centuries. As the story develops, Love protects Poppea from Octavia's attempt to have Poppea's suitor Ottone assassinate her. When Nero learns of the plot, he banishes Octavia and Ottone from Rome and crowns Poppea his new empress, a seeming victory of Love over Virtue (adultery over fidelity). The opera ends with a touching love duet between Nero and Poppea, a harbinger of three centuries of florid love duets in the operatic tradition. In this scene Poppea reveals her hope that Nero will favor her over Octavia and that Fortune and Love will protect her from the resulting troubles. Her old nurse Arnalta is worried, however, and tries to dissuade her from her plan, expressing no trust in the powers of these imaginary gods to protect her "daughter" if her ambitions become known.

 Listen to the first minute of the recording.

How Does It Work?

Timbre

A female and male singer, a recorder, and bowed and plucked stringed instruments create the timbres of this performance. A typical opera ensemble of the time might have employed one or two keyboard instruments called harpsichords, two violins, a cello, and a variety of plucked string instruments, including a lute and a **theorbo**, a bass lute with an enormously long neck and fourteen courses of strings capable of playing low-pitched bass pitches.

Texture

The singers and the recorder perform melodies to the accompaniment of the bowed and plucked strings, which play chords and a bass line.

Rhythm

The rhythm varies from nonmetrical declamation of the text by the male singer (Arnalta) to metrical dance and song melodies by the recorder and female singer (Poppea).

Melody

The melodies use both stepwise motion and **arpeggios**, that is, leaps through the pitches of a triad.

Harmony

The harmony moves clearly from a triad on the tonic to authentic cadences (V–I) at the end of each phrase.

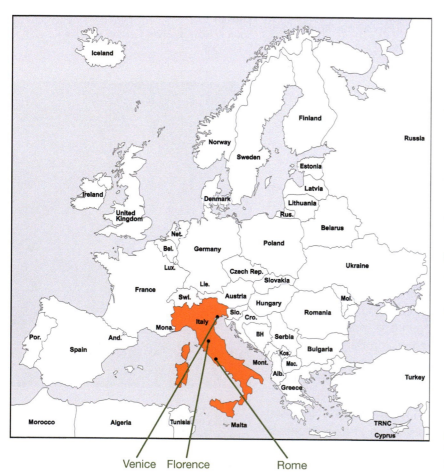

Venice Florence Rome

FIGURE 5.5

Map of Italy with the cities of Venice, Florence, and Rome

Form

The form consists of alternations between three different styles: (1) repeated instrumental interludes, called *ritornellos* (returns); (2) the female singer's aria, which consists of three short metrical tunes, each of which repeats a number of times; and (3) the recitatives of the male singer.

Performance Techniques

The female singer trills on a few notes, showing off her vocal technique, and both male and female singers manipulate the loudness and tempo of their singing to express their thoughts.

 Listen to the first thirty seconds of this recording for its timbre and texture.

What Does It Mean?

One aspect of the meaning of this music emerges in the way Monteverdi continues the Renaissance principle of text painting to express, in musical gestures, important words and ideas in the text. The singers help make this connection between text and music as well, singing loudly or softly, forcefully or gently, slowly or quickly, to express the text or convey their character's inner thoughts, which might reflect the text or be slightly at odds with it.

Listen to the entire recording. Follow this timed listening guide to understand the link between the lyrics and the music.

FIGURE 5.6
Lady with a theorbo c. 1680
Source: Painting by John Michael Wright (1617–1694). Columbus Museum of Art, Wikimedia Commons.

 LISTENING GUIDE 5.1

TIME	SECTIONS	LYRICS	TRANSLATION	DESCRIPTION
0:00	*Ritornello*			A small ensemble of bowed strings, harpsichord, and recorder play three short melodic phrases in duple meter.
0:12	Poppea:	*Speranza, tu mi vai il cor accarezzando*	Hope, you caress my heart	A female vocalist sings two phrases at a middle loudness (*mezzo forte*), ending with a ritard, an expression perhaps of her wistful emotional state. She is accompanied by cello and harpsichord in this section and throughout.
0:20	*Ritornello*			The instrumental melody returns.
0:32	Poppea:	*Speranza, tu mi vai il genio lusingando*	Hope, you come to me like an alluring gift	The singer repeats the first phrase, this time loudly (forte) as if reassuring herself, and then through an octave range.

continued

TIME	SECTIONS	LYRICS	TRANSLATION	DESCRIPTION
		e mi circondi intanto di regio sì, ma immaginario manto.	and envelope me in a royal but imaginary cloak	
0:52		*No, non temo, no, di noia alcuna (2x)*	No, I am not afraid of any trouble	She sings loudly with a steady beat in short arc-shaped phrases that rise in sequence, all these elements expressing her confidence and affirming her lack of fear at what may befall her.
1:06		*per me guerreggia Amor, e la Fortuna.*	Because fighting for me are Love and Fortune.	She shifts to triple meter to explain why she is so confident. The short melody repeats with slight variants in something like AAAAB form, but she ends on the second degree of the scale, as if her reverie is interrupted. (It is, by the entrance of Arnalta, her old nurse.)
1:30	*Ritornello*			The instrumental melody returns.
1:45	Arnalta:	*Ahi figlia, voglia il cielo, che questi abbracciamenti non sian un giorno i precipizi tuoi.*	Ah, daughter, I wish to heaven that these embraces do not one day cause your downfall	Arnalta, a female role sung by a male tenor, sings in a nonmetrical declamatory style accompanied by just the harpsichord playing chords. The style allows her to express her ideas at almost the same tempo as ordinary speech.
1:56	Poppea:	*No, non temo, no, di noia alcuna,*	No, I am not afraid of any trouble.	Poppea repeats her words and melody rather loudly, suggesting her optimism.
2:06	Arnalta:	*L'imperatrice Ottavia ha penetrati di Neron gli amori, ond'io pavento e temo ch'ogni giorno, ogni punto sia di tua vita il giorno, il punto estremo.*	The Empress Octavia has discovered Nero's loves and I am terribly afraid that some day, some moment Will bring your life to an extreme end.	Arnalta resumes her recitative with a melody that rises in pitch and words that go faster and faster as a way to express her rising concern and fear for Poppea's Fortuna).
2:24	Poppea:	*per me guerreggia Amor, e la Fortuna.*	But fighting for me are Love and Fortune.	Poppea repeats her melody and words, this time a little softer, as if Arnalta's worries have given her pause.

TIME	SECTIONS	LYRICS	TRANSLATION	DESCRIPTION
2:46	Arnalta:	*La pratica coi regi è perigliosa, l'amor e l'odio non han forza in essi, sono gli affetti lor puri interessi.*	The company of kings is perilous Love and hate have no strength against them. Love and hate have no strength against them.	Arnalta argues that Love and Fortune do not have the power Poppea hopes they have, singing "for-" of *forza* (strength) on a loud, singing high-pitched tone that mirrors in music the idea of strength.
3:06	*Ritornello*			A new instrumental tune is introduced.
3:14	Arnalta:	*Se Neron t'ama, è mera cortesia,* *s'ei t'abbandona, non te n' puoi dolere.* *Per minor mal ti converrà tacere.*	If Nero loves you, it is merely a courtesy If he abandons you, it should not make you regret it. It would be better for you to remain silent.	Arnalta's recitative continues, slowing briefly on three held, descending pitches that emphasize and express the meaning of the three syllables of "do-le-re" (regret).
3:33	*Ritornello*			The new instrumental tune returns.
3:40	Arnalta:	*Con lui tu non puoi mai trattar del pari, se le nozze hai per oggetto e fine, mendicando tu vai le tue ruine.*	You are not his equal, and if your goal is to marry him, it will be your ruin.	Armalta continues her recitative, ending with a descent over more than an octave to a very low pitch, an icon of Poppea's impending fall from the heights of her ambitions to the depths of ruin if she continues in her hope to marry Nero.
3:59	Poppea:	*No, non temo, no, di noia alcuna.*	No, I am not afraid of any trouble.	Poppea repeats her melody, this time loudly and quickly as if her resolve has returned and she is unpersuaded by Arnalta's arguments
4:05	Arnalta:	*Mira, mira Poppea.*	Be careful Poppea.	Arnalta abandons her recitative in favor of an aria in triple meter. The cello enters to accompany her.
4:09		*dove il prato è più più ameno e dilettoso, stassi il serpente ascoso.*	Where the grass is most pleasant and delightful there the snakes hide.	Arnalta sings the words *ameno i dilettoso* (pleasant and delightful) with light melismas on some of the syllables, a musical gesture that mirrors the meaning of the words.
4:22		*Dei casi le vicende son funeste.*	Some choices can be deadly.	On the word *funeste* (deadly), Arnalta moves suddenly down a

continued

TIME	SECTIONS	LYRICS	TRANSLATION	DESCRIPTION
				half step, a move that expresses the word's meaning but, in its surprising abruptness, might have earned the epithet "baroque" from critics of the period.
4:32		*la calma è profezia delle tempeste.*	The calm comes before the storm.	To paint the text, Arnalta sings the word "calm" quietly and the repeated word "storm" (*tempeste*) very loudly.
4:42	Poppea:	*No, non temo, no, di noia alcuna,*	No, I am not afraid of any trouble,	Poppea repeats her position loudly, still unconvinced by Arnalta's arguments.
4:50		*per me guerreggia Amor, e la Fortuna.*	because Love and Fortune defend me.	
5:02	Arnalta:	*Ben sei pazza, se credi che ti possano far contenta e salva un garzon cieco ed una donna calva. Ben sei pazza, se credi.*	You are crazy if you think you can be made contented and safe by a blind boy and a bald woman. You are crazy if you think so.	Arnalta expresses her frustration with a melody containing a series of equal-length staccato tones jumping around in disjunct motion. She then exits the stage abruptly, defeated by Poppea's continuing expressions of hope and confidence in Love and Fortune.

AESTHETICS

At first listening, the lack of a regular beat and repeating melody in Arnalta's recitatives might sound a bit strange to newcomers to opera. Perhaps the links between the music and the text in the timed listening guide help explain its logic and expressive possibilities. The singers cultivate a vocal technique that is loud enough to be heard without amplification in large opera houses. In doing so, they produce vocal qualities that some listeners new to the genre may find off-putting because they are so different from the sound of popular singers today and what some consider "natural." Opera fans, on the other hand, enjoy the vocal quality of the singers. They listen for subtle differences in tone quality among them, and they have their favorites.

SOCIAL BEHAVIOR

One of the striking features of this performance is that a man sings the role of Arnalta, Poppea's aging female nurse. This reflects conventions of the seventeenth and eighteenth centuries, when men often sang female roles. Opera directors today sometimes exploit this seeming contradiction for its humorous potential, giving Arnalta exaggerated breasts or having her act out stereotypical female behaviors in the manner of a contemporary drag queen.

Conversely, during the seventeenth and eighteenth centuries lead male roles, like those of Nero and Ottone, were often sung by male sopranos and altos. Today these roles are sung by counter-tenors, men who sing in a high-pitched, head-resonated falsetto voice. In the seventeenth century they were sung by a *castrato*, a male singer castrated before puberty to prevent his voice from changing from soprano to tenor or bass. There is some evidence that this practice began in the church. Palestrina, in 1558, probably had both *castrati* and boys in his Sistine Chapel choir, where women would not have been allowed to sing. Castration, approved for this purpose by the pope in the late sixteenth century, allowed outstanding boy sopranos to continue their careers as adults, singing the soprano parts of Renaissance sacred four-part polyphony. In Baroque opera, *castrati* were much prized for their spectacularly powerful voices, and no opera could attract an audience without at least one in a lead role. Much stronger than female sopranos or a countertenor's falsetto, the sound of a *castrato* was interpreted as an icon of masculine power and associated with heroic male roles. Changing social and artistic values contributed to the decline in the popularity of *castrati* by the end of the eighteenth century. Italian law and papal orders put an end to the practice by the late nineteenth century, although some *castrati* lived into the early twentieth century. When male countertenors sing these roles today, the timbre of their voices sounds more feminine than heroic, inviting the audience to reconcile male and female stereotypes in new ways.

What Is Its History?

Opera was a harbinger of enormous changes in musical practice during the period from 1600 to 1750. Some of these changes responded to the implications for music of "reborn" (Renaissance) texts about music by Plato and other Greek philosophers. New thinking about vocal music began in Italy, first in Florence and later in Venice, cities full of wealthy bankers and merchants who had enriched themselves through trade with the Ottoman Empire and along the shores of the Mediterranean Sea. In Florence during the late sixteenth century a group of composers and intellectuals called the Florentine camerata ("the club of Florence") began debating Greek ideas about the expressive power of music. As they read about the powerful effects on the emotions and on ethics of Ancient Greek monophonic music, they began to doubt whether the polyphonic, contrapuntal motets and madrigals of their own time were capable of achieving the same effects as the Ancient Greeks had claimed for their monophonic music. They theorized that the reported power of Ancient Greek melody must have lain in its ability to express the emotional meanings inherent in sung lyrics.

The Florentine intellectuals wondered whether polyphonic music obscured the meaning of the text and limited the possibilities for expressing the full extent of the meaning and emotion in it. They theorized that, if a single line of melody hewed closely to the contours and rhythms of speech and emotion in the text, perhaps it could replicate the powerful expressive quality of music that the Greeks had written about. They experimented with creating melodies in a nonmetrical, declamatory rhythm that mimicked the rhythm of speech, in the process creating the genre called recitative. If someone, while speaking during an emotional moment, would likely stutter or stop and start again, then music, they argued, should do so as well. If the text changed dramatically in emotion, then the melody should as well. But the Florentines could not seriously advocate for the abandonment of harmony and counterpoint in favor of Ancient Greek monophony. What to do?

Their solution is called monody. This is a confusing term because it sounds like monophony and might seem to be another label for a texture with only one voice. Monody reduces the texture of Renaissance-period polyphony with four equal vocal parts for soprano, alto, tenor, and bass to an emphasis on the melody. **Monody** has a three-part texture: a vocal melody (or sometimes a duet); an instrumental bass line called the ***basso continuo***; and chords improvised by a keyboard or lute player. In the new practice the chords were not written out. The player was expected to supply them, to figure them out from the bass part. If the chord was difficult to deduce from the bass note, Baroque composers added numerals called "figures" above or below the pitches of the *basso continuo*, creating a **figured bass**. The numbers indicate the number of scale degrees above the bass note that the player should play. For example, if the bass note is C with no figures, the player, by implication, would play a triad on C: C-E-G. If the numerals 6 and 4 are written below C, the player would play six notes above C, which is A, and four notes above C, which is F. The resulting triad would be C-F-A. Playing such a bass line with figures is called "realizing a figured bass." Music students today are often taught how to do it. It is one of the principal achievements of the Baroque

FIGURE 5.7
Piazza San Marco by Canaletto (1697–1768) in 1720, with Saint Mark's Cathedral in the background
Source: Metropolitan Museum of Art, Wikimedia Commons.

period in music history, one that echoes today in the song notations (sheet music) and chord-based improvisations of jazz and popular music.

Although the composers of the Florentine camerata tried their hand at writing in this new style, their first works in this new genre, opera, have been largely forgotten today. Claudio Monteverdi is considered its first master. He was an outstanding madrigalist before turning his hand to the new style of monody advocated by the Florentine camerata. He wrote four books of Renaissance-style polyphonic madrigals at the end of the sixteenth century while working at the court of the Duke of Mantua, a region west of Venice. Book Four, published in 1603, contains one of his most frequently performed polyphonic madrigals, "Sì, ch'io vorrei morire" (Yes, I would welcome death), notable for its exquisite painting of the text. In his fifth book of madrigals (he wrote a total of eight), published in 1605, he introduced the new style of monodic vocal composition. In one of his most performed madrigals in this new style, "Zefiro torna e di soavi accenti" (Return, O Zephyr [a breeze] with gentle motion), published in 1632, Monteverdi set two voices, a duet, against the *basso continuo*. This new style enabled virtuosic singing in the form of fast runs, trills, and other ornaments because the voices are not tethered to contrapuntal relations among the parts. In opera, this style of metrical, melodic singing was given a new genre name: aria.

ECONOMIC ACTIVITY

Monteverdi's first opera, *Orfeo* (1607), produced at the court of Mantua, is regarded as the first successful opera, and it and *Poppea* are still performed occasionally today, especially by musicians dedicated to the revival of early music. *Orfeo* tells the famous story of the Greek mythical musician Orpheus, who used music to save his beloved Euridice from death in the underworld. Later in his career Monteverdi moved from Mantua to Venice, where he became the music director at St. Mark's Cathedral. Opera, aimed at public audiences of wealthy merchants rather than at courtly or religious ones, combined humor, sexuality, and overwrought emotional scenes. It appealed to a broad public, and by 1700 Venice, a city of 140,000 people at the time, had sixteen opera houses. Today Santa Monica, California, a city of about the same size, has about the same number of movie theaters. Venetian opera productions, in other words, were forms of entertainment similar in their cultural impact to films today.

EMOTIONAL RESONANCE

While emphasizing single melodic lines gave Monteverdi and other Baroque composers new tools to express the emotion and meaning of sung texts, they continued to use familiar musical conventions developed in Renaissance and Italian polyphonic madrigals to paint the meaning of texts. In Arnalta's recitatives Monteverdi combines Renaissance expressive conventions with the new monodic style to underline the meaning of the words *forza* (strength), *funeste* (deadly), *ruine* (ruin), and *dolere* (regret).

AESTHETICS

This stylistic innovation, monody, did not eliminate contrapuntal polyphony from European music. During the Baroque period these two practices existed side by side and both were valued. Musicians of the period distinguished these two musical styles with their own labels: the older contrapuntal polyphony was called *prima prattica* (first practice) and the newer monodic style with figured bass was called *seconda prattica* (second practice), terms that reflected the order in which these styles emerged in European music history.

Operas in this period were performed once or perhaps a few times and then disappeared from the repertoire in favor of new operas, a bit like movies do today. The score of *Poppea* was lost for nearly 250 years, until it was rediscovered at the end of the nineteenth century. Baroque operas, and indeed a lot of Baroque music, were forgotten for a time as European musical style changed over the next two centuries. It was revived during the nineteenth century when European intellectuals and musicians became interested for the first time in the history of their musical traditions. Modern performers have to reconstruct *Poppea* from fragmentary evidence, and performances can differ significantly. Early revivals used a modern orchestra. Later ones, based on musicological research, used small ensembles typical of the period. Directors, too, have a great deal of freedom in how they stage the opera and which sexes sing the roles. Although opera originated during the Baroque period, Baroque operas are today rare flowers on the fringes of the modern opera repertoire.

WHERE DO I GO FROM HERE?

* Watch a video performance or two of "Speranza, tu mi vai." Note the costuming and stage action, particularly the way men dress and act the role of Arnalta.

* Compare the effects of three videos of the final love duet from L'incoronazione di Poppea: "Pur ti miro, pur ti godo" (I gaze at you, I possess you), one with a countertenor singing the role of Nero, one with a bass singing the role, and one with a woman singing the role.

* Listen to a performance of Monteverdi's monodic madrigal, "Zefiro torna e di soavi accenti" (Return, O Zephyr [a breeze] with gentle motion), published in 1632. Note the florid, melismatic singing style.

GATEWAY 18
BAROQUE ORCHESTRAL MUSIC

What Is It?

Our gateway to Baroque orchestral music is the first movement of Antonio Vivaldi's (1678–1741) Violin Concerto in E Major, RV 269, "Spring." Vivaldi lived and worked in Venice, Italy, and was one of the most prolific and influential composers of the Baroque period. A **concerto** is a composition that pits an orchestra, called the *ripieno* from Italian for "full" or "stuffed," against a soloist or a small group of soloists, in this case, one or two violinists. Concertos typically have three movements: fast tempo, slow tempo, fast tempo. RV 269 is a recent catalog number assigned to this piece by a scholar making a complete list of Vivaldi's compositions. "Spring" is a name Vivaldi gave the piece, one of four concertos in a set that came to be called "The Four Seasons."

The term "E Major" in the title requires some explanation. It is shorthand for a longer phrase: "in the key based on an E major scale." A major scale is a mode with the intervals of a scale with a final on C (C D E F G A B C). During the Baroque period the major mode and the minor mode, a mode that can be written with a final on A (A B C D E F G A), replaced the old system of Medieval church modes (Dorian, Phrygian, Lydian, and Mixolydian). By Vivaldi's time the major and minor modes could, in principle, each be played with a final on any of the twelve pitches of the dodecaphonic scale (C C♯ D D♯ and so on). When a major scale is played with a final on C, it is called "the key of C major,"

FIGURE 5.8
Antonio Vivaldi
Source: Museo internazionale e biblioteca della musica di Bologna, Wikimedia Commons.

not the mode of C major. When a major scale is played with a final on E, as in this concerto, it is called "the key of E major" or simply E major. When minor scales are played on A or B, they are called the key of A minor and the key of B minor, respectively. The result is a collection of twelve major and twelve minor keys. When a major and minor key share the same set of pitches, as C major and A minor do for example, they are said to be relatives of one another: the relative major and the relative minor.

An aside: In this system of major and minor keys, the terms major and minor are also applied to the intervals between scale degrees. The interval of a half step is called a **minor second** and the interval of a whole step is called a **major second**. Each of the other intervals in a diatonic scale, except fourths and fifths, also have two sizes: major and minor thirds, major and minor sixths, and major and minor sevenths.

This performance is by the Venice Baroque Orchestra, conducted by its founder and violinist Andrea Marcon, with violinist Giuliano Carmignola in the lead solo role.

 Listen to the first thirty seconds of the recording and note the contrast between the full orchestra and the solo violins.

How Does It Work?

Timbre

The timbre contrasts a small string orchestra plus harpsichord with the sound of solo violins, sometimes just one and sometimes two in duet.

Texture

The texture features a melodic line accompanied by bass and chords. Sometimes the violins play alone in counterpoint.

Rhythm

The meter is duple. The rhythm of the orchestra employs a constant pulse, sometimes at two levels: a fast pulse subdivides a slower constant beat. This type of pulsating rhythm is one of the hallmarks of Baroque musical style. During some of the violin solos the pulse seems to disappear and the music sounds nonmetrical.

Melody

The melodies are diatonic and move in stepwise motion, but some of the solo violin passages are chromatic.

Harmony

The movement starts in E major, shifts to the relative minor (C♯ minor), and returns to E major.

Form

The form alternates a *ritornello*, a returning melody played by the *ripieno* (the full orchestra), with passages for solo violin. The *ritornello* is in European dance form: AABB. Most times the *ritornello* consists only of the B part returns, played one time.

Performance Techniques

The violin part, played by Giuliano Carmignola, features many melodic ornaments and trills.

 Listen to the first thirty seconds of the recording for the AABB form of the *ritornello*.

What Does It Mean?

The concerto, and its cousin the sonata, join opera as the most important and long-lasting contributions of the Baroque period to European classical music genres. (A **sonata**, from the Latin word for sound, is an instrumental composition for a soloist or a small group of soloists.) Concertos and sonatas were the first instrumental compositions in the history of European music meant for listening in concert or church settings rather than for dancing, the amusement of amateur players, or as instrumental versions of vocal works. The question of what instrumental compositions for listening could mean, that is, how listeners are meant to understand and interpret them if they do not dance to them and if they have no lyrics, was vexing to some listeners in the seventeenth and eighteenth centuries and remains so today. One interpretation is that instrumental music is meant for purely musical enjoyment, a type of pleasure explainable through description and analysis of their musical elements. Many, perhaps most, Baroque concertos and sonatas, can be understood this way. Certainly the musical names "concerto" and "sonata" seem to focus on their musical sound and its properties.

AESTHETICS

For example, the timed listening guide below indicates the way the first movement of the concerto **modulates** (changes keys) from its "home key" of E major to other keys for a significant time, in particular to the major key on the fifth degree of the scale (B major) and the relative minor key (C♯ minor). During the Renaissance, the dominant and tonic relationships (V–I) were established within musical phrases and expressed in cadences at the end of phrases. During the Baroque the dominant pitch became a "key area" that composers could travel to and live in musically before returning to the tonic in a large-scale V–I movement. These movements to closely related keys, often achieved through melodic sequences, allowed composers to expand the length of their works beyond the confines of relatively short dance tunes.

Another interpretation of these purely instrumental works argues that they carry with them associations and iconic musical gestures developed in sixteenth-century vocal polyphony and early seventeenth-century opera, with echoes going back even earlier to Hildegard's religious chants and the English round "Sumer is icumen in." In this interpretation, the long history of associations between happy texts, fast tempos, rising melodies, and the major mode and between sad texts, slow tempos, falling melodies, and the minor mode carries over into instrumental music. Thus, the moods and emotions in particular instrumental compositions can be explained in terms of their musical elements, without any direct references to a text. Those associations are implicit in purely instrumental music. Similarly, ornamentation and other instrumental devices may be icons of sounds in nature, such as bird song, because musical icons of textual meaning, emotion, and references to natural sounds were developed in Renaissance vocal music.

EMOTIONAL RESONANCE

Concertos and sonatas and other forms of purely instrumental European music can be enjoyed in both ways: as abstract music and as expressions of mood and emotion. Vivaldi's Violin Concerto in E major is a good example. Its title bears its strictly musical meaning and suggests listening to it for its musical properties: in this case a featured solo instrument (violin), a genre (concerto, implying a contrast between soloists and a string orchestra), and a key (E major).

Vivaldi gave this concerto the additional name "Spring," clearly implying that this concerto could be understood as referencing something external to the music itself, in this case something in nature. Each concerto in "The Four Seasons" has a poem, which Vivaldi may have written, printed in the score. This suggests that the concertos may be interpreted to express, or to paint, the words and moods of the poem. This is an early instance of what came to be called, during the nineteenth century, **program music**: music composed to express the emotions, moods, and meanings of an unperformed verbal narrative.

CULTURAL LINKAGES

Listen to the entire first movement of Vivaldi's Violin Concerto in E major, "Spring," and follow the timed listening guide to understand the link between Vivaldi's poem about spring and the way his music expresses the poem's text. The guide is preceded by the poem.

LISTENING GUIDE 5.2

Giunt' è la Primavera e festosetti *La Salutan gl' Augei con lieto canto,* *E i fonti allo Spirar de' Zeffiretti* *Con dolce mormorio Scorrono intanto:* *Vengon' coprendo l' aer di nero amanto* *E Lampi, e tuoni ad annuntiarla eletti* *Indi tacendo questi, gl' Augelletti;* *Tornan' di nuovo al lor canoro incanto:*	Springtime is upon us and the birds celebrate their return with festive song, and murmuring streams are softly caressed by the breezes. Thunderstorms, those heralds of Spring, roar, casting their dark mantle over heaven, and then they die away to silence, and the birds take up their charming songs once more.

TIME	SECTION	DESCRIPTION
0:00	*Ritornello*	"Springtime is upon us." The *ripieno* plays the *ritornello* (AABB). The major key and the spritely dance tempo in a meter of four suggest the optimism of spring.
0:32	Solo violins & *ritornello*	Two solo violins play "songs of the birds," a phrase in the score, using a wide variety of iconic articulations including trills and melodic gestures followed, at 1:03, by the B melody of the *ritornello*.
1:10	Solo violins & *ritornello*	The violins play constant rapid pulses and then longer tones softly in parallel thirds to paint the poem's reference to "murmuring breezes," followed, at 1:30, by the B melody of the *ritornello*.
1:37	Solo violins & *ritornello*	Loud, low-pitched tremolos in the violins alternate with rapid ascending runs and arpeggios to paint the poem's reference to "thunderstorms roaring." The passage modulates to the relative minor key, now associated with the darkness of a storm, followed, at 2:00, by the return of the *ritornello* in the relative minor key.
2:09	Solo violins	"The birds take up their charming songs once more." Now their songs are in a minor key and use ascending chromatic melodic lines as icons of an unsettled state.
2:27	*Ritornello*	A variant of the A melody returns softly, beginning in the minor key and and starts to modulate to the major key from the beginning of the piece.
2:40	Solo violins & *ritornello*	The solo violin plays an ascending melody with a few references to bird song and completes the modulation back to the major key, followed, at 2:53, by the BB part of the *ritornello*, ending with ritard.
3:13	End	

The slow second movement of this concerto paints this text: "And then, on the flower-strewn meadow, with leafy branches rustling overhead, the goatherd sleeps, his faithful dog beside him." Low-pitched droning strings suggest the rustling branches, a slow melody with long tones suggests the sleeping goatherd, and two tones played over and over "very loudly" imitate, humorously, the bark of a dog. The third movement text, "Led by the festive sound of bagpipes, nymphs and shepherds lightly dance beneath the brilliant canopy of spring," is painted with imitations of the drone of a rustic bagpipe and a set of fast danceable melodies in European dance form (AABBCCDD).

The sound of a string orchestra is commonplace in our culture today. Coupled with the dance tempos, the constant pulse of the music, the clear and familiar tonal harmony, the repeating *ritornello* melodies, and the virtuosic violin playing, many listeners today find this and other examples of Baroque orchestral music quite pleasing.

What Is Its history?

During the Renaissance two families of bowed string instruments competed for the affection of professional and amateur musicians. The violin family, with fretless necks, seems to have been a favorite of professional musicians. The viol family, whose fretted necks made it somewhat easier to play, was favored by wealthy and courtly amateurs. By the seventeenth century the violin family was flourishing in the hands of master musicians and craftsmen, and the viol family disappeared from common use until it was revived during the twentieth century as part of the early music movement. During the sixteenth century, the small Northern Italian town of Cremona, Monteverdi's birthplace about 150 miles west of Venice, was home to the best violin makers (luthiers), among them members of the Amati and Guarneri families. Today professional violinists greatly admire and seek out violins made in Cremona during the late seventeenth century and early eighteenth century by contemporaries of Monteverdi and Vivaldi: Nicolò Amati (1596–1684), his apprentice Giuseppe Guarneri (1698–1744), and another possible apprentice Antonio Stradivari (1644–1737), whose Latinized name, Stradivarius, is a metaphor for excellence in all fields and whose violins are valued today in the millions of dollars.

Orchestral music intended for listening at indoor concerts, like this Vivaldi violin concerto, was an outgrowth of the instrumental *ritornello* of opera. At first operas were accompanied by small string ensembles with harpsichord accompaniment playing a figured bass. By the first half of the 1700s the increasingly rich and powerful European monarchies of France, Britain (formed in 1707 by the union of England and Scotland), Austria, and Prussia (formed in northern Germany in 1701) could afford to hire large numbers of musicians for elaborate courtly ceremonies, concerts, and opera productions. The most famous, admired, and imitated early orchestra was the "24 Violins of the King," an orchestra that played for Louis XIV of France, who reigned from 1643 to 1715. By the end of the seventeenth century, large churches, which had long trained priests and clerics as composers and choristers, hired musicians to accompany services in the new style of monody called *seconda prattica*. St. Mark's Cathedral in Venice, where Monteverdi had worked toward the end of his life, had perhaps the largest church orchestra in Europe by the end of seventeenth century. Court and church orchestral musicians included not only string players, who doubled the soprano, alto, tenor, and bass parts of four-part tonal harmony but also players of recorders, transverse flutes, oboes, bassoons, "natural" (valveless) horns and trumpets, and **timpani** (single-headed, bowl-shaped kettle drums). Neither the number nor the kinds of instruments in an orchestra was standardized during this period, and composers were skilled in creating, and rewriting, music to suit the size and instruments of the orchestras they had at their disposal for a particular occasion.

The term concerto to designate these orchestral compositions is a cognate of the term consort, used during the Renaissance for small instrumental ensembles. *Concerto* in Italian refers to playing "in concert," that is, playing together, retained in the English expression "let's work in concert on this problem." There are three principal types of Baroque concertos: the solo concerto, the concerto grosso, and the *ripieno concerto*.

- The solo concerto features a contrast between a solo instrumentalist and the orchestral ensemble, the *ripieno*.

TECHNOLOGY

ECONOMIC ACTIVITY

TECHNOLOGY

AESTHETICS

- The **concerto grosso** contrasts a small group of soloists called the *concertino*, with the *ripieno*.
- The *ripieno concerto* features the entire ensemble and eliminates the contrast between orchestral and solo timbres.

A *ripieno concerto* was sometimes called *sinfonia*, from the Greek "sounding together." Some of Vivaldi's later compositions in this style were forerunners of the orchestral compositions called symphonies in the late eighteenth century. At the macro level of form, concertos have three movements: fast, slow, and fast. Within each movement concertos borrowed the *ritornello* principle from opera as the main formal structure. The instrumental soloist or small ensemble mimicked the role of the singers in opera and performed an evolving set of new music, while the *ripieno* played a melody that returned. In this way instrumental works balanced familiarity and stability against variety and change. This formal principle was later called **rondo form**: ABACAD, and so forth.

Two Italian composers are credited with developing some of the structural principles that Vivaldi used in his concertos. Arcangelo Corelli (1653–1713), a noted violin virtuoso, wrote many sonatas that allowed soloists, including himself, to show off their technique. His formal excursions into related keys, such as the relative minor and the dominant key, were also models that Vivaldi followed. Jean-Philippe Rameau (1683–1764), an important French composer of operas and keyboard sonatas and the most important music theorist of the time, used Corelli's works as models for his explanations of the new system of tonal harmony in his 1722 book *Traité de l'harmonie réduite à ses principes naturels* (Treatise on Harmony Reduced to its Natural Principles), an explanation still influential today. Another Venetian composer, Tomaso Albinoni (1671–1750), gave the concerto its three-movement form. Vivaldi's consistent use of this form, coupled with his renown around Europe, ensured that the concerto (and the sonata) would have this form for centuries to come.

> **CULTURAL LINKAGES**

Antonio Vivaldi, a priest and virtuoso violinist, composed around 500 concertos during his lifetime, most of them at a school in Venice for young girls, some of them orphans. Judging by the demands of the music, they were exceptionally well trained. In Venice during the fourteenth century, the Catholic Church had established four "hospitals" for orphans, the children of indigent parents, and those with incurable illnesses. One, the Pio Ospedale della Pietà, functioned as a conservatory of music for girls, who were trained as singers and instrumentalists in an early form of music therapy. From 1703 to 1740, Vivaldi supervised their teaching and composed sacred and secular music for them to play and sing. Not allowed to play outside the *ospedale*, even if they left it for marriage, they gave public concerts for admiring visitors from all over Europe, including the pope. A French visitor around 1740 described a concert performed by "about forty girls," who "sing like angels," dress like nuns, have a leader with "a bouquet of pomegranate flowers over her ear," and play with a precision rivaling the famous professional orchestras of Paris.[38]

Vivaldi's father taught him to play violin, and they concertized together throughout much of his life. The younger Vivaldi's violin technique, reflected in the virtuoso violin solos of his concertos, awed contemporary admirers. The *ospedale* contracted with him to produce two masses a year and two motets and two concertos each month. In 1717 he obtained the prestigious post of *maestro di cappella* at the court of the Duke of Mantua, where Monteverdi had worked more than a century earlier. There he wrote "The Four Seasons," whose references to nature were perhaps inspired by the countryside around this small town or the taste of his noble patron. The European aristocracy of the time was particularly enamored of nature and the countryside, which painters, novelists, and Vivaldi idealized in their creations. Of course peasants who lived close to nature suffered no such illusions. They suffered great poverty and misery. For local theaters Vivaldi wrote and produced more than forty operas, the most popular genre of the day. At least one was performed in Prague, and they enjoyed enough success for him to dream of a commission from the Austrian emperor Charles VI. He failed in his quest, however, and died in poverty in Vienna at the age of sixty-three after an extraordinarily successful and prolific career.

Vivaldi's instrumental concertos were published during his lifetime, and in that form they spread around Europe. They proved enormously influential among German composers including Johann Sebastian Bach, who taught himself to compose in Vivaldi's "Italian style" and transcribed some of Vivaldi's concertos for keyboard. On the other hand, his operas, like most Baroque operas, are rarely performed today, having been supplanted by those of Wolfgang Amadeus Mozart in what came to be called "the Classical style." But his energetic and virtuosic concertos retain their charm, and many modern players and listeners are devoted to them.

WHERE DO I GO FROM HERE?

- Listen to a performance of another concerto ("Fall, "Winter," or "Summer") from Vivaldi's "The Four Seasons." Try to find the accompanying poem and listen for the way Vivaldi "paints" the text in that concerto.

- Listen to a solo concerto by Vivaldi for an instrument besides the violin: the recorder, oboe, bassoon, or mandolin.

- Listen to Johann Sebastian Bach's Brandenberg Concerto No. 5 in D Major, a *concerto grosso* featuring a *concertino* section of violin, transverse flute, and harpsichord. It was probably composed between 1717 and 1723.

- Listen to George Frideric Handel's Organ Concerto, Op. 4, No. 5, IV: Presto, composed in London in 1735 or 1736.

GATEWAY 19
BAROQUE SACRED MUSIC

What Is It?

Our gateway to Baroque sacred music is the "Hallelujah" chorus from George Frideric Handel's oratorio, *Messiah*, first performed in Dublin, Ireland, in 1742 and London, England, in 1743. An **oratorio** is a multi-movement composition that tells a biblical story in the vernacular (local) language rather than in the Latin of the Catholic liturgy. To do so, it uses many of the conventions of opera (recitatives, arias with orchestral and *basso continuo* accompaniments, and choruses), but it is performed in concert settings minus the acting, costumes, and scenery of opera. *Messiah* contains more than fifty sections, including recitatives, arias (called "airs" in English), choruses, and two instrumental *sinfonias*. It takes about two and a half hours to perform and has three parts: (1) the Christmas story, including Old Testament prophecies of the coming of a Messiah; (2) the Easter story of Christ's suffering and death; and (3) his resurrection and the redemption of Christians through faith. The "Hallelujah" chorus, from Hebrew for "Praise God," ends Part 2. The English text was created by Charles Jennens, a gentleman farmer and friend of Handel's, who cobbled the text together from passages in the King James Bible and the Anglican *Book of Common Prayer*. In this performance John Eliot Gardiner, the conductor and a noted specialist in Baroque performance practice, the Monteverdi Choir, and the English Baroque Soloists try to recreate the choral sound of the first performance of *Messiah*, which had a choir of thirty men and boys from Dublin's two cathedrals as well as two women as soloists.

 Listen to the first thirty seconds of the recording.

How Does It Work?

Timbre

The sound is created by a small string orchestra with the addition of trumpets and timpani and a chorus of men and boys.

FIGURE 5.9
George Frideric Handel
Source: Painting by Balthasar Denner
(1685–1749). National Portrait Gallery,
London, Wikimedia Commons.

Texture

Handel used all the textures available to him: monophony, monody, polyphony of voices singing rhythmically independent parts and parts in the same rhythm, and imitative polyphony.

Rhythm

The meter is in four and moves along with a strong pulse and short, crisp rhythmic devices, for example, on the many repetitions of the word "Hallelujah."

Melody

The melody is diatonic in a major key, employing many leaps through the pitches of major triads, including ascending leaps of an octave.

Harmony

The harmony is tonal, in a major key.

Form

The form consists of four sections based on the text and features the repetition and return of many short melodic ideas.

Section 1: Hallelujah (repeated)

Section 2: For the Lord God omnipotent reigneth.
            Hallelujah (repeated)

Section 3: The kingdom of this world is become
            the kingdom of our Lord and of his Christ.

Section 4: And he shall reign for ever and ever,
            King of kings and Lord of lords.
            Hallelujah (repeated)

Performance techniques

The performers change dynamics from soft to loud at important moments.

Listen to the entire performance following this timed listening guide, which explains the way the musical elements change as the text changes.

LISTENING GUIDE 5.3

TIME	SECTION	TEXT	DESCRIPTION
0:00		Instrumental overture	The string orchestra begins softly, its rhythm anticipating the rhythm of the word "Hallelujah."
0:07	1	Hallelujah (repeated)	The chorus, singing in four-part harmony, repeats "Hallelujah" five times softly on the tonic chord and then five more times loudly on the dominant chord.
0:26	2a	For the Lord God omnipotent reigneth. Hallelujah	The chorus sings in octaves on the V chord until "Hallelujah" returns in harmony, this time joined by the trumpets and timpani.

TIME	SECTION	TEXT	DESCRIPTION
0:38	2b	For the Lord God omnipotent reigneth. Hallelujah	The chorus repeats the words, this time on the tonic chord.
0:49	2c	For the Lord God omnipotent reigneth. Hallelujah	The melody of "for the Lord . . ." and the chorus on "Hallelujah" are sung by rhythmically independent parts, with the melody passing from the sopranos to the basses to the tenors.
1:16	3a	The kingdom of this world is become	The chorus sings softly in four-part harmony to the accompaniment of the string orchestra.
1:27	3b	the kingdom of our Lord and of his Christ.	The chorus sings a variant of the melody, this time loudly and with trumpet and timpani accompaniment, the contrast a musical icon of the difference between the plain earthly world (soft) and the glorious heavenly kingdom (loud).
1:36	4a	And he shall reign for ever and ever,	This section features imitative polyphony, with the basses, tenors, altos, and sopranos each entering in turn on the melody.
1:59	4b	King of kings, and Lord of lords.	One part declaims the words on a single pitch while the chorus responds with "forever and ever, Hallelujah, Hallelujah" in harmony. The pitch rises with each repetition, an icon of the growing intensity of faith, joy, and praise.
2:40	4c	And he shall reign for ever and ever,	The chorus sings in counterpoint.
2:51	4d	King of kings, and Lord of lords.	The chorus sings a varied repeat of 4b.
3:00	4e	And he shall reign for ever and ever, King of kings, and Lord of lords. Hallelujah (repeated)	The chorus, accompanied by the trumpet and timpani, concludes loudly and triumphantly in four-part harmony.
3:44		End	

What Does It Mean?

In this chorus Handel has absorbed the text painting possibilities of Italian opera, sonically illuminating the text with signs of association and similarity. He uses rising pitch to express the intensification of faith. Trumpets and timpani, associated for centuries with royal and aristocratic festivities, create a feeling of majesty in the revelation of Christ as Lord and king. Softness reflects the ordinariness of secular life, while loudness conveys the glories of a religious life. The major key, long associated with positive and joyous moods, and short, punchy melodic phrases reinforce the brightness of the message. Doubt, which would have been expressed in an excursion to the relative minor, is banished from this movement.

EMOTIONAL RESONANCE

What Is Its History?

George Frideric Handel was born Georg Friederich Händel in 1685 in the prosperous German trading city of Halle, about 100 miles southwest of Berlin, where his father worked at the court of a local duke. His musical talent was evident at a young age, and he was sent to study organ and counterpoint with the organist at the town church. There he learned to play and compose in all the genres of music required in the Lutheran liturgy of the time, including elaborate contrapuntal organ compositions, four-part hymn accompaniments, and performances of recitatives and arias on sacred texts, styles and techniques he eventually put to use in his English oratorios. By the age of eleven or so, he was nearly the equal of his teacher and already composing music for services and giving organ lessons.

> **CULTURAL LINKAGES**

The Lutheran musical traditions he learned in Halle have their roots two centuries earlier in the Protestant Reformation of the sixteenth century. Martin Luther, a trained musician, ignited the Protestant Reformation in 1517. To make religious lessons and worship more accessible to local congregations, he translated many Latin liturgical texts into German and wrote his own hymn melodies to new German texts he also composed. His most famous hymn in this vein, "Ein feste Burg ist unser Gott" (A mighty fortress is our God), became an anthem for Protestants in their battles against the Catholic Church in the early seventeenth century. The Thirty Years War, which began as a conflict between Protestant and Catholic states in Europe, raged from 1618 to 1648 and killed eight million people. Lutheran services encouraged congregational singing of hymns, with organists supplying organ accompaniments in the four-part harmony of the Renaissance. As musical styles changed, so did the harmonies of these hymns. Johann Sebastian Bach's hymn harmonizations in the early eighteenth century are the most well known. They are still used to teach tonal harmony to music students. During the seventeenth century, the new style of opera was also introduced into Lutheran religious services in a multi-movement genre called **cantata** (from Italian for "to sing") to distinguish them from the new instrumental genre sonata. By the eighteenth century the church cantata had become a set of pieces that might include an instrumental overture, an opening contrapuntal chorus, two recitative-and-aria sets, and a concluding chorale with all four parts moving in the same rhythm and suitable for congregational singing. Taken together, the cantata told a story or expressed a religious sentiment suitable for the day in the church calendar for which it was composed. The most famous of these were composed by Handel's contemporary Johann Sebastian Bach, born in the same year as Handel, 1685, and who lived nearly as long, to 1750. Between 1723 and 1750 Bach composed more than 200 cantatas for the Lutheran St. Thomas Church in Leipzig, about twenty-five miles southeast of Halle. Among his most famous are "Ein feste Burg," "Wachet auf," and "Ich habe genug." Handel, who by the time Bach moved to Leipzig was living in England, never met Bach or heard his cantatas.

After a year at the University of Halle, Handel moved to Hamburg, where the first opera house in Germany had been established in 1678. There, in 1705 at the age of twenty, he composed and produced his first two operas. These works caught the attention of the wealthy Medici family, who, in 1706, invited him to Florence. In 1709 his opera *Agrippina*, about the plotting of Nero's mother to have him installed as Emperor of Rome, premiered in Venice, the home of opera. In Rome a group of cardinals and a wealthy patron close to the church invited him to compose oratorios. Oratorios have their origin in the sixteenth-century Catholic Counter-Reformation and the reforms of the Council of Trent (1545–1563). Responding to the Protestant challenge to educate believers in Biblical teaching, wealthy parish churches built church halls called oratorios (oratories) as places for the education of the faithful through classes, lectures, and concerts in the local language, Italian. These concert pieces based on Biblical stories were called **oratorios** after the place where they were performed. For Easter Sunday, 1708, Handel composed an oratorio titled *La resurrezione* (The Resurrection), performed not in an oratorio but in the wealthy patron's home. Arcangelo Corelli, a famous violinist and composer, conducted a large orchestra of more than forty musicians.

Handel's operas and oratorios were much loved in Italy, attracting the notice of the German prince Georg, Elector of Hanover. The ruler of the principality of Hanover in northern Germany was called Elector because he had the right to vote in an electoral college of princes for the Holy Roman Emperor, successors to Charlemagne, who from the fifteenth to the early nineteenth century were the rulers of lands in present-day Germany, the Czech Republic, Hungary, and Austria. In 1711 Prince Georg invited Handel to become the *Kapellmeister* of his court musicians and singers for a princely sum that Handel could not refuse. However, Handel's reputation as an opera composer had also reached London, where in 1711 his new opera *Rinaldo*, about a knight during the First Crusade against Muslims in Jerusalem in 1099, was a huge hit with the British. In 1712 Handel left his German prince in the lurch and decamped permanently for London, where he lived until his death in 1759.

In London Handel quickly became a favorite of the nobility, including Queen Anne, who gave him a royal stipend in 1713 after he composed an *Ode for the Birthday of Queen Anne*, a setting of a long poem in her honor for soloists, chorus, and orchestra. When she died without a male heir in 1714, an act of the British Parliament designed to ensure successions to the throne only by Protestants led to the enthronement of her second cousin, Prince Georg, Elector of Hanover. Handel's erstwhile patron became King George I of Great Britain until his death in 1727. He apparently bore Handel no grudge for leaving his previous court and increased his royal stipend. Perhaps he enjoyed the company of a fellow German speaker.

ECONOMIC ACTIVITY

In 1720 Handel founded an opera company called the Royal Academy of Music with the financial aid of aristocrats who were obsessed with Italian operas. Importing excellent singers from Italy, he wrote and produced more than thirty operas in Italian, one or two each year, for the next twenty-one years. He revived his most successful ones in later years, among them *Giulio Cesare in Egitto*, first performed in 1724 with eight recitatives and arias for a *castrato* in the lead male role. Handel's first opera company failed in 1729, apparently the victim of the success of an English-language satirical musical review called *The Beggar's Opera*, which omitted recitatives in favor of spoken dialogue, folk songs, arias, and familiar hymn tunes with new words. Handel continued to write and produce operas until 1741 in the face of growing disinterest in them from the English middle-class. They were, after all, in a language the English didn't understand and usually about Ancient Greeks and Romans distant from them in time, place, and social status.

After 1741, to attract the growing London middle-class audience to paid performances of music, Handel abandoned opera composition and devoted himself with equal energy to oratorios in English. Before 1741, he had already composed English oratorios based on, and named after, Old Testament stories about *Esther*, *Deborah*, *Saul*, and *Israel in Egypt*. *Messiah*, written in 1741 and premiered in Dublin in 1742, was his only oratorio based on the New Testament. Its first performance was a benefit for Dublin hospitals and to aid those thrown in prisons as debtors. After that success he returned to Old Testament stories, writing fifteen oratorios between 1742 and 1752, a pace of one or two each year, including *Hercules*, *Judas Maccabaeus*, *Joshua*, and *Solomon*. His oratorios exploited the musical conventions of Italian operas, especially solo recitatives and arias, but they included masterful choruses, perhaps a legacy of his upbringing in the liturgy of German Lutheran Churches. English audiences found their settings of familiar Biblical stories in English much more accessible than the myths and histories of Ancient Greeks and Romans in Italian operas.

CULTURAL LINKAGES

Oratorios in Italy and in England were performed during the Lenten season, the forty days before Easter, a time of religious contemplation when the performance of Italian opera, with its sensual, hedonistic themes, was either expressly forbidden or considered inappropriate. During Lent, Handel would supervise the performance of ten or so of his oratorios, sometimes playing an organ concerto during intermission, and end the season with *Messiah*. Often they were benefits for charitable institutions. This link between his oratorios and charities turned them into much admired civic as well as religious events. In 1759 he collapsed while attending a performance of *Messiah* and died a few days later, on the day before Easter.

FIGURE 5.10

A nineteenth-century painting imagining George Frideric Handel, right arm outstretched, with King George I during a performance of *Water Music* in 1717; in fact, Handel was probably on the barge directing the musicians!

Painting by Edouard Jean Conrad Hamman (1819–1888). Wikimedia Commons.

Although Handel is best known for his oratorios and operas, he composed many vocal and instrumental works for civic occasions, including *Water Music*, which consists of three suites of short dance tunes and airs for orchestra. It was commissioned by King George I for a boat trip in 1717 up the Thames River with his guests. An orchestra of fifty musicians on a barge traveled with the royal party, attracting an audience of boaters and strollers along the shore. In 1749 he composed a similar suite of five movements called *Music for the Royal Fireworks* at the request of King George II, who was George I's son and the grandfather of King George III, who lost the American colonies. For his contributions to British civic and musical culture Handel was honored with burial in Westminster Abbey, the child prodigy from Halle joining Queen Anne, King George I, many British royals, and the leading lights of British cultural and political history before and since.

Most Baroque operas, sonatas, concertos, and religious works fell into disuse shortly after their first performances, especially when new styles made them sound musty and obsolete. But not *Messiah*. It is one of the few compositions from the Baroque period that has been continuously performed since Handel's day.

CULTURAL LINKAGES

Indeed, it is one of the most beloved and often performed compositions in the entire European classical tradition. By the end of the eighteenth century it had reached the European continent. In Britain and abroad, large amateur choruses performed it throughout the nineteenth and twentieth centuries, sometimes rearranged for a large modern orchestra rather than the small Baroque orchestra with trumpet and timpani that Handel used. In 1859 a *Messiah* performance celebrated the centenary of his death with a choir of nearly three thousand, an orchestra of more than four hundred, and an audience of 10,000 in the Crystal Palace, a gigantic hall built from wood, iron, and newly invented plate glass for the Great Exhibition of 1851, one of the earliest World's Fairs. In the twentieth century the Mormon Tabernacle Choir kept the nineteenth-century tradition of large-scale performances alive with a chorus of 360 and a large string orchestra with two flutes, two trombones, and two French horns added to what would have been a Baroque orchestra of the period. Every Advent season, the weeks leading up to Christmas Day, hundreds of choruses and orchestras all over the world perform it, some in concerts halls, some in churches, and some in sing-a-long versions with the audience singing the choruses with professional soloists and an orchestra. In the 1960s a new edition of the written score, plus the research of music historians, led to a revival of small-scale performances, such as this one, more in line with the sound that Handel's audiences heard in the 1740s and 1750s.

The "Hallelujah" chorus, as a stand-alone movement, has long infused popular culture. Its short, repeated melodies, straightforward harmonies, constant rhythmic pulses, and repeated statements of "Hallelujah," have made it instantly recognizable—and useful, often as a musical joke. In a TV commercial or a movie, when something unexpected and wonderful happens, the opening measures of the "Hallelujah" chorus might pop up right on cue when a customer gets a great deal on a car loan or when, in the 1989 comedy *National Lampoon's Christmas Vacation*, suburban dad Clark Griswold—after much frustration—finally manages to illuminate his massive lighting display of 25,000 twinkle lights that blinds the neighbors and causes a blackout for the rest of his town.

WHERE DO I GO FROM HERE?

- Compare a performance of the "Hallelujah" chorus by the Mormon Tabernacle Choir to the one in this gateway recording by John Eliot Gardiner.

- Listen to other movements of *Messiah*. Powerful choruses in the vein of "Hallelujah" include:

    Part I, 3: "And the glory of the Lord"; and
    Part I, 12: "For unto us a child is born."

    Virtuosic arias written to showcase the skills of the singers give some idea of the florid, melismatic singing style of early eighteenth-century Baroque opera:

    Part I, 2: "Ev'ry valley shall be exalted" for tenor;
    Part I, 5: "But who shall abide" for countertenor;
    Part I, 16: "Rejoice greatly, o daughter of Zion" for soprano; and
    Part II, 38: "Why do the nations so furiously rage together" for bass.

- Listen to selections from Johann Sebastian Bach's cantatas:

    "Ein feste Burg ist unser Gott" (BMV 80)
    Chorale: "Und wenn die Welt voll Teufel wär";
    Chorale: "Das Wort sie sollen lassen stahn."
    "Wachet auf" (BMV 140)
    Chorale: "Zion hört die Wächter singen";
    Chorale: "Gloria sei dir gesungen."
    "Ich habe genug" (BMV 146)
    Aria: "Ich habe genug";
    Aria: "Schlummert ein, ihr matten Augen."

- Watch or listen to a recording of Handel's *Water Music*.

GATEWAY 20
BAROQUE KEYBOARD MUSIC

What Is It?

Our gateway to Baroque keyboard music is Prelude and Fugue in C major from *The Well-tempered Clavier*, Book I, by Johann Sebastian Bach (1685–1750). **Keyboard** is a generic term used for all types of instruments that employ the layout of long, usually white, keys for the seven-pitch diatonic scale and short, usually black, keys for the five additional chromatic pitches of European music. Modern keyboard instruments include the piano and electronic synthesizer. During the Baroque period, the principal keyboard instruments were organ, harpsichord, and clavichord. The word prelude suggests a piece before another piece.

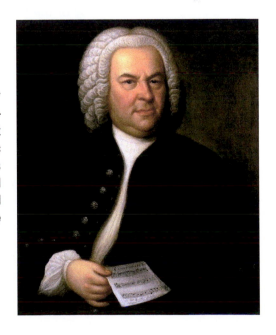

FIGURE 5.11
Johann Sebastian Bach
Source: Painting by Elias Gottlob Haussmann (1695–1774). Bach-Archiv Leipzig, Wikimedia Commons.

Bach's **preludes** are short, free-form pieces spun out from a single melodic or rhythmic idea. A **fugue**, from Latin for "flight" or "fleeing from," is a tightly organized piece featuring imitative counterpoint. *The Well-tempered Clavier*, published in 1722, is a collection of twenty-four preludes and fugues in each of the twelve major and twelve minor keys of the tonal system. **Clavier** means keyboard in German. Bach probably performed them on all the keyboard types available to him. **Well-tempered** means well-tuned, that is, tuned in a way that allows pieces in all keys to sound reasonably good. Bach worked his entire life in the towns, churches, and courts of what is today central Germany. He published *The Well-tempered Clavier* while in service to a prince who was an amateur musician. These preludes and fugues had, and continue to have, a pedagogical function, as Bach wrote on the title page of *The Well-tempered Clavier*: "for the benefit and use of studious musical youth, and also for those in this studio already well skilled in this special pastime." It is played on the harpsichord by American harpsichordist and church organist John Paul.

 **Listen to the first thirty seconds of the recording.**

How Does It Work?

Timbre

The timbre of the harpsichord is created by a quill attached to the end of a lever on a key. It plucks a single string. Each tone has a metallic quality that decays rather quickly, although the low-pitch bass tones sustain a bit longer than do the high-pitched ones.

Texture

The texture of the prelude is monophonic. The fugue, starting at 2:11, begins with imitative polyphony and continues with four rhythmically independent voices throughout.

Rhythm

The meter of both pieces is quadruple and features constant pulsation without pauses.

Melody

The melody of the prelude is based on ascending arpeggiated chords and moves mainly through leaps of a third. The opening melody of the fugue begins in ascending stepwise motion before adding leaps that curve up and down.

Harmony

The harmony is tonal, but with the addition of occasional chromatic pitches.

Form

Overall the form contrasts two movements, the first monophonic and free-flowing, the second contrapuntal and tightly wound. Both are based on the continuous repetition of a short musical idea: in the prelude, ascending arpeggios; in the fugue, a short melody repeated over and over in different polyphonic contexts.

Performance Techniques

The performer plays with a steady pulse, neither speeding up nor slowing down, except at the ends of sections, and with no pauses in the phrases. There are no crescendos or decrescendos, because harpsichords cannot produce them even if players vary the force with which they hit the keys.

🔊 **Listen to this recording and notice the contrast between the monophonic texture of the prelude and the imitative polyphony of the fugue, which begins at 2:11.**

What Does It Mean?

Bach had four goals in mind for the preludes and fugues in *The Well-tempered Clavier*. First, as he indicated on the title page, they were exercises for beginning students and the amusement of more advanced players. They were not meant for public performance though musicians today perform them in concert. Second, by composing a pair in each of the major and minor keys of the tonal system, he demonstrated a musical solution to the problems of pitch and key that had bedeviled the tonal system, problems not evident in the older system of melodic modes but one that Chinese and Arab theorists had discovered centuries earlier. Third, modulating to different key areas within a prelude or fugue, he illustrated some of the chromatic complexities of the tonal system. Fourth, he demonstrated his unsurpassed skill at counterpoint, especially imitative counterpoint, a technique basic to Baroque musical style and required of all church organists of the time. Although Bach, like Monteverdi, Vivaldi, and Handel, was a master of text painting and its uses in vocal and instrumental music for evoking scenes and sentiments, such expression is not at issue in these keyboard pieces. They are purely musical creations at a level of complexity that delights players and listeners today and leads many classical music critics to regard Bach as one of the greatest composers in the history of European music.

> AESTHETICS

In this C major prelude, and in others in the *The Well-tempered Clavier*, Bach creates a sense of unity by repeating the same melodic and rhythmic device in every single measure. He provides internal structure in short sections that move away from and return to the tonic chord via the dominant chord (I–V–I). Along these chordal pathways he introduces dissonant-sounding chords that enrich the palette of tonal harmony.

The fugue is a Baroque-period instrumental extension of imitative vocal polyphony developed during the Renaissance. As a genre, the common defining feature of a **fugue** is the opening **exposition** of a single musical melody, called the **subject**, in imitation. The texture may have three, four, or five parts, called "voices," a term borrowed from vocal polyphony. The voices may enter in any order. In Bach's Fugue in C Major, they enter in this order: alto, tenor, bass, soprano. The first entry is called the statement and the second entry is called the answer. The resulting four-part texture can be graphed like this, with the passage of time from top to bottom and left to right:

alto voice subject and continuation _____

    tenor voice subject and continuation_____

        bass voice subject and continuation_____

           soprano voice subject and continuation

After all the voices have entered in imitation, the exposition ends. Bach exercised quite a bit of freedom in what he did next in the development or restatement of the subject and its movement through related key areas. He might reintroduce the subject somewhat veiled in a thick contrapuntal texture, as he does here, or he could continue with counterpoint without the subject in sections called **episodes**. Bach's Fugue in C major has no lengthy episodes; the subject continues to enter in different voices throughout the fugue, creating a strong sense of unity with little of the subject–episode contrast that characterizes some fugues. These developments after the exposition modulate to other key areas such as the dominant and the relative minor.

Listen another time to Bach's Prelude and Fugue in C Major, following this timed listening guide, which describes the formal principles outlined above.

LISTENING GUIDE 5.4

TIME	SECTION	DESCRIPTION
0:04	**Prelude**	The prelude repeats an ascending arpeggio on different chords throughout. The occasional V-I cadences create an internal sense of closure or arrival from time to time.
0:04	Section 1	The lowest pitch in each arpeggio can be heard as a bass line, creating an inherent polyphony within a monophonic texture, something heard in Shona *mbira* music. In this section the bass line descends through an octave plus a fourth, arriving at a low C, an octave below the starting pitch.
1:08	Section 2	The bass line descends again, eventually settling on low G on the fifth degree of the C scale, where it stays, creating a drone texture called a "pedal point," a reference to an organist holding down a foot pedal to create a continuous low pitch.
1:47	Section 3	The pedal point on G, which has created a dominant effect and anticipation of resolution on the tonic, resolves to low C, two octaves below the starting pitch, establishing another pedal point to the end. The chord on G just before C is a **dominant seventh chord**. While a triad has three pitches, a **seventh chord** adds a fourth pitch to the chord, the seventh scale degree. A dominant seventh chord adds the flatted seventh degree to the dominant triad (V): G-B-D-F.
2:09	End	
2:11	**Fugue**	A contrapuntal texture of rhythmically independent voices throughout with the almost continuous presence of a short melody, the fugue subject.
2:11	Section 1	The exposition: Each voice (alto, soprano, tenor, bass) enters in turn in imitative polyphony. The alto starts on C, but the soprano and tenor enter on G, creating a modest sense of movement from tonic to dominant. The bass enters on C, returning to the tonic.
2:43	Section 2	The exposition complete, the subject returns in the soprano voice within the four-part texture, followed almost immediately by the tenor, and then the alto and bass. Bach introduces chromatic pitches for two additional statements of the subject in the alto and then the tenor, as the voices modulate to the relative minor key, which the player marks with a slight ritard to end this section with a V-i (E major to A minor) cadence. (Lowercase Roman numerals [i, iv, v] are used to indicate minor chords on their respective scale degrees.)
3:20	Section 3	Returning to C major, each voice enters before the previous voice finishes the subject, a speeding or tightening up of the imitative polyphony, a technique called *stretto*, from Italian for "close," "tight," or "fast." Attention shifts quickly from voice to voice as each enters in turn with the subject. Sometimes the subject is hard to hear in the thick four-voice texture. The player ends the section with a slight pause on a cadence on the tonic.
4:13	Section 4	A pedal tone on the tonic in the bass supports one last point of imitation with tenor, alto, and soprano voices entering in *stretto*.
4:34	End	

For centuries the intellectual complexity of Bach's fugal counterpoint has amazed composers and music students learning to compose in this style. It is even more amazing to think that Bach and other church organists of the period could improvise fugues. Most listeners find the constant pulsation of the prelude and fugue, and indeed of Baroque musical style, attractive. Taking the genre name fugue literally, we could hear a fugue as a musical game of tag in which the first voice to enter is "it" and tags the next voice, while all the other voices are "flying around" and "fleeing from" it.

AESTHETICS

The musical terms used to describe the elements of a fugue also provide clues to its meaning. They are borrowed from language and literature: subject, statement, answer, exposition, episode, and development all suggest that musical form can be explained as a metaphor for literary form. The familiar expression "musical phrase" is another example in this vein. When music seems abstract and not expressive of the content and emotions of an associated lyric or painting or natural scene, musical theorists since the Baroque period made sense of it using the forms of literature rather than the thematic content of literature. Such metaphors are a common feature of human thought. We tend to explain most things in our world metaphorically, as if they were something else, a process that connects different parts of our world together and makes them feel coherent and "natural."

CULTURAL LINKAGES

What Is Its History?

Like the violin family, the keyboard instruments so familiar to us today, pianos and synthesizers, came into their own during the Baroque period. The organ has the longest history, and Bach, like Handel, was a virtuoso player of the instrument. The organ began as a type of panpipe, a set of whistle pipes of different lengths. Unlike, say, the 'Are'are mouth-blown panpipes in Chapter 1, Gateway 3, an organ's pipes vibrate when pressurized air, controlled by a lever or key, is blown over the pipe's edge. The oldest organ, called *hydraulis*, was invented in Greece in the third century BCE, with water pressure forcing air over the pipes. Portable organs employing a bellows instead of water pressure figured prominently in the secular musical life of the Byzantine Empire. In 812 Charlemagne, whose father had received an organ from the Byzantine Emperor, placed the first church organ in his chapel at Aachen. In 1361 a church in Halberstadt, Germany, not far from Handel's birthplace of Halle, installed the first permanent church organ. By the seventeenth century, nearly every Lutheran and Catholic Church in Europe had a permanently installed organ with most of the features of modern organs, including elaborately decorated cases in Baroque style for the pipes.

TECHNOLOGY

An enormously complex instrument, the Baroque organ consists of hundreds, even thousands, of flute and reed pipes of different lengths (and therefore different pitches) into which air is forced by a bellows. The pipes are organized into sets called ranks, each covering different octaves and having different timbres. The movement of the air into the pipes and ranks is controlled from a console containing two or more keyboards, called manuals; a pedalboard played with the feet; and a set of knobs called stops. A stop opens and closes the passage of air to one of the ranks of pipes. The player pulls out a stop to play a particular rank and pushes it in to stop the flow of air to the pipes in the rank. By changing the stops and the manual, the player can alter the timbre, loudness, and octave of the organ's sound. "Pulling out all the stops" means every rank sounds, creating a huge, loud sound, and the phrase has become a metaphor for a grand gesture in any human endeavor. Lutheran organists accompanied congregational singing on the organ with harmonic accompaniments. They also composed more elaborate polyphonic chorale preludes built around the melody of the hymn tune. Today these are played before and

FIGURE 5.12

Byzantine pipe organ, tuned bells, aulos, and kithara (lyre) in a Byzantine mosaic from Syria from c. fifth century CE

Source: Hellenic Society for Near Eastern Studies, Wikimedia Commons.

FIGURE 5.13
Baroque organ in a Catholic Church in Wuppertal-Beyenburg, Germany
Source: Beckstet, Wikimedia Commons.

after the service, during the collection of offerings, and sometimes during the last **verse** of a hymn—and at organ concerts.

The **harpsichord** is a plucked zither. Its shape is anticipated by the Arab *qanun* (Chapter 3, Gateway 9). The oldest surviving example is from the early seventeenth century, when harpsichords provided chordal *basso continuo* parts for solo recitatives and arias. Composers directed their own orchestral compositions often while playing the harpsichord. By the eighteenth century harpsichords had one or two manuals (keyboards) covering five octaves (60 keys or so) of multi-string courses. The timbre could be altered with stops that selected all the strings or a single string of the course to be played. In this recording, the player chose to play just a single course. Along with Bach, Domenico Scarlatti (1685–1757), an Italian composer who worked in royal courts in Spain and Portugal and composed more than 500 solo sonatas for the instrument, launched the harpsichord and its descendant, the piano, as a solo instrument.

The **clavichord**, from Latin meaning "key," was invented about the same time as the harpsichord. The keys raise metal blades to stop the strings, producing a very quiet sound not suitable for concert performances. It was used primarily at home for the amusement of the player, something like the Chinese *qin* in that regard, and as a composer's tool.

In 1685 Johann Sebastian Bach was born 100 miles southwest of Halle, in the town of Eisenach, where Martin Luther had attended school. His father worked there as a professional musician. The region was a hotbed of Protestant organ music. His forefathers going back four generations were the most numerous and famous professional town and church musicians in the area. Taught by his father and brother as a boy, he was sent to a prestigious Latin school in northern Germany, where he studied organ with leading musicians and established himself as a virtuoso organist. In contrast to Handel, the cosmopolitan life and international fame of an itinerant opera composer was not for the young Bach, and he never composed operas, the most popular genre of the age. Instead, at seventeen this devout young man returned home to take up the family craft: musical composition, performance, and teaching for towns, courts, and churches.

Compared to Handel, who traveled from Germany to Italy to England during his career, Bach worked his entire life in a relatively small, forested area of Germany about the size of the state of Vermont. He held positions in local churches and courts and was relatively unknown outside that region:

FIGURE 5.14
A modern organ console with four manuals, pedalboard, and stops
Source: Wikimedia Commons.

FIGURE 5.15
A single-manual harpsichord
Source: Tomwsulcer, Wikimedia Commons.

FIGURE 5.16
Clavichord from *c.* sixteenth century
Source: Gérad Janot, Wikimedia Commons.

- Arnstadt (1703–1707) as a church organist;
- Mühlhausen (1707–1708) as a church organist;
- Weimar (1708–1717) as an organist and court composer;
- Köthen (1717–1723) as a court composer; and
- Leipzig (1723–1750) as a church composer and town musician.

In each of these places he composed what was required of him by contract. As a church composer in Arnstadt and Mühlhausen, he improvised and composed chorale preludes and hymn harmonizations. As a court composer in Weimar and Köthen he composed concertos, dance suites for orchestras, and the preludes and fugues in Book I of *The Well-tempered Clavier*. In Leipzig he was in charge of music for the town's four Lutheran Churches and an ensemble of university students called the *collegium musicum*. For the largest church, St. Thomas Church, he was required to produce a multi-movement cantata for soloists, choir, and string orchestra for each Sunday of the liturgical calendar. He wrote more than 200 of them. He also wrote more ambitious religious works too long for a Sunday service. His *Christmas Oratorio* (1734) combines six cantatas, each performed on a different Sunday during Advent. Today it is sometimes performed in a concert lasting about three hours. He also wrote a number of Passions based on the Easter story as told in the Gospels; the *St. Matthew Passion* (1727) and the *St. John Passion* (1724) survive and are still performed today in concert. Surprising perhaps for a Protestant, at the end of his life, in 1749, he wrote a complete mass, his Mass in B Minor. The work is massive. Each few lines of the Credo, for example, have their own recitative and aria. Evidently, he never heard a performance of the complete mass, today regarded as one of his greatest and most moving achievements.

In these modest circumstances Bach lived a dutiful domestic life, especially compared to Handel, who never married, and Vivaldi, who was a priest. In 1707, after moving to Mühlhausen, he married

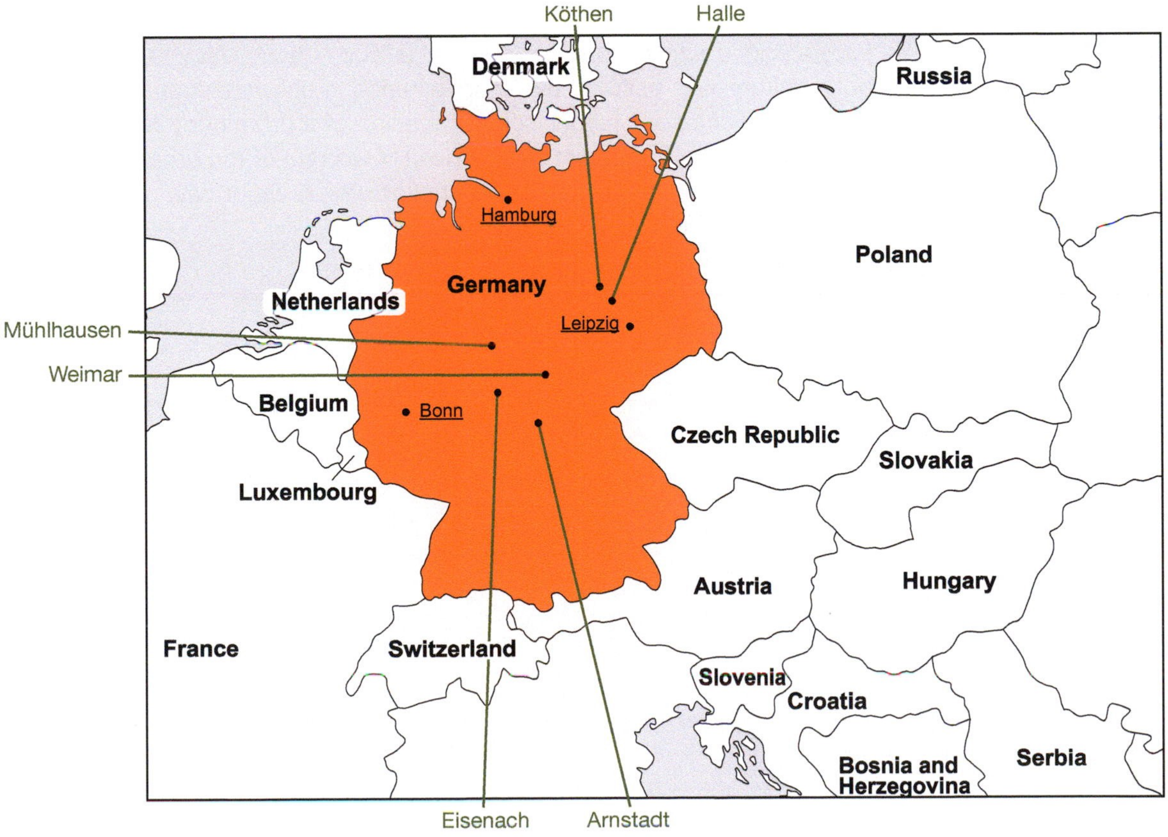

ECONOMIC ACTIVITY

FIGURE 5.17
Map of Germany

his second cousin, Maria Barbara Bach, who gave birth to six children, only three of whom lived beyond their first birthday. While he was working in Köthen, she fell ill and died suddenly in 1720. The following year he married a young court singer, Anna Magdalena Wilcke. She gave birth to thirteen children, but only six of them survived. Bach continued his family's tradition, dutifully teaching all his sons to play keyboard music and compose. Four of them became distinguished composers of the next generation, continuing their father's craft and contributing to the development of the new musical styles of the mid-to-late eighteenth century.

AESTHETICS

Bach's compositions were composed for church and court, rather than the concert and opera stages, and so during his lifetime his renown was quite limited compared to Handel's or Vivaldi's. As a consequence, and as musical styles changed, his work ceased to be performed for many decades, his legacy living on mainly in the skills he bequeathed to his sons and in musical manuscripts that the next generation of composers studied. Mozart, Beethoven, and other composers of the late eighteenth and early nineteenth centuries studied his scores to learn tonal harmony and fugal and contrapuntal technique. Although they rarely wrote fugues, they inserted fugal passages within some of their compositions as icons of seriousness.

CULTURAL LINKAGES

Bach's music lay mostly unperformed for nearly eighty years, except occasionally in Leipzig, until 1829, when the composer and organist Felix Mendelssohn (1809–1847), at the age of twenty, produced and conducted an abridged version of the *St. Matthew Passion* in Berlin. A child prodigy, Mendelssohn had written his first full symphony at fifteen and his famous *Overture to A Midsummer Night's Dream* at sixteen. His family owned manuscripts of Bach's compositions, and his principal teacher had studied with two of Bach's sons. From an early age Mendelssohn found Bach's music inspiring. He eventually took Bach's old position at the St. Thomas Church in Leipzig and directed the town's leading civic musical organizations, as Bach had done. Mendelsohn also revived some of Bach chorale preludes and other keyboard music, including Bach's Toccata and Fugue in D Minor, which he played in concert in 1840. That piece became probably the most famous work in the entire organ repertoire. During the silent-movie era, theater organists improvising accompaniments to silent films played its opening unison descending minor melody followed by an ascending arpeggio during scary scenes. That association found its way into an early talking film, *Dr. Jekyll and Mr. Hyde* (1931). Its position in popular culture was assured by its appearance in an orchestral arrangement for the 1940 Disney animated film *Fantasia*. Mendelssohn, the scion of a prominent Jewish family that had renounced Judaism, secured the Protestant Bach's position as one of the great composers of the European classical musical tradition, a position he has held to the present day.

WHERE DO I GO FROM HERE?

- Listen to recordings of Bach's Prelude and Fugue in C Major played on piano and on organ and compare them to the harpsichord performance in this gateway. Which do you prefer and why?

- Listen to a recording of Bach's Prelude and Fugue in C Minor, the second one in *The Well-tempered Clavier*. How are its elements similar to and different from those in the C Major Prelude and Fugue?

- Listen to Bach's organ prelude on the hymn tune "Wachet auf" and notice the way he treats the tune within a contrapuntal texture of rhythmically independent parts.

- Listen to a performance of Bach's Toccata and Fugue in D Minor.

- Listen to one or more of the keyboard sonatas of Domenico Scarlatti and compare them to Bach's keyboard style in the Prelude and Fugue in C Major.

GATEWAY 21
JAVANESE COURT MUSIC[39]

What Is It?

Our gateway to Javanese court music is a composition for gamelan called "Ketawang Puspawarna Laras Slendro Patet Manyura." Java is the most populous island in the archipelago of islands that form the country of Indonesia in island Southeast Asia. The majority of Javanese are Muslims, but Hinduism and Buddhism, which Islam had superseded by the sixteenth century, still resonate in its musical theater accom-panied by the gamelan. The **gamelan** is a large orchestra of around forty instruments made of bronze gongs or metal keys, plus drums and a bowed fiddle. In this recording female soloists and a male chorus perform with the gamelan. The composition is played at the opening of concerts at two Javanese princely courts. Its long name places it within a well-developed musical system and includes the name of the piece, its form, its tuning system, and its melodic mode.

FIGURE 5.18

A Javanese gamelan with two female soloists
Source: Gunawan Kartapranata, Wikimedia Commons.

- *Ketawang* is a musical form based on a rhythmic cycle of 16 beats.
- *Puspawarna* is the name of this composition in the *ketawang* form: it means "kinds of flowers."
- *Laras* means tuning system.
- *Slendro* is one of two tuning systems in Javanese music: it has five approximately equidistant pitches in an octave.
- *Patet*, also *pathet*, means melodic mode.
- *Manyura* is one of three melodic modes in the *slendro* tuning system.

The composition is called "Puspawarna" for short.

"Puspawarna" is based on a poem with nine stanzas. Each stanza describes a flower in a way that makes a metaphorical connection between floral beauty and attractive female qualities:

Flower of the *kencur* plant, always spoken of with admiration, her body is well-shaped and her movements graceful, she is so charming in speech that one feels carried away.

Flower of the starfruit tree, when picked soon comes back; she shines sweetly indeed like a precious jewel, she is the queen of flowers and the essence of women.

Flower of the durian tree, one stops to look at it amazed at her shape; her sweet smiles and her elegant speech embrace the senses.

Flower of the sugar palm bends over the durian branches; whenever I am looking at you and thinking of the flower, I become wistful.

Flower of the banana tree hangs down over a pond; it is fitting for those of noble descent to have a demure expression and unaffected manners.

Flower of the teak tree, scattered around the house, I stand and look out, waiting for you endlessly, not knowing if I will match.

Flower of the betel palm opens fragrantly in the evening; I am overwhelmed to receive your visit, hoping that you will grant your favor.

Flower of the cotton plant, constantly cut, I strongly desire to adore you, to fulfill your wishes unresistingly.

Flower of the pandanus plant, scattered on the floor, when you come down to my place do not be anxious, I will surrender.

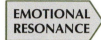

The liner notes to this recording say, "the mood it evokes is of ripeness or fulfillment. The text refers to different kinds of flowers, each symbolizing a different *rasa* (mood)." The mood of ripeness is presumably created by the association between the lyrical references to many fruit-bearing plants and the music. This performance contains two of the nine stanzas.

 Listen to the first thirty seconds of the recording.

How Does It Work?

Timbre

The piece employs a variety of timbres. At the core is the sound of bronze gongs and metal bars, an obviously metallic sound very rich in overtones. Drums, a bowed lute called *rebab*, xylophone, bamboo flute, plucked zither, female soloists, and a male chorus add to the timbral opulence.

Texture

The texture is a complex weave of many melodic lines produced by the gongs, a bowed lute, the female voices, and the male voices, with drum accompaniment. Sets of low-, mid-, and high-pitched gongs mark the rhythmic structure. Keyed metallophones, gongs, xylophone, and zithers play heterophonic elaborations of the melody at higher pitches.

Rhythm

Three kinds of rhythm interact in this performance. Forming the foundation are the gongs, each of which play tones of a single duration in a steady pulse. Over this steady pulse, the female soloists sing nonmetrically, the male singers sing a metrical melody with a variety of long and short tones, and the flute and bowed fiddle play a mix of metrical and nonmetrical phrases.

Melody

The men's vocal melody is broken up into a series of descending phrases with a variety of steps and leaps in a pentatonic scale of approximately equidistant intervals.

Harmony

The piece is a polyphonic, heterophonic weave of many melodic lines, but harmony in the European sense is not present.

Form

The form is a strophic song with two strophes. A *rebab* solo begins the piece. An instrumental section precedes each of the two strophes.

Performance Techniques

The drummers control the tempo and tempo changes. The male singers supply vocal calls that add to the excitement during the instrumental sections.

Listen to the first thirty seconds of the recording focusing on its layered texture and rich timbre.

Timed Listening Guide

The form of this piece is supported by a series of ten rhythmic cycles whose beginnings and ends are marked most audibly by the sounding of the gamelan's lowest-pitched knobbed gong. This lowest-pitched gong is named *gong ageng* (the word gong comes into English from Indonesia). Each rhythmic cycle, called a *gongan*, consists of sixteen beats, many marked by the sounding of knobbed gongs at different pitches. In the chart below, pitch is represented vertically, time horizontally. The names of the gongs sounding on each beat, from low to high, are: G = gong, N = *kenong*, P = *kempul*, T = *ketuk*, p = *kempyang*.

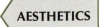
AESTHETICS

16	1	2	3	4	5	6	7	8	9	10	11	12	13	14	15	16
	p		p		p		p		p		p		p		p	
		T				T				T				T		
				–								P				
								N								
G N																G N

This elaborate cyclical rhythmic structure, called *bentuk* in Javanese, sounds beneath the melody, marking its phrase structure. In English it is called the **colotomic structure**, from Latin meaning "to cut." These gongs cut up time into beats or pulses. The gamelan's texture consists of three layers: (1) a rhythmic, cyclical (colotomic) structure played on knobbed gongs; (2) a mid-pitched, mid-tempo melody played on metallophones; and (3) high-pitched, fast-tempo elaborating parts.

Listen to the entire recording following this timed listening guide, which describes the formal principles outlined above. Count the beats and notice the sounding of the gong and *kenong* on beat 16 and the *kenong* on beat 8. Each one marks the end of the men's melodic phrases.

LISTENING GUIDE 5.5

TIME	DESCRIPTION
0:00	The piece begins with an eight-beat introduction, first on the *rebab*, followed by the drums.
	Instrumental interlude:
0:07	*Gongan 1:* The full orchestra enters on the low gong in a fast tempo with the female soloists singing and calls by the male chorus. The tempo gradually slows.
0:22	*Gongan 2:* The tempo is established with the melody and elaborating instruments marking, in a clock-like manner, each of the 16 pulses of the cyclical structure. Notice the vocal calls. The female soloists sing, somewhat buried in the texture. In another recording they might sound quite prominently.
	First strophe:
0:46	*Gongan 3:* The male chorus enters two and a half beats before the *kenong* sounds, the halfway point in the *gongan*. Their melody cadences on the *gong ageng* at the end of the cycle. The female soloists continue to sing.

continued

TIME	DESCRIPTION
1:13	*Gongan* 4: The male chorus enters with the second phrase of the melody, which cadences half way through the cycle on the *kenong*. The third phrase enters and cadences on the *gong ageng* at the end of the cycle.
1:40	*Gongan* 5: The male chorus continues with the fourth and fifth phrases of the song, the fourth phrase cadencing on the *kenong* and the fifth on the *gong ageng*, as in *gongan* 4.
	Instrumental interlude:
2:08	*Gongan* 6: Instrumental interlude with male vocal calls.
2:37	*Gongan* 7: Instrumental interlude with male vocal calls and females singing in the background.
	Second strophe:
3:04	*Gongan* 8: Men begin the second strophe of the song with the first phrase as in *gongan* 3. Women continue to sing in the background.
3:37	*Gongan* 9: Men sing the second and third phrases of the song melody as in *gongan* 4. The tempo speeds up slightly toward the end of the *gongan*.
3:58	*Gongan* 10: Men sing the fourth and fifth phrases of the song as in *gongan* 5. Note the dramatic ritard before the final *gong ageng* sounds.
4:33	End: The *gong ageng* sounds. Notice how long the low gong continues to ring, taking ten seconds to decay into silence at 4:44.

What Does It Mean?

The forty or so bronze instruments of a gamelan are not owned by individuals, as most instruments of the European orchestra are. Rather, the entire orchestra is owned by a prince, a wealthy individual, a broadcasting company, or a music conservatory. New owners commission the making of all the instruments as a set and place them in their palace, home, or institution. The largest gongs, gong, *kenong* and *kempul*, hang on wooden frames. The melody instruments consist of two rows of tuned, knobbed gongs that are set on strings within a wooden frame; metal keys arranged over individual bamboo resonators within a wooden frame; and xylophone, zithers, flute, and *rebab*. Musicians come empty-handed to rehearsals and performances to play on the set of instruments the patron provides.

Gamelan music is played in one of two tuning systems. To play in these two different scales, some gamelans have two sets of instruments, one for each of the pitch systems. Both are arranged together on the floor, each set at a ninety-degree angle to the other set. The musicians, seated on the floor, shift their positions to play in the tuning system appropriate to each composition. One tuning system is called *slendro*, the five-tone equidistant pentatonic scale heard in "Puspawarna." It has intervals about halfway between a major second and a minor third. The other tuning system, called *pelog*, is a seven-tone heptatonic system from which five (but sometimes six or seven) main pitches are chosen. The distance between the five main pitches in *pelog* varies from roughly a half step to about a major third. Unlike Baroque music, with its keys and tempered tunings, there is no external standard against which to measure pitches and intervals in this tradition. Although every gamelan adheres to the principles of the two tuning systems, each gamelan possesses its own unique set of pitches and intervals and thus a unique sound. At the time of its making, the maker, the owner, or the leader of the orchestra may give the gamelan a name that captures its particular sound quality. During the eighteenth century, a female poet at a Javanese prince's court mentioned gamelans with the names "Swept Away,"[40] "Smile," and "Misty Rain." Gamelans in the United States at UCLA, the University of Michigan, and Oberlin College are named "Venerable Dark Cloud," Venerable Lake of Honey," and "Venerable Diamond," respectively.

The master blacksmiths who forge these beautiful bronze instruments are held in extraordinarily high regard not least because, through their mastery of fire, they infuse each instrument of the gamelan, and the gamelan itself, with a living spirit. Because they believe the gamelan contains a living being, some musicians approaching the most venerated gamelans to take their seats do not step over any of the instruments, believing that to be disrespectful. Instead they may bow and say "excuse me" to the spirit of the gamelan as they pass between the instruments to reach their position.

Not only is the gamelan embedded in Hindu/ Buddhist culture, so are compositions like "Puspa-warna." Its cyclical rhythmic structure may represent Java's Hindu and Buddhist past. Hinduism and Buddhism came to Java from India as early as the fourth century CE and flourished there until the sixteenth century, when Islam became the dominant religion. The cyclical rhythmic structure of Javanese gamelan music can be understood as an icon of Hindu/ Buddhist beliefs in the cyclical nature of life. In contrast, Christianity emphasizes the progression of life from birth to adulthood to death to a life after death, for which the Baroque concept of fugal development may be an icon.

Although "Puspawarna" is a concert piece, gamelan accompanies the many forms of musical theater in Java. The characters in these plays may be humans, three-dimensional rod puppets, paintings on a scroll, or two-dimensional shadow puppets made from water buffalo hide. The last, a type of theater called *wayang kulit*, is perhaps the most famous.

Shadow-puppet theater accompanied the spread of Hinduism to Java. Performances tell romantic stories from the Ancient Hindu Sanskrit epics, the *Ramayana* and the *Mahabharata*. The *Ramayana* tells the story of Prince Rama, whose wife Sita, is kidnapped and whom he, with the help of the monkey king Hanuman and his army, rescues. The *Mahabharata*, the longest epic poem ever created at nearly two million words, is nearly ten times longer than Homer's *Iliad*. It tells the story of a conflict between two families competing for power after the death of the king. Both feature ideal representatives of fidelity, filial loyalty, evil, greed, and other human qualities. They teach Hindu philosophy

FIGURE 5.19
A Javanese *wayang kulit* performance in Wellington, New Zealand. The Javanese *dhalang* Budi Surasa Putra controls the puppets with attached rods
Source: Dave Wilson.

FIGURE 5.20
The same *wayang kulit* performance from the audience's perspective
Source: Dave Wilson.

and values and suffuse Javanese culture in ways analogous to the Bible stories in Christian cultures. The association of gamelan with these stories gives its sounds some of its meaning.

Wayang kulit performances are conducted by a single puppeteer (*dhalang*), who manages all the puppets, speaks the parts of all the characters in a language and vocal quality appropriate to each one, and cues the gamelan musicians, who sit behind him, by tapping on a wooden box or striking some metal plates with his foot. A large white cloth screen separates him and the musicians from the audience. A light casts the puppets' shadows onto the screen so the audience sees what may appear to be magical images from the mythological past whose origin in human activity is hidden from view. Today most people prefer to watch from the side of the *dhalang* and the gamelan. The performances begin around eight in the evening and end an hour or so before dawn. *Dalangs* learn the epic stories in aural tradition and extemporize rather than memorize many of their lines. While telling the ancient stories, they give voice to clown figures and, through them, improvise references to contemporary politics and culture, criticizing current politicians and celebrities in an entertaining way that draws on Ancient Hindu philosophy. In this way, gamelan music for *wayang kulit* shares in making Javanese history and its religious and cultural values relevant in the modern world. Unfortunately, some *dhalang*s have crossed a line and been imprisoned and even executed for inserting political criticism in their storytelling.

What Is Its History?

The history of the gamelan begins in the Bronze Age, a period from around 3000 BCE to 1200 BCE, when bronze, an alloy of copper and tin, was the hardest and most useful man-made material. The Bronze Age superseded the Stone Age when humans learned to make tools and decorative items by melting (smelting) and combining copper and tin ores and pouring the hot liquid mixture into wax casts. Even after 1200 BCE, when humans learned to smelt iron to make an even harder metal for tools, bronze remained a favorite material for sculptures and musical instruments. Working with bronze was known to all the ancient civilizations from Mesopotamia, Egypt, and Greece to India, Southeast Asia (Indonesia and Thailand), East Asia, and Africa. Beautiful items from these cultures have been preserved to the present. In these areas, gongs and bells made of bronze have long been associated with religious rituals. Gongs and bells are classified as three-dimensional struck **idiophones**. An idiophone is a class of instrument in which material other than strings, stretched skin, or columns of air vibrates. A metallic idiophone is a **gong** if it has a surface diameter greater than its depth, a **bell** if it has a depth greater than its surface diameter, and a **cymbal** if it is a flat plate with no depth.

Tuned Chinese bell chimes date from between 3000 and 2000 BCE. In Europe church bells, once believed to exorcise demons and keep the devil at bay, have been used since the Medieval period for signaling calls to worship and funerals (the death knell). The oldest surviving European church bell chimes are from the fifteenth century. Indonesian bronze gongs date from around the first century BCE. These were flat gongs like the gongs called tam-tams played today in symphony orchestras. They produce a shimmery white noise rather than a specific pitch. The gongs of the gamelan have a central raised "boss" or "nipple" that produces a specific pitch when struck.

Java is an extraordinarily fertile land, and the cooperation required to grow rice has been a part of the culture since ancient times. Accumulated wealth from rice cultivation led to the formation of regional kingdoms from the fourth century CE onward. Hinduism was the main religion of these kingdoms and *wayang kulit* performances were accompanied by small ensembles, some containing bronze bossed gongs. In the sixteenth century Islam became the dominant religion, and a powerful sultanate gained control of most of central Java. At about the same time, the Dutch East India Company arrived in western Java in search of expensive spices to send back to Europe. The company, acting on behalf of the Dutch crown, was able to extend its influence to the central Javanese sultanate by the early eighteenth century. Two princely courts survived as regional

ECONOMIC
ACTIVITY

POLITICAL
ACTION

administrators in the towns of Surakarta and Yogyakarta. They believed themselves to rule with divine authority at the same time their contemporary, King Louis XIV of France, was proclaiming the divine right of kings. Ironically, the first large gamelans became aural symbols of royal power just when Javanese princes' real-world political power was waning. "Puspawarna" is part of the legacy of this seventeenth- and eighteenth-century tradition. Again, from the liner notes: "The piece is performed for the entrance of the prince. ... The text and melody are attributed to Prince Mangkunegara IV of Surakarta (reigned 1853–1881), to commemorate his favorite wives and concubines." Perhaps there were nine of them, each one honored by a stanza of the poem. This piece is introduced in this chapter because it is played in an orchestral tradition that developed about the same time as the European Baroque orchestra and for largely the same reasons: the patronage of kings, princes, and the clergy made rich by a new European-initiated system of world trade across the vast oceans of the world. After Indonesia declared independence in 1945, only Yogyakarta managed to retain its status as a kingdom within the Republic of Indonesia. Today wealthy businesses, state broadcasting companies, and educational institutions in Java have joined the Yogyakarta prince in the patronage of this musical tradition.

"Puspawarna" seems to float along without any dramatic changes. It does not get louder or softer, although it slows down and speeds up gradually. It doesn't modulate to other scales or modes. It goes in a circle rhythmically. This floating quality of gamelan music impressed the French composer Claude Debussy (1862–1918) when he heard a Javanese gamelan at a World's Fair in Paris in 1889. At the end of the nineteenth century and the beginning of the twentieth century European composers were seeking alternatives to the very directed nature of European tonal music, which moves through a series of chord progressions and key areas from the tonic key to other keys to the dominant key and back to the tonic key. Some composers in the early twentieth century chose to abandon tonality altogether. Debussy was so impressed with gamelan music that he wrote at one point that "Javanese music obeys laws of counterpoint which make Palestrina seem like child's play."[41] Without abandoning tonality completely, he experimented in some of his compositions with mimicking what sounded to him like the gamelan's floating sound. In a solo piano sonata entitled *Pagodes* (Pagodas), composed in 1903, Debussy created a musical icon of Javanese gamelan music on the piano by employing a pentatonic scale rather than the usual European diatonic, heptatonic scale. Low pitches mimic the deep gongs and very high pitches suggest the metallic timbre of the gongs and metallophones. In many sections of the piece the music moves along in constant pulsating rhythm as the gamelan does. And like "Puspawarna," Debussy's composition sits in one tonal place, created in this case by long-held drone tones as the melodies move up and down in stepwise runs, essentially going nowhere. The effect, like the sound of the gamelan, can be transfixing.

> **AESTHETICS**

During the 1960s, when programs in ethnomusicology in the United States began to invite visiting artists from abroad to teach their musical traditions, American universities became patrons of the Javanese gamelan tradition. A UCLA professor, Mantle Hood, who had written his doctoral dissertation on *patet* in Javanese music, brought the first university gamelan to the U.S. (A Western Javanese gamelan was played at the Chicago World's Fair of 1893. It is exhibited at Chicago's Field Museum and in the late 1970s helped spawn a still-active gamelan ensemble tradition in that city.) Robert Brown, an ethnomusicology Ph.D. from UCLA, made this recording of "Puspawarna" in Java and wrote the liner notes. In 1977 it was included on a "golden record" that NASA sent into space on the Voyager 1 space probe. The golden record was intended for any extraterrestrial beings that might find it in the distant future. It contained greetings in fifty-five human languages, a whale "greeting" and environmental sounds, and a sampling of some of what the producers regarded as the greatest music in the world, including "Ketawang Puspawarna," Bach's Prelude and Fugue in C Major, Bulgarian bagpiping with a singer, the Chinese *qin*, Mbuti hunter gatherers from Central Africa, North Indian classical music in *rag bhairavi*, and recordings of Beethoven, Chuck Berry, Louis Armstrong, and others.

> **CULTURAL LINKAGES**

WHERE DO I GO FROM HERE?

- Watch a video performance of Javanese gamelan in Java (many of the available videos are of American and European gamelan ensembles) and listen for the complex structure of colotomic instruments marking time, melodic instruments, and elaborating instruments. Does watching the ensemble in action affect the way that you understand how the music works?

- Watch part of a performance of Javanese *wayang kulit* with gamelan accompaniment. To what extent does your understanding of gamelan shift when hearing it in this setting?

- Listen to a performance of Claude Debussy's *Pagodes*. In what ways does it resemble a gamelan performance? In what ways is it different?

- Listen to the sound recordings on NASA's "golden record" and comment on the choices.

CLOSING

The period from 1600 to 1750 represents an important turning point in the history of European court and church music. Some of the most important new developments include:

- the use of dissonance to express sorrow and anguish;
- the showcasing of vocal and instrumental virtuosity and improvisation;
- the cultivation of music to express affects in the text, and of instrumental music that used those devices to express emotions or pastoral scenes;
- the emergence of a "second practice" of playing bass and chords to accompany melodies, alongside the older "first practice" of multipart polyphony;
- the invention of a new vocal style called recitative that allowed for the creation of a new genre of theatrical storytelling with music called opera;
- a shift from having the harmony follow from counterpoint to the writing of chordal harmony, which the counterpoint needed to reflect;
- the development of instrumental music, specifically the orchestra and the keyboard solo, as the rival of vocal music;
- the development of the tonal system as a set of 24 keys (12 in each of the major and minor modes) to replace the modal system of Medieval and Renaissance music;
- the use tonality and its directional movement from tonic (I) to dominant (V) and back to the tonic (I); and
- the development of musical notation in its present form.

All of these musical devices, ensembles, and genres are still with us today. For that reason, the Baroque period is considered to be the start of what is called the "common practice period." What is common between Baroque music and European classical music that came later is the underlying principle of tonality, the concerto, the string orchestra, solo keyboard works, and opera. Otherwise little of the vast repertoire of Baroque music is performed today by major orchestras and soloists. Its performance has been championed by specialized groups and individuals dedicated to its "authentic," "historically informed" performance and to piano students and composers-in-training interested in learning compositional techniques that represent one of the high points of European contrapuntal practice.

Although many of today's musical practices have their roots in the Baroque period, we cannot project back in time all the features of today's musical culture onto music of the Baroque period. For example, composers today are considered artists who create unique works of art. Baroque composers

ECONOMIC ACTIVITY

were, instead, artisans and craftsmen who wrote music to satisfy the demands of their patrons. That is why Vivaldi wrote hundreds of concertos and Bach hundreds of cantatas and keyboard pieces. They were paid to produce them, and to do so quickly.

This chapter focused on only four composers of the Baroque period: Monteverdi, Vivaldi, Handel, and J. S. Bach. The rise of the power of church and court created a patronage system that supported dozens of excellent and productive musical craftsmen during this period. All of these composers were men, which surely reflects the mores of the time. It would have been almost impossible for a woman during this period to hold sway at court or in the church. One woman who did manage to carve out a composing and performing career for herself was Barbara Strozzi (1619–1677). She did so in the confines of the homes of wealthy merchants in Venice, where Monteverdi was living and working early in her life. Under the patronage of her father, she composed many madrigals and cantatas and had them published.

Even though today we regard the prodigious output of these men and women as works of art,

FIGURE 5.21
Barbara Strozzi holding a bowed viol
Source: Painting by Bernardo Strozzi (1581–1644). Gemäldegalerie Alte Meister, Wikimedia Commons.

SOCIAL BEHAVIOR

EMOTIONAL RESONANCE

their art was the by-product of a cultural system with an insatiable demand for new, quickly produced works. Composers did not have the time to worry about making great art, and, as a consequence, they often copied tunes and other devices from their own earlier work and from other composers. Similarly, today we assume that, in their performances, musical performers are expressing emotions that they actually feel. This is true, for example, of popular songs. Audiences often interpret them as reflecting the autobiographical experiences of the writer or singer. And in classical music performers close their eyes and sway as they play, as if they themselves are in the throes of the emotions they are expressing. During the Baroque period, the affects were in the music and the musical gestures—it was the sound of the music itself that stirred emotions in listeners and not the biographies of the composers or the antics of the performers. Musical composition as art and performance as the expression of internal emotions would have to wait for later periods of European music history.

THINGS TO THINK ABOUT

- Compare the way different societies and institutions (courts in Europe and Java, and the Catholic and Protestant Churches) during this period directed their patronage of music and of related traditions and rituals. Who benefited from these systems of patronage? Who were left out of this system?

- Given the global circulation of goods and resources during this period, what are some of the ways that music circulated from its place of origin to other places? Give specific examples if you can.

NEW TERMS

aria	episode	oratorio
Baroque	exposition	prelude
basso continuo	figured bass	program music
bell	fugue	recitative
cantata	gamelan	*ritornello*
castrato	gong	rondo form
clavichord	harpsichord	sonata
clavier	idiophone	subject
colotomic structure	keyboard	theorbo
concerto	modulate, modulation	timpani
concerto grosso	monody	verse
cymbal	opera	well-tempered

MUSIC FROM THE AGE OF ENLIGHTENMENT AND REVOLUTION (1750–1800)

THE EUROPEAN COMPOSERS featured in this chapter, Franz Joseph Haydn, Wolfgang Amadeus Mozart, and Ludwig van Beethoven, all worked in or near Vienna, a city somewhat, but not completely, removed from many of the major social, political, and intellectual currents of the day. These included political revolutions in the United States in 1776, France in 1789, and Haiti in 1791. These revolutions were inspired, in part, by a philosophical movement known as the Enlightenment. The Enlightenment advocated reason over adherence to tradition and opposed both religious dogma and monarchies like those in France and England. Intellectuals of the period engaged in spirited debates while consuming new drinks made possible by global trade (coffee, tea, and cocoa) served in a new institution: the coffeehouse. By around 1710 London had nearly 500 of them. Over a favorite drink and a smoke the leisured and literate classes all over Europe gathered in coffeehouses to talk politics and discuss the exciting new developments in science, philosophy, and literature, gatherings that fueled open-minded and reasoned discussions. Coffeehouses even hosted occasional musical performances as they do today. Against this backdrop of teeming new political ideas, aristocratic musical patronage entered its last stage in the city of Vienna, capital of a large multi-ethnic empire in central Europe.

The social and political drivers of these revolutions were dissatisfaction with the status quo, whether taxation without representation in the American colonies, food scarcity in France, or slavery in Haiti. The institution of slavery was in turn driven, to some extent, by Europeans' newfound love of tea, coffee, and cocoa. All bitter drinks, they created an enormous demand in Europe for sugar to sweeten them. Sugar plantations in the New World required vast numbers of field hands to supply

FIGURE 6.1
An English tavern or coffee house, mid-eighteenth century
Source: Painting by Joseph Highmore (1692–1780). Yale Center for British Art, Wikimedia Commons.

the need for it. Since Europeans' germs had killed as much as 90% of the native population in the Americas, plantation owners turned to Africa as a source of slave labor. Between the sixteenth and nineteenth centuries, millions of Africans were kidnapped, shipped across the Atlantic, and enslaved to work on the sugar and tobacco plantations of the Caribbean and Brazil and the rice fields of the North American colonies. Under brutal and horrific conditions, at least five million people died either on the way to ships after being kidnapped, on the ships during the passage across the Atlantic, or within the first year of being enslaved. The fruits of their labors were shipped from the Americas and the Caribbean to England and the continent. By the eighteenth century there were twice as many Africans in the Americas as Europeans. By the time the slave trade ended in the middle of the nineteenth century an estimated twelve million Africans had been shipped in bondage to supply labor in the New World and millions more had died en route. It is estimated that more than 50 percent of all enslaved Africans came to the Americas during the 1700s, which coincides with what has been called the Classical period of European music history, one of the subjects of this chapter. In this chapter we will also look at the new religions that enslaved Africans created in the new world, religions that combined African traditional and Catholic beliefs and practices: *Candomblé* in Brazil, *Santería* in Cuba, and *Vodou* in Haiti. The drum music of these religions is one of the inspirations for the rhythms of Latin popular music today. Many devotees of *Vodou* participated in the revolt of self-liberated slaves against the French in Haiti in 1791, a revolt that led to national independence in 1804.

In the domain of culture, important thinkers in this period, especially in France, argued for the power of reason and logic as keys to understanding human and physical nature. The French mathematician René Descartes (1596–1650), called by some the "father of modern philosophy" and famous for his dictum *cogito ergo sum* ("I think, therefore I am"), wrote in 1628 that "if . . . anyone wishes to search out the truth of things in serious earnest, he ought . . . to think how to increase the natural light of reason." By the eighteenth century Europeans understood themselves to be living in an "enlightened" age free of the dictates of religious dogma. They sought to spread this light not only to highly educated churchmen and aristocrats but to merchants and others at the middle levels of society as well. In newspapers and books and at cafés, coffeehouses, salons in wealthy homes, and even in public theaters, they discussed universal human rights, disputed Louis XIV's assertion of the divine right of kings, and argued against the religious intolerance between Catholics and Protestants that had held Europeans hostage to a devastating Thirty Years War in central Europe from 1618 to 1648. This sense of a new world order based on republicanism, that is, the rule of the people rather than of a monarchy, undercut the power of the aristocracy and enabled revolutionary ambitions.

FIGURE 6.2
University of Virginia Rotunda
Source: Aaron Josephson, Wikimedia Commons.

The Enlightenment gave birth to a new age of science and scholarship. Isaac Newton (1643–1727) created the scientific method to help distinguish fact from fiction in the natural world. French thinkers like Voltaire (1694–1778), Jean-Jacques Rousseau (1712–1778), and Denis Diderot (1713–1784) created, starting in 1751, an *Encyclopédie* ("a circle of knowledge") of twenty-eight volumes that included signed articles written by some of the greatest thinkers of the period. It included vast amounts of material on the world that traders, explorers, scientists, and inventors were unfolding before their eyes. Beginning in 1712, Rousseau wrote a *Dictionnaire de musique*, which covered not only European classical music but also what we call today world music. It is intellectual activity like this that characterized the Enlightenment.

Although the power of reason and the scientific method and the new discoveries in physics, biology, and astronomy are often celebrated as a scientific revolution, in fact there was no clear victory for the forces of "enlightened" reasoning. Religion retained tremendous power over people's thinking, although, influenced by Enlightenment thinking, religious tolerance seems to have improved during the eighteenth century. Women's position in society also improved somewhat during this period. A number of women became well-educated and productive writers, composers, thinkers, and leaders of the salon culture, especially in Paris, where Enlightenment ideas were discussed.

The politics of the Enlightenment, its championing of the rights of man, and the political revolutions that followed in its wake had the effect, in the musical domain, of encouraging composers to regard themselves as autonomous artists with some independence from wealthy patrons. The lives of Haydn, Mozart, and Beethoven, in sequence, read like a parable of the transition in European music from courtly and church patronage of musical craftsmen to the emergence of the independent, self-employed musical artist. Mozart and Beethoven, in particular, began to think of themselves not so much as artisans, as Baroque composers had, but as independent artists who could legitimately seek the freedom to compose as they wished. Of course practicing these ideals, that is, not having the support of wealthy patrons, put them in grave economic jeopardy. It meant that they had to rely on other sources of income such as giving instrumental and composition lessons, receiving royalties on their published works, and producing and selling tickets to their own public concerts at which they played or conducted their new compositions.

ECONOMIC ACTIVITY

One Enlightenment idea, that the natural, rather than the supernatural, world is the controlling force in people's lives, led to aesthetic changes in music as well. Some composers after 1750 regarded the ornamentation, elaborations, and imitative counterpoint of the Baroque period as excessive, "artificial," and "unnatural." Some patrons and musicians of the period favored, instead, artistic styles that they thought of as simple, balanced, and "natural." This can be seen clearly in the domain of architecture, where the elaborate filigree and wavy lines of Baroque buildings, fountains, and sculptures were replaced by the regular "rhythm" of columns and unadorned facades characteristic of Greek architecture. This borrowing of architectural style from (Ancient) Greece is what gives the music and art of this period its designation: classical. Thomas Jefferson (1742–1826) was the leading exponent of this style in the new United States. His designs of buildings at the University of Virginia set the style for government buildings in Washington, D.C. and state capitals for years to come.

AESTHETICS

Some composers turned away from the expression of emotion and affect in the Baroque manner to what they considered a more elegant style. They stripped their music of excessive dissonance, elaborate counterpoint, and virtuosic ornamental display. They favored, instead:

- shorter musical phrases in balanced, "periodic" four- or eight-measure lengths;
- clear melodies in the top voice with subservient polyphonic accompaniments in the lower voices;
- new instrumental forms with repeats of a small amount of melodic material; and
- the inclusion within a single movement of contrasting, even rapidly changing, affects.

Composers and critics during this period regarded these new practices as less artificial than Baroque styles and thus truer in spirit to the simplicity and balance of nature.

Musicians today still regularly perform the compositions of just three composers: Franz Joseph Haydn (1732–1809), Wolfgang Amadeus Mozart (1756–1791), and Ludwig van Beethoven (1770–1827). All

FIGURE 6.3
The U.S. Capitol Building in 1846
Source: John Plumbe, Wikimedia Commons.

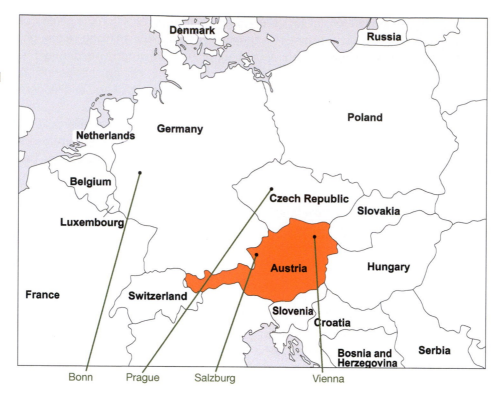

lived and worked in or near Vienna, the capital of the Austrian Empire, which controlled much of central Europe until its defeat by Napoleon in 1806. As a thriving imperial capital, Vienna provided ample opportunity for patronage by the emperor, the nobility, wealthy merchants, and foreign embassies. At the time, many other composers besides these three were famous, particularly in the genre of Italian opera, which continued to be an extraordinarily popular entertainment. But only the operas of Mozart are still frequently performed in the repertoire of modern opera companies.

Haydn, Mozart, and Beethoven composed far less religious music (masses, oratorios, and cantatas) than their Baroque predecessors had. Instrumental music dominated vocal music for the first time in European music history, although opera remained extraordinarily popular and influenced the aesthetics of instrumental music. The principal instrumental musical genres of the Classical period were: (1) the symphony; (2) the solo concerto; (3) the string quartet; and (4) the solo sonata, especially the piano sonata. The symphony and the concerto were continuations of Baroque practices. The piano sonata was an outgrowth of Baroque solo harpsichord compositions but in new forms. The string quartet (two violins, viola, and cello) was a new genre of chamber music. The gateways of this chapter are a string quartet by Haydn, an opera and a symphony by Mozart, and a piano sonata by Beethoven. All were created at the height of the transatlantic slave trade, and so we include an example of music from Brazil, a genre called *Candomblé*, which took shape during this period.

GATEWAY 22
CLASSICAL-PERIOD CHAMBER MUSIC

What Is It?

Our gateway to chamber music of the Classical period is Franz Joseph Haydn's (1732–1809) String Quartet No. 62 in C Major, Op. 76, No. 3, "Emperor," Movement II. He composed it around 1797.

For nearly thirty years during the second half of the eighteenth century, Haydn served as the court composer to a wealthy land-owning Hungarian family in the Austrian Empire (also named the Habsburg Empire after its ruling family), a huge multinational territory in central Europe. It included present-day Austria, Hungary, and parts of the neighboring Slavic-speaking nations of Slovenia, Croatia, Slovakia, the Czech Republic, and Ukraine. A **string quartet** consists of four players performing on instruments of the violin family: two violins, viola, and cello. A string quartet is a type of **chamber ensemble**, an ensemble designed for performances in intimate settings such as small rooms (chambers). **Op.** is short for **opus** ("work" in Latin). Some composers and publishers used opus numbers to identify their compositions in chronological order. No. 3 refers to this string quartet's placement in a set of six string quartets in Opus 76. "Emperor" is an epithet that musicians and publishers have assigned to this quartet. It refers to the theme of this movement, an anthem Haydn composed to honor the Habsburg emperor, Franz II. Movement II is the second movement of four in a typical Classical-period string quartet. This performance is by the Kodály Quartet from Hungary.

 Listen to the first thirty seconds of the recording.

How Does It Work?

Timbre

Two violins, a viola, and a cello playing over about a four-octave range create a rather warm sound.

Texture

The texture has two, three, and four lines moving mostly in the same rhythm with the melody mainly in the highest part.

Rhythm

This movement is in a slow duple meter.

Melody

The melodies tend to move in conjunct motion but with occasional leaps.

Harmony

The movement is based on tonal harmony in the key of G major, the dominant key of the quartets key of C major.

Form

This movement is cast in **theme and variations form**. Compositions in this form present a melody, called a theme, followed by repeats of the theme but with varied treatments of the texture, rhythm, and harmony. The form of this movement can be written A A' A'' A''' A''''. The A theme of this movement has five phrases and the form aabcc.

Performance Techniques

The players employ vibrato on long-held tones to warm the sound, and alternate between legato and staccato articulation.

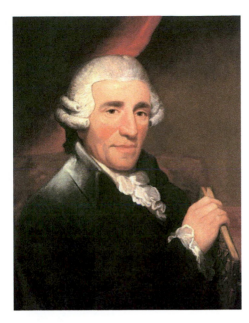

FIGURE 6.5

Franz Joseph Haydn looking a bit like his contemporary, George Washington (1732–1799)

Source: Painting by Thomas Hardy (1757–c. 1805). Royal College of Music Museum of Instruments, Wikimedia Commons.

FIGURE 6.6

Map of the lands ruled by the Habsburg family from 1282 to 1815

Source: Andrein, Wikimedia Commons.

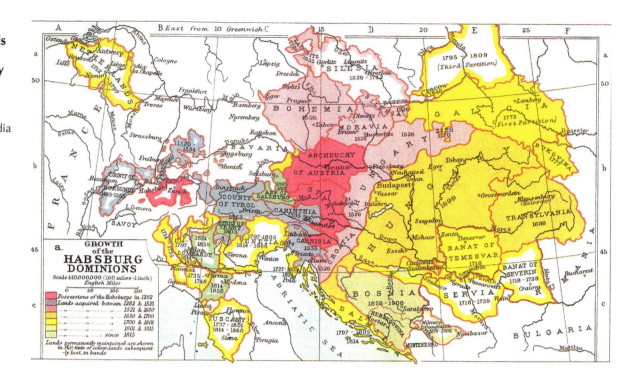

Listen to the first 1:35 of the recording, the first statement of the theme, for the slow duple meter, the four parts moving in nearly the same rhythm, and the aabcc form.

Listen to the entire recording following the timed listening guide and notice the way Haydn varies the theme in a set of four variations.

LISTENING GUIDE 6.1

TIME	FORM	DESCRIPTION
0:00	A	In the first statement of the theme, played by the first violin, the accompanying three instruments play other lines in more or less the same rhythm, a style associated with Protestant four-part chorale harmonizations, thus giving this first section a somewhat sacred quality.
1:36	A'	In the second statement of the theme, the counterpoint is reduced to two parts. The second violin plays the melody, while the first violin plays a faster-moving, higher-pitched part that is melodically and rhythmically independent of the melody.
2:54	A''	The low-pitched cello plays the melody in the third statement of the theme. The first violin supplies a contrapuntal melody, and the second violin and viola fill in the pitches of the chordal harmony.
4:24	A'''	The mid-pitched viola plays the melody. The other instruments weave contrapuntal lines, many of them syncopated, around the melody. At first the first violin accompanies the viola in a two-part texture. The second violin enters almost immediately to create a three-part texture. The cello enters at 5:01 to create a four-part texture to the end.
5:55	A''''	In the final variation, a slightly different version of the four-part texture of the first variation returns to the end the piece with the hymn-like character of the first section. The first violin jumps up an octave on the repeat of a in the aabcc form and remains there throughout this section until it descends stepwise during a *codetta* (a little coda or tail) that ends the whole movement.

What Does It Mean?

Understanding the meaning of string quartets and their close relatives, symphonies, at the end of the eighteenth century requires a return to the problem posed by Baroque instrumental sonatas and concertos of the early eighteenth century. What does purely instrumental music mean? As a French commentator of the time asked, in a somewhat complaining voice, "Sonata, what do you ask of me?" In other words, how am I to understand purely instrumental music without lyrics? The meaning of Movement II of Haydn's String Quartet, Op. 76, No. 3 can be understood in terms of the similarities of its musical elements to those of sacred hymns and anthems; its association with the court of the Austrian emperor (the "Emperor" quartet); its textural and rhythmic contrasts with Baroque style; and the way its style mirrored courtly and architectural styles of the period.

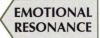

To begin, the slow tempo and four-part harmony of the opening and closing sections of this movement resemble the style of religious hymns sung and played during church services. These similarities in musical style infuse this secular instrumental composition with a quasi-religious feeling.

In fact, this melody is taken from a secular hymn or anthem that Haydn composed in honor of Austrian Emperor Franz II. Haydn got the idea for this secular hymn while visiting England during the early 1790s. After three decades of service as a court composer and conductor of one of the best orchestras in Europe, his employer reduced his obligations to provide the court with new music on a nearly daily basis. He now had the freedom to travel abroad. His fame as a composer had spread all the way to England, where he was invited to compose a set of symphonies for public performance. There he heard the hymn sung to King George III against whom American colonists had successfully concluded their War of Independence in 1783: "God Save the King" and sung as "My Country, 'Tis of Thee" in the U.S. Haydn felt that the Austrian Empire needed a similar patriotic anthem, and in 1797 he and a compatriot were commissioned to write the tune and lyrics for an Austrian national anthem in praise of the emperor. The result was "Gott erhalte Franz den Kaiser" (God save Francis the Emperor).

God save Francis the Emperor, our good Emperor Francis.
Long live Francis the Emperor in the brightest blissful splendor.
May laurel branches bloom and make a wreath of honor for him wherever he goes.
God save Francis the Emperor, our good Emperor Francis.

The same year he used the anthem's tune as the theme for this movement.

Although the tune Haydn composed for this anthem was originally associated with the benevolent Austrian emperor and was used to inflame Austrian patriotic sentiments for decades afterward, over time it has taken on new meanings through new associations. During the mid-nineteenth century a German poet set new words to Haydn's tune in support of those seeking the unification of small principalities into a unified German state. The words were "Deutschland, Deutschland über alles" (Germany, Germany, above all else). In 1922 the tune and poem became the German national anthem. After Adolf Hitler came to power in 1933, that anthem became strongly associated with evils of his Third Reich. After World War II the Germans kept Haydn's tune but eliminated the opening line, which by then had very negative connotations. Instead, the current German national anthem begins with the third verse: "Unity and justice and freedom for the German fatherland!" The tune has also been used for Christian hymns and for university anthems called alma maters.

Haydn's tune, with its changing lyrics or with no lyrics as in this string quartet, is a good example of a musical index that develops new meanings over time. Starting life as the tune for a paean to a benevolent Austrian emperor, it has served as the national anthem of peaceful German states, the aggressive expression of the worst of Nazism, Christian hymns, and college songs. Listeners will have very different emotional responses to this tune depending on the associations they have with it. Those who associate the tune with a hymn or their school's song will have positive feelings about the tune, while those who remember the tune's association with Hitler's Germany may have a negative reaction. For those who make none of these associations, it may simply be a nice tune with perhaps a religious feel to it. One of the interesting questions that arises when the tune is heard as an instrumental without words, as in this string quartet movement, is what meanings are retained from a listener's previous associations. Can they erase completely the tune's negative connotations as Hitler's anthem or its positive connotations as a Christian hymn or school song? Perhaps, but maybe those associations are unavoidable and appear in the background of their understanding of this movement, forever coloring their response to it as instrumental music.

AESTHETICS

In the late eighteenth century, when this quartet was composed, listeners were no longer familiar with the early eighteenth-century music of Bach, Vivaldi, or Handel in the so-called Baroque style. Hadyn and others of his generation had created a new musical style that had superseded the older style of Bach and his contemporaries. Music lovers today have the luxury of comparing the two styles and, in doing so, adding meaning to the sound of instrumental music. Music historians refer to Haydn's style, and those of his younger colleagues Mozart and Beethoven in the late eighteenth century, as the Classical style. In this movement the two most obvious stylistic differences between Baroque and Classical style concern rhythm and texture. In the Baroque style the rhythm, especially of fast movements, moved in a constant pulsation with few pauses, a technique that instilled the music with a certain relentless energy. In this movement, and in the Classical style in general, Haydn, Mozart, and Beethoven favored melodies and textures that combined notes of many different durations, along with pauses, to create a variety of effects: energy to be sure, but also drama, tenderness, elegance, lightness, and sadness. In terms of texture, Haydn and other Classical-period composers dispensed with the harpsichord, which had provided the chords in Baroque-style instrumental ensembles. Instead, they wrote out all the interior parts between the melody and bass line to create their harmonies. They reduced the importance of the bass part and simplified the harmonies, especially compared to J. S. Bach's elaboration of them. Distinguishing Classical from Baroque style gives some modern listeners pleasure and adds to the meaning they find in eighteenth-century instrumental music.

CULTURAL LINKAGES

Listeners in the late eighteenth century understood this style to be an elegant reflection of their courtly lifestyle and the new style of architecture in the buildings going up around them. The regular, repeating melodies of the Classical style and the avoidance of long, spun-out melodies and elaborate ornamentation seemed to mimic the spare, clean look of the colonnaded buildings of the Neo-classical architectural style of the period, a striking contrast to the ornate, passionate style of Baroque exteriors and interiors (Figs. 6.2 and 6.3). Some called the resulting elegant and graceful musical style *galant*, a French word used to describe a stylish, fashionable man (*galant homme*) or, in German, *empfindsamer stil* (sensitive style). To audiences of the time, this musical style seemed particularly pleasing, its elegance a mirror of the powdered wigs, silver shoe buckles, brocaded jackets, ruffled collars, and tight leggings worn during this period by men of fashion all over Europe and in the American colonies. Its relative simplicity, compared to Baroque style, fit well with the carefree courtly life of central Europe during the late eighteenth century. And it was attractive to a growing audience of wealthy merchants, bankers, and tradespeople who sought the trappings of aristocratic life.

What Is Its History?

Haydn was born in 1732 about thirty miles southeast of Vienna in a small Austrian town where his father and grandfather had been mayors. He grew up with the sound of local folk songs and dances in his ears. Later in life those melodies and the drones of bagpipes popped up occasionally in his compositions. His father, an amateur musician, recognized his interest in music and sent him, at the age of six, to study violin and keyboard with a relative in a nearby town. At eight the choir director at St. Stephen's Cathedral in Vienna heard his beautiful singing voice and invited him to join the cathedral choir, where he remained until his voice changed and he was dismissed at age seventeen.

ECONOMIC
ACTIVITY

Penniless and relatively poorly educated, Haydn became a freelance musician, playing violin in local bands hired by serenaders and in the Emperor's court orchestra as an extra player when needed. "I barely managed to stay alive by giving music lessons to children for about eight years,"[42] he told an early biographer. Although he had not received systematic training in composition at St. Stephen's, after he left the cathedral he taught himself to compose by studying the works of J. S. Bach's son, C. P. E. Bach, one of the most popular composers of the time. He taught himself counterpoint using the treatise, mentioned in the previous chapter, written by the Viennese composer and theorist Johann Joseph Fux (c. 1660–1741) titled *Gradus ad Parnassum*.

In 1757 a local nobleman hired him to compose and play music with three musicians he had at his disposal: two violinists and a cellist. Haydn, who played viola, composed his first string quartets for this engagement. In 1759 his success as a freelancer finally landed him his first paying job as *Kapellmeister* for a Czech nobleman with a small orchestra for whom he composed his first symphony. His marriage in 1760 produced no children. In 1761, at age twenty-nine, his work caught the attention of Hungarian Prince Paul Anton Esterházy, one of the richest noblemen in the Austrian Empire. He hired Haydn as assistant musical director, and for the next twenty-nine years the prince and, after his death in 1762, his brother Prince Nikolaus provided Haydn with steady employment.

Both princes were keen musicians; their grandfather had been a composer. In his role as a liveried servant, Haydn had to inquire of the prince each morning and afternoon whether any musical entertainment was required that day for his and his guests' entertainment. Prince Nikolaus, a military officer, was demanding but kind to his servants, including Haydn, providing them with occasional gifts, financial support, and medical care. He occasionally reprimanded Haydn for his carelessness or inattention to his duties, but he gave Haydn the money to hire fine virtuoso instrumentalists and singers for musical productions at the family's palace in the city of Eisenstadt about thirty-five miles south of Vienna and at Esterháza, their country estate. One of the largest and most impressive palaces in Europe, it was another seventy miles from Vienna and its teeming musical life. Esterháza had 126 rooms and featured two concert halls, an opera house, and a marionette theater. To serve the prince's enthusiasms, Haydn produced a stunning quantity and range of compositions. A catalog created in the twentieth century lists more than 700 works in thirty-two genres, including operas.

Prince Nikolaus loved to entertain hundreds of guests at a time. For their amusement Haydn wrote ninety symphonies, which were played by his relatively small orchestra of fifteen or so players. **Symphonies** are works for string orchestra with the addition of wind instruments and percussion. The term symphony is the English word for *sinfonia*, an Italian name for the instrumental overture at the beginning of operas and also for a *ripieno concerto*. Symphonies lack the contrast of the Baroque solo concerto and concerto grosso. Symphonies came into their own during the Classical period, and Haydn worked out many of their features. As Haydn told a biographer about his work in the relative isolation of a Hungarian rural estate:

> Not only did I have the encouragement of constant approval, but as conductor of an orchestra I could make experiments, observe what produced an effect and what weakened it, and was thus in a position to improve, alter, make additions or omissions, and be as bold as I pleased. I was cut off from the world, there was no one to confuse or torment me, and I was forced to become original.

Haydn's early symphonies composed for the Esterházy family had three movements (fast–slow–fast), just like Baroque concertos. His early string quartets had five movements: to the original three he added two dance movements called minuets. The minuet, a graceful and stately dance in triple meter, was a popular social and court dance during the eighteenth century (Figure 6.7). Alexander Hamilton's wife Eliza reported that the slow minuet was the favorite dance of the rather formal George Washington at the balls he reluctantly had to host and attend after his inauguration in 1789 as the first U.S. president. By the end of the 1760s, Haydn had settled on a four-movement form

FIGURE 6.7
Minuet danced at a ball given by French king Louis XV in 1755
Source:
Lebrecht Music and Arts Photo Library / Alamy Stock Photo.

for both genres, fast–slow–minuet–fast, the standard form for compositions in these genres ever since. His Opuses 1, 2, and 3, composed between 1762 and 1765, are all sets of six string quartets. All in major keys and with many movements in triple meter, these quartets are excellent examples of the courtly *galant* style popular in the middle of the eighteenth century. Each has five movements. His next set of six string quartets, Opus 9, composed in 1769, had the four-movement form that became standard for the genre and contained his first one in a minor key. He continued to compose string quartets throughout his life, often in sets of six, a practice that Mozart and Beethoven and some later composers imitated.

In addition to music for the entertainment of guests at Esterháza, Haydn also wrote music for his patron to play for his own enjoyment. Prince Nikolaus played an instrument called the baryton. Rarely played today, it is a large bowed viol with a fretted neck and some additional strings that could be plucked by the thumb. Haydn wrote more than a hundred trios for baryton, viola, and cello for the prince to play with Haydn and other staff musicians. The instrument fell into disuse until it was revived during the twentieth-century early music movement. Later in life the prince turned his attention to opera, and for some years Haydn produced more than a hundred opera performances a year for him, including a dozen or so of his own composition. For less grand occasions the prince seems to have had an insatiable appetite for chamber music performances, and for these Haydn wrote string quartets, duos, and trios; keyboard sonatas; keyboard trios for violin, cello, and keyboard; and songs. And for the prince's chapel he wrote religious music.

In his own time, and today, Haydn was much admired in Vienna and around Europe for his string quartets and symphonies. Visitors to Esterháza from all over Europe reported on his music, and the prince gave him permission to publish some of it, spreading his fame further. After the death of Prince Nikolaus in 1791, Nikolaus' son and grandson were much less interested in music and disbanded the palace orchestra, keeping Haydn on with a sinecure and the duty to write a Mass each year. Having achieved an international reputation as an outstanding composer, he accepted invitations for two lengthy sojourns in England, where he wrote and performed the last twelve of his symphonies (the so-called "London Symphonies," nos. 93–104). Regarded in England as a musical genius, Haydn was able for the first time to mingle socially with high society. He even received an honorary degree from Oxford University. Thus, Haydn experienced in his own lifetime a transformation from musical servant to treasured artist, a transition characteristic of the Classical period in European music history.

When Haydn returned to Austria from his London successes, he visited his birthplace and was touched to find a statue in his honor placed there. After writing his Opus 76 string quartets around 1797, he turned his attention to the composition of Masses and two oratorios, *The Creation* (1798) and *The Seasons* (1801), before ill health stopped him. He died in 1809.

Haydn's legacy in European classical music is vast. He made fundamental contributions to the symphony, the string quartet, and a musical form known as sonata form, discussed in the next gateway. These three musical innovations of the Classical period have resonated in European classical music ever since. The young Wolfgang Amadeus Mozart much admired Haydn's string quartets and wrote them in sets of six as Haydn had. Mozart dedicated his Op. 10 string quartets of 1785 to Haydn. Ludwig van Beethoven studied with Haydn for a time after he arrived in Vienna in 1792 at the age of twenty-two, and his eighteen string quartets are among the most admired in the repertoire. Because of these Classical-period composers' interest in the genre, the string quartet joined the symphony as one of the most important genres of European classical music. From the nineteenth century to the present, many composers have written substantial numbers of string quartets, including Franz Schubert, Antonín Dvořák, Béla Bartók, and Dmitri Shostakovich.

Haydn's string quartets began as small-scale entertainment in the palaces of the wealthy and for the self-amusement of professional and amateur musicians. Haydn and Mozart enjoyed playing them, and some stories suggest they may have played together on at least one occasion. String players today enjoy playing them not least because, unlike in an orchestra where they must bow to the demands of the conductor, they work together in a sensitive musical conversation among equals. Toward the end of the eighteenth century and during the early nineteenth century, something like modern-day professional string quartets were forming and performing sometimes in concert halls, as they do today. Recently some string quartets, like the Kronos Quartet in the U.S. and the Soweto Quartet in South Africa, have taken the genre into new areas of fusion with world music, popular music, and jazz.

WHERE DO I GO FROM HERE?

- Listen to Movement III, the minuet and trio, of Haydn's String Quartet Op. 76, No. 3. Listen for the overall form (A = minuet 1; B = the trio = minuet 2; A = minuet 1).
- Listen to Haydn's String Quartet, Op. 33, No. 3, "The bird," Mvt. 4 for the way he imitates bird songs, one way to introduce iconic meaning into the abstract form of Classical-period instrumental music.
- Listen to one or more contemporary fusion compositions for string quartet commissioned by the Kronos Quartet.
- Listen to the Soweto Quartet from South Africa playing versions of local popular songs.

GATEWAY 23
CLASSICAL-PERIOD SYMPHONIES

What Is It?

Our gateway to Classical-period symphonies is Wolfgang Amadeus Mozart's Symphony No. 40 in G Minor, Movement I, written in 1788 (Figure 6.8). A **symphony** is a multi-movement composition for orchestra, one that lacks the contrast between soloist and orchestra of a concerto. The orchestra for this work consists of four sections: a string section of multiple violins, violas, cellos, and basses; a woodwind section with pairs of flutes, oboes, clarinets, and bassoons; a brass section with horns, and a set of timpani (kettle drums). Like nearly all Classical-period symphonies and string quartets, Mozart's Symphony No. 40 has four movements: fast tempo, slow tempo, minuet and trio, and fast tempo. In this performance James Levine (b. 1943), music director of New York's Metropolitan Opera from 1976 to 2016, conducts the Chicago Symphony.

 Listen to the first thirty seconds of the recording.

How Does It Work?

Timbre

The sound is created by an orchestra. The melody is played by the strings, then the woodwinds, and then the whole orchestra playing together.

FIGURE 6.8
Wolfgang Amadeus Mozart as a child, by his keyboard
Source: Painting by Anonymous, possibly by Pietro Antonio Lorenzoni (1721–1782). Mozarteum, Salzburg, Wikimedia Commons.

Texture

The texture emphasizes the melody with the other parts supporting it with a variety of contrapuntal lines.

Rhythm

The meter is duple.

Melody

The movement employs two contrasting themes: the first is built from a rapid three-note motive, the second from a long note followed by a descending melodic line.

Harmony

The harmony is tonal in the key of G minor.

Form

The form of this movement is called **sonata form**, an extended ABA' form in which two themes (melodies) appear in the A section, are "developed" in various ways in the B section, and return in a slightly different manner in the A' section.

Performance Techniques

Sudden contrasts between loud and soft passages and crescendos from soft to loud create considerable drama in the music.

 Listen to the first minute of this performance for the way the first theme is constructed from a short three-note motive.

What Does It Mean?

AESTHETICS ⟩

The meaning of this performance is intimately linked to the formal principles at work in this movement. Mozart, Haydn, Beethoven, and other composers of the Classical period developed a new form different from Baroque-period instrumental music. The Baroque concerto featured an orchestra playing two melodies (AABB), a section called the *ritornello*, in alternation with contrasting melodic material played by a soloist or small group. In Classical-period symphonies (and string quartets) the contrasting material was eliminated. Instead, the AB melodies were repeated (ABAB). This became the A section of what came to be called sonata form. Then these melodies were "developed" in a variety of ways in the B section. Then the opening ABAB melodies returned in slightly altered form (A'). The resulting ternary form (ABA') is based on a much more limited, some would say economical, amount of melodic material than in the Baroque concerto. At a more detailed level, the form of this movement in particular, and of sonata form in general, can be written this way:

||:AB:||"motives" of melody A and B are "developed"||AB'||.

The double parallel lines mark off sections and the colons indicate that the section is repeated.

Another important new compositional technique of the Classical period is the division of melodies into short segments called motives. Melodic motives are then "developed" by repeating them in sequence, using them to modulate or transition to closely related keys, and setting them in different forms of counterpoint, sometimes putting the two melodies, or their motives, in counterpoint with one another. Using their skill at counterpoint and the potential of the tonal system to move melodies to other keys, Classical-period composers used melodic motives to extend the length and internal coherence of instrumental music in a logical and coherent way.

Mozart and Haydn and other composers of the late eighteenth century worked out these new formal procedures in their compositions without reference to a written theory or explanation. During the nineteenth century, music theorists looking back on their compositions gave these procedures the name sonata form. They borrowed terms from literary analysis to name its main sections and melodies. They called the opening section of sonata form, ||:AB:||, the **exposition**. They called the melodies of sonata form the **themes**: A is the first theme, B is the second theme. They labeled the section with modulating melodic motives and elaborate counterpoint the **development** and the return of the opening themes the **recapitulation**. Using nineteenth-century music theory, the form of this movement and of sonata form can be rewritten like this: ||: Exposition :|| Development | Recapitulation ||.

One more term is commonly applied to descriptions of sonata form: **transition**. Classical-period composers wrote extended material when they transitioned from the first theme to the second theme, from the exposition to the development, from the development to the recapitulation, and often when they modulated from key to key. With this terminology, music theorists metaphorically linked the meaning of sonata form ("sonata, what do you ask of me?") to a three-part literary argument: the exposition of a couple of ideas (themes), their development and logical relationship, and their recapitulation or conclusion. Or, as a high-school English teacher might say: "Tell 'em what you're gonna tell 'em, tell 'em, and tell 'em what you told 'em."

Sonata form developed first as a practice without a theory. It became a common device in the opening movements of instrumental music in the late eighteenth century, and it was sometimes used in other movements as well. The expectations created by these formal procedures gave the music a coherence that audiences appreciated. Late eighteenth-century listeners began to expect that, after the first theme, they would hear a second, contrasting theme. After these two themes repeated, their motives would "develop" through sequences, counterpoint, and modulation to related keys. And then the movement would conclude with a return or recapitulation of the two themes. This alternation of expectation and the satisfaction of expectation generated a certain kind of aesthetic pleasure, a meaning distinct from the iconic meaning music had gained for many centuries through similarities between musical elements and ideas expressed in poetry and painting and imagined pastoral scenes and sounds.

> **CULTURAL LINKAGES**

> **AESTHETICS**

Listen to the entire performance following this timed listening guide, which outlines the sonata form of this particular movement.

TIME	SECTION	DESCRIPTION
0:00	**Exposition**	
0:00	First theme	The first theme is presented in the violins, with lower strings accompanying. The theme is based on a repeated three-note motive. This short motive is the basis for much of the musical material in the movement. The entrance of all the instruments marks the end of this section.
0:22	First theme repeats	The first theme is repeated, with winds playing sustained chords. Suddenly the whole orchestra enters and the music quickly begins to modulate (transition) towards the relative major before a cadence and a pause.
0:47	Second theme	The second theme is in the relative major (B-flat major). This theme, with its contrast of long-held notes and shorter runs, has a gentler, more lyrical character than the first theme, a typical thematic contrast in music of the Classical period.

LISTENING GUIDE 6.2

TIME	SECTION	DESCRIPTION
0:56	Second theme repeats	The theme repeats with clarinets taking the lead and almost immediately begins to transition and crescendo to a climax.
1:19	Transition	The motive from the first theme repeats in the major key as part of the transition back to the repeat of the exposition. The music alternates between loud and soft passages and again crescendos to a dramatic conclusion.
1:48	**Exposition repeats**	
3:36	**Development**	The development begins with two loud block chords. Motives from the first theme are subjected to quick modulations based on sequences and chromatic pitches. The phrases overlap with each other to create a much busier polyphonic texture than in the exposition. As the motivic material is passed around the orchestra, loud passages create intensity in alternation with soft passages that relieve the tension. The music decrescendos in anticipation of the recapitulation.
4:46	**Recapitulation**	
4:46	First theme	The first theme reappears as in the exposition.
5:06	First theme repeats	The repetition of the first theme is altered almost immediately. Whereas in the exposition this music served to transition and modulate to the second key area, in the recapitulation it serves to move away from and then back to the home key. This transition to the second theme is more "developed" than in the exposition. It ends, as in the exposition, with an abrupt pause.
5:52	Second theme	The second theme, originally in B-flat major, is now in G minor, so that the movement can end on its original tonic key.
6:01	Second theme repeats	The second theme repeats as before but crescendos to a climax in G minor.
6:29	Transition	The first theme motives return and crescendo to a climax and cadence.
6:58	**Coda**	Instead of ending at this point as the cadences suggest, the first theme returns and Mozart tacks on a short **coda** (tail) to extend and underline the ending of the movement with three loud block chords.
7:12	End	

EMOTIONAL RESONANCE   Mozart, Haydn, and other Classical-period composers used major keys to create elegant-sounding works to entertain and please their wealthy patrons. Minor keys were rarely used, but they seem to have had more expressive possibilities, including, as in this movement, the mimicking of the rapidly changing emotions of a fraught situation. Mozart expresses these emotions in this movement with his restless, active first theme whose minor key and short rhythmic motive convey a slightly agitated quality in contrast to the relaxed, elegant second theme. The crescendos and decrescendos, the abrupt and unexpected changes in dynamic levels, and the dramatic pauses add to the emotional swirl and clearly mark the formal organization of the movement. The emotions portrayed are very general, however, and leave listeners to make of the music what they will.

At a very detailed level, Mozart subtly alters the timbre of the melodies, motives, and counterpoints throughout the movement. He uses the three-note motive of the first theme in all manner of transformations: as melodies, as accompaniments, and sometimes just as a short–short–long rhythm on a single pitch. The constant changes, filigrees, and internal complexities suggest an unendingly creative musical mind at work. His older contemporary Haydn commented, "posterity will not see such a talent again in 100 years."[43] On the other hand, the musical richness caused some critics of the time to find Mozart's compositions too complicated to understand and fully enjoy. Emperor Joseph II of Austria, one of Mozart's otherwise supportive patrons, supposedly complained of another of Mozart's works, "there are too many notes," to which Mozart responded "there are just as many as there should be."

 Listen another time to this performance for pleasure, paying attention to as many of these elements as you can: shifts in key and mode, changes in loudness and softness, appearances of the three-note motive in the melody and the accompaniment, and repetitions and returns of melodies.

What Is Its History?

Early in the eighteenth century, music for string orchestras took two principal forms: concertos and *sinfonias*. Concertos were played in instrumental concerts and featured a contrast between a soloist or a small number of soloists and the full orchestra (Chapter 5, Gateway 18). *Sinfonias*, symphonies in English, used the full orchestra for the preludes (overtures), interludes, and postludes of operas, cantatas, and oratorios. Around 1730 the symphony began to escape the confines of vocal music and became a popular instrumental concert genre in its own right. Courts competed for the best orchestras to play them and the best composers to write them. The most famous orchestra in the mid-century performed at the court of a prince-elector of the Holy Roman Empire in the city of Mannheim in southwest Germany along the Rhine River.

Its most celebrated and innovative composer, Johann Stamitz (1717–1757), worked there after 1741. He and his orchestra are credited with many of the innovations that characterize the classical symphony, including the abandonment of the harpsichord, the change of the Baroque melody–chord–bass texture to melodies with four-part contrapuntal accompaniment, the expansion of the three-movement concerto form to four movements with the inclusion of the minuet and trio, and the addition of wind instruments as an obligatory feature of what had been the Baroque string orchestra (Figure 6.9).

Many of the features of Mozart's Symphony No. 40 started as innovations of the Mannheim school, including sudden changes in dynamics, abrupt pauses, and a rising arpeggiated theme at the beginning of a movement (called a "Mannheim rocket"), which Mozart uses in Movement IV of this symphony. During the 1750s J. S. Bach's son, C. P. E. Bach, working in Berlin for the court of Frederick the Great, the King of Prussia and an avid flute player, also contributed a few symphonies.

In 1759 Haydn wrote his first symphony, and during the 1760s he wrote nearly forty of them for Prince Nikolaus and his guests. Mozart composed the first of his forty-one

FIGURE 6.9

The Dublin Philharmonic Orchestra in a form typical of the nineteenth century: first row, from left to right, first violins, second violins, cellos, violas, and basses; second- and third-row risers, from left to right, four horns, piccolo, two flutes and two clarinets, two oboes and two bassoons, and three trumpets; back row, left to right, four percussionists including bass drum and timpani, three trombones, and one tuba

Source: Derek Gleeson. Wikimedia Commons.

AESTHETICS

symphonies in 1764 at the age of eight or nine. An astonishing child prodigy, he set the European music scene ablaze during a brief thirty-five-year lifetime before illness doused his spirit and his unparalleled musical gifts in 1791. His father, Leopold, a violinist and court musician for the Prince-Archbishop of the Salzburg region 200 miles west of Vienna, taught music to Wolfgang and his older sister Maria Anna (nicknamed "Nannerl"), his two surviving children. Both proved to be enormously talented. He called Wolfgang a "gift from God." He was a keyboard virtuoso by the age of five, when he began dictating solo keyboard pieces and violin sonatas to his father. In 1762 Leopold took leave of his court responsibilities and led his children on a tour of the royal courts of Europe including those of Maria Theresa, Empress of Austria, and her daughter Marie Antoinette and of King George III in London, where J. C. Bach's (1735–1782) music impressed the young Wolfgang. Not only did this trio create a sensation, with Nannerl often receiving top billing as a keyboard virtuoso, young Wolfgang absorbed like a sponge the latest musical styles around western Europe. Once Nannerl reached her teens and marriageable age, Leopold no longer allowed her to tour and perform, and she was forced to live the domestic life typical of women of the time (Figure 6.10). Father and son continued to travel for more than a decade in search of fame and a suitable position for the youthful phenom as a court *Kapellmeister*. In 1770 they traveled to Italy, where, at the age of fourteen, Wolfgang composed his first opera and then two others in the next three years. His most famous work of this period is a motet called "Exultate, Jubilate," composed in 1773 in Milan for orchestra and the *castrato* starring in one of his operas. His Italian successes did not lead to the hoped-for position at Maria Theresa's imperial court in Vienna. She lumped Mozart and other composers into a category of "useless people" who would "degrade" the court by "go[ing] around the world like beggars."[44] Evidently, aristocratic support for musicians was not universal.

ECONOMIC ACTIVITY

Nowhere was this more evident than in the Salzburg Archbishop's court, to which Leopold and Wolfgang returned in 1773. Wolfgang's fame, including the composition of some twenty symphonies, earned him only a relatively low-paying position at court. He was especially frustrated that the Archbishop did not support opera, which he loved. He continued to compose symphonies, keyboard works, and religious music, but yearned for a more suitable position. In 1777 he and his mother embarked on another trip to the musical centers of Europe in search of a patron. Sadly, his mother died in Paris in 1778, no jobs were offered, and he returned to the Salzburg court in 1779. In 1781 he had a final falling out with the Archbishop on a visit they made to Vienna for the coronation of Maria Theresa's son, Emperor Joseph II. There the Archbishop treated him like a lowly servant rather than like the musical celebrity he had become in the rest of Europe. He quit the Archbishop's service in a huff and stayed in Vienna, determined to make it on his own as a freelance musician. In those years in Salzburg from 1773 to 1780 he had composed another dozen or so symphonies, bringing the total to thirty-four.

For the next eleven years, from 1781 until his death in 1791, Mozart tested the limits of an independent artist in a European musical culture where most outstanding composers, including Haydn, J. S. Bach, C. P. E. Bach, Stamitz, and Vivaldi, had depended on employment at aristocratic courts or in wealthy churches and religious institutions. The one genre where a composer might make it on his own was opera, the most popular genre of music among the moneyed bourgeoisie and the aristocracy. Handel had made a similar decision seventy years earlier when he left the employ of the Elector of Hannover in 1712 for the world of Italian opera in London.

FIGURE 6.10
The Mozart family with a portrait of Mozart's mother, Anna Maria, in the background
Source: Painting by Johann Nepomuk della Croce, c. 1780. Artexperts, Mozarteum, Salzburg, Wikimedia Commons.

Luckily for Mozart, Joseph II loved music, especially a type of musical theater called ***Singspiel*** (singing play), which was sung in German rather than Italian and which eschewed recitative in favor of spoken dialogue between arias. Leopold founded a company dedicated to its performance, and in 1782 Mozart composed one its first successes, a *Singspiel* called *Die Entführung aus dem Serail* (The Abduction from the Seraglio), set inside Topkapı, the *seray* or palace, and *harem*, the domestic space for women, of the Ottoman sultan. Exploiting the Austrian fascination with the Ottoman Empire at its southeastern border, Mozart added percussion instruments from Turkish military bands into the percussion section of the orchestra: bass drum, cymbals, and triangle. An enormous success, this *Singspiel* secured Mozart's reputation as a composer in Vienna, allowing him access to the salons of the local aristocracy.

Unlike Handel, who shared in the production and profits of his London operas, Mozart was paid a very modest flat fee, not enough to sustain him and his new wife, Constanze, a singer. (They had six children, two of whom survived to adulthood.) To support himself, Mozart turned to the production of his own public concerts. A virtuoso keyboard player, he organized well-attended subscription concerts to show off his and his students' skills. They performed his keyboard sonatas and concertos on the new instrument, the fortepiano (see Gateway 25), which was replacing the harpsichord in popularity. During his eleven years in Vienna he wrote some sixteen piano concertos, nine piano sonatas, seven symphonies, and many string quartets, six of them published as Opus 10 and named in honor of Haydn, whom he had met (and briefly studied with) in Vienna and whose compositions he much admired. Said Mozart, "He alone has the secret of making me smile and touching me to the bottom of my soul." He also received commissions to write five more operas during these years, including two in the year of his death: *The Magic Flute*, a *Singspiel*, and an Italian opera, *La Clemenza di Tito* (The Clemency of Titus). Sadly, in September of 1791 he fell ill from an unknown infection while in Prague for the premiere of *La Clemenza di Tito*. Although well enough to conduct the premiere of *The Magic Flute* in October in Vienna, his condition soon worsened, and he died on December 5, 1791.

A morbid footnote to his illness and death was a composition he was working on, but never finished, at the time of his death: a Requiem Mass commissioned by a nobleman in honor of his recently deceased wife. Much fictional license was made of this story in the 1984 movie *Amadeus*, which won the Academy Award for Best Picture. It dramatizes stories Constanze told claiming that Mozart had received the commission from an unidentified messenger and had come to believe he was writing his own Requiem. It also focuses on Mozart's financial trials as a freelance musician and his supposed rivalry with Antonio Salieri (1750–1825), the director of Italian opera at the Habsburg Court. His compositions of his last year (the two operas, the Requiem, and his Clarinet Concerto) are today among his most admired works. Mozart loved the clarinet and is often credited with securing its position in the woodwind section of the orchestra.

Coincidentally, Haydn spent 1791, the year of Mozart's death, in London, where he wrote and performed his first six "London Symphonies," Nos. 93 to 98, to great acclaim. He returned in 1794 and 1795 to perform his last six symphonies, Nos. 99 to 104. Some critics hear the influence of Mozart's Vienna symphonies, Nos. 35 to 41, in Haydn's last contributions to the symphony. Mozart's symphonies of the 1780s and Haydn's of the 1790s are, with a few exceptions, the oldest symphonies still commonly performed today.

In the early nineteenth century the symphony joined opera as the most prestigious genres of European classical music, and composers from Beethoven to the present have built on the legacy of Haydn and Mozart. Among other nineteenth-century contributions was the expansion of the size of the orchestra and of the variety and range of woodwind, brass, and percussion instruments. The sound of the symphony orchestra, particularly its string section, has become a sonic index of the upper classes, which have patronized symphony orchestras since the late eighteenth century. It has become a sign of "class," that is, of refinement. As a consequence, jazz, popular, and world-music musicians have often used the sound of the string section of a symphony orchestra when they have wanted to suggest "classiness." Some listeners' emotional response to symphonic timbre may depend, at least a bit, on their attitudes toward the social classes this sound signifies (indexes).

> ECONOMIC
> ACTIVITY

> EMOTIONAL
> RESONANCE

WHERE DO I GO FROM HERE?

- Listen to James Levine and the Chicago Symphony performing Movements II, III, and IV of Mozart's Symphony No. 40 in G minor. Follow the formal organization of each movement.
- Listen to Franz Joseph Haydn's Symphony No. 101 in D Major, Mvt. II. Nicknamed "The Clock" for the way this movement imitates a clock's ticking, it represents the sort of humor in Haydn's music that amused Mozart and many other admirers since then.
- Listen to Haydn's Symphony No. 100 in G Major, "Military," Mvt. II, for his use of the "Turkish" battery of percussion instruments (timpani, bass drum, cymbals, and triangle), which Mozart introduced in *The Abduction from the Seraglio*.

GATEWAY 24
CLASSICAL-PERIOD OPERA

What Is It?

Our gateway to Classical-period opera is Act I, Scene 1 from Wolfgang Amadeus Mozart's opera *Le Nozze di Figaro* (The Marriage of Figaro) composed in 1786 in Vienna. Called "Cinque . . . dieci" (Five . . . ten) after the first sung words, it is a "little duet" (*duettino*) between Figaro, valet to Spanish Count Almaviva, and Susanna, maid to Countess Almaviva. The scene begins with Figaro and his fiancée Susanna each distracted by preparations for their wedding. Figaro is measuring their new apartment in the palace, presumably thinking of what delights are in the offing, while Susanna is going on about her pretty new wedding cap (in modern terms, her veil).

FIGARO
misurando
Cinque. . . dieci. . . venti. . . trenta. . .
trentasei. . .quarantatre

SUSANNA
specchiandosi
Ora sì ch'io son contenta;
sembra fatto inver per me.
Guarda un po', mio caro Figaro,
guarda adesso il mio cappello.

FIGARO
Sì mio core, or è più bello,
sembra fatto inver per te.

SUSANNA e FIGARO
Ah, il mattino alle nozze vicino
quanto è dolce al mio/tuo tenero sposo
questo bel cappellino vezzoso
che Susanna ella stessa si fe'.

FIGARO
measuring [the wedding bed]
Five . . . ten . . . twenty . . . thirty . . .
Thirty-six . . . forty-three

SUSANNA
gazing into a mirror
Yes, I'm very pleased with that;
It seems just made for me.
Take a look, dear Figaro,
Just look at this cap of mine.

FIGARO
Yes, my dearest, it's very pretty;
It looks just made for you.

SUSANNA and FIGARO
On this morning of our wedding
How delightful to my (your) dear one
Is this pretty little cap
Which Susanna made herself.

In this recording the English bass Thomas Allen plays Figaro, the American soprano Kathleen Battle sings the Susanna role, and the Italian conductor Riccardo Muti leads the Vienna Philharmonic, an international cast typical of opera performances today.

 Listen to the first thirty seconds of the recording.

How Does It Work?

Timbre

A full Classical-period orchestra accompanies a hardy operatic bass voice and a light soprano voice.

Texture

The texture combines the orchestra with vocal parts that vary from solos to singing independent melodic lines to parallel thirds.

Rhythm

The meter is in four. The rhythm is varied and changeable, including constant pulsation in the bassoon accompaniment at one point.

Melody

The scene contrasts Figaro's melody, built from a two-pitch descending motive, with Susanna's, which consists of longer phrases in stepwise motion.

Harmony

The harmony is tonal in a major key.

Form

The scene begins with an orchestral introduction followed by Figaro's solo and then Susanna's. The two then sing independent melodic lines until joining together in parallel thirds.

Performance Techniques

The most striking technique is the operatic vocal sound, one capable of filling a large opera house without amplification.

 Listen to the first thirty seconds of this recording again, this time paying attention to the timbre and texture of the two singing voices.

What Does It Mean?

This scene is filled with musical gestures suggestive both of the text and of the characters' thoughts and their genders. In this scene Mozart links the unspecified emotional contrast of the two themes in sonata form to the particular emotions of the two characters' words, thoughts, and actions. Whereas in the Classical-period symphony and string quartet the two themes engage in a metaphorical dialogue through close proximity and counterpoint, in opera the combination of words and themes creates a theatrical dialogue between two characters. The scene can also be understood formally to work out a truncated version of the three parts of sonata form:

1. Exposition = ‖: AB :‖, the first theme sung by Figaro and the second theme sung by Susanna;
2. Development = Motives of A in counterpoint as the characters converse;
3. Recapitulation = B – transition – B; the first theme is omitted since Figaro adopts Susanna's melody and her point of view and abandons his preoccupations and his melody.

FIGURE 6.11
Figaro and Susanna in a performance of *The Marriage of Figaro* in St. Petersburg
Source: ITAR-TASS News Agency/Alamy Stock Photo.

FIGURE 6.12
Soprano Kathleen Battle as Susanna in *The Marriage of Figaro* at the Metropolitan Opera
Source: Johan Elbers, The LIFE Images Collection/Getty Images.

Listen to the entire recording following this timed listening guide, which examines the iconic links between music, text, action, and the thinking of Figaro and Susanna.

LISTENING GUIDE 6.3

TIME	FORM	SECTION	TEXT	TRANSLATION	DESCRIPTION
0:00	**Exposition**	Orchestral prelude			
0:00	A	first theme			The strings play short phrases beginning with repeated pitches and ending with a descending, disjunct leap
0:16	B	second theme			The oboes play a contrasting narrow-range, undulating, stepwise melody with bassoon on the bass part.
0:32	A′	Figaro	*Cinque . . .* *dieci . . .* *venti . . .* *trenta . . .* *trentasei . . .* *quarantatre*	Five . . . ten . . . twenty . . . thirty . . . thirty-six . . . forty-three	The strings play the first part of the first-theme phrase and Figaro sings the numbers on the descending leaps at the ends of phrases, the punchy, short motive an expression of his masculinity in this case. The rising pitch over the course of his solo represents his increasing excitement at the prospect of marriage.
0:53	B′	Susanna	*Ora sì ch'io son contenta;* *sembra fatto inver per me.* *Guarda un po', mio caro Figaro,* *guarda adesso il mio cappello.*	Yes, I'm very pleased with that; It seems just made for me. Take a look, dear Figaro, Just look at this cap of mine.	Susanna sings her solo to the second-theme melody, its undulating, stepwise motion now an expression of her femininity.
1:03	**Development**	Susanna and Figaro	They repeat their words	Repeat	The A theme is broken apart and set in counterpoint: Figaro repeats his descending leaps, while Susanna sings the repeated

TIME	FORM	SECTION	TEXT	TRANSLATION	DESCRIPTION
					pitches of the first half of the first theme. In this case, the counterpart, with each character repeating what they sang before, suggests that the two of them are not listening to one another. They are preoccupied with their own thoughts.
1:26	**Recapitulation**				
1:26	B″	Figaro	*Sì mio core or più bello sembra fatto in ver per te.*	Yes, my love, it is very pretty. It seems just made for you.	Figaro finally hears Susana, expressed literally by echoing her words and metaphorically by singing her theme.
1:37	transition	Susanna and Figaro	They sing previous text	Repeat	They sing back and forth in conversation briefly until finally they sing, in parallel thirds, an icon of their love, and a melodic sequence that rises in pitch, an icon of their increasing passion.
2:03	B‴	Susanna and Figaro	*Ah, il mattino alle nozze vicino quanto è dolce al mio/tuo tenero sposo questo bel cappellino vezzoso che Susanna ella stessa si fe'.*	On this morning of our wedding How delightful to my (your) dear one Is this pretty little cap Which Susanna made herself.	Figaro and Susanna sing her theme in parallel thirds, a musical portrayal of Figaro's devoted attention to Susanna's delight in her wedding cap.
2:42	End				

This example illustrates the way the conventions of vocal music lent meaning to instrumental music and vice versa. In instrumental music a punchy, loud two-note motive represents some sort of strength. Once Figaro or some other masculine character in opera sings such a motive, the strength becomes masculine, and similar gestures in instrumental music might, as a consequence, be interpreted as masculine, rather than vaguely strong. A soft undulating melody in instrumental music represents a lilting, delicate feeling. Once sung by Susanna or another attractive female character in opera, similar instrumental melodies might be interpreted as feminine as well. This back-

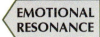

EMOTIONAL RESONANCE

and-forth between instrumental and vocal music allowed the specific emotions of musical gestures in opera to be interpreted as general emotions in instrumental music and vice versa. Haydn's String Quartet Op. 76, No. 3, Mvt. IV, written a decade after *Le Nozze di Figaro*, illustrates this point (see Chapter 6, Gateway 22). The theme of the fourth movement consists of two motives: a loud, forceful, staccato three-pitch gesture followed by a soft, delicate, undulating six-note melodic phrase. They may be nothing more than a musical representation of a vague contrast between strength and weakness, vigor and fragility. After Mozart's *Figaro*, it is hard not to interpret these melodic motives as a conversation between a man and woman; he perhaps angry and powerful, she perhaps defensive and powerless.

Although Act I, Scene 1 establishes the sincere love of Figaro and Susanna for one another, we can predict that there may be some trouble in their future since the opera lasts three hours. The problems begin in the next scene, when Susanna confides in Figaro that she has heard that Count Almaviva, who "scours the countryside for fresh beauties," hopes to exercise the privilege supposedly accorded Medieval lords to bed their servants, a *droit du seigneur* (right of the lord). Figaro, outraged, hatches a plot to expose and embarrass the Count with the aid of Susanna, the Countess, and the Count's young page, Cherubino, played by a woman in what is called a "pants role." Structured as a classic French farce, all manner of silliness ensues, with people entering rooms as others hide in closets or jump out of windows to escape detection. Mistaken identities abound, many of them playing with Cherubino's male/female character, creating continual confusion and mirth. At play's end the Count's lechery is exposed for all to see. He begs the Countess to forgive him and she agrees, all promise to be happy, and they set out "to the sound of a gay march" to celebrate the wedding of Figaro and Susanna.

CULTURAL LINKAGES

Although modern audiences enjoy Mozart's music and the farcical elements of the opera, at the time the opera was understood as an indictment of the nobility and its exploitation of the lower classes. The opera's source was a popular French play composed in 1778 by Pierre Beaumarchais (1732–1799), a remarkable figure whose influence included the invention of a reliable mechanism for pocket watches, music instructor at the French court, playwright, spy, diplomat, and arms dealer. In the latter three capacities he advocated for the entry of France on the side of the colonists in the American Revolution and supplied the revolutionary army with weapons, uniforms, and other provisions. King Louis XVI immediately understood the play, titled *La Folle Journée* (The Follies of a Day), *ou Le Mariage de Figaro*, as an indictment of the aristocracy and his government, and he refused to allow its public performance, even over the objections of his queen, Marie Antoinette. Beaumarchais's play finally premiered to enormous success in 1784 at an important public theatre in Paris.

The Austrian Emperor Joseph II also objected to the public performance of the play, but his court librettist for Italian operas, Lorenzo da Ponte (1749–1838), working with Mozart, omitted Figaro's angry denunciation of the Count and the nobility at the end of the play and turned it into a comparatively harmless comedic romp about jealousy and male arrogance. Their version passed the censors and entered public performance in Vienna just two years after the play's public debut in Paris. The opera was so successful that Mozart and da Ponte received a commission for a second opera, which premiered in Prague the next year, 1787, just a month after the signing of the new U.S. Constitution. Titled *Don Giovanni* and based on a seventeenth-century Spanish story about Don Juan, a shameless womanizer, this lord commits murder, refuses to repent, and goes to hell, a much darker, more devastating critique of aristocratic privilege than *The Marriage of Figaro*.

POLITICAL ACTION

In 1789, just five years after the premiere of Beaumarchais's play, desperately poor peasants, urban laborers, and women ignited the French Revolution against the wealth and privilege of the aristocracy. Perhaps Louis XVI was right to worry about the play's potential effect. Georges Danton, a leading figure in the revolution, said the play "killed off the nobility," and Napoleon, who came to power in the wake of the revolution, thought the play had "already put [the Revolution] into action." Evidently, Louis XVI, Danton, and Napoleon believed in the power of art to alter social and political conditions.

The play and the two operas by Mozart and da Ponte also captured the libertine spirit of the time. Catherine the Great, Empress of Russia from 1762 to 1796 and the Venetian roué Giacomo Casanova (1725–1798) were just two of the most notorious avatars of eighteenth-century libidinous license. Reflecting the spirit of the age, wealthy slave-owning landowners of the southern American colonies also took advantage of their own version of the *droit du seigneur*. In 1787, the year of *Don Giovanni*'s premiere, Thomas Jefferson's fourteen-year-old enslaved maid, Sally Hemmings, joined him in Paris, where he had been the American minister to the French court since 1784. They returned to the new United States in 1789, she having borne him a child.

CULTURAL LINKAGES

What Is Its History?

By the early eighteenth century, opera had conquered all of Europe. It had developed into a highly structured form featuring a contrast between recited speech (recitative) accompanied by the harpsichord and an often florid aria accompanied by the full orchestra. Composers wrote arias to show off the skills of the singers, especially the castrati playing the lead male roles. The action proceeded in a rather artificial way (the term Baroque is practically synonymous with artifice), each character impressively declaiming their position and then, after showing off their vocal skills, exiting the stage to wild applause. Although opera was public entertainment in Monteverdi's Venice and Handel's London, it was especially beloved by the aristocracy, not least because the plots of Baroque-period operas told the stories of Ancient Greek gods and Roman emperors, who, when they acted benevolently, were exemplars of noble virtue.

This type of opera continued to be a court favorite until the end of the eighteenth century. However, by the 1730s it was declining in popularity among the general public. This was one of the reasons Handel turned to the composition of oratorios intended for that audience (Chapter 5, Gateway 19). Mid-eighteenth-century composers began to write in a new style, de-emphasizing the virtuosity of arias and writing more duets and choruses. The plots shifted from tales of ancient times to stories about contemporary ordinary people, often caught in comic situations. Castrati ceded popularity to a new kind of character, the *basso buffo* (the bass buffoon). People began to distinguish between two types of Italian opera: *opera seria* (serious opera), the older style; and *opera buffa* (comic opera), the newer style. *Le Nozze di Figaro* is an *opera buffa*.

Yet a third type of musical drama competed with Italian opera for the public's attention. Called *ballad operas* in English and *Singspiel* in German, these productions were sung in the local language and dispensed with recitative in favor of spoken dialogue, features appealing to audiences with little or no knowledge of Italian. Mozart's first success as a freelancer in Vienna was a *Singspiel*, composed in 1782, called *Die Entführung aus dem Serail* (The Abduction from the Seraglio).

Over the course of his life Mozart composed more than twenty works, many of them very short, in these three genres of musical theater: *opera seria*, *opera buffa*, and *Singspiel*. His first three operas, composed in Italy in his teens, were *opera seria*. His seven mature operas, composed

FIGURE 6.13
Teatro La Fenice ("The Phoenix"), built in the 1790s in Venice and restored in 2004 to a mid-nineteenth-century style after a fire
Source: Youflavio, Wikimedia Commons.

FIGURE 6.14
Soprano Diana Damrau singing "The Queen of the Night" from *The Magic Flute* in Salzburg in 2006

between 1780 and 1791, all enjoyed fantastic success at the time. Some remain among the most admired and frequently performed works in the opera repertoire:

1. 1780: *Idomeneo, re di Creta* (Idomeneus, King of Crete), an *opera seria* composed while still in Salzburg at the court of the Archbishop, on commission from the Elector of Bavaria and premiered in Munich;
2. 1782: *Die Entführung aus dem Serail* (The Abduction from the Seraglio), a *Singspiel* premiered in Vienna for the Emperor's "national theater";
3. 1786: *Le Nozze di Figaro* (The Marriage of Figaro), an *opera buffa* premiered in Vienna for the Emperor's Italian opera company;
4. 1787: *Don Giovanni*, an *opera buffa* premiered in Prague;
5. 1790: *Così fan tutte* (Thus do all [women]), an *opera buffa* premiered in Vienna at the Emperor's theater;
6. 1791: *La Clemenza di Tito* (The Clemency of Titus), an *opera seria* premiered in Prague for the coronation of Emperor Joseph II as King of Bohemia;
7. 1791: *Die Zauberflöte* (The Magic Flute), a *Singspiel* premiered in Vienna.

Mozart's *opera buffa*s and *Singspiel*s are the oldest operas in the standard repertoire, although Monteverdi's *Orfeo*, Handel's *Rinaldo*, and a few others are heard occasionally. The two *opera seria*s have been less performed, their old-fashioned style militating against their popularity with modern audiences attuned to the "natural" style of musical dialogue and emotional expression that Mozart perfected in *Le Nozze di Figaro*.

WHERE DO I GO FROM HERE?

- Watch three different video performances of *Le Nozze di Figaro*, Act I, Scene 1, the *duettino* between Figaro and Susanna, and compare the variety of ways modern opera directors stage the scene.

- Listen to performances of these arias from *Le Nozze di Figaro* to get some idea of their lyrical quality, which contrasts with the virtuosity of Baroque opera: Figaro's "Non piu andrai"; Countess Almaviva's "Porgi, Amor"; and Cherubino's "Voi, che sapete che cosa e amor."

- Listen to "Der Hölle Rache kocht in meinem Herzen" (Hell's Vengence Boils in My Heart), also known as The Queen of the Night aria, from *The Magic Flute* and written in the florid, virtuosic style of *opera seria*.

- Listen to "Là si darem la mano," a *duettino* from *Don Giovanni* between the Don and Zerlina, a peasant girl. Structured much like "Cinque . . . dieci," its musical gestures signal first her resistance to his advances and then her acquiescence.

GATEWAY 25
CLASSICAL-PERIOD PIANO MUSIC

What Is It?

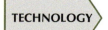

Our gateway to Classical-period piano music is Ludwig van Beethoven's (1770–1827) Piano Sonata in C Minor No. 8, Op. 13 (Pathétique), Mvt. I: Grave – Allegro molto e con brio. A **piano** is a keyboard instrument on which hammers attached to the keys strike the strings. It is a successor to the harpsichord, on which plectra attached to the keys pluck the strings. Invented around 1700, it largely had replaced the harpsichord by the end of the eighteenth century and was the preferred keyboard instrument of Mozart and Beethoven, both of whom were concertizing virtuoso performers on it. *Grave* means very slow and solemn. *Allegro molto e con brio* means very fast and with spirit. *Pathétique* (sadness, poignancy) is an epithet assigned to the work by Beethoven's publisher based on his assessment of the feelings the work created. In this performance Geoffrey Lancaster (b. 1954), an Australian pianist, conductor, and specialist in late eighteenth-century music, plays the fortepiano. The **fortepiano** (literally, loud–soft) is the predecessor of the modern piano. Unlike on the harpsichord, players of the fortepiano and the modern piano can play loudly or softly by altering the force of their touch on the keys. Compared to the modern piano, which has a range of more than seven octaves, eighteenth-century fortepianos had a range of five or six octaves and a much lighter, thinner sound.

 Listen to the first thirty seconds of the recording.

How Does It Work?

Timbre

The timbre of the fortepiano varies according to the register and the loudness or softness of the playing. In this movement Beethoven employs a pitch range of more than five octaves, nearly the entire range of the instrument, which creates a variety of timbres. Loud sounds in the lower register have a buzzing sound reminiscent of the harpsichord, and higher register pitches sound a bit metallic. Middle-register pitches are relatively round.

Texture

Textures vary considerably, including:

- block chords;
- melody with an octave **tremolo** in the bass part (the pianist rocks back and forth rapidly between two low pitches an octave apart);
- melody with bass and chords;
- melody with arpeggiated chords.

Rhythm

The meter is duple with a variety of rhythms including rapid runs, long-held tones, and long–short–long rhythms.

FIGURE 6.15
Ludwig van Beethoven in 1820
Source: Painting by Joseph Karl Stieler (1781–1858). Beethoven-Haus Bonn, Wikimedia Commons.

Melody

There are four melodies in this movement:

1. The opening slow section has an ascending stepwise motive with a long–short–long rhythmic pattern.
2. The fast section opens with a "rocket" theme, a rapid ascent over two octaves.
3. The second melody contrasts long tones with a stepwise descent using trills (a **trill** consists of rapid movement between two adjacent pitches in a scale).
4. The third melody features an ascending stepwise line with arpeggiated chords in the bass.

Harmony

The harmony is tonal. The harmonies of the first three melodies are in minor keys; the harmony of the fourth is in a major key.

Form

The piece opens with a slow introduction before launching in a fast movement in sonata form with three, rather than the usual two, melodies. The melody of the slow introduction returns at the beginning of the recapitulation and of the coda.

Performance Techniques

The playing features rapid alternation of loud and soft tones. Notice the rapid decay of the long chords in the slow opening. The modern piano has a much more sustained decay. The trills, rapid runs, tremolos, and arpeggiated chords require a high level of skill from the performer.

Listen to the first thirty seconds of the recording for the minor key and the texture of melody with block chords.

Listen to the entire recording following this timed listening guide, which outlines the form of the movement.

LISTENING GUIDE 6.4

TIME	SECTION	DESCRIPTION
0:00	**Slow Introduction**	A short six-note melodic motive in block chords is repeated in sequence a number of times ending with a rapid chromatic descent.
1:43	**Exposition**	
1:43	First theme	A "rocket" theme in C minor accompanied by rapid octave tremolo in the bass.
1:55	Transition	Descending runs contrast with ascending variants of the rocket theme.
2:14	Second theme	Still in minor, the new melody starts with long tones followed by descending trilled tones.
2:45	Third theme	This theme, in the relative major of E-flat, has a stepwise ascent accompanied by arpeggiated chords.
3:04	Transition	Fast descending runs lead to a restatement of the rocket theme, now in E-flat major.
3:26	**Exposition repeat**	
5:09	**Development**	Begins with three statements of the slow introduction motive before launching into variants of the rocket theme, the octave tremolos, and the arpeggios of the exposition. After moving through a number of key areas, it ends with a rapid descending solo run.
6:44	**Recapitulation**	A varied repeat of the exposition, except the second theme is in a major key and the third theme is in the home key of C minor rather than E-flat major as it was in the exposition.
8:14	**Coda**	After a dramatic pause, the coda reintroduces a variant of the introductory motive without the dramatic sustained first chord. The movement ends with one more statement of the first, rocket theme and four concluding loud block chords.
9:06	End	

What Does It Mean?

AESTHETICS

Many of the features of this movement would have been familiar to audiences of the time, including the slow introduction. Although the first movements of most late eighteenth-century symphonies, string quartets, concertos, and sonatas were in fast tempos, it was not unusual for them to begin with a slow **introduction**, as in this example. The contrast between loud and soft, which players of the fortepiano could execute, mirrors similar contrasts in symphonic music, such as in the first movement of Mozart's Symphony No. 40 (Chapter 6, Gateway 23). Even the appearance of three themes rather than the archetypal two was not unknown. What may have seemed striking about this work to audiences of the time is its unrelenting intensity. Gone are much of the lightness, lyricism, and elegance of Haydn's and Mozart's compositions. No sooner has a passage like the first, rocket theme started softly (piano) than it crescendos to extreme loudness (forte) by the end. Accompanying tremolos, pulsating beats, and arpeggios, even for the somewhat lilting second theme, create an unceasing, restless, driving energy. The *pathétique* epithet probably derives from the opening slow introduction, with its low pitches, block chords in a minor key, and dramatic pauses, as if sighing.

🔊 **Listen one more time to this performance for pleasure, paying attention to the drama in the work created by these musical elements.**

Part of the meaning of a work like this is social and economic. Like Mozart, Beethoven was a fine pianist and supported himself by giving piano recitals for which he composed five piano concertos and thirty-two piano sonatas. These works make up an important part of his legacy. Lacking a permanent position at a court, he also made money from the publication of these works, which were commissioned by wealthy patrons and purchased and played by amateur pianists, a few of whom Beethoven taught. Learning to play his and many other composers' piano sonatas became an important indicator of cultural and educational attainment for home-bound women during this time. Before the invention of recording devices and the possibility of passive enjoyment of music, playing piano sonatas and singing to the accompaniment of a piano were one of the principal forms of entertainment in middle-class homes throughout the nineteenth century. Amateur pianists to this day usually learn at least a few of Beethoven's simpler piano sonatas as they develop their skills. His more virtuosic sonatas, along with his piano concertos, are among the earliest to provide professional pianists with brilliant and expressive show pieces.

> ECONOMIC
> ACTIVITY

> CULTURAL
> LINKAGES

What Is Its History?

The invention of the fortepiano, with its hammering rather than plucking mechanism, was the work of Bartolomeo Cristofori (1655–1731). Born near Venice in the same region where the violin was perfected, he was hired in 1688 by the wealthy Medici family in Florence to care for its large collection of musical instruments. In their workshops he made important contributions to harpsichord design before creating his first piano, "which makes soft and loud [sounds]," in 1700. Interest in the new instrument spread slowly and mainly among the nobility. It entered public performance around 1760, just in time for Mozart, who made it his favorite instrument. Mozart's fortepianos had about five octaves of keys with the hammers striking two strings tuned in unison. During Beethoven's life the sustaining power of the piano's tones was improved considerably and its range extended to six and then seven octaves. In 1843 the Chickering & Mackays company of Boston patented a piano with an iron frame, which supported thicker and tenser strings and thus a richer and more sustained sound. The modern grand piano was born. During the 1860s a German immigrant to New York founded the Steinway & Sons piano company, which today accounts for a huge percentage of piano sales.

> TECHNOLOGY

Beethoven, like J. S. Bach and his sons, was born into a multigenerational musical family. His grandfather, born in Flanders (the Dutch-speaking area of Belgium), became the *Kapellmeister* to the Elector of Cologne, whose palace was in Bonn. His father Johann, a court singer, keyboardist, and Ludwig's first music teacher, recognized his son's prodigious talent and organized his first public concert at the age of seven. Perhaps thinking of Leopold and young Wolfgang Mozart, he claimed young Ludwig was only six. At ten Ludwig began studying with the court organist and at fourteen

FIGURE 6.16

A modern replica of an 1804 pianoforte, made by Paul McNulty. Note the reversed color of the black and white keys from the modern piano

Source: Paul McNulty and Viviana Sofronitzki, Wikimedia Commons.

was employed as assistant organist in the court chapel. Around this time he composed three piano sonatas, today listed without opus numbers, for the Elector. At seventeen he traveled to Vienna hoping to study with Mozart, but stayed only two weeks before returning to Bonn. His mother had fallen ill and soon died. In 1791 he met Haydn when the famous composer passed through Bonn to and from his first trip to London. In 1792, at the age of twenty-two and with the financial support of the Elector, he headed once more to Vienna, this time to study with the old master. He remained there for the rest of his life.

Beethoven's first three years in Vienna were occupied mainly with the study of composition. Unfortunately Mozart had died the year before he arrived, and Haydn was preoccupied with his second trip to London and could not give him much attention. He soon made the acquaintance of wealthy members of the nobility, who admired his talent. They invited him to display his keyboard skills, especially his ability to improvise, at their salons, and they commissioned compositions from him. In 1795 he gave his first public concert at which he played a piano concerto to showcase his keyboard skills. He also published his first chamber works, pieces he labeled his Opus 1, three piano trios (compositions for violin, cello, and piano), and Opus 2, his first three piano sonatas, dedicated to Haydn. Over the next five years he published mainly chamber sonatas in various combinations of instruments for the amusement of professional and amateur players in the elite Viennese social scene. His first eleven piano sonatas and first six string quartets, the latter also dedicated to Haydn, date from this period. He also wrote cello sonatas (cello and piano), violin sonatas (violin and piano), more trio sonatas, and a string quintet (two violins, two violas, cello).

By 1800 the Viennese public had recognized the thirty-year-old Beethoven as the city's finest piano virtuoso and improviser (improvisation contests were popular in Vienna) and a worthy successor to the compositional legacy of Haydn and Mozart, whose style he had absorbed. In 1800 he debuted his Symphony No. 1 in concert, launching an artistic trajectory that would establish his own legacy as one of the greatest composers in the history of European classical music. The story of his symphonies, his most well-known pieces today, is told in Chapter 7, Gateway 27. On a more ominous note, by 1798 he was experiencing hearing loss and tinnitus, a harbinger of calamity to come.

WHERE DO I GO FROM HERE?

- Listen to one or more of the three movements of Beethoven's Piano Sonata No. 8, Op. 13, played on a modern grand piano and compare that sound to the sound of the fortepiano in this gateway recording. Which do you prefer and why?

- Listen to Beethoven's Piano Concerto No. 1, Mvt. III for some idea of the way he showcased his piano technique in concert and the way his style in this piece captures the elegance typical of the style.

- Listen to some of Mozart's piano works, such as his Piano Concerto No. 24 in C minor, supposedly a favorite of Beethoven, or his Sonata No. 11 in A major, whose three movements are in theme and variations form, minuet and trio form, and rondo form, defying the convention of including sonata form in the first movement of a piano sonata. Compare the motives, forms, and other musical features to those of Beethoven's piano music. What are the similarities and differences? Do you have a preference for one or the other of these compositions?

- Listen to Beethoven's String Quartet, Op. 18, No. 3, Mvt II: Minuet and Trio and compare it to the Haydn Minuet and Trio in Chapter 6, Gateway 22. Both were composed within a year or two of one another.

GATEWAY 26
MUSIC OF THE ATLANTIC SLAVE TRADE[45]

What Is It?

Our gateway to music of the Atlantic slave trade is a recording of a song for an African-derived Brazilian religion called ***Candomblé*** (pronounced kahn-dom-BLEH). This religion focuses on a pantheon of male and female deities called ***orixás*** (pronounced o-ri-SHAZ). Each *orixá* controls a domain of nature or human life (water, war, thunder and lightning, disease, and so forth) and has favorite colors, foods, songs, percussion rhythms, and dances. This recording is titled *Ijexá for Oxum. Ijexá* (pronounced ee-zhe-SHA) is a dance and percussion rhythm named for a town in Nigeria where the Yoruba people live. *Oxum* (pronounced oh-SHOON) is a female *orixá* associated with water, fertility, beauty, and vanity. Her color is yellow. Jorge Alabê (ZHOR-gee a-la-BEH), a well-known master drummer and *Candomblé* initiate from Brazil who lives in San Francisco, leads a small ensemble with a two-pitch bell player and three drummers, who also sing. Alabê is an honorific name for a master of the tradition. He plays the lead, low-pitched drum and sings the lead solo part.

 Listen to the first thirty seconds of the recording.

How Does It Work?

Timbre

The sound consists of three barrel-shaped drums (*atabaque*, pronounced a-ta-BA-kee) of different sizes (low, medium, and high pitched), a two-pitch (low and high) iron bell (*agogô*), solo male voice, and male chorus.

Texture

The texture consists of a soloist and unison chorus singing over an accompaniment of four interlocking percussion parts.

Rhythm

An eight-beat meter is expressed in different rhythms (polyrhythms) on the bell and three drums. The singers sing syllabically without a lot of rhythmic variety. The rhythm of the bell can be written like this, where H = the high pitch; L = the low pitch; and - = rest:

1 &	2 &	3 &	4 &	5 &	6 &	7 &	8 &
H H	- L	- L	L -	H -	H -	L -	L -

Melody

The melodies consist of short descending phrases moving stepwise through a narrow-range, four-pitch or five-pitch (pentatonic) scale.

Harmony

There is no harmony. The singers sing solo and in unison.

FIGURE 6.17
Modern oil painting by Joseph Nunes of *Oxum* portraying her personality (vanity), color (yellow), and the water she controls
Source: Wikimedia Commons.

FIGURE 6.18
Jorge Alabê playing a drum (*atabaque*)

Form

The drummers play repeating rhythmic patterns with variations by the lead drummer, who plays the lowest-pitched drum. The singers sing a set of six slightly different songs, each based on one line of text. Each song has a solo-and-chorus, call-and-response structure.

Performance Techniques

The drums are played with the hands using damped and ringing sounds in the center and edge of the drumhead.

 Listen to the first thirty seconds of this performance with attention to the call-and-response structure of the performance and polyrhythmic drum part.

Timed Listening Guide

The six songs in this recording are in a language called Anago, which is descended from a dialect of the Yoruba language in Nigeria. Using a rich set of metaphors and allusions within a complicated theology, the songs evoke ideas and stories about *Oxum* and the town, spelled Ijesha, and the Ogun region of Nigeria where these practices are believed to have originated. After the bell and drums enter one at a time, the lead singer salutes *Oxum*, calling her "mother" (*ye ye*). The songs call her mother of the river and a princess from the town of Ijexá (Ijesha) in the Ogun region, and they ask the devotees to behold her beauty. The x is pronounced like sh in English.

Listen again to the performance following this timed listening guide.

LISTENING GUIDE 6.5

TIME	SECTION	DESCRIPTION	WORDS
0:00	Instrumental intro	The bell enters followed by the three drums in turn from highest to lowest pitch	
0:13	Salutation to *Oxum*	The lead singer enters with a short descending phrase of two pitches a minor third apart (G-E)	*Ye ye O*
0:17	Song 1	The lead singer sings a four-pitch solo melody (B-A-G-E) followed by chorus. They sing the song four times.	*Ye ye o ye ye xolodo*
1:06	Song 2	The solo singer introduces a new melody, adding new pitches higher in the range to create a descending pentatonic scale (E-D-B-A-G-E). The chorus responds, and they sing the song five times.	*A da ba o umafe*
1:38	Song 3	The singer starts a new song with choral response, sung four times.	*[I]jexa moro bogum*
2:04	Song 4	A new melody with choral response, sung six times.	*Ojo ma tindo lara ojo*
2:43	Song 5	After a brief pause a new melody is introduced a half-step higher with choral response, sung six times.	*A oro um maleixe are orô mimoriô*
3:26	Song 6	A final new melody is introduced a half-step lower on the original pitch. The chorus responds, and the song is sung three times.	*Orixalá coma kenké*
4:01	End		

CULTURAL LINKAGES

What Does It Mean?

This recording takes on meaning in a number of ways: (1) in relation to an elaborate religious system, *Candomblé*; (2) in relation to the religious rituals in which this song, and others like it, might be performed; and (3) in relation to the history of the tradition, which devotees trace to similar religions along the west coast of Africa, home to the present-day countries of Nigeria, Ghana, Benin, and Angola. *Candomblé* is concentrated in the cities of Salvador and Recife along the northeastern shore of Brazil. Enslaved Africans were brought to this region to work on sugar and tobacco plantations during the seventeenth and eighteenth centuries. Devotees, called *povo de santo* (people of the saint), originally were of African descent, but today they may be of any race.

Candomblé devotees undergo years of spiritual training after which they may be able to go into trance and be possessed by the *orixá* who has become their spiritual "mother" or "father." Performances of songs like "Ijexá for Oxum" occur during ceremonies called *festas* held in ceremonial houses (*casas*) or yards (*terreiros*), each controlled by a spiritual "family." There may be a hundred or more of these in a large city like Recife. *Festas* begin in the early evening and last into the morning hours. Forty or more participants wear white clothing, some with colored accessories associated with their deity. During the ceremony the drummers, called by the honorific title *alabê*, perform a variety of songs and rhythms each one associated with a particular *orixá*. While the lead drummer sings and the drummers drum, the participants dance and sing the choral responses, sometimes in improvised harmony. If conditions are right, some devotees may become visibly emotional while dancing to and singing the songs of their *orixá*. At that point the drummers and lead singer intensify their performance, hoping that the devotee will quickly become possessed. Those possessed

CULTURAL LINKAGES

FIGURE 6.19
Map of Brazil with the cities of Recife and Salvador

FIGURE 6.20
Map of the slave-trading regions of Africa

typically cry out and fall to the ground, at which point caretakers surround them, wipe off sweat, hold them, and stand them up so they may dance while possessed. For devotees, possession is a hoped-for result of participation in the ceremony. Emotional attachment to their spiritual father or mother functions as a psychological and emotional release from the tensions of everyday life, in a safe place surrounded by other devotees.

Lyrics, melodies, drum rhythms, and dances are associated with the potential presence of a particular *orixá*. Some of the rhythms are iconic signs: a slow tempo may represent the movements of an *orixá* in the form of an old man. Normally only those devotees who have pledged themselves to a particular *orixá* become possessed when they hear, sing, and dance to that *orixá*'s song. Occasionally an uninitiated person will go into trance, but musicians never do while performing.

FIGURE 6.21
Candomblé
possession
Source: Sylvia
McIntyre-Crook.

What Is Its History?

Devotees and most Brazilians understand *Candomblé* as having its roots in West African religious practices, which have an analogous set of deities, many with similar names. The language of "Ijexá for Oxum" contains words and phrases transmitted from a dialect of the Yoruba language of Nigeria. By the same token, many Brazilians interpret these religious practices as symbols of Brazilian national identity.

The Portuguese initiated the transatlantic slave trade in 1526, and over the next three centuries nearly five million enslaved Africans were brought to Brazil, the most of any country in the Americas. Brazil abolished slavery in 1888, the last country in the Americas to do so. Of the estimated twelve million Africans shipped to the Americas, 50 percent arrived during the eighteenth century. Many worked on the Caribbean islands in present-day Cuba, Puerto Rico, the Dominican Republic, Jamaica, and Trinidad and Tobago. Around 450,000 ended up in the United States.

Enslaved Africans brought with them knowledge, skills, aesthetic preferences, and religious beliefs learned in Africa and, to the extent possible, kept them alive in the New World. Similar African-derived religious practices, including call-and-response singing with African words accompanied by polyrhythmic drum ensembles in honor of deities, survive in Cuba under the name *Santería*

**CULTURAL
LINKAGES**

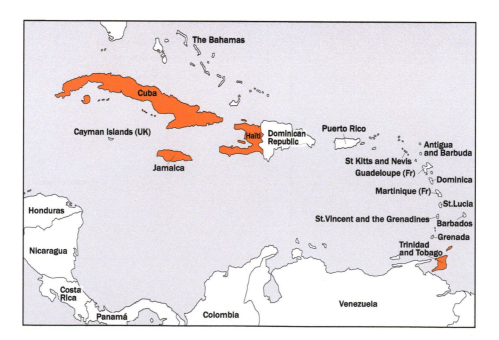

FIGURE 6.22
**Map of the
Caribbean**

(the worship of saints) and in Haiti with the name *Vodou* (from the name of a similar West African religion, *Vodun*). The Catholic Church condemned these African religious practices as witchcraft and at various times banned them. But the enslaved Africans kept them alive. One way to gain the acceptance of the church was to link the Africans' pantheon of deities to the names and symbolism of Catholic saints, hence the name *Santería*. For example, *Oxum* (*Ochún* in *Santería*) is linked to the Virgin Mary and shares some of her symbology; *Oxóssi*, the deity of the hunt is linked to St. George, who slayed a dragon in return for a kingdom's conversion to Christianity; and *Omolu*, the deity of disease and medicine is linked to St. Lazarus, whom Jesus raised from the dead. The historical record contains references to these practices, including one observer in 1790 who wrote, "the blacks divided by Nations dance with the instruments unique to each one."[46] The word "Nations" refers to African ethnic groups brought to Brazil. Today those nations are preserved not as ethnic groups but as slightly different religious practices under the umbrella of *Candomblé*, a term that appeared in print in 1807. Although the songs, rhythms, dances, and beliefs of *Candomblé* clearly have their roots in Africa, all these elements have surely changed over the nearly five centuries since enslaved Africans were first brought to Brazil.

FIGURE 6.23
Dancing Ogun, the *orixá* of iron, blacksmiths, warriors, and drivers
Source: Toluaye, Wikimedia Commons.

The African musical legacy in Brazilian culture, especially the polyrhythmic drum rhythms, continues to resonate in various forms of popular music up to the present. The most ubiquitous genre, **samba**, permeates Brazilian musical life: at the pre-Lenten Carnival and at patron saint festivities, marches, birthday parties, and soccer matches. In the 1920s and 1930s popular dance bands modeled on U.S. jazz bands referred to their music, some based on samba rhythms, as *samba-canção* (samba-song). One of the most famous of these samba singers, Carmen Miranda (1909–1955), "the ambassador of samba," starred in American movies in the 1940s. In the 1950s Brazilian musicians combined samba rhythms, transposed onto the guitar, with the smooth vocal style of jazz to create a genre called *bossa nova* (new thing). Successor genres include *música popular brasileira* (Brazilian popular music) or *MBP*, noted for its political lyrics, and *samba/pagode* (samba/celebration), a contemporary commercial music. Under the rubric "Latin music," the legacy of the transatlantic slave trade, especially its rhythms, permeates the popular music not just of Brazil but of Spanish- and French-speaking Central and South America as well in such genres as *son cubano* from Cuba, *cumbia* from Colombia, *merengue* and *bachata* from the Dominican Republic, *zouk* from Haiti, and cosmopolitan genres such as Latin jazz, salsa, and *música tropical*.

WHERE DO I GO FROM HERE?

- Listen to a hip-hop group called Opanijé performing a tune called "Se diz."

- Listen to a jazz orchestra called Rumpilezz (also Letieres Leite & Orkestra Rumpliezz) who play a tune called "Feira de Sete Portas," which uses the *ijexá* rhythm but alters the meter to 7.

- Watch a video of a *Candomblé* ceremony.

- Listen to famous samba singer Clara Nunes (1942–1983) sing the song "Ijexá (Filhos De Ghandi)," a song that uses the *ijexá* rhythm. Filhos De Ghandi (Sons of Gandhi) is a famous "street *Candomblé*" group (*afoxé*) from Salvador.

- Listen to the song "Beleza pura" (Pure Beauty) written and sung by composer and guitarist Caetano Veloso (b. 1942), noted for his contributions to *bossa nova* and *MPB*.

CLOSING

During the second half of the eighteenth century, European composers elevated tunefulness, straightforward homophonic accompaniments, and the expression of multiple affects in a single movement over such elements of Baroque musical style as imitative counterpoint, elaborate figuration, and the expression of a single affect in a single movement. Instrumental music competed with vocal music, especially opera, for the favor of audiences by absorbing many of opera's expressive conventions. Secular music surpassed religious music as the principal medium of compositional practice. And public concerts, music lessons for the wealthy merchant and bourgeois classes, and royalties from published compositions began to supplant courtly patronage as the means of support for composers, who began to regard themselves, and were regarded by their audiences and critics, as artists and not merely as servants and craftsmen.

During the nineteenth century the compositions of Haydn, Mozart, and Beethoven came to be viewed as the finest representatives of the European musical tradition. They became the "classics" and the masterpieces against which all future composers and their works would be measured. And the African-derived religious music of Catholic countries in Latin America and the Caribbean provided the roots of the proliferation of Latin popular music styles beginning in the nineteenth century and continuing to the present. Both the European music and the African-derived music of this period might be said to represent triumphs of human creativity, one supported by unimaginable wealth and the other in response to unimaginable degradation.

THINGS TO THINK ABOUT

- Nearly all cultures have used music to connect humans to the supernatural world. Compare the way *Candomblé* devotees use music in their religious ceremonies to the way Medieval Christians, Muslims, Tibetan Buddhists, and the Shona people have used it. Are there any patterns in the use of music in these different religious traditions?

- Some of the music of this period is meant to be pleasurable in an abstract way that depends on the attractive combination of its musical elements, and some of it is meant to express emotions in some way. Do you favor one or the other of these approaches in the music you listen to? If so, which one and why do you favor it? If not, why not?

NEW TERMS

Candomblé	minuet and trio	sonata form
chamber ensemble	opus (Op.)	string quartet
development	*orixás*	symphony
downbeat	piano	syncopation
exposition	recapitulation	theme
fortepiano	rondo form	theme and variations form
melodic motive	samba	
minuet	*Singspiel*	upbeat/offbeat

MUSIC FROM THE EARLY NINETEENTH CENTURY (1800–1850)

EUROPEANS SPENT MUCH of the nineteenth century working through the political and social implications of the American, French, and Haitian revolutions. These revolutions had opened the Pandora's box of freedom and the right of the public to rule itself free of monarchical tyranny. As a result, the political life of nineteenth-century Europe and the United States was quite volatile. Antagonism to the old order sprang up from many quarters, fueled by opposition to slavery and the horrid working conditions for laborers in the new factories of the Industrial Revolution. This political ferment fueled musical ferment as well. As radicals challenged monarchs, emperors, and slave-owners, the elegant style of the late eighteenth century was no longer adequate for the times. Mozart had perhaps anticipated the French Revolution in *The Marriage of Figaro* and Beethoven's emotional *Pathétique* sonata was suggestive of musical changes to come. But an even more emotional, occasionally unhinged mode of making music was needed to express the growing experience of instability in the economic and political spheres of nineteenth-century Europe.

Another revolution, the **Industrial Revolution**, was less a single revolutionary moment and more a long period that began in the U.K. in the late eighteenth century at about the same time as the American, French, and Haitian revolutions. Its innovations in manufacturing, transportation, and communication had many practical and musical consequences. The invention of the steam engine, in 1775, powered looms that wove textiles much more quickly than before and enriched producers who sold vast quantities of material for clothing. By mid-century locomotives for trains had lessened travel times between, and knitted together, far-flung communities. The installation of gas lighting indoors and outdoors allowed factories to stay open after dark and be even more productive. And nightlife developed along well-lit city streets. More efficient and precise methods of casting iron led to a stronger metal and to the building of massive structures including iron bridges, the first in 1778 in England, and the Eiffel Tower in 1889. Cast iron and steel frames for pianos allowed more strings to be held under greater tension, which increased the piano's range, enriched its tone quality, and lengthened the decay of each tone.

The deployment of these production aids allowed large numbers of workers to gather in one factory and for factory owners to accumulate great wealth through manufacturing. Factory workers' wages inspired people to move from the countryside to the city in search of wage labor. Cities became the home to three new urban social classes: (1) the **bourgeoisie** (a French word denoting a city dweller), consisting of lawyers, insurance agents, accountants, bankers, and financiers, to serve (2) **capitalists**, the new class of factory-owning manufacturers who needed the management skills of the bourgeoisie to run their businesses, who hired (3) the **proletariat**, the laborers who produced the goods manufactured in newly efficient factories. Capitalists seeking to make cities more livable formed civic symphonic societies, built concert halls, and patronized classical concerts. The bourgeoisie had the money to buy tickets, fill the halls, and hire professional musicians as music teachers for their daughters, for whom playing the piano became a sign of education and good

TECHNOLOGY

ECONOMIC ACTIVITY

FIGURE 7.1
Steam locomotive *Hibernia*, built in 1834
Source: Wikimedia Commons.

breeding, a "social accomplishment." In the United States the bourgeoisie and the proletariat constituted the audience for a new form of popular entertainment, the minstrel show, which we will introduce in this chapter. Improved manufacturing techniques and advanced engineering led to the addition of valves to brass instruments, which increased their versatility for performing in all the keys of tonal music and led to their integration into large orchestras that filled the grand concert halls built in the nineteenth century with sound and with adoring audiences.

Early-nineteenth-century music was also influenced by a new worldview and theory of art called Romanticism, which developed toward the end of the eighteenth century and flourished during the first half of the nineteenth century. Today the word romantic has two common meanings. It refers to expressions and displays of affection for another person and to suggestions that are unrealistic or too idealistic. During the early nineteenth century, the terms **Romantic** and **Romanticism** referred to expressions in literature, music, and painting of an artist's interior experiences of passion, restlessness, longing, and striving. This chapter explores the emotionality and Romanticism of the period through three gateways: a symphony by Ludwig van Beethoven, a symphony by the Frenchman Hector Berlioz, and a short piano piece by Polish emigré to Paris Frédéric Chopin. In addition the chapter includes a first look at American popular music and the way it responded to the institution of slavery during the first half of the nineteenth century.

GATEWAY 27
BEETHOVEN'S SYMPHONIES

What Is It?

Our gateway to Ludwig van Beethoven's (1770–1827) symphonies is the first movement of his Symphony No. 5 in C Minor, Op. 67. Premiered in 1808 at a concert he produced to showcase his compositions and piano skills, it is the most famous composition in all of European classical music. Hungarian-born conductor Sir Georg Solti (1912–1997) leads the Vienna Philharmonic in this recording.

 Listen to the first thirty seconds of the recording.

How Does It Work?

Timbre

The sound is created by an orchestra. In addition to the strings, the clarinet, horn (sometimes called the French horn), bassoon, flute, and oboe sound prominently in brief solo roles and trumpet and timpani create excitement at various points.

Texture

The textures are rich and varied and feature important unison and solo passages.

Rhythm

The meter is duple. A striking four-note rhythmic motive (short–short–short–long), marked by a pause, opens the movement and is heard throughout, creating a strong sense of unity.

Melody

The opening melody is built up from the opening motive. The second theme is longer and dissolves into its constituent motives, in one point to a single tone.

Harmony

The harmony is tonal, starting and ending in C minor with excursions to other keys.

Form

Sonata form organizes the work at the macro level. At the micro level the opening rhythmic motive, heard throughout as melody and accompaniment, is also an important formal element.

Performance Techniques

Dynamics provide perhaps the most striking performance element. Long crescendos build excitement, as do sudden changes from loud to soft and soft to loud.

Listen to the first fifty seconds of the recording and notice the different treatments of the opening four-note motive.

Listen to the entire recording following this timed listening guide, which outlines the form and some of the features of the piece.

LISTENING GUIDE 7.1

TIME	SECTION	DESCRIPTION
0:03	**Exposition**	
0:03	First theme (A)	The movement opens with two forte statements by the strings of a short–short–short–long motive in sequence followed by a soft melody built on that motive. After a dramatic crescendo, the theme ends with a long-held tone played by the violins.
0:22	First theme (A')	A varied repeat of the first theme with another long crescendo ending in two loud chords. The short–short–short–long motive is introduced as an accompaniment figure in the basses.
0:47	Second theme (B)	A horn call announces the second theme, a soft, lyrical melody played first by the orchestra, then the clarinet, then the orchestra, finally ending with another long crescendo and some transitional material.
1:09	Third theme (C)	A new melody in pulsatile rhythm is introduced ending with a loud cadence based on the short–short–short–long rhythmic motive, followed by a pause.
1:28	**Exposition repeats**	
2:55	**Development**	
2:55	Section 1	A solo horn plays the opening motive answered by the orchestra. The opening motive is then traded, like a question and answer, among the instruments of the orchestra ending in a long crescendo.
3:31	Section 2	The strings enter with the same melody from the second theme horn call, which during this section is reduced to two tones and then to one tone with a decrescendo to piano.
4:04	Section 3	The opening motive re-enters suddenly and loudly and alternates with the soft horn motive followed by another long crescendo.
4:17	**Recapitulation**	The opening motive returns, this time very loudly and played by the full orchestra including trumpets and timpani. At the end of the first statement of the first theme, instead of the violins' held tone,

continued

TIME	SECTION	DESCRIPTION
		an oboe holds the tone and plays a short unaccompanied melody. The second theme horn call is played by the bassoon instead of the horn. The recapitulation ends with a rush to the now familiar cadence introduced in the exposition.
5:56	**Coda**	Instead of stopping at the cadence as expected, the full orchestra continues loudly playing what amounts to a second development section.
5:56	Section 1	The full orchestra plays the opening motive loudly in different ways until some new melodic material is introduced.
6:26	Section 2	A new, ascending theme is introduced and varied.
7:00	Section 3	The recapitulation, with full orchestra, seems to begin again but is abruptly cut short with three forte playings of the opening motive and ten loud cadential block chords.
7:24	End	

What Does It Mean?

AESTHETICS

Part of the meaning of this piece resides in its relationship to the expectations of eighteenth-century audiences steeped in the music of Haydn and Mozart and the elegant style they had developed. It fulfills those expectations by working within the conventions of sonata form and the fast-tempo opening movement of a Classical symphony. But Beethoven stretched those conventions in new ways, deepening the expressive possibilities of the style. He expanded the coda, the tail at the end of the movement, from a slightly extended ending to a lengthy second development, even introducing a new theme almost halfway through the coda. His cadences at the end of the movement, and at the end of the entire symphony, are loud and long, as if he felt that the excursions to other keys created such instability that they required the insistent reiteration of the tonic key. His long crescendos from piano to forte add drama, as do the sudden pauses and abrupt shifts from loud to soft. Finally, Beethoven took the Classical-style practice of breaking melodies into their constituent motives to a new extreme in this movement: he started with a motive and built not only a melody, but many melodies, accompaniments, and the entire movement from a single tiny melodic and rhythmic cell. He may have learned this from Haydn, and it is anticipated in the first movement of Mozart's Symphony No. 40.

Part of the explanation of the dramatic elements in this movement in C minor, and the related drama in his *Pathétique* Piano Sonata, No. 8 (Chapter 6, Gateway 25), might be the drama in Beethoven's life. His childhood in Bonn was marred by his father's alcoholism. In 1789, at age eighteen, he sued to receive half his father's salary to support him and his two younger brothers, whom he cared for. In Vienna, his letter of introduction from the Elector of Cologne gave him access to the salons of the aristocracy, including their daughters of marriageable age. But any romantic interest he might have had in them, including one he addressed in a letter as "Immortal Beloved," went unrequited. Their families would not allow them to marry a commoner and a musician of modest financial means. If those refusals were not galling enough, Beethoven, although he depended on wealthy nobles for financial support, regarded himself as their equal as a human being. Inspired by the French Revolution's ideals of *liberté, egalité,* and *fraternité,* he deeply resented any demands or interference his patrons made on his art, a position that Haydn was not free to take with his patron, Prince Nikolaus Esterházy. Finally, his hearing worsened significantly between 1798 and 1808. In 1801 his letters to a friend described his anguish and his reluctance to engage others socially lest they discover his growing deafness.

Another understanding of the dramatic quality of this movement of Beethoven's Fifth Symphony is a Romantic one, that is, as a representation of the internal personal anguish and loneliness he was feeling at this time in his life. For example, one common interpretation of the opening short–short–short–long motive is as an icon of knocking at the door, specifically fate knocking at the door. Whose fate? Beethoven's? Presumably. The roiling character of the movement created by the changes in dynamics and its minor key seem to suggest a fate beset with personal problems. The horn call and second theme may represent one hoped-for solution to the problem. In 1802 his doctors recommended that he retreat to the countryside for the sake of his mental and physical health. He sought refuge from his troubles by walking and working outside Vienna from time to time. Horn calls in European classical music had long referenced rural hunting horns, and the lyrical second theme suggests a hoped-for respite from inner turmoil in the outdoors. The overall arc of the movement, in which the first theme dominates throughout and at the end, suggests that the cure was only temporary. On the other hand, the symphony ends with a fourth movement in C major rather than the more conventional C minor of the first movement. Beethoven, referencing centuries of associations between mode and mood (major = happiness, minor = sadness), fended off any criticism of his choice of key by saying, "Joy follows sorrow, sunshine [follows] rain."[47]

🔊 *Listen one more time to this performance for pleasure, paying attention to the shifting drama in the music and the possibility of its expression of Beethoven's inner life.*

Beethoven occasionally wrote in his scores that a movement should be played "with innermost feeling," an indication that he understood his music as the expression of those feelings. In fact, Beethoven's music is often interpreted as perhaps the earliest example of music as an externalization of the inner emotional life of the composer or musician. Dating back to the Medieval period, European classical music had developed the ability to represent exterior natural scenes and sounds, the contents of a painting, and the emotions and ideas of a poem, song lyric, or opera libretto. The theory of art called Romanticism, which developed during Beethoven's lifetime, claimed that literature, painting, and music was at its best when it expressed an artist's interior emotions. The interpretation of Beethoven's compositions and an expression of his emotional life was something new for European music, something that made Beethoven an early exemplar of Romanticism in music.

FIGURE 7.2
Bell Rock Lighthouse
Source: Painting by J. M. W. Turner (1818). Scottish National Gallery, Wikimedia Commons.

Although Beethoven may have sought some solace during pleasant strolls outside Vienna, the Romantics prized the complexity, irregularity, volatility, and fierceness of nature as a mirror of inner human turmoil, and they valued an artist's ability to represent those qualities in art. For example, paintings of country scenes and sunsets were called Romantic. The turbulent, brooding landscapes and seascapes of the English painter J. M. W. Turner (1775–1851) exemplify Romanticism in visual art. Beethoven was to do something similar in his Sixth Symphony, also premiered in 1808.

In German literature, one of the progenitors of Romanticism was Johann Wolfgang von Goethe (1749–1832), a polymath famous today as the author of the epic two-part "closet play" (meant to be read rather than staged) *Faust*, about a doctor who made a tragic deal, "a Faustian bargain," with the devil. (A performance takes about fifteen hours to read!) The first part was published in 1808, the year Beethoven's Symphony No. 5 debuted in concert. His earlier novel, *The Sorrows of Young Werther* (1774), helped to launch Romanticism as a literary movement. In it, a passionate young man's unrequited love for a woman who marries another man (reminiscent of Beethoven's life) leads him to suicide. The book seems to have emerged from Goethe's own emotional turmoil at the age of twenty-four: as an old man he wrote of it, "That was a creation which I, like the pelican, fed with the blood of my own heart."[48] This link between inner passion and outer creativity was one of the hallmarks of Romanticism. The English poet-laureate William Wordsworth (1770–1850), born the same year as Beethoven, argued that poetry should spring from "the spontaneous overflow of powerful feelings."[49] He and other Romantic poets fed the idea that poetry, and by extension of music and painting, were expressing the poet's, composer's, or painter's emotions. In this intellectual environment, the works of Beethoven were interpreted in much the same way. In 1810, just two years after the premier of Beethoven's Symphony No. 5, the German writer and composer E. T. A. Hoffmann (1776–1822) wrote that Beethoven's music expresses human pain and longing in a "concord of all the passions."

CULTURAL LINKAGES ▷ Many of the ideas about music that people take for granted today have their origins in the Romantic view that works of literature, music, and painting express the inner world of the artist. At least four ideas associated with the Romanticism of this period continue to resonate in European classical music to this day: (1) the concept of the genius, (2) reverence for the work of art, (3) the notion that musicians are expressing their "innermost feelings" when they perform, and (4) musicians' obligation to perform a composer's music just as he (and nearly all European composers were men) intended them to. In Romantic terms, a genius was an artist who could create a completely original work not indebted to previous work. Until the end of the eighteenth century, composers were considered skilled craftsmen. Under the unceasing demands of secular and religious patrons, they routinely borrowed from their own previous work, and that of other composers, and fit their compositions into well-established stylistic norms if only to meet their deadlines. Haydn, Mozart, and Beethoven were probably the first composers accorded the exalted status of "genius."

EMOTIONAL RESONANCE ▷ If a musical genius was expressing his "innermost feelings" in the composition, it followed that the musicians who played the work must access their own innermost feelings to produce them in sound. This idea gave rise to the sorts of performance mannerisms typical of solo and chamber recitals today: closed eyes, furrowed brows, serious faces, and swaying bodies. Audiences are supposed to understand these as external signs of internal emotions. And they probably help musicians and their audience feel those emotions.

AESTHETICS ▷ In addition to interpreting Beethoven's compositions as highly personal expressions of his own inner states rather than as mere text painting or entertainment, early nineteenth-century music critics began to regard his work as art, a concept given new meaning during this period by Enlightenment philosophers. For most of their history, Europeans regarded art as the skillful making of something. Art was synonymous with mastery of a craft whether painting, cabinet making, or playing and composing music. Today these master makers of things are called craftspeople and artisans, and their work is called artisanal. This definition puts a great deal of emphasis on the makers of art and their ability to create something useful and well made. This equation of art and craft was challenged during the Enlightenment when the German philosopher Immanuel Kant (1724–1804), in his *Critique of Judgment* (1790), linked art to aesthetic judgments of the beautiful, the sublime, the good, and the agreeable. Kant was interested less in the making of art and more in art's supposed ability to generate sensory experiences that could be judged aesthetically as beautiful or ugly, tasteful or crude, good or bad. Such aesthetic verdicts, he suggested, could be based on substantive qualities in the work of art itself, qualities such as elegance, balance, complexity, and the like. Written during Beethoven's lifetime, this Enlightenment view of art affected the reception of Beethoven's work as art in this new sense.

If the composed work was an example of art, it followed that the performer's principal obligation was to render it as accurately as possible according to the composer's artistic intentions. This was a new idea in the history of European music. Up to this point, some solo instrumentalists and opera singers had treated the composer's written music as a template on which to add their own interpretations through ornamentation, variation, and improvisation. Kant's ideas suggested that the composer was the true artist, and artisanal performers were reduced to servants of the composer's art. One of the most influential figures to take this tack with respect to the works of Beethoven was E. T. A. Hoffman, perhaps best known for his novella *The Nutcracker and the Mouse King* (1816), which became the basis for Tchaikovsky's ballet *The Nutcracker* (1892). He argued that musicians had a "sacred" duty to perform the compositions of Beethoven with reverence, as if Beethoven were a musical god. This view of the obligation of performers to the compositions of composers is now a standard feature of much modern thinking about European classical music performance practice, but it was not always so.

What Is Its History?

A story goes that when a young music student was asked how many symphonies Beethoven composed, he answered, "Four: the third, the fifth, the sixth, and the ninth." Today, these four symphonies are his most admired, performed, and written about, and the child's answer speaks to a historical phenomenon known as canonization. **Canonization** is a selection process by which scholars, critics, performers, and audiences at a particular time in history come to regard certain works of art, literature, and music as the most important, the most influential, and possessing the greatest artistic merit. The selected works then form what is called a "canon," a word that originally meant "rule." Within the European classical music canon, some composers are judged, at particular moments in history, more worthy than others, and some of their compositions are judged more important than others. Canon makers include critics, music historians, and musicians. Over the years they have judged Beethoven's nine symphonies as among the most important and influential in the history of European classical music. Among these nine symphonies conductors and audiences have responded most positively to his third, fifth, sixth, and ninth symphonies. Musical canons and their subdivisions are not immutable, however, and they change as taste in music and other cultural values change.

European classical music enthusiasts routinely refer to this repertoire as "Great Music." Important works of European literature and philosophy are called "Great Books." These two canons, plus the European canon of great art, form the **Western canon**, a term that puts these works at odds with music, literature, and art from non-European traditions and new work by women, minorities, and people living outside the European cultural orbit. Thus, canonization has implications for cultural politics as, for example, when teachers and professors argue over which works of literature, art, and music, especially those outside the Western canon, deserve to be included in school and college curricula.

Beethoven waited until five years after he had published his Opus 1 in 1795 to premier his first orchestral works for a concert in 1800: a piano concerto, which he played, and Symphony No. 1 in C Major, which he conducted. He wrote these works in the elegant style of Haydn and Mozart, but, as if to announce that he was prepared to stretch the boundaries of the style, he began his first symphony with an ending, a cadence from V to I rather than the usual statement of the theme in the tonic key. A musical joke, it was perhaps a nod to his teacher Haydn's fondness for little musical jokes like this. Symphony No. 2, premiered in 1803, also closely adhered to the conventions of the Classical symphony.

Symphony No. 3 was written in 1804, the year Napoleon declared himself emperor of France. Beethoven had welcomed the French Revolution against ruling-class privilege, which he abhorred. Believing Napoleon to be the Revolution's savior after the murderous excesses of the early revolutionaries, he had planned to dedicate this symphony to "Buonaparte." The news of Napoleon's tyrannical ambitions infuriated the composer. He ripped up the title page and in 1806 published it with the dedication *Sinfonia Eroica . . . composta per festeggiare il sovvenire di un grand Uomo* (heroic symphony . . . composed to celebrate the memory of a [once?] great man). That story—with its drama seemingly expressed in the music—and its length (at fifty minutes of performance time, it is about twice as long as the typical Classical-period symphony and his own Symphony No. 1)

> CULTURAL
> LINKAGES

> POLITICAL
> ACTION

FIGURE 7.3
Beethoven in 1804
Source: Painting by Josef Willibrord Mähler (1778–1860). Museen der Stadt Wien, Wikimedia Commons.

AESTHETICS

have led many music historians to regard his Third Symphony as the opening salvo of a new period in European music history: the Romantic period. Symphony No. 4 debuted in 1807 and, although full of Beethoven's characteristic energy, retreats to the conventions and length of the Classical-period symphony.

The concert in 1808 at which Beethoven conducted his Symphony No. 5 lasted four hours, twice as long as a modern classical concert. The program consisted of eight pieces, including his Symphony No. 6 before intermission and his Symphony No. 5 in the second half. Both probably startled listeners. They would have expected the Fifth Symphony, in the key of C minor, to begin and end in C minor; instead its final movement is in C major, as if the veil over Beethoven's feelings in the first movement had lifted. The Sixth Symphony, begun in 1802 during his retreat to the countryside for his health, evokes pastoral scenes and sounds and came to be known as Beethoven's Pastoral Symphony. In a manner reminiscent of Vivaldi's Four Seasons concertos, he wrote descriptions of the references to natural sounds at the beginning of each of the five movements: (1) awakening of cheerful feelings upon arrival in the countryside; (2) scene by the brook; (3) merry gathering of country folk; (4) thunderstorm; and (5) shepherd's song; cheerful and thankful feelings after the storm. The Fifth and Sixth Symphonies, performed together at the same concert, must have made quite the contrasting impression: the sixth portraying a peaceful and calm, if unpredictable, external world, the fifth expressing agitated internal feelings.

After a pause of a few years, Beethoven presented his Symphony No. 7 in 1813 and Symphony No. 8 in 1814. Both are rather conventional in style and length. The Seventh Symphony features many sprightly dance melodies, and the second movement of the Eighth Symphony employs a constant pulse suggestive of both Baroque style and the second movement of Haydn's Clock Symphony (No. 101).

Ten years passed before Beethoven appeared again in public with his final symphony, Symphony No. 9 in D Minor, in 1824. In 1815 his personal life took a wretched turn when his brother Carl died, and Beethoven fought his widow for custody of their teenage son. He won, but the boy, miserable without his mother, attempted suicide in 1826. Isolated by his deafness and preoccupied with family troubles, Beethoven retreated from public life to compose his final, most profound works during this stressful period: three piano sonatas, his gigantic *Missa Solemnis*, and his Ninth Symphony.

Beethoven's Symphony No. 9 broke the bounds of the instrumental symphony with the addition, in the fourth movement, of four vocal soloists and a chorus singing "Ode to Joy," his adaptation of a poem by the Romantic poet Johann Christoph Friedrich von Schiller (1759–1805). It is the longest of his symphonies and takes about an hour to perform. The fourth movement alone takes twenty-five minutes, the length of a typical Classical-period symphony. The movement begins with a restatement and musical rejection of each of the themes of the first three movements before the melody of the poem "Ode to Joy" is introduced, accepted, and played in four variations. But at the point that might have ended a typical Classical-period symphony, a baritone soloist announces, "Oh friends, not these sounds! Let us instead strike up more pleasing and joyful ones!" And the chorus responds "Joy! Joy!", an indication that Beethoven had reached the end of his ability to express his emotions in music and sought the help of words. The ode is a Christian-inspired strophic hymn to the brotherhood of man that Beethoven elaborates through an extended set of vocal and instrumental variations.

In 1825 and 1826 Beethoven composed his last four of sixteen string quartets, considered by some the apotheosis of that genre, before dying in 1827. His nine symphonies, thirty-two piano sonatas, five piano concertos, a violin concerto, sixteen string quartets, and duets and trios for violin, cello and piano are among the most beloved in the standard repertoire of classical music today.

For the rest of the nineteenth century and into the twentieth century Beethoven's symphonies echoed in the consciousness of many classical composers, including Johannes Brahms, Anton Bruckner, and Gustav Mahler working in Vienna; Hector Berlioz in Paris; and Pyotr Ilyich Tchaikovsky and Dmitri Shostakovich in Russia. The scenic "painting" in his Sixth Symphony inspired many similar symphonies during the nineteenth century and a new symphonic genre called a **tone poem** or **symphonic poem**, a one-movement work in which the music tells a story or describes a scene. The Hungarian composer Franz Liszt called this kind of musical representation **programmatic music**, that is, music that expresses a textual narrative or program.

Beethoven's Fifth Symphony has assumed a prominent place in popular culture since its premier in 1808. The New York Philharmonic included it in its first concert in 1842. When Morse code, a combination of dots and dashes representing letters, was developed in the 1840s to send telegraphic signals, the pattern short–short–short–long was assigned to the letter V. During World War II the Allies began using the V sign, made with the fingers, to signal the hoped-for victory over the Germans. The opening of Beethoven's Fifth Symphony became an iconic sign of victory (V is also the Roman numeral for five). In the 1970s the first movement was included on the Voyager Golden Record sent into outer space. Nowadays the organist at Los Angeles Dodgers baseball games plays the two statements of the opening motive whenever a Dodger pitcher achieves victory by striking out a batter.

FIGURE 7.4
Beethoven in 1823
Source: Painting by Ferdinand Georg Waldmüller (1793–1865). Kunst Historisches Museum, Wien, Collection of Ancient Instruments.

WHERE DO I GO FROM HERE?

- Listen to a performance of the first movement of Beethoven's Symphony No. 5 by Leonard Bernstein and the New York Philharmonic and compare its emotional effects to those in this gateway recording. What in the performances creates those effects? Which do you prefer and why?

- Listen to the other three movements of Beethoven's Symphony No. 5. Notice the way the opening motive of the first movement returns in various forms in movements III and IV, creating a sense of unity across the entire symphony.

- Listen to a performance of the fourth, choral movement of Beethoven's Symphony No. 9, sometimes listed as Movements IV and V.

GATEWAY 28
PROGRAMMATIC ORCHESTRAL WORKS

What Is It?

Beethoven's symphonies inspired a century of symphonic music that is called programmatic, that is, it tells a story. The first and fourth movements of Hector Berlioz's (1803–1869) *Symphonie Fantastique: Épisode de la vie d'un artiste . . . en cinq parties* (Fantastical Symphony: An Episode in the Life of an Artist, in Five Parts) are our gateways to this tradition. Berlioz composed and first performed *Symphonie Fantastique* in 1830, just three years after Beethoven's death. A symphony in five movements, it combines the Romantic idea of art as an outward expression of inner passions with the idea, exemplified in Beethoven's Symphony No. 6 ("Pastoral"), that music can describe scenes and tell stories, in this case the composer's fantasies about the fate of his love for a famous English actress named Harriet Smithson.

 Listen to the first thirty seconds of the fourth movement.

FIGURE 7.5
Hector Berlioz in 1832
Source: Painting by Emile Signol
(1804–1892). Villa Medici, Rome,
Wikimedia Commons.

FIGURE 7.6
An ophicleide
Source: Crosby Brown Collection of
Musical Instruments. Metropolitan
Museum of Art, Wikimedia Commons.

How Does It Work?

Timbre

Berlioz expanded the Classical-period orchestra to include a larger string section, four instead of two bassoons, four timpanis, and instruments rarely used before in symphonic music: the ophicleide (a low-pitched, keyed brass instrument invented in 1817 and replaced later in the century by the tuba), two harps, and the **English horn** (a low-pitched relative of the oboe). He also created new timbral effects, such as having the violinists strike the strings with the wood of their bows (*col legno*, with wood) to create a rustling sound. Berlioz combined these instruments in new ways to create a variety of sonic effects capable of rendering his fantasies in music.

Texture

The polyphonic texture varies greatly, but Berlioz uses monophonic unisons and octaves to great effect.

Rhythm

The tempo and meter of the movements follow the conventions of the Classical symphony up to a point. Mvt. I begins with a slow introduction before the fast, main part of the movement. Mvt. IV is a march.

Melody

Each movement of the symphony has its own melodies, but one melody appears in varying forms in all five movements. That melody, played first in Mvt. I, represents the beloved, Harriet Smithson. Berlioz calls it his **idée fixe**, his obsession or mania. It is a long melody with an ever-rising pitch contour that seems to express his yearning for her love.

Harmony

The harmony is tonal with occasional loud dissonances to express the composer's troubled emotional life and fantasies.

Form

The first movement has some of the features of sonata form. The fourth movement march has some features of European dance form and some of theme and variations.

Performance Techniques

In addition to the *col legno* technique, Berlioz requires very high-pitched and low-pitched playing from the musicians and **glissandos** (slides) from the wind instruments, among other techniques. In the score he provides very detailed signs for crescendos and decrescendos for individual notes and phrases, all designed to increase the emotional impact of the music. His long crescendos and sudden changes from loud to soft are reminders of Beethoven's use of these techniques for expressive purposes.

What Does It Mean?

How Berlioz's *Symphonie Fantastique* works is inextricably tied to what it means. What it means is in turn linked to the shape of the entire symphony and its relationship to an "episode" in Berlioz's life.

As a music student in Paris, Berlioz attended performances in 1827 of Shakespeare's *Hamlet* and *Romeo and Juliet* by a traveling English theater company. He fell in love with Shakespeare, eventually learning English to be able to read the plays, and with the actress Harriet Smithson, who played Ophelia and Juliet. He bombarded her with love letters to no avail. In 1830 he composed his *Symphonie Fantastique* as an imaginary expression of his love sickness. For the symphony he wrote a **program**, a narrative describing the internal passions and thoughts represented in the music. In the timed listening guides for each movement, his program is given before the description of each movement, beginning with this preface:

> The composer's intention has been to develop, insofar as they contain musical possibilities, various situations in the life of an artist. The outline of the instrumental drama, which lacks the help of words, needs to be explained in advance. The following program should thus be considered as the spoken text of an opera, serving to introduce the musical movements, whose character and expression it motivates.

The timed listening guides that follow are for the first and fourth movements with some descriptions of the way the *idée fixe* appears in the other movements.

Mvt. I: Reveries. Passions (Largo, Allegro)

The author imagines that a young musician, afflicted by the sickness of spirit which a famous writer (François-René de Chateaubriand, 1768–1848) has called vague passions (*le vague des passions*), sees for the first time a woman who unites all the charms of the ideal person his imagination was dreaming of, and falls desperately in love with her. By a strange anomaly, the beloved image never presents itself to the artist's mind without being associated with a musical idea, in which he recognizes a certain quality of passion, but endowed with the nobility and shyness which he credits to the object of his love.

FIGURE 7.7
Harriet Smithson
Source: George Clint, Wikimedia Commons.

EMOTIONAL RESONANCE

This melodic image and its model keep haunting him ceaselessly like a double *idée fixe* (a musical and a psychological obsession). This explains the constant recurrence in all the movements of the symphony of the melody which launches the first allegro. The transitions from this state of dreamy melancholy, interrupted by occasional upsurges of aimless joy, to delirious passion, with its outbursts of fury and jealousy, its returns of tenderness, its tears, its religious consolations—all this forms the subject of the first movement.

Listen to the first 5:30 of Mvt. I, until the second theme is introduced, following this timed listening guide, which indicates the link between musical gestures and the composer's program.

TIME	SECTION	DESCRIPTION	PROGRAM
0:00	**Slow Introduction**		
0:00	Section 1	The opening is very quiet.	"melancholy reverie"
1:38	Section 2	A very fast melody enters and the music continues with a long crescendo followed by rising and falling melodies, pauses, and sudden changes in dynamics, all reminiscent of Beethoven's dramatic style.	"interrupted by a few fits of groundless joy"
4:53	**Allegro in quasi sonata form** **Exposition**		
4:53	Theme 1	A long melody with long phrases, each higher than the first. This is the *idée fixe*,	

LISTENING GUIDE 7.2

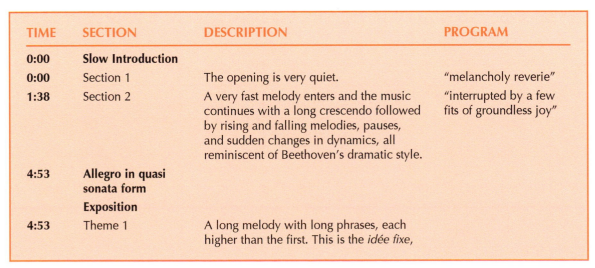

continued

TIME	SECTION	DESCRIPTION	PROGRAM
		whose rising pitches suggest increasing yearning for the beloved.	
5:30	Theme 2	New melodic ideas and thicker textures are introduced.	

The second movement, "A Ball," is a waltz, a popular triple-meter couple dance during the nineteenth century. Two sprightly melodies convey a carefree scene, but then the third melody, the *idée fixe*, enters quietly in the flute and oboe. They are accompanied by the strings playing motives from the waltz theme to suggest that his obsession with his beloved cannot be erased even on such a light-hearted occasion. The third movement, "Scene in the Countryside," uses the oboe and English horn, long symbols of the outdoors in European orchestral music, to evoke a peaceful pastoral scene. The *idée fixe* returns even in a setting where the artist has sought relief from his obsession.

Mvt. IV. Marche au Supplice (March to the Scaffold) (Allegretto non troppo)

Convinced that his love is unappreciated, the artist poisons himself with opium. The dose of the narcotic, too weak to kill him, plunges him into a sleep accompanied by the most horrible visions. He dreams that he has killed his beloved, that he is condemned and led to the scaffold, and that he is witnessing his own execution. The procession moves forward to the sound of a march that is now somber and fierce, now brilliant and solemn, in which the muffled noise of heavy steps gives way without transition to the noisiest clamor. At the end of the march the first four measures of the *idée fixe* reappear, like a last thought of love interrupted by the fatal blow.

Listen to the entire fourth movement following this timed listening guide.

LISTENING GUIDE 7.3

TIME	SECTION	DESCRIPTION
0:05	**Introduction**	Timpani open the movement, with punctuations in the low strings and muted horns.
0:31	A	The low strings leap up an octave and then play a descending stepwise minor-scale melody over nearly two octaves to create a musical picture of the composer's descent into hell and his slow steps to the gallows.
0:44	A'	The violas join the cellos and basses for a repeat of the theme, accompanied by a countermelody in four unison bassoons.
0:57	A''	The violins take the theme, now in major, while the lower strings play a countermelody of their own.
1:09	A'''	This treatment of the melody repeats.
1:21	A''''	Accompanied by the bassoon countermelody, the low strings play the descending theme in its original form, while the upper strings play it in inversion, that is, ascending, all of the strings playing *pizzicato*.
1:41	BB	The brasses, including the very low tuba, erupt with a syncopated marching tune in major, representing the triumph of justice for the artist's imagined evil deed. The section ends on a dissonant chord, suggesting the composer's disturbed emotional state.
2:05	**Repeats from the beginning**	

TIME	SECTION	DESCRIPTION
4:08	A	The A theme returns, this time with each note of the melody (or small groups of notes) being assigned a different group of instruments—including the bass drum and cymbals! This technique is called tone color melody. Its use here is one of the earliest examples in orchestral music.
4:19	BB	The marching tune returns, slightly re-orchestrated in the winds, and with an active accompaniment in the strings.
4:50	A	Berlioz repeats the tone color melody, but continues on with a driving statement of the A theme in the brass. The theme continues, gradually rising in both pitch and tension.
6:12	C	Just as the movement seems about to end, the orchestra abruptly stops as the clarinet sounds the *idée fixe*, the artist's final thought. It is interrupted by a loud attack from the full orchestra, representing the fall of the guillotine, followed by descending *pizzicato* pitches that depict the bouncing of the artist's severed head after its fall. The movement ends with triumphant chords signaling the delivery of justice and relief from the nightmare.
6:39	End	

The fifth movement, called "Dreams of a Witch's Sabbath," is full of unusual timbral and expressive effects that place the artist in a hell full "of a frightful troop of ghosts, sorcerers, monsters of every kind, come together for his funeral." The *idée fixe* is heard one final time, this time played by a clarinet in a high-pitched manner with glissandos that seems to mock the artist and his obsession.

What Is Its History?

Berlioz was born near the southeastern French town of Grenoble to a well-educated doctor. At twelve, relatively late in life for a future composer, Hector began studying guitar, but never learned to play piano or violin, the standard tools of most composers. The orchestra became his instrument. Sent by his father to study medicine in Paris but repulsed by the dissection table, he soon abandoned his medical studies in favor of long hours studying musical scores in the library of the Paris Conservatoire. Largely self-taught in counterpoint, he began private study of composition and was admitted to the conservatory in 1826 at the age of twenty-three. In 1828 he first heard Beethoven's symphonies, whose expressive range he expanded in his *Symphonie Fantastique*. In his memoirs he wrote, "I saw the giant form of Beethoven rear up. The shock was almost as great as that of Shakespeare had been. Beethoven opened before me a new world of music, as Shakespeare had revealed a new universe of poetry."[50]

In 1830, as a revolution broke out that would depose the French king (the monarchy had been restored after Napoleon's fall in 1814), he won the conservatory's prestigious composition prize, the Prix de Rome, which gave him a five-year stipend and the opportunity to study in Italy for two years. In 1833 Harriet Smithson finally agreed to marry him. They had a son the next year, but the marriage did not fulfill his Romantic dreams. They separated after a few years, but he continued to provide for her until she died in 1854.

Berlioz supported himself by organizing concerts of his works, much as Mozart and Beethoven had. But because he desired such large performing forces, these efforts were expensive and exhausting. To earn money, he turned to writing musical criticism and to conducting, at both of

FIGURE 7.8
"Cajetan," a caricature by Anton Elfinger lampooning Berlioz's grandiose effects and noisy instrumentation. Its title: "Fortunately the hall is solid . . . it can stand the strain!"
Source: Wikimedia Commons.

FIGURE 7.9

An unhappy Hector Berlioz in 1863 at age sixty
Source: Photograph by Pierre Petit (1832–1909). Biblioteque National de France, Wikimedia Commons

which he was extraordinarily gifted. He traveled around Europe, to England, Germany, and Russia, conducting his own work and those of others to great acclaim. Today he is regarded as one of the first great orchestral conductors. Although he enjoyed successes in Paris and around Europe, he seems to have felt underappreciated by the French public. Illness brought his composing to a halt in 1862, and he died, embittered, in 1869.

Composers outside France greatly admired Berlioz's compositions for the depth of their emotional expression and their innovative treatment of the orchestra. The Hungarian Franz Liszt (1811–1886), the German Richard Wagner (1813–1883), and Russians Pyotr Ilyich Tchaikovsky (1840–1893) and Nikolai Rimsky-Korsakov (1844–1908) all heard him conduct his works in concert. They carried his Romantic ideas and orchestral techniques into the second half of the nineteenth century. Liszt, for example, composed more than a dozen one-movement orchestral pieces he called symphonic poems, works that express emotions and tell stories through instrumental music. These in turn inspired a generation of late-nineteenth-century composers to write similar one-movement programmatic tone poems.

In 1844 Berlioz, having created all manner of new orchestral sounds in his compositions, published his *Grand traité d'instrumentation et d'orchestration modernes* (General Treatise on Instrumentation and Modern Orchestration), an influential book on **orchestration**, the art of composing for orchestral instruments singly and in combination. Composers studied it for decades. Like his compositions, it contributed mightily to the flowering of orchestral tone color in the late nineteenth century.

Until the first half of the nineteenth century, orchestras as permanent performing organizations existed mainly in commercial opera houses and the courts of wealthy aristocrats. Beethoven and Berlioz had to draw on those resources and freelance musicians to produce concerts of their orchestral music. The collapse of aristocratic patronage and the growing interest in instrumental music for orchestra during the first half of the nineteenth century led wealthy citizens in many cities in Europe and the United States to form civic organizations to support orchestras dedicated to instrumental music. The Philharmonic Society of London, formed in 1813, commissioned Beethoven's Ninth Symphony. They also invited the German composer Felix Mendelssohn (1809–1847) to visit many times. He wrote his Scottish Symphony and Hebrides Overture for performances there. The Royal Liverpool Philharmonic Orchestra was founded in 1840, and the Vienna and New York Philharmonic Orchestras were created in 1842. Today many orchestras in the United States carry the name "civic" to indicate their origins as organizations founded and supported by a city's community leaders.

Conservatories of music were another new source of patronage for orchestral music. The first was the Paris Conservatoire, founded in 1795 in the wake of the French Revolution. The Vienna Conservatory was founded in 1819 and The Royal Academy of Music in 1822. In 1828 The Concert Society of the Paris Conservatory was founded to support performances of symphonies by Beethoven, Mozart, and Haydn.

Conservatories spread widely in the second half of the nineteenth century, and in the 1860s conservatories were established in St. Petersburg and Moscow, as well as the first in the United States at Oberlin College in 1865.

WHERE DO I GO FROM HERE?

- Find a program for, and listen to a recording of, Modest Mussorgsky's (1839–1881) *Night on Bald Mountain* (1867), a tone poem.
- Find a program for, and listen to a recording of, Nikolai Rimsky-Korsakov's (1844–1908) *Scheherazade (1888)*, a four-movement programmatic orchestral suite.
- Find a program for, and listen to a recording of, Richard Strauss's (1864–1949) *Till Eulenspiegel's Merry Pranks* (1895), a tone poem.

GATEWAY 29
ROMANTIC-PERIOD PIANO MUSIC

What Is It?

Our gateway to Romantic piano music is Frédéric Chopin's (1810–1849) Waltz in C-sharp Minor, Op. 64, No. 2 composed in 1847. Born in Poland, Chopin lived his adult life in Paris. A **waltz** is a ballroom dance for couples in triple meter. This waltz is performed by Artur Rubinstein (1887–1982), who, like Chopin, was born in Poland. He was one of the most famous pianists of the mid-twentieth century.

 Listen to the first thirty seconds of the recording.

How Does It Work?

Timbre

A solo modern grand piano, with its relatively pure tone quality, plays throughout.

Texture

The texture consists of a high-pitched melody accompanied by alternating bass tone and chords.

Rhythm

The meter is triple. Artur Rubinstein plays some sections with a steady beat and some with **rubato** ("robbed time" in Italian), an unsteady beat or pulse created by slightly lengthening certain beats and slightly shortening others. In this performance the second of the three beats is sometimes slightly held and the third beat is sometimes slightly rushed. The melodic rhythms are quite varied: one melody uses long and short tones; another is pulsatile; and a third features syncopation.

Melody

The melodies consist of long, undulating phrases in minor and major keys with some chromaticism.

FIGURE 7.10

This photograph of Frédéric Chopin in 1849, the year of his death, by Louis-Auguste Bisson (1814–1876) may be the oldest photograph, using a technology called daguerreotype, of a European composer

Source: Music-Images/Alamy Stock Photo.

Harmony

The harmony is tonal with two sections in a minor key and one in a major key.

Form

The form is a version of European dance form: AABBCCBBAABB.

Performance Techniques

Rubinstein uses rubato in some sections but not others, and occasionally employs **accelerandos** (speeding up the tempo) and ritardandos or ritards (slowing down the tempo). The playing is *legato* throughout.

Listen to the first thirty seconds of this recording for the triple meter played with rubato.

Listen to the entire recording following this timed listening guide.

LISTENING GUIDE 7.4

TIME	FORM	DESCRIPTION
0:00	AA	The first melody features ascending leaps and descending scalar passages. Rubinstein plays the waltz meter relatively slowly. The triple meter is clear from the alternation of bass note and chords (bass–chord–chord), but the beat is not steady. He plays it with *rubato*.
0:46	BB	A new pulsatile melody alternating arpeggios with chromatic scales is introduced at a faster tempo with no *rubato*. The beat is steady. At the end of this section, Rubinstein slows the tempo, that is, he plays a *ritardando* or ritard, to signal the end of the section.
1:14	CC	A third melody is introduced in a slower tempo than the second section. The melody, which contains many tiny subdivisions of the beat, is syncopated against the triple meter in the left hand. Quite often an accented melody tone occurs on the third, weak beat of the triple-meter pattern. Try counting the 1-2-3 meter performed with *rubato* and hearing the accented note from time to time on beat 3.
1:54	BB	
2:18	AA	
3:06	BB	Rubinstein starts through the second (B) melody at a slower tempo than he did previous times and employs *accelerando* to speed up and then ends the performance with a ritard to a very high pitch.
3:40	End	

What Does It Mean?

AESTHETICS

Chopin, who arrived in Paris from Poland in 1831, the year after the premiere of Berlioz's *Symphonie Fantastique*, was in some sense Berlioz's opposite. Whereas Berlioz did not play the piano and wrote lengthy works for large orchestras with or without voices, Chopin, a virtuoso child prodigy on the piano in the mold of Mozart and Beethoven, wrote exclusively for the piano in very short forms, some pieces less than a minute long. Like Mozart and Beethoven, he used his piano compositions to show off his prodigious keyboard skills. But unlike them, he felt out of his element in public concerts and composed only two piano concertos, one set of variations for piano and orchestra, and three piano sonatas. He preferred the intimate atmosphere of Parisian salons, gatherings of the wealthy elite of Paris for performances and discussions of the arts and politics. For these occasions, he composed dozens of very short, single-movement works.

One of the meanings Chopin's listeners might have attributed to such salon performances was indebted to the Romantic theory that the performer, in this case also the composer, was expressing his inner feelings in the music. In the Romantic atmosphere of the time, his performances, filled with fluctuating tempos, *rubato*, and melodic twists and turns both sweeping and subtle, may have been interpreted as the sensitive expressions of Chopin's inner life, including the suffering of a refugee from wars in Poland, nostalgia for his homeland, and perhaps more intimate desires. Young women were reported to have been so overcome with emotion while hearing him play that they fainted.

Chopin eschewed sonata form in favor of a multitude of solo piano genres, some of them in dance meters (waltzes, *mazurka*s, *polonaise*s), some suggesting a mood (ballades, nocturnes, impromptus, scherzos), and some implying abstract musical content (études, preludes). Each of these genres had its own associated meanings. The waltz, for example, had its roots in the Austrian countryside. By the early nineteenth century it had replaced the courtly minuet as the most fashionable ballroom dance among the upper classes of Europe. Young people were drawn to it because it was faster than the staid minuet. They could dance facing one another, their arms around one another's shoulders and waists, while spinning rapidly around the dance floor. Dancing face to face as opposed to holding hands side by side as in the minuet and other Baroque dances shocked the sensibilities of the older generation, even though one dance tutor published in 1816 shows dancers at arm's length in rather dignified poses. In the same year the *Times of London* described an aristocratic ball with a rather less modest dancing style, apparently not at arm's length but with bodies "compressed":

FIGURE 7.11
Nine positions of the waltz from Thomas Wilson's Correct Method of German and French Waltzing (1816)
Source: Wikimedia Commons.

FIGURE 7.12
Frédéric Chopin playing for the Radziwiłłs, an aristocratic Polish family, at a Berlin house party in 1829
Source: Painting by Henryk Siemiradzki, 1887.

We remarked with pain that the indecent foreign dance called the Waltz was introduced (we believe for the first time) at the English court on Friday last . . . it is quite sufficient to cast one's eyes on the voluptuous intertwining of the limbs and close compressure on the bodies in their dance, to see that it is indeed far from the modest reserve which has hitherto been considered distinctive of English females. So long as this obscene display was confined to prostitutes and adulteresses, we did not think it deserving of notice; but now that it is attempted to be forced on the respectable classes of society by the civil examples of their superiors, we feel it our duty to warn every parent against exposing his daughter to so fatal a contagion.

Chopin composed more than a dozen waltzes, but they were not intended to accompany dances. He played them in the salons of Paris high society, where he was a fixture at their soirées. If he had played his waltzes for dancers, he would have had to maintain the beat very strictly. But Chopin's waltzes were meant for listeners not dancers, and so Rubinstein, following Chopin, uses contrasting tempos, *accelerando* and *ritardando*, *rubato*, and syncopation to evoke the sentimental possibilities in what otherwise is a dance genre.

What Is Its History?

Chopin was born Fryderyk Franciszek Chopin in a small town west of Warsaw, Poland, and spent his youth in Warsaw studying music. His father, a French *emigré*, played flute and violin and tutored the children of local nobles in French. His Polish mother played and taught piano. He gave his first public concert and composed his first piece, a Polish dance called *polonaise*, at age seven. During his teenage years he studied piano, composition, and counterpoint at the Warsaw music conservatory, founded in 1810 and now named in his honor *Uniwersytet Muzyczny Fryderyka Chopina*. His teachers proclaimed him a genius. In 1829, after attending a concert in Warsaw by the most famous violin virtuoso of the day, Niccolò Paganini (1782–1840), Chopin dedicated a set of piano variations titled *Souvenirs de Paganini* to him. Paganini's 24 Caprices for Solo Violin, Op. 1, a set of short studies exploring the technical demands of the violin, inspired Chopin to begin composing a similar set of 24 études for the piano, Op. 10 (12 études) and Op. 25 (12 études) between 1829 and 1836.

After graduating from the Warsaw conservatory in 1829, he spent the next two years traveling around Europe giving concerts that included his only works for piano and orchestra: a set of variations on the theme of the *duettino* "Là ci darem la mano" from Mozart's *Don Giovanni* (mentioned in Chapter 6, Gateway 24) and two piano concertos. While traveling abroad in 1831, Chopin learned that an uprising to depose Tsar Nicholas I of Russia as king of Poland had failed. Warsaw had been reduced to a military outpost of the Russian Empire. Chopin decided to remain with other members of the Polish upper classes in exile in Paris, where he lived for the rest of his life.

When he arrived in Paris at the age of twenty-one, Chopin had learned that concertos and sonatas intended for performances in large concert halls were not for him. He was physically slight and had been a sickly child, and his delicate piano style did not seem suitable for those large venues and genres. He preferred the intimate surroundings of evening parties in the homes of the wealthy, where he often improvised new work. Among his first patrons was Jakob Mayer Rothschild, one of five brothers with banks in Paris, London, Frankfurt, Vienna, and Naples. The family had accumulated the largest fortune in history to that point. Chopin, grateful for Rothschild's early and continued patronage, dedicated his Waltz in C-sharp Minor, Op. 64, No. 2 to Rothschild's daughter Charlotte. Other than these small events, he gave very few public concerts, and, when he did, they were often in the small recital hall of the Pleyel piano company, which supplied his pianos. Otherwise, he supported himself by giving piano lessons to the children of the wealthy and with royalties from his published works.

His nostalgia for Poland was given voice in compositions in two Polish dance rhythms. The *polonaise* is a dance in a slow triple meter with sharp staccato rhythms. Chopin wrote ten of these. The *mazurka* is a dance in a fast triple meter, and he wrote more than forty of these. In 1836 Chopin's contemporary, the important German composer and music critic Robert Schumann (1810–1856), wrote about Chopin's *mazurka*s in a manner recalling Confucius's and Plato's beliefs in the power of music: "If the mighty autocrat in the north [Tsar Nicholas I of Russia and Poland's nemesis] could know that in Chopin's works, in the simple strains of his *mazurka*s, there lurks a dangerous enemy, he would place a ban on his music. Chopin's works are cannon buried in flowers!"[51] Like the waltz, the *mazurka* spread across Europe and to the Americas. Today in Sweden, the folk dance genre *polska* (Polish dance) is based on the meter and rhythm of the *mazurka*.

Chopin wrote in many other genres as well. Among them are a set of twenty-four miniature preludes in each of the twelve major and minor keys, an homage to J. S. Bach's *Well-tempered Clavier*, which he admired (Chapter 5, Gateway 20). He also composed some twenty nocturnes (evening serenades). The invention of the genre called nocturne is credited to John Field (*c.* 1782–1837), a composer born in Ireland but active in Russia later in his life. Unlike the generally cheery dance pieces, nocturnes evoke sad moods of lonely nights and the sense of foreboding in the face of unconquerable natural forces, ideas pervading early nineteenth-century Romanticism. Field's eighteen nocturnes feature slow-tempo, song-like melodies played with *rubato* in the right hand over

CULTURAL LINKAGES

ECONOMIC ACTIVITY

POLITICAL ACTION

AESTHETICS

arpeggiated chords in the left hand but with none of the technical brilliance Chopin would bring to them. Field used the pedal on the newly resonant piano to allow the tones to ring without being dampened. These techniques combine to create icons of watery, dream-like experiences and a rather somber mood popular in the early nineteenth century. His nocturnes influenced similar ones by many more famous composers of the nineteenth century, including Chopin.

Chopin had serious relationships with two women during his life in Paris. The first was Maria Wodzińska (1819–1896), the daughter of a Polish count. A painter who studied piano with John Field, she met Chopin, who composed two waltzes for her, at the age of fourteen. They were engaged for a year when she was sixteen, but her father broke it off, ostensibly because of Chopin's ill health. She painted his portrait in 1836, when he was twenty-six years old. The second affair was with the notorious George Sand (1804–1876), a woman writer who scandalized Parisian society by taking a man's name, wearing men's clothes, smoking in public, and leaving her husband for a number of prominent lovers, including Chopin. She lived with him for nearly ten years after his break-up with Maria Wodzińska in 1837. In 1841 she published a novel called *A Winter in Majorca* about their miserable sojourn on that Mediterranean island in an effort to cure Chopin's tuberculosis.

FIGURE 7.13
Frédéric Chopin in 1836
Source: Watercolor by Maria Wodzińska (1819–1896). National Museum, Warsaw, Wikimedia Commons.

As his illness grew worse after 1842, his productivity diminished though he occasionally rallied to perform. In February, 1848, he gave his last concert in Paris. Later in the year, during a visit to England, he played for Queen Victoria and her consort, Prince Albert. At his last concert, in London in November, 1848, he reportedly weighed less than one hundred pounds. A year later, some three thousand people from all over Europe attended his funeral in Paris. Among the pieces performed was Mozart's Requiem (mentioned in Chapter 6, Gateway 23).

During his life, Chopin met and knew personally many of the leading figures of European music, including Hector Berlioz, who was seven years his senior. Among his contemporaries were three outstanding piano virtuosos and composers, among them Franz Liszt (1811–1896). He and Chopin lived near one another and were close friends during the 1830s. Liszt was a more flamboyant personality than Chopin, and he, unlike Chopin, concertized widely throughout Europe for many years. His theatrical performances, in which he embellished the scores he was performing, including Chopin's, with ornaments and new chords, created a sensation, especially among young women, and made him, in twentieth-first-century terms, a rock star. Liszt's piano compositions were partly inspired by Chopin's and are even more virtuosic.

Before Chopin left Warsaw he met another young contemporary, also a child prodigy, Felix Mendelssohn (1809–1847), in Berlin. A child of a wealthy Jewish family that had converted to Christianity, Mendelssohn's piano miniatures, a set of forty-eight *Songs without Words* written from 1832 to 1845, are much admired today. Unlike Chopin, Mendelssohn composed in all the major genres of the day, including five symphonies, concertos for piano and for violin, string quartets, oratorios, cantatas, and one opera. His most famous work is probably an orchestral overture and suite of pieces composed as incidental music for a production of Shakespeare's *Midsummer Night's Dream*. The most famous of them is the ubiquitous "Wedding March."

Felix's older sister Fanny Mendelssohn (1805–1847) was also a prodigious, if less well-known, musical talent. She composed more than six hundred pieces, most of them songs and short piano pieces, many with associated poems. One impressive collection, called *Das Jahr* (The Year), is a set of twelve pieces, each named for a month of the year. Because of prevailing views of women's roles in those days, her family tolerated but did not encourage her composing. Her father wrote to her in 1820, when she was just fifteen and Felix was eleven, "Music will perhaps become his [Felix's] profession, while for you it can and must be only an ornament."[52] Because of the limitations placed

SOCIAL BEHAVIOR

on her as a woman composer, she wrote only one orchestral work, an overture, and only began publishing her works in 1846, the year before her death. Her reputation as a composer languished until recently, when modern scholars and performers have discovered and championed her work.

Robert Schumann (1810–1856) rounds out this group of famous contemporary pianist/composers. Born in Germany to a father who was a writer and publisher, he demonstrated an early love of music. For much of his life he remained enthralled with literature and writing and with playing and composing music. His teacher, Friedrich Wieck (1785–1873) of Leipzig, believed he could become the greatest pianist of the age. During his twenties, from 1830 to 1838, he composed only piano works, including programmatic suites of short pieces with evocative titles like *Papillions* (Butterflies), *Carnaval*, *Kinderszenen* (Children's Scenes), *Novelletten* (Novellas), and *Nachtstücke* (Night Pieces). In 1834 he indulged his literary side by creating a musical magazine, *Neue Zeitschrift für Musik* (New Journal for Music), in which he joined Berlioz to become one of the most important music critics of the day. A generous soul, in an 1836 essay, he declared Chopin a genius. When an injury to his left hand ended his performing ambitions, he turned in 1839 and 1840 to composing songs, and in 1841 he composed the first of four symphonies. In 1852 he wrote the last work published during his lifetime, like Mozart, a Requiem mass. In 1854, after suffering mental health problems for years, he unsuccessfully attempted suicide, after which he asked to be committed to an insane asylum, where he died in 1856 at the age of forty-six.

> **SOCIAL BEHAVIOR**

While Schumann was studying with Friedrich Wieck, he fell in love with his teacher's daughter, Clara Wieck (1819–1896). A piano prodigy, she started touring Europe with her father in 1830 at the age of eleven. Even the redoubtable Paganini was taken with her virtuosity, and Liszt and Chopin praised her performances. Robert and Clara married in 1840 over the strenuous objections of her father. They had eight children, yet through it all, as Clara Schumann, she continued her career as one of the most celebrated piano virtuosos of the nineteenth century, performing more than 2000 concerts in a sixty-year career that ended in 1891. In her concerts, she championed the work of her husband and played compositions by Bach, Beethoven, Mozart, Chopin, and others. In that way she was a model for a new kind of piano virtuoso, not the composer/performer but one who was principally a vessel for the faithful performance of other composers' works. But because it was still expected of soloists that they would play some of their own works for solo piano in concert, something not expected of modern pianists, Clara composed many solo piano pieces, including, in 1853, *Variations on a Theme by Robert Schumann*. Today she is recognized, along with Fanny Mendelssohn, as an important composer of the nineteenth century.

WHERE DO I GO FROM HERE?

- Listen to these short piano pieces by Frédéric Chopin: Étude in G-flat Minor, Op. 10, No. 5; Prelude in G Major, Op. 28, No. 3; Nocturne No. 8 in D-flat Major, Op. 27, No. 2; *Souvenir de Paganini*; Mazurka No. 5 in B-flat Major, Op. 7, No. 1; Polonaise No. 3 in A Major, Op. 40, No. 1 ("Military").

- Listen to a Swedish *polska* and compare its style and form to a Chopin dance piece.

- Listen to John Field's Nocturne No. 1 in E-flat Major and compare it to one by Chopin.

- Listen to Franz Liszt's *Grande études de Paganini*, S141: No. 3 in G-sharp Minor ("La Campanella," The Little Bell) and compare its style to an étude by Chopin.

- Listen to Felix Mendelssohn's *Songs without Words*, Op. 62, No. 6 ("Spring Song").

- Listen to Fanny Mendelssohn's *Das Jahr: No. 2. February*.

- Listen to Robert Schumann's *Kinderszenen*, Op. 15, VII: *Träumerei* (Daydreaming).

- Listen to Clara Schumann's *Variations on a Theme by Robert Schumann*.

GATEWAY 30
EARLY AMERICAN POPULAR MUSIC[53]

What Is It?

During the early nineteenth century the banjo was a ubiquitous presence in American popular culture. Our gateway to American music of the early nineteenth century is a modern song that evokes, and opens a door to, this era of American music. African American singer/songwriter and multi-instrumentalist Rhiannon Giddens (b. 1977) composed and sang the song, titled "Julie," on her 2017 album *Freedom Highway*. In this recording she also plays the banjo and is accompanied by fiddle and bass. Giddens composed "Julie" in the old-time style of rural Appalachian music in an old European genre called the **ballad**, a short song that tells a story. The modern **banjo** is a fretted, long-necked plucked lute with four strings running along the neck and a fifth, shorter string running halfway up the neck. The sounding body consists of a wooden hoop with animal skin or plastic stretched over it. In this recording Giddens plays a fretless banjo, an older construction style of the nineteenth century.

FIGURE 7.14
Rhiannon Giddens plays the fretless banjo
Source: Wikimedia Commons.

Giddens composed "Julie" after reading Andrew Ward's 2008 book, *The Slaves' War: The Civil War in the Words of Former Slaves*. The lyrics are cast in the form of a dialogue between Julie, an enslaved servant, and her owner, her "mistress."

 Listen to the first thirty seconds of the recording.

How Does It Work?

Timbre

A relaxed female solo voice sings in her mid-range with the muted sound of the plucked banjo, fiddle, and bass.

Texture

The texture is heterophonic, as the voice, banjo, and fiddle all perform slightly different versions of the melody. The banjo's short fifth string sounds a syncopated, high-pitched drone, and the bass adds an intermittent, plucked drone tone.

Rhythm

The meter is duple with occasional syncopations as in the long–short–long rhythm on the opening syllables, "Ju-lie oh."

Melody

The melody is based on a pentatonic scale with flat third and flat seventh, the same scale as the *Candomblé* example in Chapter 6, Gateway 26. It consists of four phrases each with a slightly different shape.

Harmony

The harmony is drone-like on the pitches of the pentatonic scale.

Form

This is a **strophic song** with seven verses: AAAAAAA. Each strophe (verse) consists of four lines of text and four melodic phrases: abca. Each verse repeats a textual refrain, either "Julie, oh Julie" or "Mistress, oh mistress." An instrumental introduction introduces the melody. A short instrumental interlude based on the first melodic phrase breaks up each exchange between Julie and her mistress. Between each pair of exchanges, Giddens and the fiddle player play the complete verse melody. The performance ends with two instrumental renditions of the tune. The performance increases subtly in intensity as it moves from no bass accompaniment to a bass tone every four beats, then every two beats, then every beat.

Performance Techniques

Slides from pitch to pitch are heard in the singing and in the banjo playing. She plucks the banjo's string using an old technique called clawhammer style, which comes from West Africa.

Listen to the entire performance following this timed listening guide.

LISTENING GUIDE 7.5

TIME	SECTION	DESCRIPTION	SENSE OF THE LYRICS
0:00	Instrumental introduction	The banjo plucks the rhythm, and then the banjo and fiddle play the four-phrase verse melody hetero-phonically. Just before the verse the bass enters with a long bowed drone on the tonic pitch that continues almost uninterrupted until the beginning of the third verse.	
0:25	Verse 1	The singer enters and sings the first verse accompanied heterophonically by banjo and fiddle.	Julie, oh Julie, see the [Union] soldiers have come to free you.
0:43	Short interlude	The banjo and fiddle play the first (a) phrase of the verse melody.	
0:47	Verse 2	Same as Verse 1	Mistress, oh mistress, I see the soldiers and I am waiting until they come for me.
1:04	Long interlude	The banjo and fiddle play all four phrases (abca) of the verse melody.	
1:25	Verse 3	The bass joins the voice, banjo, and fiddle with a plucked tone every four beats.	Julie, oh Julie, don't leave this house and everything you have ever known.
1:43	Short interlude	The bass becomes slightly more active, almost outlining the melody with its own addition to the heterophony.	
1:46	Verse 4	The bass adds a "pick-up note" before the first beat of each measure.	Mistress, oh mistress, I will leave with what remains of my family.
2:04	Long interlude	The bass plays an ostinato that oscillates between the lower tonic pitch, the fifth, and the tonic an octave higher. This continues through Verse 5.	

TIME	SECTION	DESCRIPTION	SENSE OF THE LYRICS
2:24	Verse 5		Julie, oh Julie, please tell them the money belongs to you.
2:41	Short interlude		
2:48	Verse 6	The bass plays the pick-up note and main note every two beats, all on the tonic. The singer ends with a decrescendo on a long-held tone and the bass transitions back to playing one tone every four beats.	Mistress, oh mistress, I will not lie, because you got that money by selling my children.
3:14	Verse 7	The singer sings more softly and slowly than before. She ends on a long-held tone and then crescendos on it until the instrumental postlude starts.	Mistress, oh mistress, best wishes but "I'm leavin' hell."
3:47	Postlude	The instruments play the verse melody, this time with bass plucking a drone tone on the tonic on every beat.	
4:04	Postlude	The instruments play a repeat of the verse melody.	
4:22	End		

What Does It Mean?

Beyond the meaning of the lyrics, which capture one of the horrors of slavery, the tearing of children from their parents to be sold for profit, and the sometimes affectionate bond between owners and the enslaved people working in their households, part of the meaning of this song is Rhiannon Giddens' reclaiming of the string band tradition of the Appalachian Mountains as her own. Fiddle and banjo music and the singing of songs in this style were, for most of the twentieth century, associated almost exclusively with those mountains and the rural white musicians who have kept it alive into the present. In this recording Rhiannon Giddens makes the point that enslaved African American

CULTURAL LINKAGES

musicians contributed to this tradition as soon as they arrived in North America during the seventeenth century. From Africa they brought with them memories of three-stringed, long-necked, fretless plucked lutes with a skin-covered gourd or wooden body. One such instrument is called *ekonting* and is played today by the Jola people of the West African countries of Senegal, The Gambia, and Guinea-Bissau. Each of the *ekonting*'s three strings is a different length.

By the eighteenth century enslaved African Americans had reconstructed a modified fretless version of the instrument in the United States and the Caribbean, and contemporary accounts refer to it as banjer and banjo, which almost surely are African-derived names. The number of strings on these early American gourd banjos varied widely and was eventually standardized at five. Frets were added to the neck in the late 1800s. Giddens' fretless banjo is a nod to the older style of fretless banjo played by enslaved

FIGURE 7.15
Musa Diatta plays *ekonting* in Bijilo, Gambia
Source: Scott V. Linford.

African Americans in the early nineteenth century, and its wooden hoop body is typical of banjos of the late nineteenth century.

The playing style Giddens employs also has its roots in Africa. It is called **clawhammer style**. She curls the four fingers of her right hand into a claw shape and strikes the strings with the fingernail of her index finger in a downward motion. She plucks the short fifth string (and sometimes the other strings) with her thumb. This technique is similar to one observed today among players of the *ekonting*. Her playing technique differs from the modern three-finger picking style most white banjo players use today. This performance gains its meaning in part from the fact that a black woman is playing the banjo in a style that contrasts with the way many rural white musicians have played it since the 1940s. By doing so, she affirms the multifaceted roots of American rural music in Africa.

> **SOCIAL BEHAVIOR**

Enslaved populations in the United States were also exposed to the violin. They took to the instrument quickly because it was similar to bowed, gourd-bodied instruments in West Africa. On it they played with a raspy timbre favored in African music (Chapter 3, Gateway 10). By the eighteenth century artwork depicted fiddlers playing at the dances of their white masters. Runaway slave notices mentioned that some of them could play "remarkably well on the violin."[54] Some rural white fiddlers have reported that they learned from black fiddlers.

FIGURE 7.16
Elizabeth Cotten, who plays the guitar left handed without changing the order of strings, with her guitar "Stella" in 1977
Source: Alamy Stock Photo.

The song style and story-telling form of "Julie" are rooted in the American versions of old Scottish, Irish, and English songs that European settlers, including the frontiersman Daniel Boone (1734–1820), brought with them to the Appalachian Mountains in the eighteenth and early nineteenth centuries. Many of their songs employ pentatonic scales and feature dialogue between characters, usually a man and a woman. In writing "Julie," Giddens adopted both these stylistic elements to create a new song that sounds as old as the hills and valleys of Appalachia in a manner that black and white singers of the region have shared for three centuries.

One of Giddens' inspirations was Elizabeth Cotten (1893–1987), a black singer, guitarist, and banjo player born in Chapel Hill, North Carolina. She became famous during the folk music revival of the 1960s, when, in her sixties, folk singers Peggy and Mike Seeger, half siblings of Pete Seeger, discovered her and brought her to public attention. Her most famous song, "Freight Train," was recorded by Peter, Paul, and Mary, Bob Dylan, and Joan Baez, among many others. Giddens has recorded Cotten's song "Shake Sugaree" in tribute.

What Is Its History?

Rhiannon Giddens was born in North Carolina and received her bachelor's degree in opera performance from the Oberlin Conservatory, founded in 1865 and the first college and conservatory to welcome black students. In 2005 she formed the Carolina Chocolate Drops with three other musicians. Their 2010 album *Genuine Negro Jig* won the Grammy for Best Traditional Folk Album. They learned some of their repertoire from Joe Thompson (1918–2012), one of the oldest of the old-time black fiddlers, who played with his cousin, the banjo player Odell Thompson. In 2015 Giddens released her first full-length solo album, *Tomorrow is My Turn,* and she received a MacArthur "Genius" Fellowship in 2017, the same year she released "Julie" on the album *Freedom Highway.*

The Appalachian fiddle and banjo tradition seems to have started among African Americans during the eighteenth century. During the nineteenth century a popular entertainment known as the minstrel show may have helped spread its popularity among white musicians. By the twentieth century, and before the intervention of Rhiannon Giddens and the Carolina Chocolate Drops, the tradition had become an index of rural white communities in the southeastern United States. Later additions to white rural musical ensembles were plucked zithers, guitar, mandolin, and bass. In 1939 Bill Monroe (1911–1996), a mandolinist from Kentucky, formed a group called the Blue Grass Boys, consisting of mandolin, banjo, fiddle, guitar, and bass and featuring singing in tight three- and four-part vocal harmonies. When other southern groups began to imitate their lineup and sound, a new genre was born, taking its name from the name of Monroe's group: **bluegrass**. Bluegrass added to rural styles a great deal of syncopation, improvisation, and fast tempos—elements from jazz and popular music. Bluegrass began alongside other styles at the roots of country music (Chapter 11, Gateway 45), but since the 1940s it has had a history of its own that, while always intertwined with country music, has produced its own stars and generated its own audiences.

In 1954 Elvis Presley recorded one of the well-known songs of the Blue Grass Boys, "Blue Moon of Kentucky," as the B side of his first successful 45 rpm recording, an up tempo rhythm and blues number called "That's All Right" by Mississippi blues singer Arthur "Big Boy" Crudup (1905–1974). Folk music revivalists of the 1960s, including Bob Dylan, Joan Baez, and Judy Collins, were steeped in the Appalachian song, fiddle, and banjo tradition. Among its most famous regional exponents were Jean Ritchie (1922–2015), a singer and zither player from Kentucky, and Doc Watson (1923–2012), a blind singer and guitarist from North Carolina. Many singers of commercial country music have roots in this tradition as well. Mainly an amateur form of music making today, as it was in its heyday, summer festivals of "string band music" or "ole time (or old-time) music" take place across the country.

FIGURE 7.17
Ben and Lew Snowden of the The Snowden Family Band from Clinton, Ohio, playing from the gable of their home; they played professionally from 1850 to 1920
Source: Ohio Historical Society, Wikimedia Commons.

FIGURE 7.18
Bill Monroe and his Blue Grass Boys in 1973
Source: Getty Images.

Bluegrass enjoyed a resurgence with the soundtrack to the Hollywood film *O Brother, Where Art Thou?*, released in 2000. Vocalist-fiddle player Alison Krauss (b. 1971) was one of the driving forces on that album. As of 2018 Krauss has received twenty-seven Grammy awards, second only to the famed orchestral conductor Sir Georg Solti (the producer Quincy Jones also has twenty-seven Grammys). Mandolin virtuoso Chris Thile (b. 1981) grew up winning bluegrass competitions and experimenting with the sounds of pop and other genres with his fellow prodigy bandmates in the group Nickel Creek, siblings Sara and Sean Watkins. In 2017 alone he released an album of sonatas and partitas by J. S. Bach with cellist Yo-Yo Ma and a duo album with jazz pianist Brad Mehldau, bringing bluegrass sensibilities and improvisation into dialogue with a number of other musical styles. His five-member band Punch Brothers is said to be a contemporary version of the Blue Grass Boys that explores overlaps between bluegrass, classical music, jazz, and popular music idioms.

During the first half of the nineteenth century, the banjo emerged from the Appalachian Mountains and the rural countryside to become the featured instrument of the most popular form of public entertainment in the period, the minstrel show. **Minstrel shows** presented white entertainers,

> CULTURAL LINKAGES

mainly from the north, masked in "blackface" makeup. They imitated and ridiculed both free and enslaved African Americans in ostensibly black styles of speech, dance, and music: "stump speeches," humorous dialogues, skits about life under slavery on the plantation, step dancing, cake-walking (an exaggerated high-stepping dance), and songs and instrumental tunes on the fiddle and banjo, tambourine, and bones (two pairs of animal bones or wooden sticks held in each hand and rattled together in rhythm). Stereotypical characters in minstrel shows included "Sambo," an enslaved man who was happy-go-lucky and musical; "Zip Coon," a freedman (former slave) speaking and dressing in an elegant, dandyish style undercut by malapropisms and other displays of ignorance in "stump speeches"; "Jim Crow," who moved and danced in an exaggerated style and who would eventually give his name to repressive segregationist laws in the South after Reconstruction in the late nineteenth century; comic dialogues between "Tambo" (the tambourine player) and "Bones" (the bones player); "Mammy" or "Auntie," an older woman who raised and loved the children of her mistress; and "Uncle," the elder of a happy enslaved family and friend of his master. The minstrel show is arguably the source of negative stereotypes about African Americans that persist to this day.

The cover of a song book published by Christy's Minstrels, founded in 1843, shows a fiddle, two banjos, tambourine, and triangle, and lists "Jim Crow Polka" as one of its songs. A common theme of the songs and skits of minstrel shows was the happy lives of enslaved workers on the plantation, a gross misrepresentation that helped to justify the mandatory return of runaway slaves discovered in northern states under the draconian Fugitive Slave Act of 1850. "Julie," whose lyrics are borrowed from the oral narrative of a freedwoman after the Civil War, reveals the kind of painful experiences that minstrel shows suppressed. Rhiannon Giddens' playing of the banjo restores the instrument's dignity within traditional African American culture after the ignominy it suffered in minstrel shows.

Despite the racist stereotypes they created, minstrel shows launched the careers of many African American performers, who initially were forced to wear blackface makeup so that audiences would believe they were white performers pretending to be black—a cruel irony. African American banjoist Horace Weston (1825–1900) began his career that way but was later able to create a dignified image by playing his own complex and virtuosic compositions. The Rabbit's Foot Company was a minstrel troupe of black performers founded by a black entrepreneur. It toured in the South during the first half of the twentieth century and launched the careers of Ma Rainey, Bessie Smith, Ida Cox, Brownie McGhee, Big Joe Williams, and other later stars of the classic blues (Chapter 9, Gateway 39).

Minstrel shows also provided a venue for the performance of new popular songs. The most important and enduring composer of these songs was Stephen Foster (1826–1864), who, like Chopin, lived a remarkably short life. From Philadelphia and called by some "the father of American music," he wrote more than two hundred songs, some which have achieved anthem-like status: "Oh, Susanna" for the California gold rush of 1848; "Old Folks at Home" ("Swanee River," 1851) for the South as a whole; and "My Old Kentucky Home" (1853) for the state of Kentucky in particular. Other well-known songs of his include "Camptown Races" (1850), "Jeannie with the Light Brown Hair" (1854); and "Beautiful Dreamer," published posthumously in 1864. Foster wrote many his most famous songs for Christy's Minstrels. Although he avoided the most crude, racist, and degrading aspects of minstrel shows, he did use typical epithets of the period for African Americans ("darkies") and parodied African American dialects in the lyrics, as in "Camptown races, sing dis song, do dah do dah." Unable to make a living from the royalties from his songs (printers printed his songs without paying him any royalties), he died in poverty in New York having bequeathed to America a rich legacy of popular song sung and played by both white and black singers and musicians until well past the middle of the twentieth century. His songs were taught in schools throughout the twentieth century, becoming something like American folk songs. Some still are taught with the lyrics stripped of their faux black dialect and some with only their melodies in elementary school instrumental classes. His songs raise interesting ethical questions for educators today, given their original association with minstrel shows. Should those meanings be erased or can they be used for educational purposes today?

Despite the racism at its core, the imagery of minstrel shows has been remarkably persistent in American culture to the present. In 1927 the famous Jewish American entertainer Al Jolson (1886–1950) sang in blackface a song called "Mammy" in the first "talking picture," *The Jazz Singer*. From 1928 to 1960 the radio show "Amos 'n' Andy" featured white actors voicing the roles of black characters in dialogues similar to those of Tambo and Bones. Musical films from the 1930s through the 1950s featured historical evocations of minstrel shows, with such famous stars as Fred Astaire, Bing Crosby, and Judy Garland performing in blackface. On the Fox network the animated TV series *The Cleveland Show* (2009–2013) about a black family relied on negative stereotypes for its humor and used white actors to voice some black characters. Even today Aunt Jemima's breakfast food and Uncle Ben's rice products reproduce the racist iconography of minstrel shows.

African American music, including the banjo, was also the subject of short character pieces for the piano by early nineteenth-century American composer Louis Moreau Gottschalk (1829–1869). Another short-lived composer of the period, he was born in New Orleans to a Jewish father and a Creole (the French- and Spanish-speaking communities of Louisiana) mother. He had five half-siblings (the children of his father's mistress) of mixed black and white descent. From them and from the general musical atmosphere in New Orleans, he gained an appreciation of African American musical styles and incorporated them into his piano character pieces. He toured widely as a piano virtuoso throughout North and South America, often playing his own compositions based on the African American tunes he heard growing up in Louisiana. He was widely admired in Europe as well as in the United States. He gave a sensational concert in Paris in April of 1849, a few months before Chopin died in the same city. At the concert he debuted a composition named "Bamboula: Danse des Nègres," dedicated to an admirer, the Queen of Spain. In 1853 he published another popular showpiece called "The Banjo," which imitates the plucking style and ostinato rhythmic patterns of banjo players.

Thus, whether it was the instrumental and vocal traditions of the Appalachians, parodies of black music and dancing in minstrel shows for northern urbanites, accompaniments to the popular songs of Stephen Foster, or the classical, virtuosic piano miniatures of Louis Moreau Gottschalk, the banjo, a gift of enslaved Africans to American culture, and its associated song repertoire, were central features of the American musical scene during the first half of the nineteenth century.

FIGURE 7.20
Stephen Foster
Source: Getty Images.

FIGURE 7.21
Louis Moreau Gottschalk
Source: Brady-Handy Photograph Collection. Library of Congress, Wikimedia Commons.

WHERE DO I GO FROM HERE?

- Listen to a recording of black North Carolina fiddler Joe Thompson to a recording of "Old Joe Clark" played by Oscar Jenkins, Fred Cockerham, and Tommy Jarrell, white fiddlers and fretless banjo players from North Carolina.
- Listen to the Carolina Chocolate Drops' recording of "Snowden's Jig (Genuine Negro Jig)."
- Listen to a recording of "The Banjo" by Louis Moreau Gottschalk. What elements of this piano music convey the sound of a banjo?

CLOSING

AESTHETICS

Among the principal economic and intellectual factors shaping European music of nineteenth-century Europe and the United States were the Industrial Revolution and a literary and philosophical movement known as Romanticism. Because of this last factor, music historians have commonly referred to the early nineteenth century as the **Romantic Period** of European music history, but it could, to equally good effect, also be called the Industrial Period. In the domain of European classical music today, a number of practices and ideas have their roots in the first half of the nineteenth century.

- The modern piano, with its steel frame and taut strings, starts to take shape.
- The celebration of virtuoso performers and of the musical interpretations of commanding symphony and opera conductors originate in this period.
- The notion that some composers are geniuses and that performers must honor their compositional intentions is also a product of the early nineteenth century.
- The idea that instrumental music could have a narrative thrust and convey a verbal story became a taken-for-granted feature of European classical music.
- In the United States African American music entered the mainstream of white popular culture for first time, not in the bodies of black musicians, singers, and dancers, but in the imaginations of white performers with little but a stereotypical and deeply racist understanding of African American culture. These stereotypes have persisted in popular entertainment and product branding to the present.

THINGS TO THINK ABOUT

- Compare the effects of the Industrial Revolution on each of the worlds of music opened up by the gateways in this chapter.
- Given what you now know about Romanticism, how do those ideas about music compare to your own beliefs about the nature of music and what music is capable of expressing?

NEW TERMS

accelerando	clawhammer style	orchestration	Romanticism
ballad	English horn	pizzicato	*rubato*
banjo	Enlightenment	program	song, strophic
bluegrass	glissando	programmatic music,	tone poem
bourgeoisie	*idée fixe*	program music	tritone
canonization	Industrial Revolution	proletariat	waltz
capitalist	minstrel show	Romantic Period	Western canon

MUSIC FROM THE LATE NINETEENTH CENTURY (1850–1900)

8

DURING THE SECOND HALF of the nineteenth century the Industrial Revolution produced a parade of new inventions that changed the way people lived and communicated, including the sewing machine (1850s), telephone (1876), incandescent light bulb (1879), and, most importantly for music, the phonograph (1877). The famous Italian opera composer Giuseppe Verdi (1813–1901), who lived through most of the century, would have experienced a nearly constant stream of new, life-altering technologies during his lifetime. The Industrial Revolution and the continuing domination in the European political sphere of aristocratic families led to two radical responses. First, the doctrines of socialism and communism, elaborated most famously by the German philosopher and economist Karl Marx (1818–1883), sought solutions to the growing disparity between rich and poor and the degraded conditions of workers (the proletariat) in the new factories of Europe. Second, **nationalism**, the notion that each European ethnic group had the right to its own nation-state, challenged the imperial regimes of central and eastern Europe: the Russian, Austro-Hungarian, and Ottoman Empires.

The contribution of socialism and communism to nineteenth-century musical life seems to have been limited to a few marching songs for laborers to use in their protests and to the institution of brass bands, which represented labor unions, factories, and both left and right political parties in mass demonstrations (Chapter 9, Gateway 36). The same cannot be said for the other radical response to the political status quo in Europe: nationalism. At the end of the eighteenth century German writers brought a radical new concept to the idea of the nation. Previously, the revolutions in the United States and France had posited the notion that all those defined as "men" living in a nation had "certain inalienable rights," including the right to govern themselves and to be full-fledged "citizens" of a republic rather than subjects of a king ruling by divine right. In the United States and

FIGURE 8.1
South Australia (Adelaide) Police Band in 1907
Source: Wikimedia Commons.

France, for example, all citizens have these rights, regardless of their ethnic origins or when they or their families arrived in those countries. This type of nationalism is today known as **civic nationalism**, "civic" referring to a society and its citizens.

The German writers of the late eighteenth century proposed another form of nationalism: **ethnic nationalism**. Ethnic nationalists reject citizenship and residency as the basis for political participation. Instead, they believe that each ethnic group has a right to its own nation-state. Under this doctrine an ethnic group becomes a nationality. This philosophy arose in a geopolitical environment in which there were very few nation-states defined by nationality. Many of the nation-states in Europe today (Germany, Italy, Greece, Poland, and so on) did not exist at the beginning of the nineteenth century. Instead, many Europeans lived either in a small duchy, principality, or city-state, or they lived in a large empire that contained many nationalities. The map of Europe around 1815 illustrates this point. Russia was a huge empire that included the present-day countries of Poland, Ukraine, Finland, Latvia, and many others. The Ottoman Empire included present-day Turkey, Greece, Bulgaria, Romania, and others. The Austro-Hungarian Empire included present-day Austria, Hungary, Croatia, Slovakia, the Czech Republic, Ukraine, and the northern part of Italy. Great Britain comprised four "nationalities": the English, Scottish, Welsh, and Irish. Sweden and Norway were governed by a common king, and Iceland was a colony of Denmark. At the other extreme, present-day Germany and Italy were a jumble of small territories. In 1815 only a few countries resembled modern nation-states, among them France, Spain, Portugal, and the Netherlands. Much of the political history of Europe in the nineteenth century can be understood as a battle, led by writers, philosophers, and political activists with the aid of some military men, for the sovereignty of particular nationalities within the boundaries of nation-states. Among these intellectuals were composers and performers, who used instrumental music, plus songs and operas with words in "national languages," to rouse national sentiments and encourage these political movements.

POLITICAL ACTION

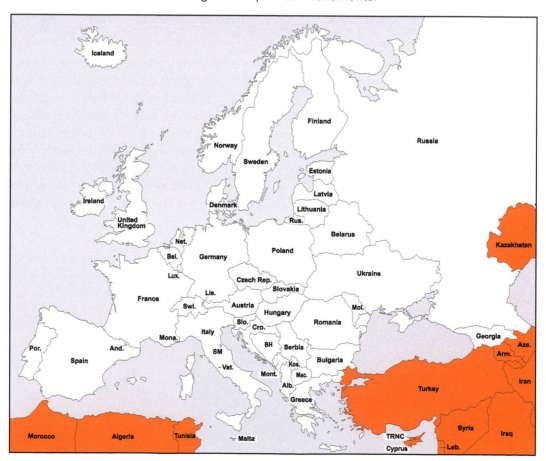

FIGURE 8.2
Map of European nations today

In this chapter the German composer Richard Wagner and the Czech composer Bedřich Smetana represent nationalism in music. Neither Germans nor Czechs lived in nation-states in 1850. During the second half of the nineteenth century, both composers' compositions contributed to the intellectual and artistic agitation for German and Czech national status. The third composer we discuss in this chapter, Claude Debussy from France, was distinctly French in his artistic tastes, but France had been a nation for many centuries with an already strong sense of its national identity. His compositions at the very end of the nineteenth century seem at once the last flowers of Romanticism and harbingers of new styles in the twentieth. Nationalism as part of the spirit of the times also had a life in the United States, as those under the sway of nationalism wondered what form the national music of this relatively new nation would take. When formerly enslaved African Americans from the south began appearing in the north performing classical concerts of "negro spirituals," the nationalist Czech composer Antonín Dvořák, who lived in the United States for a few years in the 1890s, argued that their music, as well as that of Native Americans, could provide the basis for an American national music.

Though slavery had been abolished in 1865 in the United States, many African Americans in the following years continued to work as sharecroppers under conditions similar to slavery. Gruesome acts of violence continued as well, and lynchings of African Americans became frequent in the South as a way of intimidating black communities and promoting the notion of white supremacy. After the Reconstruction Era (1865–1877), white lawmakers began to pass "Jim Crow" laws mostly (but not only) in the American South, the name Jim Crow borrowed from the name of a character type in blackface minstrelsy. For nearly a hundred years, until the passage of the 1964 Civil Rights Act, Jim Crow laws legalized racial segregation in public facilities, relegating African Americans to separate facilities for education, public transportation, and other public spaces such as restaurants, hotels, bathrooms, and drinking fountains. These facilities were inferior and poorly funded in comparison to those for whites, and in many instances they were not available at all. Until the passage of the 1965 Voting Rights Act, Jim Crow laws also suppressed the voting rights of African Americans and disenfranchised black citizens through poll taxes and literacy tests. In this late nineteenth-century culture of segregation, violence, and oppression, African American spirituals entered the mainstream of American culture. In this chapter we look at their origins under slavery and their legacy in this period and beyond.

GATEWAY 31
NINETEENTH-CENTURY OPERA

What Is It?

Ever since its invention around 1600, opera in the Italian language, even when composed by an Austrian like Mozart or a German like Handel, had been the most popular musical genre in Europe. Even Beethoven, whose creations were in an entirely different style and spirit, admired the operas of his younger contemporary Gioachino Rossini (1782–1868), who composed nearly forty operas in a seventeen-year period from 1812 to 1829. During the second half of the nineteenth century German composer Richard Wagner (1813–1883) reacted strongly against this style of Italian opera. He believed that the emphasis on virtuosic arias and the contrast between recitative and aria broke up the dramatic flow to deleterious effect. Writing in a more flowing style that obliterated the distinction between recitative and aria, he wrote his librettos in German and ceased to call his creations operas. He called his works **music dramas**. Today they are considered among the most important artistic creations, not just musical creations, of the late nineteenth century.

Our gateway to Wagner's music dramas and late-nineteenth-century Italian opera is the orchestral Prelude and final aria, *Liebestod*, from his music drama titled *Tristan und Isolde*, composed between 1857 and 1859. Unlike most opera composers, who relied on librettists for the story and lyrics, Wagner wrote both the libretto and the music for his music dramas. The story of Tristan and Isolde originates in twelfth-century Medieval **romances**, written stories about mythical and legendary figures. The most famous in English are the stories of King Arthur, Sir Lancelot, and Guinevere and the Knights of the Round Table. Wagner knew the story of Tristan and Isolde, about a similar love triangle, through its retelling by German poet Gottfried von Strassburg (died *c.* 1210).

Isolde was an Irish princess engaged to be married, but Tristan, a young knight from Cornwall on the southwest coast of England, killed her lover in battle. In Act I Tristan travels to Ireland to convince Isolde to marry his uncle, King Marke of Cornwall. On the sail from Ireland to Cornwall, Isolde, a master of magic potions, tries to poison Tristan to revenge his killing of her fiancé and to commit suicide herself. Her handmaid, realizing her intent, substitutes Isolde's love potion for the poison, and Tristan and Isolde fall madly in love. In Act II, while King Marke leads an evening hunting party, Tristan sings to Isolde that their passion can flourish only at night (remember the nocturne) not in the light of day and of reason and responsibility, which they are flouting under the potion's spell. Upon his return King Marke discovers Tristan's betrayal of their friendship, and one of his knights mortally wounds Tristan. In Act III Tristan has been taken to Brittany in northern France to die, but he longs for Isolde to arrive and comfort him. She does, just in time. He dies in her arms. She faints and, after awakening, sings a final aria recounting her vision of the two of them in the other world, a transfiguration that will, through death, allow their love to live forever.

FIGURE 8.4
Richard Wagner composing at the piano, 1843
Source: AF Archive/Alamy Stock Photo.

How Does It Work?

Timbre

Wagner required a very large orchestra and then wrote for its entire range from very low to very high pitches. Flutes and horns are prominent.

Texture

The texture is a wash of chords in the background with melodies emerging out of the mass of sound. Sometimes orchestral and vocal melodies sound in counterpoint.

Rhythm

The melodic rhythms often consist of very long notes, so the tempo seems slow, an expression of languorous, deep emotion. If the duration of the entire work is considered an aspect of rhythm, then *Tristan und Isolde* is very long by operatic standards, running to nearly four hours compared to the more usual three.

Melody

The Prelude, like Classical-period sonata form, has two recurring themes. Wagner called such recurring themes **Leitmotifs** (guiding or leading motives). Unlike a Classical-period symphony, the *Leitmotifs* of the Prelude do not represent contrasts between strong (possibly masculine) and weak (possibly feminine) themes. Rather, both have similar yearning qualities, the first created by chromaticism and the second through a sequence of rising pitches. If they represent the yearning of Tristan and Isolde, then that yearning is not gendered. The *Liebestod* aria also has two *Leitmotifs*, the first one referred to as the "*Liebestod* [Love-Death] *Leitmotif*" and the second one the "bliss *Leitmotif*" in the timed listening guide.

Harmony

The harmony is tonal but highly chromatic, moving continuously through many keys and thus sounding rather unstable and resembling shifting emotions. Occasional dominant seventh chords suggest an imminent release of tension to the tonic chord, a characteristic of tonal music. But Wagner avoids their resolution throughout the opera until the very end, maintaining their tension and creating a sense of yearning through what he called "endless melody."

Form

The form of both the Prelude and *Liebestod* aria features frequent repeats and returns of the *Leitmotifs*, but not in a predictable or regular pattern.

Performance Techniques

Frequent crescendos and decrescendos of varying length are the most striking performance techniques. In the *Liebestod* aria, the orchestra, at certain points, becomes so loud that it is no longer simply an accompaniment to the voice. It becomes something like a character in the drama and almost drowns out the singer.

What Does It Mean?

As in Berlioz's *Symphonie Fantastique*, how this opera works and what it means are inextricably interwoven. The Prelude has an implicit program or meaning as it anticipates the love story of the opera: the uncontrollable amorous yearning of Tristan and Isolde for one another.

Timed Listening Guide: Prelude

Listen to the entire recording of the Prelude following this timed listening guide.

TIME	DESCRIPTION
0:00	The cellos open quietly in unison on a melodic motive designed to create a sense of unfulfilled yearning: an upward leap followed by a chromatic descent and chromatic ascent. The woodwinds enter on the fourth tone with a chord not belonging to traditional tonal harmony. It is made up a perfect fourth (D#–G#) and an augmented fourth (F–B) and has been called "the Tristan chord." The phrase ends, unresolved, on a dominant seventh chord and is followed by a long pause.
0:28	The phrase repeats in sequence at higher and higher pitches, creating a musical image of rising passion. The melody is reduced to two pitches a half-step apart, creating a sense of "leading" somewhere until the full orchestra enters loudly but inconclusively.
1:51	A new yearning theme is introduced in the cellos: three phrases rising in sequence to a final large ascending leap followed by orchestral crescendos and diminuendos as the melody "develops," creating a sense of churning emotions.
3:26	The second yearning theme returns and develops rather quietly for a while until it gradually increases in loudness.
5:25	The second yearning theme returns a third time loudly followed by the churning orchestra and a fourth time in the brasses. The violins begin playing an ever higher set of scales, and then reintroduce the second theme again. The orchestra crescendos to an almost unbearable level of intensity.
7:31	The climax ends, and the orchestra gradually descends in pitch and loudness. The first yearning theme returns in the cellos and the two themes interweave in counterpoint through louder and softer passages.
9:17	The timpani plays a roll, and the English horn plays the first "yearning" theme. The roll continues and the bass clarinet plays the theme very softly, ending with the double basses in unison to silence, followed by two soft plucked tones.
10:32	End

EMOTIONAL RESONANCE

The combination of the contrapuntal interweaving of the yearning quality of the two melodies, the continuous surging of the music through degrees of loudness and softness, and the crescendo to the loudest possible sound and gradual decrescendo creates probably the most intense musical expression of passionate sexual love in the history of European music. Critics in the late nineteenth century noticed this, and some seemed embarrassed by it. A critic for the *Allgemeine musikalische Zeitung* (General Musical Journal) reported in 1865 of *Tristan und Isolde*:

> Not to mince words, it is the glorification of sensual pleasure, tricked out with every titillating device . . . We think that the stage presentation of the poem *Tristan und Isolde* amounts to an act of indecency.

After a performance in 1882 in London a critic in *The Era*, a weekly magazine, wrote:

> We cannot refrain from making a protest against the worship of animal passion which is so striking a feature in the late works of Wagner . . . The passion is unholy in itself and its representation is impure, and for those reasons we rejoice in believing that such works will not become popular . . . Wagner's music, in spite of all its wondrous skill and power, repels a greater number than it fascinates.

Clara Schumann wrote that *Tristan und Isolde* was "the most repugnant thing I have ever seen or heard in all my life."

There are many duets in *Tristan und Isolde*, but *Liebestod* is the only section resembling an aria. The music paints the lyrics in a European musical tradition that is hundreds of years old. The orchestra represents Isolde's emotions as she sings, at times overwhelming the sense of her words with the intensity of her feelings of love and joy at her vision of their radiant transfiguration into an eternal spiritual state of love after death.

Timed Listening Guide: Liebestod

Listen to the entire recording of the *Liebestod* following this timed listening guide, which explains the meaning of the music in relation to its musical elements and the text.

FIGURE 8.5

Tristan and Isolde in the first 1865 production, photo by Joseph Albert (1825–1886)

Source: Wikimedia Commons.

TIME	GERMAN TEXT	ENGLISH TRANSLATION	DESCRIPTION
0:00	*Mild und leise wie er lächelt*	How mild and tenderly he smiles	The *Liebestod Leitmotif*, sung very softly and slowly, consists of two short, four-tone, arch-shaped phrases, the second one slightly higher than the first.
0:16	*wie das Auge hold er öffnet,*	How sweetly he opens his eyes.	The *Liebestod Leitmotif* repeats on the second line of text, getting slightly louder.
0:30	*seht, ihr's, Freunde? Seht ihr's nicht?*	Do you see, friends? Do you not see?	Isolde sings new material as the *Liebestod Leitmotif* is taken up by the orchestra.
0:42	*Immer lichter, wie er leuchtet,*	How brightly he shines,	The melody rises to near the top of Isolde's vocal range, painting the words "shines" and "soars high among the stars."
	stern-umstrahlet hoch sich hebt?	How high he soars among the stars?	
1:14	*Seht ihr's nicht?*	Do you not see?	The *Liebestod Leitmotif* is heard in the orchestra.
1:20	*Wie das Herz ihm mutig schwillt,*	How valiantly his heart swells,	Isolde sings the *Liebestod Leitmotif* again.
	voll und hehr im Busen ihm quillt?	Beats fully and sublimely in his breast?	
1:44	*Wie den Lippen, wonnig mild,*	How lips, soft and gentle	The orchestra brings the *Liebestod Leitmotif* into the foreground before Isolde enters with another melodic line.
2:04	*süsser Atem sanft entweht?*	softly exhale sweet breath?	Isolde sings the *Liebestod Leitmotif*, and the flutes enter

continued

LISTENING GUIDE 8.2

TIME	GERMAN TEXT	ENGLISH TRANSLATION	DESCRIPTION
			in counterpoint with a new motive signifying bliss: an upward leap followed by a rapid scalar descent.
2:20	*Freunde! Seht! Fühlt und seht ihr's nicht?*	Friends! Look! Do you not feel it and see it?	The music becomes louder and more agitated.
2:41	*Höre ich nur diese Weise,*	Do I alone hear this melody,	Isolde sings again the *Liebestod leitmotif* as the orchestra interjects the bliss motive from time to time.
	die so wundervoll und leise,	which so wonderfully and tenderly	
	Wonne klagend, alles sagend,	Softly mourning, saying all,	
	mild versöhnend aus ihm tönend,	gently forgiving sounds from him,	
3:24	*in mich dringet, auf sich schwinget,*	penetrates within me, rising up,	Isolde's singing "rises up" louder and higher in a scalar ascent.
	hold erhallend um mich klinget?	Sweetly echoes and rings around me?	
3:49	*Heller schallend, mich umwallend,*	Sounding clearly, surrounding me	The orchestra rises higher and higher in sequence, burying Isolde's singing as she "dives" into its "roaring . . . surging swell" and "ringing sounds."
	sind es Wellen sanfter Lüfte?	Are they waves of soft breezes?	
	Sind es Wogen wonniger Düfte?	Are they clouds of wondrous fragrance?	
	Wie sie schwellen, mich umrauschen,	As they swell and roar around me,	
	soll ich atmen, soll ich lauschen?	Shall I inhale them, shall I listen to them?	
	Soll ich schlürfen, untertauchen?	Shall I sip them, dive into them?	
	Süss in Düften mich verhauchen?	Sweet scents shall I exhale?	
	In dem wogenden Schwall	In the surging swell	
	in dem tönenden Schall	in the ringing sounds,	
5:17	*in des Welt-Atems wehendem All*	In the world's breath encompassing all	The music begins to "sink" in pitch and loudness, and the "bliss" motive returns.
	ertrinken, versinken	To drown, to sink	
	unbewusst höchste Lust!	Unconscious, what utter bliss!	

TIME	GERMAN TEXT	ENGLISH TRANSLATION	DESCRIPTION
6:14			A crescendo returns to the Prelude's opening, "yearning" *Leitmotif*, which ends on the dominant seventh chord.
6:25			This time, four hours after the Prelude, the dominant seventh chord at the of the first phrase of the Prelude resolves to the tonic for the first time in the opera, the release from love's yearning in death. The music drama ends on a long crescendo and diminuendo to silence.
7:00	End		

Wagner's musical style in *Tristan und Isolde* stands in marked contrast to the style of Italian opera, which had been the most popular genre of European classical music for the previous 250 years. During the first half of the nineteenth century three Italian composers dominated the opera scene in Europe. During the teens and twenties of that century, Gioachino Rossini (1792–1868) wrote nearly forty operas before retiring from opera composition in 1829, in his late thirties. Among his most famous is *Il barbiere di Siviglia* (The Barber of Seville), composed in 1816. During the 1830s Gaetano Donizetti (1797–1848) and Vincenzo Bellini (1801–1835) were prolific and important. Donizetti wrote seventy operas over a long career. It was not unusual for him, and for Rossini, to produce three, four, or five operas a year. Bellini lived a very short life but he composed eleven operas during his eleven-year career. All worked within the conventions of a style of Italian opera called **bel canto**, which emphasizes show-stopping virtuosic singing and beautiful tone quality.

All this activity set the stage for Giuseppe Verdi (1813–1901), born the same year as Wagner and the greatest nineteenth-century composer of Italian operas. During the 1840s he composed fifteen of them, and during the 1850s, when Wagner was composing *Tristan und Isolde*, Verdi composed another ten. Verdi's compositional pace slowed considerably after those two frenetic decades, but he wrote his last opera, *Falstaff*, based on Shakespeare's larger-than-life character, in 1893, at the age of ninety. In 1896 Giacomo Puccini (1858–1924) composed *La Bohème* and continued this Italian tradition into the early twentieth century. Altogether these five composers boast about forty operas in the modern standard operatic repertoire, with Verdi alone having written about twenty of them.

Wagner found these composers' treatment of the orchestra stunted. He once commented sarcastically that Verdi used the orchestra like a guitar. Indeed, to showcase the vocalists, Verdi often wrote orchestral accompaniments consisting of little more than bass and block chords in alternation—like a guitar. If in Italian opera the music seems to serve the singers, Wagner wanted the music to serve the drama. To this end he composed in a musical style without a strong distinction between recitative and aria. He developed the orchestra not as an accompaniment to the singing but as a character capable of conveying the psychological reality behind the singers' words.

> AESTHETICS

What Is Its History?

The romance of Tristan and Isolde, two people whose love violates social conventions (Tristan's loyalty to King Marke) in a way that can only be resolved in death, is a Medieval love story that

> CULTURAL LINKAGES

reverberates through the history of European literature and music. At the end of the sixteenth century Shakespeare retold a version of it in *Romeo and Juliet*, even including a magic potion that the Friar gives to Juliet to mimic death. Goethe's *The Sorrows of the Young Werther* (1774) is another version, resolved by the death of the male lover, who shoots himself. In 1827 Hector Berlioz, under the spell of Shakespeare and Harriet Smithson, wrote *Symphonie Fantastique*, whose male protagonist, like young Werther agonizing over unrequited love, dies from an overdose of another magic potion, opium. Thirty years later Wagner brings the story full circle in his music drama *Tristan und Isolde*. The Romeo-and-Juliet version of the story continues to reverberate in American popular culture, including Leonard Bernstein's Broadway show *West Side Story* (1957) and even the Disney film *High School Musical* (2006).

Richard Wagner was born in 1813 in Leipzig, where Bach lived and worked during the last twenty-seven years of his life. He was raised by a family of thespians and imagined that he would become a writer and poet until he heard the music of Beethoven. He studied composition for a few years, but never developed great skill as a performer. Like Berlioz, his instrument was the orchestra. After numerous disappointments, Wagner's first success was an opera called *Rienzi* written in German in the Italian opera style on an Italian historical theme: the people of Rome rising up against the nobility. Produced in Dresden, Germany, in 1842, its success led to his appointment as director of the opera there, his first job and one that gave him the security to write and produce his next three operas, all with his own poetry and all on Germanic themes: *Der fliegende Holländer* (The Flying Dutchman, 1843), a story of love ending in death; *Tannhäuser und der Sängerkrieg auf Wartburg* (Tannhäuser and the Singers' Contest at Wartburg, 1845), a Medieval tale about sacred and profane love; and *Lohengrin* (1850), from a Medieval romance about the son of Percival, a knight of King Arthur's Round Table charged with finding and keeping the Holy Grail.

In his Dresden operas after *Rienzi*, Wagner abandoned the style and stories of Italian opera and began to develop the hallmarks of his personal style: his own poetic librettos based on Medieval Germanic myths, legends, and romances; a vocal writing style called **arioso** between the florid, melodic arias and the recitatives of Italian opera; *Leitmotifs* as indexes of characters, thoughts, emotions, objects, and places; chromaticism and unresolved harmonies played over long stretches of "endless melody" as expressions of rising and falling emotional states; and the orchestra and its palette of colors as a character in the drama equal to the vocalists.

POLITICAL ACTION

Wagner was not able to attend the premiere of *Lohengrin* in 1850 because in 1849 he had fled Dresden under threat of arrest for his participation in an uprising in 1848 against the tyranny of German princes and dukes and in favor of the unification of Germany's many principalities into a German state. In 1848 Europeans of all classes, including the nobility, urban workers, and rural peasants, were suffering economic hardships and chafing against autocratic rule, whose end was the promise of the French Revolution. The Irish potato famine was causing a million deaths and another million to emigrate. Karl Marx and Friedrich Engels published their *Communist Manifesto* in February of that year. Revolutions began in January in Sicily against Spanish rule. In February the French toppled their constitutional monarch. In March German students and intellectuals, including Wagner, engaged in mass demonstrations in favor of national unity and freedom of the press. The authorities issued a warrant for Wagner's arrest, and he escaped to Zurich, Switzerland, where he lived for a decade.

CULTURAL LINKAGES

In Switzerland, cut off from support for his musical compositions, he wrote essays on his views of music and art, including *The Artwork of the Future* (1849), in which he outlined his ideas for the way a **Gesamtkunstwerk** (total artwork) could unite all the elements of drama (poetry, music, stage design, and acting); *Judaism in Music* (1850), an anti-Semitic screed in which he claimed that Jews like Felix Mendelssohn, born and working in Germany, could not express the German national spirit but could only produce entertainment for money rather than great art, as ethnic Germans could; and *Opera and Drama* (1851), in which he outlined the methods he was using to create what would become his magnum opus: a set of four operas called *The Ring of the Nibelung*, also known as the

Ring Cycle or simply The Ring. Based on old Viking sagas written down from oral tradition in Old Norse, a Germanic language, and on a Medieval German romance, Wagner began writing it during the 1850s, when he had no hope of its being produced. It tells a multigenerational story of a world inhabited by humans, gods, and underworld creatures (Nibelungs [dwarves] and mermaids), all greedily seeking power and wealth symbolized by a golden ring. In the end, their avarice comes to nothing, and everything is destroyed. Wagner abandoned writing the third opera of the Ring when he fell under the spell of his patron's wife, Mathilde Wesendonck (1828–1902). Their affair angered Wagner's wife Minna, but it inspired *Tristan und Isolde*, a story of love, like his own for Mathilde, obliterating social convention.

Wagner's interest in Germanic myths, legends, and romances, his desire for a unified German state, and his anti-Semitism had its origins in a new philosophy, ethnic nationalism, created by German writers at the end of the eighteenth century and developed by Wagner and others during the nineteenth century. In its virulent form, ethnic nationalists believed that the nation-state should contain only members of the nationality that defined it. Other nationalities resident in the nation, especially Jews, should be expelled from its territory.

> **CULTURAL LINKAGES**

When the arrest warrant for Wagner was lifted in 1862, he returned to Germany. In 1864 the eccentric eighteen-year-old King Ludwig II of Bavaria invited him to Munich. The eighteen-year-old king's patronage allowed Wagner to produce *Tristan und Isolde* in 1865, his first premiere since *Lohengrin* in 1850. The premiere was conducted by his good friend Hans von Bülow, whom Wagner repaid by having a child the same year with his wife, Cosima, one of three illegitimate children of Franz Liszt. They would have two more children before Wagner's wife Minna died and Cosima was granted a divorce so they could marry. Wagner resumed composition of the last two operas of the Ring with King Ludwig's patronage. Ludwig also supported the production of the first two operas of the cycle, *Das Rheingold* (The Rhine Gold) in 1869 and *Die Walküre* (The Valkyries) in 1870. At this time King Ludwig was also building a dream castle designed in the imagined style of a Medieval castle with interior decor based on the romances that had inspired his beloved Wagner.

FIGURE 8.6
Bavarian King Ludwig II's *Schloss Neuschwanstein* (New Swanstone Castle), the inspiration for Disneyland's Sleeping Beauty Castle
Source: Library of Congress, Wikimedia Commons.

In 1871 Wagner, Cosima, and their three children moved to the small town of Bayreuth near Munich, where they began building an opera house suitable for the production of his Ring cycle. With the help of King Ludwig, as well as "Wagner societies" formed in Berlin, Vienna, Leipzig, and London, the Ring premiered in its entirety in 1876 at a music festival at the new Bayreuth opera house, including the last two operas of the cycle: *Siegfried* and *Götterdämmerung* (The Twilight of the Gods). One of the great cultural events of the nineteenth century, Wagner's festival was attended by kings and many of the most famous composers of the day. Wagner died of a heart attack in 1883. Until her retirement in 1906, Cosima managed the annual or bi-annual festival, adding Wagner's other music dramas, but not *Rienzi*, to the program. The festival immediately became a pilgrimage site for Wagner's legions of fans, and the Wagner family has continued to manage it up to the present. Wagner's operas, including *Rienzi*, have entered the standard repertoire of opera houses around the world. *Tristan und Isolde* is especially popular, and performances of individual operas from the Ring Cycle are regularly performed. Mounting the entire cycle is an enormously costly, ambitious, and rare undertaking. All productions of it are treated by the press as major, newsworthy cultural events.

> **CULTURAL LINKAGES**

AESTHETICS

Wagner's musical style, with its "endless melodies," chromaticism, harmonies liberated from the need to cadence regularly, and its rich orchestration, was enormously influential. Austrian and German composers Gustav Mahler (1860–1911), Richard Strauss (1864–1949), and Arnold Schoenberg (1874–1951) adopted many of its elements, while Frenchmen Claude Debussy (1862–1918) and Maurice Ravel (1875–1937) and Russian Igor Stravinsky (1882–1971), working in France, reacted against it in their compositions. It became the basis for American movie music, which is full of Wagnerian orchestral evocations of the emotions the characters are experiencing. And it set the stage for the eventual dissolution, during the twentieth century, of tonality as the harmonic basis for European classical music.

CULTURAL LINKAGES

The artistic impact of Wagner's music has always stood in relief against his deplorable personal life: his unpaid debts to his many benefactors, his infidelities, and his anti-Semitism, which lost him friends and admirers during his lifetime. Wagner's anti-Semitism continues to present a dilemma for some performers and audiences and raises the question of whether art can or should be separated from the artist. His music, a favorite of Adolf Hitler, became associated with an even-more-appalling form of anti-Semitism than he espoused. Even so, a number of important Jewish musicians, during his lifetime and since, have loved and championed his music. His operas have never been produced in Israel, although in 1981 conductor Zubin Mehta played a selection from *Tristan und Isolde* as an encore after announcing that audience members and musicians who objected to its performance could leave. A few left, but most stayed. Wagner's "Wedding March" (aka "Here Comes the Bride") from *Lohengrin* is probably more used today than Mendelssohn's, and "The Ride of the Valkyries" from *Die Walküre* enlivened a scene of attacking helicopters in Francis Ford Coppola's Vietnam-war film *Apocalypse Now* (1979).

WHERE DO I GO FROM HERE?

- Watch a few videos of the *Liebestod* and compare the ways it has been staged. Does it affect your perception of the music? Do you prefer one of the stagings over the others?

- Listen to "The Ride of the Valkyries" from Wagner's *Die Walküre*. Other than its appearance in *Apocalypse Now*, can you find other appearances of this composition in popular culture? How have those added to or changed its meaning, from your perspective?

- Listen to one or more of the following nineteenth-century Italian opera scenes. How do their musical elements compare to those heard in Wagner's work? "Largo al factotum della città" (Make Way for the Servant of the City) from *Il barbiere di Siviglia* (1816) by Gioachino Rossini; "Casta diva" (Chaste Goddess) from *Norma* (1831) by Vincenzo Bellini; "Ohimè! Sorge il tremendo fantasma e ne separa" (Alas! The Terrible Ghost Rises and Separates Us) from *Lucia di Lammermoor* (1835) by Gaetano Donizetti; "Libiamo ne'lieti calici" (Let's Drink from the Joyful Chalices) from *La Traviata* (1853) by Giuseppe Verdi; and "Quando me'n vo soletta per la via'" (When I Walk Alone in the Street) from *La Bohème* (1896) by Giacomo Puccini.

GATEWAY 32
EUROPEAN MUSICAL NATIONALISM

What Is It?

During the late nineteenth century the most powerful political current and one of the most important sources of musical inspiration in Europe was **ethnic nationalism**. At a time when large parts of Europe were either controlled by large, multi-ethnic empires or divided into small principalities and city-states, ethnic nationalists argued that every "ethnic group" had a right to its own nation-state (see map of Europe in 1815—Figure 8.3. After lengthy struggles for national unity, Italy was formed in 1861 and Germany in 1871. The Slavic, Hungarian, and German ethnic groups of the Austro-Hungarian Empire fought for their independence, as did the people of the Balkans, who sought independence from the Ottoman Empire. In this inflamed political environment many composers wrote music expressing nationalist sentiments in the hope of inspiring their people.

Our gateway to European **musical nationalism** is a symphonic tone poem called *Vltava* (also *The Moldau*), premiered in 1875 by the Czech composer Bedřich Smetana (pronounced BED-reekh SME-ta-na) (1824–1888). Vltava is the name of a river running through Czech lands in central Europe. The river's name in German is Moldau, and so in English this work is commonly known as *The Moldau*. It is one of a collection of six symphonic poems Smetana wrote to represent Czech history, culture, and landscape titled *Má Vlast* (My Homeland). Of these, *The Moldau* is the most frequently performed today. Noted Czech conductor Karel Ančerl (1908–1973) and the Czech Philharmonic perform it.

FIGURE 8.7
Bedřich Smetana around 1880, by Jan Vilímek (1860–1938)
Source: Wikimedia Commons.

 Listen to the first thirty seconds of the work.

How Does It Work?

Timbre

A variety of orchestral colors, featuring flutes and horns, express each moment in the story of the river's flow through Czech lands.

Texture

The textures are contrapuntal throughout with occasional block chords, especially at cadences.

Rhythm

A variety of duple, triple, and compound meters are deployed. **Compound meters** combine duple and triple meters, for example, a measure of six pulses can be grouped into two beats of three pulses each: 3+3.

Melody

Melodies feature stepwise motion. The main theme, representing the Moldau, has an arch shape and a recurring long–short–long–short rhythm; a contrasting "water" theme features rapid runs with an undulating, "wavy" shape.

Harmony

The harmony is tonal in both major and minor keys.

Form

The piece employs something like rondo form, with the Moldau and water themes returning after contrasting excursions to other material.

Performance Techniques

The performance features long crescendos and decrescendos and sudden contrasts of loud and soft in a manner reminiscent of Beethoven's symphonic style.

Listen to the first 1:30 of this performance for the way the opening "rippling" melodies come together in the "broad" Moldau theme.

FIGURE 8.8

Prague's Vyšehrad Castle on the Moldau River (Vltava).
Smetana and another famous Czech composer Antonín
Dvořák (1841–1904) are buried in the Vyšehrad cemetery
next to the church in this photo by Stanislav Jelen
Source: Wikimedia Commons.

What Does It Mean?

The meaning of the performance derives partly from the way the music expresses the program that Smetana wrote for it.

The composition describes the course of the Vltava, starting from the two small springs, the Cold and Warm Vltava, to the unification of both streams into a single current, the course of the Vltava through woods and meadows, through landscapes where a farmer's wedding is celebrated, the round dance of the mermaids in the night's moonshine: on the nearby rocks loom proud castles, palaces and ruins aloft. The Vltava swirls into the St John's Rapids; then it widens and flows toward Prague, past the Vyšehrad (the high castle on a hill above the Vltava), and then majestically vanishes into the distance, ending at the Labe (Elbe, in German).

He inserted text labeling each section into the score.

Listen to the entire performance following this timed listening guide with quotes from the score suggesting the meaning of the music.

LISTENING GUIDE 8.3

TIME	FORM AND PROGRAM	DESCRIPTION
0:00	Introduction: "The source of the Vltava"	Two solo flutes, accompanied by pizzicato strings, play undulating phrases representing the flowing and turning streams that will join to form the great Moldau River. The tension gradually increases until the flutes in parallel thirds form an icon of the sources of the Moldau coming together. The arrival of the streams at the Moldau is signaled by a sudden drop in register, with the undulating melody played by the strings.
1:05	AABC	The Moldau theme (A) in E minor, triple meter, and three stepwise phrases is played by the first violins, with the undulating, rolling river gesture continuing below it as accompaniment. The undulating accompaniment transitions back to a repeat of the Moldau theme.
2:01	ABCA	A varied repeat of the Moldau theme. A third playing of the Moldau theme is abruptly interrupted after the A phrase by the brass section, playing loudly.
2:57	"Hunt in the Woods"	A brass fanfare begins, played by horns and trumpets. Fanfares based on the overtone series of a natural, valveless horn are common musical icons of a hunt in symphonic music. The fanfare eventually breaks down into a single, repeated pitch and decrescendo, which serve to predict a transition to the next section.
4:01	"Country Wedding"	A village dance melody, with narrow range, frequent short, repeated notes, drone-like accompaniment, and steady pulsatile rhythm. The music gets louder, and then quickly fades away, as if passengers on a boat sailing along the

TIME	FORM AND PROGRAM	DESCRIPTION
		Moldau are moving out of earshot of the village dancing scene.
5:32	"Moonlight Dance of the Nymphs"	The bassoons announce a new section with long-held notes before the flutes, harp, and strings, muted to suggest a distant, eerie sound, enter quietly with the undulating water theme. A new melody with long-held notes enters punctuated by the horns. The music grows louder in anticipation of a new section, and the undulating water theme returns in the flutes and strings.
8:15	ABCA	The Moldau theme returns, mostly unchanged.
9:03	"St. John's Rapids"	Loud brasses, accompanied by running lines in the strings and woodwinds, portray the winding, churning rapids. Beyond its pastoral iconicity, it may represent the challenging struggle for national recognition. A scalar descent to a sudden pianissimo is followed by an ascending scalar passage presaging a new section.
10:24	A': "The broad flow of the Vltava"	A variant, faster rendition of the first (A) phrase of the "Moldau" theme returns in the parallel major key with quick arpeggiated accompaniment figures in the strings. The challenge has been met; the nation will prevail against the forces arrayed against it.
10:56	Coda	Fortissimo block chords segue into a Beethoven-like extended set of V-I cadences to emphasize the triumph of the nation ending in a decrescendo return to soft references to the undulating river theme. The piece ends abruptly with a very loud two-chord V-I cadence.
12:26	End	

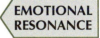

EMOTIONAL RESONANCE

In *The Moldau* Smetana, like Beethoven in his Sixth Symphony and Berlioz in the third movement of *Symphonie Fantastique*, paints a pastoral scene in music. But in this case it is not a generalized rural scene, as in those works, but a specific place in the territory where Smetana was born, a province of the Austrian Empire called Bohemia and today part of the Czech Republic. Using the techniques of programmatic music and evoking the spirit of Romanticism, Smetana was expressing in *The Moldau* his love of his homeland (*vlast*). Two interrelated phenomena awakened his patriotism: nationalism as a political philosophy and an uprising in 1848 in Prague by Czech nationalists against the Austrian Empire.

Smetana and many other composers living in empires and in small principalities used programmatic instrumental music like *The Moldau*, plus songs and operas with texts in their "national language" about the "nation's" historical events, rural legends, and tales, to rouse national sentiments and encourage these political movements. Programmatic music proved exceptionally useful, since the program could specify references to particular places like "St. John's Rapids" and the Vltava River. Rural peasant song and dance tunes, as in the section of *The Moldau* labeled "country wedding," also provided icons of the national culture and soundscape. Smetana's *The Moldau* has long captivated Czech listeners and those beyond the Czech lands.

What Is Its History?

Bedřich Smetana was born in 1824 in a provincial Bohemian town. His father, a beer brewer and amateur musician, spoke mainly German, the language of the Austrian Empire. A gifted pianist,

Smetana gave his first public performance at age six. Throughout his youth he was a popular figure at salons of the wealthy German-speaking elite. He moved to Prague in 1843 and began his study of composition there. His early works were mainly for solo piano until 1848, when nationalistic revolutions broke out across Europe. Beginning in March, 1848, nationalists in Bohemia and Hungary, seeking cultural autonomy or independence, rose up against the conservative, repressive government of the Austrian Empire. The revolutionary activities in Prague galvanized the twenty-four-year-old Smetana, who joined his comrades on the barricades in June and composed his first patriotic works, a *National Guard March* for piano and *Song of Freedom* for chorus. The Bohemian revolution, along with most of the others around Europe, was crushed. Luckily, Smetana was neither killed nor jailed.

After 1848 Smetana's life had its ups and downs. The 1850s were an unhappy decade for him. Locals interpreted his compositions as too progressive, too influenced by those of Berlioz, Liszt, and Wagner, and so he found a conducting job in Gothenburg, Sweden, something of a backwater. His wife, whom he married in 1849, died in 1859, and three of his four daughters died in childhood. In 1862 Smetana returned to Prague when the imperial government in Vienna loosened its policies concerning the Czech language. A Czech-language newspaper and a theater producing plays and operas in Czech were allowed to start up. Over the next twenty years Smetana enjoyed considerable success as he established the Czech nationalist style of composition in eight Czech-language operas based on Czech stories, the most famous of which is *The Bartered Bride* (1870). Between 1872 and 1879 he composed his *Má Vlast* cycle of six tone poems. Many of these operas and most of *Má Vlast* were composed after Smetana, suffering the same fate as Beethoven, went deaf in 1874. By 1879 he began to fear going insane, and in 1884 at the age of 60 he, like Robert Schumann, died in an insane asylum, both possibly from syphilis.

Smetana was only one of many European composers inspired by nationalist ideology and political activity during the nineteenth century. Some even turned to the collection of rural peasant songs in the national language. The songs and dances of these rural farmers, along with tales in oral tradition like those collected in Germany by the Brothers Grimm, were idealized as the perfect, ancient, unadulterated expression of the nation, *das Volk* (the folk, the people) in German. Their songs came to be called **folk songs** in English. Some collectors were particularly interested in the lyrics of the folk songs as expressions of the "national soul" of a particular nationality, but composers were mainly interested in their melodies and rhythms. They used folk music in many ways. They adopted folk tunes as themes for their symphonies, tone poems, and operas. They abstracted modal, metrical, rhythmic, and textural features (like drones) from folk tunes to write their own themes. And they used flutes, oboes and English horns, clarinets, and horns, all associated with the outdoors and the countryside, to "paint" pastoral village scenes in music.

These European nationalist composers can be divided into two groups: those who sought to arouse national sentiment in favor of national identity and nation-state status in opposition to a dominating political regime; and those who sought a basis, usually in folk tunes, for creating national sentiment in music in contrast to the prevailing "international" style coming mainly from Vienna and Paris. Besides Smetana, the first group includes:

Country	Composer	Composition
Hungary vs. Austria	Franz Liszt (1811–1886)	*Hungarian Rhapsody* No. 2 in C Sharp Minor (1847)
Bohemia/Czech vs. Austria	Antonín Dvořák (1841–1904)	*Slavonic Dances* (1878, 1886)
Norway vs. Sweden	Edvard Grieg (1843–1907)	*Peer Gynt Suite* No. 1 (1875)
Finland vs. Russia	Jean Sibelius (1865–1957)	*Finlandia* (1899)

The second group includes composers from Russia, which had an empire that subsumed many national groups, and from Spain, which for centuries had been a kingdom. In Russia and Spain composers attempted to create a sense of national identity different from that of neighboring nations.

Nation	Composer	Composition
Russia	Alexander Borodin (1833–1887)	*In the Steppes of Central Asia* (1880), tone poem
Russia	Modest Mussorgsky (1839–1881)	*Boris Godunov* (1874), opera
Russia	Pyotr Ilyich Tchaikovsky (1840–1893)	*Marche Slave* (1876), tone poem
Russia	Nikolai Rimsky-Korsakov (1844–1908)	*Russian Easter Festival Overture* (1888)
Spain	Isaac Albéniz (1860–1909)	*Suite Española* No. 1, Op. 47 (1886), piano solo

While ethnic nationalism was a central aspect of the political, cultural, and musical life of Europe during the late nineteenth century, its application in the United States was not obvious. The population of an idealized, nationalist European nation-state consisted of a single nationality, which could be represented and evoked in music by the rural "folk music" of that nationality. The United States, however, was, and is, noisily multiethnic. What music could a classical composer use to represent its supposed national soul? In the 1890s Czech nationalist composer Antonín Dvořák supplied one possible answer after he accepted an invitation to become the director of the National Conservatory of Music in New York City. New York philanthropists had founded the National Conservatory in 1885 with the goal of providing a low-cost music education to the needy including women, minorities, and the disabled. Their hope for federal funding, on the model of the Paris Conservatoire, was unfulfilled, and the conservatory eventually closed after donors lost their fortunes in the stock market crash of 1929. But in 1893 the offer of a substantial salary attracted one of the most admired composers in Europe at that time. Once in America, Dvořák set about to discover the basis for an American national style. One of his African American students, Harry Burleigh (1866–1949), introduced him to "Negro spirituals," which Dvořák championed, along with Native American music, as the musical sources of American classical music. Burleigh, a baritone who went on to compose classical arrangements of spirituals, became one of the first important African American composers. In 1893 Dvořák employed pentatonic scales characteristic of both African American and Native American music for some of the themes of his Symphony No. 9 in E Minor, "From the New World," Op. 95. It was an immediate hit with orchestras all over the world and is still regularly performed. Neil Armstrong took a recording of it to the moon in 1969.

In 1895 homesickness took Dvořák back to Prague. In his wake two Jewish composers born in Brooklyn kept the flame of American musical nationalism alive in the twentieth century: George Gershwin (1898–1937) with his orchestral one-movement composition *Rhapsody in Blue* (1924) and opera *Porgy and Bess* (1935), based on African American and Jewish melodic elements; and Aaron Copland (1900–1990), whose scores for ballets *Billy the Kid* (1938), *Rodeo* (1942), and *Appalachian Spring* (1944) evoke the landscape and culture of rural white America (see Chapter 10, Gateway 43). For nearly thirty years, from the 1970s to early 2000s, numerous bills were introduced in Congress to designate the Appalachian square dance the national dance of the United States. They failed, an illustration of the difficulty of applying European notions of musical and ethnic nationalism in a nation defined by civic nationalism and multiculturalism.

CULTURAL LINKAGES

HARRY T. BURLEIGH

FIGURE 8.9
Harry Burleigh
Source: Wikimedia Commons.

WHERE DO I GO FROM HERE?

- Listen to *Eight Slavonic Dances*, Op. 46, No. 1 by Antonín Dvořák. Note similarities to the melody of Smetana's "country wedding" in *The Moldau*.

- Listen to *Hungarian Rhapsody* No. 2 in C-sharp Minor by Franz Liszt. Which melodies, rhythms, or types of ornamentation may come from folk music?

- Listen to one of the pieces listed above by a Russian musical nationalist composer. What musical elements suggest that this composition is in a national style?

- Listen to Symphony No. 9 in E minor, "From the New World," Op. 95, Mvt. II by Antonín Dvořák. Where else have you heard these themes?

GATEWAY 33
CLASSICAL MUSIC AT CENTURY'S END

What Is It?

At the end of the nineteenth century, German and Austrian composers were absorbing the lessons of Beethoven and Wagner. Johannes Brahms (1833–1897), working in Vienna, was enthralled by Beethoven's art. He wrote four symphonies, two piano concertos, and many piano works in a conservative style compared to Wagner's. They extended the tradition of non-programmatic orchestral composition going back to the mid-eighteenth century. Others worked in the more progressive vein of Wagner's harmonic innovations: Richard Strauss (1864–1949) in programmatic tone poems in the manner Liszt; and Gustav Mahler (1862–1911) in ten influential symphonies, the last incomplete.

> **CULTURAL LINKAGES**

In Paris Wagner's operas were popular, but at the same time artists and writers were creating a new movement that came to be called modernism. **Modernism** refers, among other things, to the rejection of traditional boundaries and rules in art. In this vein, some late-nineteenth-century French artists were imagining new ways, sometimes literally blurring boundaries, to paint the natural world, a movement called **impressionism**. And some French writers were abandoning logic and narrative in favor of evocation and suggestion, a movement called **symbolism**. Our gateway to music at the end of the nineteenth century is a one-movement orchestral work by French composer Claude Debussy (1862–1918) titled *Prélude à l'après-midi d'un faune* (Prelude to the Afternoon of a Faun), first performed in 1894. This work draws, to some extent, on Wagner's models as it renders in music a poem by an important symbolist poet: *L'après-midi d'un faune* by Stéphane Mallarmé (1842–1898) in a style some historians interpret as an early foray into modernism.

Mallarmé's poem relates the thoughts of a faun awakening from a dream. A faun is not a young deer (fawn) but the Roman analog of the Greek god Pan, a horned half-man-half-goat creature (*satyr* in Greek) who roamed the forests playing his panpipes in search of pleasure with wine and young female deities (nymphs). The poetry is full of evocative, surprising, and contradictory poetic images of the sights and sounds of the forest: "stifling with heat the cool morning struggles"; "an arid rain"; "scintillating flowers"; "frivolous shade." Against this sylvan backdrop, in language that is direct but elusive,

FIGURE 8.10
Claude Debussy
Source: Nadar. Paris, Wikimedia Commons.

the faun tries to remember his love making with two nymphs—or, as he says, "Did I love a dream?" His flute-playing, from which flow rain and breezes and breath, provides a "prelude" to his amorous adventures. But the effort proves too much and, addressing the nymphs, he concludes, "With no more ado . . . I must sleep . . . and . . . open my mouth to wine's true constellation! Farewell to you, both: I go to see the shadow I have become."

 Listen to the first thirty seconds of the recording.

How Does It Work?

Timbre

Debussy uses timbre, for which tone color is an apt synonym, to paint in music Mallarmé's depiction of the changing sensations of the forest scene and the faun's desultory mood. A flute solo represents Pan's flute and horn calls suggest the outdoors. The sound of woodwinds, long associated with the outdoors in European classical music, is featured prominently. The strings play **tremolos** (on strings, short, rapid, back-and-forth bowing) softly to suggest the rustling of breezes through the forest leaves and the changing, dappled light. The timbres change continuously but gradually to suggest the faun's flow of memory and sensation.

FIGURE 8.11
A faun in the form of the Greek god Pan teaches young Daphnis, the son of Hermes and a nymph, to play the panpipes
Source: Virtusincertus, Wikimedia Commons.

Texture

The piece begins with an unaccompanied flute solo. Often the strings play soft murmuring sounds in the background to woodwind and horn solos.

Rhythm

A sense of pulse is almost completely absent. The music flows along, like a breeze or a brook, unconstrained by a beat or meter.

Melody

The opening flute melody has an inverted arch shape and uses a mainly chromatic scale.

Harmony

The harmony is tonal, but cadences are spaced far apart, and so the feeling of tonality is considerably weakened.

Form

The piece has an ABA form. The A sections are based on the inverted arch-shaped, chromatic flute melody. In the B section a new melody is introduced.

Performance Techniques

The most striking performance techniques involve the use of mutes to quiet the horns and the strings and create a muffled sound. In one section the strings bow over the fingerboard rather than near the bridge, as usual, to create a new tone color. The score directs the flute player to play "sweetly and expressively."

Listen to the first minute of this performance for the melodic shape of the solo flute melody and the shimmering timbre of the orchestra when it enters.

Listen to the entire recording following this timed listening guide.

LISTENING GUIDE 8.4

TIME	FORM	DESCRIPTION
0:00	A	A section
0:00	a	A solo flute enters with a chromatic, inverted arch-shaped melody in its low register.
0:25	b	The orchestra enters with a harp arpeggio suggesting shimmering forest light followed by horn calls.
0:57	a	The flute melody returns, this time accompanied by soft, long tones in the orchestra.
1:36	c	The orchestra enters on a dominant seventh chord. It seems to suggest light rather than tension, followed by a new melody based on thirds which "develops" into a three-tone motive.
2:04	a′	The orchestra enters quietly on a sustained chord and then the flute plays its melody. It continues to play variants of the melody in a way that sounds improvised.
2:43	a″	The flute plays a faster version of the melody over the shimmering sound of harp arpeggios. The section resolves on a major chord and a slight pause, suggesting a new section is coming.
3:22	B	Second section
3:22	Melodic runs	The tone color (timbre) of the orchestra changes, followed by rapid runs by different instruments.
3:51	d	A new melody is introduced by the oboe followed by a series of gentle crescendos and decrescendos and changing tone colors in the orchestra, the first time the traditional timbre of a string orchestra asserts itself.
5:10	ee′e″	The orchestra plays a new melody with a series of descending phrases, followed by a varied repeat, and then a short motive from the melody.
6:57	A′	A variation of the A section returns.
6:57	a′a″a‴a⁗	The flute plays the opening melody but more slowly than at the beginning, followed by suggestions in the oboe and flute of forest sounds. The oboe plays a repeat of the melody followed by the flute playing it twice more. The oboe plays the very end of the melody.
9:27	cadence	A cadence on a major triad followed by the horns playing the opening melody in parallel thirds to a soft ending on a major triad.
10:07	End	

What Does It Mean?

CULTURAL LINKAGES

For the French musical public in 1894, *Prélude à l'après-midi d'un faune* meant something in relation to nearly a century of expressive Romantic music by Beethoven, Berlioz, Chopin, Wagner, and Smetana and in relation to the current artistic climate in France. Just as Debussy did in *Prelude to the Afternoon of a Faun*, Beethoven, Berlioz, and Smetana had painted rural scenes in their music, one indicator of the Romantic fascination with the wildness and restorative qualities of nature as opposed to the regulated intensity of urban life. Chopin had modeled a dreamy, rhythmically fluid expressivity. And Wagner's *Tristan und Isolde* was just one example of the Romantic interest in

Ancient and Medieval myths and legends like the story of Pan. Debussy, and Mallarmé, could be interpreted as following in that long Romantic tradition.

As a young musician Debussy was fascinated by Wagner's music, which was all the rage in the Paris of his youth. In 1888 and 1889 he attended the Bayreuth festival and absorbed Wagner's new approach to "endless melody." The opening phrase of Wagner's *Tristan* Prelude echoes eerily in the opening of Debussy's *Prelude*, each with their solo opening lines, shared chromatic, inverted arch-shaped melodies (much extended in Debussy), and opening, unstable, non-tonic chords. In the B section the strings enter and play subdued echoes of the sweeping crescendos and decrescendos so prominent in the *Tristan* Prelude. On the other hand, in *Prelude to the Afternoon of a Faun*, Debussy, while absorbing aspects of Wagner's style, rejects its dramatic, emotional character. Rather than expressing the surging passions of characters in a drama or the composer's unrequited love as in *Symphonie Fantastique*, Debussy paints, following Mallarmé's text, a gentle picture of an idyllic forest afternoon in a manner somewhat reminiscent of the pastoral quality in some symphonic movements by Beethoven and Berlioz but in a musical style partly indebted to Wagner's innovations.

Debussy's dreamy, gauzy, gentle music matches the artistic and literary milieu of France during the late nineteenth century. Mallarmé was one of a group of French poets breaking the formal boundaries of poetic tradition in elusive, free-form, illogical ("arid rain") poetry devoid of traditional poetic meters and rhyme schemes. This group has been collectively called **symbolist poets** because of their striking verbal symbols of a real world, perhaps experienced in dreams, rather than the Romantic expressions of the inner, emotional life of the poet. In addition to Mallarmé, who was an acquaintance of Debussy's (he studied piano with Mallarmé's mother), other famous symbolist poets include Charles Baudelaire (1821–1867), Paul Verlaine (1844–1896), and Arthur Rimbaud (1854–1891).

French painters of the period were also challenging the conventions of their art. In 1874, while Debussy was a student at the Paris Conservatory, Camille Pissarro (1830–1903), Claude Monet (1840–1926), and Auguste Renoir (1841–1919) mounted an exhibition that scandalized the artistic establishment. Although their paintings of rural landscapes and seascapes continued the Romantic fascination with nature, they did so in a new style that erased the formality and energy of traditional representations in favor of suggestions of the shapes they were viewing, the colors they were seeing, and the way light illuminates an ever-changing, fluid natural world. One critic, responding negatively to the exhibit, seized on a painting by Monet called *Impression: Sunrise* and sarcastically dubbed the style impressionism. The name stuck. Debussy's *Prélude à l'après-midi d'un faune* represents the sonic expression of the late-nineteenth-century French literary and artistic world, and his style is often called musical impressionism, although Debussy disliked the epithet, probably because of its negative connotation at the time.

FIGURE 8.12
Impression: Sunrise **by Claude Monet**
Source: Musée Marmottan Monet, Wikimedia Commons.

 Listen one more time to *Prélude à l'après-midi d'un faune* for the pleasure of Debussy's "impressionistic" painting of a dreamy, wine-soaked summer day.

What Is Its History?

Debussy was born in 1862 to a family of shopkeepers in a small town a few miles west of Paris. He began studying piano at seven years old and, at age ten, entered the Paris Conservatoire, where he studied for the next eleven years. An accomplished pianist who might have had a concert career, he spent the summers of his late teens in Russia serving the musical needs of a wealthy businesswoman who was a patron of composer Pyotr Ilyich Tchaikovsky. In 1884 Debussy won the Conservatory's prestigious Prix de Rome for composition in spite of music that pushed against the boundaries of traditional musical style. He spent two unhappy years in Italy, unimpressed by the operas of Donizetti and Verdi. A few years later, at the Bayreuth festival, he found the style, Wagner's, that would influence his early work. In 1889 he attended the Paris *Exhibition Universelle*, a world's fair for which the Eiffel Tower was built. Cultural exhibits and shows from various parts of the world included a "negro village," which displayed people as if in a zoo; Buffalo Bill's "Wild West Show" with sharpshooter Annie Oakley; and performances by a Javanese gamelan (Chapter 5, Gateway 21). The sound of the gamelan, with its approximately equidistant pentatonic scale, made a profound impression on Debussy. He began using equidistant chromatic scales and equidistant six-pitch (hexatonic) **whole-tone scales** (e.g. C-D-E-F♯-G♯-A♯), both of which eliminate the directionality of half steps (leading tones) in European major and minor scales and chords. His piano miniature "Pagodes" (1903) uses a pentatonic scale and extreme high and low pitches to suggest the sound world of the Javanese gamelan.

Debussy's chaotic personal life involved a series of affairs and two marriages. Both a girlfriend and his first wife attempted suicide by shooting themselves when he left them. He had his only child, a girl, with his second wife. When the child was three, he wrote a famous set of six piano pieces called *Children's Corner Suite* (1908), not to be played by children but to evoke playfulness of childhood. He died of cancer in 1918 during World War I.

Debussy was not especially productive. In addition to *Prelude to the Afternoon of a Faun*, his most famous symphonic work, he wrote others in this genre, including *Nocturnes* (a set of three), *La Mer*, and *Images* (a set of three). Other highly regarded works include a ballet premiered in 1912 in Paris by the *Ballets Russes* called *Jeux* (Games), an often-played string quartet (1893), numerous suites of miniatures for solo piano (the most famous of which is "Clair de lune," based on a poem by Paul Verlaine), and many songs setting the poetry of Mallarmé, Baudelaire, and other symbolist poets. His large-scale masterpiece is an opera titled *Pelléas et Mélisande*, which eschews arias in favor of a speech-like recitative style that would become the norm of twentieth-century operas.

Debussy's innovations were enormously influential in France and the United States in the early twentieth century. He knew all the most important composers in the French musical scene, all of whom had to react in one way or another to his work. Among the champions of his revolutionary musical style were French composers Erik Satie (1866–1925) and Maurice Ravel (1875–1937) and three foreign composers residing in Paris: Manuel de Falla (1876–1946) from Spain, Igor Stravinsky (1882–1971) from Russia, and Arthur Honegger (1892–1955) from Switzerland. In the United States composers Duke Ellington (1899–1974) and George Gershwin (1898–1937) studied Debussy's orchestrations and harmonies, which included, for example, ninth chords (chords built in thirds that include scale degrees 1, 3, 5, 7, and 9) moving in parallel motion. This type of chord movement is not technically allowed in traditional classical harmony, but it became a common feature of jazz. Later in the century German composers adopted some of his innovations, and the dreamy, fluid quality of his music resonates in New Age music, which first came to prominence in the 1960s and 1970s.

FIGURE 8.13
Debussy and Igor Stravinsky in Paris
Source: Bettmann/Getty Images.

WHERE DO I GO FROM HERE?

- Compare the elements of Debussy's *Estampes*: 1. "Pagodes," which imitates the Javanese gamelan, to the elements of the Javanese gamelan performance heard in Chapter 5, Gateway 21.
- Compare the elements of Debussy's *Children's Corner Suite*: VI. "Golliwog's Cake Walk," which mimics ragtime piano rhythms, to a recording of a rag by composer Scott Joplin.
- *Suite Bergamasque*, 3. "Clair de lune" (Moonlight) is featured at the end of the 2011 film *Ocean's Eleven* in an orchestral version. Where else have you encountered this composition?
- Listen to one or more of the *Trois Gymnopedies* (Three Dances for Naked Athletes) (1888) for piano by Erik Satie. How are they similar to and different from Debussy's piano pieces?
- Listen to *Jeux d'eau* (Play of Water) (1901) for piano by Maurice Ravel. How does this music resemble and differ from the piano music of Debussy and Satie?

GATEWAY 34
AFRICAN AMERICAN RELIGIOUS MUSIC

What Is It?

After the Civil War ended in 1865, a number of social activists began to record in musical notation the songs of newly freed African Americans. Among these "slave songs" were many religious songs called **spirituals**. Another group of activists, members of the American Missionary Association, an antebellum Protestant abolitionist organization, founded Fisk University in Nashville in 1866, just a year after the end of war, with the stated purpose to educate "the most helpless and neglected class [freed slaves]" on the model of northeastern universities like Harvard and Yale. The founders believed that "the reign of equal educational privileges and equal rights . . . if successful, would revolutionize the state" of Tennessee. They argued that education, modeled on the private colleges of New England, was indispensable if the south in general, and newly freed African Americans in particular, were to flourish after the Civil War.

CULTURAL LINKAGES

One of those northern college traditions was the glee club. Glees, descendants of the English madrigal (Chapter 4, Gateway 13), were popular *a cappella* songs in three- and four-part harmony sung by gentlemen members of English social clubs (glee clubs) between 1750 and 1850. In the U.S. during the second half of the nineteenth century, glee clubs morphed into all-male collegiate choirs, starting with the Harvard Glee Club in 1858, the University of Michigan Men's Glee Club in 1859, and the Yale Glee Club in 1861. They performed a wide repertoire of classical and popular music that rarely included old English glees. Among these collegiate choirs was a vocal ensemble of men and women at Fisk University called the Fisk Jubilee Singers. They formed in 1871. Nearly forty years later, in 1909, another incarnation of the ensemble, a male quartet, recorded "Swing Low, Sweet Chariot," the first spiritual ever recorded. Our gateway to African American religious music of the late nineteenth century is a recording of "Swing low, sweet chariot" by the Fisk Jubilee Singers in the early 1980s.

FIGURE 8.14

The Fisk Jubilee Singers in 1882, with Ella Sheppard at the keyboard

Source: Deep Roots Magazine, Wikimedia Commons.

 Listen to the first minute of the song, the first verse and chorus.

How Does It Work?

Timbre

A female soloist sings in the falsetto manner of a classically trained singer alternating with a choir of male and female voices.

Texture

The texture alternates solo singing with a chorus singing block chords.

Rhythm

The meter is duple with some **syncopation** (offbeat accents), as in the opening short–long–short rhythm on the words "swing–LOW–sweet."

Melody

The melody has an undulating shape in a pentatonic scale.

Harmony

The harmony is triadic with a V–I cadence at the end of each phrase.

Form

This is a strophic song. It begins with a refrain, and then each strophe alternates a verse and a refrain. Each verse and each refrain is performed in solo-chorus, call-and-response form.

Refrain:
Swing low, sweet chariot (solo)
Coming for to carry me home (chorus)
Swing low, sweet chariot (solo)
Coming for to carry me home (chorus)

Verse 1:
I looked over Jordan and what did I see (solo)
Coming for to carry me home (chorus)
A band of angels coming after me (solo)
Coming for to carry me home (chorus)

Verse 2:
If you get there before I do (solo)
Coming for to carry me home (chorus)
Tell all my friends I'm coming too (solo)
Coming for to carry me home (chorus)

Verse 3:
I'm sometimes up and sometimes down (solo)
Coming for to carry me home (chorus)
But still my soul seems heavenly bound (solo)
Coming for to carry me home (chorus)

Performance Techniques

The female soloist sings with vibrato in a classical style with almost no variation from strophe to strophe.

Listen to this recording with these elements in mind, following this timed listening guide.

LISTENING GUIDE 8.5

TIME	SECTION	DESCRIPTION
0:00	Chorus	Soloist and chorus sing the refrain "Swing low . . ." in tonal harmony.
0:32	Verse 1	"I looked over Jordan" sung to the same melody as the refrain. In the second line of text, "A band of angels . . .," the choir hums the choral harmony.
1:02	Chorus	"Swing low . . .," the second time through with the choir humming the chords.
1:36	Verse 2	"If you get there . . ."
2:08	Chorus	"Swing low . . .," the second time through with the choir humming the chords.
2:40	Verse 3	"I'm sometimes up . . ."
3:13	Chorus	"Swing low . . .," sung a little more softly and slowly than before, ending with a ritard.
4:02	End	

What Does It Mean?

Many meanings have been associated with "Swing low, sweet chariot" and other spirituals. Some of the meanings derive from the words, some from the style of performance, some from the performers, some from the sources of the spiritual songs, and some from their unique position in American society.

Spirituals entered the repertoire of college choirs like the Fisk Jubilee Singers after the Civil War from transcriptions (notations) of the singing of formerly enslaved Africans, including some of the original members of the choir. Created by the enslaved, spirituals registered, in a highly distilled fashion, the cruelty and suffering they endured and their hope for freedom either in this world or the next. The lyrics borrow their imagery from Biblical stories they heard at outdoor religious services called camp meetings, some of which were about the exodus of the Israelites from Egypt and their crossing the Jordan River to Canaan, the promised land. From readings of Deuteronomy 12:10, they heard, "But when ye go over Jordan, and dwell in the land which the Lord your God giveth you to inherit, and when he giveth you rest from all your enemies round about, so that ye dwell in safety . . ." These enslaved men and women created spiritual songs based on this Biblical imagery as coded messages of encouragement and resistance: the chariot that took the prophet Elijah to heaven (from 2 Kings chapter 2) as their mode of transportation to the promised land of freedom, "over Jordan," where other runaways had gone before, but "I'm coming too." Other spirituals evoke a trip to freedom on a boat ("Michael, row the boat ashore") or a metaphorical train ("I hear the gospel train is coming . . . get on board, children") on the underground railroad; reference the Biblical story of a plea to the Egyptian Pharaoh to release the enslaved Israelites ("Tell old Pharaoah . . . let my people go"); convey hope of salvation from the misery of slavery ("Children, we shall all be free," "Steal away, steal away to Jesus, I ain't got long to stay here," and "Didn't my Lord deliver Daniel"); and express their sorrows and woes under the master's lash ("Nobody knows the trouble I seen," "I'm troubled in mind," and "I've been buked and I been scorned").

Enslaved African Americans originally sang spirituals in a call-and-response style with hand-clapping, stamping, and dancing. They sang in unison and in parallel harmonies typical of some African singing styles. But the Fisk Jubilee Singers followed a different performance model, one

CULTURAL LINKAGES

AESTHETICS

ECONOMIC ACTIVITY

consistent with the mission of the university. The Fisk University treasurer George L. White (1838–1895) had a modest music education and believed that choral concerts by a group of Fisk singers might be able to raise money for the college, which was in dire need of financial support. He and his students adapted the unison, improvised tradition of slave songs to the contemporary, notated, classical style and harmonies of university glee clubs. Adding choral arrangements of Stephen Foster's popular songs to their repertoire, a group of eleven male and female students, along with White and a white female principal of a black school in Alabama, set out in October of 1871 on what they thought would be a month-long tour of the northern states to give concerts and raise $20,000 for the university.

CULTURAL LINKAGES

The project was beset with difficulties, not least the resistance and prejudice they endured. Maggie Porter, a singer with the group, reported that "There were many times when we didn't have a place to sleep or anything to eat. Mr. White went out and brought us some sandwiches and tried to find some place to put us up."[55] White hoped that churches would sponsor his students' concerts, filled as they were with sacred songs. But northern audiences knew African American culture mainly through the distorting lens of minstrelsy (Chapter 7, Gateway 30). White's hoped-for sponsors, members of polite, religious society, viewed such performances dimly and sometimes refused to sponsor their concerts. When they did sponsor one, they were poorly attended until word of mouth and favorable newspaper reviews attracted larger audiences. A contemporary account of their trip includes these descriptions of the reception and the meaning northern listeners attached to their singing of spirituals:

EMOTIONAL RESONANCE

Was there not so much odium attached to negro concerts, as represented by burnt cork minstrels, that people of taste and character did not think it becoming to rush in crowds to a paid concert by negroes? . . . People came to despise, to ridicule, to wonder, but remained to admire, and to bury their foolish prejudices. . . .[56] Once under the magnetism of their music, prejudice melted away, and praise of their performance was upon every tongue . . . The music carried the people with ecstasies of sympathy and pleasure . . . Gray-haired men wept like little children . . . Our people can now listen to the genuine soul music of the slave cabins [sung by] living representatives of the only true, native school of American music.

In this period of segregation, racial violence, and Jim Crow laws, the weeping of these northern concert audiences may reveal a complex mix of emotions: sympathy and compassion for the experiences of these singers; pleasure at their musical skill; grief for the hundreds of thousands of lives lost in the civil war that ended slavery; and perhaps repentance for their own attitudes towards race. Such is the power of music.

CULTURAL LINKAGES

These old songs in their new form, coupled with the positive reception of northerners, led the Fisk singers themselves to change their understandings of the songs. Many of them were freed men and women who only after their emancipation had "learned their letters," some self-taught. Those who hadn't been enslaved knew about life under slavery from parents and grandparents. The father of Ella Sheppard (1851–1914), the group's pianist and the best educated among them, lived in Nashville and "had bought himself for $1800," meaning that he had purchased his own freedom (see Figure 8.14). He then bought his daughter Ella from her mother's owner in Mississippi and moved to Ohio to escape slavery. There Ella was able to study voice and piano. She wrote that the spirituals "were sacred to our parents, who used them in their religious worship and shouted over them . . . It was only after many months that gradually our hearts were opened to the influence of these friends and we began to appreciate the wonderful beauty and power of our songs."[57]

Her ambivalence toward the songs was anticipated in *My Bondage and My Freedom*, a book written in 1855 by Frederick Douglass (1818–1895), freed from slavery before the Civil War and an ardent and influential abolitionist and social reformer:

I did not, when a slave, understand the deep meanings of those rude, and apparently incoherent songs. I was myself within the circle, so that I neither saw or [sic] heard as those without might see and hear. They told a tale which was then altogether beyond my feeble comprehension; they were tones, loud, long and deep, breathing the prayer and complaint of souls boiling over with the bitterest anguish. Every tone was a testimony against slavery, and a prayer to God for deliverance from chains. The hearing of those wild notes always depressed my spirits, and filled my heart with ineffable sadness. The mere recurrence, even now, afflicts my spirit, and while I am writing these lines, my tears are falling. To those songs I trace my first glimmering conceptions of the dehumanizing character of slavery. I can never get rid of that conception. Those songs still follow me, to deepen my hatred of slavery, and quicken my sympathies for my brethren in bonds.

> **EMOTIONAL RESONANCE**

Because of the difficulties in attracting an audience to their concerts, the Fisk Jubilee Singers' first tour lasted five months rather than the planned one month. They returned to Fisk University in March of 1872 to a warm welcome, having, at great personal sacrifice, met their goal of raising $20,000. "The permanency of the university was assured,"[58] a chronicler of their trip wrote. The first building on the Fisk campus was named Jubilee Hall.

> **ECONOMIC ACTIVITY**

What Is Its History?

> **CULTURAL LINKAGES**

The term "spiritual" for a religious song dates to the early 1700s and a Protestant religious movement called the Great Awakening. Some Protestants advocated for a new kind of personal religious experience based on redemption from sin and personal salvation. Preachers traveling in the South sought both black and white converts, and some white ministers invited blacks into their congregations. New religious and social movements almost always require new songs, and so in 1707 Dr. Isaac Watts (1674–1748), a minister in England, published a collection of new *Hymns and Spiritual Songs* with tuneful melodies and rhyming poetry in a contemporary language designed to be appealing and easily understood. Among Watts' hymns were "Joy to the world, the Lord is come" and "When Isra'l, freed from Pharoah's hand/left the proud tyrant and his land," which resonated in the spiritual "Go Down, Moses": "When Israel was in Egypt's land/Let my people go/Oppressed so hard they could not stand/Let my people go." Other composers added more hymns to this tradition later in the eighteenth century, including "Amazing Grace (how sweet the sound)" and "On Jordan's stormy banks I stand/and cast a wishful eye on Canaan's fair and happy land/I am bound for the promised land." In black spirituals Canaan stands for Canada, the northernmost stop on the underground railroad.

During the first half of the nineteenth century a Second Great Awakening among Baptists and Methodists in the south spread Christianity to the "unchurched," both whites and blacks, at camp meetings and revival meetings where the enslaved heard these hymns and spiritual songs and transformed them in aural tradition into their own language and musical style. The style echoes African elements also preserved in *Candomblé* (Chapter 6, Gateway 26), such as pentatonic scales with a minor third and a minor seventh and improvised call-and-response singing. Watts' lyrics about sin and personal salvation were made to reference salvation from the harsh reality of slavery.

Something close to the original performance style of African American spiritual songs is preserved today by performers from the Georgia and South Carolina Sea Islands. During the eighteenth century these mosquito-infested, malaria-infected places sent plantation owners scurrying to higher, healthier ground on the mainland. Enslaved Africans were left in charge of growing rice using tidal flows of water, knowledge of which they had brought with them from the west coast of Africa. Left to their own devices, blacks living on or near the islands preserved musical styles closer to their African roots than did mainland black populations in contact with white culture. Recent recordings by Bessie Jones and the Georgia Sea Island Singers and The McIntosh County (Georgia coast) Shouters give some idea of the antebellum style of singing by blacks. These groups perform **ring shouts**, which originated among enslaved African Americans as religious rituals featuring dancing in a circle, hand claps, and call-and-response singing. A modified, subdued version of this style is conveyed in a performance of the spiritual "Roll, Jordan, Roll" in the 2013 movie *12 Years a Slave*, which won the Academy Award for Best Picture.

The first printed collection of African American songs, titled *Slave Songs of the United States*, was published in 1867 by three white abolitionists from the north who had worked in South Carolina to aid the enslaved during the Civil War. The Fisk Jubilee Singers took some of their songs from that collection but also learned from other sources. After a white minister heard them sing in Nashville, he taught them "Swing low, sweet chariot," which he had heard sung by workers at his school in Mississippi and which he attributed to a recently freed African American named Wallis Willis.

CULTURAL LINKAGES >

Choirs at other black colleges founded by missionaries in the 1860s and 1870s took up this glee-club style of spiritual singing and have enjoyed considerable fame since then. Choirs from Morehouse College, a male college founded in Atlanta in 1867, Hampton University, founded in 1868 in Virginia, and Tuskegee University, founded in 1881 in Alabama with freed slave Booker T. Washington (1856–1915) as its first president. R. Nathaniel Dett (1882–1943), a composer and director of the Hampton Singers, and William L. Dawson (1899–1956), a choral conductor and composer at Tuskegee, both produced sophisticated arrangements of the spirituals. These "concert spirituals" have long been a point of pride in the black community and a staple of the music programs in black colleges and universities. In the twentieth century they entered the repertoire of white college and high-school choirs and became an important genre in the pantheon of American classical music.

That movement of spirituals into the mainstream of American music was aided in no small part by Henry T. ("Harry") Burleigh, whose grandfather had bought his own freedom in 1835. Raised in Erie, Pennsylvania, his grandfather taught him to sing spirituals. Burleigh studied voice and gained some fame locally as a classical singer before he was accepted at the National Conservatory of Music in New York in 1892, just in time to meet its new director, Antonín Dvořák, and introduce him to spirituals as "the only true, native school of American music." Burleigh arranged spiritual songs for voice and piano and toured the country as a concert artist, spreading the popularity of spirituals. Since then, under his influence, many African American classical singers have included spirituals, along with European opera arias and art songs, in their repertoire. Among them were Roland Hayes (1887–1977), who had studied at Fisk and had sung in the Fisk Jubilee Singers; Marian Anderson (1897–1993), who in 1939 sang a famous concert for 75,000 people at the Lincoln Memorial after being denied access to segregated concert halls in Washington, D.C.; and Paul Robeson (1898–1976), a famous Broadway actor and singer. More recently African American opera singers Kathleen Battle, Jessye Norman, and Leontyne Price have included spirituals in their recitals.

In 1874, just as the Fisk Jubilee Singers were spreading excitement about African American spirituals at home and abroad, American composer Philip Bliss (1838–1876) published *Gospel Songs: A Choice Collection of Hymns and Tunes*, with the goal of updating the style and language of Protestant religious music, including Dr. Watts' spirituals. White and black composers linked to the Pentecostal movement have created **gospel songs** ever since. In the 1930s black **gospel quartets**, in some sense descendants of the Fisk Jubilee Singers, gained fame on the radio, including such groups as the Dixie Hummingbirds, the Five Blind Boys of Alabama, and the Soul Stirrers. In the same decade a blues singer from Georgia named Thomas A. Dorsey (1899–1993), the so-called "father of black gospel music," composed "Take My Hand, Precious Lord," made famous by Mahalia Jackson (1911–1972), the most important mid-twentieth-century gospel singer. The favorite gospel song of Dr. Martin Luther King, Jr., she sang it at his funeral in 1968.

TECHNOLOGY >

One of the characteristic sounds of gospel music has long been the organ, used as a solo instrument and to accompany large choirs of singers in church services (see Chapter 5, Gateway 20 for more on the pipe organ). Beyond its historical association with religious services, several features of the organ make it ideal for accompanying the sounds of large groups of singers. Typically an organ has at least two keyboards played with the hands, along with a pedal keyboard played by the feet in a very low-pitch register. This setup allows the organist to play over a very wide pitch range, from very low pitches on the pedal keyboard to very high pitches at the top of the range of the keyboards played with the hands. In addition, organs also have a wide dynamic range. Playing loudly is necessary when accompanying the great volume of sound produced by many people singing together. Playing softly accompanies moments of prayer and contemplation. After 1935 many American churches that had used the piano as an accompaniment instrument, because they couldn't afford to install a permanent pipe organ, purchased the new electric Hammond B-3 organ. One of the main features of the Hammond B-3 organ is that the player can change its timbre quickly by moving sliding drawbars to increase or decrease

FIGURE 8.15
A Hammond B-3 organ
Source: Cliff, Wikimedia Commons.

the volume of different components of the sound in a way that changes the timbre. Bright timbres are valued because they can cut through the timbre and volume of a large choir.

During the 1950s and 1960s black gospel music, with its optimistic themes of salvation, provided the soundtrack of the Civil Rights Movement along with a new genre it inspired: soul music. **Soul music**, the creation of Ray Charles (1930–2004), James Brown (1933–2006), Aretha Franklin (1942–2018), and other singers raised on black gospel music, combined gospel's stylistic elements with secular lyrics that expressed the hope for freedom from Jim Crow laws, segregation, and racial discrimination, as well as themes of love, relationships, and sex. Today gospel and popular singers such as Mavis Staples have applied the singing style of gospel music to the performance of spirituals. And black gospel choirs have introduced the general public to the style of African American religious singing. Today the Fisk Jubilee Singers and other black college vocal groups perform both spiritual and gospel songs as well as elements of jazz in their programs.

WHERE DO I GO FROM HERE?

- Listen to the 1909 recording of "Swing low, sweet chariot" and some of the other early recordings of the Fisk Jubilee Singers. What similarities and differences do you notice among them?

- Watch a video of Bessie Jones and the Georgia Sea Island Singers or the McIntosh County Shouters singing songs of slavery and performing ring shouts. Which musical elements connect to spirituals and which musical elements are reminiscent of examples of African music and *Candomblé*?

- Listen to a performance of a spiritual by Marian Anderson or Paul Robeson.

- Listen to a performance of the gospel song "Precious Lord, Take My Hand" by Mahalia Jackson.

- Find some recordings of field hollers, work songs, ring shouts, and spirituals. What musical elements do they share?

CLOSING

During the late nineteenth century composers kept alive the Romantic spirit of the early years of the century by writing tone poems and other instrumental music designed to express in music the emotions inherent in poetic images, philosophical ideas, fictional narratives, and works of art. Their orchestral and piano music took on a fuller sound due to changes in the manufacture of metals and musical instruments and to the willingness of wealthy capitalist patrons to take the place of the aristocracy in support of extravagant and expensive forms of music making. And nationalism unleashed a new *raison d'être* for composers: serving the aspirations of their national community for a sovereign, independent nation-state. The musical legacy of this period includes:

- school and military brass bands;
- the modern piano;
- the current size of the large symphony orchestra;
- the public concert in a large concert hall; and
- music conservatories (and university schools of music).

Finally, African American music continued to enter the mainstream of American musical life, not with the parodied banjo, but in the form of spirituals arranged in a European manner for college choirs.

THINGS TO THINK ABOUT

- Compare the way the musical worlds opened by the four gateways in the chapter respond to the ambitions of ethnic nationalism.
- Compare the reaction of audiences to each of the four gateway compositions. How do these reactions compare to your own response to "new music," that is, new musical genres and styles? Do you seek it out, welcome it, or avoid it?

NEW TERMS

arioso	gospel songs	soul music
bel canto	impressionism	spirituals
civic nationalism	*Leitmotifs*	symbolism
compound meter	Modernism	symbolist poets
ethnic nationalism	music drama	syncopation
field holler	musical nationalism	whole-tone scale
folk songs	Nationalism	work song
Gesamtkunstwerk	ring shout	
gospel quartets	romances	

Music History during the Long Twentieth Century

THE LONG TWENTIETH CENTURY begins around 1890, with the sale of the first musical recordings, and continues to the present. The use of electricity and electronics to record, produce, and transmit music is the defining feature of this era of music history. People all over the world now enjoy the ability to hear music whenever they want and in the absence of the musicians who perform it. Recordings have revealed a vast repository of human music making that previously was largely unknown to people who could not hear it live. Recordings have captured virtually the entire history of twentieth-century musical life, especially those traditions that, before the advent of recording technology, were transmitted in aural rather than written tradition. Recordings have helped to knit together people and societies around the world who are able to hear and see each other sing, play, and dance and imagine worlds far beyond their own.

During the twentieth century the United States replaced Europe as the dominant force in world affairs, its military and economic muscle matched by its influence in music, movies, and fashion. As a consequence, Part III shifts focus to American music. Each of its six chapters contains gateways representing the four major categories of musical life today: popular music, jazz, classical music, and world music.

PART III

MUSIC FROM THE TURN OF THE TWENTIETH CENTURY (1890–1918)

9

IN 1877 THOMAS EDISON invented the phonograph, making recording and playback of sound possible for the first time. Though early phonographs were recorded to fragile tinfoil and later wax cylinders, by the 1890s recordings were being made to flat discs that could be used to make many duplicates. For the first time, it became possible to mechanically reproduce a musical performance, and to hear it in a time and place distant from where it was originally performed. This technology ushered in an era that transformed the ways that people experienced music. Musical performances could be preserved, musical sounds could be distributed widely, and recordings could be bought, sold, and owned. Edison and his contemporaries surely could not have imagined the multi-billion-dollar music industry that developed after recordings and radio replaced sheet music as the main way people consumed popular music in the 1920s. Thanks to recordings we can construct detailed histories of jazz, all kinds of popular music, and folk and classical traditions from rural America and around the world dating back to around 1900. This chapter traces the beginning of these histories for the long twentieth century in the period between 1890 and the end of World War I in 1918, the turn of the twentieth century.

The phonograph and the mechanical reproduction of sound were some of the many technological innovations that occurred from 1890 to 1918, innovations that were just one aspect of other rapid changes in social, economic, and cultural life in many parts of the world. Many people moved to cities, where the availability of electricity transformed many aspects of daily life. Industrialization accelerated rapidly, especially in the United States. European power in world affairs continued to decline, a process begun in the nineteenth century as European imperial powers lost colony after colony to independence movements in the Americas.

In 1890 traditional European monarchies were firmly in place in much of the continent, but after a devastating World War from 1914 to 1918 Europe lay in economic ruin, with many of its imperial rulers, who had been the source of so much musical patronage for centuries, deposed. The United States, in contrast, had enjoyed extraordinary industrial and economic growth in the 1890s. In 1917 it intervened decisively in what Americans at the time called the European War on the side of Britain, France, and the Russian Empire against Germany, the Austro-Hungarian Empire, the Ottoman Empire, and Bulgaria. World War I was the first war conducted with weaponry produced on an industrial scale, including newly invented tanks and airplanes. It resulted in more than nine million

FIGURE 9.1

Thomas Edison in 1878 with an early model of his phonograph. Photo by Levin C. Handy
Source: Bardy-Handy Collection. Library of Congress, Wikimedia Commons

dead and countless millions wounded. During and immediately after the war, the Russian Empire had become the Soviet Union, and the Austro-Hungarian and Ottoman Empires had dissolved into a plethora of small nation-states. At the end of the war in 1918 the United States had emerged as the most economically powerful country in the world. The twentieth century has been called the "American century" for the scope of the United States' global reach and influence in politics, economics, and culture, including music.

Between 1890 and 1918, European stability was challenged not only by political strife among nations and empires but by social and economic unrest as well. Misery among working-class industrial workers coupled with poverty in rural villages caused a flood of emigrants to the United States, Argentina, and Australia (some six million people immigrated to the United States from Europe between 1901 and 1910 and American cities grew enormously in size). There was growing resistance to European colonialism and imperialism in the Americas, Africa, India, and Southeast Asia. This political and economic malaise stimulated new thinking and creativity among European artists and intellectuals, who began to question the inevitability of European progress and cultural superiority. Their work contained radical departures from the cultural, intellectual, and artistic traditions of the nineteenth century.

Intellectuals began to question the nature of human psychology and the physical world. Sigmund Freud (1856–1939) theorized that unlocking the unconscious was the key to understanding human behavior, and he developed a process of therapeutic interventions for psychologically troubled individuals that he called psychoanalysis. Albert Einstein (1879–1955) undermined the previously taken-for-granted dichotomy between energy and matter, arguing that matter could be transformed into energy in his famous equation $E = mc^2$. As scientists showed that the psychological and the material worlds were more complex than initially thought, movements in the visual arts like impressionism, surrealism, and cubism shifted away from realistic representations of the world and towards capturing sensory experiences and psychological states. In his cubist works Pablo Picasso showed ways to do that, beginning with early paintings like his 1907 *Les Demoiselles d'Avignon* (The Damsels [young women] of Avignon). The content of the painting, five nude prostitutes (the Avignon in the title is a reference to a street in Barcelona known for its brothel) facing unabashedly toward the viewer, was scandalous in its time. Its form was equally surprising for its elimination of three-dimensional perspective in favor of two dimensions; its treatment of the human body as a set of geometrical shapes; and its drawing of the two faces on the right to resemble African masks he had seen in a French ethnographic museum. This last move captured the turn-of-the-century fascination with Asian, African, and Middle Eastern cultures, whose works of art were on display in museums and in world's fairs in major cities in Europe and the United States.

Collectively these artists came to be called modernists and their work examples of modernism. Modernists wanted to liberate themselves from traditional artistic norms in ways analogous to revolutionaries trying to bring down the old economic and political order in Europe. The notion of modernism in music also arises at this time. Like visual artists, modernist European composers began to move away from musical sounds that were considered pleasing and easily understood and towards music that called those values into question and demanded deeper engagement from listeners. Tonal music, the basis for European classical music for the previous two centuries, began to fade among European composers. Modernist musical aesthetics changed the course of classical music in the long twentieth century.

The period from 1890 to 1918 is also a time when popular culture emerged as a significant force in the world's cultural life. The term popular is used to reference the taste of the general public (the populace) and refers both to large numbers of people (popularity) and to the lower and middle classes. The idea of popular culture for large masses of people became possible only with the late-nineteenth-century growth of cities and the expansion of education to nearly all segments of the general population. Until this time, cultural production (books, folklore, art, music) in Europe was not widespread, that is, popular. Rather, each class or stratum of society (the church, the courts of the aristocracy, the urban bourgeoisie, and the rural peasantry) had its own kind of music. Universal education and masses of people living and earning wages in towns and cities created a new literate audience with modest amounts of money and leisure time to spend on cultural activities such as reading, visiting museums to view art, acquiring copies of paintings rather than originals, attending sports events, buying tickets to vaudeville shows and motion pictures, and purchasing newly invented phonographs to play music at home. Not everyone lived in cities, of course. Some people in the United States still lived in the countryside. They farmed the land in conditions that demanded hard work and barely met their needs for daily subsistence. Arguably the most significant musical genre that emerged under these conditions was the blues, a genre created by African American communities in rural areas of the South where Jim Crow laws institutionalized the suppression of black voting rights, and lynchings and other violent legacies of slavery persisted. The blues, along with vaudeville songs, outdoor band concerts, and the new genre of ragtime, were all part of the dynamic popular musical culture in the United States during this period.

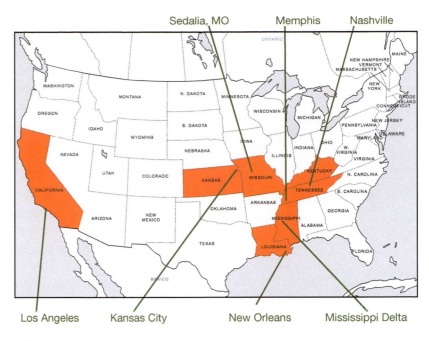

FIGURE 9.2
Map of the continental United States

This chapter includes several gateways to types of music that were products of these changing times, spanning European classical music, jazz, popular music, and world music:

- the blues, one of the precursors to jazz and a genre that has enjoyed a rich history in its own right;
- American band music, which proliferated in this period as a popular music;
- American popular piano music, through the example of ragtime, a genre showing influence from a number of musical traditions;
- early modernism in European classical music; and
- Balinese gamelan playing a genre that emerged in this period in the wake of Dutch conquest of the island of Bali.

 GATEWAY 35
THE BLUES

What Is It?

The musical genre known as the blues provides the foundation for much of American popular music and jazz during the long twentieth century. Historians trace its roots to African American culture at the turn of the twentieth century. Our gateway to the blues is "Backwater Blues" by the vocalist Bessie Smith (1892–1937). Even though it was recorded in 1927, in some of its musical elements and lyrical themes it is an example of a blues with roots in the period from 1890–1918. The blues came to prominence during this period and was widely performed in rural and

FIGURE 9.3
Bessie Smith in 1936
Source: Everett Historical, Shutterstock.

urban African American communities, though rarely recorded. A **blues** is a strophic song most typically in a repeating AAB form of 12 bars. The blues were (and are) an entertainment music for enjoyment, dancing, and partying. They also were (and remain) a way for performers and audiences to deal with hardships and struggles that are related to economic oppression, racism, sexism, infidelity, domestic abuse, and other perils of daily life. As a genre name it derives from phrases like "I've got the blues" used when people are feeling down.

One of the defining features of the blues is what has come to be called **blue notes**. These are pitches on the third, fifth, or seventh scale degree of the major scale that are lowered to pitches either in the minor mode or otherwise outside the major scale, even if the underlying harmony is major. Blue notes seem to give the blues a characteristic sad quality, perhaps because they are often part of a minor mode. This example, and many examples of the blues, has a swing feel. In a swing feel beats are subdivided unequally with the first note longer than the second note. Sometimes this is approximated by suggesting an underlying triple subdivision of the beat. The relative length of notes in swing often depends on the tempo of the music, and a uniform swing feel is best achieved when musicians playing together listen to one another and synchronize the ways that they are swinging the rhythmic durations.

 Listen to the first thirty seconds for the overall sound and the swing feel.

How Does It Work?

Timbre

This recording features a female vocalist with a particularly bright tone along with a piano. The recording technology of 1927 results in the timbre of both the voice and the piano sounding slightly muffled.

Texture

The texture can be described as melody with accompaniment, where the vocal carries the melody most of the time and piano provides the accompaniment.

Rhythm

The song has a steady beat in a duple meter maintained by the piano. The vocalist and the pianist incorporate a swing feel throughout the performance. They also incorporate a good deal of syncopation.

Melody

The melody is based on a major mode with a great deal of microtonality as the vocalist slides between pitches. It also relies heavily on blue notes.

Harmony

The piano establishes the harmonic structure, which features chords based on thirds, each one with a duration of either two or four bars.

Form

After a two-bar piano introduction, the song takes the form of a strophic song where each verse lasts twelve measures. The lyrics of each of the seven verses have an internal form of AAB, where one line of text (A) is repeated once, albeit with different underlying harmony and usually a different melody, followed by a new line of text (B).

Performance Techniques

In addition to sliding between pitches, Bessie Smith is very flexible with her phrasing, one of the markers of a master of the blues style. For some of the phrases, she seems to rush slightly and sings slightly ahead of the beat. For others, she seems to slightly delay and sings the lyrics slightly late or behind the beat. Sometimes she sings the phrases directly on the beat. In addition, after each line of text the piano plays a short improvised phrase, which means each line of text is a call and response between the vocalist and the pianist.

Listen to the first thirty seconds, the first verse, for the way Bessie Smith slides into pitches and anticipates or delays beats.

Listen to the entire example following this timed listening guide.

LISTENING GUIDE 9.1

TIME	FORM	INTERNAL FORM	LYRICS	DESCRIPTION
0:00	Instrumental introduction			A piano plays a rolling repeated pattern in the low register of the piano, setting up a swing feel and a steady pulse maintained throughout the recording.
0:04	Verse 1	A	When it rains . . .	The vocalist sings the opening verse. She slides upwards to the pitch on the "five"
0:13		A	When it rains . . .	and "skies" in the first line and "rains" in the second line. She slides downwards
0:23		B	Then trouble's . . .	at the end of the pitch when she sings "night" in both of the first two lines. The piano remains in the background while she is singing, but responds to each line with an improvisation. The improvisation after the first "B" line is a good example of syncopation.
0:32	Verse 2	A	I woke up . . .	
		A	I woke up . . .	
		B	That's enough trouble . . .	
1:00	Verse 3	A	Then they rowed . . .	
		A	Then they rowed . . .	
		B	I packed . . .	
1:28	Verse 4	A	When it thunders . . .	In verse 4 between the first and third lines, the left hand of the piano shifts from its rolling repeated pattern to a more active, descending low-register line emphasizing a swing feel, which is featured in place of the high register improvisations that have been happening so far. This perhaps serves as an icon of the low sound of thunder referenced in the lyrics.
		A	When it thunders . . .	
		B	There's thousands . . .	

continued

TIME	FORM	INTERNAL FORM	LYRICS	DESCRIPTION
1:54	Verse 5	A	Then I went . . .	Verses 5, 6, and 7 feature a new
		A	Then I went . . .	style in the piano accompaniment
		B	Then looked . . .	where the left hand plays only on
				the beat in punchy, accented
				notes that resemble a march.
2:21	Verse 6	A	Backwater blues . . .	The improvised piano responses in
		A	Backwater blues . . .	Verses 6 and 7 are generally in a
		B	Cause my house . . .	lower register and less active than in
				previous verses, perhaps reflecting the
				mood of the lyrics that conclude the
				vocalist's story of hardship without
				resolution of that hardship. At the same
				time, they continue an upbeat, swinging,
				danceable rhythm.
2:49	Verse 7	A	Mmmmmmmm . . .	
		A	Mmmmmmmm . . .	
		B	There ain't no . . .	
3:11				The piano plays its final response and ends
				the song on an accented major chord.
3:16	End			

What Does It Mean?

CULTURAL LINKAGES

The lyrics of this blues tell the story of a flood that destroys the home of the song's protagonist and the homes of many others. Each verse tells part of the story, which includes a five-day rainstorm (verse 1), the protagonist getting trapped in her house by the flood waters and evacuated in a rowboat (verses 2 and 3), the displacement of many other people (verse 4), a reflection by the protagonist on her now-destroyed house (verse 5), and a lament on having nowhere to live (verses 6 and 7). These devastating lyrics are set to a bouncy, rhythmic feel on the piano. While these musical elements seem contradictory, they demonstrate some of the nuances of the blues. For black communities subject to segregation, discrimination, and violence under Jim Crow laws, the blues was music for coping with racial oppression and music for dancing and having a good time. "Backwater Blues" embodies both purposes with its danceable rhythms and lyrics that comment on the suffering of a community after natural disaster and, more subtly, the way that racism and economic oppression exacerbated that suffering.

Flooding in areas of the American South near the Mississippi River and other waterways has long been an inevitable consequence of weather patterns. When heavy rains come, floodplains (lowlands) are often flooded with backwater, stagnant water that is not part of the main flow of the river. This less desirable (and less valuable) land was typically the home of blacks, subject as they were to a lack of access to equal pay and steady employment, and of lower-class whites.

"Backwater Blues" was recorded and released in 1927 in response to a flood in Nashville that forced nearly ten thousand people, mostly African Americans, from their homes. The recording became popular in the aftermath of the catastrophic Mississippi flood later that year, where over 90 percent of the flood victims were African Americans. Although white flood victims were entitled to receive relief services for free, black flood victims were forced to pay for food and other services and in some cases take loans from landowners in a version of slavery that continued more than sixty years after the end of the Civil War. The blues provided one way to deal with this oppression at an individual and collective level.

Since the lyrics do not mention these issues directly, finding the meanings of "Backwater Blues" involves interpreting the lyrics as a coded reference to oppression and shared adversity. In her study of Bessie Smith and other blues singers, scholar and activist Angela Davis has argued that the blues is not merely a series of complaints about life's challenges, but a way of strengthening a collectivity and offering glimpses of the possibility of moving beyond oppression.[59]

 Listen again to "Backwater Blues," paying special attention to the lyrics as both a personal and a collective story.

The AAB form of each strophe of the blues is an important part of what makes the blues both an effective means of catharsis amidst adversity and a vehicle for fun and entertainment. It can be understood as a pattern of tension-release-resolution. The first line of each strophe of a blues introduces a situation or problem (tension) and is typically sung over a harmony based on the tonic chord (I) for the full four measures of the line. When the first line of each strophe's lyrics is restated in the second line, the underlying harmony moves to the IV chord for two measures before returning to the I chord for the next two measures. The singer also alters her performance of the melody, sliding on different words, modifying the duration of particular notes and the rhythm of the line, or changing pitches of certain notes of the melody, often microtonally. The second line, then, is not simply a repeat of the first but rather it often shifts the emphasis of the first line because of harmonic, melodic, and expressive changes. For example, when Bessie Smith sings in verse 5 "then I went and stood upon a high and lonesome hill" the first time, she ascends to a high sustained pitch on the word "went." When she repeats the line over the IV chord, she remains in a lower, relaxed register and stretches out the pitch on the word "I." With its emphasis on "went," the first line could be interpreted as expressing the strain and anxiety in the act of going. The second line's lower register perhaps makes it sound more "blue," and by stretching out the word "I," Smith might be accentuating the loneliness of leaving a destroyed home, and in a sense releasing the tension of the first line.

> EMOTIONAL RESONANCE

Listen again to the first strophe of "Backwater Blues." Listen for the changes in harmony and the ways that Smith alters her performance of the melody.

These repeated lines in the typical form of the blues set up the resolution that the third (B) line of text brings. This part of the blues form typically occurs over a V chord for the first two bars, which, as a dominant, leads strongly back to the I chord for the final two bars, giving the harmony a sense of resolution. The B line in verse 5, "then looked down on the house where I used to live," answers the question of why the protagonist went to the top of the lonesome hill, an answer that brings this blues to an even darker image of the results of the flood, the image of homelessness. Blues singers employ a number of narrative strategies connecting the B lyrics of the blues to the preceding repeated A lyrics. They move the storyline along, interpret the A lyrics in a surprising way, introduce humor, or make the struggle of the story even heavier. The harmony and lyrics work together to bring a brief moment of resolution to each strophe of the blues. The resolution in the lyrics is often not a happy one, and the cyclical, strophic nature of the blues prevents the resolution from being too final, providing an immediate opportunity to continue dealing with the issue at hand in the next strophe.

A number of musical elements of the blues have their roots in African music and the music of African slaves in the American south. Two of these are clearly heard in this example: call and response and microtonality. The call and response here involves Bessie Smith presenting each line as a "call" characterized by her expressive use of pitch and rhythmic flexibility and the pianist, James P. Johnson, offering "responses" as short, improvised phrases. With its roots in a number of musical traditions of Africa, call and response by definition requires collective interaction. Call and

> CULTURAL LINKAGES

response among musicians and between musicians and audience members is common in the blues, as well as in forms of music making that became common during and after the time of slavery in the U.S., such as work songs, ring shouts, field hollers, and spirituals (Chapter 8, Gateway 34). The call and response elements of these genres offered a communal, shared experience where many participants were interacting in musical ways. This collective participation served to foster community, communication, and solidarity among African Americans in the time of slavery and in the oppressive times of Reconstruction and Jim Crow.

 Listen again to several strophes of "Backwater Blues" for the way the vocal and piano perform call and respond with one another.

> AESTHETICS

The microtonality that we hear in Bessie Smith's performance can be traced through the transatlantic slave trade to many musical traditions of the Americas (Chapter 6, Gateway 26). Though many other musical traditions around the world share this trait, in the case of the blues it is a marker of an African American aesthetic that appears alongside musical elements drawing on European roots such as harmony based on thirds and the fixed equal temperament of the piano.

What Is Its History?

The blues emerged in impoverished African American communities of the American South, mostly likely in the period after the Civil War at the beginning of the Jim Crow era. Documentation of the blues from the turn of the twentieth century is scarce because the blues was not originally written down and recording technology was not yet prevalent. Blues songs were first published as sheet music in 1912. "Backwater Blues" and many of Bessie Smith's songs were not recorded until the 1920s.

FIGURE 9.4
Gertrude "Ma" Rainey
Source: Wikimedia Commons.

> CULTURAL
> LINKAGES

"Backwater Blues" is an example of what is known as the classic blues. The **classic blues** was usually sung by a black female singer accompanied by a band, or a pianist. Because there were at least two people performing together, forms, meters, and harmonies had to be established or more or less agreed upon in advance. Bessie Smith was a protégé of Gertrude "Ma" Rainey (1886–1939), who was known as "The Mother of the Blues" since she was one of the first African American women to perform blues music professionally. Mamie Smith (1883–1946, no relation to Bessie) was the first to record the blues in 1920. Rainey became well known through her extensive tours in minstrel shows (Chapter 7, Gateway 30), where she performed the blues as early as 1902.

The classic blues was usually performed in theaters, tents, and "juke joints" (informal entertainment houses that were a big part of African American social life) where audiences paid to attend organized performances. These settings created a space for black female singers and their audiences to deal with topics that were considered off limits in public, topics such as domestic violence, marital infidelity, and homosexuality intertwined with the struggles of racial discrimination and economic oppression. Rainey's "Prove it on Me Blues" (1928), for example, articulates female homosexuality. In Bessie Smith's graphic "Send Me To the 'Lectric Chair" (1927), Smith sings as a protagonist who catches her man with another woman, kills him in retribution by cutting his throat, and remorselessly asks a judge to give her the death penalty. Blues like these gave voice to the lived experiences of their audiences, especially those of black women, sometimes in the form of exaggerated fantasies. When recording technology became more readily available in the early 1920s, recordings of the classic blues were popular among black audiences on what were known as **race records**: phonograph recordings produced between the 1920s and 1940s that record labels marketed to African Americans.

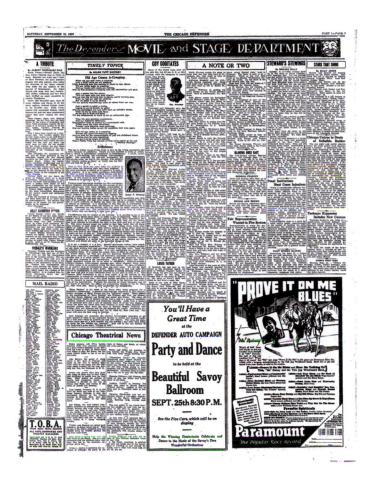

FIGURES 9.5A AND 9.5B
An advertisement for Ma Rainey's "Prove it on Me Blues" in the September 22, 1928 national edition of the African American newspaper *The Chicago Defender*
Source: Courtesy of Alex van der Tuuk.

Bessie Smith, known as "The Empress of the Blues," was born in Chattanooga, Tennessee.[60] Her rise to prominence began in 1909 when she began to perform in black theater and tent shows in the South, Midwest, and East Coast. Along with Rainey, she enjoyed widespread popularity starting in the early and mid-1920s with the advent of race records and their promotion of classic blues. Smith sold over four million records between 1924 and 1929, starred in the short film *St. Louis Blues* (1929), performed on Broadway, and became an international symbol of the classic blues singer. The 1920s also witnessed the rise of jazz to great popularity, and Smith recorded and performed with some of the most well-known jazz musicians of her time such as Louis Armstrong, Coleman Hawkins, and James P. Johnson (the pianist on "Backwater Blues"). These collaborations demonstrate that, though the blues was in many ways a precursor to the development of jazz, there was a great deal of exchange among musicians of these genres as each contributed to the development of the other.

In the late 1920s and 1930s, the popularity of classic blues records inspired the recording of the country blues or rural blues, which had developed at the end of the nineteenth century. The **country blues**, as its name suggests, emerged in rural areas. It typically involved a male singer accompanying himself on the guitar, fiddle, or banjo. The performer could adjust the form, tuning, and harmonies of a given song to better suit the lyrics of the song, the vocal range of the singer, or his mood or whims, since he did not have to depend on coordinating with other instrumentalists or the pre-set tuning of a piano. In many cases, the country blues was not divided neatly into three four-bar phrases per strophe, but rather it varied by strophe depending on the lyrics. W. C. Handy (1873–1958), the composer of the popular "St. Louis Blues" (published as sheet music in 1914), said that he was inspired by a country blues singer that he witnessed in 1903 performing at a train station in Tutwiler, Mississippi, in the Mississippi Delta region. Though no one can say for certain where or when the blues first developed, this region is today considered the birthplace of the blues. In the late 1920s a number of country blues musicians began to release race records including Blind Lemon Jefferson (1893–1929), Charley Patton (1891–1934), and Eddie "Son" House (1902–1988).

FIGURE 9.6
Robert Johnson, with guitar, and blues musician Johnny Shines (1915–1992) c. 1935
Source: Getty Images / Robert Johnson Estate.

One of the best-known country blues musicians is Robert Johnson (1911–1938), whose recordings from 1936 and 1937 inspired innovations in guitar performance by countless performers including Jimi Hendrix, Stevie Ray Vaughan, Eric Clapton, and the Rolling Stones. His most influential songs include "Sweet Home Chicago" (1936), "Love in Vain" (1937), and "I Believe I'll Dust My Broom" (1937). Like other country blues musicians, a robust mythology arose around Robert Johnson both during and after his life. The central story about Johnson is that he met the devil at a crossroads at midnight and sold his soul in exchange for an incredible ability to play the guitar, a Faustian bargain. Though many have sought to attribute this legend to the fantasies of passionate fans, Johnson recorded several songs that also propagated this myth such as "Me and the Devil Blues" (1937) and "Cross Road Blues" (1936). Myths about great musicians can be found in musical traditions almost everywhere. These myths serve to explain the seemingly unbelievable virtuosity of a musician or elevate a musician to a god-like status and great renown. Johnson died one year after his final recordings, but his recordings continue to inspire blues musicians and those exploring the roots of guitar-based popular music genres.

The blues has continued to develop as a genre in its own right alongside jazz and continues to be relevant in people's lives today. Blues musicians like Muddy Waters, B. B. King, and Taj Mahal have continued the legacy of Robert Johnson and others as guitarist-singers of the blues. There are blues clubs and blues festivals all over the world. Chattanooga has dedicated both a museum and a performance venue to Bessie Smith. The film director Martin Scorsese directed a seven-part documentary series *The Blues* (2003) that traces the history of the blues. In 2015 actor-rapper-singer Queen Latifah starred as Bessie Smith in a biographical film titled *Bessie*. Over the last century, the blues has served people everywhere as a vehicle for entertainment, dance, the expression of emotion, and the experience of collective solidarity in the face of struggle.

WHERE DO I GO FROM HERE?

- Listen to a Robert Johnson recording and explore its sound and meaning. What issues do the lyrics approach? What aspects of form or meter vary in each strophe, if any? How does his style connect to other styles of popular music that you are familiar with? Are there any more recent recordings of this particular song that you could compare with Johnson's recording?

- Listen to some 1920s or 1930s recordings from other blues singers Mamie Smith, Gertrude "Ma" Rainey, Blind Lemon Jefferson, and Eddie "Son" House. Compare the musical elements of these examples share with those of "Backwater Blues."
- Watch *Bessie* (2015) starring Queen Latifah. How does this film depict Bessie Smith? Does it mythologize her in any way? Which aspects of her life and music are emphasized and which are minimized?

GATEWAY 36
AMERICAN BAND MUSIC

What Is It?

In the nineteenth century, municipal bands, large ensembles of wind instruments and percussion, played an important role in the popular culture of the United States and Europe. At the turn of the twentieth century, recording and radio technology had not yet transformed the way people listened to music (that happened about twenty years later). Bands in the U.S. thrived because they provided popular entertainment across the country. The most prominent composer of band music was John Philip Sousa (1854–1932). Our gateway to American band music is his composition "The Stars and Stripes Forever" (1896). Sousa composed more than a hundred marches, many of which are still played today. "The Stars and Stripes Forever" is his best-known march, and was declared by an act of Congress in 1987 to be the National March of the United States of America.

Bands are sometimes called wind ensembles, symphonic bands, concert bands, or, when the musicians play while marching or performing coordinated movements, marching bands. In the United States today band music is performed most often in high schools, college and university music programs, military ensembles, and competitive drum and bugle corps. This recording of "The Stars and Stripes Forever" is by the "The President's Own" United States Marine Band, which Sousa raised to national prominence during his time as its conductor (1880–1892). Today the U.S. Marine Band is considered one of the premier bands in the United States.

FIGURE 9.7
John Philip Sousa
Source: Elmer Chickering, Wikimedia Commons.

 Listen to the first twenty seconds of this recording.

How Does It Work?

Timbre

A variety of timbres are produced by the ensemble of brasses, woodwinds, and percussion in different combinations.

Texture

Several versions of melody with accompaniment appear throughout the piece, with the final section of the piece adding an **obbligato**, which in band music means a second melody played simultaneously and in counterpoint with the main melody. Sections of homophonic rhythm are interspersed throughout.

Rhythm

Duple meter, characteristic of marches, is heard throughout, with prominent syncopations in the melody and "oom-pah" (low–high) accompaniments.

Melody

The melodies are generally in a major mode with some chromaticism.

Harmony

The piece uses tonal harmony throughout, plus quickly shifting chromatic harmonies in several sections.

Form

The form is a version of the typical American march form, which Sousa helped to standardize. It follows a variation of the European dance form, AABBCC'DCC'DCC'.

- Introduction: a fanfare (4 bars).
- First strain, or section (A): the first melody (16 bars), with balanced four-bar phrases (repeated once).
- Second strain (B): the second melody (16 bars). It is common for the second strain to be played softly once, and then repeated loudly, a performance practice tradition that is often not notated on the score.
- Trio (C): the third melody, played legato (16 bars). March trios are often in a secondary key: the subdominant for major-key marches (like in this example), and the relative major for minor-key marches. The trio here is repeated with some variation in the harmony and melody (C').
- Break strain, or "dogfight" (D): the fourth strain is often the most exciting music of a march and contrasts sharply with the more reserved trio melodies (24 bars).
- Repeat of the trio: the repetition of the trio features an added obbligato, played by a solo piccolo (CC').
- Repeat of the break strain (D).
- Grandioso: the final repetition of the trio melody (CC'), played at a loud dynamic, a fuller texture, with the obbligato (this time with all of the piccolos playing together), and with an additional countermelody in the trombones.

FIGURE 9.8
"The President's Own" United States Marine Band in 2017
Source: GySgt Rachel Ghadiali.

Performance Techniques

This performance by "The President's Own" United States Marine Band features great dynamic contrast among the various strains of the form. It also demonstrates the way that musicians in large wind ensembles precisely match articulations so that a given note played by multiple musicians is played uniformly in both accent and length.

Listen to the first minute or so and notice the slightly contrasting timbre between the first and second time through the first strain (A) and the contrast between the relatively strong quality of the first strain and the more lyrical second strain (B).

Listen to the entire recording following this timed listening guide.

LISTENING GUIDE 9.2

TIME	SECTION	FORM	DESCRIPTION
0:00	Introduction	I	A four-bar fanfare in octaves, with the full ensemble playing. Notice the syncopation in the second measure and the ascending chromatic line in the third measure.
0:04	First Strain	A	The major-key melody, in E-flat major, features a rhythm where a beat is divided into a long note followed by one or two short notes. This is typical of American march style and is less used in, for example, British marches.
0:19	Repeat of First Strain	A	
0:34	Second Strain	B	A more lyrical melody, with long held notes, is played softly the first time. Notice the playful, off-beat octave displacements in the upper winds.
0:50	Repeat of Second Strain	B	Second strain repeat, played loudly the second time, with the addition of full brass and percussion. Such changes provide variety to music that is otherwise notated as a literal repeat.
1:06	Trio	C	The trio modulates to the key of the IV chord (A-flat in this case) and presents a stately melody of long-held tones played by the saxophones and clarinets. This phrase ends on the dominant of the new key in a half-cadence.
1:24		C'	The melody repeats in the second half of the trio with some variation and the harmony ventures into more distant territory before ending with a full authentic cadence.
1:39	Break Strain	D	Lasting 24 bars, the "dogfight" has the first uneven phrase structure in the march (three eight-bar phrases), the only real departure from the archetypal American march form. This is also the most chromatic and exciting music in the march, the purpose of which is to contrast with the majestic trio melody. The downward chromatic lines seem to reference and invert the upward chromatic line from the introduction.
2:04	Repeat of Trio	C	The solo piccolo obbligato is added to the trio.
2:22		C'	Second half of the trio.

continued

TIME	SECTION	FORM	DESCRIPTION
2:37	Repeat of Break Strain	D	The break strain is repeated exactly.
3:03	Final Trio ("grandioso")	C	The trio is played with full brass and percussion, including a new countermelody in the trombones and the obbligato played by the entire piccolo section.
3:18		C′	Second half of the final trio.
3:34	End		

What Does It Mean?

CULTURAL LINKAGES

As a march, "The Stars and Stripes Forever" has its roots in one of the main activities for military and community bands of the nineteenth century—marching—though bands were known to play both on parade and in concert performances. The typical form for earlier marches was more repetitive than the form Sousa later used for "The Stars and Stripes" and many of his other marches. This earlier march form would proceed through an introduction (I) and two repeated strains (IAABB) and a trio with two repeated strains (CCDD) before returning to the introduction and first two strains again (IAABB). When bands played these marches in parades, an audience member might hear the first two strains first at a distance and they would sound different minutes later when the band was much nearer. In this context a march full of repeats would not sound repetitive to audience members, since they would be experiencing a shift in dynamics and perhaps the overall sound because of the shifting location of the band. The American modernist composer Charles Ives (1874–1954) was inspired by this kind of listening experience. His composition for symphony orchestra *Three Places in New England* (1911–1914) includes in its second movement, "Putnam's Camp," sections where the orchestra is divided into multiple groups, each performing its own tune in its own key and meter, mimicking the sound of multiple community bands in a parade.

AESTHETICS

Sousa, in his marches written for the U.S. Marine Band and for his own professional touring band towards the end of the nineteenth century, expanded the form of the march to better suit concert performances. The form for "The Stars and Stripes Forever" does not return to the beginning and repeat the first two strains, but instead proceeds sequentially from the first two repeated strains (AA, BB) to the trio (CC′), and then to a final section where the break strain alternates with the trio, with one repetition (DCC′DCC′). For concert music, it was more compelling to bring the composition to a climax, creating the effect of a general crescendo from the beginning of the piece to the end. Sousa's march form concludes with the exciting break strain and the thick texture of the final trio featuring a melody and two countermelodies. These techniques created a sense of linear, forward momentum (as opposed to a repeating, more cyclical motion) and gave marches a welcome variety.

🔊 **Listen again to "The Stars and Stripes Forever" and try to identify the sections of the form without relying on the timecodes given in the listening guide.**

What Is Its History?

Europeans first learned about military bands in their battles with the Ottoman Empire during the seventeenth century. Ottoman armies were accompanied into battle by a *mehter*, a band of valveless trumpets, **shawms** (loud, double-reed aerophones), drums, and cymbals and other idiophones. Early European and American military bands employed **fifes** (high-pitched, side-blown flutes), bagpipes (in Scotland), and drums. By the mid-nineteenth century, brass instruments had added valves that made it possible for them to play chromatic melodies in all keys, rather than being confined to the pitches of the overtone series. Bands began to feature the brass and sometimes eliminate woodwinds, and most towns in Europe, the U.S., and Latin America had their own municipal bands. From the first half of the nineteenth century through World War I, bands of brass, woodwinds, and percussion were an important part of popular culture in Europe, the United States, and Latin America. Manufacturers, labor unions, high schools, and universities sponsored marching and concert bands to represent them on various occasions. In all these contexts, bands were used to create an emotional bond to the group they represented, whether the military unit (morale), the country (patriotism), the labor union (solidarity), or the school (pride).

Although the repertoire of brass bands is rooted in military marches, bands of the late nineteenth and early twentieth centuries played a wide variety of music, including popular dance music of the period (waltzes, polkas, and the cakewalk) and arrangements of classical music. During the nineteenth century, melodies from classical operas entered Italian popular culture when municipal brass bands played them for outdoor festivities. The Union Army in the American Civil War is said to have had 500 bands.[61] By 1890 virtually every town in the United States had a band and a park or town square with a bandstand for bands to play on. The total number of bands likely exceeded ten thousand. As America prospered and began pursuing its own imperial ambitions in the Philippines and Latin America in the 1890s, the patriotism indexed by brass bands playing military marches and the national anthem became an important feature of American musical life. That tradition continues today at sporting events where school bands promote enthusiasm for country and team before, during, and after games and matches.

FIGURE 9.9
Ottoman-era Turkish military band called *mehter*
Source: Painting by Arif Pasha 1939. National Library. Ankara, Wikimedia Commons.

FIGURE 9.10
Three sousaphones of the UCLA Marching Band
Source: UCLA Marching Band.

John Philip Sousa was born in Washington, D.C. His father, a Marine band musician, enlisted him in an apprentice program run by the U.S. Marine Band at age thirteen. After serving as its conductor, Sousa formed his own band in 1892 and concertized around the world for nearly forty years, becoming known as "The March King." Sousa also helped to design the **sousaphone**, a version of the tuba that players support on their shoulders and that sounds over the rest of the band.

One of the other well-known bandleaders of the period was James Reese Europe (1880–1919), a leading musician in the African American music scene of New York City in the 1910s. His large ensembles of African American musicians performed arrangements of marches, popular songs, spirituals, and blues songs in many settings, including Carnegie Hall, where he performed a number of times between 1912 and 1915. During World War I, he served as a lieutenant, and led the band of the 369th Infantry Regiment of the New York National Guard (an all-black regiment known as the "Harlem Hellfighters"). When the Hellfighters were deployed to France in 1918, Reese and the Infantry Band performed extensively for military and public audiences and became famous throughout

Europe. One of the main features of the music of all of his ensembles was the prominence of a syncopated style and repertoire drawn from a genre of piano music called ragtime, which African Americans had pioneered at the end of the nineteenth century. A forerunner to jazz, ragtime and its history are the subject of the next gateway.

CULTURAL LINKAGES

Bands have continued to be an important part of musical life of the United States throughout the long twentieth century. Most high schools and universities have both concert bands that perform sit-down concerts and marching bands that perform in parades and in support of sports teams. Each high school and university has what is known in the U.S. as a "fight song," a song that is closely associated with the school team and played as a way to encourage fans to cheer for their team. The marching band halftime show has become a standard feature at high school and university football games. In many cases these shows involve elaborate displays of musicianship and field marching. Some high school bands work on one show per year and enter competitions against other high school bands throughout the school year.

Independent non-profit musical organizations called drum and bugle corps have also developed annual elaborate field performances for a competition season that occurs in the summer. Many of these ensembles were formed around the middle of the twentieth century sponsored by local Boy Scout troops or by local veterans' organizations such as the VFW or the American Legion. By the 1970s, many drum and bugle corps had separated from their original sponsors and formed their own organizations and governing bodies including DCA (Drum Corps Associates, founded in 1964) and DCI (Drum Corps International, founded in 1972). Today, DCI organizes a summer tour of competitions for over forty drum and bugle corps whose members are between the ages of thirteen and twenty-two. These ensembles put on spectacular shows featuring complex musical arrangements and compositions, intricate movements by the musicians on the field, large stationary percussion and keyboard sections called "pits," dazzling sets and special effects, and choreography performed by non-playing members of the ensemble known as the "auxiliary" or "color guard."

Music for marching bands now includes a broad number of styles and a large repertoire in addition to the marches of Sousa and others. For drum and bugle corps and competitive high school marching bands, duple meter is still used in some of the music for marching, but compound and additive meters of great complexity now also serve to inspire intricate movements of musicians as they march through complicated formations on the field. Musical compositions for concert bands since Sousa's time also employ twentieth- and twenty-first-century classical musical styles.

WHERE DO I GO FROM HERE?

- John Philip Sousa composed 136 marches during his lifetime. Find a recording of a march other than "The Stars and Stripes Forever" and figure out the form of that march. How is it similar to and different from the form of "Stars and Stripes"?

- Find a video recording of a performance by a drum and bugle corps at a recent DCI competition. What is the musical repertoire used for this particular performance? How do the music and visual elements relate to one another?

- Did your high school have a fight song? Research that fight song, or the fight song of another high school, college, or university, and find out when it was written, who composed it, and whether it has undergone any changes in its history. What is the form of the fight song?

- Find some recordings of James Reese Europe's band and compare them to recordings of a band playing Sousa marches.

- Listen to Charles Ives' "Putnam's Camp" from *Three Places in New England*. How does the composition achieve the effect of the sound of multiple ensembles playing at the same time?

GATEWAY 37
RAGTIME

What Is It?

Nearly a half century after Louis Moreau Gottschalk became the first important American classical composer and performer by sometimes borrowing from African American traditions, African American musicians began to develop a new approach to composing for and performing on the piano. Called ragtime, this new style was all the rage in this period. The most famous of these compositions, "Maple Leaf Rag" (1898) by Scott Joplin (c. 1868–1917), is our gateway to ragtime and American popular piano music at the turn of the twentieth century. **Ragtime** features a "ragged" or syncopated rhythm accompanied by a steady bassline with regular accents in duple meter. The texture, meter, and form of this and many other rags (the name for compositions in the ragtime style) mirror those same musical elements in the popular marches of the nineteenth century. This recording is by Richard (Dick) Zimmerman (b. 1937), a ragtime historian and performer who is one of the key figures associated with a revival of ragtime that began in the second half of the twentieth century.

 Listen to the first thirty seconds of "Maple Leaf Rag."

How Does It Work?

Timbre

The timbre is the sound of a solo piano.

FIGURE 9.11
Scott Joplin
Source: Pictorial Press Ltd / Alamy Stock Photo.

Texture

The piano performs a number of textures, including a melody in the right hand with an accompaniment of the left hand alternating between a bass note and a chord; arpeggios through both hands; and block chords in both hands. The alternating bass note-chord in the left hand mimics the "oom-pah" accompaniment style of a march.

Rhythm

The piece is in a duple meter with highly syncopated rhythms throughout.

Melody

The melody includes stepwise motion as well as motion through arpeggiated chords in a major key.

Harmony

The harmony is tonal throughout. As in a Sousa march, after the first two strains in one key (A-flat), the trio modulates to the key of the IV chord (D-flat). Unlike a Sousa march, the final strain returns to the original key.

Form

"Maple Leaf Rag" is a multi-strain ragtime march, with related repeating sections whose form follows almost exactly the common form of Sousa's and other classic American marches. Here the form is AABBACCDD, a variant of European dance form similar to the form of "The Stars and Stripes Forever" (Chapter 9, Gateway 36).

Performance Techniques

This recording by Dick Zimmerman features quite a bit of deviation from the notated score of "Maple Leaf Rag" in terms of rhythm and pitch. Zimmerman adds syncopation where none is notated in some cases, plays an octave higher in the right hand in two different strains, and adds arpeggios and other ornamentation in a number of instances. In the trio Zimmerman plays with a slight swing feel at a few brief moments, but most of the performance is played "straight," a term used by musicians to describe equal subdivisions of the beat in contrast to a "swing feel." Such variations on the notated version of the piece were typical of the performers of the early twentieth century.

Listen to the first thirty seconds of "Maple Leaf Rag" and notice the three contrasting textures and the syncopated melody.

Listen to the entire piece following this timed listening guide.

LISTENING GUIDE 9.3

TIME	SECTION	FORM	DESCRIPTION
0:00	First Strain	A	The melody of the first strain includes arpeggiated chords and some stepwise motion in a syncopated, "ragged" rhythm. The texture varies quite a bit during the strain, including bass note-chord alternation, block chords, and arpeggios.
0:20	Repeat of First Strain	A	The first strain is repeated with slight ornamentations and variations introduced by the performer that do not appear in the notation.
0:40	Second Strain	B	The second strain introduces a different arpeggiated melody accompanied by a regular "oom-pah" gesture that alternates between a bass note and a chord. This became a common pattern for a jazz style known as "stride piano," as the left hand "strides" between the low bass note and the higher chord. In this performance the right hand is played one octave higher than written, and the performer introduces more variations and syncopations that do not appear in the notation. This mimics what participants in the stride piano scene and historians have reported about the performance practice of the time, in which skilled players would compete in what were called "cutting contests" to show off their improvisatory and technical skills while playing a composed rag or other popular song.
1:01	Repeat of Second Strain	B	The second strain repeats, this time with the right hand in the written octave, but again with a number of variations on the notation introduced by the performer.
1:21	Return of First Strain	A	A repeat of the opening strain, but with some changes added by the performer. One change can be heard at the end of the first two phrases, where the performer adds an ascending arpeggio in the right hand (1:23–1:26).
1:42	Trio	C	The stride piano pattern continues in the trio, with one interruption for an arpeggiated pattern. Similar to in the second strain, the right hand is played an

TIME	SECTION	FORM	DESCRIPTION
			octave higher than written for most of this first statement of the trio. For the trio, the key moves to the subdominant (D-flat major).
2:02	Repeat of Trio	C	The trio is repeated with the right hand playing in the notated octave.
2:23	Fourth Strain	D	The fourth strain for the most part abandons the alternating bass-chord stride piano pattern in favor of a pattern where the bass note on the downbeat in each measure is generally followed by two chords and then another bass note. It also returns to the original key (A-flat).
2:43	Repeat of Fourth Strain	D	The fourth strain repeats, with a slight ritardando in the final few bars.

What Does It Mean?

The hallmark of the ragtime style is its rhythmic syncopation. In "Maple Leaf Rag" the melodies in the right hand accent various offbeats while the left hand plays a constant stream of single notes and chords on the beat. The "oom-pah" pattern in much of the left hand derives from the popular marches of the nineteenth century and a popular ballroom dance called the two-step. The syncopation in the right hand, however, is a departure from these influences.

AESTHETICS

The name "ragtime" comes from a practice known as "ragging," where a performer would take a known melody and add syncopated, "ragged" rhythms. Compositions with melodies featuring these ragged syncopations became known as "rags." During the time of ragtime's initial popularity between the mid-1890s and around 1918, this kind of syncopation was heard as a feature of African American music, perhaps because it was related to the rhythmic patterns typically played on the banjo, the most common instrument used in minstrel shows (Chapter 7, Gateway 30). As the syncopated ragtime melodies interlock with the regular, on-the-beat bass rhythm, this music embodied traces of the African practice of superimposing multiple rhythms on top of one another. Another rhythmic influence adding to the syncopation in ragtime compositions is the Cuban **habanera rhythm**, a syncopated rhythm that, in a bar of four beats, accents the first beat, the offbeat after beat two, and the fourth beat. It appeared in George Bizet's opera *Carmen* in 1875 and later in the tango, a popular dance from Argentina that swept through Europe and the United States during this period. This rhythm, along with other musical elements with roots in Latin America, was part of what the ragtime and early jazz pianist Ferdinand "Jelly Roll" Morton (1890–1941) called the "Spanish tinge" in jazz. He considered the "Spanish tinge," which writers later called the "Latin tinge," to be an integral part of the jazz sound, as is evident in his performances and published compositions, the first of which, "Jelly Roll Blues" (1915), is arguably the earliest published jazz composition. The melody in the trio of "Maple Leaf Rag" begins with two repetitions of the habanera rhythm.

🔊 **Listen to the Trio (C) of "Maple Leaf Rag" at 1:42 to identify the habanera rhythm.**

Many types of ensembles played ragtime during its heyday, including dance bands, brass bands, banjo and mandolin ensembles, and symphony orchestras (the ensembles of James Reese Europe from the previous gateway are some of the most famous examples). In many cases, ragtime was music for dancing in settings like juke joints, and the moderate tempo of "Maple Leaf Rag" certainly lends itself to dance. Publishing ragtime compositions as sheet music for solo piano meant that ragtime could also be played at home. Pieces like "Maple Leaf Rag" sold thousands of copies.

FIGURE 9.12
Front cover of the sheet music to "Maple Leaf Rag"
Source: Scott Joplin (public domain), Wikimedia Commons.

FIGURE 9.13
James P. Johnson
Source: Granamour Weems Collection / Alamy Stock Photo.

"Maple Leaf Rag" can be performed exactly as notated in the 1899 sheet music, but its melodies, rhythms, and harmonies can also be embellished and adapted as they are in this recording.

This practice of embellishing existing popular songs was common among ragtime and early jazz pianists such as Jelly Roll Morton, James P. Johnson, and Willie "the Lion" Smith (1897–1973). They elaborated on well-known songs to showcase their virtuosity and musical creativity for audiences and fellow musicians. Each had his own style, which was sometimes associated with a geographical region (e.g., Morton in New Orleans style, Johnson and Smith in East Coast style, and Scott Joplin in Midwestern style). In the 1910s Johnson, Smith, Fats Waller (1904–1943), and others developed a piano style known as **stride piano**. It featured the left hand "striding" between bass notes and chords, along with heavy syncopation and many other virtuosic techniques. In many cases the stride pianists performed "Maple Leaf Rag" and other compositions at blistering tempos, which either led to extremely fast technical dancing or settings where audiences did not dance but instead listened to and appreciated the skills of the performer. In this recording of "Maple Leaf Rag," the pianist Dick Zimmerman embellishes the melody, rhythm, and harmony of "Maple Leaf Rag" to give some idea of what a live performance of this composition might have sounded like in the early years of the twentieth century. For example, he plays the melody of the second strain (B) an octave higher than written during its first repetition and begins the second repetition with an arpeggiated chord that doesn't appear in the first repetition or in the notated score.

🔊 **Listen to both repetitions of the second strain (B) of "Maple Leaf Rag" (0:40–1:21) for the shift in octave in the first repetition and the arpeggio ornamentation at the beginning of the second repetition.**

What Is Its History?

Ragtime became a popular style around the mid-1890s, and by the time Scott Joplin published "Maple Leaf Rag" in 1899 (it was composed in 1898), over one hundred rags had already been published. The word "rag" first appeared in published sheet music in 1896, and the first instrumental song with "rag" in the title, *The Mississippi Rag* by bandleader William H. Krell, was published in 1897. "Maple Leaf Rag" was and remains the most famous rag. It started the craze for amateurs to learn to play composed rags from sheet music. During the heydey of ragtime, American marches and ragtime borrowed ideas from one another, so that marches often sound like rags and rags often sound like marches.

Scott Joplin was born in Texas, began playing piano as a teenager, and was educated by a German teacher in classical music theory. He traveled as a musician throughout the South and Midwest before settling in 1895 in Sedalia, Missouri, where he earned a living teaching piano. Like other black pianists of his time, he developed a style of piano playing where he would "rag" popular songs and marches by improvising and adding syncopation. While in Sedalia, he composed the "Maple Leaf Rag," named after the town's "Maple Leaf Club," a social club where he often played. He wrote more than forty rags, in addition to other compositions including two operas, *A Guest of Honor* (1903, now lost) and *Treemonisha* (1911). Joplin died in 1917 and, by the early 1920s, ragtime had begun to fall out of popularity as a new popular music, jazz, was gaining favor among dancers and listeners. In reality, early jazz, with its syncopations and dance-friendly tempos and styles, sounded very similar to ragtime, so this change was at first one of terminology rather than of style.

Though it was no longer popular, Joplin's music and the ragtime style enjoyed several revivals during the twentieth century, the most significant in the 1970s as the result of increased attention from classical musicians and scholars. The pianist and musicologist Joshua Rifkin released an album of Joplin rags in 1970, performed exactly as they were notated on the sheet music without embellishment, treating them, in other words, like classical music. Arrangements of Joplin rags constituted the score to the popular 1973 film *The Sting*. Several collected editions of piano rags also appeared in the 1970s, making the sheet music broadly available to the public (most rags had until that point fallen out of print). Dick Zimmerman recorded a five-LP set titled *Scott Joplin: His Complete Works* in 1974. *Treemonisha* was performed for the first time in 1972 by the Atlanta Symphony and fully staged by the Houston Grand Opera in 1976. A novel named *Ragtime* was published in 1975. It served as the inspiration years later for a Broadway musical of the same name, premiered in 1996. These and other revivalist activities brought Joplin's music and ragtime to broader public attention. Joplin was awarded a Special Citation by the Pulitzer Prize board in 1976, nearly sixty years after his death at age 49. Since then ragtime has continued to inspire musicians and composers in jazz and classical music as well as in many other musical scenes and genres.

> **CULTURAL LINKAGES**

WHERE DO I GO FROM HERE?

- Find a recording of Joshua Rifkin performing "Maple Leaf Rag." Notice the differences between his precise performance of the notated score and Dick Zimmerman's performance filled with embellishments and adaptations. What contrasting values do these two performance styles represent?

- Choose one of the stride pianists, either James P. Johnson, Willie "the Lion" Smith, or Fats Waller, and investigate his musical and personal biography and the context for the development of the stride piano style.

- The Broadway musical *Ragtime* (1996) and its subsequent revivals feature ragtime as a musical style along with a number of other styles. Look into the storyline of the musical and its soundtrack. How does its use of ragtime and other styles line up with the history of these styles? How does the use of ragtime serve the storyline? What musical elements of ragtime do you hear in the soundtrack?

GATEWAY 38
MUSIC OF EARLY EUROPEAN MODERNISTS

What Is It?

During the late nineteenth century Richard Wagner and Claude Debussy, among others, tested the limits of tonal music. During the first two decades of the twentieth century, Igor Stravinsky (1882–1971) from Russia and Arnold Schoenberg (1874–1951) and his students Anton Webern (1883–1945) and Alban Berg (1885–1935), working in Vienna, pushed tonality aside in favor of new approaches to musical harmony and melody. Our gateway to the music of these early European modernists is

FIGURE 9.14
Igor Stravinsky
Source: George Grantham Bain Collection
at the Library of Congress. Wikimedia
Commons.

The Rite of Spring (*Le Sacre du Printemps*), a 1913 composition by Russian composer Igor Stravinsky.[62] Originally including the subtitle *Scenes from Pagan Russia*, it was composed as a ballet for the Ballets Russes, a company of Russian dancers, choreographers, and visual artists in Paris. Today it is commonly performed as an orchestral concert piece. In this composition, Stravinsky explores alternatives to tonality, one of the common traits of the music of the early European modernists. Since its debut this composition has been frequently performed by symphony orchestras the world over, and there are over 100 recorded versions of it. This recording, by the London Symphony Orchestra conducted by Claudio Abbado, was released in 1997.

 Listen to the first thirty seconds of the recording.

How Does It Work?

Timbre

The Rite of Spring features wide palette of timbres from the instruments of a large symphony orchestra. The opening section features many woodwind timbres in a number of combinations, and an astounding twenty woodwind players are required to perform the piece.

Texture

This piece includes a variety of textures from solos to thickly layered contrapuntal parts.

Rhythm

The rhythmic elements are varied, including nonmetrical sections, sections with steady duple meter, and sections with changing and irregular meters. There are also many instances of **polyrhythms** (multiple parts with different rhythms), especially where beats are divided into two equal subdivisions by some members of the orchestra and into three equal subdivisions by others at the same time.

Melody

The melody is mainly in a minor mode.

Harmony

The harmony has many dissonant, modern-sounding chord clusters based on seconds and thirds.

Form

The form is based on solos and small groups alternating with contrasting dynamics.

Performance Techniques

Ornamentations such as trills are played throughout the piece by many of the instruments. Some of the musicians, such as the bassoonist who plays the opening solo, are required to play pitches that are extremely high or low for their particular instruments.

🔊 Listen to the recording of *The Rite of Spring* with these elements in mind.

The Rite of Spring has two parts: Part I, titled "The Adoration of the Earth"; and Part II, titled "The Sacrifice." This timed listening guide includes the first two sections of Part I: the orchestral introduction and "The Augurs of Spring."

Listen another time and follow along with the timed listening guide.

TIME	SECTION	DESCRIPTION
Track 1:		
0:00	Orchestral Introduction	The piece begins with an unaccompanied bassoon playing at the upper limit of its range. This is a Russian folk melody in a minor mode.
0:10		Other wind instruments gradually enter with non-triadic chordal harmony. Stravinsky's use here of wind instruments continues their centuries-long use as signifying the outdoors.
0:54		The melody disappears, replaced by a multi-layered texture featuring undulating chromatic lines in the winds as well as a number of sustained pitches. Solo lines, characterized by fast-moving notes, emerge from this texture. Some moments of a steady pulse appear periodically and then disappear.
2:08		The thickness of the layering and the loudness of the orchestra builds, accompanied by a steady pulse in the low strings.
2:39		The orchestra suddenly stops and the solo bassoon restates the opening melody, transposed down a half-step.
2:48		Other winds enter with trills and triplet flourishes. The violins begin softly playing a four-note *pizzicato* ostinato.
Track 2:		
0:00	The Augurs of Spring: Dances of the Young Girls	The strings, accented by the horns, play a repeating pattern of pulsating chords. The violin, violas, and four of the horns play a dominant seventh chord and the cellos, basses, and other four horns play a major chord based on a tonic one half-step higher than that of the dominant seventh chord. This seems to create a new kind of chord made of adjacent pitches called a **chord cluster**. These chord clusters are played loudly and in a driving rhythm, providing some of the piece's most memorable material, which was perhaps shocking to the ears of its first listeners.
0:08		The english horn plays the four-note ostinato originally played in the *pizzicato* violins as a solo, accompanied by bassoons playing staccato repeating figures and cellos playing a *pizzicato* eight-pitch repeating figure.
0:13		The string ostinato accented by the horns returns. It continues to alternate with sections featuring the eight-pitch repeating figure from the low strings and the four-note ostinato originally played by the *pizzicato* violins and then the english horn. The trumpets introduce triplet rhythm, creating a polyrhythm with the duple-meter strings ostinato. The trumpets play a short melody that descends chromatically. This motif and others are introduced and developed as they are played by different instruments and in different permutations and variations throughout the orchestra.
1:38		A solo horn introduces a folk melody in a major mode. This melody is then taken up by a flute soloist as it is combined with variations on earlier motifs and ostinatos.
2:11		The trumpets and cellos present a chant-like theme in a minor mode.
2:27		The music becomes suddenly softer, and the texture builds again, thickening and adding layers as the folk melody introduced by the horn is developed across the orchestra and a climax of loudness and thick texture is reached to introduce the next section of the piece, titled "Ritual of Abduction."
2:54	End	

FIGURE 9.15

An example of costumes and sets from the original production of *The Rite of Spring*

Source: Public domain, Wikimedia Commons.

What Does It Mean?

As an orchestral ballet, the storyline of *The Rite of Spring: Scenes of Pagan Russia* depicts a series of imaginary Ancient Slavic rituals, beginning innocently with traditional line dancing, but culminating in the sacrificial death of a young girl, ordered by a tribal elder. Each of its scenes, with titles like "Ritual Abduction," "Spring Round Dances," "Mystic Circles of the Young Girls," and "Ritual of the Ancestors," is meant to evoke a part of the storyline, emphasizing ideas of the "primitive," something old, ancient, and mystical imagined to be connected to rural village or "folk" culture. The recordings of the orchestral introduction and "The Augurs of Spring" present some of the musical sounds connected to notions of rural life. The bassoon opens the introduction with a Russian folk melody at the top of its register in a minor mode, performing a timbre that sounds unfamiliar and perhaps strange to those who have not heard the extreme high range of the bassoon or Russian rural folk melodies. When the horn plays another folk melody during "The Augurs of Spring" section (this one in a major mode), it continues the horn's association with the pastoral in European classical music. This relatively simple folk melody is later heard in the flute and a number of other instruments, played in contrast to the many rhythmic and harmonic complexities occurring throughout the piece. Stravinsky took these melodies from published collections of folk music. The opening bassoon melody, for example, came from a song in an anthology of Lithuanian folk songs published in 1900.

CULTURAL LINKAGES

 Listen again to the opening to Track 1 of *The Rite of Spring* as well as Track 2 at 1:38 to identify these melodies.

AESTHETICS

Polyrhythms, asymmetrical patterns of accents, and frequently changing meters occur throughout the piece. These techniques create instability, tension, and excitement, as their irregularity and unpredictability would not have been something audiences were accustomed to hearing. In addition, they would have opened up new possibilities for choreography that did not depend on movements grouped in regular patterns of two, three, or four.

For harmony, Stravinsky stacks layers of pitches and melodies, often in multiple keys, to create dense, dissonant musical textures. An example of this is the opening to "The Augurs of Spring" where two different chords are played simultaneously in the strings and horns, a harmonic technique called **polytonality**. Polytonality provides particular sets of dissonances and consonances depending on which keys are sounding at the same time. They may share some pitches in common, some of the pitches of one of the keys may be in consonant intervals with pitches of the other key, or the pitches of one key may be in dissonant intervals with those of another. These simultaneities form new types of harmonies that may be built not only on intervals of thirds, but also on intervals of seconds, fourths, or any number of others. This is one example of the way modernist composers of this period sought to move away from the traditional tonality of European classical music. Another was Arnold Schoenberg, who, after the turn of the century, turned away from the expansive Romantic style he had composed in during the late nineteenth century and began to espouse **atonality**, which abandons the concept of a tonal center and other hierarchical structures of the tonal system.

🔊 **Listen to the opening of Track 2 of *The Rite of Spring* again for these features of harmony and rhythm.**

In *The Rite of Spring*, Stravinsky's modernist explorations of polytonality draw on material from musical folklore for inspiration, just as nationalist composers of the nineteenth century did. Since he extended the harmonic vocabulary of many Russian nationalist composers (Chapter 8, Gateway 32), his folklore-inspired works have been retrospectively considered "neonationalist." Even folk melodies, such as the bassoon solo or the pastoral horn melody, are enmeshed in modernist harmonic structures that may have been inspired by additional folk music sources as well, which music historians have traced to anthologies of folk music that would have been available to Stravinsky. These additional folk sources are masked by harmonies that push the boundaries of tonality while modernist harmonies are masked by the diatonic folk motifs that appear throughout the composition. This "fusion" of the modern and the folkloristic is one of the features that has made *The Rite of Spring* a perennial favorite for orchestras and audiences long after its debut in Paris with the Ballets Russes.

The departure from tonality in *The Rite of Spring* (and other modernist works of this period) was, in some ways, a response to broader shifts in European society. The political order dominated by European empires and monarchs was declining, revolutions were springing up in soon-to-be former European colonies, and new understandings of the complexities of the psychological and material worlds were emerging in the work of intellectuals like Sigmund Freud and Albert Einstein. In European classical music, this broader crisis of confidence in older ways of thinking can be heard in the music of composers who questioned the value of tonal music that was meant to express or induce emotion and to be relatively easily understood. One way to interpret the modernist shift away from tonality in *The Rite of Spring* is that it reveals a questioning of the philosophical and social underpinnings of nineteenth-century European society and an exploration of new, more complex musical terrain.

What Is Its History?

Igor Stravinsky was born near St. Petersburg, then the capital of the Russian empire. His father was a professional opera singer. Although Stravinsky studied piano and music theory in his youth, his parents encouraged him to study law when he began his university studies in 1901, and he did. His most significant training as a composer began in 1902 under the mentorship of the Russian composer Nikolai Rimsky-Korsakov (1844–1908), who advocated for the development of a national Russian style of composition in the last decades of the nineteenth century, and, toward that end, notably published two collections of Russian folk songs in 1974. Stravinsky took private lessons at the home of Rimsky-Korsakov until the latter's death, where he learned orchestration and other compositional skills and about Rimsky-Korsakov's nationalist style and its reliance on musical folklore.

In 1909, Stravinsky's composition *Fireworks* was heard at a concert in St. Petersburg by Sergei Diaghilev (1872–1929), a Russian impresario who, starting in 1907, was presenting the best Russian concert music, operas, and ballets in Paris. Diaghilev was impressed and commissioned the young Stravinsky to compose first *The Firebird* (1910), and later *Petrushka* (1911) and *The Rite of Spring*, all three of which drew on elements of musical folklore. Diaghilev's company, the Ballets Russes, spotlighted the most famous Russian dancers of the period including Anna Pavlova and Vaslav Nijinsky. The company was a locus of modernist innovation. Diaghilev commissioned new scores from the leading French composers of the period, including Claude Debussy (*Jeux*, 1913), Maurice Ravel (*Daphnis et Chloé*, 1912), and Erik Satie (*Parade*, 1917). His set designers included leading modernists Pablo Picasso (1881–1973) and Henri Matisse (1869–1954) as well as the fashion designer Coco Chanel (1883–1971). Many of the ballets, including *The Rite of Spring*, played to the fascination at the time with the exotic, the folkloric, and the primitive. For *The Rite of Spring*, Nijinsky invented an entirely novel choreography focused on stomping and lurching movements, which

CULTURAL LINKAGES

CULTURAL LINKAGES

imagined an ancient pagan way of life and attempted to capture a sense of village dance traditions and the ways that peasants are rooted to the earth. The Russian designer, painter, and writer Nicholas Roerich (1874–1947) designed the sets and costumes. In the context of a broader revival affirming Russian national identity through folk arts, Roerich was an avid student of folk culture. He was particularly interested in archeology as a way to understand what such an ancient Slavic culture might have looked (and sounded) like. He worked closely with Stravinsky and introduced him to a good deal of folk music, some of which formed the basis for the musical material of *The Rite of Spring*. Roerich's costumes and sets conjured an imaginary "primitive," ancient Russia along with Nijinsky's choreography and Stravinsky's score, all reflections of a "neoprimitive" movement in the visual and performing arts.

The premiere of *The Rite of Spring* on May 29, 1913 incited one of the most famous riots in the history of European music. In the full house of Théâtre des Champs-Élysées in Paris, what began as boos and hisses in the opening measures soon devolved into shouting, fistfights, and people throwing vegetables and other objects at the stage. Accounts vary as to whether the police were called in, but, in any event, forty people were removed from the theater and order was largely maintained through the rest of the evening. While Stravinsky later boasted that it was his music that had driven the audience into hysterics, others have claimed that Nijinsky's controversial choreography provoked the violent response, with its stomping and rootedness in the ground perhaps offending the sensibilities of a Parisian crowd accustomed to balletic elegance and a seeming ability to defy gravity. Musicologist Richard Taruskin has even speculated that the riot may have been pre-arranged by Diaghilev in order to generate publicity.[63, 64]

Regardless of the cause of the riot, *The Rite of Spring* was only performed as a complete ballet and orchestral work seven times before the outbreak of World War I in 1914, though it was performed as a concert piece (without a ballet) for the first time just before the war, receiving positive reviews. After the war, Diaghilev revived the performance with a new choreographer, and it began to be performed as a concert work as well. In 1940 it was included in the Disney animated film *Fantasia*, the only work by a living composer to appear in a score full of well-known classical orchestral compositions. In the decades that followed, *The Rite of Spring* became a standard part of the orchestral repertoire, even though Stravinsky for the most part left behind this particular style of Russian neonationalist-modernist composition after 1920. There have been a wide variety of choreographic interpretations over the years. In 1987 the choreographer Millicent Hodson worked with Chicago's Joffrey Ballet to reconstruct Nijinsky's choreography, and the Joffrey performers danced in replicas of Roerich's costumes.

Like Stravinsky, other composers from the turn of the twentieth century were also exploring ways to extend and depart from tonality. The French composer Claude Debussy (1862–1918) turned to scales that were not diatonic, as well as to music cultures outside of European classical music, such as the Javanese gamelan (Chapter 8, Gateway 33). The composer Erik Satie (1866–1925), a friend of Debussy, included material based on the scales and ornamentation of Romanian and Hungarian Romani ensembles, which he heard at the 1889 world's fair in Paris, in some of his seven *Gnossiennes* (composed between 1889 and 1897) for piano.

AESTHETICS

During this period the Austrian composer Arnold Schoenberg extended the expressionism and emotion of Wagner and other German and Austrian composers of the late nineteenth century. He explored atonality and the boundaries between speech and singing in his work *Pierrot Lunaire* (1912). In the early 1920s, Schoenberg pioneered a practice of composition based on the organization of the twelve chromatic pitches into ordered non-repeating sequences known as **tone rows**. This approach, which became the basis for **serialism**, was explored by Schoenberg and his students Alban Berg, Anton Webern, and Hanns Eisler (1898–1962). Stravinsky, Schoenberg, and other early modernist composers took new pathways away from tonality and other conventions of European classical music that would be further developed throughout the twentieth century. Stravinsky himself took a number of directions as a composer, after 1920, entering what some have called his "neoclassical period" (c. 1920–1951), which was followed by his "serial period" (c. 1952–1968). After living in Russia, Switzerland, and France in the 1920s and 1930s, Stravinsky moved to the United States at the outbreak of World War II in 1939, where he became a citizen and lived until his death in 1971.

Modernism only goes so far in explaining European classical music in the period from 1890 to 1918. Many European composers continued to compose using the lush chromatic harmonies, programmatic content, and large operatic, symphonic, and concerto forms of the nineteenth century, including Gustav Mahler, Richard Strauss, Jean Sibelius (1865–1957), Sergei Rachmaninoff (1873–1943), and many others. Their tonal compositions, more than Schoenberg's atonal and twelve-tone ones, are still frequently performed for contemporary concert audiences, along with Stravinsky's *Rite of Spring*.

WHERE DO I GO FROM HERE?

- Listen to some compositions by Debussy, Satie, and/or Schoenberg from the period 1890–1918. What musical elements in their works challenge traditional boundaries, one of the definitions of modernism?

- Find an orchestral work from 1890–1918 by Mahler, Richard Strauss, Sibelius, or Rachmaninoff, and compare that work to *The Rite of Spring*. Consider as many elements of music as you can. What are some of the broad similarities and particular differences?

- *The Rite of Spring* and other compositions by Stravinsky have inspired the musical soundscape of many twentieth- and twenty-first-century orchestral Hollywood film scores. Bernard Herrmann (1911–1975), a frequent collaborator of Alfred Hitchcock, seems to have drawn on some elements of *The Rite of Spring* for his iconic score to the Hitchcock film *Psycho* (1960). Watch the film and see if you can identify any similarities between *The Rite of Spring* and Herrmann's score. What effect does the music have on the mood of the film?

GATEWAY 39
BALINESE GAMELAN

What Is It?

In 1908 the Dutch conquered the Hindu island of Bali in present-day Indonesia after having first invaded the island with their military in 1846. In the wake of the collapse of traditional Balinese political structures, music for gamelan orchestras similar to those of Java (Chapter 5, Gateway 21) changed dramatically, beginning around 1915. Our gateway to this new kind of Balinese gamelan music is a piece from later in the twentieth century titled "Tabuh Sekar Jepun" (1968) arranged by the Balinese composer I Wayan Gandera (1945?–2002). It is an example of a performance of a **gamelan *gong kebyar***, the most popular type of Balinese gamelan orchestra for much of the twentieth century. Like Javanese gamelans, gamelan *gong kebyar* is composed mainly of bronze percussion instruments and is played by several dozen musicians. "Tabuh" is the word for an individual composition and "Sekar Jepun" means "Japanese flower," referring to a West Indian jasmine flower said to have been brought to Bali by the Japanese and commonly used both for ceremonial offerings and for decoration on headdresses for dance and other performances. It is common in Bali to name a composition after a flower.

🔊 **Listen to the first thirty seconds of this recording to get some idea of this type of gamelan sound.**

FIGURE 9.16
Map of Bali

Bali

How Does It Work?

Timbre

A Balinese gamelan *gong kebyar* orchestra consists of hanging knobbed gongs, rows of knobbed gongs set in wooden boxes called *reyong*, and a number of slab-key metallophones, called *gangsa*, struck with hammers. Each individual *gangsa* instrument has a two-octave range, and together the *gangsa* instruments cover a range of four octaves. Altogether, the gamelan *gong kebyar* collection of idiophones spans a five-octave range. Gamelan *gong kebyar* also includes a pair of *kendang* (two-headed, barrel-shaped drums), *ceng-ceng* (cymbals), a *suling* (bamboo flute), and a *kempli*, a knobbed, kettle-shaped gong used to keep the pulse. These timbres can be heard in various combinations during the recording of "Tabuh Sekar Jepun."

AESTHETICS

The gongs and metallophones of gamelan *gong kebyar* are made in pairs to have a slight difference in pitch between the gongs or keys of the two instruments in each pair. Each pair of instruments is thought of as male and female, with female instruments having the slightly lower pitch. This difference in pitch causes a beating effect that is called *ombak*, which means "waves." The speed of the beating is designed to be absolutely consistent over the entire range of the orchestra. Without *ombak*, the sound is considered dead. Each gamelan orchestra is tuned to itself, not to match other gamelans. There is no standard tuning. Instead, each orchestra is a unique entity.

Texture

Although played by several dozen musicians, a Balinese gamelan acoustically pulsates as if a single instrument. The texture of a Balinese gamelan has been called "stratified polyphony." In this texture, the lowest-pitched instruments move slowly and provide the foundations for the faster, more complex ornamentation of the higher-pitched instruments. In this modern composition, however, I Wayan Gandera highlights several instru-ments and instrumental sections of the gamelan, either by featuring them unaccompanied or by assigning them a pattern that stands out in relation to the other instruments.

Rhythm

This piece is composed in sections. Some phrases have even numbers of beats (2, 4, 8, or 16), some are nonmetrical. In the second half of the piece, these phrases are expressed as regular, repeating cycles. The use of repeating cycles is one of the

FIGURE 9.17
Balinese gamelan, with musicians playing an instrument called *reyong* **in the foreground**
Source: travelib Indonesia / Alamy Stock Photo.

most recognizable elements of gamelan performance. The largest gong marks the *last* beat of each cycle, not the first, and coincides with the last note of the melody. Sometimes, however, melodies can span multiple gong cycles. "Tabuh Sekar Jepun" features several examples of multiple-cycle melodies.

Melody

Balinese melodies (*pokok*) are played by *gangsa* metallophones with a lower pitch range and elaborated upon by those with a higher pitch range. Like the gong cycles, they are regular and repetitive. The melody that ends the piece, which is based on a popular Javanese song, is sixteen beats long. It is ornamented in three different ways (by the *gangsa*, *reyong*, and *kendang*) at various times in the piece, and played in two different speeds, each of which provides different opportunities for musical expression.

This piece uses a five-note subset of the seven-note "parent" scale system known as *pelog*. The gamelan can only play these five pitches, which are irregularly spaced: three notes close together, then a large gap, then two more closely spaced notes.

Harmony

Groups of different notes sounding at the same time often occur in Balinese music, but these are usually not intended to be heard as chords. One of the only times something analogous to chords happens is during *gangsa* parts, when a player who usually would play an interlocking part stops playing that part and instead plays the melody line three notes higher than usual. This yields an interval somewhat equivalent to a fifth.

Form

Traditional Balinese pieces follow a three-part form often described as head (exposition), body (the central movement, often played at a slow tempo), and feet (the exciting conclusion). This piece only roughly follows this model. The main melody is in fact the *last* movement, not the middle, which is instead occupied by an extended section showcasing the sounds of the *reyong* and the *kendang*. This final section has its own internal form of fast, slow, fast.

Performance Techniques

One of the more striking techniques heard in this piece is called **kotekan,** in which two parts interlock while playing figures too fast to be played alone. Instead, they are divided between two partners in a variety of configurations, sometimes involving a pattern where partners alternate playing every other note. Players dampen the ringing of each note so that it does not overlap with the notes of their partners. On the *gangsa*, this is accomplished by striking a key with a mallet in one hand and then quickly grabbing the key with the other hand to stop the vibration. On the *reyong*, however, a cylindrical mallet must be held in each hand. The dampening, then, must be done by the *same* hand that has just struck the note, at lightning-fast speeds.

Listen to the first thirty seconds of this performance with these timbral and textural elements in mind.

Listen to the entire recording following this timed listening guide, which gives the Balinese name of each section.

LISTENING GUIDE 9.5

TIME	SECTION	GONG CYCLE	DESCRIPTION
0:00	*kebyar*	N/A	The entire ensemble plays short phrases in unison, with no clear meter or steady tempo. The last note of each phrase is marked with a stroke of the largest gong.
0:08	*reyongan*	N/A	*Reyong* "solo." This one instrument is played by four musicians. In this section, the *reyong* plays *kilitan*: melodic patterns each consisting of four adjacent tones divided between a pair of interlocking players, and doubled an octave higher by the second pair. Several times in this section, the "harmonization" of two pitches simultaneously sounding at an interval of a "fifth" can be heard. Around 0:41 the largest gong can also be heard, marking the end of this section.
0:43	*genderan*	N/A	This section showcases the *gangsa* (metallophone) instruments and features a combination of interlocking and unison phrases. At 0:56 the *kempli* is heard for the first time, dictating a pulse. At 1:08 the largest gong clearly resounds, marking the end of the phrase. After the striking of the gong, the *ombak* beating effect from the tuning of the instruments can be heard clearly as well.
1:10	*reyongan*	N/A	Similar to the previous *reyongan* section.
1:26		*bapang* (8 beats)	The *reyongan* continues, but now a steady gong cycle is introduced and the pulse implied in the earlier *reyongan* is made explicit. The *reyong* phrases are interposed with short unison phrases from the *gangsa* section.
2:52	*kendangan*	*bapang* (8 beats)	*Kendang* (drum) duet. The gong cycle is reinforced with an eight-beat *pokok* (base melody). The *reyong* and *ceng-ceng* (cymbals) mirror the drums' patterns and variations which unfold over numerous iterations of the cycle. The end of this section exits the gong cycle with a group solo by the *gangsa*, which is concluded with a sounding of the largest gong.
4:02	*genderan*	N/A	Similar to *genderan* section above.
4:34	A (3x)	*lelonggoran* (16 beats)	This melody, played together by the full ensemble here, is derived from the popular Javanese song "Suwe Ora Jamu."
4:49	A' (*genderan*, 3x)	*lelonggoran* (16 beats)	The *pokok* continues while the *gangsa* elaborate it with an interlocking ornamentation called a *kotekan*.

TIME	SECTION	GONG CYCLE	DESCRIPTION
5:06	A (2x)	*lelonggoran* (16 beats)	Repeat of A.
5:17	A'' (9x)	*lelonggoran* (16 beats)	The *pokok* is the same as the previous section although it is played twice as slow. The *reyong* plays a melodic elaboration of the melody, while the *kendang* (accompanied by the *ceng-ceng*) play a pattern that repeats every three gong cycles (a total of three times). In this section the *suling* (bamboo flute) is heard clearly for the first time. It plays the *pokok* and adds some ornamentation to the melody.
6:32	A''' (3x)	*lelonggoran* (16 beats)	The same *pokok* is played at the faster original tempo from A. The *gangsa* plays the *kotekan* from A' in addition to the rhythmic elements from A.
6:49	End		

What Does It Mean?

On the island of Bali the performing arts have long been an important part of everyday life. Many Balinese learn and perform gamelan as part of their normal lives, and there are more than twenty-five varieties of gamelan in Bali that perform regularly, of which six or seven are common throughout the island. Gamelan *gong kebyar* is one of the most frequently performed types of gamelan in Bali. The meanings of gamelan *gong kebyar* can be as complex as its musical organization, and this gateway focuses on just two of its many facets of meaning: (1) the way that gamelan performance in general is an emblematic and experiential example of the value for collectivity in Bali; and (2) the ways that gamelan *gong kebyar* is meaningful as a modern, twentieth-century form of gamelan performance.

> CULTURAL LINKAGES

Today, the main settings for gamelan performance are rituals that mark either the life cycle (e.g., marriages, birthdays, cremations) or temple festivals. Gamelan performances also occur on national holidays, for village events like fundraisers, and in presentation for tourists. Gamelans of all types perform on these occasions. In many cases they are intertwined with dance, theater, and other performing arts such as shadow puppetry. With the dozens of musicians required to perform gamelan, often in cooperation with dancers and puppeteers, the performing arts in Bali are almost always communal efforts. This is an expression of the value Balinese society places on cooperation and community spirit.

Balinese villages are divided into sections, each one called a *banjar*. Community organizations called *sekaha* are formed within the *banjar* to execute integral tasks, including organizing religious rituals, managing the cultivation of rice, and playing gamelan for temple ceremonies. When a community has a need, the appropriate *sekaha* gathers and finds a way to meet that need to sustain the life of the community. Gamelan musicians organize themselves into these collective groups, and they perform for celebrations and other occasions that require gamelan performance. Their goal in participating in rituals, ceremonies, and other performances is not to showcase individual musicians, but rather to create a sense of oneness within the group. Certainly some individuals are more proficient than others in gamelan performances, but these qualities serve to elevate the overall quality of the ensemble rather than showcase the skills of one person over the others.

> SOCIAL BEHAVIOR

The communal aspect of gamelan *gong kebyar* performance in "Tabuh Sekar Jepun" is evident throughout the piece as the musicians remain coordinated with one another through many different tempos, several elaborations of the *pokok* melody, and the *kotekan* technique where players' parts precisely interlock to form fast melodic and rhythmic passages. The very opening *kebyar* section of the piece features a few short nonmetrical unison phrases played with precision by the entire

> AESTHETICS

ensemble, without the guide of a steady beat. The final section of the piece contains a clear example of the *kotekan* technique in the first elaboration of "Suwe Ora Jamu" in the *gangsa* (A'). The extremely fast line is played through close coordination of multiple musicians as they interlock their parts with one another. These challenging and virtuosic performance techniques are part of the reason that gamelan *gong kebyar* is one of the most popular styles of gamelan for musicians and audiences. In order for these techniques to be performed properly, they require extensive training and practice.

ECONOMIC ACTIVITY

Devoting so much time to music (as well as dance and other arts) is made possible by an environment perfectly suited to agriculture. People need to spend only about half of their time working in the fields to produce enough food to sustain themselves. There is also a great demand in Bali for the arts, artistic production, and artists. The arts are vibrant in Bali as highly respected and valued elements of society because they are integral to religious practice, sources of popular entertainment, and the basis of a great deal of cultural tourism. Gamelan is a pervasive aspect of the arts in Bali, and though most Balinese people do not regularly produce art as adults, those that participate in gamelan find themselves among communities, organizations, and audiences that are supportive of their work.

 Listen to the *kebyar* section at the beginning of the piece as well as the A' section featuring the *kotekan* technique (beginning at 4:49), keeping in mind that this level of precision is accomplished by a number of musicians working together.

AESTHETICS

The word *kebyar* means "to burst open" or "to flare up suddenly." It refers to the explosive sound of the gamelan when all of the metallophones, gongs, and drums are struck together at once. This sound, encompassing a range of more than five octaves, produces piercing high frequencies, rich pulsating metallic timbres in the mid-range, and booming low frequencies from the larger gongs. *Kebyar* passages that feature this sound may occur throughout a piece, and often appear at the beginning (heard in this example from 0:00 to 0:08). Gamelan *gong kebyar* is best known for repertoire featuring these types of explosive moments that highlight the dynamic qualities of its component instruments, often involving sudden shifts in tempo, dynamic, texture, or pitch material.

This so-called *kebyar* style differentiates it from much of the ritual ceremonial gamelan music from before the emergence of gamelan *gong kebyar* in the early twentieth century. This earlier ritual repertoire could be considered "continuous," meaning that the music continues in a steady flow of tempo, texture, and dynamics without abrupt or sudden changes. Pieces used for rituals and ceremonies are typically not attributed to individual composers. Soon after the emergence of gamelan *gong kebyar*, individual composers began to be recognized as the composers of new compositions. These pieces are termed *kreasi baru* or "new creations," a term used for gamelan *gong kebyar* compositions since the early twentieth century. Composers today continue to produce *kreasi baru* for gamelan *gong kebyar*, exploring new possibilities for the *kebyar* style.

CULTURAL LINKAGES

The virtuosity, dramatic contrast, and other features of gamelan *gong kebyar* have fascinated Balinese musicians and composers, as well as tourists, researchers, and composers from outside of Bali. While gamelan *gong kebyar* performances continue to serve ritual functions and remain an integral part of community life, they also serve as entertainment for tourists as tourism has become an integral part of the Balinese culture and economy over the last one hundred years. Today, over four million tourists visit Bali per year, many of whom are interested in experiencing aspects of Balinese culture such as its music. Many gamelan *sekaha* perform for tourist groups regularly in villages, outside temples, on stages at hotels, at restaurants, or at festivals. Tourism has generated more revenue and interest in all forms of gamelan, inspired the composition of even more new repertoire, stimulated the creation of new ensembles, and encouraged the revival of pieces that had become nearly obsolete. In tandem with the rise of tourism, festivals and competitions between gamelan *sekaha*, as well as a robust conservatory system for music and the performing arts, have also risen to prominence in Bali. These institutions actively promote gamelan throughout Bali and beyond, and their activities and devotion to gamelan result in the continuation of existing repertoires, excellence in performance, many new compositions that explore the sonic possibilities in gamelan, and high levels of virtuosity that are especially notable in gamelan *gong kebyar* performances like "Tabuh Sekar Japun."

What Is Its History?

Hinduism has been the predominant religion in Bali since around 500 CE, when the religion came to Southeast Asia from India and fused with the local animist religion. Islam spread to the region beginning in the thirteenth century. By the sixteenth century some Javanese Hindu aristocrats began relocating to the neighboring island of Bali, taking their courts and their court gamelan orchestras with them. From this time until the beginning of the twentieth century, eight courtly centers in Bali served as patrons of a flourishing arts tradition perhaps unparalleled anywhere in the world. Gamelans played for Hindu temple ceremonies and court functions and accompanied shadow puppet theater and court dancing, all in elegant, slow-tempo music, as they once did in Java.

> CULTURAL LINKAGES

The imperial ambitions of European powers between the sixteenth and early twentieth centuries had enormous impact in areas of the world they sought to colonize and on the lives of people who lived in those places. By the nineteenth century the Netherlands controlled much of this part of Asia, but they had not completely conquered the southern part of the island of Bali. In 1906 and 1908 the Dutch mounted decisive military campaigns that succeeded in deposing the remaining traditional kings (*rajas*) of southern Bali and imposing colonial control over the whole island. Both of these battles had horrifying ends. Unable to defend themselves against European rifles and cannons with their swords and knives, the Balinese faced certain defeat. To preserve their honor, they met the Dutch army passively, with a ritual suicide, called *puputan*. Here is an account of the first of these battles:

> On September 14, 1906, an overwhelming Dutch force landed at Sanur beach; there was no significant resistance and the force marched to Denpasar, Bali, as if in a dress parade. They passed through a seemingly deserted town and approached the royal palace, noting smoke rising from the *puri* [palace] and, most disquietingly, they heard a wild beating of drums coming from within the palace walls. Upon reaching the palace, a silent procession emerged, led by the *Raja*, borne by four bearers on a palanquin. The Raja was dressed in traditional white cremation garments, wore magnificent jewelry, and was armed with a ceremonial *kris* [dagger]. The other people in the procession consisted of the Raja's officials, guards, priests, wives, children and retainers, all of whom were similarly attired. When the procession was a hundred paces from the Dutch force, they halted and the Raja stepped down from the palanquin and signaled a priest who plunged his dagger into the Raja's breast. The rest of the procession began killing themselves and others. A "stray gunshot" and an "attack by lance and spear" prompted the Dutch to open fire with rifles and artillery. Women mockingly threw jewelry and gold coins at the troops. As more people emerged from the palace, the mounds of corpses rose higher and higher. Approximately 1,000 Balinese died. The soldiers stripped the corpses of the valuables and sacked the ruins of the burned palace.[65]

Balinese traditional religion sanctions such ritual suicides, which have their analogs in village rituals accompanied by gamelan music. In these rituals the evil witch Rangda, with her hideous tongue, threatens the villages. The villagers, in trance, rush to attack her in defense of the village, but she turns their daggers against them and they try to stab themselves in the chest with their own weapons. Fortunately the benevolent *barong*, a shaggy, friendly, ox-like beast, prevents the suicides, defeats Rangda, and the village is saved. In the *puputan*s of 1906 and 1908, the power of the *barong*

FIGURE 9.18
The Balinese witch Rangda as dramatized today
Source: Niradj, Shutterstock.

was no match for the Dutch army. The suicides were carried out and the Balinese went down to a staggering defeat that, in its mass, self-inflicted violence, shocked the world, the Dutch public, and the Balinese themselves.

In the area of culture and music the *puputan*s had three important consequences.[66] First, the Dutch government decided to support the arts in Bali and turn the island into a tourist destination, which it remains today. Second, gamelan orchestras moved from the now-defunct courts into village social life, where *sekaha* devoted to music, theater, and dance became the sources of patronage. Third, a new genre of music emerged—gamelan *gong kebyar*.

The origins of gamelan *gong kebyar* can be traced to the northern coastal town of Singaraja, the Dutch colonial capital in the mid-nineteenth century.[67] It was a locale with much contact with broader Southeast Asian and European culture. In the first decade of the twentieth century at the time of the complete Dutch takeover of the island, a literary revival was underway in the north of Bali centered on a new awareness of Hindu texts. People formed *sekaha pepaosan* (reading clubs), and groups from different *banjar* began to compete against one another, singing Hindu poetry in front of audiences at temple ceremonies and night markets. The excitement of audiences for these kinds of competitions led *sekaha* to explore new formats. Gamelan *gong kebyar* came about as these competitions began to experiment with the addition of gamelan accompaniment. The poetry performances in these settings alternated with gamelan music, which resulted in the abrupt and rapid shifts in the music that have come to characterize gamelan *gong kebyar*. By this time music, dance, and drama were already frequently integrated in Balinese performing arts, but this juxtaposition of discontinuous and different musical sounds one after the other was something new. There is evidence that some of the exciting

FIGURE 9.19
The *barong* protects the entranced villagers, who are trying to commit ritual suicide
Source: theskaman306, Shutterstock.

techniques of gamelan *gong kebyar* may have had antecedents in earlier styles of gamelan, but this was the first time they had been used in a competitive display of virtuosity, creating what must have been an exhilarating effect for performers and audiences alike. *Sekaha* soon began to cultivate the *gong kebyar* style and to invent new techniques of musical surprise and ingenuity, and competitions between groups became popular, even at times sponsored by the Dutch.

In the 1920s and 1930s, tourism began to develop in Bali,[68] and its reputation for being a hotbed for traditional culture and performing arts spread, with some gamelans performing regularly at hotels and one being sent to perform at the 1931 Paris Colonial Exhibition. Musicians became aware of how they were contributing to perceptions of the island because of the enthusiastic responses of international audiences. Gamelan ensembles of older genres began to absorb some of the stylistic straits of *gong kebyar*, though some Balinese were critical of this challenge to older traditions. Balinese society was undergoing drastic changes under Dutch colonial rule, and the musical changes embodied in gamelan *gong kebyar* and other genres it affected are expressions of these changes.

Since Indonesia declared its independence at the end of World War II in 1945, gamelan *gong kebyar* has continued to develop both in Bali and around the world. Conservatories, competitions, and festivals have fostered performance and innovation, and tourism has become a significant source of patronage for many *sekaha*, especially after the opening in 1969 of an international airport on the island. Universities, museums, and community groups in the United States, Europe, and Australasia have purchased complete Balinese gamelans—there are over one hundred gamelans in the United States alone. Universities offer courses that teach students how to perform gamelan *gong kebyar* and other styles. Gamelan ensembles outside Indonesia are also often connected to the community life of Indonesian people living abroad or to Indonesian embassies, consulates, and cultural institutions, and outside attention has contributed to the preservation and valuing of these traditions by the Balinese. Today both inside and outside Bali, gamelan *gong kebyar* continues to thrive as it captivates performers and audiences in a multitude of settings.

> **CULTURAL LINKAGES**

WHERE DO I GO FROM HERE?

- Find a college or university near you that has a gamelan—maybe there is one in your school. What kind of gamelan is it? Is it Balinese? Is there an active ensemble learning gamelan *gong kebyar*? Attend a concert and experience the sounds of gamelan in person. Or, even better, see if you can get permission to attend a rehearsal of this ensemble to see how a group of people learns and rehearses gamelan performance techniques.

- Locate a video online of the *koketan* technique. Do the performers make it look easy, or does its complexity and technicality seem evident?

- Have you encountered musical performance as a tourist anywhere before? What are some of the ways that you think tourism may have affected the genre of music you encountered as a tourist?

- Look into some of the other vibrant Balinese arts today. When did these arts emerge, and how do their meanings relate to gamelan *gong kebyar*, if at all?

CLOSING

The gateways to music between 1890 and 1918 in this chapter include three examples from music for popular audiences in the United States, one example of European classical music, and one example of music under European colonial rule. All these examples illustrate the increasing interconnectedness of the world, which was in part related to the ways that European powers had colonized much of the world over the preceding four centuries. The blues arose as African Americans suffered during Reconstruction and the Jim Crow era, when new forms of oppression continued the legacy of slavery. American band music grew out of industrial-era instrument technologies and European dance forms, with even deeper roots in Ottoman military music. Ragtime drew on the form of marches as well as African American and Latin American rhythmic sensibilities to inspire a widely popular music and dance phenomenon. Stravinsky pursued musical modernism in *The Rite of Spring* by infusing material from traditional folk music into European classical forms. Balinese gamelan *gong kebyar* sprang up almost immediately after the Dutch conquered Bali, drawing on new sources of patronage, new audiences, and new forms of social organization as it became a world-renown genre.

All of these forms of music making could also be called modern in the sense that they are to some extent breaking with traditions of the past as they engage with changes occurring in the world. At the same time, however, each of these gateways remains to some extent grounded in the traditions of the past. This struggle between remaining connected to tradition on the one hand and innovation free from the constraints of the past on the other is a hallmark of the music of this period, and indeed of most forms of music making since then. Musical continuity and transformation is evident in the meanings and histories of the music explored in this chapter, and these themes will continue through the rest of the chapters exploring the music of the long twentieth century.

THINGS TO THINK ABOUT

- The blues, ragtime, and gamelan *gong kebyar* all emerged among communities who had been oppressed, exploited, or conquered by European colonial powers. Compare the various ways that these communities grappled musically with, contested, and negotiated the challenges they faced.

- The musical styles and genres in this chapter all represent either something new or something old that changed to something new. Compare the social and cultural factors that stimulated change in these cases.

NEW TERMS

atonality	gamelan *gong kebyar*	ragtime
blue notes	habanera rhythm	serialism
blues	*kotekan*	shawm
chord cluster	*mehter*	sousaphone
classic blues	obbligato	stride piano
country blues	polyrhythm	swing feel
fife	polytonality	tone row

MUSIC FROM THE INTERWAR PERIOD (1918–1939)

THE PERIOD BETWEEN the end World War I in 1918 and the beginning of World War II in 1939 can be divided into two decades. The first, sometimes called the Roaring Twenties, featured unprecedented economic growth in the U.S. and among the victorious European nations in World War I. An epic stock market crash on Oct. 24, 1929 ushered in the second decade of the interwar period, the Great Depression.

While the economic prosperity of the Roaring Twenties is often celebrated in contrast to the widespread despair of the Great Depression, it was enjoyed by a minority, as at least 60 percent of American families lived on an income below the standard of what could provide for the basic necessities of life. A growing middle class and wealthy elite in North America and Europe could afford the new inventions of the pre-war generation, such previously unheard-of luxuries as an automobile, a telephone, and electricity-powered radios and phonographs. Music of all kinds could now be heard at home in this sector of the population, not just in a concert hall or the salons of the wealthy. To sell to this market, record companies recorded classical music, jazz, popular music, and ethnic and regional music targeted at particular communities.

The Roaring Twenties also coincides with the first Great Migration, the movement of roughly 1.6 million African Americans from the rural American South to cities of the West, Midwest, and Northeast between 1916 and 1930. They relocated to pursue economic opportunities and to seek escape from segregation, rural poverty, and lynching. In New York City the Great Migration contributed to the "Harlem Renaissance," a national flourishing of African American arts and literature named for an African American neighborhood north of Central Park in New York City. It included the work of writers like Langston Hughes and Zora Neale Hurston, musicians like Duke Ellington, and other black intellectuals.

The press, along with writers such as F. Scott Fitzgerald (1896–1940), dubbed The Roaring Twenties "The Jazz Age." Jazz was a slang word that had a number of meanings before it became the name of a musical genre. In print it was first used on the west coast in writing about baseball, meaning "lively" or "energetic," with its first known published appearance describing a baseball pitch (a curveball called a "jazz ball") in the *Los Angeles Times* in 1912.[69] By 1915 it was being used in Chicago newspapers to describe a new lively kind of music, and by the end of World War I it was being used to refer to sex. In the 1920s, jazz was used to describe these things and more, including virtually all dance music, a great deal of which would probably not be categorized as "jazz" today. With all that the word jazz encapsulated at the time, calling the 1920s "The Jazz Age" seemed an apt way to describe an American society energized by the end of war and moving on from a deadly flu epidemic in 1918 that had killed as many as 100 million people worldwide. By the end of the interwar period, the word jazz was being used around the world as a name for a musical genre that enjoyed mass popularity. Two gateway recordings are devoted to jazz in this chapter: one by Louis Armstrong (1901–1971) and his Hot Five that demonstrates musical innovations of black migrants

FIGURE 10.1
A flapper
Source: Bain News
Service, Wikimedia
Commons.

from the South in urban settings such as Chicago and New York City, and one by the big band of Duke Ellington (1899–1974), one of the great American composers of the twentieth century.

Victory in World War I also inspired a new American confidence in the role of the U.S. in the world. President Woodrow Wilson claimed that the United States had fought a just "war to end all wars." Patriotism spread through the population, not least among the children of Jewish immigrants who had fled economic and political oppression in eastern Europe before the war. Some of them became the most prominent composers of popular songs, including Irving Berlin (1888–1989), who wrote "God Bless America" in 1918. Another one, George Gershwin (1898–1937), a popular songwriter influenced by Jewish traditions and emerging jazz styles, also wrote a classical tone poem called *Rhapsody in Blue* in the nationalist vein, which is the subject of a gateway in this chapter.

The victory over war and disease gave many something to celebrate. One more victory also got the party started. In 1918, after a long struggle, women in the United States were given the right to vote. They felt a new confidence, and some of them, called flappers, adopted unconventional behaviors, including wearing daring, uncorseted, knee-length dresses, cutting their hair in short bobs, and drinking and smoking in public. These women, from the class of white middle-class and wealthy elites, felt free to participate on their own terms in the jazz-soaked social life of the times.

Disposable income was spent not only at clubs with live music and on home entertainment like radio and phonographs, but on spectator sports. Sports heroes became part of the cultural landscape for the first time, including boxer Jack Dempsey, college football player Red Grange, and the "wonder horses" Man o' War and Seabiscuit. Baseball became the national sport (though the "jazz ball" never caught on), and huge new stadiums were built for fans to follow their favorites, like the New York Yankees' slugger Babe Ruth.

All this entertainment flourished in spite of the passage in 1920 of the Eighteenth Amendment to the U.S. Constitution banning the sale of alcoholic beverages. This unleashed a wave of smuggling from Canada, Mexico, and the Caribbean run by gangsters whose internecine rivalries raised the noise level of the Roaring Twenties. Prohibition finally ended with the passage of the Twenty-first Amendment in 1933.

After the 1929 stock market crash, for most of the second decade of the interwar period the Great Depression brought on suffering for the bulk of the population of not only the United States but also most of the world. A drought wiped out farmers in the Midwest, another source of misery. Poverty and inflation in Germany made the demagoguery of Adolf Hitler appealing to the masses.

FIGURE 10.2
A dust storm in Texas in 1935
Source: NOAA George E. Marsh Album, Wikimedia Commons.

After he came to power in 1933, the specter of war hung over Europe. Threatened by Hitler, many Jews emigrated to the United States, invigorating musical life in classical music circles. Most prominent among them was the Austrian composer Arnold Schoenberg.

In spite of economic hardship during the Depression of the 1930s, the United States and Mexico enjoyed a "golden age" of cinema. In 1927 the first "talking picture," tellingly titled *The Jazz Singer*, anticipated vast numbers of "musicals," films in the 1930s that featured the popular singing and dancing stars of the day, including Bing Crosby, Fred Astaire, Ginger Rogers, and Judy Garland. In Mexico, mariachi music figured prominently in films with singing stars like Jorge Negrete and Pedro Infante. A gateway in this chapter is devoted to this genre. People also flocked to large ballrooms to listen and dance to the music of big bands led by Duke Ellington and other bandleaders, whose recordings they also bought to listen to at home and heard on the radio. This escapist fare in movies, Broadway shows, big band dance music, and sound recordings was eagerly consumed by audiences seeking relief from economic desperation.

GATEWAY 40
EARLY JAZZ

What Is It?

The word "jazz" had a number of meanings in the interwar period, referring to dancing, sex, and music of many styles. As the genre of music known as jazz today developed in the course of the long twentieth century, musicians and historians have looked back to the 1910s and 1920s, when the word jazz was first associated with music, and have called some styles of music in this period "early jazz." Our gateway to early jazz is "Struttin' with Some Barbecue" (1927) composed by Lillian (Lil) Hardin Armstrong (1898–1971) and performed by Louis Armstrong and His Hot Five. In a style of what is known today as **New Orleans jazz**, a rhythm section (in this case piano and banjo) backs up three melodic instruments (usually trumpet or cornet, clarinet, and trombone) that play together in polyphony and call and response, and also as improvising soloists. Louis Armstrong (1901–1971) grew up in New Orleans, performing on the cornet (similar to the trumpet) as a teenager. This and other recordings of Louis Armstrong and His Hot Five from the late 1920s were recorded in Chicago, a destination for Armstrong and many other black musicians from the South and Southwest in the course of the Great Migration. The recording's emphasis on single soloists improvising with a rhythm section accompaniment is an example of the innovations of black musicians who had migrated from the south to urban centers like Chicago, New York, and Los Angeles.

FIGURE 10.3

Louis Armstrong and His Hot Five. From left: Louis Armstrong (trumpet), Johnny St. Cyr (banjo), Johnny Dodds (clarinet), Kid Ory (trombone), and Lil Hardin Armstrong (piano)

Source: Getty Images / Gilles Petard.

This gateway is also an early example of one of the most common forms in jazz performance, in which a **head** (melody) is played, followed by a number of improvised solos over the internal form and underlying harmony of the head and a concluding repetition of the head. Each improvisation based on the structure of the head is called a **chorus**. So, if an improvised solo lasts for two repetitions of the basic form, it lasts for two choruses.

 Listen to the first thirty seconds of the recording.

How Does It Work?

Timbre

The timbres of the cornet, clarinet, trombone, banjo, and piano can all be heard clearly.

Texture

The texture includes both individual and collective improvisations by the cornet, clarinet, and trombone over a chordal accompaniment played by the banjo and piano.

Rhythm

The song is in a duple meter, with a swing feel. The banjo and piano for the most part play steady pulsatile chords, while the other instruments add syncopated and swung rhythms.

Melody

The melody is generally in a major mode, and tends to arpeggiate among chord tones rather than move stepwise through a scale.

Harmony

The chord progressions in this composition follow tonal harmony through a number of major and minor triads as well as some dominant seventh chords. Some chromaticism can be heard from time to time.

Form

After a 12-measure intro, a repeating 32-bar form is introduced, which has an internal form of ABA'C, with each section lasting eight bars. The first time, or during the first chorus, this 32-bar form is a statement of the melody. The second chorus features a clarinet and then a trombone solo, and the third chorus features a cornet solo. The final chorus is a restatement of the head.

Performance Techniques

During each statement of the melody in the cornet, the trombone and clarinet can be heard simultaneously improvising with the cornet. After the head, however, the clarinet, trombone, and cornet each perform solo improvisations over the form. Each of these three instruments performs microtonally, bends the start or end of pitches, and adds various types of ornamentation as they imitate the sound of a human voice singing the blues.

Listen to the introduction and the head (to about 0:32) and pay attention to the polyphonic, simultaneous lines of the trumpet, trombone, and clarinet.

Listen to the entire performance, following this listening guide, which describes each chorus.

LISTENING GUIDE 10.1

TIME	SECTION	FORM	DESCRIPTION
0:00	Introduction		The song starts with a twelve-bar introduction, featuring a prominent melody in the cornet and improvisation in the clarinet and trombone. Bars 1-4 and 9-12 feature an accompaniment with a steady beat, while in bars 5-8, the banjo, piano, clarinet, and trombone play sustained chords on beat one of each measure while the cornet plays eighth notes and syncopated figures.
0:14	Head (first chorus)	A	The cornet begins the melody or "head." This melody generally ascends up an arpeggio and then partially descends along the same or a similar arpeggio. The clarinet and trombone improvise while the cornet plays the head, and their parts are more active in between the cornet phrases, in a call and response of sorts. The banjo provides a steady pulse on every downbeat. The piano performs a bass line on beats one and three, reminiscent of the "oom-pah" bass line of marches and the bass line as performed in ragtime solo piano.
0:24		B	The harmony in the second eight bars of the head shifts to a series of chords that tend to be minor, but are still in the original key. The texture remains constant here and throughout the head.

TIME	SECTION	FORM	DESCRIPTION
0:34		A'	The first four bars of A' are just about the same as the first four bars of A, but in the second four bars, the harmony and melody are different from A.
0:44		C	At the end of these last eight bars of the head, the banjo plays two bars solo, ascending chromatically on a series of chords, one on each downbeat.
0:54	Clarinet Solo (second chorus)	A	The clarinet improvises solo over the first sixteen bars of the form, accompanied by a new texture in the piano and banjo where the piano abandons its "oom-pah" bass line and joins the banjo in playing a chord on each downbeat. The accompaniment stops for the last two bars and the clarinet plays on its own.
1:04		B	The clarinet continues improvising with the accompaniment, though the accompaniment stops for the last two bars and the clarinet plays on its own in a brief section called a **break**, since it is a break in the continuity of the chugging rhythmic playing of the rhythm section.
1:13	Trombone Solo (second chorus continues)	A'	The trombone begins its improvised solo, taking advantage of the instrument's slide mechanism to perform ornamentation that slides between pitches. The accompaniment also shifts again. The banjo continues to play chords on every beat, but the piano is now playing chords only on every other beat, beats two and four. This emphasis on beats two and four is a typical feature of the swing feel.
1:23		C	The solo continues, and again the last two bars occur with no accompaniment and the trombone plays the end of the solo on its own.
1:33	Cornet solo (third chorus)	A	The full-chorus cornet solo begins. The improvised melody Armstrong plays draws not only on the major mode, but also on the blues, especially the lowered third blue note. His playing is also highly syncopated throughout. The accompaniment changes once again, where now the banjo and piano are both only playing chords on beats two and four.
1:43		B	The solo continues, and again last two bars occur with no accompaniment as the cornet plays a break at the end of this section.
1:53		A'	The solo continues over the harmony of A'.
2:03		C	In this, the final solo before the return of the head, the final two bars of the form are replaced with four bars of an unaccompanied, syncopated rhythm played in harmony by the cornet, clarinet, and trombone together.
2:15	Head (final chorus)	A	The head returns, this time with the cornet adding some improvised flourishes that distinguish this statement of the head from the one at the beginning. The texture is the same as in the initial statement of the head.
2:26		B	The clarinet takes a particularly active role in the improvisation in this B section. The last two bars break once again for a solo banjo rhythmic figure.
2:36		A'	A' is similar to its appearance in the initial statement of the head, with more active clarinet and trombone improvisations.
2:46		C	For the last C section, the accompaniment drops out, and the clarinet, cornet, and trombone play in homophonic rhythm. They repeat the final two bars of this figure and hold a sustained chord to finish the performance.
3:02	End		

What Does It Mean?

AESTHETICS

Louis Armstrong and His Hot Five play "Struttin' with Some Barbecue" with some musical elements of music rooted in the entertainment scene in New Orleans before 1918, music that came to be called jazz, while hinting at some of the directions that jazz would take in the years following this recording. The instrumentation of three wind instruments (cornet, clarinet, and trombone) and a rhythm section (in this case banjo and piano) plays the head in a polyphonic texture that was common for this kind of ensemble. The cornet plays a main melody, adding some embellishment and ornamentation. The clarinet plays a countermelody that is much more active than the cornet part, which seems to fill in the gaps in the cornet melody. In the initial head the clarinet is generally playing lower than the cornet, while in the final head the clarinet plays extensively in a range that is higher than the cornet melody. The trombone plays a less active countermelody than the clarinet, emphasizing the important pitches in the harmony and often using the slide of the trombone to slide from one note to the next in a technique sometimes called "tailgating," a reference to bands playing on the backs of trucks during Mardi Gras and other festive parades.

This manner of several musicians playing together in polyphony is called **collective improvisation**, since each of the players would be improvising to some extent, even if it meant they were embellishing pre-composed melodies. In some forms of New Orleans jazz dating back to this period and earlier, the texture is primarily heterophonic, as all of the musicians simultaneously embellish pre-composed melodies in different ways. One of the effects of this texture is that listeners' attention is not necessarily focused on the primary melody alone, but can be drawn to other elements such as the countermelodies, the rhythmic breaks at the end of some of the choruses, and the syncopated rhythms.

SOCIAL BEHAVIOR

This texture is also an enactment of collectivity, a way of making music where the focus is on the group as a whole, as musicians play embellished or improvised individual parts simultaneously. This kind of collective interaction has its roots in several older forms of African American music and dance from the United States including spirituals, ring shouts, and work songs (Chapter 8, Gateway 34). Many scholars suggest that it is also a legacy of polyphonic practices from a number of African musical traditions, such as the polyphony of Central African foragers (Chapter 1, Gateway 1) or the inherent polyphony created by the interlocking parts of *mbira* players (Chapter 3, Gateway 10). Though this kind of polyphony is based on harmonies rooted in the tonality of European classical music, the collectivity heard in this polyphonic texture is also a thread that can be traced through several African and African American musical practices.

TECHNOLOGY

Lil Hardin Armstrong composed "Struttin' with Some Barbecue" with the intention that it would be recorded. Technological limitations in recording at the time meant that the maximum duration of one side of a record was around three minutes, and so the composition and the number of choruses had to fit within that time constraint. New Orleans jazz, however, was often music for dancing, and single songs would often last much longer than three minutes. The polyphonic or heterophonic texture of the style developed in New Orleans and other cities would continue for longer periods of time, engaging with dancers at social and other community events such as funeral processions that typically

SOCIAL BEHAVIOR

involved dance. The collectivity in the improvisation of the musicians and the social collectivity in the places the music was played reinforced one another; the polyphonic musical texture is in many ways an icon of the communal dance and social interaction that goes along with it. When black musicians from New Orleans and other areas of the South moved to places like Chicago, they adapted their

TECHNOLOGY

musical styles and innovated new ones to work with new technology like recordings, which allowed listeners to hear their performances in places far distant from where they were recorded.

🔊 **Listen again to "Struttin' with Some Barbecue" and compare the polyphonic interaction of the lines of the cornet, clarinet, and trombone at the beginning with those at the end of the recording.**

Though the recording of "Struttin' with Some Barbecue"—especially the head—provides some clues into what this kind of entertainment music in New Orleans and elsewhere might have sounded like before this period, it also demonstrates the emergence of the improvised solo as a key element of jazz performance that was happening as musicians migrated to northern urban centers. The clarinet and trombone solos, each lasting half of a chorus, mainly outline the underlying chords played by the piano and the banjo. By contrast, Louis Armstrong plays a longer cornet solo lasting a full chorus, demonstrating his virtuosity as a soloist. His solo includes extensive syncopation and microtonal blue notes like the lowered third over major harmonies, revealing influences of the blues and ragtime in his improvisation. This texture of an improvising soloist with rhythm section accompaniment was a new development in jazz during this period. Even in the context of the head, Armstrong's cornet features more prominently than the other instruments, whose polyphonic lines seem to be in supporting roles of his melody. Louis Armstrong's recordings of this era helped set the stage for jazz to become a setting for soloists to demonstrate their skill in improvising, usually with a rhythm section accompaniment in musical dialogue with the soloist. This focus on solo improvisation became one of the hallmarks of jazz, and is one of the main characteristics today in most types of jazz.

🔊 **Listen again to the solos in "Struttin' with Some Barbecue." Identify where the soloists use syncopation and listen for the blue notes in the cornet solos.**

What Is Its History?

The word jazz was first used to describe music in 1915 in Chicago newspapers. The first recording to use a form of the word jazz was "That Funny Jas Band from Dixieland" (1916) by a white duo named Collins and Harlan who recorded in the style of minstrelsy, singing in an exaggerated stereotype of what was considered a "black dialect." In 1917 a group of white musicians from New Orleans with the name "The Original Dixieland Jass Band" (ODJB) recorded the song "Livery Stable Blues" in New York, and it became a hit. Some of the members of ODJB had previously played in white brass marching bands in New Orleans, bands whose repertoire included popular minstrel songs and ragtime songs. As a result, elements of ragtime and minstrelsy were featured in the music of ODJB, as were blues and other popular songs of the day. In part because of their name and the popularity of their recording, audiences began to refer to these kinds of music as jazz, and

they associated it with New Orleans. Although the band tried to take credit for inventing jazz as a new style of popular dance music, the roots of jazz had been growing deeply among African American and Creole (mixed-race, French- and Spanish-descended) musicians from the blues and ragtime music scenes of New Orleans and throughout the South during the decades before 1917.

Although no recordings exist of New Orleans bands before 1917, photographs suggest that these bands featured lineups similar to that of the ODJB. The ODJB performed with a "front line" of cornet or trumpet, clarinet, and trombone accompanied by a rhythm section of piano and a drum set. Similar to the head of "Struttin' with Some Barbecue," the frontline musicians in ODJB recordings improvised simultaneously, creating a polyphonic texture of independent musical lines. The piano and drum set provided a constant pulse and the oom-pah, bass-chord accompaniment of a marching band. Though African American and Creole musicians were playing something like this style of dance music

FIGURE 10.4
A promotional postcard for the Original Dixieland Jazz Band
Source: Getty Images / GAB Archive.

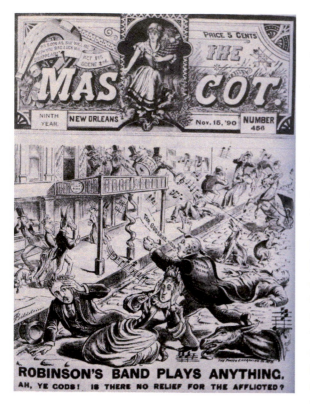

FIGURE 10.5
The front page of an 1890 edition of *The Mascot*, a New Orleans newspaper, depicting a caricature of well-to-do white bypassers reacting negatively to the sounds of an African American band, perhaps playing a precursor to jazz
Source: F. Bildestein (public domain), Wikimedia Commons.

FIGURE 10.6
The modern drum set
Source: Dave Wilson.

in New Orleans, throughout the South, and in the northern and western cities they were moving to as part of the Great Migration, recording technology enabled the spread of this music. It must have sounded incredibly fresh to dancers in New York clubs and elsewhere in 1917. They were familiar with dance bands playing conventional arrangements that featured the melody plus harmonic accompaniment on piano and bass. Chances are the simultaneously improvised three-part polyphony of this New Orleans style, coupled with the rhythmic drive of a drum set, would have knocked them off their feet.

Early New Orleans jazz musicians have said that "jazz" was not used to describe their music, which they viewed as a version of ragtime that included improvisation. But the well-documented musical life of New Orleans before the explosion of jazz as a musical genre helps in understanding some of the music that developed later in places like Chicago among musicians like Louis Armstrong, Lil Hardin Armstrong, and the rest of the Hot Five. New Orleans had a lively outdoor brass-band music scene tied to Carnival (Mardi Gras) celebrations and funerals in the African American community. In Africa, funerals are in many cases a time to celebrate the life of the deceased, and this tradition endured in New Orleans. Street bands played, and still play, a mournful tune on the way to the cemetery, but a joyful one on the way home. These street brass bands feature both bass drum and snare drum along with sousaphone and other wind instruments, and the Rebirth Brass Band, the Dirty Dozen Brass Band, and many others are still a lively part of the New Orleans music scene today.

New Orleans also boasted a lively indoor musical culture that featured bands playing for respectable dances in all the ethnic communities of the city (black, Creole, and white) plus, to some extent, in the many brothels that served sailors and others in this port city. When the brass bands came indoors and sat down on stage to play for dancers, the changes they made resembled an early jazz band lineup. The string bass substituted for the sousaphone in some cases. Piano, guitar, and banjo were added to provide chordal accompaniment. And, in perhaps the most important innovation, a drummer for one of the New Orleans dance bands named Dee Dee Chandler invented a contraption (a pedal he could "kick" with his foot to play the bass drum) that allowed him to play both bass and snare drums simultaneously while sitting down. Musicians called this combination a drum kit or drum set or a trap set (short for contraption), and the bass drum a "kick drum" after the way it was played. An important later addition to the drum set, common in the 1930s, was the **hi-hat**, a pair of similar cymbals mounted on a stand with a foot lever that, when depressed, crashed the cymbals together. Drum sets may include one or more "tom-tom drums" or "toms" attached to the bass drum or standing on the ground, as well as a number of single cymbals mounted on stands.

The Creole musicians who played this early kind of dance music belonged to the middle class in the integrated French quarter of the city. They had music educations and could read the music of John Philip Sousa, Scott Joplin, and other composers of band music and ragtime. They maintained and developed the syncopations of ragtime and the polyphonic principles

AESTHETICS

of band music, applying them to their performances. They also continued the ragtime performance tradition of improvisation, a legacy of African and other musical traditions from the time of slavery. These traditions overlapped with one another for centuries in places like New Orleans, with its rich multiplicity of cultures and its ties to the Caribbean and Latin America. In this setting, musicians, as a matter of course, improvised over popular dance music, rags, and blues.

By the time World War I had ended, black and Creole musicians were already leaving New Orleans and other parts of the South for New York, Chicago, California, and Paris, bringing their ragtime- and blues-inflected music to join already vibrant music scenes in those cities and to plant the seeds of what would become known as the "Jazz Age" in the cultural life of the U.S., Europe, and Asia. New Orleans-born Jelly Roll Morton relocated to Los Angeles in 1917 before moving to Chicago in 1923 and then New York in 1928. While in L.A., he performed there and on tour up and down the west coast with other black musicians who had migrated from Texas, Mississippi, and other parts of Louisiana. In these urban environments, and as bands began to travel around the country and the world and record their music using new and developing recording technology, musical styles began to change and develop in a number of ways. One of the significant developments was a focus on solo improvisation.

Louis Armstrong's innovative solo improvisations were influential in his time and laid a foundation for much of the improvisation in jazz that would come after him. Born to a poor family in New Orleans, he received formal musical training in school and real-world musical experience playing in the bands of Joe "King" Oliver (1881–1938), one of the leading cornet players and bandleaders of the period and his mentor. In 1922 Armstrong followed Oliver to Chicago to play in Oliver's Creole Jazz Band, leaving the South for a northern city like so many other African Americans had at the time. Armstrong's technique was stronger than the other trumpeters in Chicago, and Oliver began to give him space in the band's arrangements to expand solo breaks, like the ones in "Struttin' with Some Barbecue," into longer solos. Encouraged by his future wife, the pianist Lil Hardin, who played in Oliver's band, Armstrong began to form his own bands. In 1927 he recorded Hardin's "Struttin' with Some Barbecue" with his Hot Five, a recording that illustrates this new version of New Orleans jazz with collective improvisation and Armstrong's brilliant solo playing. Between 1925 and 1928, Armstrong completed several dozen recordings with his Hot Five and his Hot Seven, which added a drum set and a tuba to the Hot Five instrumentation. Like "Struttin' with Some Barbecue," other recordings from these sessions such as "West End Blues" (1928) and "Potato Head Blues" (1927) showcase the ground-breaking melodic, rhythmic, and timbral elements of Armstrong's soloing, along with ensemble playing characteristic of New Orleans jazz.

Armstrong's long career after the 1920s departed from the New Orleans jazz style as he performed in many settings as an instrumentalist and as a vocalist. As a vocalist he was highly influential in the development and popularity of **scat singing**, vocal improvisations using vocables to imitate the sounds of musical instruments. In the 1930s and early 1940s, he performed almost exclusively as a soloist with big bands, both on trumpet and as a singer. During and after this time,

FIGURE 10.7
Photo of King Oliver's Creole Jazz Band. From left: Johnny Dodds (clarinet), Baby Dodds (drum set), Honoré Dutrey (trombone), Louis Armstrong (2nd trumpet), King Oliver (1st trumpet), Lil Hardin (piano), William Johnson (bass, also holding banjo)
Source: Getty Images / Bettmann.

FIGURE 10.8
Armstrong (right) appearing on a television program with trumpet player and music executive Herb Alpert in 1967
Source: Getty Images / David Redfern.

FIGURE 10.9
The Preservation Hall Jazz Band in action, 2010
Source: Philip Scalia / Alamy Stock Photo.

CULTURAL
LINKAGES

he became well known for recording and performing popular Broadway and other songs that became known as the Great American Songbook, though he also returned to a New Orleans-style format beginning in the late 1940s. For much of his life, he was one of the most famous individuals in the United States and served as a cultural ambassador of the U.S. abroad as a performer. His 1964 release of the song "Hello Dolly" (from the Broadway musical of the same name) was his last recording to hit number one on the charts. When it reached number one on the *Billboard* charts, it unseated the Beatles' unprecedented three-month run in the number one position with their string of three hits: "I Want to Hold Your Hand," "She Loves You," and "Can't Buy Me Love." In 1967, Armstrong released "What a Wonderful World." Included in popular films such as the 1978 film *Good Morning Vietnam*, it has become a standard for events like first dances at wedding receptions and has been re-recorded in new arrangements by such artists as Nick Cave, Sarah Brightman, and Rod Stewart, who recorded the song in a duet with Stevie Wonder.

Louis Armstrong's influence in jazz and popular music during his life (and after his death) cannot be under-estimated. Though in the 1930s he first departed from his performance of the styles categorized today as New Orleans jazz, these styles have had a history of their own since then, independent of Armstrong. In the 1930s styles of New Orleans jazz became less popular and gave way to big bands, the subject of our next gateway. Since then, however, New Orleans jazz has enjoyed several revivals in the United States and around the world, the first of which gained a broad audience in the 1940s and 1950s in the U.S. and Europe. In New Orleans today New Orleans jazz caters to both tourists and locals. The Preservation Hall Jazz Band has been performing in New Orleans and on tour around the world since its inception in the early 1960s. The band also collaborates with contemporary popular bands such as The Foo Fighters, My Morning Jacket, and Arcade Fire. They seem to be continuing, in a different form, the mixing of musical influences and cultures that characterized New Orleans in the first half of the twentieth century, when jazz first became a national and international musical phenomenon.

WHERE DO I GO FROM HERE?

- Listen to "West End Blues," "Potato Head Blues," or another recording from the Hot Five or Hot Seven sessions. How would you describe Armstrong's and other musicians' soloistic playing? How are they interacting in their collaborative improvisation? What elements do these recordings share with examples of the blues and ragtime discussed in Chapter 9, Gateways 35 and 37? How do they differ?

- Listen to "Livery Stable Blues" by the Original Dixieland Jazz Band. What elements does this recording share with minstrelsy? What elements of ragtime and the blues does it contain?

- Find a band that is today actively performing something related to early jazz in New Orleans. Listen to a few of their recordings, or maybe even a complete album. What can you learn from their promotional materials about the audience for this band (e.g., is the music geared towards tourists, aficionados, or some other demographic)?

- Select three or four recordings made by Louis Armstrong in different eras of his life. To what extent are they connected to jazz of this early period?

GATEWAY 41
SWING

What Is It?

Swing was one of the most popular styles of music during the 1920s and 1930s. It was played by large jazz ensembles called **big bands** (sometimes called dance bands). They filled large ballrooms with their sound, entertaining dancers in energetic dance styles such as the Lindy Hop, the Charleston, and dozens more. Both swing music and the dances that emerged along with it were part of a craze that took the United States and much of the world by storm. By 1935, "swing" was being used consistently by the music industry as a musical genre name, marking the beginning of what is known as "The Swing Era." Big bands of the swing era had a typical instrumentation of five saxophones, four or five trombones, four or five trumpets, and a rhythm section typically including drums, bass, piano, and guitar. One of the most influential musicians and composers in the development and popularity of swing was Edward Kennedy "Duke" Ellington (1899–1974), whose big band, beginning in the late 1920s, was one of the most well known. Our gateway to swing is a composition by Ellington and trumpet player Bubber Miley (1903–1932) called "Black and Tan Fantasy." Composed and recorded in 1927 during the period leading up to the swing era, "Black and Tan Fantasy" demonstrates some of the classic sounds and cultural meanings that characterize Ellington's music and the music of the big band swing sensation.

FIGURE 10.10
Duke Ellington in 1946
Source: William Morris Agency (management), Wikimedia Commons.

 Listen to the first thirty seconds of this recording.

How Does It Work?

Timbre

This composition features the big band timbres of saxophones, trombones, and trumpets, along with piano, banjo, bass, and drums. In addition, trumpet and trombone timbres are frequently altered with the addition of mutes.

Texture

Several textures can be heard, including several versions of melody with block-chord accompaniment, solo piano, and some brief moments of contrapuntal texture.

Rhythm

The meter is a quadruple meter, and a swing feel is heard throughout. The tempo of the pulse ranges between about 108 and 112 beats per minute, which makes it suitable for dancing.

Melody

The melody begins in a minor mode, then shifts into a major mode. In both minor and major modes, blue notes are emphasized from time to time. Sometimes the melody is improvised by soloists.

Harmony

The harmony follows minor and major tonal chord progressions, usually in triads and seventh chords.

Form

The form begins with a 12-bar minor blues, followed by a 16-bar section in the parallel major key and five choruses of a 12-bar blues, the last one with a two-bar extension.

Performance Techniques

Performers in this composition frequently play microtonally. The brass instruments bend pitches and use mutes in a way that helps them mimic the sounds of a human voice. In the final chorus, we also hear call and response between the trumpet and the full band.

Listen to the first thirty seconds again and pay attention to the muted trumpet sound, pitch bends, and the underlying, accompanying pulse.

Listen to the entire recording following this timed listening guide.

LISTENING GUIDE 10.2

TIME	SECTION	DESCRIPTION
0:00	1st Chorus	The piece begins with a muted trumpet playing a minor melody along with a muted trombone playing in harmony. The trumpet and trombone are accompanied by pulsing block chords in the rhythm section. The end of this 12-bar minor blues section and the beginning of the next section is marked with a cymbal crash played by the drummer.
0:27	16-bar interlude	An alto saxophone plays a 16-bar composed solo that is actually two repetitions of an eight-bar phrase in an AA form reminiscent of a European dance form. The saxophone is accompanied by the pulsing banjo and piano as well as sustained chords played by the other wind players and the bass player playing with a bow. The harmony in this section is characterized by chromaticism, especially in the two bars at the end of the first eight-bar phrase where the harmony changes on every beat.
1:02	2nd Chorus	The trumpet plays an improvised solo over a 12-bar major blues form, beginning with a sustained high-pitched tone on the tonic for the first four bars. The trumpet player, Bubber Miley, is playing through a straight mute and is using a "plunger mute," which he moves with his hand to adjust the timbre and pitch as he plays. A prominent growling effect in the trumpet can be heard in the second half of this chorus.
1:29	3rd Chorus	The trumpet timbre shifts again as it improvises over another chorus of a major blues, emphasizing pitch bends and the lowered-third blue note.
1:55	4th Chorus	The piano plays a solo, drawing on characteristics of stride piano such as the "oom-pah" figure where the left hand alternates between low bass notes and a higher-pitched chord.
2:21	5th Chorus	The trombone plays an improvised solo, again with a muted sound that affects the timbre. About halfway through, the trombone performs an effect that sounds like laughter or the imitation of a whinny of a horse.
2:48	6th Chorus	The trumpet returns, beginning with two bluesy two-bar phrases that are answered by accented chords played by the full band in a call-and-response style. This chorus begins as a major blues, but on the eleventh bar, the harmony returns to the minor key from the beginning of the piece. This final phrase is a quotation from the "Funeral March" theme of Frédéric Chopin's Piano Sonata No. 2, Op. 35 in B-flat minor (1839), and extends the length of the 12-bar blues form by two bars to a total of 14 bars.
3:23	End	

What Does It Mean?

The musical elements of "Black and Tan Fantasy," reveal much about the experience of big band music and swing in the 1920s and 1930s as well as about its roots in the blues, early jazz, and music of Africa and the African diaspora.

"Black and Tan Fantasy," like much big band music of this period, features a swing feel with an emphasis on beats two and four of a four-beat measure. The label on the initial recording of "Black and Tan Fantasy" lists "Duke Ellington and His Orchestra" as the performing ensemble and includes the dance name "Fox Trot," a well-known couple dance.

Big bands like Duke Ellington's orchestra functioned primarily as live entertainment for dancing. Dancing to the swinging rhythms of big bands in large ballrooms full of dancers as well as smaller dance clubs became wildly popular in the 1920s and 1930s in New York, throughout the United States, and around the world. Beginning in 1927, Ellington's band performed regularly at New York's Cotton Club, a venue in Harlem that catered almost exclusively to white patrons and relied on the legacy of minstrelsy, setting black musi-

FIGURE 10.11
Cab Calloway leading his big band and an audience of dancers at the Cotton Club in 1937
Source: Getty Images / Bettmann.

cians on a stage that replicated a mansion on a southern plantation, complete with a backdrop that depicted weeping willows and slave quarters. Other clubs in Harlem were frequented predominantly by African Americans, excluded from white venues like the Cotton Club. "Black and tan" clubs, a third type, were small cabarets, usually in black neighborhoods, that attracted both black and white patrons, though they were sometimes segregated inside. As one of the few public spaces where whites and African Americans could socialize in close proximity, black and tan clubs were experienced by many white patrons as erotic, dangerous, and playful places where they could go "slumming," living out their fantasies of pushing against the boundaries of segregation. Ellington's "Black and Tan Fantasy" plays on the sexual anxieties and desires of his white audiences, musically placing "black" and "tan" elements in close proximity to one another and featuring sounds of the blues and timbral effects that would be titillating for much of his paying public at the time.

The form of "Black and Tan Fantasy" juxtaposes the 12-bar blues of each chorus and the 16-bar interlude that appears after the first chorus. The blues sections draw on microtonality, blue notes, timbral effects added by mutes, and other musical elements that mark the music as distinctly African American. These musical elements—especially the growling timbres of muted brass instruments—were distinctive aspects of Ellington's music and led to his style being called "jungle music." While this term reinforced racist stereotypes about African Americans likely held by the Cotton Club's white patrons, Ellington himself also used the term, recognizing that it served to promote and advertise his unique style as a composer and arranger. The 16-bar interlude departs from the "jungle" sound, drawing instead on some of the conventions of ragtime such as the syncopated melody with an "oom-pah" accompaniment and the adoption of a European dance form (AA) as its internal form. It also adopts the chromatic harmonies of the late-nineteenth-century European classical tradition. Ellington seems to be creating a musical icon of the black and tan ideal by situating the formal, timbral, and melodic elements of the African American roots of the blues in close proximity to the 16-bar interlude and its European musical roots in texture, form, and harmony.

> **AESTHETICS**

Listen again to "Black and Tan Fantasy" and pay attention to the contrasts between the 12-bar blues sections and the 16-bar interlude.

CULTURAL LINKAGES

Ellington's musical commentary in "Black and Tan Fantasy" also has a few more layers adding to its rich and complex meaning. The melody in the first chorus is a modification of a spiritual titled "The Holy City," a composition that co-composer and trumpet player Bubber Miley said that he learned from his mother. This spiritual was commonly sung in both black and white Christian churches at the beginning of the twentieth century. The original melody of "The Holy City" is in a major mode, and the lyrics state: "Jerusalem, Jerusalem; lift up your gates and sing." This is a tribute to the holy city of Jerusalem, often used in Christianity as a metaphor for heaven where unity with God is achieved and the perils of life on earth—such as Jim Crow and other racial discrimination—have disappeared (see Chapter 8, Gateway 34). In "Black and Tan Fantasy" there are no lyrics and the melody is transformed into a minor mode and into a blues. Ellington's transformation of a Christian hymn tune into a blues symbolically unites African Americans' religious and worldly experiences, as if their Christian belief in life after death is reaching into their daily experiences of racial injustice and suffering as a danceable blues that can offer a moment of entertainment and pleasure and, perhaps, a black and tan fantasy that imagines a future without racial injustice.

The final phrase of "Black and Tan Fantasy" references Frédéric Chopin's Piano Sonata No. 2 in B-flat minor, Op. 35, known as the "Funeral March" (Chapter 8, Gateway 33). By including this musical quotation, Ellington draws a strong connection to the European classical tradition, which he studied. At the same time, he closes his "Black and Tan Fantasy" with a signifier of death—a funeral march—indicating with a playful dash of humor that the fantasies of the black and tan clubs, whatever they are, certainly have not been realized in any satisfactory way.

 Listen to "Black and Tan Fantasy" once more, this time considering how references to the afterlife in "The Holy City" and Chopin's "Funeral March" might give the composition deeper significance.

What Is Its History?

CULTURAL LINKAGES

The history of "Black and Tan Fantasy" can be connected to both the emergence of big bands and swing music in the interwar period and the personal biography of Duke Ellington. The development of many swing dance styles can be traced to Harlem's Savoy Ballroom, which opened in 1926. This enormous space filled an entire city block and had a 4000-person capacity. It boasted a lavishly

adorned interior and provided a high-class experience for a relatively low entrance fee. It was open to both white and black guests but, unlike the Cotton Club, its primary patrons were from the surrounding black neighborhoods. Big bands and styles of swing dancing were widespread by the late 1920s, and with the mid-1930s adoption of swing as a genre label by the music industry, the swing era began, with big band swing and dance dominating the popular culture of the United States until the mid-1940s. Hundreds of bands toured the country, some with black band leaders like Fletcher Henderson (1897–1952), Jimmie Lunceford (1902–1947),

FIGURE 10.12
The Savoy Ballroom in 1942
Source: Getty Images / Weegee (Arthur Fellig) / International Center of Photography.

Cab Calloway (1907–1994), and Chick Webb (1909–1939), and some with white leaders like Benny Goodman (1909–1986), and Glenn Miller (1904–1944).

As the 1920s came to a close, the stock market crash of 1929 and the ensuing Great Depression left many people struggling to make ends meet. Most Americans certainly did not have the means to purchase records, and record sales plummeted. As a live experience of music and dance, big bands and swing provided an escape and a distraction from the anxieties of the Great Depression rather than a way to engage with or reflect on those anxieties. If they couldn't afford to attend live performances, fans could hear the music on the radio, and restaurants and nightclubs played it on jukeboxes. These were coin-operated record players that later on ended up playing a role in rejuvenating the recording industry.

As swing became a popular music in the mid-1930s, jazz vocalists such as Ella Fitzgerald (1917–1996) and Billie Holiday (1915–1959) played important roles in big bands and swing. Carrying on Armstrong's legacy as a jazz vocalist, their solos were creative interpretations of popular songs, some of which became massively popular hits. In 1935 Fitzgerald began performing with a big band led by Chick Webb (1905–1939) on recordings and at venues like the Savoy Ballroom. She later became known for masterful scat singing that incorporated elements of bebop, a style of jazz that emerged in the 1940s. Holiday, known for her original and expressive interpretation of song melodies and the distinct timbre of her voice, first recorded with the Benny Goodman big band in 1933. Her 1939 recording of "Strange Fruit" was an emotional and graphic account of a lynching in the American South, and it remains one of the most influential examples of jazz directly engaging with racial injustice.

FIGURE 10.13
Billie Holiday studio portrait in 1939
Source: Getty Images / Gilles Petard.

While many sophisticated whites in New York enjoyed traveling uptown to hear and see what they viewed as exotic shows at the Cotton Club and other venues in Harlem, prevailing racist attitudes meant that white audiences in much of the rest of the country did not hire black bands to play for their dances. Instead of dancing to the style of "hot" big bands coming out of Harlem, they danced to "sweet" bands, like Paul Whiteman's (Chapter 10, Gateway 43), who were known for playing popular songs in styles that featured slower tempos and less improvisation. Many white musicians, however, loved the "hot" jazz they were hearing in clubs and on recordings and taught themselves to play it. The first of these white musicians to break into the national consciousness playing hot jazz was Benny Goodman. Born in Chicago to a Jewish immigrant family from eastern Europe, he studied classical clarinet as a child and continued to play it throughout his life. But he found New Orleans clarinet players who he heard in Chicago nightclubs in the early 1920s equally fascinating. A prodigy, Goodman was playing professionally by the age of thirteen. When he was still a teenager, he moved to New York in the late 1920s and played in bands and small groups and recording sessions with many of the outstanding musicians of the day, including black musicians.

By the early 1930s he was leading his own big band. John Hammond, a music producer for Columbia Records who was tuned in to the music of the African American community, heard Goodman and suggested that he use the "hot" arrangements of black bandleader Fletcher Henderson (1897–1952), who was having trouble keeping his band together during the Depression. The Goodman band's new arrangements, featuring improvisation and the driving rhythms of black bands, became a sensation in the first half of 1935 when Goodman's band was regularly featured in a national radio broadcast. White youth flocked to hear and dance to Goodman's band. Other white jazz musicians quickly followed suit, forming their own popular bands, among them Glenn Miller, Tommy Dorsey, Woody Herman, and Artie Shaw.

While Goodman's big bands made him a household name at the time, he also made contributions to the history of jazz and American popular music that were quieter but just as profound. Goodman is usually credited with being the first white bandleader to perform on stage with African American musicians, a radical move in the midst of the harsh racial segregation of the time. He did so in small

> CULTURAL
> LINKAGES

> SOCIAL
> BEHAVIOR

FIGURE 10.14
Benny Goodman and his big band
Source: Getty Images / Bettmann.

combos (trios, quartets, and sextets) that would become the model for jazz for generations to come. These ensembles featured much more improvisation than his and other big bands did. They included, in addition to Italian-American drummer Gene Krupa (1909–1973), three of the most important black jazz musicians of the day: the pianist Teddy Wilson (1912–1986), the vibraphonist Lionel Hampton (1908–2002), and the guitarist Charlie Christian (1916–1942). Goodman and his integrated combos were performing an imagined future without the legal racial segregation that characterized American society at this time.

Two bandleaders, Count Basie (1904–1984) and Duke Ellington, transcended the swing era. They continued performing long after the 1930s and 1940s as their music influenced the development of jazz far beyond the dance hall. Basie's band came from Kansas City, which, like many cities throughout the United States, played host to **territory bands**, big bands that performed in a geographic area within a day trip of their home city. As an active center for several such bands, Kansas City served as a home base in the 1920s and 1930s for other influential musicians such as bandleader Bennie Moten (1894–1935) and Mary Lou Williams (1910–1981), a gifted pianist, talented arranger, and prolific composer. Basie and his band relocated to New York and enjoyed great popularity there and on a national scale. But as the popularity of swing waned after World War II, he and other bandleaders struggled to keep their groups working, and Basie had to break up his band. In the 1950s he re-formed his band, which toured the country and accompanied popular vocalists like Frank Sinatra, Tony Bennett, and Sarah Vaughan until his death in 1984.

Duke Ellington is regarded as one of the most significant American musicians of the twentieth century. He was born in Washington, D.C., where he was raised in a middle-class family. He formed his first dance band as a teenager in the 1910s, drawing on the formal musical training he had received as a child as well as on music he had heard in his younger years, in particular the Harlem stride piano style he heard from pianists James P. Johnson and Willie "the Lion" Smith when they performed in D.C. on tour. The stride style significantly shaped Ellington's compositions and arrangements for big band from his first composition at age fourteen, "Soda Fountain Rag" (based on James P. Johnson's "Carolina Shout") to the stride piano fourth chorus in "Black and Tan Fantasy" to his 1964 recording "Second Portrait of the Lion," dedicated to Willie "the Lion" Smith.

After moving to New York in 1923, he formed his band, the Washingtonians. By 1926, he had begun to develop his own style in compositions such as "East St. Louis Toodle-O" (1926, also co-composed with Bubber Miley), a ragtime dance, and "Black and Tan Fantasy." His renown as a composer beyond the world of big band swing was recognized at his debut at Carnegie Hall in 1943. There, he and his band premiered his three-movement composition *Black, Brown, and Beige*, an instrumental work that Ellington said was a musical parallel to the history of African Americans.

Ellington kept his band together in the face of the declining popularity of swing after World War II, often subsidizing his musicians out of his own pocket. Ellington was admired for creating and adapting compositions to suit and highlight the individual styles and skills of the musicians in his band. This meant that his compositions and arrangements were constantly evolving, with many of the adaptations worked out with the musicians themselves shaping individual parts, and then scrawling changes on sheet music or committing them to memory. Most other big bands had standing repertoires with arrangements that would be performed in the same manner even if a musician was replaced with another. Many of these arrangements contrasted the sections of the big band: the five saxophones would play together in unison or in harmony, and the trombones and trumpets would do the same. Ellington took a different approach. He combined instruments from different sections together at various points of a given composition, creating timbres that contributed to his distinctive sound.

In the course of his life, Ellington composed music both as a sole composer and collaboratively with other musicians. He was known for carrying a pencil and paper with him on the road, composing music as it came to him on trains, on buses, in hotels, or wherever he found himself. His body of work includes not only popular songs and compositions for big band, but also ballets, scores for film and television, and symphonic works for orchestra. All of his music contains elements of jazz, though Ellington himself was ambivalent about the word "jazz," finding the label confining and having been known to say that the music he composes is instead "the music of humankind" or "Negro folk music." Under any label, Ellington's work is interrelated with the history and contemporary life of black Americans, musically express-

FIGURE 10.15
(From left) Lionel Hampton, Teddy Wilson, Benny Goodman, and Gene Krupa
Source: United Archives GmbH / Alamy Stock Photo.

ing struggles against racial injustice, providing sounds for celebration and entertainment, and embodying the creative contributions of African Americans to the fabric of American life.

Duke Ellington's most significant collaborator, Billy Strayhorn (1915–1967), joined Ellington in 1938 as a fellow composer and arranger. Strayhorn contributed significant works of his own to the Ellington band repertoire, most notably "Take the 'A' Train" (1939), which became one of the theme songs for the band. Another one of Strayhorn's best known compositions is "Lush Life," most of which was written when Strayhorn was a teenager, though its first performance was not until 1948 with the Ellington band. "Lush Life," with music and lyrics by Strayhorn, features complex chromatic harmony and an angular melody, both of which pushed the limits of conventional practices in jazz at the time. These unconventional practices were welcomed by Ellington as he embraced the exploration of boundaries between European classical composition, jazz, the blues, other African American musical traditions, and music cultures he encountered from various parts of the world. The lyrics of "Lush Life" speak of isolation, romantic loss, and loneliness, and they gesture to Strayhorn's experience as a black gay man.

In the 1950s and 1960s, many compositions from this period bear both of their names. In the mid-1960s, Strayhorn developed esophageal cancer and his health declined steadily until his death in 1967. One of his last compositions was titled "Blood Count" (1967), a piece whose title refers to blood tests he was receiving in the hospital. It features passionate and emotional solo playing by alto saxophone player Johnny Hodges. This piece and other Strayhorn compositions and arrangements were featured on the Ellington album . . . And His Mother Called Him Bill (1968), an homage from Ellington to his compositional partner of nearly thirty years.

Duke Ellington's renown stretched beyond the boundaries of the United States for much of his career. Between 1963 and 1973, he performed on a number of tours sponsored by the U.S. State Department. Through "jazz diplomacy" the U.S. government hoped that live performances by American jazz musicians would produce in audiences abroad warmer affinities for the United States and for its foreign policy. Many jazz musicians participated in these tours, but none more frequently than Ellington, who performed throughout the Middle East, Africa, Asia, the Soviet Union, eastern Europe, and Latin America. He often composed music specifically about the

CULTURAL LINKAGES

FIGURE 10.16
Billy Strayhorn in the late 1940s
Source: William P. Gottlieb Collection. Library of Congress.

CULTURAL LINKAGES

city or country he was visiting. The results were albums with titles like *Far East Suite* (released in 1967, inspired by a 1963 tour and co-composed with Strayhorn) and *Latin American Suite* (released in 1972, inspired by a 1968 tour). He was also known to meet and collaborate with local musicians, many of which were national (or international) stars in their own right. On his final tour in 1973, he performed with the established Ethiopian jazz composer and vibraphonist Mulatu Astatke in a concert with Astatke's ensemble, featuring Ethiopian traditional instruments, sharing the stage with Ellington's big band. At this time Ellington was already suffering from lung cancer, which would take his life months later in the spring of 1974. Since his death, he has been memorialized in countless ways including streets, bridges, and parks named after him, three posthumous Grammy awards (he received nine during his life), and a posthumous "Special Citation" by the Pulitzer Prize board for his lifetime of work in 1999. Stevie Wonder's hit song "Sir Duke" (1976) was a tribute to Ellington, and hundreds of other artists have composed homages to him and his work with Billy Strayhorn.

WHERE DO I GO FROM HERE?

- Listen to *Black, Brown and Beige* and see if you can identify the musical elements that it shares with "Black and Tan Fantasy," with the blues, with ragtime, or with any other music that you know. What are those elements?

- Listen to "Blood Count" and other Billy Strayhorn compositions on the album . . . *And His Mother Called Him Bill* and compare them to pieces where Ellington is the sole composer.

- Listen to one or two pieces from *Far East Suite* or *Latin American Suite* and describe the way Ellington engages with musical traditions from those parts of the world.

GATEWAY 42
AMERICAN POPULAR SONG

What Is It?

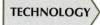

TECHNOLOGY

Before the recording industry and radio took off in the 1920s, popular music was distributed across the United States and around the world as "sheet music" and in the form of player piano rolls. New York City had long been a hub for the printing of popular songs as sheet music and the production of live shows full of songs on Broadway, the name of the theater district in midtown Manhattan, home to dozens of theaters. Our gateway to American popular song in the interwar period comes from New York's world of popular song production, a song written for the 1930s Broadway musical *Girl Crazy* called "I Got Rhythm" (1930), with music by George Gershwin (1898–1937) and lyrics by Ira Gershwin (his brother, 1896–1983). In *Girl Crazy*, "I Got Rhythm" was initially performed by the famous vocalist Ethel Merman, whose brassy voice often brought down the house. A **Broadway musical** is a sometimes comic, sometimes serious play with singing and dancing added to the spoken dialogue. As with opera arias, songs underline emotional moments in the narrative. Unlike opera and like the German *Singspiel*, spoken dialogue substitutes for recitative. During the interwar period, George Gershwin, Irving Berlin (1889–1989), Jerome Kern (1885–1945), Cole Porter (1891–1964), and Richard Rodgers (1902–1979) each wrote hundreds of songs, some for Broadway musicals and others for sale as individual songs sold as sheet music to professional performers and to amateurs for home entertainment. Sheet music was bought and produced along a single block on 28th Street, where songwriters, sometimes aided by skilled pianists known as "song pluggers," came to plug their songs to publishers and professional singers looking for new material. The street was known as Tin Pan Alley for the cacophonous street sound of dozens of pianos simultaneously playing different songs from the publishers' offices, and songs of this era are often called Tin Pan Alley songs. Tin Pan Alley and Broadway shows were closely intertwined before and during the interwar period, and many of the most popular Tin Pan Alley songs were also songs used in Broadway musicals in a mutually beneficial arrangement. "I Got Rhythm" was widely recorded by many artists soon after it was first published. This gateway recording is from the soundtrack of the 1943 film version of *Girl Crazy* and features vocalist Judy Garland and the Tommy Dorsey big band with added orchestral strings.

 Listen to the first 1:29 of the recording.

How Does It Work?

Timbre

The main timbre featured on this recording is Judy Garland's voice, smooth and rich, along with the timbres of the piano, orchestral strings, woodwinds, brass, and some light percussion.

FIGURE 10.17
Ira (left) and George Gershwin at work on a film score (c. early 1930s)
Source: Everett Collection Historical / Alamy Stock Photo.

Texture

The texture is primarily melody with accompaniment. In the refrain, several countermelodies constitute much of the accompaniment.

Rhythm

As you might guess from its title, the main feature of "I Got Rhythm" is its rhythm. The song follows a strict duple meter throughout, with four beats to a measure. The verse has a rubato, slow tempo. The refrain follows a quicker, danceable tempo with a swing feel, and is where things get interesting. The melody is mostly constructed of a series of four-note phrases, where only the third note of the phrase lands on a strong beat. The other notes are on weak beats and are syncopated. In European-derived classical music, beats one and three of a measure are "strong beats," and were the beats emphasized in marches. Beats two and four are "weak beats." In jazz and much American popular music, however, the swing feel emphasizes two and four, and syncopation accents many different beats, both of which give the music a "rhythm." In "I Got Rhythm," these rhythmic elements of jazz and popular music are featured. The first note of the melody's four-note phrase begins on beat two. This and each of the notes in the phrase has a duration of one and a half beats. The second note of the melody occurs between beats three and four of the first measure, the third note occurs on beat one of the second measure, and the fourth note occurs between beats two and three of the second measure. This pattern can be visualized like this:

```
1   2   3   4   |   1   2   3   4

    x   x       x       x
```

This syncopated pattern beginning on beat two and, based on notes of the same length, happens several times in "I Got Rhythm": three times in each A section and three times in the B section for a total of twelve repetitions in the course of the AABA' form.

FIGURE 10.18
Judy Garland and Mickey Rooney dancing in the 1943 film
Girl Crazy
Source: Pictorial Press Ltd / Alamy Stock Photo.

Melody

The verse, which introduces the song, is primarily in a minor mode. The mode of the melody of the refrain, or main part of the song, is major and relies heavily on a pentatonic scale.

Harmony

The harmony is relatively straightforward with some chromaticism in the verse. In the refrain, the A section follows a repeating chord progression in the tonic key (E-flat major) that cycles through a series of closely related chords. The B section of the refrain departs from the tonic key and features a cycle of dominant chords that last two bars apiece, moving from harmonies distant from E-flat major through a cycle based on the circle of fifths, which leads back to the key of E-flat for the repeat of the A section.

Form

This recording begins with a twelve-bar verse before continuing into the refrain or main part of the song, which has an internal form of AABA'.

Performance Techniques

In live performance at a Broadway show this song would include many visual elements, especially dancing.

Listen to the entire performance following the timed listening guide.

LISTENING GUIDE 10.3

TIME	SECTION	INTERNAL FORM	DESCRIPTION	LYRICS
0:00	Introduction		A piano plays an introduction accompanied by sustained brass chords. The melody and rhythm of this introduction foreshadow the upcoming refrain. The brass take over to conclude the introduction with a fanfare-type phrase that is based on a fragment of the melody of the refrain.	
0:13	Verse	a	The vocalist enters, singing a four-bar melody in a minor key at a relatively slow tempo, accompanied by an orchestra of strings, brass, and woodwinds.	Days can be sunny . . . .
0:25		a'	The melody of "a" repeats with a different set of lyrics, more or less the same harmony and orchestra parts, and a slightly different ending.	Birds . . .
0:38		b	A new melody and harmony enters at the same slow tempo. This section, like the previous two, has a duration of four bars, but it is divided into two parts that begin similarly and end differently. At the end of the final two bars, a fast tempo in a	I'm chipper . . .

TIME	SECTION	INTERNAL FORM	DESCRIPTION	LYRICS
			swing style begins, which sets up the ensuing refrain.	
0:55	Refrain 1	A	The vocalist begins the "refrain," or the main part of the song, which features syncopation.	I got rhythm . . .
1:03		A	The melody of A repeats with a different set of lyrics, but more or less the same harmony and orchestra parts.	I got daisies . . .
1:11		B	The harmony shifts for the B section, and the melody follows suit. The rhythm, however, is nearly exactly the same as in the A section.	Old man trouble . . .
1:19		A′	The melody of A repeats with yet a different set of lyrics, and two extra measures are added to the form at the end.	I got starlight . . .
1:29	Interlude		The piano trills for four measures as the orchestra, featuring muted brass, performs a series of short phrases in a crescendo.	
1:33	Refrain 2	A	The piano takes over the lead and plays a version of the A melody that is similar to the introduction at the beginning of the recording. In the fifth and sixth bars the harmony moves briefly to another key before returning to the usual chords of the A section.	
1:42		A	The piano and orchestra play a variation on the melody that is not syncopated.	
1:49		B	The orchestra plays the melody while the piano plays an accompanying part.	
1:57		A′	The piano plays another less syncopated version of the A section. The accompaniment features saxophones playing a sustained countermelody with a pronounced vibrato, reminiscent of big band saxophone section performance.	
2:07	Refrain 3	A	The vocal enters again, singing the same lyrics from the first iteration of the refrain.	I got rhythm . . .
2:16		A	The vocalist sings the second repetition of A, varying some of the pitches of the melody with phrases emphasizing the microtonality of the blues.	I got daisies . . .
2:23		B	The vocalist sings the B section, also with some elaboration of the melody and lyrics.	Old man trouble . . .
2:33		A′	Instead of repeating the lyrics of the final A section, the vocalist holds the last pitch of the B section for the first half of the final A section. The last line of the song repeats as a "tag" and the orchestra plays at full strength to give the ending a sense of finality.	
2:49	End			

What Does It Mean?

"I Got Rhythm" demonstrates some of the typical characteristics of Broadway and Tin Pan Alley songs of the interwar period and the way they had changed over the years, in part to keep pace with the development of recording technology. In earlier decades, the verse lyrics tended to describe a lengthy narrative often over several repetitions with new text each time. By the 1920s, verses became shorter and their lyrics functioned more as a dramatic setup for corresponding refrains. This shorter length of popular songs responded to the three-minute limit that technology imposed on recording. The verse in "I Got Rhythm" follows this convention as its lyrics can be taken to pose a question ("Why do I feel so carefree and happy?"), which the refrain answers with "because I got rhythm."

The verse and refrain of songs of this period contrast in a number of ways, as in "I Got Rhythm." The verse, with its slower, rubato tempo, is not particularly rhythmic and its melody is in a minor mode. The lyrics of the verse express happiness—which is usually expressed with a melody in a major mode—but they have not yet disclosed the source of that happiness. The major mode, lively tempo, and syncopated rhythms are reserved for the refrain, where the lyrics (and the music) reveal the first of several sources of happiness: rhythm.

> 🔊 **Listen to "I Got Rhythm" again, noticing the many contrasts between the verse and the refrain.**

The four-note syncopated melodic phrase first appears on the words "I got rhythm," which, if performed correctly, demonstrate that the vocalist actually has got the rhythm to sing in a syncopated manner in between beats using four notes of the same rhythmic duration. The third note of the melody first occurs on the first syllable of the word "RHY-thm" and is the only one that lands on a strong beat, driving home that the vocalist has rhythm and can land on the beat when necessary. With each of the notes of the four-note rhythmic motive lasting a beat and a half, the vocalist in a sense performs in a slower tempo than the pulsing tempo of the musicians backing her up. Maybe this reveals even more about the vocalist's state of mind—not only is she carefree because she has rhythm, she can execute complicated syncopation and perform at a slower, more relaxed tempo than the musicians with whom she is performing. The last phrase of each A section, the only phrase that doesn't follow the four-note rhythmic motive pattern, provides a sense of release. The lyrics here are also typical of Tin Pan Alley songs of the 1930s—they do not deal with the challenges of life during the Great Depression, but focus on lighter topics like how dancing and love can make a person happy.

> 🔊 **Listen to "I Got Rhythm" once more, paying close attention to the rhythm of the refrain. See if you can follow along with the syncopated rhythm, maybe by tapping your foot to the steady beat and saying or singing the lyrics along with the vocalist during the A section.**

The internal form of the refrain is also typical of Tin Pan Alley songs, many of which follow an AABA form or a close variation of it. In this form, new lyrics are typically used for each section, even though the melodies of the A sections are more or less the same. This provides an opportunity for the lyrics in the second A section to elaborate on those in the first, and for the B section to approach new territory melodically, harmonically, and lyrically. The melody of the B section in "I Got Rhythm" enters a higher register, and features repeated notes over the four-note rhythmic motive, which contrast the ascending and descending shape of the melody in the A section. The B section also enters completely new harmonic territory, beginning on a dominant seventh chord on the third scale degree before cycling back to the original key for the restatement of the A section. Because a B section typically departs from yet connects the second and final A sections of a song in AABA form, it is also referred to as the **bridge**.

What Is Its History?

ECONOMIC ACTIVITY

The history of "I Got Rhythm" as a popular song is wrapped up in the history of both Tin Pan Alley and Broadway musicals. From the nineteenth century through the 1920s popular songs were mainly distributed as sheet music, that is, as the musical scores of individual songs with piano accompaniments. Tin Pan Alley became the hub of sheet music sales, and vaudeville singers and amateurs came to the stores on 28th Street looking for new songs to sing. The 1920s and 1930s are known as the "golden age" of Tin Pan Alley, as the new popular songs from this period almost completely eclipsed the American popular songs of the nineteenth-century composer Stephen Foster and other early-twentieth-century songwriters. The songs of this era borrowed from the inflections of blues and jazz, and their popularity was spread through sheet music sales, performances in live Broadway shows and by dance bands, the relatively young recording industry, and the brand new medium of radio. Many of these songs have continued to be performed, recorded, and enjoyed by audiences decades after they were first written. Songs with this kind of ongoing circulation are called **standards** or **jazz standards**, and they are most often performed today either by jazz musicians as vehicles for improvisation or by vocalists from any number of genres. Standards from this era by composers like Gershwin, Kern, and Berlin make up what singers of this music today call the Great American Songbook.

CULTURAL LINKAGES

During the early twentieth century, Jewish immigrants or their children living in New York City, among them Irving Berlin, Jerome Kern, and George Gershwin, played a significant role in the entertainment industry. They were the fruit of a massive immigration to the United States of some twenty-five million Europeans from central, eastern, and southern Europe beginning in the late nineteenth century. Among them were nearly four million Jews, many of whom settled in New York. Most of these immigrants, young, poor, and from rural areas, were sent scurrying from Europe for new opportunities in the new world by the economic and political upheavals of the late nineteenth century. In Russia the Christian population, believing incorrectly that Jews were responsible for the assassination of Tsar Alexander II in 1881, subjected their Jewish neighbors to violent, riotous attacks, called pogroms. After losing their homes and livelihood, many Jews had little choice but to seek a new life elsewhere in the world. Restricted by law to what was called the Pale of Settlement (and the source of the expression "beyond the pale"), a region that today includes the countries of Ukraine, Belarus, Poland, and Lithuania, many left Europe for a new life in America. Without property or education or much English, they opened small businesses in the Jewish community and some became entertainers in Yiddish and vaudeville theaters. By 1910 a quarter of New York City's population was Jewish, among them performers, managers, publishers, and other entrepreneurs in the entertainment industry. Because of the strong Jewish presence in this industry, young aspiring performers and songwriters likely did not experience the level of anti-Semitism common in other types of businesses.

Born in Brooklyn to Russian-Jewish immigrant parents, George Gershwin was inspired to pursue music at the age of ten, after hearing fragments of a recital at school by eight-year-old Maxie Rosenzweig (1900–1956), who went on, under the name Max Rosen, to become one of the leading violinists of the period. Under Maxie's spell, George began to play and study piano at home. At age fifteen he left school to play piano for a music publisher in Manhattan's Tin Pan Alley. In addition to "plugging" other people's songs to performers, he began writing his own songs.

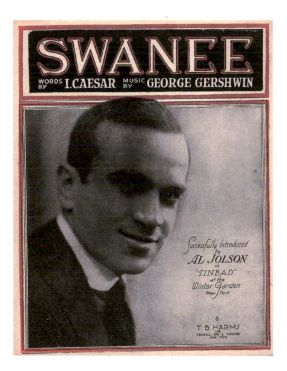

FIGURE 10.19

The sheet music for George Gershwin's "Swanee," his first hit (1919) and the best-selling hit song of his career, with Al Jolson (1886–1950), the most famous entertainer of the 1920s, on the cover

Source: George Gershwin and Irving Caesar (public domain), Wikimedia Commons.

FIGURE 10.20
Irving Berlin
Source: Pictorial Press Ltd / Alamy Stock Photo.

FIGURE 10.21
Jerome Kern in 1934
Source: Alfredo Valente, Wikimedia Commons.

In 1916, "Swanee" was picked up by Al Jolson and became George's first big hit. Over the course of his short life—he died of brain cancer at the age of 38—Gershwin, with his brother Ira as his lyricist, wrote many of the most popular and enduring songs of the interwar period, mainly for Broadway shows. Many of his compositions have become standards and are still performed frequently by jazz musicians today, including songs like "Someone to Watch Over Me" (1926), "Summertime" (1935), and "Love is Here To Stay" (1937). He also became renowned for a number of his classical compositions explored in the next gateway.

In addition to sheet music, records, radio, and dance bands, the popular songwriters of this period wrote their songs for plays with music referred to collectively as the "American musical theater," "Broadway musicals" after the theater district in New York, "musical comedies," or simply "musicals." These American musicals were descendants of nineteenth-century musical theater productions in Europe called operetta, comic operas, or light opera. They were distinguished from opera by their use of spoken dialogue instead of musical recitative, which made them more accessible to a mass audience. In the late nineteenth century the most famous producers of English-language operettas were the composer Arthur Sullivan (1842–1900) and the librettist W. S. Gilbert (1836–1911). Gilbert and Sullivan's most famous comic operas, including *The Pirates of Penzance* (1879) and *The Mikado* (1885), toured Britain, Europe, and North America to great acclaim and provided one of the models for the American musical theater.

Early American musicals featured songs and dancing with little regard for a story line. Shows like *Girl Crazy* were basically musical revues in which new songs could often replace older ones without seriously disrupting the flow of a silly plot. For this reason, "I Got Rhythm" and many other songs of the 1920s and 1930s are better remembered today as standards or as part of the Great American Songbook than as songs from particular Broadway musicals. The Broadway musical came into its own when composers, lyricists, and librettists (the people who write the story, the libretto or "book" of the musical) found a way to integrate songs and dance numbers into an engaging storyline. The first convincing example of this type was a show called *Show Boat*, premiered in 1927 and written by Jerome Kern and lyricist Oscar Hammerstein II (1895–1960). *Show Boat* tells the story of white performers on a paddlewheel steamboat working the Mississippi River from the 1880s to the 1920s and of the black dockworkers who served them. It was notable for one of the earliest instances of a mixed-race cast, the depiction of the divisions between black and white society, an interracial marriage, and a mixed-race character trying to "pass" as white.

This daring approach to contemporary social issues, which has been both lauded as revolutionary and criticized as trading in racial stereotypes, characterized much of the work of Oscar Hammerstein II. Although born into a German-Jewish family of theater entrepreneurs, he was raised an Episcopalian. After *Show Boat*, Hammerstein co-wrote other shows with Kern and a number of other composers. His place in music history, however, was sealed with he teamed with Richard Rodgers in the 1940s and 1950s to write some of the most beloved Broadway musicals of all time, including *Oklahoma!* (1943), *Carousel* (1945), *South Pacific* (1949), *The King and I* (1951), and *The Sound of Music* (1959), using the formal conventions of the popular songs of the 1920s and 1930s. *South Pacific* and *The King and I* continued Hammerstein's interest in interracial romance and marriage, testing the waters of social convention in a way similar to Benny Goodman and his integrated bands.

Many Broadway musicals were also made into films that turned performers into widely popular stars. In the 1936 movie of *Show Boat*, Paul Robeson (1898–1976), an All-American college and professional football player, valedictorian of his Rutgers University class, Columbia Law school grad, social activist, actor, and powerful bass-baritone, sang "Old Man River," perhaps the most popular song from *Show Boat*. The film industry in Hollywood also produced a plethora of its own musical films, escapist fare for a population suffering during the Depression. The virtuosic dancing of Fred Astaire (1899–1987) and Ginger Rogers (1911–1995) and the dazzling choreographies of Busby Berkeley (1895–1976) for masses of dancers were immensely popular with movie-going audiences of the period.

FIGURE 10.22
Paul Robeson, center, with the chorus of longshoremen in *Show Boat*
Source: Ronald Grant Archive / Alamy Stock Photo.

"I Got Rhythm" as a hit song emerged from Broadway and Tin Pan Alley, but its popularity transcended both scenes as it and its form became common in several musical spheres almost immediately. Big band leaders began to compose melodies over the form and melody of the song's refrain for new compositions, including Fletcher Henderson's "Yeah Man" (1933), Jimmie Lunceford's "Stomp It Off" (1934), Chick Webb's "Don't Be That Way" (1934), Count Basie's "Blow Top" (1940), and Duke Ellington's first three choruses of "Cotton Tail" (1940). In the 1940s and 1950s, musicians playing bebop and other later styles of jazz wrote songs based on the AABA refrain that became standards in their own right, such as "Anthropology" (also known as "Thriving on a Riff") by Charlie Parker, "Oleo" by Sonny Rollins, and "Rhythm-a-ning" by Thelonious Monk. Compositions based on "I Got Rhythm" (or portions of it) are likely in the hundreds, and jazz musicians today continue to improvise and compose new material based on this song, often challenging themselves to do so at blistering tempos. It has become the most common vehicle for improvisation in jazz other than the 12-bar blues. Perhaps it is the song's deceptive simplicity in melody, form, and harmony that has made it an ideal means for musicians to unlock their inventiveness as composers and improvisers. In any case, it allows musicians to showcase that they not only have "got rhythm," but also can demonstrate many other forms of musical virtuosity.

WHERE DO I GO FROM HERE?

- What is the most current recording of "I Got Rhythm" that you can find? When was it recorded? Listen to it and compare the performance of the melody (and the rhythm of the melody) to Judy Garland's performance. Is the syncopated rhythm of the A section the same? What are other similarities and differences in the performance of the melody?

- Listen to a number of recordings of songs based on "I Got Rhythm," such as "Anthropology" by Charlie Parker, "Cotton Tail" by Duke Ellington, or "Oleo" by Sonny Rollins. Can you follow the form and its chord progression throughout the recording? How does a faster (or slower) tempo affect the way you perceive the song?

- Find some other recordings of George Gershwin songs composed in the 1920s and 1930s. Some examples include "Someone to Watch over Me" (1926), "Summertime" (1935), and "Love is Here To Stay" (1937). How many versions of a given song can you find? How does its form compare to the form of "I Got Rhythm"? What other musical elements common in Tin Pan Alley songs or in songs from Broadway musicals of this era can you hear?

GATEWAY 43
AMERICAN SYMPHONIC NATIONALISM

What Is It?

One of the trends in classical music in interwar America was the development of a repertoire that had a particularly "American" sound. One of the most-performed symphonic compositions in this American nationalist vein is *Rhapsody in Blue* by George Gershwin, our gateway to American symphonic nationalism and a work written originally for piano and jazz band in 1924. It was later scored for piano and symphony orchestra. A **rhapsody** is a one-movement composition that has a free-flowing, improvisatory character and that often evokes national sentiment through the use of folk or newly composed folk-like melodies. This performance is by the Columbia Symphony Orchestra conducted by Leonard Bernstein.

FIGURE 10.23
"A portrait of George Gershwin at a piano" [in concert attire] by Edward Steichen
Source: Getty Images / Edward Steichen.

🔊 **Listen to the first thirty seconds of the recording and notice the bent notes and timbre of a jazz orchestra at the beginning of this piece of classical music.**

How Does It Work?

Timbre

The piece alternates solo piano with full orchestra, with episodes for solo clarinet, horns, and muted solo trumpet playing "wah-wah" sounds reminiscent of Bubber Miley's playing in "Black and Tan Fantasy" by Duke Ellington and His Orchestra.

Texture

The texture is chordal and contrapuntal, although the opening unaccompanied clarinet solo is a striking and memorable feature of the piece.

Rhythm

The meter is in four with syncopated rhythms, rubato, and varied tempos.

Melody

Many of themes are based on a blues scale, in alternation with major-mode melodies.

Harmony

Traditional tonal harmony with jazz-inspired chords.

Form

The piece presents six main themes, each played by the orchestra in alternation with piano solos that show off the pianist's virtuosity in both classical and jazz styles.

Performance Techniques

The upward clarinet slide over nearly two octaves, called a glissando, and other "bent notes" characteristic of jazz and blues are featured in what is otherwise a composition in the classical tradition.

Listen to the entire recording following this timed listening guide.

TIME	SECTION	DESCRIPTION
0:00	Introduction	The work opens with an arresting solo clarinet playing an upward *glissando*, a signature element of the piece, but one suggested by the first clarinetist to play the piece and later adopted by Gershwin.
0:07	A (orch)	The clarinet, joined by the orchestra, continues with the first theme, which descends through a scale that includes chromatic tones and blue notes (flat 7th, flat 6th, flat 5th, and flat 3rd) with jazz-like slides into pitches.
0:41	B (orch)	The horns introduce a second melody built on a motive of a single pitch played four times and repeated on blue notes (1111 ♭7 ♭7 ♭7 ♭7 1111 ♭3 ♭3 ♭3 ♭3) before descending through a scale that features blue notes mixed in with some tones of a major scale.
0:55	A (orch)	Muted trumpets play the first theme creating "wah-wah" effects evocative of early jazz.
1:05	C (piano) A (orch)	The piano enters with a short third theme before the full orchestra returns to the first theme.
1:29	C (piano)	The piano plays a solo beginning with the third theme followed by arpeggiations and chords in a style derived from nineteenth-century classical pianism followed by a series of sequential modulations to new keys.
2:16	A (piano) C (orch)	The piano plays the A theme in a rubato tempo, and sections of the orchestra play aspects of the C theme in response, featuring a bass clarinet. More nineteenth-century-style arpeggiations, chords, and modulations in the piano follow.
3:44	A (orch)	The orchestra enters grandly and loudly with the first theme.
4:13	D (orch)	A long growl in the brass (created by a self-explanatory technique called "flutter-tongue") signals a transition to something new: the growling brass introduces a short, up-tempo, arc-shaped, major-mode melody accompanied by flourishes on the piano.
4:40	B (orch)	The solo clarinet plays parts of the B melody, interspersed with grand arpeggio gestures on the piano.
4:56	B (orch)	The second theme returns grandly and loudly in the full orchestra before fading into soft melodic fragments ending in four syncopated chords and a pause.
5:42	B + A (piano)	A second piano solo returns to the second theme, accompanied at one point by the horns holding long tones. The piano introduces a swing rhythm and continues with the first theme played *fortissimo*.
7:56	E (Piano)	The piano solo continues by introducing a fifth theme featuring many blue notes softly in a slow, rubato tempo. Soon the melody in the right hand is syncopated against pulses in the left hand, creating a jazz feel. Plenty of nineteenth-century piano flourishes follow.
10:14	F (orch)	The sixth theme, in a major mode, features longer-held tones than the previous themes. Combined with a medium tempo and medium dynamic level and played by the full orchestra with dynamics swells and brief responses from the horns, the effect is broad, romantic, and occasionally majestic.
12:13	F + C (piano)	A fourth piano solo features the sixth theme with mainly classical piano gestures. The C theme briefly returns.
14:15	F (orch)	The brass section enters with the sixth theme, this time with rapid dynamic changes on individual pitches, while the piano continues its

continued

TIME	SECTION	DESCRIPTION
		flourishes. The orchestra increases in loudness and slows down to signal a change.
15:14	B + A (orch)	The second theme in full orchestra and piano (played with a swing feel!) are followed by the first theme crescendoing to a grand finale with a brief reference to the third theme.
16:25	End	

FIGURE 10.24
Aaron Copland conducting
Source: Pictorial Press Ltd / Alamy Stock Photo.

What Does It Mean?

Much of the meaning of *Rhapsody in Blue* comes from its combination of jazz and classical styles. The swing rhythms, syncopation, melodies using blue notes, and jazz harmonies are performed by a classical symphony orchestra, with its wide timbral palette, and pianistic techniques borrowed from classical music. The result is a musical icon of the union of European and American, specifically African American, musical sensibilities. Czech nationalist composer Antonín Dvořák, during his sojourn in the United States in the 1890s, suggested that African American music, specifically spirituals, could provide the basis for a unique American national style of classical music (Chapter 8, Gateway 34). By 1924 other African American genres, especially ragtime, blues, and jazz, had exploded into the national consciousness. Gershwin used jazz to fulfill Dvořák's prediction that African American music could provide the basis for an American national style, creating in *Rhapsody in Blue* a composition that responded to the tradition of nineteenth-century European nationalist classical music but that sounded uniquely American.

Another important American nationalist composer of the period, Aaron Copland (1900–1990), worked in a similar vein but turned to various rural traditions for inspiration. Copland grew up, like Gershwin, in New York City and was exposed to jazz even as he studied European classical music. His early work combined jazz with the gnarly dissonances of modernist compositions such as those of Igor Stravinsky's *Rite of Spring*. However, the Depression of the 1930s strengthened Copland's commitment to leftist causes and ideas. That commitment, along with an increased interest in ballet, film, and children's music, motivated him to to develop a simplified style for many of his compositions beginning in the 1930s and 1940s. These compositions reached a wide audience, including not just aficionados of modernist music or the bourgeois audience for traditional classical music but the "common man" as well. His style in these compositions employed the same technique as nationalist composers in Europe had. He borrowed folk tunes or created folk-like melodies, maintained the tonality of traditional classical compositions, and introduced modern harmonies and techniques judiciously in a manner guaranteed to be accessible to many people. As result, his compositions in this more accessible style, like those of Gershwin, retain their appeal today. Often played on patriotic occasions, they have become icons and indexes of American national identity and sentiment. Among his most famous compositions are *El Salon Mexico* (1936), *Billy the Kid* (1938), *Rodeo* (1942), *Fanfare for the Common Man* (1942), *Appalachian Spring* (1944), and *Clarinet Concerto* (1948), a classical work commissioned by jazz clarinetist Benny Goodman.

CULTURAL LINKAGES

Part of the social meaning of the music of Gershwin and Copland is related to their ethnicity. Both were the children of Jewish immigrants from eastern Europe (Russia, Ukraine, and Lithuania). During the interwar period, they and other American Jews were at the center of American musical life in classical and popular music. Irving Berlin (1888–1989), for example, immigrated as a child with his family to New York. His love for his new country inspired his song "God Bless America" (1918) and numerous others that have entered the so-called Great American Song-book. With the exception of Cole Porter, virtually all the popular song writers of the interwar period were Jewish.

In addition to popular and classical music in the interwar period, music composed for the new "talking pictures" became central to the American musical experience. The first successful feature-length "talkie," was *The Jazz Singer*, starring Al Jolson in 1927. Movie "musicals" were filled with the popular songs of the day. But classical composers also provided background music to bring out the dramatic, romantic, or comedic character of scenes. One of the pioneer composers of movie music in this interwar period was another Jewish immigrant, originally from Hungary, Max Steiner (1888–1971). A child prodigy born to a well-to-do theater impresario and inventor, Steiner was

FIGURE 10.25
Max Steiner conducting a film score in a recording studio for large orchestras, called a "scoring stage"
Source: RGR Collection / Alamy Stock Photo.

invited to London at the age of eighteen to conduct musical shows and operettas. Stranded as an enemy alien in London at the beginning of World War I, he immigrated to the United States, where he continued his work as a conductor and arranger for Broadway shows. In 1929 he moved to Hollywood to do the same for the new talking pictures.

During the silent film era, pianists and organists improvised musical accompaniment to **under-score** the emotional quality and action of the scene. They applied the programmatic clichés of nineteenth-century orchestral music to match the character of the images on the screen. In the early years of talking films, producers and directors eschewed this kind of background music in favor of something they could not have in silent films, diegetic sound only. **Diegetic sound and music**, from a Greek word meaning narration, is the sound that the characters in a play or film actually perform or hear: a lullaby sung to a child, a dance band playing on screen, or the sound of a news broadcast coming from the radio. Diegetic sound is an integral part of the narrative structure of plays and movies. Diegetic songs defined the movie musicals of the interwar period, performed by such stars as Fred Astaire, Ginger Rogers, and Bing Crosby. In 1932, when a film producer unhappy with a sequence in a new film complained to Steiner, the composer suggested that he could add an underscore to the sequence to see whether it would improve its impact. Steiner did, the producer was happy, and a new era in film composition was born. Steiner, who has been called "the father of film music," went on to compose more than 300 film scores including for three of the classic films of the period: *King Kong* (1933), *Gone with the Wind* (1939), and *Casablanca* (1942). For the last eighty years the emotional impact and success of films has depended as much on an indispensable musical underscore (or "score") as on the cinematography, plot, action, acting, dialogue, and visual effects. Much film scoring today still uses the iconic, expressive conventions of nineteenth-century orchestral music, pioneered by classical composers like Max Steiner. Today we can add another "c" to the definition of European classical music: music for church, court, concerts, and cinema. Thanks to composers like George Gershwin, it is also common for film composers to use jazz and popular-music styles in their film scores.

What Is Its History?

The word "rhapsody" in the title of *Rhapsody in Blue* comes from the Greek word for a reciter of epic poetry, the most famous of whom was Homer in his *Iliad* and *Odyssey*. The word eventually became associated with literary expressions of emotion. Under the spell of Romanticism during the early nineteenth century the term was used in the titles of compositions, especially for piano, that expressed musical emotions. During the late nineteenth century nationalist composers began writing

CULTURAL LINKAGES

FIGURE 10.26
Paul Whiteman and his orchestra, c. 1925
Source: Getty Images / Chicago History Museum.

one-movement symphonic works that evoked national sentiment. Some were tone poems, like Smetana's *The Moldau,* but many were called rhapsodies. Among the most famous are Franz Liszt's nineteen *Hungarian Rhapsodies* for solo piano, Maurice Ravel's *Rapsodie espagnole* (1908) for orchestra, Ralph Vaughn Williams' three *Norfolk Rhapsodies* for orchestra (1906), and Pancho Vladigerov's (1899–1978) *Bulgarian Rhapsody "Vardar,"* for violin and piano (1928). Gershwin's *Rhapsody in Blue* falls squarely in this tradition of these evocative nationalist compositions.

Gershwin loved classical music. He regularly attended concerts of new compositions by his contemporaries. He studied with various piano and composition teachers in his youth and, after becoming well established as a composer of both popular songs and classical music, traveled to Paris in 1926 and 1928 hoping to study with Maurice Ravel. Ravel much admired jazz, and Gershwin's treatment of it, but he refused to take him as a student, famously writing to his American admirer, "Why become a second-rate Ravel when you're already a first-rate Gershwin?" *Rhapsody in Blue* was his first and most popular classical orchestral composition, but his Concerto in F (1925) and a tone poem called *American in Paris* (1928), written after his first stay in Paris, are still frequently performed, as is his opera *Porgy and Bess* (1935), based on a novel by DuBose Heywood (1885–1940) about black life on Catfish Row, a tenement on the waterfront in Charlotte, South Carolina.

Rhapsody in Blue was the result of a commission from Paul Whiteman (1890–1967) to write a "jazz concerto." Born in Denver, Whiteman believed that jazz, with its roots in black communities, could be made respectable for white audiences if it were classicized. In 1924 he organized a famous concert in New York in which he contrasted his version of what he regarded as the undisciplined, free-wheeling style of nightclub jazz with what he called symphonic jazz. Among other pieces played that evening, *Rhapsody in Blue* debuted with Gershwin as piano soloist and a jazz band augmented with a string section. The audience included many contemporary stars of the classical music scene including Russian composer and piano virtuoso Sergei Rachmaninoff. The concert created a stir, and Whiteman became known for a time as "the king of jazz." Whiteman was a friend of many black musicians in New York, some of whom he hired to write arrangements for his band. Given the racial segregation of the times, however, he did not hire them to play in his bands. Eventually his brand of "symphonic jazz" lost favor, and by the 1930s bands of a different sort, such as those of Fletcher Henderson, Duke Ellington, and Benny Goodman had achieved a different kind of synthesis between improvisatory jazz and the compositional tradition of European classical music, though Henderson and Ellington saw Whiteman's music as an important precursor to their compositional styles.

After Gershwin's death, the composer Ferde Grofé (1892–1972), who had arranged *Rhapsody in Blue* for Whiteman's jazz orchestra, rearranged it for symphony orchestra in 1942. *Rhapsody in Blue* is structured episodically in the manner of nineteenth-century tone poems, and, though it lacks the careful motivic development of eighteenth- and nineteenth-century European classical music, it became an enduring, popular, and respected addition to the classical music repertoire, one with a distinctly American flavor. At the opening ceremonies of the 1984 Olympic Games in Los Angeles, eighty-four pianists played *Rhapsody in Blue,* creating an indexical relationship between the work and American culture for all the world to hear. In 1987 United Airlines started using *Rhapsody in Blue* in its advertising, onboard safety announcements, and its terminal at Chicago's O'Hare Airport. This commercial use has been so ubiquitous that it may have altered the way people understand the piece today, perhaps erasing for them its meaning as a musical symbol of American national identity.

CULTURAL LINKAGES

WHERE DO I GO FROM HERE?

- Listen to George Gershwin's *American in Paris* and compare its musical elements and form to *Rhapsody in Blue*.

- Listen to Aaron Copland's *Appalachian Spring*, "Doppio Movimento." Are you familiar with this piece from any other source? What about it to you sounds "American," if anything?

- Listen to some of the most well-known songs (arias) from Gershwin's opera *Porgy and Bess*, including "Summertime," "I Got Plenty O'Nuttin'," It Ain't Necessarily So," and "I Loves You, Porgy." Can you find both versions of the arias from the opera itself *and* arrangements of them by singers in different styles? What about these arias do you think makes them appealing as stand-alone songs independent of the original opera?

GATEWAY 44
MEXICAN AND MEXICAN AMERICAN MARIACHI MUSIC[70]

What Is It?

Mexican mariachi music is one of the best known folk traditions in the world, a sonic symbol (or index) of Mexico everywhere and of Mexican American culture and identity in the United States. Mariachi music today, played by musicians who call themselves mariachis (the origin and literal meaning of the term is obscure), varies from one or two musicians singing and accompanying themselves on guitar while serenading diners in a restaurant to a large ensemble of two trumpets, three or more violins, guitar, **vihuela** (a small guitar-shaped instrument), **guitarrón** (a large guitar-shaped instrument), and harp, with the musicians wearing sombreros and the decorative *traje de charro*, suits that were the traditional attire of wealthy nineteenth-century Mexican landowners. Though mariachi emerged at the end of the nineteenth century, it assumed something like its present sound when it was included in Mexican movie musicals of the 1930s and 1940s. Today the repertoire of mariachi ensembles includes a diverse collection of old regional, rural songs in a genre called *son* (literally "sound" or "style"), songs composed for musical films of the 1930s and 1940s in a genre called *canción ranchera* (ranch songs), popular songs in a genre with roots in Cuba called *bolero ranchero* (ranch boleros), regional folk genres like *huapango* from eastern Mexico, polkas,

FIGURE 10.27
Mariachi Sol de Mexico performs with Espinoza Paz (center) at the 2015 Latin Grammy Awards. From right, the instruments are guitar, *vihuela*, *guitarrón*, harp, trumpets, and violins
Source: Getty Images / Kevin Winter.

and arrangements of classical pieces and the latest popular songs. Our gateway to mariachi is "La Negra," the best known song in the rhythmically active style known as *son jalisciense* (*son* from the Mexican state of Jalisco), performed by Mariachi Vargas de Tecalitlán.

 Listen to the first thirty seconds of this recording.

How Does It Work?

Timbre

Bowed violins, trumpets, plucked and strummed accompanying instruments (*vihuela, guitarrón, guitar,* and harp), and male vocals in an almost operatic style contribute to the timbre.

Texture

The rhythmically active accompaniment by the *guitarrón, vihuela,* harp, and guitar (together they are called the *armonía* or "rhythm section") supports the melody on violins and trumpets (which together form the *melodía* or "melody section"), and vocals.

Rhythm

Triple meter (2+2+2) in alternation with, or at the same time as, compound duple meter (3+3). Much of the underlying rhythm of mariachi is created by the *armonía.* The various rhythmic patterns of the *guitarrón, vihuela,* harp, and guitar interlock with one another, and they function as a single unit that provides the rhythmic foundation for the group. In mariachi, the rhythmic patterns played by the *armonía* distinguish one style from another, and the rhythmic patterns played by the *armonía* in "La Negra" indicate that it is in the *son jalisciense* style.

Melody

The melody is in a major mode throughout, with one exception in the D section where the beginning of the vocal line lowers the seventh scale degree of the major mode.

Harmony

Most of the melodies are performed in parallel thirds and are played and sung over a harmony that includes I, IV, and V chords, sometimes in a repeating chordal ostinato. Mariachi musicians today refer to the I chord as *primera* (first), the V chord as *secunda* (second), and the IV chord as *tercera* (third), perhaps a ranking of their importance or the frequency of their occurrence. When teaching a new song to musicians, sometimes leaders of a group will hold up one, two, or three fingers to indicate which chord comes next. Just as it provides the rhythmic foundation, the *armonía* also provides the harmonic foundation for the group.

Form

"La Negra" has five distinct sections that alternate between verses with vocals and instrumental-only interludes: A (instrumental), B (with vocals), C (instrumental), D (vocal), and E (instrumental). Each section is made up of a series of several short repeating melodic phrases (labeled a, b, c, and so forth).

Performance Techniques

Throughout this recording we hear *gritos*, high-pitched shouts in the falsetto range, from members of the ensemble. In live performance musicians and audience members often perform *gritos* to express their excitement and increase the intensity and enthusiasm of the performance. Mariachi Vargas de Tecalitlán includes *gritos* in this recording to emulate the live experience of mariachi music and to feature all of the sonic elements that make songs like "La Negra" exciting for listeners.

Listen to the first thirty seconds of this recording and pay attention to the texture of the melody over a bass line, the parallel thirds in the *melodía* (trumpets and violins), and the *gritos*.

Listen to the entire recording following this timed listening guide.

LISTENING GUIDE 10.5

TIME	SECTION	PHRASES	DESCRIPTION	LYRICS
0:00	Instrumental Prelude		The trumpets and violins begin in a slow rubato tempo, but are soon joined by the *guitarrón*, *vihuelas*, guitars, and harp, though the harp may be difficult to hear. Together they establish a triple meter (2+2+2) and gradually perform an accelerando, repeating the I chord over and over before switching to the V chord. As they switch to the V chord, the first of many *gritos* (shouts) from ensemble members adds to the building excitement of the music.	
0:13			The group begins a pattern of two measures in triple meter followed by one measure in compound duple meter (3+3) and another in triple meter. This pattern happens twice and is outlined by strong accents, especially in the trumpets and violins, at the start of each measure in triple meter, and on beats one and four of the measures in compound duple meter.	
0:21		a	The violins play a major-key melody (a) in thirds, and the trumpets respond with the same melody in thirds.	
0:23		a		
0:25		b	The violins and trumpets play a new major-key melody (b) together, repeating it three times.	
0:28		b		
0:30		b		
0:32		c	Another new major-key melody (c) in thirds begins, with the first half played by the violins and the second half by the trumpets.	
0:36		c′	The phrase repeats, this time with the second half played by the violins and trumpets together with an extended ending that sets up the entrance of the vocals. The bright plucking of the high-pitched strings of the harp may be faintly audible in the background.	
0:42	Song Verse	d	The male vocals enter, singing a new two-phrase major melody (d) in thirds. They repeat this melody four times, which emphasizes the compound duple meter, while the accompaniment in the plucked and strummed strings continues with a triple meter. The lyrics sing of a beautiful woman that causes sorrows (*pesares*) for the singer because she seems to show romantic interest in him, but she hasn't told him when she'll want to be with him. The trumpets and violins respond to the singers' phrases, almost as if to agree with their sentiment.	*Negrita de mis pesares . . .*

continued

TIME	SECTION	PHRASES	DESCRIPTION	LYRICS
		d		*Negrita . . .*
		d		*A todos . . .*
		d		*Así me . . .*
0:59	Instrumental Interlude		The violins return to the repetition of the I chord in a similar fashion to the opening of the recording, but maintaining the fast tempo that has been established.	
1:03		e	The violins play yet another new melody (e) that repeats three times and maintains a strong triple meter.	
1:06		e	The harp can be heard faintly playing in between beats one and two in a syncopated rhythm.	
1:10		e	On the third repetition, the rhythm shifts to emphasize the compound duple meter.	
1:14		f	Another new melody appears (f) that repeats three times. The first half is played by the violins, and the second half by the trumpets. In each second half of the melody, the *armonía* strongly accents every note of the melody.	
1:18		f		
1:22		f	For the last repetition of this melody, the violins join the trumpets on the second half. They are joined by some *gritos* that raise the excitement going into the next section.	
1:27		g	The violins play long sustained tones (one per measure) that follow the chordal ostinato of IV-I-V-I for a new melody (g) that includes two repetitions of the pattern.	
1:35		g'	The trumpets join the violins on the chordal ostinato and together they emphasize a compound duple meter while the rest of the band plays the triple meter. Some high-pitched *gritos* help build the intensity.	
1:43		g''	The entire ensemble plays the chordal ostinato together on an accented triple meter, ending with an accent on beat two of the final measure, which sets up the entrance of the vocals in the next section.	
1:51	Song Verse	h	The vocals enter with a new, two phrase melody (h). This time the melody ascends to a pitch that is not in the major mode ($\flat$7), but is a half-step lower than the seventh pitch of the major scale. The lyrics here ask when the beautiful woman will be brought to the singer, and the brief change in mode suggests the uncertainty, stress, and longing behind the question.	*¿Cuándo me traes . . .?*
1:59		h	The melody repeats with the same lyrics.	*¿Cuándo me traes . . . ?*

TIME	SECTION	PHRASES	DESCRIPTION	LYRICS
2:06	Instrumental Closing	f	The call and response melody f returns and repeats three times.	
2:10		f		
2:14		f		
2:18		i	One last new melody (i) enters, where the violins and trumpets outline two repetitions of the chordal ostinato (IV-I-V-I) in a triple meter.	
2:27		i'	The same melody repeats, but this time the entire ensemble plays only accents on the beats.	
2:35		i''	The ensemble plays the same melody once again, playing two accented pitches for every beat. The chordal ostinato repeats two and a half times before the pulse stops. The violins and trumpets play an unaccompanied, slower, three-note ascending melody, and the recording ends with the ensemble playing two final accented I chords all together.	
2:50	End			

What Does It Mean?

"La Negra" is a song in the musical subgenre called *son jalisciense. Son* is a larger genre category, literally meaning "sound" or "style," and *jalisciense* refers to Jalisco, the region in central-west Mexico where the genre and mariachi itself both emerged. One of the most striking elements of "La Negra" and music in the *son jalisciense* and other *son* subgenres is its fast tempo and energetic rhythm suitable for dancing. "La Negra," the best known *son jalisciense* in the mariachi repertoire, showcases this spirited rhythmic aspect of the genre with its constant fast tempo, shifting accents in the interlocking patterns of the *armonía,* and alternating and layered combinations of triple and compound duple meters. This kind of high-energy rhythm is important in mariachi music, which is often used for celebrations and festive occasions, such as weddings, fifteenth birthday celebrations called *quinceañeras* (in the U.S.) or *quince años* (in Mexico), baptisms, company parties, and more. Not all mariachi music is fast, but the rhythmic energy of songs like "La Negra" helps to create a celebratory atmosphere at these kinds of events. It is quite the challenge for musicians to successfully perform the various syncopated interlocking patterns by the *armonía* and the quickly shifting and overlapping meters by the entire ensemble. If these are not executed well, the performance loses its rhythmic drive and the appropriate atmosphere is more difficult to achieve. If they are performed excellently by master musicians like Mariachi Vargas, they can help induce the positive emotions of celebration that audiences are looking for.

Other sounds that make "La Negra" perfectly suited for celebratory events are the major mode, which is understood to be a "happy" sound, and the *gritos* that occur throughout the recording. The musicians utter *gritos* in the instrumental sections of the recording, often when one repeated phrase is transitioning to another (e.g., the transition from phrase f to phrase g between 1:24 and 1:27). They help ramp up the energy through the transition. When mariachi is performed at celebrations, ensemble members and audience members alike shout out *gritos* as they express their pleasure in the music and the festivities, and they inspire others to feel the same way. Even when mariachi is performed on stage at large concerts or at formal events, *gritos* shouted out by members of the

AESTHETICS

CULTURAL LINKAGES

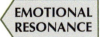

FIGURE 10.28
A map of the state of Jalisco in Mexico
Source: Wikimedia Commons.

group and the audience are part of making the performance more exciting. Of the hundreds of songs in the mariachi repertoire, "La Negra" is considered the unofficial anthem of mariachi. Most groups begin or end performances with "La Negra," and they are often asked to begin with this song to set the tone for an event.

🔊 **Listen to "La Negra" and follow the musical elements that add to the celebratory nature of the music, such as meter shifts from triple to compound duple, changes in the *armonía* pattern, and *gritos*.**

The lyrics of "La Negra" are also full of meaning. The lyrics sing of longing for a particular woman who in the first line is called "Negrita," an endearing diminutive version of "La Negra," which means simply "the beautiful woman," or "the dark-haired one." The poetic lines are arranged in *coplas*, poetic stanzas of four lines that rhyme in a pattern of a-b-a-b. In "La Negra," each of these lines has precisely eight syllables. Many of the lines are repeated in the course of the song, a feature common to mariachi lyrics. At certain points, the vocalists seem to express the meaning of the lyrics in the ways they perform the melody.

EMOTIONAL RESONANCE ▷

For example, the second line metaphorically describes how this beautiful woman flirtatiously bats her eyes by describing them as "flying paper" (*papel volando*). When they sing the word *volando*, they slide up into the pitch of the second syllable and seem to slightly stretch out that syllable (*vo-LAN-do*) in a way that almost mimics what might be the rhythm of the batting of the eyes. As the first section continues, they perform the same slide-up and sustained pitch on the rhyming words *cuando* (when) and *penando* (suffering). Through the lyrics, the singer laments that, even though the woman has agreed to be with him, no one knows *when* this will happen, and, as a result, he is *suffering*. Slightly stretching out the word *CUAN-do* seems to subtly indicate a sense of longing, and lengthening *pe-NAN-do* into the next measure could be an expression of a feeling of suffering. Many mariachi songs also have double meanings. "La Negra" is also understood to refer to locomotives (and their black color) that took young soldiers off to battlefields during the Mexican Revolution in the early twentieth century, inducing sorrow and suffering for different reasons. As "La Negra" pairs these lyrical and musical expressions of sadness, longing, and suffering with the major key, driving rhythm, and celebratory atmosphere, the song's performance may suggest that it is best to deal with the perils of love, heartbreak, and war by coming together with friends to celebrate, rather than wallowing in despair. Then again, many audience members might not think much about the lyrics at all, but instead simply enjoy hearing a familiar song sung in an emotive style by a talented group.

🔊 **Listen to "La Negra" one more time and notice how the singers stylize the ways they sing the ends of their rhyming phrases (such as *volando*, *cuando*, and *penando*), and how the meanings of other lyrics might be enhanced by the vocal style of the singers.**

CULTURAL LINKAGES ▷

Like all mariachi music, "La Negra" is also a symbol of Mexican and Mexican American identity. The combination of timbres, the textures of the mariachi trumpets and violins, the vocal style of singing in thirds, and the rhythmic patterns of the *armonía* combine to create the mariachi sound, a sound that is identified as distinctly Mexican. Wearing sombreros and *charro* suits, singing lyrics in Spanish, and performing known repertoires associated with certain regions and life cycle events, mariachi ensembles are recognized in Mexico, the United States, and all over the world as musical and visual symbols of Mexico and Mexican and Mexican American identity.

What Is Its History?

Some of the mariachi repertoire and some of the instruments used in mariachi date to the earliest decades of the Spanish conquests of the Americas and the Caribbean in the sixteenth century. Conquistadors, missionaries, and colonists brought Spanish singing styles, musical rhythms, and musical instruments to what they called New Spain, which is today's Mexico. Among the instruments were the violin, the harp, and plucked lutes with waisted bodies like the guitar and the small *vihuela* (Chapter 4, Gateway 15). The Spaniards of New Spain played their songs on them and taught the local native population to play them as well. For centuries fiestas and dances in the Mexican countryside have resounded with the timbres of these instruments in various combinations, together with the sharp vocal quality of southern Spain and rhythms switching between triple (2+2+2) and compound duple (3+3) meters common in Spanish folk songs. Those rhythmic sensibilities continue to play a prominent role in mariachi music.

The modern sound of mariachi as a large ensemble, and of mariachi music as both an urban and a rural phenomenon, began in the very early twentieth century when small four- and five-piece groups calling themselves mariachis came from the countryside of Jalisco to Mexico City to perform on special occasions for Mexican president Porfirio Diaz (1830–1915), who ruled as a virtual dictator from 1876 to 1911. President Diaz boosted the Mexican economy for the wealthy but not for the poor, many of whom began to migrate to Mexico City in search of a better life, bringing their rural mariachi music with them and transforming it over time into a popular urban music. From 1910 to 1917 Emiliano Zapata (1879–1919) and Pancho Villa (1878–1923) led a peasant revolution, forcing President Diaz to resign in 1911. When a new group of populist leaders and intellectuals came to power in 1917, their version of nationalism celebrated the music and culture of the rural folk as symbols of national identity, just as Europeans had done in the late nineteenth century (Chapter 8, Gateway 32). As a popular urban music with roots in rural Mexico, mariachi by this time was perfectly situated to take on this role as a symbol of Mexican national identity.

Beginning in the 1930s, Mexican motion pictures, with diegetic music that was performed with sound on screen, portrayed rural life and music in a positive light. Actors and singers in the mariachi tradition became huge media stars. The movie-music version of mariachi music, controlled by music producers and arrangers more than the musicians themselves, began to change. Through the new media of gramophone records and talking pictures, jazz and American popular music had spread to many corners of the world, and the instruments of jazz, especially the trumpet and clarinet, influenced the modernizing sounds of many folk traditions, including mariachi. Trumpets, clarinets, and more violins were added to the ensemble to increase the dramatic impact of the music on screen. Although we can hear the deep historical roots of mariachi in some of its rhythms and other musical elements, the modern mariachi sound, born out of the film music of the 1930s and 1940s, is a far cry from the regional, rural music that inspired it.

CULTURAL LINKAGES

There are a number of mariachi ensembles based in Mexico and the United States that boast their own long histories. The story of Mariachi Vargas de Tecalitlán provides an example of the changes to mariachi music since the beginning of the twentieth century. Its history began in 1898 in a town in the southern part of Jalisco called Tecalitlán where Gaspar Vargas (1880?–1969) formed the group. Until 1931 when Gaspar's son Silvestre took over the group, the instrumentation included harp, a five-string guitar called *guitarra de golpe*, and two or three violins. Silvestre Vargas expanded the group to include *guitarrón*, guitar, and more

FIGURE 10.29
Mariachi Vargas in the early 1930s
Source: Silvestre Vargas Museum, Wikimedia Commons.

FIGURE 10.30
Mariachi Vargas around 1950
Source: Iván Lenovy, Wikimedia Commons.

violins, and under his leadership the group moved to Mexico City where they were featured in many films in the 1930s and 1940s. In the early 1940s they also added a trumpet player to the group, Miguel Martínez Domínguez (1921–2014), who established many of the stylistic conventions for mariachi trumpet playing.

The group also added classically trained violinist Rubén Fuentes (b. 1926) to the group. He became musical director in 1950 and continued to transform the mariachi sound to better suit stage performance and mainstream consumption. For example, performances of *sones* like "La Negra" previously might have lasted twenty or thirty minutes, but after they were recorded in short three-minute commercial versions during this period, shorter versions based on recordings became standard. Since the 1950s Mariachi Vargas has influenced mariachi performance styles around the world, releasing dozens of albums and performing extensively in Mexico and the United States, sometimes with symphony orchestras in formal settings—a type of performance Gaspar Vargas perhaps would have never imagined. In 1987 they famously collaborated with the pop singer Linda Ronstadt (b. 1946) on the Grammy-winning double-platinum album *Canciones de mi Padre*, a tribute to Ronstadt's Mexican heritage. Today Mariachi Vargas is one of the best mariachi ensembles in the world and promotes mariachi through educational initiatives, festivals, and competitions. While rooted in the traditions of mariachi they helped establish, they are—as they have been throughout their history—constantly adapting their music in dialogue with developments in technology, the emergence of new audiences, and ways of passing along the music of mariachi to younger generations.

CULTURAL LINKAGES

In the United States mariachi music has become an important marker of Mexican American identity. One of the groundbreaking groups in this regard has been Mariachi Los Camperos de Nati Cano from Los Angeles, another group with a long history. Natividad (Nati) Cano (1933–2014), the founder of the group, was born in the small town of Ahuisculco, Jalisco, the son of a mariachi musician. As a young musician he made his way to Guadalajara, the capital city of Jalisco, where as a teenager he played violin in the Guadalajara Symphony. He eventually settled in Los Angeles, and became one of the central figures in Mexican American mariachi. After World War II, immigration to the United States from Mexico greatly increased, and audiences were hungry for entertainment that connected them to their Mexican identity. In the late 1960s and 1970s the Chicano movement

FIGURE 10.31
Mariachi Los Camperos de Nati Cano from Los Angeles. Nati Cano is holding a *vihuela* in the center of the group
Source: Courtesy of Smithsonian Folkways Recordings.

FIGURE 10.32
Mariachi Las Alteñas from San Antonio, Texas. Las Alteñas refers to women who work in the highlands of Jalisco and the musicians' goal to reach the highest artistic standard
Source: Mariachi Las Alteñas

had followed the Civil Rights Movement in advocating for the rights of Mexican Americans. By then mariachi had already become a cultural symbol and served as a point of pride for the community. Led by Nati Cano beginning in 1961, Mariachi Los Camperos de Nati Cano captivated this new generation of Mexican Americans and helped transform mariachi into a widely respected form of artistic performance. Tens of thousands of people have heard Mariachi Los Camperos in concert in the nearly six decades of its existence, and the group has performed at concert venues such as the Kennedy Center in Washington, D.C. and Lincoln Center in New York City, as well as at the White House. Other mariachi groups from the United States have their own histories and great followings, including Mariachi Sol de México, Mariachi Reyna de Los Angeles, Mariachi Los Galleros, Mariachi Divas de Cindy Shea, and many more.

While mariachi was originally a predominantly male tradition, it has opened up to many women performers and even all-women ensembles. Women have long been performing mariachi, but in the 1970s women began to perform in some of the leading mariachi ensembles for the first time. The violinist and singer Rebecca Gonzales began performing with Mariachi Los Camperos de Nati Cano, and set the stage for further prominent female participation in mariachi including the award-winning all-women groups Mariachi Divas de Cindy Shea and Mariachi Reyna de Los Angeles, and Mariachi Las Alteñas from San Antonio, Texas.

> SOCIAL BEHAVIOR

As mariachi ensembles perform on some of the most prestigious stages of the world today, many mariachi musicians continue to perform in restaurants, at private parties, and at other celebratory events. The music is now taught in many high schools throughout the American southwest from California to Texas, where school mariachi ensembles compete in festivals modeled on the music competitions of high school concert and marching bands, symphony orchestras, and choirs. In Chicago, César Maldonado, the son of Mexican immigrants, started a non-profit in 2013 called the Mariachi Heritage Foundation. This organization partners with local public schools to teach mariachi to low-income youth, many of whom come from immigrant families. In 2017, an auditioned group of eighteen of these students (nine boys and nine girls) aged eleven to eighteen released the album *Nuestra Herencia* (Our Heritage) under the ensemble name Mariachi Herencia de México. *Nuestra Herencia* became one of the best selling mariachi albums of all time, reaching #2 on the iTunes Top Latin Album charts and garnering a Latin Grammy nomination for Best Ranchero/Mariachi Album.

> CULTURAL LINKAGES

WHERE DO I GO FROM HERE?

- Find a video of Mariachi Los Camperos de Nati Cano performing "La Negra" and compare it to the version of "La Negra" by Mariachi Vargas.
- Find some videos of Mariachi Divas de Cindy Shea. In what types of live settings do they perform?
- Find a video of an American high school or university mariachi group performing at a competition. Identify similar rhythmic patterns to those heard in "La Negra" and explain why there are such similarities.

CLOSING

The interwar years from 1918 to 1939 were a time of great change in the world's music. Jazz became a central element of popular music alongside popular songs from Broadway and Tin Pan Alley. Popular songs, in turn, absorbed the influence of jazz and of Jewish music, bequeathing a body of classic songs and jazz standards to the popular music of today. America's European-derived classical music made its mark on the European classical tradition with compositions that sounded distinctly American. Finally, aurally transmitted rural folk performances, like Mexican mariachi, entered music history for the first time, preserved not in musical notation but on the new popular media of phonograph recordings and "talking" motion pictures. The film and record industries spread music of all kinds to millions of listeners near and far. The history of music was forever changed by these new developments, which continue to play a prominent part in the music of today.

THINGS TO THINK ABOUT

- Compare the way new technologies of this period (records, radio, and movies) affected the musical sound and meaning of the genres in the chapter.
- Compare the way immigration from abroad and internal migration within the United States affected the musical worlds introduced in this chapter.

NEW TERMS

big band	diegetic sound and music	rhapsody
break	*guitarrón*	scat singing
bridge	head	territory bands
Broadway musical	hi-hat	underscore
chorus	jazz standard	*vihuela*
collective improvisation	New Orleans jazz	

MUSIC DURING WORLD WAR II AND ITS AFTERMATH (1939–1950)

WORLD WAR II was one of the darkest periods of the long twentieth century. In spite of the devastating loss of life, a remarkable amount of the music listened to and performed today has its roots in this period. One of the greatest symphonists of the twentieth century, Dmitri Shostakovich, wrote four of his fifteen symphonies during this time, and today orchestras all over the world regularly perform them. The avant-garde compositions of the Frenchman Olivier Messiaen for organ, orchestra, and chamber ensembles are still much admired and performed. Jewish composers of this period suffered greatly, some losing their lives in Nazi death camps and others forced to emigrate from central Europe to the New World. Much of their music was neglected until recently, when some performers began to champion their works. Among those performers is James Conlon, conductor of the Los Angeles Opera, who has been performing operas and symphonic and choral works of World War II-era Jewish composers under the rubric "Recovered Voices." In jazz this period saw the emergence of a new style, bebop, which was the first in a long line of new styles sometimes called, collectively, modern jazz. Jazz musicians and fans still learn from and enjoy the recordings made in this period by musicians like trumpeter Dizzy Gillespie, alto saxophone player Charlie Parker, pianist Bud Powell, drummer Kenny Clarke, and singer Ella Fitzgerald. The harmonic principles developed in this era by musicians playing bebop are arguably the basis of so-called straight-ahead jazz today.

The earliest recordings of rhythm and blues, the precursor of rock and contemporary R&B, come from this period, and country music emerged from its regional home in the southern United States to enter the mainstream of American popular music. Finally, today many tropical-themed restaurants, vacation resorts, and cruise ships employ a steel pan player as an index of fun in the sun. Transcending its roots in the society and culture of wartime Trinidad, steelband music has become an important local art form, a global party music, and a national symbol for Trinidadians both at home and abroad.

Even before Adolf Hitler usurped power in Germany in 1933, he had developed a racist theory in which the German people and others of Nordic descent were superior to all other races, including the Slavs, Jews, and Gypsies (today called Roma). Based on earlier theories of white supremacy, Hitler's theory was implemented by his Nazi Party in the form of a policy called *Lebensraum* (living space). It argued that if a supposedly superior race like the Germans were suffering from overcrowding and a shortage of

FIGURE 11.1
Ella Fitzgerald performing in 1947, with Dizzy Gillespie (right) admiring her performance
Source: William P. Gottlieb Collection. Library of Congress.

food, it had the right to extend its territory by conquering the land of a neighboring inferior people. Using that pretext, on September 1, 1939, Hitler ordered his army to invade Poland, a land of Slavic people across Germany's eastern border. Britain and France declared war on Germany a few days later.

Japan had already invaded China in 1937, ostensibly to end European imperialism in East Asia, an invasion the Chinese resisted bitterly. The United States, at the time reluctant to enter other people's wars, waited to declare war on Japan and Germany until a few days after the Japanese attacked the U.S. naval base at Pearl Harbor in Hawaii on December 7, 1941. The world, not just Europe, was now engulfed in a global war that lasted until the middle of 1945. The scale of death and destruction during World War II is beyond comprehension. The total of military and civilian deaths linked to combat, disease, and famine was between sixty and eighty-five million people, including six million Jews exterminated in a Holocaust administered by Hitler's Nazi regime. After the war, a new geopolitical "three-world order" developed. The United States and its capitalist allies in western Europe, Canada, Australia, and Japan constituted the "first world"; the Soviet Union, its eastern European communist client states, China, Vietnam, and North Korea became known as the "second world." Countries that possessed neither communist nor well-developed capitalist economies were labeled the "third world."

Soon the U.S. and the Soviet Union, the two "superpowers," were pitted against each other in a nuclear arms race called the Cold War because it never erupted into open conflict. When the Soviets tested their first atomic bomb in 1949 to match the ones the United States developed and used during World War II, the tension of the Cold War escalated dramatically. With ballistic missiles to deliver their nuclear weapons, both superpowers had the means to destroy the other, and fear of nuclear annihilation gripped the people of the world, affecting popular culture for years to come.

By 1945 third-world countries had had enough of European and American imperialism, and strong anti-colonial movements developed in Latin America, Africa, and Asia. Although a hot war never destroyed the U.S. and the Soviet Union and their allies, each began to support internal conflicts in countries of the third world in "proxy wars," arming and sometimes intervening on one side or the other in a bid to gain the sympathy of the communist or non-communist side in local, anti-colonial revolutions. In 1946 Vietnam, led by the French-educated communist Ho Chi Minh (1890–1969), declared its independence from France. The Vietnamese fought a bloody war until 1954 to drive the French out and then another war to rid themselves of the Americans from 1955 to 1975. In 1947 Pakistan and India declared their independence from British rule. After Britain withdrew from its occupation of Palestine in the Eastern Mediterranean in 1947, Israel declared its independence in 1948, engaging in subsequent violent conflicts with Arab countries over their right to a state on land also claimed as a homeland by Palestinians. The Chinese communists won their anti-colonial battle against nationalist forces in 1949, inspiring many in the third world. Ghana, the first of the African countries to declare its independence, did so peacefully in 1957, and many parts of Africa followed suit in the 1960s. A communist revolution was successful in Cuba in 1959.

Such an all-encompassing world war, and the ensuing anti-colonial struggles, severely disrupted musical life all over the world. But the need to create and enjoy music is unstoppable, and musical life endured throughout this period. Soldiers and their supporters on the home front still needed entertainment, and popular, mass culture continued in service to the morale of the troops and their families during

FIGURE 11.2
The Glenn Miller band performing in 1940 or 1941
Source: Public domain, Wikimedia Commons.

the war. In the United States the USO (United Service Organization) was formed in 1941 to provide a "home away from home" for soldiers. If they were not already serving in the military themselves, stars of the music and movie industries volunteered to provide shows for soldiers stationed at home and abroad. The camp shows were held well behind the frontlines, but the service was dangerous. Glenn Miller (1904–1944), the leader of the one of most popular swing-era big bands of the 1930s, was too old to engage in combat, so he enlisted to lead military marching bands and dance orchestras. In a flight from Britain to France across the English Channel in 1944, six months after the Allied invasion of Normandy, he and his plane disappeared, never to be found. Jewish composers and musicians who had not left central Europe in the 1930s were sent to Nazi death camps, where they were exterminated or died from starvation, cold, or psychological distress. Many Jewish and non-Jewish composers during and after the war wrote deeply moving compositions expressing their, and their compatriots', experience of this horrible conflagration. Around the world new genres and styles of music emerged to reflect the economic and political life of the postwar period. This chapter deals with key developments in American popular music, jazz, European classical music, and world music during a period torn by war, ideological differences, and nationalist, anti-colonial aspirations.

GATEWAY 45
COUNTRY MUSIC

What Is It?

During and after World War II, popular music started to shift. The popularity of swing was declining, the economy had recovered from the Great Depression, and young people, labeled "teenagers" for the first time in 1941, began to purchase records. A new genre called "country and western," today called "country," gained great popularity after the war. Its most significant figure at the time was guitarist and singer/songwriter Hank Williams (1923–1953), whose 1949 song "I'm So Lonesome I Could Cry" is our gateway to country.

 Listen to the first thirty sections of the recording to get an idea of the sound.

Country music is a commercial genre of popular music rooted in early twentieth-century rural music, mostly from white communities of the American South. Definitions of country can vary widely even among country fans, but it historically has been associated with the image of the cowboy, sung narratives about working-class life, and an underlying (or overt) Christian theology and values. Country often draws on references to symbols of work in rural settings (trucks, farms, ranches, horses), family relationships of many kinds, heterosexual love relationships and struggles, and collectivities like churches and small towns. The sound of country features vocals that often perform with a Southern accent or other vocal techniques like yodeling associated with locations in the rural South. It is also associated with instruments such as fiddles, banjos, and steel guitars, even though some country music doesn't include any of those timbres. "I'm So Lonesome I Could Cry" features a fiddle and a steel guitar. Alongside Hank Williams, the musicians appearing on this recording are Jerry Byrd (1920–2005) on lap steel guitar, Louis Innis (1919–1982) on rhythm guitar, Tommy Jackson (1926–1979) on fiddle, Ernie Newton (1908–1976) on bass, and Zeke Turner (1923–2003) on lead guitar. About a year before recording "I'm So Lonesome

FIGURE 11.3
Hank Williams
Source: WSM radio (public domain), Wikimedia Commons.

FIGURE 11.4
Natalia Zukerman playing lap steel guitar at a festival in Brooklyn, NY in 2012
Source: Getty Images / Al Pereira.

FIGURE 11.5
Steve Fishell playing the pedal steel guitar in 2013
Source: Getty Images / Guitarist Magazine.

Could Cry," they began playing together as a unit they called "The Pleasant Valley Boys." These musicians all had active careers as country performers on stage and on hundreds of recordings. Most of these songs were recorded in Nashville, which has been the center of the country music industry throughout most of its existence.

How Does It Work?

Timbre

The timbres of the recording include Hank Williams' voice, a strummed acoustic guitar, an electric lap steel guitar, an upright bass, a lead electric guitar, and a fiddle.

Texture

The texture features Williams' solo voice over an accompaniment of the other instruments. The bass plays on beat one of every measure (and sometimes other beats), the acoustic guitar strums percussively on every beat, and the lap steel guitar and the lead guitar complement the melody with background riffs and lines played in between phrases. The fiddle enters only for its solo, which is accompanied by the bass, acoustic guitar, and lead guitar.

Rhythm

Each beat of the waltz-like triple meter is subdivided into three, which give the song a rhythmic feel similar to swing. The tempo is anchored by the rhythmic strumming of the acoustic guitar on each beat. It continues slowly and steadily until the very end of the song, when it slows down even more.

Melody

Williams' melody is in a major mode and outlines chord tones of the underlying harmony. While many of the phrases start with Williams ascending and sliding into a long note, each phrase ends with descending interval, sometimes a large leap.

Harmony

Each strophe follows basically the same harmonic structure based on a major key. The harmony alternates between the I and the V chords, with the IV chord making an appearance at the start of the third phrase in each strophe.

Form

After a short introduction, the form is strophic. Two verses are followed by a strophe for a steel guitar solo, a third verse, a fiddle solo, and a fourth and final verse. Each verse has four phrases (AA'BC), the last one sung to the refrain "I'm so lonesome I could cry" in all cases except for the second verse.

Performance Techniques

Williams' voice, the lap steel guitar, and to a lesser extent, the fiddle, can be heard sliding into and out of pitches. Vocalists in country (and many other genres) use this kind of microtonality to express a variety of emotions, similar to the ways that Bessie Smith and other early blues singers had (Chapter 9, Gateway 35). On the lap steel guitar, musicians lay the instrument on their laps, pluck the strings with metal pics that they attach to the fingers of the right hand, and use a steel bar in the left hand to adjust the pitch (the steel bar is where the steel guitar gets its name). The sliding of the steel bar up and down the strings produces the characteristic "twangy" sliding sound of the lap steel guitar that is so common in country music and other associated genres. A related instrument is the pedal steel guitar, which produces a similar sound, but with many more possibilities for melody and harmony. The pedal steel guitar today typically has two necks of ten strings each that rest on a frame, like a table. Attached to each neck is a set of pedals and knee lever mechanisms that adjust the pitches of various strings to make even more glissandos and pitch bends possible than with the steel bar alone.

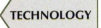

Listen to the introduction and first two verses with these elements in mind.

TIME	FORM	DESCRIPTION	LYRICS
0:00	Introduction	The electric guitar leads into the introduction with a few pickup notes on the guitar's lower strings. These few notes set up the tempo, the triple meter, and the subdivision of the beat into three. On beat one, the bass, the strummed acoustic guitar, and the lap steel guitar enter together to play four bars that set the stage for the first verse.	
0:06	Verse 1	Williams sings the first verse, which has an internal form of AA'BC. Williams stretches out and slides into the long notes of the melody on "hear," "*lonesome,*" and others, which tend to be the highest pitches in each phrase.	Hear that lonesome . . .
0:32	Verse 2 guitar solo	Williams sings the second verse in a similar manner to the first. In this verse the lead guitar can be heard clearly responding to the vocal lines with short improvised phrases in a call and response manner.	I've never seen . . .
0:58	Lap steel	The steel guitar takes a solo, a relatively simple improvisation that paraphrases the melody. This solo showcases the way the steel guitar can perform large and small glissandos, sliding up to and between pitches.	
1:24	Verse 3	The third verse continues the style of the first two verses, with more call and response from the lead guitar.	Did you ever hear . . .
1:50	Fiddle solo	The fiddle plays an improvised solo that is a variation on the melody. Throughout the solo, Tommy Jackson plays on two strings at once with his bow, a technique called a "double stop." He also occasionally slides between pitches by sliding his left finger along the string on the fingerboard of the fiddle to ornament his melody in a way characteristic of fiddle playing in country music.	
2:16	Verse 4	In the final verse the lap steel guitar is more prominent, playing in a higher register as it	The silence . . .

LISTENING GUIDE 11.1

TECHNOLOGY

continued

TIME	FORM	DESCRIPTION	LYRICS
		complements the vocal line along with the lead guitar. The last lines of the lyrics address an absent lover, revealing the source of loneliness expressed by the song. The tempo gradually slows down on the last phrase and the band plays the final major chord together.	
2:45	End		

What Does It Mean?

"I'm So Lonesome I Could Cry" has become one of country music's best-known songs, and its sound reveals some of the broader historical conventions of country music as well as the ways that lyrics help create personas that audiences can connect with.

The most obvious markers of country music in this recording are the fiddle and the steel guitar. The fiddle, which is just another name for a violin, has been associated with forms of rural music and country since long before Williams' time. Its sound and the ways that Tommy Jackson plays double stops and adds ornamentation connect this recording to fiddle playing of earlier iterations of country. The presence of the steel guitar also provides a specific "twang" with its "crying" glissandos and slightly nasal timbre that characterizes it as country. The strophe where the steel guitar plays a solo also enriches the meaning of the recording, as Jerry Byrd avoids virtuosic or intricate improvisation in favor of a simple adapted version of the melody. It seems as if the crying sound of steel guitar is too lonely and depressed to play anything but a simple line whose notes stretch out for long durations without showcasing any of the technical capabilities of the instrument that a more lively and happy emotion might inspire.

 Listen again to "I'm So Lonesome I Could Cry" for the sounds of the fiddle and the steel guitar in both solo sections and during the verses.

CULTURAL LINKAGES

EMOTIONAL RESONANCE

Like many country songs and most popular music, the lyrics of "I'm So Lonesome I Could Cry" are at the center of the song's meaning. The poetic lyrics gesture towards rural life with their references to nature, but they relate those references to loneliness and isolation. Birds—and even the moon—are crying, time moves slowly through a night that is long and dark, leaves are dying in autumn, and stars are, like tears, silently falling out of the sky. Through these evocations of a shared rural life, the song invites the audience to join the vocalist in his (or her, if a woman sings this song) despondence. The first three verses address the audience directly, telling them to listen to lonesome birds and asking them rhetorical questions that seem to indicate that this experience of loneliness is one that can be understood and shared. It is not until the end of the last verse that Williams turns to address his lover, whose absence reveals the reason for his loneliness. Unlike many of Williams' other songs, which express emotions in a straightforward way, the song doesn't describe feelings about a breakup or tension in a relationship, but rather draws the audience into solidarity with the singer through extended metaphors. It provides the possibility for listeners to experience loneliness along with someone else who understands. The lyrics also construct an image of Williams as a person experiencing hardship, living in a world of loneliness that extends beyond his personal heartbreak to an experience shared even with animals, the moon, and the stars.

When a singer in popular music is thought to be genuinely experiencing and expressing the meanings of his or her lyrics, that singer is often said to be "authentic." Personal authenticity is often a desired value in a performance of country and other popular music genres, especially when a vocalist is also the songwriter, as in the case of Hank Williams. The audience interprets the lyrics as an expression of feelings actually felt or events truly experienced by the performer, regardless of whether that is the case or not. In fact, Hank Williams did come from a life of poverty, hardship, and adversity, and his songs deal with those themes. In some cases, though, a singer-songwriter might write a song about a broken relationship and later, even if she is single or happily in a relationship, she will sing the song as if she is experiencing the pain and sorrow of a broken relationship all over again. This kind of personal authenticity is particularly intriguing in cases where, for example, a wealthy, successful performer might sing about economic hardship and challenges like struggling to pay the bills, or a star known to live in a big city sings about life working on a farm and living in a small town.

In country music, authenticity is also grounded in the notion of tradition, that is, a perception of "the old way." Country music perceived as authentic relies on timbres and performance styles of the fiddle, steel guitar, and acoustic guitar to sound old, paradoxically rejecting commercial trends and borrowings from pop music even as artists seek commercial success. Performers can also help build audience perceptions of authenticity through what they wear (for example, cowboy hats and boots) and other aspects of their appearance, how they visually market their albums, and, for the more famous, how they manage their public image with the media.

> CULTURAL LINKAGES

In addition to song lyrics, other elements of vocal performance can help construct a persona that is perceived to be authentic. In "I'm So Lonesome I Could Cry," for example, at the end of the first and third verses, Williams' voice breaks into a higher register when he sings the word "lonesome" (around 0:27 and 1:44). This vocal break (and others like it throughout the song) resembles the sound of crying itself, which helps listeners perceive that Williams actually is feeling sad and lonely. The sound of the vocal break is also reminiscent of a yodel, a vocal technique common in earlier iterations of country and some of the rural musical traditions that form parts of country's roots. This, in combination with Williams' southern drawl, heard in the way he stretches out the long notes of each phrase, adds to the perception of Williams as an "authentic" country singer, singing honestly—and in an old, traditional way—about a rural experience of loneliness.

> EMOTIONAL RESONANCE

🔊 **Listen once more to "I'm So Lonesome I Could Cry,"** listening for the breaking of Williams' voice at various points of the song and other ways that his interpretation of the melody express the emotion described by the poetic lyrics.

What Is Its History?

As the gateway to the blues in Chapter 9 illustrated, during the 1920s record companies began marketing recordings of the blues and other genres popular among black audiences as "race records." In the 1920s and 1930s record companies were also making records that targeted a niche market of rural whites that they called **hillbilly records**. These recordings initially featured musicians playing styles and repertoires, such as ballads and folk songs, that had developed in rural areas of Appalachia and the south among immigrants from the British Isles. Early hillbilly records often played up stereotypes of rural life, especially in their visual marketing, which might feature the performers sloppily dressed with floppy hats and worn-out, rolled-up overalls. But the influence of urban music like Tin Pan Alley songs was quite present in the hillbilly repertoire, and many fans of hillbilly music were people who had migrated to cities from rural areas. One of the first successful musicians to record on hillbilly records was Fiddlin' John Carson (1874–1949), a fiddle player who had moved with his family to Atlanta in 1900 to work at Exposition Cotton Mills. He became well known in the Atlanta area by winning a number of

FIGURE 11.6
Fiddlin' John Carson in the 1920s
Source: Wilbur Smith, Wikimedia Commons.

FIGURE 11.7
The Carter Family c. 1931 (from left): Maybelle, Sara (with autoharp), and A. P.
Source: Getty Images / Michael Ochs Archives / Stringer.

fiddle competitions, and his 1923 recordings became the first commercially successful hillbilly records. Early hillbilly musicians like Carson and the banjo player Uncle Dave Macon (1870–1952) were seasoned musicians by the time recording technology became widespread, and their commercial records played a role in what would later become country music.

Younger musicians recording hillbilly records in the late 1920s were even more influential in the styles of country that Hank Williams and other country artists later performed, and they were part of a shift in hillbilly records from a focus on instrumental music to one on vocals. Hailing from Clinch Mountain in western Virginia, Sara Carter (1898–1979), her husband Alvin Pleasant (A. P.) Carter (1891–1960), and her cousin Maybelle Carter (1909–1978), began recording hillbilly records as the Carter Family in 1927, with Sara on lead vocals and autoharp (a strummed zither), Maybelle on supporting harmony vocals and guitar, and A. P. on bass vocals. Their 1928 hits "Wildwood Flower" and "Keep on the Sunnyside" and subsequent recordings established the guitar in hillbilly and later country music. Also setting standards for the style were Sara and Maybelle's style of vocal harmony and Maybelle's guitar-picking style, later called "The Carter Scratch," which alternated between a melody in the bass strings and rhythmic strumming in the higher strings. They performed together through the early 1940s and began an ongoing four-generation legacy of hit-making Carter family members including Maybelle's daughter June Carter (1929–2003) and June's husband Johnny Cash (1932–2003).

In 1927 Mississippi-born Jimmie Rodgers (1897–1933) recorded his first hit song, "Blue Yodel," which borrowed from black blues singers a variation on the AAB blues form in which the first two lines repeated the same text over two different harmonies (Chapter 9, Gateway 35). He also added a phrase of yodeling on vocables inspired by vaudeville acts that imitated Austrian yodelers. His 114 recordings and the Carter Family's nearly 300 recordings and years of radio performances established much of the early repertoire and singing and guitar playing styles that would have a lasting influence on country music for years to come.

TECHNOLOGY

Beyond hillbilly records, other media also played a role in the spread of the roots of country music in the United States. In 1925 WSM radio in Nashville, Tennessee, began broadcasting a regular "barn dance" featuring live performances of rural white popular songs, comedy, and storytelling. Uncle Dave Macon was one of its first stars, appreciated for both his songs and his humorous banter. This program was later renamed the Grand Ole Opry, a show that continues today as a legendary institution attracting the best established and aspiring country performers. Hollywood "westerns" featured singing cowboys, like Gene Autry (1907–1998) and Roy Rogers (1911–1998), in the 1930s and 1940s, bringing rural music to a mass audience.

SOCIAL BEHAVIOR

After the war, in 1949, *Billboard* magazine changed the name of the chart that kept track of record sales for hillbilly records from "hillbilly" to "country" or "country and western." In the meantime, a more raw version of country music had been brewing in bars called "honky tonks" frequented by the working-class in the Southwest, especially in Texas, Oklahoma, and California. Featuring fiddle, acoustic rhythm guitar, bass, electric lead guitar, and lap steel guitar, it was clearly absorbing the influence of jazz and another genre emerging among African American musicians and audiences by the 1950s, called rhythm and blues. This music became known as **honky-tonk music**, and the lyrics of its songs focused on personal relationships and heartbreak in laments like "I'm So Lonesome I Could Cry."

The most important songwriter and performer of honky-tonk country music was Hank Williams. Born in Alabama, he began his professional career on the radio in 1937 at the age of fourteen. He was plagued by alcoholism, prescription drug abuse, and instability in his personal life. He died at the age of twenty-nine, officially of heart failure, though details of his death remain mysterious and are the stuff of myth among country music fans. The hard times and heartache that he sang about may have been so intense that they led to Williams' death. In his short life he wrote more than 160 songs, thirty-five of which made the country and western *Billboard* chart's Top Ten, with eleven of them climbing to number one.

Country music is defined as a genre of popular music because it is music produced commercially and meant to be enjoyed by people in their everyday lives—to be, well, popular. "Pop music," another genre of popular music that arose around this time, is usually used to describe music and performers who have been embraced by a large, young, mainstream audience. Since the 1950s, the relationship between pop and country is something that fans, artists, managers, and others involved in the country music industry have debated and experimented with in many ways.

In country music the "Nashville sound" emerged at the end of the 1950s. It featured vocalists such as Patsy Cline (1932–1963) and Jim Reeves (1923–1964) along with textures created in the recording studio borrowed from pop recordings of the time. These textures included a drum set, piano, orchestral string sections, and sweet-sounding "oohs" and "aahs" in background vocals. It eliminated instruments traditionally associated with country such as the solo fiddle and the banjo. The steel guitar was still present, but more as a supporting timbre blending into the texture of

the recording and without the distinctive "crying" sound in "I'm So Lonesome I Could Cry." During the 1950s and 1960s a contrasting style, the "Bakersfield sound," developed in honky-tonks in and around Bakersfield, California, a hundred miles north of Los Angeles. Bakersfield sound recordings featured a shuffle rhythm derived from rhythm and blues and an instrumentation of electric guitar, electric bass, steel guitar, rhythm guitar, and drums, creating the same sound on recordings that would be heard in a honky-tonk rather than one dreamed up in the studio. Merle Haggard (1937–2016) emerged from the Bakersfield scene and is now regarded as a legend of country music. During the 1970s singers like Dolly Parton (b. 1946), Tammy Wynette (1942–1998), and Loretta Lynn (b. 1932) performed in a style known as "classic country," which combined the Nashville sound with a return to instruments like the crying slide guitar and the fiddle associated with twang and honky-tonk. These singers are known for their superb vocal skills, successful songwriting, business acumen, and songs that resonated with the day-to-day concerns of working-class and middle-class white women in America.

Over the last thirty or forty years, the tension in country music between staying close to the signs of its "authentic" past and engaging with pop music has persisted. Since the 1980s George Strait (b. 1952) has emulated Hank Williams in his honky-tonk musical style and appearance. He appeals to audiences drawn to country artists they perceive as authentically connected to country music's traditions. Strait's neo-traditional style was one inspiration for the biggest country star in history, and one of the best-selling musicians of all time, Garth Brooks (b. 1962). Brooks became the face of modern country in the 1990s by combining honky-tonk styles with the high-tech entertainment showmanship of pop and rock stadium concerts. He attracted a large and fiercely loyal fan base, even though many country fans have

FIGURE 11.8
Taylor Swift performs onstage during the 42nd Annual Academy of Country Music Awards in 2007
Source: Getty Images / Ethan Miller.

condemned him for what they see as an abandonment of tradition and selling out for commercial gain. In 2005, Carrie Underwood (b. 1983) won the second season of the reality singing competition *American Idol* by performing in a variety of pop styles and was embraced by country fans to become one of today's most successful country singers. One of the world's biggest pop stars today, Taylor Swift (b. 1989), began her career as a teenage country singer-songwriter. In the years after her 2010 country album *Fearless* won the Grammy for Album of the Year, she left the sounds of country behind to team up with pop producers and songwriters and released some of the best-selling pop hits of the 2010s.

WHERE DO I GO FROM HERE?

- Find a recording by Fiddlin' John Carson or Uncle Dave Macon from the 1920s and compare it to either "Keep on the Sunnyside" (1928) by the Carter family or "Blue Yodel" (1927) by Jimmie Rodgers. How are they similar and different? What elements in each one may have influenced later country musicians like Hank Williams?

- Listen to some other Hank Williams recordings such as "Your Cheatin' Heart" and "Lovesick Blues." How do they compare to "I'm So Lonesome I Could Cry"? Can you identify the form and connect it to Tin Pan Alley songs or the blues? How do these or other Hank Williams recordings support the narrative of authenticity that arose about him and his life?

- Look into the roots of the steel guitar, some of which go through Hawaiian music, and trace them through to the embrace of the instrument by country music. Can you find recordings of steel guitar playing earlier than the 1940s? In what genres and styles was it prominent? How is it used today outside country music? How does understanding the instrument's roots influence your view of it?

- How many sub-genres of country music today can you find? Choose a recording from each of two or three different sub-genres and listen for the difference between them based on their sound. How do they relate to other popular music genres?

- Take a look at the book *Country Music: A Cultural and Stylistic History* by Jocelyn Neal, upon which much of this gateway is based. Are there other artists, styles, or eras of country music that capture your imagination? Which ones and why?

GATEWAY 46
BEBOP

What Is It?

During the 1940s a new style of jazz challenged the musical conventions of swing and big band jazz. Called **bebop**, it featured solo improvisation and harmonic complexity, at often very fast tempos. "Ko Ko" (1945) by Charlie Parker's Re-Boppers is our gateway to bebop. Alto saxophonist Charlie Parker (1920–1955) was one of the most virtuosic and innovative bebop musicians, and "Ko Ko" gives a taste of his sensational skills in improvisation. He worked closely with trumpet player Dizzy Gillespie (1917–1993), also heard on this recording. Parker (known as "Bird"), Gillespie (known as "Diz"), and other bebop musicians shifted the focus of jazz to the solo improviser, a legacy of the brilliant solos of Louis Armstrong and others. This recording features a typical bebop ensemble, known as a jazz combo. **Jazz combos** usually consist of one or two instrumental soloists with a **rhythm section** of drums, bass, and piano or guitar. In this case, the combo includes an alto saxophone and a trumpet accompanied by a rhythm section of piano, bass, and drums. The rhythm section musicians here include Curley Russell (1917–1986) on bass, Argonne "Dense" Thornton

(1919–1983) on piano, and Max Roach (1924–2007) on drums. There is some dispute about whether Dizzy Gillespie actually played piano *and* trumpet on this recording, or whether Gillespie played the piano part and Miles Davis (1926–1991) played the trumpet part. Regardless of who actually appears on the recording, it is a classic example of many of the characteristics of bebop, features virtuosic performance, and provides a window into the history of bebop and jazz since the 1940s.

How Does It Work?

Timbre

This recording features Parker's bright alto saxophone and Gillespie's muted trumpet. Also heard is the rhythm section of upright bass, piano, and drum set, featuring the sound of a nearly constant shimmering cymbal called the "ride cymbal."

Texture

The main texture consists of solo saxophone with rhythm section, but there is also a drum solo and a few moments where the trumpet and saxophone play solos and duets accompanied only by the drums.

Rhythm

"Ko Ko" has a blistering tempo of around 300 beats per minute (a march, for example, is around 120 beats per minute). Because of this fast tempo, the steady bass drum beat often heard in swing was impractical in the bebop style. Instead, the beat is kept in the ride cymbal with the drummer playing almost constantly in a stream of pulses and swung subdivisions of the pulse that lay the foundation for the fast swing feel. Max Roach also adds syncopated hits on the snare drum and the bass drum to complement the soloist and the other members of the rhythm section. The bass plays steady pulsatile notes that move mostly stepwise in what is called a **walking bass line**. The piano plays sparingly, adding mostly sustained chords that fill out the harmonic structure of the song in support of the soloist and other members of the rhythm section. On top of this rhythm the pre-composed and improvised melodies in the saxophone and the trumpet consist of many lines of quick notes in a swing feel, interspersed with accents and rhythmic variations that are highly syncopated.

FIGURE 11.9
Charlie Parker in 1947
Source: William P. Gottlieb Collection. Library of Congress.

FIGURE 11.10
Dizzy Gillespie in 1947
Source: William P. Gottlieb Collection. Library of Congress.

Melody

The melodies played in the introduction seem to imply a minor mode, but the improvised melodies played by Parker are generally based on major modes and follow along with the harmony of the underlying chord progression. The melodies move by steps, by leaps, and often chromatically as they move in and out of consonance and dissonance with the harmony.

Harmony

After the harmonically ambiguous introduction, the harmony follows the chord progression of the jazz standard "Cherokee," an instrumental song with an AABA form composed by Ray Noble in 1938. The harmony of the A section remains closely related to the key of the tonic, but the harmony of the B section moves in more adventurous directions to some distant keys.

Form

"Ko Ko" begins with a pre-composed introduction. There are then two choruses of saxophone improvisation over an AABA form, followed by a drum solo that lasts for a shorter duration than the full AABA form and a repeat of the introduction.

Performance Techniques

Virtuosic improvisation is one of the main features of this recording. In the course of his improvised solo, Parker plays characteristic blues phrases and melodic lines that vary greatly in length and rhythm, and he even quotes a well known melody from a New Orleans march. He and Dizzy Gillespie also employ a technique where they play certain notes in a line so softly that these notes can hardly be heard at all, but are implied. These notes are said to be "ghosted," and "ghosted notes" play a crucial role in creating exciting, dynamic, and rhythmic complexity within long strings of quick notes in a swing feel.

Listen to the first thirty seconds of the recording with these elements in mind.

Listen to the entire recording following this timed listening guide. Feel free to pause and repeat sections as you read and listen if they seem to be going by quickly.

LISTENING GUIDE 11.2

TIME	SECTION	INTERNAL FORM	DESCRIPTION
0:00	Introduction		Parker and Gillespie play a pre-composed line in octaves, accompanied by drums only. This line is fast and syncopated, and it ends with a sudden octave drop by both musicians, accented by the drums.
0:06			Gillespie's trumpet, accompanied by the drums, plays a solo improvised line of nearly all quick notes, some of which are ghosted.
0:12			Parker takes a turn with a solo improvisation on saxophone, playing three phrases of running quick notes that are broken up with longer notes.
0:19			The introduction closes with the trumpet and saxophone playing a line in harmony with one another before the drums drop out and they play one last phrase in octaves.
0:25	Chorus 1	A	A crack on the snare drum launches Parker's improvised solo. He plays in steady stream of quick tones for much of the solo. At 0:28 he plays two short phrases and then plays them again with some of the pitches modified to suit the changing harmony. In a sense he is performing call and response with himself as an improviser.
0:38		A	In this A section, we hear Max Roach responding and interacting with Parker's solo more actively, mostly through accents he is playing on the snare drum. Here and throughout the saxophone's dizzying lines, Parker varies the way that he accents some notes and ghosts others, creating the effect of a rhythm that is constantly shifting on and off the beat.
0:50		B	The harmony of the bridge moves to its more distant key, and Parker's first two phrases outline the harmony while including some slight microtonal sliding of the pitch at the end of each phrase. His last phrase here continues into the beginning of the next A section.

TIME	SECTION	INTERNAL FORM	DESCRIPTION
1:03		A	Parker continues to play in long streams of quick tones with syncopated accents, before ending this chorus with a long sustained pitch that is picked up by the piano and accents in the bass drum.
1:16	Chorus 2	A	The first phrase of this chorus is a quotation from the New Orleans march "High Society," a demonstration of Parker's familiarity with the roots of jazz.
1:28		A	The fast chromatic gesture in the high register of the saxophone that starts this A section is one that Parker uses in many improvisations, and is one of a number of his signature phrases.
1:41		B	Parker plays a dance-like repeating syncopated rhythm that interlocks with the sustained on-the-beat chords of the piano, the walking bass, and the constant swing feel of the drums.
1:54		A	The phrase begun at the end of the B section again continues through to the start of this final A section. The most clear reference to the blues can be heard in one of Parker's last phrases at 2:05, where he quickly slides up to the flatted third, a blue note.
2:07	Drum solo		Roach plays an improvised drum solo that starts out as a sort of syncopated, accented conversation between the bass drum and the snare before the bass and snare gradually begin playing together. The drum solo is shorter than a full AABA chorus.
2:29	Introduction (restated)		The introduction from the beginning of the recording repeats, with a greater emphasis on the cymbals from Roach. The recording ends after the harmonized line between Parker and Gillespie, concluding with an octave drop and punctuated with a hit on the bass drum.
2:53	End		

What Does It Mean?

Bebop musicians built on the musical foundations of jazz built by musicians like Bessie Smith, Louis Armstrong, and Duke Ellington, but they also forged new musical pathways that were exciting for them as players and for the audiences they were attracting. Those audiences were focused on listening rather than dancing, and they were smaller than the large audiences that enjoyed dancing to the music of big bands in large ballrooms. Some musical elements of bebop heard in "Ko Ko" are familiar from earlier styles of jazz such as an emphasis on syncopation, solo improvisation, a swing feel, and the microtonality and call and response characteristic of the blues. But bebop musicians like Charlie Parker put even more focus on solo improvisation, pushed tempos to extreme speeds, and favored complex harmonies and small combos of four or five musicians. These elements stand in stark contrast to the swing music and big bands of the 1920s and 1930s.

AESTHETICS

"Ko Ko" showcases many of the musical features of bebop, even though it is limited by the recording technology to about three minutes. Perhaps the most striking element is that the majority of the recording is devoted to Parker's solo improvisation. Parker's solo takes place over a 32-bar AABA form featuring the chord changes to an existing song, "Cherokee." This is an example of how

TECHNOLOGY

bebop musicians took well-known songs of their time and turned them into vehicles for exploring ideas in improvisation, a practice still common in jazz today. In this case, the melody of "Cherokee" is absent, either because the musicians did not want to have to sacrifice royalty payments to the song's composer or so that there could be more time in the recording dedicated to Parker's improvisation. Instead, the recording starts with an introduction that includes both pre-composed and improvised lines in the saxophone and the trumpet that returns at the end of the recording. This is an example of the melody-improvisation-melody (or head-solos-head) form that characterizes the vast number of small group jazz recordings and performances not only in 1940s and 1950s bebop, but in the decades since.

Another striking feature of this recording is its tempo, with the beat clipping along at around 300 beats per minute—much too fast for dancing. This music is meant for listening and to be appreciated as art, especially the art of improvisation over complex harmonic progressions. Musicians playing in a bebop style listen to one another improvise, they respond to each other musically in a kind of musical conversation, and they sometimes even verbally encourage one another. When bebop was emerging in the 1940s, its audiences were fascinated by musicians' displays of virtuosity and musical interaction as they enjoyed the music in small, intimate clubs and bars that did not always have room for dancing.

At several points in this recording, Parker plays long phrases that abruptly end with two eighth notes that descend by a leap—one example is the opening phrase of Chorus 1, around 0:26. When singers like Ella Fitzgerald improvised bebop solos while scat singing, they might have sung those two-note descending leaps on the syllabes "re-bop" or "be-bop," which gave the style (and Parker's Re-Boppers) its name. Interaction among the musicians can also be heard at several points in the recording. For example, at the end of Parker's first chorus he concludes the final A section with a sustained pitch—a stark contrast to the flurry of notes that have preceded it. The piano echoes Parker by performing the same pitch, sustaining it and repeating it several times into the beginning of the second chorus. The drummer plays three consecutive accents in the bass drum, almost to punctuate the way Parker decisively ends his first chorus. This accent pattern outlines the habanera rhythm heard in Scott Joplin's "Maple Leaf Rag" (Chapter 9, Gateway 37), a rhythm that comes up throughout this recording of "Ko Ko" and pervades bebop and other styles of jazz. The "Latin tinge" of jazz continues in bebop even as musicians take it and other existing jazz styles in new directions.

🔊 **Listen again to "Ko Ko," paying attention to the end of the first chorus and the interaction among the piano, saxophone, and drums and the habanera rhythm played in the bass drum.**

Bebop musicians were particularly interested in exploring harmony through their virtuosic improvisations. The melodic lines that Parker plays in his "Ko Ko" improvisations could be said to be outlining or implying the underlying harmony, even though his melodic lines often move in a stepwise motion. For example, at the beginning of the bridge of the first chorus (0:50), he plays two phrases one after another that are basically identical, but the second one is lower in pitch than the first by a whole step. The underlying harmony for the second phrase is one whole step lower than that of the first, and Parker is clearly following that harmonic motion in his improvised solo. The pitches he chooses to emphasize in this phrase also demonstrate how bebop musicians tended to explore more adventurous harmony. The simplest harmonies consist of triads, which include the first, third, and fifth degrees of a scale or mode. Dominant seventh chords, which add the flatted seventh degree of the scale to the triad, represent the next level of complexity. Here, on Parker's repeated phrases a whole-step apart, he gives weight to the final pitch of each of these two phrases, which happen to be the ninth degree of a major chord. When jazz musicians talk about chord tones like the ninth, the eleventh, or the thirteenth, they call them the **upper extensions** of the chord, because they do just that—they extend the chord upwards. Sometimes these pitches can be altered by being raised or lowered a half step, which results in upper extensions called **altered extensions** like the flat nine, the sharp eleven, and the flat thirteen. These upper and altered extensions add complexity to the harmony, create dissonance in a given chord, and open up possibilities for improvisations that can melodically explore these dissonances and complexities in new ways. In this example, when Parker lands on "the nine" of a major chord, he is essentially a whole step away from both the tonic pitch and the third of the chord. This results in three simultaneous pitches a step apart from one another, producing a brief dissonance that is desirable in this setting and indicates mastery of improvising over quickly changing harmonies.

Complex harmonies based on intervals of both seconds and thirds were not new contributions of bebop musicians to jazz. Composers and musicians in the jazz of the 1920s and 1930s, Duke Ellington in particular, relied heavily on these kinds of harmonies in their compositions and improvisations. With bebop and its focus on virtuosic improvisation, however, explorations of harmonic complexity became the norm in jazz composition and improvisation.

> **Listen one more time to "Ko Ko" for pleasure, and see if you can enjoy the ways that Parker's solos express the chord changes. Pay attention to moments of harmonic dissonance. Do you find them pleasing or disturbing?**

Beyond its musical meaning, bebop was embedded in the social life of the times. The innovators of bebop were, for the most part, black musicians. Most big bands were still segregated at this time, and in the early 1940s, more high-profile jobs were going to white musicians and bands. This segregation of bands and the shared experience of black musicians brought these musicians together as they developed new ways of making music. As a result of jobs going to whites and young male musicians being drafted to fight in World War II, some African American bandleaders reduced the size of their bands and musicians found it more difficult to find work performing. At the same time, racial tensions in Harlem were growing. In 1943 a policeman shot a young black soldier, which resulted in a night of rioting along 125th Street and the death of six people. As black and white soldiers fought abroad on the side of the United States in World War II, African Americans grew increasingly frustrated with a world at home where they were still experiencing segregation, inequality, and injustice. There seemed to be a dissonance between the freedoms soldiers were fighting for and the conditions of everyday life for African Americans in the United States. Bebop can be understood as a way for black musicians to consciously—but non-verbally—express something revolutionary in response to the racial, economic, and political issues permeating African American communities during and after World War II. Black musicians showcasing virtuosity, creativity, and innovation in a bebop style drawing on the blues, swing, and other music with roots in the African American experience made a strong musical statement about their place in the broader American artistic landscape.

> SOCIAL
> BEHAVIOR

What Is Its History?

Bebop developed in the early 1940s, and its exciting new approaches to harmony, melody, and rhythm have their roots in the music and lives of musicians playing in swing bands. In addition to Charlie Parker and Dizzy Gillespie, some of the main musicians involved in the development of the bebop style were pianists Thelonious Monk (1917–1982) and Bud Powell (1924–1966), bassist Oscar Pettiford (1922–1960), and drummers Max Roach and Kenny Clarke (1914–1985). These musicians were all actively playing either in territory bands or in New York swing bands and became accomplished instrumentalists by performing night after night in these groups. Historians have a few different interpretations of how bebop developed among these skilled musicians. One of the most common interpretations is that it developed in after-hours jam sessions in New York, where big-band musicians would gather after their evening performances to play together in small Harlem nightclubs such as Monroe's Uptown House and Minton's Playhouse. These kinds of informal jam sessions

FIGURE 11.11

(From left) Pianist Thelonious Monk, trumpet player Howard McGhee, trumpet player Roy Eldridge, and bandleader and Minton's Playhouse manager Teddy Hill, outside Minton's in 1947

Source: William P. Gottlieb Collection. Library of Congress.

had been part of what jazz musicians and their predecessors had been doing for decades. Competitive "cutting contests" were part of this scene just as they were for stride pianists years earlier, often displays of masculine one-upmanship as much as they were demonstrations of musical prowess. At places like Minton's, musicians would challenge each other to higher levels of speed, virtuosity, and harmonic complexity as they improvised over the chord changes to well-known standards like "I Got Rhythm" and "Cherokee," as well as the 12-bar blues. In this interpretation, bebop emerged almost organically from these kinds of spontaneous settings in the early 1940s.

Another interpretation is that these musicians were intentionally developing the new approaches of bebop as they actively toured with big bands. In these contexts, musicians would play the same music multiple times a day, often with only short solos and little room for experimentation or extended improvisation. In between shows, musicians would spend time in dressing rooms to practice, hang out, write letters, and kill time. On tour with Cab Calloway's band in the early 1940s, Dizzy Gillespie avoided the monotony of this routine by either playing practical jokes on his bandmates or developing and practicing new melodic and harmonic ideas to insert into his short solos. He was known to rehearse with musicians backstage, demonstrating new ways he was hearing upper extensions and ways that more dissonant chords could substitute for existing chords of a given composition. These experiments did not always please band leaders accustomed to existing styles like Calloway, but they were attractive to certain musicians, who also participated in the development of these new approaches. For much of 1943, Parker and Gillespie played together in the big band of the pianist Earl "Fatha" Hines (1903–1983). This sustained contact between the two has been called an "incubator" for bebop, as they worked intensely together in independent practice sessions, developed new compositions for the Hines band, and helped create an environment where interest in bebop among their bandmates would also develop.

ECONOMIC ACTIVITY

It is likely that both after-hours jam sessions and the more intentional cultivation of new techniques on tour—by Gillespie in particular—played some role in the development of bebop. One of the reasons it is difficult to figure out how bebop emerged is related to the recording industry. From 1942 to 1944, the musicians' union (the American Federation of Musicians) imposed a ban on all recording by its members in a dispute with record labels over the dissemination of royalties. For this reason, this period in the development of bebop is not documented on recordings. In addition, the new innovations of musicians could not be circulated among musicians themselves (let alone to audiences) by way of records. Instead, the music spread by word of mouth, musicians playing together in big bands, and the exchange of musical ideas at jam sessions. "Ko Ko," recorded in 1945 shortly after the ban ended, is an example of a way of making music that evolved over several years of musical interaction for which there is no recorded evidence.

The history of bebop is also rooted in the lives of its innovators, in particular Charlie Parker and Dizzy Gillespie. Charlie Parker was born in Kansas and grew up in Kansas City, first playing in local bands as a teenager before relocating to New York. He was well known for practicing for more than ten hours a day to improve his playing (what is known in jazz as "wood-shedding," maybe because a person went out to a wood shed to practice). Before he was twenty years old he was widely revered for his incredible facility on the saxophone and his lightning fast improvisations with all of their harmonic and rhythmic complexity. His many recordings with Gillespie and others are full of examples of his technical and creative prowess as a saxophonist and improviser. Though bebop was not a mass popular music like big band swing had been, Parker's music was able to reach large audiences in some cases. Jazz record producer Norman Granz put together two recordings sessions, one in 1949 and one in 1950, where Parker performed standards in his distinctive style with a small orchestra. These sessions resulted in two albums, each titled *Charlie Parker with Strings*, that were the most commercially successful albums of Parker's career. The familiar sounds of a symphonic orchestra playing well known standards were more broadly appealing than the sounds of bebop, which could be shocking and hard to grasp for audiences used to the danceable music of swing. Parker, from a young age, was consumed by heroin and alcohol abuse, which led to his untimely death at age thirty-four.

Dizzy Gillespie, born in South Carolina, taught himself how to play the trumpet, studied music formally in North Carolina, and made his way north to Philadelphia and then New York, where he played in swing big bands by the age of twenty. Gillespie rejected hard drugs and enjoyed a long career as a musician, composer, and bandleader. During the 1940s he held bebop together, hosting gatherings of musicians at his apartment in Harlem and spreading to others the harmonic and musical ideas developed by pianist-composers like Mary Lou Williams (1910–1981) and Thelonious Monk. He later formed a big band, reworking bebop and other later jazz styles for the now-standard big band instrumentation.

Gillespie helped cultivate jazz as music for listening—sometimes incorporating humor and other banter for the sake of entertainment. His openness to new and different styles of music had an enormous influence on the development of Latin jazz, evident on a recording titled "Manteca," his 1947 collaboration with Cuban percussionist and composer Chano Pozo. He nurtured the careers of many musicians in his bands, including trombonist Melba Liston, saxophonist John Coltrane, pianist John Lewis,

FIGURE 11.12
Mary Lou Williams (front) also hosted events at her apartment, where bebop and other music was discussed, such as this 1947 gathering, photographed for a magazine. From left to right around Williams are Dizzy Gillespie, Tadd Dameron, Hank Jones, Milt Orent, Dixie Bailey, and Jack Teagarden
Source: William P. Gottlieb Collection. Library of Congress.

FIGURE 11.13
Dizzy Gillespie in 1991
Source: Roland Godefroy, Wikimedia Commons.

FIGURE 11.14
A sculpture celebrating Los Angeles' Central Avenue legacy in jazz
Source: Jengod, Wikimedia Commons.

FIGURE 11.15
Thelonious Monk at his home in 1963
Source: Getty Images / The Estate of David Gahr.

trumpeter Lee Morgan, and trumpeter Quincy Jones, who would go on to great success as a record producer (he produced Michael Jackson's hit 1982 album *Thriller*, for example) and enjoy a career spanning six decades and all areas of the entertainment industry. Like Duke Ellington, Gillespie led bands on world tours sponsored by the U.S. State Department, where he was simultaneously a representative of the United States and an honest critic of the state of race relations in America. He passed away in 1993 at the age of 75 after a lifetime as one of the central figures of jazz.

A number of other musicians involved in bebop's early years impacted the development of jazz through the remainder of the twentieth century and beyond. The tenor saxophonist Dexter Gordon (1923–1990) was a leading musician in bebop of the 1940s Los Angeles scene that had arisen along Central Avenue, an African American neighborhood that stretched south from downtown LA. Some of the most notable jazz musicians of the past (such as Charles Mingus and Ornette Coleman) and today (such as Kamasi Washington) have emerged from Los Angeles jazz scenes, many of which have roots in the Central Avenue scene of the 1940s and 1950s.

The pianist Thelonious Monk, famously mentored by the pianist and composer Mary Lou Williams and known as one of the house pianists at Minton's, lived into the 1980s and left a legacy of influential compositions and recordings that continues to inspire musicians today. The pianist Jason Moran (b. 1975) has been presenting an acclaimed multimedia performance examining pianist Monk's creative process at jazz festivals and concert venues since 2009. Monk's son, the drummer T. S. Monk, co-founded the Thelonious Monk Institute of Jazz in 1986 to continue the legacy of his father. The Monk Institute supports an annual competition for young jazz musicians, International Jazz Day celebrations around the world, and a variety of education initiatives.

Students learning jazz in the United States today are typically exposed to bebop as a fundamental style of performance and improvisation. They often learn to transcribe the improvised solos of musicians like Parker and Gillespie, writing down and learning to emulate these improvisations note-for-note. The bebop style is thus still performed widely in educational institutions, and continues to influence the development of musicians who are formally trained in jazz.

WHERE DO I GO FROM HERE?

- Listen to some other recordings by Charlie Parker such as "Now's the Time," "Ornithology," "Anthropology," and "Confirmation." How are they similar and different to one another?

- Listen to "Manteca" by Dizzy Gillespie and Chano Pozo. What musical elements of bebop can you hear clearly? What elements derive from Latin American sources?

- Find some Thelonious Monk recordings such as "Round Midnight," "Epistrophy," "Rhythm-a-Ning," and "Evidence." How do Monk's melodies differ from Parker's and Gillespie's recordings? Look for a video of Jason Moran's tribute to Monk, *In My Mind*. To what extent does Moran's work help you better understand or connect to Monk's music?

GATEWAY 47
CLASSICAL MUSIC AND WORLD WAR II

What Is It?

Our gateway to classical music of the World War II era is the first movement of Symphony No. 7 ("Leningrad"), Mvt. I ("War") composed in 1941 by Russian composer Dmitri Shostakovich (1906–1975). The symphony, a gargantuan work in terms of both performing forces and length, requires two separate brass sections and seventy to eighty minutes to perform. The four movements are called "War," "Recollection," "My Homeland," and "Victory." These names harken back to a tradition at least as old as the eighteenth-century symphonies and string quartets of Franz Joseph Haydn, when listeners and critics added names to his works with abstract titles like Symphony No. 101 ("The Clock) and String Quartet Op. 33, No. 3 ("The Bird"). These nicknames suggest associations or similarities between musical gestures and something outside the music. The nickname given to this Shostakovich symphony links it to the city of Leningrad, today called St. Petersburg. The "war" of the first-movement title is the World War II from 1939 to 1945. This performance is by the Leningrad Symphony led by the Latvian conductor Mariss Jansons (b. 1943).

FIGURE 11.16
Dmitri Shostakovich in 1950
Source: Roger & Renate Rössing / Deutsche Fotothek, Wikimedia Commons.

 **Listen to the first thirty seconds.**

How Does It Work?

Timbre

All the timbral resources of a modern symphony are present, with an emphasis on bass and snare drums.

Texture

The movement begins with strings playing monophonically in octaves after which a variety of textures are used for expressive purposes.

Rhythm

The meter is in four with contrasts between march-like rhythms and more tranquil passages with long-held tones.

Melody

The melodies employ quite a bit of disjunct motion, which gives the movement its modern feel compared to eighteenth- and nineteenth-century symphonies. The melodies are based on heptatonic modes with somewhat strange-sounding, accidentals in some places.

Harmony

The harmony is tonal but with a lot of chromaticism.

Form

The form is a variant of sonata form but with a lengthy march section in the middle. The internal form of the march section is based on theme and variations form.

Performance Techniques

The usual techniques of symphonic playing are on display.

🔊 **Listen to the first minute of this performance for the angular, slightly chromatic first theme.**

Timed Listening Guide

As the nicknames for the symphony and first movement suggest, listeners and critics have interpreted this movement as referencing one of the most famous battles of World War II: the siege of Leningrad. Beginning in September, 1941, the German army surrounded the city and blocked supplies and reinforcements from entering. The siege lasted more than two years, until January of 1944 and resulted in huge numbers of deaths. This movement can be interpreted as a programmatic representation of the events and feelings of the citizens of Leningrad during the siege.

Listen to the entire recording following this timed listening guide, which interprets the references to war in the music.

LISTENING GUIDE 11.3

TIME	SECTION	DESCRIPTION
0:00	**Exposition**	
0:00	First theme	The unison strings play the first theme in C major, perhaps an icon of the citizens of the city standing together in resistance. Punctuations from the trumpets and timpani suggest a martial atmosphere. The theme, built on a C major triad, adds non-chord tones in the first repetition of the theme to create a restless feeling (an icon) of unease and anxiety. Eventually the full orchestra enters in dense counterpoint to develop the theme somewhat.
1:31	Transition	The first transition features a quiet passage led by the flute.
2:03	Second theme	The second theme enters. It is an unadorned, lyrical melody in G major, iconic perhaps of the calm before the storm of war. It begins softly in the violins and then, after a short interlude in the winds, moves to the low strings.
4:36	Transition	The second transition features the piccolo playing a tranquil melody based on descending scales in sequence. The long drone at the end of the section creates a feeling of foreboding.
5:54	**March**	The march section begins with the soft sound of the snare drum. The march theme, in E♭ major (a favorite key of military wind bands), enters quietly in the strings, as if the approaching army is far away. The melody mixes conjunct scalar descents with angular disjunct leaps in the upper strings to create an awkward effect perhaps intended to mock, iconically, the approaching German forces. The theme goes through twelve variations of harmony, counterpoint, and instrumentation, growing louder and more menacing over time, an obvious icon of the approaching army. The unrelenting snare drums are particularly intense, and, by the end of the variations, crashing percussion joins them to almost drown out the melody in an iconic rendition of artillery fire.
14:52	Development	The development section begins when suddenly the key shifts from E♭ major to A major (the unusual interval of a tritone), and the brass section erupts with a variation on the march theme and passages based on fragments of the march. The polyphony, combined with the loud drums, creates an icon of the chaos of war. The section ends with a dramatic fortissimo ascending scale passage in octaves.
16:58	**Recapitulation**	
16:58	First Theme	The primary theme returns, signaling the beginning of the recapitulation. Its phrases are in a new order, with the initial melodic line entering in the low brass around 17:12. It is also now in C minor with thundering drums and brass, the melodic mode and the instrumentation constituting musical icons of the sadness of the citizens of a city in ruins after the German attack. Later in the section the unison texture that opened the symphony also returns.

TIME	SECTION	DESCRIPTION
19:11	Transition	The scalar transition material first heard in the piccolo returns in the key of F# major, a tritone away from the tonic key of C, played by the violins and flute and later the solo flute and solo clarinet, as if representing solitary figures walking amidst the ruins.
20:16	Second Theme	The bassoon plays a transformation of the second theme accompanied by the piano and *pizzicato* strings. The alternation between measures in four and measures in three suggests a person staggering through the ruins of war.
22:40	**Coda**	The first theme is heard quietly in the violins in its original major key, as if a distant memory of the city before the war. It is followed by the descending melodic lines from the second transition. The march theme returns quietly, implying perhaps that, after the bombardment, these Germans are not going away.
25:50	End	

What Does It Mean?

One of the meanings of this composition is embedded in its musical style. It combines music with stylistic roots in the Classical period of the late eighteenth century and harmonic and melodic elements that emerge in the twentieth century. The Classical, late-eighteenth-century elements include the sound of a symphony orchestra, the use of a variant of sonata form, and tonal harmony. The modern elements include the insertion into sonata form of a long set of theme and variations on a march tune, the angular melodies with some pitches outside the tonal system, and dissonant harmonies. These elements point in two directions at the same time: toward something old and traditional and something new and fresh. The composer surely hoped to create a work that an audience familiar with eighteenth- and nineteenth-century music would find familiar and attractive but that acknowledged changes in musical style dating back to Wagner, Debussy, Stravinsky, and others. This style, because of its references to elements of Classical-period music, has been labeled **neoclassicism**.

AESTHETICS

In 1942 the score of the symphony was smuggled out of Leningrad and performed in Moscow, London, and New York to great acclaim. It was understood as a defiant expression of Russian resistance to the German invasion, and it bolstered the morale of the Allies fighting Hitler. The nicknames for this symphony date from this period. After the war, however, and after the 1953 death of Joseph Stalin, the ruthless dictator who had ruled the Soviet Union since the death of Vladimir Lenin in 1924, a new interpretation of the work emerged in reports of interviews with Shostakovich and friends who knew him well. According to those reports, Shostakovich had begun to compose this symphony well before the war reached Leningrad. Its musical gestures referenced not the siege of Leningrad but Joseph Stalin's siege of Soviet life and mentality during the 1930s, when he was responsible for the deaths of millions of Soviet citizens in the murders or imprisonment of the intellectual and political elite of the country, a genocidal famine in Ukraine, and the forced relocation of entire ethnic groups from European Russia to Siberia and Central Asia. In this version the march in the center of the movement references not the invading German army but the slow and steady growth of an oppressive, suffocating political regime. While the "Leningrad" Symphony can be interpreted as representing Soviet resistance to the Nazi invasion, Shostakovich later claimed that it had a much broader scope and was dedicated, as he put it, to the city "that Stalin destroyed and Hitler merely finished off." This story illustrates the the way musical meaning depends on context and the way it can change from person to person and time to time.

POLITICAL ACTION

FIGURE 11.17
Dmitri Shostakovich as firefighter, right, on the roof on the Leningrad Conservatory during the siege of Leningrad
Source: Music-Images / Alamy Stock Photo.

> POLITICAL ACTION

> CULTURAL LINKAGES

What Is Its History?

Dmitri Shostakovich is the most important Russian composer of the Soviet era (1917–1991). Born in St. Petersburg, he was a child prodigy as both a composer and pianist. He entered the St. Petersburg Conservatory at age thirteen. His graduation piece, composed at age nineteen, was his Symphony No. 1 (1925). It was premiered to great acclaim in Berlin and Philadelphia just a few years later, and his fame as a composer in western Europe and America was assured. Shostakovich, who was paid a salary as a musical worker by the Soviet state, was astonishingly prolific. He composed fifteen symphonies, a few dozen orchestral suites and concertos, dozens of chamber works for string quartet, piano, and various other combinations, a dozen operas and ballets, and more than thirty film scores.

Shostakovich's career provides one of the most interesting examples in music history of the collision between politics and art. After the Soviet Revolution in 1917 and his graduation from the conservatory in 1919, Shostakovich loyally served the Soviet Union in various capacities throughout his life, including for nearly thirty years as a member of the Supreme Soviet of the Russian Federation and of the Soviet Union. As with so many other prominent figures during this time, however, his loyalty to the Soviet cause could not protect him from the capricious, monstrous rule of Joseph Stalin, general secretary of the Soviet Communist Party from 1922 until his death in 1953.

In 1936 Stalin launched the Great Terror, during which he liquidated or imprisoned many influential intellectuals and political leaders, including some of Shostakovich's friends and family. Stalin attended the premier of Shostakovich's opera *Lady Macbeth of Mtensk* in 1936. Shortly after that, the work was condemned in the party-controlled press as "formalist," that is, as music that focused on modern musical elements but that was not linked iconically or indexically to the tastes and needs of the proletarian masses. Although Shostakovich rehabilitated his reputation with Stalin with compositions like Symphony No. 7 written during World War II, he was again attacked as a formalist after the war in 1948. Although Stalin spared him the fate of his friends, perhaps because he recognized Shostakovich's genius, Shostakovich lived in constant fear of Stalin. Later in life, he confessed to always keeping a packed suitcase at the ready, in case he had to flee at a moment's notice.

In September 1941, Shostakovich was living in his hometown of Leningrad when Nazi forces attacked the city. During the siege of Leningrad, which lasted nearly three years and cost more than 900,000 lives by the time it ended in 1944, Shostakovich served on a fire brigade. He wrote the first three movements of his Seventh Symphony during the attack, and finished the fourth in a nearby town after he and his family were forced to evacuate. An orchestra cobbled together from the dozen or so remaining professional musicians in the city, plus as many amateurs as they could find, premiered the work during the siege in 1942.

Shostakovich was just one of many European composers who expressed their experiences of World War II in their music. Others include Olivier Messiaen from France, Viktor Ullman, a German-Jewish composer from the area today known as the Czech Republic, and Arnold Schoenberg, an Austrian-Jewish composer who immigrated to the United States in 1934, a year after Hitler came to power in Germany.

Olivier Messiaen (1908–1992) was one of the most important and innovative composers in the history of French music. A prodigy like Shostakovich, he entered the Paris Conservatoire at the age of eleven and excelled in piano and organ performance, composition, improvisation, and music history. Messiaen's avant-garde musical style, partly influenced by his having heard Javanese gamelan and other Asian traditions, avoids the narrative conventions of traditional and neoclassical European music, conventions such as harmonic cadences and passages through various key areas. Instead, he favored various mathematical devices that created static formal structures rather than progressing through time as had eighteenth- and nineteenth-century European classical music. A devout Catholic, much of his output contains theological references. Messiaen was also an expert ornithologist and traveled the world transcribing birdsong, which he then included in some of his works, including a 1953 work for piano and orchestra titled *Réveil des oiseaux* (Awakening of the Birds).

When the German military invaded France in 1940, they captured Messiaen, who was serving in a medical unit, and imprisoned him for a year in a labor camp in Poland. There he composed his *Quartet for the End of Time* for an ensemble of four professional musicians in the camp who played clarinet, violin, cello, and piano. They premiered the work for other camp prisoners in January of 1941. The eight-movement work is inspired by a passage from the Book of Revelation from the New Testament. Rather than creating icons of the sounds of war or feelings of despair, as Shostakovich did in his Seventh Symphony, Messiaen uses the biblical text to express the apocalyptic sentiments spreading across Europe during the darkest years of World War II.

Viktor Ullmann (1898–1944) was born in the Czech lands of the Austro-Hungarian Empire to a German-Jewish family that had converted to Catholicism. After serving in the army during World War I, he moved to Vienna and studied for a time with Arnold Schoenberg, whose techniques he absorbed and developed into his own style. During the interwar years he worked as a conductor in Prague and other European cities while composing an impressive array of orchestral and chamber-music works, song cycles, an opera, and music for plays. After the Germans invaded Czechoslovakia in 1939, Ullman, now classified as a Jew in spite of his family's conversion to Christianity, was sent in 1942 to Theresienstadt, one of more than 300 concentration camps the Nazis established in Germany, Poland, and Czechoslovakia for political prisoners and those deemed inferior to the "master race," like Jews, Gypsies, homosexuals, and the disabled. A few of these camps were classified as death camps, the most notorious of which was Auschwitz in southern Poland. Theresienstadt, in the Czech lands, was designated a "model community" and housed many educated, middle-class Jews from Germany and central Europe. Artists, composers, and musicians were encouraged to develop a cultural life in the camp, children were educated, and many musical performances of classical music and jazz were held there. Ullman composed nearly two dozen works while at Theresienstadt, including a one-act opera in 1944 called "The Emperor of Atlantis." In June of 1944 the Nazis, trying to conceal rumors about death camps and their plan to exterminate the Jews, invited the Danish Red Cross to inspect the facility and view the cultural life and the relatively good conditions there. After their visit Ullman was sent in October of 1944 to Auschwitz, where he was killed in the gas chambers.

The Emperor of Atlantis, subtitled *Death's Refusal*, is Ullmann's final work. Throughout his career, he had struggled to resolve his avant-garde sensibility with his desire to communicate directly to a broad audience. In his final works, he fused the atonality of Schoenberg, the accessibility of contemporary German theatre music by Kurt Weill (1900–1950) and others, and references to Bach and Beethoven. This chamber opera, composed for seven singers and thirteen instruments, is an allegorical commentary on the deep immorality of fascism and its total disregard for the value of human life. In one act with four scenes, it takes place in a world at war. The Emperor, who lives alone in a chamber without windows and rules his empire by telephone, declares total war and attempts to persuade Death to help him in his cause. Insulted, Death refuses to participate or to carry out his work at all. Soon, the Emperor begins to hear reports that no one

FIGURE 11.18
Olivier Messiaen in 1930
Source: Paul Fearn / Alamy Stock Photo.

FIGURE 11.19
A "stumbling block," a plaque commemorating the deportation and death of Viktor Ullmann laid in a street near the Hamburg State Opera in Germany, one of more than 60,000 such stones in honor of victims of the Holocaust
Source: Ajepbah, Wikimedia Commons.

POLITICAL ACTION

FIGURE 11.20
Arnold Schoenberg teaching music theory and composition at UCLA in 1951
Source: INTERFOTO / Alamy Stock Photo.

**CULTURAL
LINKAGES**

in the war is able to die, even those with grave wounds. With the world descending into chaos and the war falling apart, Death appears to the Emperor and offers to resume his duties only if the Emperor himself volunteers to be his first victim. Realizing there is no alternative, the Emperor agrees, takes Death's hand, and is led away while the other members of the cast sing a final hymn, "Come, Death, our honored guest," set in a four-part homorhythmic harmonic style reminiscent of the German Lutheran chorale tradition. When the Nazi guards saw the opera in rehearsal, they did not fail to notice its allegorical character, and the performance was canceled. It received its first performance in 1975 in Amsterdam, and has been performed fairly frequently since, including at the Long Beach Opera in 2009 and by the Los Angeles Philharmonic in 2012.

Arnold Schoenberg (1874–1951) was arguably the most influential composer of the twentieth century. In the first decade of the nineteenth century he pushed Wagner's experiments with tonality beyond their limits into **atonality**, the refusal of a tonal center and predictable key relationships that had been the guiding principle in music composition since the eighteenth century. In the 1920s he and others in Vienna developed a new system for ordering music called **twelve-tone serialism**. In this system, all twelve pitches of the European scale are treated equally without regard for hierarchies like tonic and dominant and leading tones, and the twelve pitches are arranged into a series or row of pitches that become the basis for many kinds of compositional transformations, formal structures, melodies, and harmonies. He avoided Ullman's fate when he, and many other Jewish composers, writers, and intellectuals, left Germany in the 1930s before the worst atrocities of the Holocaust began. After the war, in 1947, he wrote a cantata using twelve-tone serial techniques for narrator, male chorus, and orchestra called *A Survivor from Warsaw*, named for the Polish capital, which had a large Jewish ghetto during the war. Based on a survivor's account of wartime experiences, Schoenberg's text recounts the harrowing story of beatings at the hands of the Nazis and being marched off to the gas chambers, to which the victims respond by singing a hymn in Hebrew expressing their love for "the Lord your God." In recent years it has been performed as a prelude to pieces with related themes in the German and Austrian tradition, including Beethoven's Symphony No. 9, with its hopeful invocation of the brotherhood of man, and Mozart's Requiem.

WHERE DO I GO FROM HERE?

- Listen to the fourth movement, "Victory," of Shostakovich's Symphony No. 7. What Classical-period form does it use and what musical devices express the sense of the "title" of the movement?

- Listen to one or more movements from Olivier Messiaen's *Quartet for the End of Time* and describe the elements of music you can hear.

- Listen to one or more sections of Olivier Messiaen's *Réveil des oiseaux* and discuss the way Messiaen creates orchestral bird sounds.

- Listen to Arnold Schoenberg's *A Survivor from Warsaw* and discuss the way he uses various musical elements to express the emotional sense of the text.

- Find a recording of Viktor Ullman's *The Emperor of Atlantis* and listen to excerpts from it. Based on what you know of the storyline of this chamber opera, how do its musical elements and references to older styles of music add to its meaning?

GATEWAY 48
TRINIDADIAN STEEL PAN MUSIC

What Is It?

Steel pan music arose in Trinidad in the 1940s as Trinidadian musicians began to make instruments out of metal cans and barrels that had previously been used for other purposes. These containers were turned into pitched percussion instruments called **steel pans** (or simply "pans") by pounding or hammering the surface of the drum in a way that subdivides it into smaller areas, each of which can be tuned. Today **steelbands** are large ensembles of various types of steel pans, usually made from fifty-five-gallon oil drums, plus a rhythm section known as the "engine room" consisting of non-pitched percussion instruments including a drum set, congas, large metal scrapers, and vehicle brake drums called irons struck with metal rods. These community-based groups, often with up to 100 members each, perform sophisticated and complex musical arrangements in many styles and genres. The development of the steelband is closely linked with carnival, a festival preceding the Christian observance of Lent. Steelbands also participate in competitions against one another where they showcase their creative arrangements and compositions as well as their masterful performance skills. The most prominent steelband competition is Panorama, which began in 1963 and is held most years during carnival celebrations in Port of Spain, Trinidad's capital. Our gateway to steel pan music is a recording of the Renegades Steel Orchestra performing their winning performance from the 1993 Panorama competition. Titled "Mystery Band," it is an arrangement of a calypso (a Caribbean song genre) composition originally by Lord Kitchener (1922–2000) and arranged for the Renegades by Jit Samaroo (1950–2016).

 Listen to the first thirty seconds of the recording to get an idea of the sound.

How Does It Work?

There are steel pans of several different kinds. The highest-pitched pans, called "tenors," have thirty or more notes in a single pan and can play a chromatic scale. The deepest-pitched pans, called "basses," have only two or three notes per pan, so musicians combine several drums in one set to form a complete chromatic scale. A set of bass pans usually includes six drums, but sometimes nine, or even twelve. Since the bodies of the instruments function as resonators, the lowest-pitched instruments use virtually the entire oil drum, while the high-pitched instruments are cut so that the size of the skirt of the drum extends down less than a foot. Pans with pitches in the middle range include "guitars" and "cellos," and their size is in between that of the tenors and that of the basses. Steel pans are played with a pair of rubber-tipped mallets. Because these instruments belong to the idiophone family of tuned gongs, their overtone structure is particularly rich, producing a shimmering, sometimes piercing timbre. One of the arts of steel pan making is to shape the sections of the pan surface not only to play a given pitch in a tempered scale but also to control the overtone structure of the pans so they sound good when played together in bands.

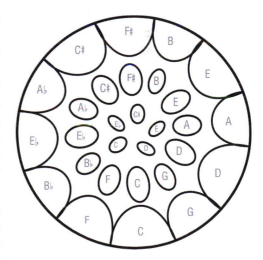

FIGURE 11.21
A drawing of the shape and pitches of the highest-pitched Trinidadian steel pan, the tenor, viewed from above
Source: Alex Sawicka-Ritchie.

Timbre

Timbres in this recording include the shimmering steel pan sound of the high-pitch tenors, the mid-range cellos, and the low-pitch basses. The non-pitched percussion of the engine room can also be heard throughout.

FIGURE 11.22
Exodus steel orchestra members performing in downtown Port of Spain for carnival in 2015
Source: John de la Bastide / Shutterstock.

FIGURE 11.23
Members of a steelband in London performing on basses (left), cellos (center, front), and tenors (center, rear)
Source: Getty Images / Mike Kemp.

Texture

This recording is an example of the typical four-layer steelband texture. The tenors play the lead melody, often doubled or harmonized by complementary lower-pitched pans called double tenors and double seconds. The background pans (including cellos and guitars) "strum" chords in a syncopated rhythmic pattern. The basses play a repetitive bass line. And the instruments of the engine room play an interlocking, polyrhythmic part that continues with a number of variations throughout the recording.

Rhythm

The rhythm is in a duple meter with interlocking polyrhythms among the instruments of the engine room, which produce a steady, nearly uninterrupted **groove** (a short, repeated musical pattern). The melodies, countermelodies, strumming, and bassline also include a great deal of syncopation.

Melody

Some melodies are in major modes and some are in minor modes. In most cases the melodies are drawn from the calypso "Mystery Band" composed by Lord Kitchener and elaborated upon. **Calypso** is a style of song that developed in Trinidad in the early twentieth century as an Afro-Trinidadian form of social commentary on living conditions in a society under European colonial rule. In calypso, a singer is backed up by a band and draws on humor and wordplay to entertain audiences.

Harmony

The harmony moves through a number of key centers, based on the harmony of the original calypso. The variations generally follow the harmony of the original themes, but additional chromatic harmonies are introduced in some of the variations.

Form

Like many arrangements for Panorama, this piece is in a theme and variations form. After an introduction, the arrangement follows the original form of "Mystery Band" (ABCDE), followed by a number of variations on that form. Some newly composed material is added in between variations at some points of the recording.

Performance Techniques

This music is being played by around 100 musicians. Each section of the band must perform with extraordinary precision and coordination with the other sections. When a large group of musicians succeeds in this endeavor it can be quite impressive. There is little variation in timbre or texture throughout the recording. Perhaps the most interesting elements to follow are the changes in the melodies and harmonies, which demonstrate the skill and creativity of the arranger, especially when expertly executed by the ensemble.

Listen to the entire recording as you follow the timed listening guide.

TIME	SECTION	DESCRIPTION
0:00	Introduction	After two percussion beats from the engine room, the introduction begins, which launches right into the thick four-part texture with the entire ensemble performing together. The melody of this introduction is heavily syncopated.
0:23		The band completely stops other than the drummer playing a pulse in the bass drum and hi-hat. Gradually the pans enter, playing an arpeggiated figure over a pentatonic scale in a massive crescendo along with the high-pitched white noise of the scrapers in the engine room. At the height of the crescendo, the band plays a unison syncopated figure on the V chord to set up the initial presentation of the themes of "Mystery Band."
0:39	A	The melody to the calypso "Mystery Band" begins with the first eight-bar phrase (A), which has an internal form of aa. The syncopated major melody is heard clearly in the tenors, supported by the strumming of the cellos, the simple repeating ostinato in the basses, and the intense driving polyrhythm of the engine room.
0:54	B	Phrase B is similarly eight bars and in a major mode, and can be distinguished by its melody, which begins with five quickly repeated pitches in succession (its internal form is bb'). The percussion group accents the rhythms of the melodic gestures, especially the syncopated phrase endings.
1:09	C	This eight-bar phrase is through-composed and, though it stays generally in a major key, begins with a chromatic harmonic progression, three slightly dissonant chords that descend by half-steps.
1:24	D	Phrase D is an eight-bar phrase in a minor key with an internal form of dd'. After a large upward leap of an octave from the end of the previous phrase, the melody descends through the minor scale with a syncopated rhythm. At the end of the phrase, the chords begin to move back towards the original major key.
1:39	E	In this sixteen-bar phrase back in the major key, each of the four-bar subdivisions of the phrase begins with two statements of a short-long-short syncopated figure.
2:10	A'	The first variation on A changes the melody quite a bit, and adds a number of syncopated accents in the engine room, cellos, and basses. The harmony becomes slightly more chromatic.
2:23	B'	This variation stays close to the original B melody at first, and then continues to elaborate on the syncopated part of the first phrase of B through a number of harmonic and melodic iterations.
2:38	C'	The initial chromatic harmonic progression of C can be heard in the cellos and basses, but the tenors perform a technical and intricate new melody over that progression.
2:54	D'	The percussion slightly thins out for this variation of D, and the drums play a series of accents while the cymbals and other high-frequency sounds of the engine room play only on the beat in a "swooshing" effect.
3:08	E'	The full engine room cranks up again, and the short-long-short motive from E returns, but not as prominently as the first time. A countermelody in the cellos descends chromatically. The entire band plays series of unison syncopated hits to end this section and change to a new major key.
3:50	A'', B'', C'', D'', E''	The melody shifts to the cellos in a new major key, while the tenors play in a supporting role. They play new variations on each section.

continued

TIME	SECTION	DESCRIPTION
5:13	F	A brief section of new material brings the tenors back to the forefront of the texture and gradually moves the tonality to a new key.
5:32	A''', B''', C''', D''', E'''	The tenors assume control of the melody, transforming it to a minor key for A''' and B'''. These variations continue to demonstrate the technical abilities of the musicians and the skills of the arranger.
6:55	G	New material enters with new harmonies and melodies. This section is called a "jam." It cyclically alternates between two chords and seems to suspend the forward linear motion of the theme and variations form.
7:12	A'''', B'''', etc . . .	More variations continue until the end of the recording, along with some sections of new material.
10:08	End	

What Does It Mean?

CULTURAL LINKAGES

Steel pan music is a cherished carnival tradition in Trinidad. Carnival is celebrated before Lent in countries with Roman Catholic heritage all over the world (in New Orleans it is called Mardi Gras). In Trinidad, its central festivities take place on the Monday and Tuesday before Lent begins on Ash Wednesday, and include parades, dancing, elaborate masquerade costumes, and a number of music competitions. Steelbands originally functioned to provide musical accompaniment to the dancing and costumed masquerades of carnival parades. The duple meter, moderately fast tempo, and complex syncopation in "Mystery Band" are all rooted in the Trinidadian style of dancing on the road at carnival. While steelbands still participate in carnival parades, today DJs with large (and loud) speaker systems on flatbed trucks provide most of the music for dancers and other carnival revelers, usually in a newer popular style of beat-driven dance music called soca. Where the extraordinary music of steelbands shines is in the context of music competitions like Panorama, an annual competition associated with carnival.

AESTHETICS

With a history stretching back over fifty years, Panorama is a competition with a number of stages (preliminary rounds, semifinals) that occur for about a month before the final competition, which typically takes place on the Saturday before carnival begins. Bands spend up to two months (the time between New Year's and Lent) preparing their ten-minute Panorama performances, which showcase the skills of both performers and arrangers. Each Panorama performance is usually based on a well-known contemporary calypso song.

Calypso has been central to the repertoire of steelbands since they first appeared. In its sung form, calypso focuses on wordplay, humor, and showmanship, and is an effective mode of storytelling and commenting on social issues of the day. In the weeks leading up to carnival, calypsonians (as calypso singers are called), accompanied by backup singers and a large backup band (drums, guitar, electric keyboard, bass, saxophones, trumpets) perform in theaters called "calypso tents" in Port of Spain to entertain audiences with their wit and masterful musical storytelling. As part of their performing personas, calypsonians take on fanciful names: some of the biggest stars have been Atilla the Hun (not Attila), Singing Sandra, Lord Invader, Lord Kitchener, and Mighty

FIGURE 11.24
Carnival masqueraders in the streets of Port of Spain, Trinidad
Source: Getty Images / Sean Drakes.

Sparrow. In addition to its storytelling function, calypso has also been popular for dancing and for the carnival parade. Before soca became the most common music in the carnival parade, calypso music provided a steady beat for people processing down the road in a dance style that moved forward with swaying short steps. The bouncing excitement created by the interlocking rhythms of calypso and the "breaks," where the entire band stops playing momentarily, can generate great energy and stimulate enthusiasm among all participants. Calypso's sometime function as a music for dancing can be clearly heard in the polyrhythms, breaks, and the overall rhythmic feel of "Mystery Band."

 Listen again to "Mystery Band" and focus on the interlocking rhythms, steady tempo, breaks, and whether you feel like it makes you want to dance or walk with a bounce in your step.

Today calypso songs deal with a wide range of topics: politics, patriotism, moral behavior, and other forms of social commentary. When steelbands perform well-known calypsos for Panorama (like Lord Kitchener's "Mystery Band"), it is important that the melody is clear, since audiences and judges will likely know the melody and the lyrics that are a big part of why the song is significant. It is also important, however, to demonstrate creativity, which is where the theme and variations form comes in. In the very first Panorama competition in 1963, an arranger named Tony Williams decided to experiment with the theme and variations form, a concept that he borrowed from the symphonies of European classical music. It enabled him to maintain the familiar calypso melody and harmony while allowing creative experimentation. He also borrowed from European classical music the concept of harmonic modulation in the form of key changes. These techniques impressed audiences and judges and remain common in Panorama performances. Arrangers today add newly composed material for introductions, transitions, and "jams." Jams, like section G of "Mystery Band" (starting at 6:55), usually repeat a pattern of two or four chords in a cycle, which suspends the linear forward motion established by the theme and variations form. On top of that pattern, the band plays an exciting and perhaps technical part. Jit Samaroo, the arranger of "Mystery Band" for the Renegades, was a master arranger known for his relatively short jams and arrangements that showcased the dexterity and high level of technical proficiency of the musicians.

FIGURE 11.25
The Mighty Sparrow performing in Amsterdam in 1989
Source: Getty Images / Frans Schellekens.

 Listen once more to "Mystery Band" and focus on the form, the ways that the variations modify the original themes and the shift in the sense of forward motion during the jam at G (6:55).

Over the past half-century, Panorama has significantly shaped the music of steelbands, not only introducing theme and variations as the most common form, but also in making steel pan music a staged (rather than a parade) performance and in emphasizing intricately pre-composed music rather than improvisation. Steelbands cover a wide repertoire beyond calypso. While Panorama has promoted the performance of calypso music, other competitions have focused on the performance of arrangements of well-known works from the history of European classical music. Steelbands also perform and record arrangements of American popular songs, adding their characteristic interlocking calypso rhythms and the rich timbres of steel pans to give the songs a new, Trinidadian sound.

What Is Its History?

The British, Dutch, Spanish, and French colonized the Caribbean islands of Trinidad and Tobago in the sixteenth and seventeenth centuries and began to bring enslaved Africans to the islands. When the British finally secured complete control of the two islands in 1797, the population was estimated at about 2000 Europeans and 10,000 enslaved people of African descent. The enslaved Africans of the French and Spanish colonists had adopted the Catholic tradition of the pre-Lenten carnival and played African drums to accompany their celebrations. After the abolition of slavery in 1834 Afro-Trinidadians became enthusiastic participants in the public carnival, bringing their own flavor and interpretation to the carnival traditions of Europeans. In the period from 1845 to 1917, thousands of immigrants from India were brought to Trinidad as indentured servants to replace the labor of the enslaved. Today Indo-Trinidadians are the largest population group in Trinidad and Tobago (nearly 40 percent), with people of African descent representing a slightly smaller percentage of the population.

TECHNOLOGY

During the 1880s the British banned the use of African-derived drums at carnival after deadly rioting among revelers. Participants quickly turned to found objects like spoons and bottles, cookie tins, brake drums, garbage-can lids, and especially an ensemble of bamboo stamping tubes called *tamboo bamboo*. Bamboo tubes of different sizes and pitches were struck on the ground and/or struck with sticks to form interlocking polyrhythms that accompanied singing. Eventually, metal instruments began to replace bamboo tubes, first because they were louder and more durable, and, later on, because they turned out to be tunable. Steelbands emerged out of this African-derived tradition of inventing musical instruments from found objects.

Early found-object containers of choice for steel pans included the steel drums used by the Bermudez Biscuit Company, caustic soda drums, garbage cans, and paint cans. Musicians figured out how to beat the bottoms of these containers into sections, each with its own pitch. The innovators of steel pan instruments were from poor communities, and the music was first associated with lower socioeconomic classes. The first steelband ensembles emerged around 1940, but during World War II carnival celebrations were banned. They were not heard again publicly until 1946. Steelbands attracted attention from Trinidadian intellectuals who, under the influence of musical nationalism, viewed the music as a kind of "urban folk" music suitable to represent the Trinidadian nation. The cultural status of steel pan music began to rise in the late 1940s as a result of government support of a steelband association and a national steel orchestra, the Trinidad All Steel Pan Orchestra (TASPO), as well as positive responses from the press in the U.K. after a 1951 TASPO performance. TASPO was one of the early groups to use another found-object container, the larger fifty-five-gallon oil drum that spread in popularity and is still the standard drum used for making steel pans today.

Oil was discovered in Trinidad in the nineteenth century, and from the early twentieth century Trinidad was an important oil producer. Discarded oil drums were a part of the environment and during the World War II Trinidad became a major oil depot (and site of American military bases) supplying the Americans and the British with fuel for their airplanes, tanks, and ships. TASPO helped the fifty-five-gallon drum become more common, but it wasn't until the invention of stands on wheels in the late 1950s that these large instruments became fully standard because they were too heavy to carry slung around the neck on the road. When the fifty-five-gallon oil drum caught on and panmen (tuners of steel pans) in Port of Spain started to tune fifty-five-gallon drums, they had to jump the fence of the American naval base at night to steal them. These larger drums were shaped into instruments of different sizes to play melody, harmony, and bass parts that eventually became the tenors, guitars, cellos, and basses used today. Other metal objects, like brake drums, became the collection of percussion instruments that make up today's engine room rhythm section.

SOCIAL BEHAVIOR

ECONOMIC ACTIVITY

By the 1970s, steelband was part of the curriculum of some schools, and by the 1980s women became integrated into the previously male-dominated membership of steelbands. Today commercial sponsors, often large corporations, support the building and maintenance of instruments for large steelbands like the Renegades. When they won Panorama with "Mystery Band" in 1993, the Renegades were sponsored by the oil company Amoco (today known as BP). These corporate sponsorships continue today as a public relations opportunity for corporations to show a commitment to the community.

"Mystery Band" is just one example of Panorama-winning performances by the Renegades, who, with their arranger Jit Samaroo, won the competition nine times in the 1980s and 1990s.

Samaroo, of Indian descent, is one of the most prominent figures in the steel pan scene today not only in Trinidad, but in steelband circles around the world. Other steelbands with ongoing success at Panorama include Phase II Pan Groove, the Trinidad All Stars, and the Desperadoes, each working with their own highly skilled arrangers.

From the 1960s through the 1990s, over half of the winning Panorama performances, including the Renegades' "Mystery Band," were based on calypsos by the calypsonian Lord Kitchener, born Aldwyn Roberts. Beginning in the 1940s, Lord Kitchener set the standard for calypso music and is one of the most highly revered calypsonians of all time. As steelbands gained prominence, Lord Kitchener (and others) began writing calypso songs with steelband performance in mind, including "pan tunes" like "Mystery Band" whose lyrics referred directly to steel pan music and whose musical elements lent themselves to performance by steelbands. Though Lord Kitchener was known for composing and performing in a variety of musical styles, his pan tunes remain classics in the calypso and steel pan repertoires.

During and after World War II calypso and steel pan music became well known in much of the world. The tradition of social and political commentary in calypso made it an ideal mode of critique of the negative impact of the American presence in Trinidad during the war. The calypsonian Lord Invader (b. Rupert Grant, 1914–1961), sang perhaps the most famous calypso song of the era, "Rum and Coca-Cola." In it he sings of how the "Yankee dollar" (spent by American military personnel stationed in Trinidad) had negative consequences for the island, including an increase in prostitution. The lyrics of the first verse open with the young girls of Trinidad giving the "Yankees" a "better price" because the Yankees "treat them nice." The chorus closes with the line "both mothers and daughters working for their Yankee dollar." In 1944 the Andrews Sisters, an American singing group noted for tight harmonies and songs about the war like "The Boogie-Woogie Bugle Boy of Company B" (1941), recorded the song with modified lyrics. Through their efforts and those of the American popular entertainer Harry Belafonte (b. 1927), who spent part of his youth in Jamaica, calypso entered the mainstream of popular music in the United States during the 1950s and 1960s.

Today steel pan music is played in cities all over the world. Panorama has inspired similar competitions in cities like New York, where Brooklyn hosts the largest and most skilled steel pan scene outside Trinidad. Many U.S. universities teach steelband ensembles, some of which were founded by well-known Trinidadian panmen. Steel pan tuner Cliff Alexis, for example, helped create the first steel pan degree program at Northern Illinois University, about a decade after he started working there in 1985. Another tuner, Ellie Mannette (b. 1926), started the University Tuning Project at West Virginia University in 1991. Arranger Ray Holman (b. 1944) started the University of Washington Steelband in 1998 during a residency there as a visiting artist. Steelband music also plays a role in tourism both in Trinidad and around the world as it has become an index of relaxing and carefree island life in the tropics, even though its emergence in Trinidad during World War II tells a different story.

FIGURE 11.26
Lord Kitchener in 1956
Source: Getty Images / Popperfoto.

CULTURAL LINKAGES

WHERE DO I GO FROM HERE?

- Listen to Lord Kitchener perform "Mystery Band" with its lyrics, and compare it to the version performed by the Renegades.

- Watch a video of the Renegades' Panorama-winning performance of "Mystery Band," paying attention to not only the technical skills of the pan players, but the overall social environment of the performance at Trinidad's carnival celebration.

- Listen to the two versions of "Rum and Coca-Cola": one by Lord Invader and one by the Andrews Sisters. Other than the differences in the lyrics, what musical elements are transformed in the Andrews Sisters' version, and to what effect?

- Find some examples of steelband performances that are arrangements of European classical works or American popular songs. How do the steelbands musically adapt the songs to suit their purposes? Which musical elements remain the same?

- Take a look at the book *Carnival Music in Trinidad* by Shannon Dudley (Oxford: Oxford University Press, 2004), upon which much of this gateway is based. How do some other musical genres contribute to Trinidadian carnival celebrations?

CLOSING

Musicians and their audiences around the world responded to and engaged with the events of World War II in countless ways. A recovering economy in the United States after the war led to a new era of business success in the music industry, and newly named genres like country attracted hordes of fans and made stars out of artists like Hank Williams. Musicians like Charlie Parker and Dizzy Gillespie created a new mode of expression in jazz—bebop—expanding the harmonic and melodic structures of their music in the context of segregated all-black big bands on the road, while other African Americans were being killed on the battlefield as they fought a war against the racist ideologies of Adolf Hitler and the Nazis. European composers wrote instrumental music that indexed and iconically represented the horrific experience of the war and offered a subtle, unspoken critique of those in power. Some, like Messiaen and Ullman, composed music in concentration camps and death camps, defiantly commenting on their conditions as prisoners with music that expressed both hope and pointed criticism of their captors. The wartime operations of the United States and Great Britain had musical consequences in Trinidad, where musicians transformed discarded oil drums into the sounds of one of today's most distinct and vibrant musical traditions.

As the war faded into the past and a new era of economic prosperity began for many, a new generation would challenge not only racial and other injustices in American society, but also the continued involvement of the American military in wars and violent conflicts abroad.

THINGS TO THINK ABOUT

- Compare the various ways that the World War II and its effects stimulated music and musicians during this period.

- National identity and nationalism appears as a theme in several of the gateways in this chapter. How and why does music become a marker of national identity in the various settings discussed here?

- Compare the ways country, bebop, and steel pan music illuminate the legacies of slavery in the Caribbean and the United States and the ways they dealt directly or indirectly with slavery in the past and discrimination and injustice in the present.

NEW TERMS

atonality	hillbilly records	steel pan
bebop	honky-tonk music	steelbands
calypso	jazz combo	upper/altered extensions
country music	neoclassicism	walking bass line
groove	rhythm section	

MUSIC FROM AN AGE OF DISENCHANTMENT AND PROTEST (1950–1975)

TREMENDOUS UPHEAVAL in American society and culture marked the period from 1950 to 1975. Singer-songwriter Bob Dylan (b. 1941) wrote "the times they are a-changin'," and musicians responded to the turmoil with new musical styles and practices. The victory on the European and Pacific fronts in World War II, postwar economic prosperity, and a baby boom created a new confidence for many that America was the greatest and most powerful country in the world. But anxieties also persisted. The United States had introduced nuclear warfare to the world and killed tens of thousands of civilians in the Japanese cities of Hiroshima and Nagasaki in the final stages of World War II. After World War II, as the Cold War intensified, the Soviet Union built its own nuclear arsenal to contend with the military power of the U.S. Americans fought in two proxy wars in efforts to stave off the perceived threat of communist expansion against Soviet-supported enemies during this period: the Korean War from 1950 to 1953 and the Vietnam War from 1955 to 1974.

The tension between optimism and pessimism about the future in the United States provided fertile ground for seeds of dissension and unrest to grow among three important segments of society: white youth, African Americans and other ethnic minorities, and women. During the 1960s, anti-war protests, race riots in a number of U.S. cities, and the assassinations of President John F. Kennedy in 1963, his brother, Senator and presidential candidate Robert Kennedy, in 1968, and civil rights activist Martin Luther King, Jr., in 1968, created a widespread sense of despair that eclipsed the optimistic national mood of the 1950s.

By this time African Americans had long been fighting against segregation and for equal rights. Organizations like the NAACP, founded in 1909, initiated legal action in the courts, organized mass protests, published and publicized key statistics, and produced artistic material. Despite progress on many fronts in the first half of the century, African Americans returning from World War II were still denied rights enjoyed by their white fellow citizens through legalized segregation, which persisted, especially in the South. They had risked their lives, and their comrades in arms had lost their lives, to protect a society that, on the one hand, had condemned an enemy that regarded certain races as inferior, and on the other hand, continued to condone unequal legal rights and violence based on race at home. In 1954 the landmark Supreme Court decision, *Brown v. Board of Education*, ruled that so-called "separate but equal" schools in the segregated South were, in fact, unequal. The next year Rosa Parks of Montgomery, Alabama, was arrested for refusing to sit in the customary place for blacks at the back of a city bus. The bus boycott that followed her defiance launched the Civil Rights Movement, which took the quest for integration and equality beyond the courts and into the streets. It featured repeated acts of civil disobedience, including sit-ins at whites-only lunch

FIGURE 12.1
Vietnam War protesters, 1967
Source: Frank Wolfe. Lyndon B. Johnson Library.

counters, peace marches, and freedom rides. The religious leaders of the movement, including Rev. Martin Luther King, Jr., Jesse Jackson, and Ralph Abernathy, advocated nonviolent resistance. But they could not control the anger and frustration that percolated in black neighborhoods in cities and that led to bloody race riots in the Watts neighborhood of Los Angeles in 1965 and in many other cities after the assassination of King in 1968. The Civil Rights Movement was, however, substantially successful in moving the country toward equality for all, as reflected in the Civil Rights Acts of 1964 and 1968 and the Voting Rights Act of 1965. The sense in the 1950s and 1960s that the rights of African Americans were at last being legally recognized led to the development of an optimistic new genre of popular music: soul music, one of the predecessors of today's contemporary R&B.

When the large numbers of babies born right after WWII entered adolescence in the 1950s and 1960s, they developed a sense of themselves as a separate group within society, a group with a new label: teenagers. Their aggressive pursuit of their own values in music, clothing, and behavior led to a "generation gap" between them and adults and contributed to the sense of tension and anxiety during this period. When in 1964 young men began to be conscripted in large numbers to fight in Vietnam, this group of young adults erupted into opposition to the war that lasted for a decade. Some took their anti-war arguments into the streets in massive public demonstrations, while others, called hippies, expressed their disgust with a mainstream flowing in the wrong direction by "tuning in [to music and alternative religions], turning on [to sex and drugs], and dropping out [of mainstream culture and society]." In addition to their opposition to the Vietnam War in the 1960s, a feeling of solidarity with the Civil Rights Movement fueled their alienation from the mainstream, and many whites joined African Americans in peace marches and freedom rides. Their taste in music, including a love of African American musical styles, coupled with their opposition to the Vietnam War, drove a dramatic change in white popular music taste away from the swing-era music of their parents and towards rock music from the mid-1950s to the mid-1970s.

The restiveness of white youth and African Americans inspired other liberation movements internal to the United States, including the women's liberation movement, the Chicano Movement, and the American Indian Movement. Each one affected music making by members of those communities. The notion of a liberation movement was taken from anti-imperialist liberation movements around the world and especially in Africa, where virtually the entire continent threw off colonial rule during this period. The gateways that follow examine major developments in popular music, jazz, European-derived classical music, and salsa. All these styles responded in one way or another to the turmoil of this period.

Two of the most important genres of American popular music today, rock and contemporary R&B, can trace their roots to the period from 1950 to 1975, a period of enormous upheaval in American society. On the other hand, much, though by no means all, of what contemporary composers in the European classical music tradition are doing today can be explained as a response to the avant-garde sensibilities of this period. In jazz, new experimental and so-called "free" styles of composition and improvisation developed alongside explorations of how jazz could be fused with a number of popular music genres. And Puerto Ricans in New York contributed a new genre, salsa, to the world music scene.

GATEWAY 49
ROCK

What Is It?

Rock music has become one of the most celebrated genres of popular music in the world. It first emerged as **rock 'n' roll** in the 1950s, when musicians like Chuck Berry (1926–2017), Elvis Presley (1935–1977), and others brought together musical elements from genres marketed to white audiences like country with those from genres marketed to black audiences like rhythm and blues. In the early 1960s, early rock 'n' roll declined and black vocal music became popular among young audiences from labels like Motown and girl groups such as the Shirelles, the Ronettes, and Martha and the Vandellas. British bands playing rock 'n' roll like the Beatles and the Rolling Stones took the U.S. by storm in the mid-1960s as part of the so-called British Invasion. In the second half of the 1960s rock audiences became associated with social movements that advocated for peace in the midst of the Vietnam War and stood in solidarity with the Civil Rights Movement and desires for racial justice in the United States. Since then, rock has spawned many subgenres that are today enjoyed by people of virtually all ages around the world.

One of the key figures in the history of rock is the guitarist, vocalist, and songwriter Jimi Hendrix (1942–1970). Hendrix came to prominence in the late 1960s and pioneered innovative technologies and new techniques and sounds for the guitar that still inspire guitarists all over the world. His group, the Jimi Hendrix Experience, released three successful albums in the 1960s and, along with Hendrix, included Mitch Mitchell (1948–2008) on drums and Noel Redding (1945–2003) on electric bass. Their 1968 recording of the Bob Dylan (b. 1941) song "All along the Watchtower" from the album *Electric Ladyland* is our gateway to rock.

 Listen to the first thirty seconds of the recording.

How Does It Work?

Timbre

One of the most fascinating aspects of this and other Hendrix performances is his experimentation with the timbre of the guitar. In the course of the recording there are many effects added to the guitar, which make its timbre gritty and rough at some points, smooth and clear at others, and nasal and cutting at others.

Texture

Throughout the recording the texture is a combination of drums and percussion, electric bass, and several layers of guitars, all of which support Hendrix's voice and his electric guitar.

FIGURE 12.2
The Jimi Hendrix Experience (from left, Mitch Mitchell, Jimi Hendrix, and Noel Redding)
Source: Pictorial Press Ltd / Alamy Stock Photo.

Rhythm

The underlying rhythm is a typical rock beat. On beat one of nearly every measure, the drummer plays the bass drum, in many cases preceded by a "kick" on the second half of beat four. The bass drum also plays a variety of syncopated rhythms underlying the beat throughout the recording. The drummer plays strong accents on beats two and four on the snare drum and other percussion, and driving pulses on other parts of the drum set and sometimes on the bass drum.

Melody

The melodies of the vocal lines and the guitar solos are largely based on pentatonic modes, which include the ♭3 and ♭7 as blue notes.

Harmony

The harmony mostly cycles through four chords over and over. It begins on a minor chord as the tonic, walks down a step to a major chord, down another step to another major chord, and up a step to the previous major chord. The cycle repeats following these chords, though sometimes, at the end of an eight-bar phrase, the last chord is replaced with a minor chord on the fourth scale degree.

Form

The form of this song is strophic, with six eight-bar verses sung in pairs by Hendrix. The verses alternate with instrumental phrases featuring guitar solos whose duration ranges from one to four eight-bar strophes.

Performance Techniques

Beyond his explorations of new timbres, Hendrix uses many innovative recording technologies in this recording, especially the ability to separate and "move" sounds between the left and right channels. Especially when listening with headphones, the guitar at times seems to move between the left and right ears.

Listen for these elements in the first thirty seconds of the recording.

Listen to the entire performance following this timed listening guide.

LISTENING GUIDE 12.1

TIME	SECTION	DESCRIPTION	LYRICS
0:00	Introduction	The introduction begins with the rhythmic pattern that accents the second half of beat three and beat four. The first eight bars introduce a groove based on this pattern in the acoustic rhythm guitar, bass, and drums. The next eight bars feature Hendrix playing a solo on lead guitar.	
0:17	Verse 1	The drums become much less active, and Hendrix's lead vocal replaces the lead guitar, which begins to respond to his blues-inflected vocal in a call and response manner. This call and response continues through each of the verses.	There must be . . .
0:35	Verse 2	Hendrix's blues-like vocal continues in a slightly higher register.	Businessmen they drink . . .
0:52	Guitar solo	After a drum fill on the toms, the drums become much louder and more active, supporting an eight-bar lead guitar solo that includes many blues references including some microtonal bent pitches.	

TIME	SECTION	DESCRIPTION	LYRICS
1:09	Verse 3	Hendrix's vocal continues for verses 3 and 4 in a similar manner to verses 1 and 2.	No reason . . .
1:26	Verse 4	At times Hendrix's vocal blurs the line between singing and speaking, such as on the lyrics "talkin' falsely now."	But you and I . . .
1:43	Guitar solo	After Hendrix shouts "Hey," we hear a lead guitar solo that starts out with similar characteristics to the previous solo.	
1:58		After eight bars, the texture thins as the drums become less active, and the guitar solo continues with a quite different timbre. We hear sustained pitches, effects such as reverb, and long slides like those typically heard on steel guitar.	
2:15		After another eight bars, Hendrix shouts "Hey" again, and the volume increases with more active drums, bass, and rhythm guitars. The lead guitar solo shifts to a more cutting timbre. Hendrix is using a wah-wah pedal, which allows him to adjust the timbre of the guitar with a foot pedal as he is playing. Waves of sharper, more nasal timbres are heard as he solos here.	
2:32		For the final eight bars of this solo, the lead guitar playing continues without the wah-wah effect and a more rhythmic approach. The solo ends with an ascending pentatonic scale that seems to be aiming for the tonic in a high register, but the solo ends before the guitar reaches that climax.	
2:49	Verse 5	Hendrix sings "All along the watchtower" in a high register, launching verses 5 and 6, which continue the texture and sensibilities of the first four verses.	All along the watchtower . . .
3:06	Verse 6	The snare drum plays a constant pulse on all four beats at many points during these verses.	Outside in the cold . . .
3:23	Guitar solo	After a final shout of "Hey" from Hendrix, this guitar solo starts with three long pitches, the first and third on the tonic, and the second one step higher. It ends with the same ascending pentatonic scale as the previous solo.	
3:39		The pentatonic lead up, this time, reaches the tonic in the high register for the climactic moment of the recording. Hendrix holds this pitch for the remainder of the recording by repeating it over and over, mostly playing a constant stream of quickly-moving notes. The pitch is also sustained by effects like reverb. In the course of these last eight or nine bars, the high sustained guitar sound shifts between the left and right channels, sometimes sounding as if it is traveling back and forth between the two. After eight bars, the overall volume begins to fade out, providing the illusion that the band continues to play as their sound gradually disappears.	
3:58	End		

FIGURE 12.3
A wah-wah pedal (right) connected to a number of other guitar effects pedals
Source: Dave Wilson.

What Does It Mean?

Understanding the musical elements of "All along the Watchtower" can help reveal much about both Jimi Hendrix and about rock in general. One of the striking elements of this recording is that guitar solos take up more than half of the time of the recording, making the lead guitar at least as important as the vocal and its lyrics. The changes in timbre, range, texture, and dynamics among the eight-bar guitar solo sections shape the overall progression of the song to a much greater extent than the lyrics do. In a sense, the verses of this song form a framework for showcasing Hendrix's guitar playing and his innovations in the sound of the guitar.

Hendrix is well known for his groundbreaking use of technology for the electric guitar, particularly his use of a pedal known as a **wah-wah pedal**. The wah-wah pedal manipulates the sound of the guitar to sound like a human voice pronouncing the words "wah-wah." The wah-wah pedal is connected by a

TECHNOLOGY ⟩ cable to both the electric guitar and the amplifier (sometimes in combination with other pedals), and takes the electronic signal from the electric guitar, modifies it, and sends that modified sound to the amplifier. Some pedals have only on-off switches or knobs that can be turned to adjust various effects. The wah-wah pedal, however, has a foot pedal that rocks forwards and backwards. As the pedal is depressed, higher frequencies in the tone are emphasized and the "wah" sound is produced as a result. The wah-wah pedal can be heard clearly at 2:15 during the third eight-bar section of Hendrix's longest guitar solo on this recording. The first wah-wah pedal was invented in 1966 just two years before this recording, and though Hendrix was not the first to use this particular pedal, he made the sound of the wah-wah pedal famous through his use of it here and in other examples, such as the opening of "Voodoo Child (Slight Return)" (1968) from *Electric Ladyland*. This kind of manipulation of timbre is reminiscent of the ways brass players use plunger mutes to produce a similar wah-wah effect, as in Duke Ellington's "Black and Tan Fantasy" (Chapter 10, Gateway 41). The wah-wah pedal and other timbral effects developed by Hendrix connect him to the legacy of African and African American experiments with timbre and added effects (such as the buzzing sound on the Shona *mbira* in Chapter 3, Gateway 10).

 Listen to Hendrix's lengthy solo on "All along the Watchtower" between 1:43 and 2:49 again, and see if you can hear him begin the use of the wah-wah pedal at 2:15.

AESTHETICS ⟩ Hendrix's guitar playing and vocals are closely linked to the blues. He knew the recordings of blues guitarist and singer Robert Johnson (Chapter 9, Gateway 35) and call and response reminiscent of Johnson can be heard between his vocal phrases and his lead guitar lines, even though "All along the Watchtower" is a strophic song and not in a blues form. In addition to Johnson's acoustic guitar playing, Hendrix also knew the music of electric blues players Elmore James (1918–1963), T-Bone Walker (1910–1975), and others he heard in his early years. This wide range of blues influences can be heard as Hendrix performs the vocal and guitar melodies with a great deal of microtonality, a lot of sliding between pitches, and an emphasis on the blues scale. The vocal sensibilities of blues singers have influenced singers and instrumentalists in countless popular music genres, and Hendrix's vocals and guitar melodies on this recording and many others are particularly clear examples of how his music—and rock 'n' roll and rock in general—is grounded in the blues.

CULTURAL LINKAGES ⟩ Echoing Bessie Smith's "Backwater Blues," "All along the Watchtower" expresses frustration with the status quo and suggests an upending of established hierarchies in society. In the first four of the song's six verses, Bob Dylan's enigmatic lyrics describe a conversation between a joker and a thief. In verses one and two the joker is looking for a "way out of here"—"here" a world where businessmen benefit from the hard work of others—and there seems to be confusion about values and priorities in broader society. The thief replies in verses 3 and 4 that the value of human life is clear to them both (life is not a joke), and that the hour is late, implying a sense of drama. Hendrix's long guitar solo builds on this sense of drama until the final verses describe the watchtower of a castle, a symbol of the seat of power, about to be stormed by the thief and the joker amidst a howling wind and the sound of a growling wildcat.

CULTURAL LINKAGES

The final section then unleashes a final growling, howling guitar solo that reaches the highest pitch of the recording on guitar, sustained for more than a full eight-bar section and moving back and forth from the left channel to the right. Hendrix expresses the subversive meaning of the lyrics in his manipulation of melodic range, timbre, dynamics, and technology, making it clear that he and his listeners are aligned with the thief and the joker against the establishment. Hendrix's guitar solos amplified, literally, the countercultural themes of Dylan's lyrics, as the audience for the song was loosely defined by opposition to U.S. involvement in the war in Vietnam and support of the Civil Rights Movement, sexual freedom, communal living, psychedelic drugs, and hope for peace and justice. Hendrix, Dylan, and their audiences are imagining a world where the current power structures are broken down, their music a metaphor of social change. Rock music in the 1960s is closely related with these kinds of desires for social change, though its history and its roots in the rock 'n' roll of the 1950s helps explain its cultural importance even more clearly.

🔊 **Listen one more time to "All along the Watchtower" from beginning to end, this time focusing on the various guitar solo sections. Notice the changes in each section, the musical elements that Hendrix uses to build and/or restrain intensity throughout the recording, and other ways Hendrix's guitar playing and voice express the meaning of the song's lyrics.**

What Is Its History?

The history of "All along the Watchtower," and rock music in general, is rooted in the emergence of rock 'n' roll as a genre in the mid-1950s. At that time, radio play and record sales fueled the popularity of country and western primarily for a white audience and rhythm and blues for black audiences. **Rhythm and blues** was a new genre label that replaced "race records" as the *Billboard* chart category in 1949. It included a range of musical styles performed mainly by African American artists and marketed to African American audiences. It featured a strong backbeat (accents on beats 2 and 4), flashy showmanship and choreography, and bands consisting of piano, electric guitar, bass, drums, and saxophone. Big Mama Thornton (1926–1984), Muddy Waters, and Ruth Brown (1928–2006) were among the best-selling rhythm and blues (or R&B) artists in the early 1950s. Their recordings served as precursors, and in some case inspirations, for what would become rock 'n' roll.

CULTURAL LINKAGES

The term "rock 'n' roll" itself comes from the common use of the words "rockin'" and "rollin'" as references to sex in the lyrics of rhythm and blues songs and race records. A radio disc jockey named Alan Freed (1922–1965) is usually credited with its first use as a commercial genre label to refer to any music that appealed to teenagers. In 1951, on his radio show, he started playing upbeat, guitar-based dance records from the rhythm and blues genre. Freed noticed that many white youngsters were calling in to request these songs. In the segregated society of time, he used the label "rock 'n' roll" to increase the appeal of the music to a white audience. Radio disk jockeys all over the country soon followed suit.

Freed began organizing concerts and tours of black artists such as Chuck Berry (1926–2017), Fats Domino (1928–2017), and Little Richard (b. 1932) to perform for mixed-race audiences. These artists were all initially R&B performers whose music—as rock 'n' roll—became wildly popular among both black and white audiences. One of the early rhythm and blues groups to appeal to both black and

SOCIAL BEHAVIOR

FIGURE 12.4
Chuck Berry
Source: Pickwick Records, Wikimedia Commons.

CULTURAL LINKAGES

white audiences was Louis Jordan and His Tympany Five, which had formed in 1938 (initially releasing race records) and served as an inspiration for Chuck Berry in particular. Berry himself was probably more influential on the future of popular music than any other rock 'n' roll musician as a songwriter, as a guitarist, and as a vocalist. While the saxophone had been the primary soloing instrument on Freed's radio shows, Berry, along with the guitarist Bo Diddley (1928–2008), made the guitar the focal instrument of rock 'n' roll. His recordings of such songs as "Johnny B. Goode" (1958), "Roll over Beethoven" (1956), and "Maybellene" (1955) helped to establish rock 'n' roll as a widely popular genre and influenced and inspired countless musicians in rock 'n' roll and rock in the 1950s and long afterwards. Though rock 'n' roll was here to stay, in 1959 Freed was brought down by a scandal in which it was revealed that he accepted bribes, called payola, from record producers in exchange for featuring their songs on his radio show. Payola was common practice across the music industry at the time, so some have argued that Freed was taken down because he was supporting the indie record labels who were promoting African American artists and was a threat to the major record labels, who weren't.

Rock 'n' roll became an age-group identity marker for a new generation of white teenagers born during and immediately after World War II in what is known as the baby boom. One of the ways they distinguished themselves from adults was in their musical taste. That white kids were going crazy at concerts and dances to the rhythmically energetic music of black artists, especially male black artists, performing in a genre named after synonyms for sex, was the perfect symbol of rebellion against the segregated and prudish social norms of 1950s American society. Many white adults hated the new music that was so different from the swing music and popular songs of the early 1950s. They found it sexually suggestive and even threatening in terms of black male performers appealing to white girls. The more they expressed their disgust, however, the more young people clung to it as an symbol of their generation and its aspiration to break with out-of-date, racist values and practices. The association of rock 'n' roll, and later rock, with rebellion against social norms was sealed in these early years.

The popularity of rhythm and blues styles under the name rock 'n' roll attracted many white artists, especially from the South, who might otherwise have become country singers. By dropping the fiddle and pedal steel guitar of country music and featuring the drums, piano, guitar, and saxophone of rhythm and blues bands, they were able to transcend their regional roots and cash in on the national popularity of rhythm and blues. They did so by producing **covers**, or new versions of existing rhythm and blues songs. Some covers closely imitated previous recordings, but others changed tempos, rhythms, and even lyrics to appeal to different or broader audiences. One of the most famous covers from this period is Elvis Presley's recording of "Hound Dog" in 1956, a song originally recorded by Big Mama Thornton in 1952. Thornton's original draws on the blues in its microtonality, its shifting syncopation, and its lyrics that use double entendre to play with sexuality and gender expectations. It was a number one hit on the R&B charts for seven weeks in 1953. Presley's version features a faster tempo, a vocal style that includes rhythmic "hiccups" common in the style called "rockabilly" (a combination of rock and hillbilly), and cleaned-up lyrics that seem to make the song about a literal hound dog without any sexual metaphors. Presley's version reached number one on the pop, R&B, and country charts after its release.

The producer Sam Phillips (1923–2003), who owned Sun Records in Memphis, Tennessee, first recorded Presley in 1954 along with other young white artists, including Carl Perkins (1932–1998), Jerry Lee Lewis (b. 1935), and Roy Orbison (1936–1988). These artists imitated the sound of black singers and mimicked their dynamic, energetic performance style. Elvis Presley's energetic movements and hip-shaking dancing amplified the excitement, enthusiasm, and sexual energy of his performances. Both white and black musicians and producers drew on influences from country music, African American and white gospel, the music of pop crooners of the time, rhythm and blues, and the blues to create a blend of styles appreciated by both black and white audiences under the marketing category rock 'n' roll.

Alongside rock 'n' roll on the pop charts of the 1950s was a genre called **urban folk**. Performed in large part by urban intellectuals, urban folk drew on rural folk music and the Depression-era protest songs of Woody Guthrie (1912–1967). The most well-known urban folk group in the 1950s was the Weavers, led by the banjo player and singer Pete Seeger (1919–2014). In the early 1960s a younger generation of artists like Bob Dylan, Joan Baez, and Peter, Paul, and Mary performed urban folk along the same lines. Their newly composed songs focused on social commentary, and their bands featured acoustic rather than electric guitars, which made it easier to hear their lyrics clearly. They looked down on rock 'n' roll since it was primarily enjoyed for fun and socializing rather than for engaging with the serious issues of the day. In 1965, however, and in the wake of the success of the Beatles, Bob Dylan began recording and performing on electric guitar with a rock band, something he had aspired to as a high school student when he dreamed about playing in Little Richard's band. Although he continued to write about the serious themes of urban folk in what became known as folk rock, many loyal fans of urban folk were dismayed at Dylan's shift away from the genre's acoustic conventions. The injection of more "grown-up" lyrical content into rock 'n' roll was a sign that the teenagers of the 1950s were themselves becoming adults, ready for their music to mature along with them. That Hendrix recorded a version of Dylan's "All along the Watchtower" is a sign not only of Dylan's enormous influence on rock, but also that rock music was, by 1968, deeply engaged in the social challenges of its time. Not incidentally, Dylan admired Hendrix's version of the song and has said that Hendrix's version was not only an improvement on the song but also an inspiration for how Dylan has performed the song in subsequent live performances.

Rock 'n' roll's start along the path to engaging with social issues of its time began in 1964, when a new generation of white musicians from Britain brought rhythm and blues back to the United States. Like their white counterparts in the southern United States a decade earlier,

FIGURE 12.5
Elvis Presley
Source: INTERFOTO / Alamy Stock Photo.

FIGURE 12.6
Bob Dylan in 1966
Source: Pictorial Press Ltd / Alamy Stock Photo.

many British rockers had been absorbing the electric guitar-based sound of black R&B artists, even covering old recordings by blues legends like Robert Johnson and Muddy Waters, whose 1950 recording "Rollin' Stone" inspired both a new band's name and a new magazine devoted to music and politics. The first of the British groups to cross the Atlantic and hit it big in the United States was The Beatles, a band from Liverpool, England. After several years performing covers as a bar band, members of the Beatles bassist Paul McCartney (b. 1942) and rhythm guitarist John Lennon (1940–1980) began to compose their own songs in imitation of the styles of the day. Eventually lead guitarist George Harrison (1943–2001) and drummer Ringo Starr (b. 1940) joined in the songwriting effort. The Beatles first achieved success in Britain with their 1963 album *Please, Please Me*, and first toured the United States in 1964, exciting thousands of adoring fans.

FIGURE 12.7
The Beatles in 1963
Source: Getty Images / Photoshot.

The success of the Beatles led to a "British Invasion" of similar groups drawing on American black music. Some, like The Rolling Stones and The Who, had an enduring impact on American popular music. In 1966, after their third and last U.S. tour, the Beatles, in parallel with the American group the Beach Boys, began to experiment with new forms, textures, and timbres they could create in recording studios. Both bands released **concept albums**, albums that were conceived as an integral whole, with interrelated songs arranged in a particular order. This revealed a shift in perspective where albums were viewed as large-scale works of art, and rock and other popular musicians as artists. The Beach Boys released the first concept album, *Pet Sounds*, in 1966 and the Beatles released *Sgt. Pepper's Lonely Hearts Club Band* in 1967. These two albums have influenced countless bands and artists who since then have created their own concept albums and experimented with new technologies and the other musical elements of rock.

Born in Seattle, Jimi Hendrix moved to New York's Harlem neighborhood in 1963 at age twenty-one after serving for a time in the U.S. Army. In New York he worked as a guitarist locally and on tour for R&B acts like the Isley Brothers and Little Richard when they played the "chitlin circuit," an informal network of performance venues in the eastern half of the U.S. where black performers entertained audiences, without fearing for their safety, during the Jim Crow era. He had built a reputation as an excellent R&B guitarist and began to perform with his own band in clubs in Greenwich Village. "The Village," as it was known, is a neighborhood in downtown Manhattan that was at the time a site of flourishing artistic activity and a home for many nightclubs that served the urban folk, folk rock, jazz, and rock scenes. Greenwich Village audiences were largely white, but by 1965 the phenomenon of white teenage audiences adoring black rock 'n' roll stars like Chuck Berry was already a thing of the past. As a black musician with extraordinary skills in blues and R&B styles, Hendrix did not seem to fit the image of what an American 1960s rock star should be.

In 1966 Chas Chandler (1938–1996), the original bass player of the British R&B and rock band The Animals, heard Hendrix play in Greenwich Village. Familiar with the scene in Britain, where great interest in R&B and the blues had persisted as audiences saw British rock bands succeeding in the U.S. and around the world, Chandler convinced Hendrix to come to London. Audiences there were thrilled to see and hear a black American musician playing rock music that clearly drew on African American traditions like the blues. Hendrix and Chandler put together the Jimi Hendrix Experience, and Hendrix experienced his first large-scale success with the album *Are You Experienced?* (1967), which spent thirty-three weeks on the charts in the U.K.

TECHNOLOGY

Hendrix developed his own version of the stage antics of R&B performers and also extended their brilliant playing with his own groundbreaking virtuosity. In his performances he played his guitar with his teeth, stroked the guitar neck as if making love to it, and, on occasion, set his guitar on fire or destroyed it on stage. While often drawing on long-established blues and R&B forms, styles, and melodies, he manipulated and transformed the sound of his guitar using a **fuzz box** (an effects pedal that distorts timbre), a wah-wah pedal, and other effects pedals along with feedback and stacked Marshall amplifiers turned up to maximum volume, producing the extreme loudness that is part of what distinguishes rock from other genres. **Feedback** happens when an audio input, like an electric guitar or a microphone, receives the sound from an audio output, like a speaker, in a loop, which often results in a high-pitched screeching sound. Though the sound of guitar feedback in his time was typically avoided as undesirable, Hendrix's innovative use of it continues today in many subgenres of rock music.

EMOTIONAL RESONANCE

At the Woodstock Festival in 1969, where hundreds of thousands of young people gathered ostensibly in the name of peace and love to hear their favorite musicians, Hendrix performed a set of music full of his songs and guitar improvisations pointing to influences from the blues and jazz. In the midst of the set he unleashed perhaps his most famous single performance, a solo guitar rendition of the American national anthem complete with gritty, loud, and distorted effects that expressed iconically the violence of "the rockets red glare, the bombs bursting in air." The sonic symbolism of patriotism in the national anthem combined with the horrible sounds of war to capture the tension inherent in the times: most people at some level love their country but many youth at the festival had come to despise their leaders, who had built a nuclear arsenal and had led the nation into a pointless and unjust war in Southeast Asia. It was as if Hendrix was reclaiming the national anthem for anti-war youth and musically redefining what it might mean to be an American.

An interest in alternative lifestyles led some rock bands and artists during the 1960s to create a subgenre called psychedelic rock, among them Big Brother and the Holding Company (featuring Janis Joplin [1943–1970]), the Grateful Dead and Jefferson Airplane of the San Francisco scene, and the Beatles starting with their album *Revolver* (1966). Produced using new studio technologies and influenced by the enigmatic lyrics of Bob Dylan, their music seemed to replicate (and often accompanied) parts of the multisensory experience induced by psychedelic drugs such as LSD, which can include such sensations as "hearing colors" or "tasting sounds." In a nod to alternative religions, some psychedelic rock musicians incorporated the the sounds of the North Indian *sitar* and *tabla* into their recordings. Among the most famous examples are the Beatles' "Love You To" from *Revolver* (1966) and the Rolling Stones' "Paint it Black" (1966) (see Chapter 4, Gateway 16).

FIGURE 12.8
Jimi Hendrix performing at Woodstock in 1969
Source: Getty Images / Barry Z Levine.

Rock music continues to be an important part of the popular music scene today. During the last forty years the Irish band U2, the American Bruce Springsteen and his E Street Band, and the British band Radiohead, to name just a few, have all enjoyed tremendous commercial success performing diverse styles of rock, selling millions of albums, and filling stadiums the world over. Many of them have engaged with the political and social issues of their times. Springsteen, for example, has given voice to the plight of the working class, including Vietnam veterans, in the United States, conferring

CULTURAL LINKAGES

on them a measure of dignity. Radiohead, realizing the negative effects that large-scale tours have on the environment, have curtailed their touring so that their carbon emissions and environmental impact are minimal. They have also experimented with business models that allow fans to download certain albums and pay whatever they think is a fair price.

Beyond the commercial mainstream, other genres have grown out of rock since the 1960s. Heavy metal and its countless subgenres emerged around 1970, and metal musicians have explored extremes in loudness, distortion, and guitar virtuosity, to the delight of their communities of fans. In the 1970s punk rock developed as a reaction against the elaborate performances of popular rock bands like Led Zeppelin and Pink Floyd. The music of punk bands like the Ramones and the Patti Smith Group from the U.S. and the Sex Pistols and the Clash from the U.K. featured a do-it-yourself ethic, stripped-down simple songs, and lyrics that were anti-establishment in nature. The independent record labels and underground scenes that developed in the wake of punk led to the umbrella term

FIGURE 12.9
The Smashing Pumpkins in 1993 (from left, D'Arcy Wretzky, Jimmy Chamberlin, Billy Corgan, and James Iha)
Source: Getty Images / Paul Bergen / Redferns.

alternative rock, which emerged in the 1980s and burst into the mainstream in the 1990s with the popularity of groups like the Seattle grunge bands Nirvana and Pearl Jam and the Chicago band Smashing Pumpkins.

Rock music was the dominant form of popular music from the mid-1950s to the mid-1970s, but it is no longer as central as it once was. Today it is one of many types of popular music enjoyed by wide audiences. Rock bands from the 1960s, 1970s, 1980s, and 1990s continue to re-form for reunion tours to perform for fans who have aged with them and for new, younger fans who have become interested in their music. Beyond these reunion tours and the commercially successful artists and bands nominated for Grammys and other major awards in rock categories each year, countless bands and audiences form smaller scenes in cities around the world as people continue to find meaning and inspiration from the rock bands of today.

WHERE DO I GO FROM HERE?

- Listen to "Johnny B. Goode" by Chuck Berry for musical elements of the blues. Does the timbre of his electric guitar sound similar to the guitar timbres of any contemporary music that you know?

- Listen to Bob Dylan's original version of "All along the Watchtower" (1967) and compare it to Hendrix's version. How does Hendrix's version enhance (or detract from) the meaning of the song?

- Listen to "Voodoo Child (Slight Return)" or some other tracks from Hendrix's *Electric Ladyland*. How does his playing mark the music as psychedelic rock? Are there connections to the blues and R&B?

- Listen to some tracks from *Nevermind* (1991) by Nirvana, *Ten* (1991) by Pearl Jam, or *Siamese Dream* (1993) by Smashing Pumpkins. To what extent does it seem like the musical elements, including the lyrics, build on the recordings and songwriting of Hendrix, Dylan, and others you might be familiar with? How do they depart from earlier versions of rock?

- Do you have any favorite groups that might be considered indie or alternative rock bands? Explore some of their interviews or social media activity and see if you can figure out how they are they connected to their predecessors in rock music.

GATEWAY 50
NEW DIRECTIONS IN JAZZ

What Is It?

During the 1950s, 1960s, and 1970s, jazz musicians reacted in a variety of ways to bebop's innovations. Some wanted to simplify its harmonic complexities, while others wanted to push those harmonic complexities to their limits. Some wanted melodies rather than harmonies to structure improvisation, while others wanted to expand possibilities in rhythm and tempo. Still others wanted to explore overlaps between jazz and popular music in ways that were exciting to both musicians and audiences. Tenor saxophonist John Coltrane (1926–1967) was involved in several of these directions in jazz, and his recording titled "Acknowledgement," the opening part to his album *A Love Supreme* (released in 1965), is our gateway to jazz in this period. *A Love Supreme* is a suite in four parts: "Acknowledgment," "Resolution," "Pursuance," and "Psalm." This recording features Coltrane on tenor saxophone, Jimmy Garrison (1934–1976) on upright bass, Elvin Jones (1927–2004) on drums, and McCoy Tyner (b. 1938) on piano. From 1962 to 1965 this group of musicians constituted John Coltrane's regular quartet, which later became known in jazz circles as Coltrane's "Classic Quartet." One of the many reasons the quartet is "classic" is that *A Love Supreme* was a widely successful album with broad appeal beyond jazz audiences. It sold a half a million copies by 1970—a great deal more than was typical for jazz albums at the time—and many more since then.

 Listen to the first thirty seconds of the recording.

How Does It Work?

Timbre

The sounds on this recording consist of John Coltrane's tenor saxophone, an upright bass, a piano, and a drum set with prominent cymbals (a gong also opens the recording). At the end of "Acknowledgement," John Coltrane's voice is heard, repeatedly singing the words "A Love Supreme."

Texture

The main texture here is solo saxophone with rhythm section accompaniment. The piano plays chords rhythmically, a process called **comping** (short for "accompanying"), the bass plays either a four-note ostinato or an improvised bass line, and the drums provide a steady groove.

FIGURE 12.10
John Coltrane in the early 1960s
Source: Everett Collection Inc / Alamy Stock Photo.

Rhythm

After a mostly nonmetrical introduction, a steady pulse is introduced by a bass ostinato and then picked up by the drums. At first the drums play a beat seemingly inspired by Afro-Latin sensibilities with elaborate syncopation in the ride cymbal. Throughout the recording, this type of groove continues, though Elvin Jones occasionally adds a slight swing feel on the ride cymbal. Coltrane's soloing sometimes lines up rhythmically with the rhythm section, but at other times he seems to be playing nonmetrically over the steady pulse.

Melody

The melodies of the saxophone are structured mostly around a minor pentatonic mode. The basis for many of the melodies Coltrane plays is a short, ascending three-note phrase that begins with an ascending minor third and an ascending whole step. He elaborates this phrase starting on various pitches at various times of the recording.

Harmony

For the most part, "Acknowledgement" is an example of improvisation over a particular mode, in this case a minor pentatonic. The musicians do not continue playing in this "home key" throughout the composition, but often modulate phrases and harmonies chromatically and to keys that are distantly related to this key. Near the end of the recording, the home key shifts down a step to set up a new harmonic structure for the following movement in the *A Love Supreme* suite.

Form

"Acknowledgment" begins with a nonmetrical introduction followed by a long, seemingly open-ended improvisation. With closer attention, however, it is evident that the improvisation is structured into five sections that are built of 4-, 8-, and 16-bar components.

Performance Techniques

The musicians can be heard responding to one another, increasing and decreasing rhythmic and dynamic intensity together, and sometimes playing in similar ranges to one another as they improvise over the structure of the composition.

Listen to the entire performance with these elements in mind while following the timed listening guide.

LISTENING GUIDE 12.2

TIME	SECTION	DESCRIPTION
0:00	Introduction	A gong, a piano chord, and a pedal tone on the bass open the recording. Coltrane enters playing nonmetrically, improvising over a pentatonic scale. He emphasizes intervals of a fourth while the drummer plays a roll on the cymbals and the piano plays a number of block chords ascending and descending through the range of the piano, also nonmetrically.
0:31		The bass enters playing a four-note ostinato. It establishes the tonality of the composition, moving from the tonic to the minor third, back to the tonic and up to the fourth. These are the first three pitches of the minor pentatonic scale.
0:40		The drums establish a pulse, playing a highly syncopated groove in an Afro-Latin style.
0:48		The piano enters, playing harmonies based on the interval of a fourth.
1:03	Section 1 (32 bars)	Even though Coltrane's improvisation may seem open-ended and completely free-form, there is a fairly regular organized structure that the musicians are creating (and following) that can be heard. Coltrane begins this first section with a three-pitch arch-shaped phrase (A). This phrase is part of a pentatonic scale and forms the basis for much of his improvisation. Sometimes in this section he is playing rhythmically with the groove; at other times he is playing quickly and nonmetrically throughout a wide range of the saxophone. He ends this section with a sustained, accented high pitch.
2:05	Section 2 (48 bars)	Coltrane introduces several statements of a new, ascending three-pitch phrase (B) based on the pentatonic scale, though he also plays it in many keys outside of the pentatonic scale. The piano follows the solo, playing chords outside of the tonic key with Coltrane. In the middle of this section Coltrane ascends to another high pitch, played with a rough, strained timbre.
3:37	Section 3 (40 bars)	Coltrane plays phrase B and fragments of phrase A in a number of keys. He ascends to a number of repeating high pitches, playing with a rough timbre and bringing his solo to a climax. At the end of this section he descends into the middle and lower range of the saxophone, improvising not as rapidly, and mostly in the home key.
4:54	Section 4 (36 bars)	Coltrane plays the opening four-note ostinato twice in the home key before a long section where he only plays this ostinato, but modulates it into all twelve keys throughout much of the register of the saxophone and plays it in a number of rhythms as well as nonmetrically before returning to repeat it in the home key.
6:03	Section 5 (20 bars)	A strong chord in the piano announces this last section, where we hear several overdubbed layers of Coltrane's voice singing the ostinato to the words "a love supreme." From here until the end of the recording, the drums intermix and sometimes alternate the polyrhythmic Afro-Latin groove with a swing feel—heard in swung subdivisions of the beat in the ride cymbal and a hi-hat closing on beats two and four. The bass also plays the ostinato as it did at the beginning of the recording and the home key shifts down a step for the whole band.
6:41	Coda	The vocal drops out, and the bass plays a three-note version of the ostinato, with the piano comping and the drums alternating between a swing feel and the Afro-Latin polyrhythmic groove. The piano fades out and then the drums, leaving the bass to a brief improvisation based on this three-note ostinato. The recording ends with the bass playing briefly in a rubato tempo before strumming an open fifth in the new home key.
7:41	End	

What Does It Mean?

There are many ways to understand "Acknowledgement" and *A Love Supreme*, but Coltrane provides a useful starting point in the liner notes to the album. He writes about a spiritual awakening in 1957 that led him to a rich, full, and productive life: "through the merciful hand of God, I do perceive and have been fully reinformed of his omnipotence. It is truly a love supreme." Coltrane was interested in a number of religions, and many believe that "Acknowledgment" points to his particular affinity for Islam. He does not specify a particular religion here, but he wants his listeners to know that this album is about a spiritual path. Its elements can be interpreted in light of that broad meaning, which also comes through in the title to each part.

The form of "Acknowledgement" is organized around the way that Coltrane approaches three short melodic phrases: the four-note ostinato, three-note phrase A, and three-note phrase B. Though the ostinato in the bass is heard for the first time after the introduction, the full statement of the four-note phrase is not revealed until the end of the recording in Section 5, where Coltrane's voice sings the ostinato with the words "a love supreme." His singing reveals that this four-note ostinato expresses this supreme spiritual love. In Section 4, Coltrane plays the "a love supreme" phrase without melodic embellishment in all keys and all around the range of the saxophone. This is the only time he performs this type of unembellished modulation of a given theme, which suggests that this is not spontaneously improvised, but part of a preconceived compositional structure.

Coltrane's saxophone solo, in broad strokes, starts with a brief fragment of the love supreme ostinato in Section 1, explores the possibilities of that fragment in search of the full statement of the ostinato in Sections 2 and 3, takes the ostinato into all possible keys in Section 4, and experiences a revelation of the full ostinato with text in Section 5. In one sense, this is an "Acknowledgement" that this spiritual "love supreme" is always present, often underlying everything he does, but only revealed in full after a period of searching and exploration. This love supreme is not only always present, but it is everywhere. It can be found in every key and it can be transformed into new and different forms. The form of "Acknowledgement" can also be understood as challenging the linear structure so often heard both in jazz when soloists improvise over a head or a repeating chord progression and in European classical music in forms like theme and variations or sonata form. Even though the bass performs the ostinato early on, the listener doesn't realize that it is the main theme, or head, until it appears at the end. This cyclical approach has antecedents in the blues and other African American forms, as well as in many African musical traditions (Central Africa in Chapter 1, Gateway 1 and Shona music in Chapter 3, Gateway 10). If the form of "Acknowledgement" is a cycle, from Coltrane's spiritual perspective it could be heard as a returning to the divine, the love supreme, over and over, with periods of search and exploration in between each return.

Other musical elements suggest Coltrane's spiritual search in "Acknowledgement." On several occasions Coltrane performs in a high register with a rough or strained timbre. The high register of the saxophone, combined with the rough timbre, sounds as though Coltrane is exerting a lot of energy, in the same way that a singer would strain to sing or shout high pitches. It may be an expression of anguish or strife, or striving connected to overcoming the difficulties and hardships encountered in the search for spiritual wholeness. The rough timbre also is a continuation of the value African and African American musicians have placed on buzzing timbres in jazz, in Jimi Hendrix's guitar effects, and in the Shona *mbira dzavadzimu* (Chapter 3, Gateway 10), where added buzzing effects connected musicians and listeners to the spiritual world.

 Listen to "Acknowledgement" again, this time listening for appearances of the "A Love Supreme" ostinato and thinking about how Coltrane explores and transforms it before it is fully revealed when Coltrane's vocal enters.

"Acknowledgement" also demonstrates one way jazz musicians were responding to the harmonic complexities of bebop. It is called **modal jazz**, that is, jazz based on improvising over melodic modes rather than quickly moving chord progressions. Some musicians wondered what might be expressed if they improvised with a given mode as the underlying framework over long periods of time. In "Acknowledgement" the minor pentatonic provides this modal basis for improvisation. Coltrane, McCoy Tyner, and Jimmy Garrison take advantage of this underlying constant mode by not only experimenting with different harmonic and melodic formulations based on the pentatonic scale, but by venturing outside of that scale while some of the other musicians may continue in the "home key." Coltrane does this many times as he takes phrases A and B to other keys chromatically distant from the home key. Sometimes Tyner and Garrison follow him to these distant tonalities, but sometimes they remain in the home key. On a few occasions, the three musicians come back together in the home key after venturing out of it for a while, in another demonstration of cyclical motion that may be an icon of a spiritual journey.

What Is Its History?

Born in North Carolina, Coltrane first learned music in community and high school bands there and in Philadelphia, where he moved in his teens. After serving in the Navy at the end of World War II, he returned to Philadelphia where he honed his musical skills and studied jazz theory, before he moved to New York. There, he started playing with some of the leading figures in the bebop scene, including Thelonious Monk. In some of his music, he was interested in developing the harmonic complexities of bebop, which he did on one of his most-admired albums, *Giant Steps* (1960). The tempo of the recording of its title track, "Giant Steps," is nearly 300 beats per minute, and the harmony changes every two beats for much of the form, sometimes between chords that are distantly related to one another in ways that would be unfamiliar to bebop players accustomed to improvising over jazz standards. This presents enormous difficulties for improvisers as they seek to play fluid lines informed by bebop sensibilities that move rapidly among harmonies that shift to distant key centers far more quickly than they ever would in bebop. Coltrane and others were pushing the conventions of bebop to its harmonic limits, and "Giant Steps" still challenges students learning how to play jazz today to be able to improvise smoothly over quickly changing chord progressions.

FIGURE 12.11
Miles Davis in 1970
Source: Pictorial Press Ltd / Alamy Stock Photo.

Coltrane recorded *Giant Steps* in May, 1959, just a few weeks after recording the most well-known album of modal jazz titled *Kind of Blue* (1959) led by trumpet player Miles Davis. "So What," the first track from *Kind of Blue*, is a modal composition in AABA form. One mode underlies the entire form. The only change is that the B section is a half-step higher than the A section. It maintains the head–solos–head overall form and the AABA form, both of which connect it to the common practices in form already established in jazz. Each of the other musicians performing on "So What" made significant contributions to various streams of jazz in this period beyond *Kind of Blue*: Paul Chambers on bass, Jimmy Cobb on drums, Bill Evans on piano, Julian "Cannonball" Adderley on alto saxophone, and John Coltrane on tenor saxophone.

In another reaction to the complexities of bebop, some jazz musicians brought elements of rhythm and blues, soul, and rock 'n' roll into their music (Chapter 12, Gateway 49). **Hard bop** is a style of jazz that featured the rhythms of gospel and rhythm and blues, memorable and simple bluesy melodies, and an aggressive, driving pulse in the drums that often accented beats two and four (known as the "backbeat") in a four-beat measure. It departed from the virtuosic fast-tempo conventions of bebop, favoring instead slower tempos and simpler melodies, though it continued the head–solos–head form and complex harmonies for improvisation that characterized bebop. These elements arguably made hard bop recordings more understandable and appealing to larger audiences, and some of these recordings sold at a much higher rate than recordings in other jazz styles.

The drummer Art Blakey (1919–1990), along with the pianist Horace Silver (1928–2014) formed a group called the Jazz Messengers in 1953. Their style of hard bop emphasized bebop harmonic elements. In 1956 Horace Silver left the group to develop his own music emphasizing the R&B and gospel elements of hard bop and enjoyed commercial success with his album *Song for My Father* (1965). Art Blakey and the Jazz Messengers continued to perform hard bop until Blakey's death in 1990, with a wide variety of musicians performing in the group in its many years of existence, including the trumpet player Wynton Marsalis. The group's recording "Moanin'" (1958) is a classic example of a bluesy, memorable hard bop head followed by bebop-oriented improvised solos. John Coltrane also participated in hard bop, and his album *Blue Train* (1958) is considered to be among his most significant contributions to that style.

FIGURE 12.12
Herbie Hancock in 1974
Source: Heritage Image Partnership Ltd /
Alamy Stock Photo.

Miles Davis was particularly active in this period. He had performed in the bebop style with Charlie Parker and others and was at the forefront of the development of several jazz styles after bebop: modal jazz with albums like *Kind of Blue* and *Milestones* (1958) recorded with his "First Great Quintet," some early iterations of hard bop, and in another style of jazz known as "cool jazz" typically associated with jazz musicians from the west coast like the pianist Dave Brubeck (1920–2012) and the baritone saxophonist Gerry Mulligan (1927–1996), as well as East Coast-based musicians such as the pianist Lennie Tristano (1919–1978), the saxophonist Lee Konitz (b. 1927), and the pianist John Lewis and his Modern Jazz Quartet. Davis' so-called "Second Great Quintet," with Wayne Shorter (b. 1933) on tenor saxophone, Herbie Hancock (b. 1940) on piano/keyboards, Tony Williams (1945–1997) on drums, and Ron Carter (b. 1937) on bass, included more open forms for improvisation that relied on a metric pulse but very little harmonic structure for improvisation on albums such as *Miles Smiles* (1966). Transitional albums with some of the same musicians, *Filles de Kilimanjaro* (1968) and *In a Silent Way* (1969), began to explore electronic sounds and demonstrate a stylistic shift towards the rhythms and timbres of rock.

Davis' album *Bitches Brew* (1970) is the most famous example of how he combined elements of rock and jazz in what became known as jazz fusion, a genre label indicating how jazz styles were blended with rock and funk (though of course musicians have explored many other types of stylistic fusions with jazz). The rhythm section for *Bitches Brew* is extensive and includes two bass players, two to three drummers, two to three electric keyboard players, and a percussionist, plus many wind players, often all playing simultaneously. On the album Davis also employed new technologies common in rock, such as effects pedals and post-recording editing techniques where he spliced together and layered recorded materials on top of one another. In using these techniques Davis took cues from innovations of the guitarist Jimi Hendrix. Though the album sold over a half million copies, some critics and audiences responded negatively to *Bitches Brew*, believing that it compromised the purity of jazz. But since jazz has always involved the overlap and influence of many

FIGURE 12.13
Wayne Shorter in 1976
Source: Heritage Image Partnership Ltd /
Alamy Stock Photo.

FIGURE 12.14
The Ornette Coleman Quartet in New York in 1971.
Left to right: drummer Ed Blackwell (1929–1992), tenor
saxophonist Dewey Redman (1931–2006), Ornette
Coleman, and bassist Charlie Haden (1937–2014)
Source: Getty Images / Val Wilmer / Redferns.

musical styles and traditions, the search for some "pure" essence of jazz is likely futile. Many musicians were inspired to take jazz fusion further in the years after *Bitches Brew*. Herbie Hancock and Wayne Shorter both pursued projects in jazz fusion, Hancock with his album *Head Hunters* (1973) and many others (Chapter 1, Gateway 1), and Shorter with his band Weather Report, active in the 1970s and early 1980s.

After *A Love Supreme*, Coltrane pursued an even more avant-garde agenda in his albums *Meditations* (1966) and *Ascension* (1966), both of which continued his expression of the spiritual in music and experimented with improvisation over a loose harmonic framework, sometimes without a constant pulse. At the same time, other musicians began to question the common formal, harmonic, and rhythmic structures in jazz as they developed what was first known as "The New Thing," and later **free jazz**. Saxophonist Ornette Coleman (1930–2015) was prominent in this movement, and his 1961 album *Free Jazz* gave the style its name. His concept of "harmolodics" gives equal weight to melody, harmony, and rhythm in the development of improvised musical ideas. Often structuring his improvisation around melodic phrase shapes, he at times departed from the harmonic structures and steady pulse that had characterized jazz since its beginnings. Coltrane hints at this kind of approach in "Acknowledgement," in which his improvisation is based on transformations and permutations of phrases A and B rather than a particular harmonic structure. But Coleman took it further in the course of a long career that continued for nearly fifty years after Coltrane's tragic death from cancer at the age of forty.

Both individual musicians and so-called collectives developed The New Thing and free jazz during the 1960s and 1970s, chief among them the pianists Cecil Taylor (1929–2018) and Paul Bley (1932–2016), the saxophonist Albert Ayler (1936–1970), the Association for the Advancement of Creative Musicians (AACM), and the Art Ensemble of Chicago. Founded in 1965 on Chicago's South Side, the AACM and its members have experimented adventurously with combining avant-garde jazz, classical music, and music of various traditions of the world into new forms. In the context of the Civil Rights Movement, the AACM was one of many examples of African American artists and communities coming together to forge pathways towards a world of equal rights. AACM cofounder

FIGURE 12.15
Art Ensemble of Chicago around 1980
Source: Getty Images / Tom Copi / Michael Ochs Archives.

and pianist-composer Muhal Richard Abrams (1930–2017) and early member trumpet player John Shenoy Jackson (1923–1985) stated in the early 1970s that part of the AACM's intention was "to show how the disadvantaged and the disenfranchised can come together and determine their own strategies for political and economic freedom, thereby determining their own destinies."[71] The Art Ensemble of Chicago, affiliated with the AACM, did so in their lengthy performances that included improvisation, climactic moments featuring blues or other forms from past iterations of jazz, and performances on dozens of whistles, bells, and percussion instruments scattered all over the stage that referenced traditional music of Africa. The musicians also used elaborate makeup and theatrical dress to show that the stage was a place where collective performance was a ritual of sorts, a special experience separate and different from everyday life.

FIGURE 12.16
Charles Mingus in the 1970s
Source: CSU Archives / Everett Collection Historical / Alamy Stock Photo.

All this experimentation with the underpinnings of jazz seems like an indirect, implicit challenge to the authority of tradition being worked out explicitly by demonstrators on the streets of America. One jazz artist who explicitly referenced the politics of the period was bassist Charles Mingus (1922–1979) in a composition called "Fables of Faubus" (1959). It includes lyrics denouncing the Governor of Arkansas, Orval E. Faubus, who in 1957 had mobilized the Arkansas National Guard to prevent the integration of nine black students into previously all-white Little Rock Central High School. In response, U.S. President Dwight Eisenhower ordered the 101st Airborne Division of the U.S. Army to protect and escort the "Little Rock Nine" to school. Mingus' composition uses humor, improvisation, and many elements of existing jazz styles to condemn Faubus' racism as "ridiculous," to use a word from the composition. Countless other recordings and performances in jazz during this period challenged racial injustice, among them Abbey Lincoln's stirring and powerful wordless vocals on "Triptych: Prayer/Protest/Peace" from Max Roach's *We Insist: Freedom Now Suite* (1960) and "Mississippi Goddam" (1964) and other music by the pianist and vocalist Nina Simone.

John Coltrane was not himself particularly politically active or vocal, but he did view his music as a conscious attempt to make change, whether that change was political, social, musical, or personal. His album *A Love Supreme* inspired many musicians, some of whom would take more overt political stances in the context of the New Thing and free jazz. Since Coltrane passed away in 1967, his life and music have touched countless musicians and audiences and the styles of jazz they enjoy as they connect music to other meaningful aspects of their lives.

WHERE DO I GO FROM HERE?

* Listen to "Pursuance" and "Psalm," two of the other three parts of the *A Love Supreme* suite. Listen for how the melody of "Pursuance" begins with statements of phrase A from "Acknowledgement," and sets up a clear 12-bar blues form at a fast tempo. The fourth part, "Psalm," has been interpreted as an expression of a poem that Coltrane wrote in the liner notes, also titled "A Love Supreme," in a recitation of the poem on saxophone, without words. Some have interpreted the way he expresses the words as melodies as analogous to how an African American preacher might phrase a line of text when addressing a congregation. Try reading Coltrane's poem along with "Psalm," beginning with the title "A Love Supreme," and match the text to the way he is expressing it on the saxophone.

* Listen to "Giant Steps" and follow along with Coltrane's improvisation over the rapidly changing harmonies. How does this compare to his playing on "Acknowledgement"? How does it compare to the kind of improvisation you heard in the gateway to bebop (Chapter 11, Gateway 46)?

- Listen to "Moanin'" by Art Blakey and the Jazz Messengers. How is the head influenced by the blues? What are the rhythmic and melodic elements that might have made this recording appealing to a wide audience? To what extent do the improvised solos share musical characteristics with bebop?

- Listen to all or part of *Bitches Brew* by Miles Davis. What are some of the elements that point to the fusion of jazz and rock in this recording?

- Find a recording of Ornette Coleman from any period. How do its harmonic structures, rhythms, pulse, or other musical elements suggest that this recording could be considered "free jazz"?

- Listen to "Watermelon Man" from Herbie Hancock's *Head Hunters* album. The introduction is a reference to hocketing among Central African foragers that we heard in Chapter 1, Gateway 1. In this example of jazz fusion, what various musical traditions or styles does Hancock seem to be fusing? Which parts of this recording are most appealing to you and why?

- Listen to "Fables of Faubus" by Charles Mingus, "Triptych Prayer/Protest/Peace" by Abbey Lincoln, and "Mississippi Goddam" by Nina Simone. Compare the musical elements the musicians use in their approaches to and expressions of protest of racial injustice.

- Read some excerpts from the book *John Coltrane: His Life and Music* by Lewis Porter, upon which much of this gateway is based. What other aspects of Coltrane's music and his life are interesting to you?

GATEWAY 51
THE CLASSICAL AVANT-GARDE

What Is It?

Avant-garde, a French word, means vanguard, the military unit placed at the front of an army, leading the way forward. Used to describe art, it has some of the sense of modernism. It refers to those artists who are pushing forward against the resistance of tradition. Between 1950 and 1975 the avant-garde in music was ascendent in classical music. Our gateway to this kind of music from 1950 to 1975 is *In C*, composed by Terry Riley (b. 1935) in 1964.

The title is an ironic reference to the history of European music since the Baroque period. In that tradition, the phrase "in C" refers to a piece in the key of C major within the system of tonality and its twelve major and twelve minor keys (Chapter 5, Gateway 20). In this piece the harmony implied by the name is static. It abandons the tension of moves to related keys and the release of a return to the tonic via an authentic cadence. Instead, the C of this piece is a fast-tempo, repeated, pulsating drone that the pianist plays on a high-pitched C throughout the entire piece. This performance features familiar classical instruments including the oboe, bassoon, trumpet (played by Terry Riley), clarinet, saxophone, flute, viola, trombone, vibraphone (a struck, keyed idiophone with metal bars), and a marimbaphone (a struck, keyed idiophone with metal bars).

🔊 **Listen to the first thirty seconds of the recording.**

FIGURE 12.17
Terry Riley around 1972
Source: Philippe Gras / Alamy Stock Photo.

How Does It Work?

Timbre

The timbre is created by the collective sound of the instruments mentioned above playing together. Overall the timbre seems quite bright and even a bit metallic.

Texture

The texture begins with a pulsating drone played solo on the piano and evolves into a complex contrapuntal texture before ending on a drone on C. All the instrumentalists play the same melody, each entering one after the other. The resulting texture is created by an odd sort of round, a particular type of imitative polyphony.

Rhythm

The rhythm consists of a constant fast pulse without a strong sense of meter. The durations the instrumentalists play range for very short to very long, held tones.

Melody

The melody consists of many very short melodic motives or patterns using nine pitches: the seven pitches of the C major scale (C D E F G A B) plus F♯ and B♭. This pitch collection is a bow to the tonal system since the F♯ is the accidental needed to produce a major scale on the dominant (V = G major) and B♭ is the accidental needed to produce a major scale on the subdominant (IV = F major).

Harmony

The harmony is based on the drone tone and chords produced by the pitches the instrumentalists play. The first harmony is the interval of a third (C-E), followed by a three-pitch chord (C-E-F), then a four-pitch chord (C-E-F-G), and so on until all nine pitches may be heard simultaneously.

Form

If musical form is a metaphor for shape, then *In C* has a temporal almond shape. It begins with a drone, thickens as the instruments enter one by one, reaches its full extent, tapers off as instruments complete their set of melodic patterns, and ends with the drone tone. The length of the performance is not specified, but recorded performances average about forty minutes and take between twenty and seventy-five minutes.

Performance Techniques

Riley gives a great deal of freedom to the performers. Instead of handing them a score that determines what they will play, as European composers had for centuries, he gives them instructions. These instructions allow them a great deal of freedom as to how they choose to play the piece. As a result, the form of the performance is unpredictable. This approach to composition is called **indeterminacy**. The players are given a score with fifty-three short melodic patterns numbered from one to fifty-three. They are instructed to enter when they like and play each pattern in its numbered order as many times as they like before going on to play the next pattern, until they have played all fifty-three patterns. They are asked to listen to the other musicians and together try to create interesting rhythmic, melodic, and harmonic musical events as the piece progresses from beginning to end. The result is a piece whose performed form is unknown in advance and varies with each performance.

Listen to the first minute of this recording for the successive entrances of each instrument.

Listen to the first six minutes of the recording following this timed listening guide.

LISTENING GUIDE 12.3

TIME	DESCRIPTION
0:00	The piano plays a constant pulse on a high-pitched C.
0:07	Marimba and trumpet enter with the first melodic pattern: an ornament on C leading to an E.
1:07	The second and third patterns are introduced, both based on EFE, EFE.
1:45	The fourth and fifth patterns are introduced, both based on EFG, EFG.
3:26	The sixth pattern is introduced: a long-held C.
4:05	The seventh pattern is introduced, a rapid rhythmic motive on C, CCC, played every nine beats.
5:16	The eighth pattern is introduced: a long-held G that descends to a long-held F.
5:57	The ninth and tenth patterns are introduced: short, fast, two-note motives on the pitches BG.
And so on	Patterns 10 to 53 are introduced in order.
41:55	End

What Does It Mean?

AESTHETICS

In C can be understood for the way it is situated within the social, political, and artistic iconoclasm of the 1950s and 1960s. Just as rock musicians and their fans railed against the social conservatism of the time and the politics of racial segregation and the war in Vietnam, Terry Riley and a few other composers carried on their own battle against the aesthetic powers that be in the world of classical music.

After World War II the composers who enjoyed the most prestige exploited Arnold Schoenberg's twelve-tone serialism and its successor system, **total serialism**, the organization of all elements of music, including timbre, texture, rhythm, and dynamics, into "rows" that provided the underlying logic of the composition. At one level these composers were creating a new balance among all these elements in a tradition that emphasized harmony and counterpoint more than all the other elements of music. At another level total serialism allowed them to control all the elements of the musical performance and to make the relationships among tones in a piece of music extraordinarily complex. That complexity can be explained, notated, and seen on paper. Unfortunately, ordinary listeners find the music baffling because, except for the timbre of familiar instruments, there are too few icons of previous musical experience. Predictable relationships among pitches, so crucial to most music, are avoided. Recognition of formal structure is almost impossible. And expressive devices such as dynamics are largely unpredictable. As a result many composers were losing their audience.

In the United States Milton Babbitt (1916–2011) was the leading exponent of total serialism. Early in his life he was equally devoted to mathematics and music and eventually become a specialist in twelve-tone composition and a pioneer of total serialism as a compositional technique. His music and that of other composers in this vein was unpopular with audiences. But in keeping with its intellectual orientation, it was, and to some extent still is, patronized by university music departments. Babbitt was an articulate spokesman for the idea that music should be the object of research in a university setting, and his work was an attempt to question the nature of music and its possibilities. In a famous essay he titled "The Composer as Specialist" published in 1958 in *High Fidelity*, a magazine for audiophiles, he argued that music was more than entertainment and a pastime. It could be the subject of the same serious study as physics and mathematics. Just as quantum mechanics and the theory of relativity had placed the understanding of physics beyond the capacity of all but a few specialists to understand, it should be possible for compositions by an "informed composer" to reach that advanced stage. To achieve this "advanced music," he suggested that:

> the composer would do himself and his music an immediate and eventual service by total, resolute, and voluntary withdrawal from this public world to one of private performance and electronic media, [away from] the public and social aspects of musical composition. By so doing, the separation between the domains would be defined beyond any possibility of confusion of categories, and the composer would be free to pursue a private life of professional achievement, as opposed to a public life of unprofessional compromise and exhibitionism.

FIGURE 12.18
Milton Babbitt with an electronic music synthesizer, *c.* 1965
Source: Getty Images / Keystone / Stringer.

Given the importance of music for the social life of humankind over many millennia, his manifesto amounts to a radical redefinition of the nature of music. Ignoring the history of music as a fundamentally social experience, Babbitt redefined music as a product of individual minds seeking to understand all the possible complexity in the world of musical sound. Since he well knew that the public would not patronize this kind of music, he welcomed the university as its patron: "such a private life is what the university provides the scholar and the scientist. It is only proper that the university . . . should provide a home for the 'complex,' 'difficult,' and 'problematic' in music." The magazine's editors captured one sense of what Babbitt was saying when they, without asking him, published his essay with the title "Who Cares If You Listen?" Although Babbitt was annoyed and claimed that that was not what he intended, his essay clearly implies that, while he may have hoped that a few souls with "special preparation can understand the most advanced work," he wanted to separate himself and his music from the readership of *High Fidelity* magazine and most music lovers. As Babbitt hoped, universities provided just that possibility: they became, and still are, the principal patrons of composers of this kind of music. He taught at Princeton University and Columbia for many years, and he and his colleagues trained generations of students in the challenges of serialism. Musicians' interest in such challenges lives on today in a movement dubbed "the new complexity."

In C was a radical reaction against the prevailing prestige of total serialism and its complexity among professional, university-based composers of the period. It is based on a drone, which creates a solid foundation for listeners, rather than either tonal harmony or the dissonant harmonies of serialism. Its pulsatile rhythm drives the music in a way that resembles the constant beat of dance music. Its melodic patterns repeat over and over, setting up a comforting familiarity. Some listeners might find its harmonic tone clusters challenging, but the total package has an oddly familiar ring to it. During the 1960s young people, including many without any interest in classical music, found the music appealing, and Riley's compositions had an immediate crossover appeal with fans of rock and jazz.

In addition to its celebration of simplicity over complexity, *In C* is also a reaction against another feature of total serialism: the desire of composers to control musicians' performance decisions. *In C* refuses complete compositional control, delegating what actually happens in a performance to

> SOCIAL
> BEHAVIOR

the performers, who are given the freedom to create the work in concert with their fellow musicians. In his "performing directions" to performers, Riley wrote, "One of the joys of *In C* is the interaction of the players in polyrhythmic combinations that spontaneously arise between patterns. Some quite fantastic shapes will arise and disintegrate as the groups move through the piece when it is properly played." In the political and social environment of the period, it is not too much of a stretch to see the indeterminacy of Riley and other composers who adopted this principle as a kind of protest against composers' desire for total control in a way analogous to the protests on the street against political leaders and old systems of social control. All the same, in this piece Riley gave some control back to performers in a gesture that may be a metaphor for ordinary citizens marching in the streets of America's cities and towns to take back a measure of control from leaders orchestrating an unpopular war and opposing racial integration.

> **CULTURAL LINKAGES**

Finally, while *In C* sounds very different from the music produced by the procedures of twentieth-century total serialism and eighteenth- and nineteenth-century tonal music, it does sound like something familiar. It sounds a bit like both Javanese gamelan music and African music, both of which were being listened to in the countercultural American music scene of the 1960s. The constant pulse of *In C* is reminiscent of the pulsation of both Javanese and African music, and the idea of musicians improvising on a given pattern is an essential element of African music. This kind of iconicity links *In C* to the musical experience of many people during the 1960s, making it an index of such countercultural values of the period as resistance to authority and the seeking of alternative lifestyles, behaviors, and belief systems.

What Is Its History?

Riley did not invent musical expressions of resistance to authority during the 1960s. One of his inspirations was the music, and the thinking about music, of John Cage (1912–1992), a Californian who, starting in the late 1940s, had articulated in his compositions and writings an extreme version of an avant-garde alternative to the traditions of European classical music. Born in Los Angeles, he studied composition with Arnold Schoenberg, who had moved to the United States from Vienna in the 1930s. Schoenberg famously remarked that Cage was his most interesting student but that he was an inventor, not a composer. Among his inventions was the **prepared piano**, a piano into which screws and other objects are inserted between the strings to alter its timbre and emphasize its nature as a percussion instrument. Cage's *Sonatas and Interludes* for prepared piano (1946–1948) explore the resulting drum- and bell-like sounds in twenty-six short "sonatas" mostly in AABB form and four "interludes."

> **CULTURAL LINKAGES**

In the 1940s Cage began to read Hindu and Zen Buddhist philosophy, whose search for quietness and stillness greatly affected his music. His two most radical moves were to eliminate the composer's intention to form and control sounds, that is, the goal of most European composers for centuries,

and to focus listeners' attention not just on musical sound but on all sounds. For his 1951 *Music of Changes* for piano, Cage created charts in notation of tones, silences, dynamics, durations, and tempos. Instead of ordering them serially as Milton Babbitt might have, he ordered the elements of his notations randomly by tossing coins based on a prophetic technique outlined in the Chinese *Book of Changes* (the *I-Ching*). In so doing, he surrendered control over the final form of

FIGURE 12.19
John Cage performing in 1966
Source: Getty Images / Rowland Scherman.

the piece. This method of composition, which leaves the final form of the composition to chance, is called **aleatory** (or **aleatoric**) **composition**.

Cage's *Imaginary Landscapes No. 4*, also from 1951, was scored for twelve radios, twenty-four players, and a conductor. The score determined the overall length of the piece and which frequency (station or static noise) on the radio would be played when and at what volume. One player changes the frequency of each radio while the other controls the volume. The conductor cues the changes. The resulting sounds are indeterminate and vary with each performance.

His most remarked-upon indeterminate piece is called *4'33"*, first performed in 1952 at an outdoor music festival near Woodstock, New York. The score called for the performer to perform three movements, all of them *tacet*, a traditional musical direction in Latin for performers to remain silent. The resulting performance, a nonperformance in fact, focuses listeners' attention on what are usually the extraneous and annoying sounds of a concert: the ambient noise of the lighting and heating systems, the audience coughing and moving in their seats, and so on. At an outdoor concert venue such as the one for the premier of the work, the sounds would have been richly varied and random, including, perhaps, bird calls, dogs barking, children crying, the wind in the trees, and rain splattering on the ground. The composition questions the very nature of music and asks whether there is not also music, and thus lessons to be learned, in the seemingly random sounds of our environment, not just in the sounds that composers and performers intentionally organize in the name of music. Cage's compositions in this vein, like those of some other composers during this period, are perhaps more interesting to think about than to listen to, but they were deeply connected to avant-garde art and the political activism of the period. All were engaged in an intense and deep questioning of the fundamental assumptions on which everyday life, art, and music are based.

Both Cage and Babbitt and many other composers of this period were fascinated by the possibilities of manipulating electronically produced sound as Cage was in *Imaginary Landscapes No. 4*. Typically, they manipulated musical, natural, and other sounds recorded on tape recordings. Recording on tapes rather than discs was invented in Germany in the 1930s. By the 1950s the commercial music industry and university laboratories were using them, and reasonably priced tape recorders were available to home users. Tape recorders allowed composers to manipulate all kinds of sounds, not just musical sounds, by changing the speed of the tape, playing the tape backwards, combining different recorders in polyphony with themselves and live performers, and cutting up the tape and splicing it back together in a new order. In 1948 the French composer, writer, and scientist Pierre Schaeffer (1910–1995) dubbed this compositional process *musique concrète*. Composers using tape recordings could disassemble the sounds they had recorded by cutting the tapes to bits and building a composition from its "concrete" foundations: the elements of music that have helped us answer the question "how does it work" throughout this book. In collaboration with composer Pierre Henry (1927–2017), he created the first piece using these procedures: *Symphonie pour un seul homme* (Symphony for One Man).

During the early 1950s sounds produced by electronic oscillators became a new possibility for creating and manipulating sounds not available on acoustic instruments and that had never been heard before. Laboratories with machines that allowed the output of oscillators to be recorded, mixed, and edited on tape were established at Columbia University in New York and a number of other major cities around the world. Soon the oscillators were linked to a keyboard, and composers could control the waveform to alter the timbre of the sound in a process called **sound synthesis** on instruments called synthesizers. Milton Babbitt, working at the Columbia-Princeton Music Center in New York, was a leader in this movement. Some early work in this vein was composed exclusively for electronic sound. In some concerts the audience was faced with nothing but a stage full of speakers. Edgar Varèse (1883–1965) composed his *Poème électronique* as a sound installation for the Philips Radio Pavillion at the 1958 Brussels World's Fair. Other composers combined live performers with electronic and recorded sound. Milton Babbitt, for example, in his 1964 *Philomel*, set to music a dramatic story of sexual violence from the Roman poet Ovid's (43 BCE–*c.* 18 CE)

> AESTHETICS

> TECHNOLOGY

Metamorphoses, a collection of over 250 myths from the Ancient Greek and Roman world. He combined a live vocal soloist with electronic sounds, including bird calls and an echo of the singer's voice. In 1967 Canadian composer R. Murray Schafer, born in 1933, created a devastating evocation of nuclear war in *Threnody* (*Japanese Children*), a composition for children's choir, orchestra, and a tape recording of the sounds of war. Collages of electronic and recorded natural sounds and synthesized sounds challenged the boundaries of traditional definitions of music, just as Babbitt's total serialism and Cage's indeterminate, chance compositions had.

CULTURAL LINKAGES

World music provided yet another inspiration for new sounds in this period. Composers borrowed instruments and ideas about tuning and scales from these traditions, and some invented their own instruments to play the new sounds and scales that interested them. If East Coast Ivy League colleges patronized the complexities of serialism and electronic music, the more laid-back culture of the West Coast, and California in particular, was home to many of these experiments. Henry Cowell (1897–1965), born in Menlo Park, California, turned to world music in the 1950s and wrote two concertos for Japanese *koto* (plucked zither) in the 1970s. Lou Harrison (1917–2003), born in Portland, Oregon, was a student of Cowell, of Arnold Schoenberg, and of K. R. T. Wasitodiningrat, an important Javanese composer who taught at the California Institute of the Arts. He wrote for combinations of Asian and Western instruments and for Javanese gamelan. Harry Partch (1901–1974), born in Oakland and inspired by the microtonal pitch systems of Middle Eastern music, invented new musical instruments that could play a 43-pitch scale that he devised. His instruments included altered forms of the guitar, the Ancient Greek *kithara* (lyre), and the African marimba (xylophone), as well as whimsical percussion instruments made from cloud-chamber bowls used in physics labs and a set of suspended gourd bells he called a gourd tree.

AESTHETICS

It is in this restless, searching, experimental cultural and artistic environment that Riley's *In C* made its initial impression. Two other American composers echoed his approach to creating compositions that feature the ceaseless, pulsating repetition of a small number of musical elements: Steve Reich (b. 1936) and Philip Glass (b. 1937). Because their work seemed simple compared to the music going on around them and the music that preceded them in the eighteenth and nineteenth centuries, it came to be labeled **minimalism**, even though the procedures they employed could be quite complex and the length of their works quite long. In a related movement in the 1960s, "minimal art" reduced painting to color, shapes, and lines. Terry Riley's *In C* from 1964 is one of the first and most admired works in this style. In the 1970s Steve Reich followed jazz and popular musicians into the domain of world music, traveled to Africa, and began to compose pieces for percussion ensemble influenced by the polyrhythms of African music. Philip Glass, inspired by the *tala*s of Indian classical music, wrote pieces with short repetitive melodies, simple harmonies, and repeated rhythms for his own ensemble. The rhythmic drive of these three composers' works returned the avant-garde to one of music's most fundamental elements, rhythm, and, as a result, attracted a much larger following among the general public and fans of rock music and jazz than any of the other innovative streams that defined European and American classical music in this period.

Little of the experimental, avant-garde music of this period was composed for symphony orchestra or opera companies, not least because their audiences, oriented as they are to "classics" and "masterpieces," were not ready for such music. Composers used small ensembles to work out their ideas. Today the music of this period, with the exception of a few pieces by Riley, Reich, and Glass, is rarely performed and, when it is, relatively small venues like museum spaces and university recital halls are its home. A new kind of performing ensemble has arisen to give life to this kind of music and its successors

FIGURE 12.20
Harry Partch's Cloud-Chamber Bowls, a percussion instrument cut from large glass bottles
Source: HorsePunchKid, Wikimedia Commons.

today: the **new music ensemble**. Most university schools of music have them, and a few have a public following, including, in the United States, the Bang on a Can All-Stars, Eighth Blackbird, the Kronos Quartet, and the Philip Glass Ensemble. At the college level, the graduates of the Oberlin Conservatory Contemporary Music Ensemble have enjoyed notable success in this field.

WHERE DO I GO FROM HERE?

- Listen to a few of John Cage's *Sonatas and Interludes* for prepared piano and describe them in terms of the elements of music, with special attention to the timbres he creates.

- Read about and watch a video of a performance of Steve Reich's "Music for 18 Musicians" and comment on what elements in the performance hold your interest.

- Read about and watch videos of Philip Glass's opera *Einstein on the Beach*. Describe some of the sounds you hear and the relationship between the sounds and images.

- Listen to, or watch a video of, Milton Babbitt's *Philomel*, composed in the same year as *In C*, 1964, and compare the musical elements of performances of these two works.

- What kinds of electronic music technologies are you familiar with from the music that you listen to? Choose one electronic instrument or technology and see if you can trace its history back to the period between 1950 and 1975 (or earlier). Can you find some examples of the use of this technology? In what kinds of styles and genres has it been featured? Why do you think it has been common in those arenas and not others?

GATEWAY 52
SALSA

What Is It?

Salsa first emerged in New York City in the 1960s and 1970s as a popular Latin American dance music. While it has roots in Cuban musical genres and influences from jazz, it was first popular among New York's Puerto Rican (or "Nuyorican") community. Its practitioners have come from a number of Latin American countries. As a result, salsa has broad appeal in a wide variety of music cultures. The word salsa can be used in a number of ways: as a musical genre or style, as a collection of musical genres or styles, or as a style of dance, not to mention its other common use in reference to a spicy sauce.

FIGURE 12.21
Tito Puente performing on the *timbales* with his band in 1985
Source: Getty Images / Robert Alexander.

Our gateway to salsa is "Oye Como Va" by Nuyorican musician and international star Tito Puente (1923–2000), a song that contributed in part to the widespread popularity of salsa in the 1970s. "Oye Como Va" first appeared on Puente's 1963 album *El Rey: Bravo*. *El Rey* means "The King," and Puente was called "The King of the *timbales*" and "The King of Latin music" throughout his career. **Timbales** are single-headed drums with shallow metal bodies, usually tuned to higher pitches than the tom-toms of a drum set. During solos *timbaleros*, players of the *timbales*, produce a wide variety of timbres. When their role is to keep time, the *timbalero* plays cowbells, cymbals, and the shell of the *timbales* rather than striking the drum heads. Traditionally *timbales* were played in sets of two, but Tito Puente added more drums to the set, and today up to seven or eight *timbales* of different sizes often appear together in a set. Although Tito Puente was associated with salsa for much of his career, he at times rejected the genre label, often instead preferring to consider himself a musician in the vein of Latin jazz or *mambo*, a dance music that developed in Cuba in the 1930s.

The phrase "*oye como va*" is a greeting that means something like "hey, how's it going?" but, together with the next line of text, it is an invitation to listeners and dancers to "listen to how my rhythm goes." It's no wonder, then, that rhythm is one of the most intriguing and captivating aspects of "Oye Como Va," and of salsa music more broadly.

 Listen to the first thirty seconds of the recording.

How Does It Work?

Timbre

Varied timbres are produced on the *timbales*, cowbell, *bongos* (small hand drums), and *congas* (barrel-shaped drums), along with male vocals, flute, saxophones, trombones, and trumpets.

Texture

The rhythm section provides a repetitive groove that supports polyphonic melodic lines and ostinatos in the flute, vocals, and saxophone and brass sections.

Rhythm

The rhythm of "Oye Como Va" is established by a repeating two-bar syncopated ostinato at the beginning of the recording. Each instrument or voice that enters introduces a new syncopated rhythm, creating a polyrhythm with many layers.

Melody

The melodies are mostly in minor and minor pentatonic modes.

Harmony

The harmony mostly alternates between a minor i chord and the IV chord, both with upper extensions of the chords.

Form

The form alternates between instrumental sections and a vocal refrain, called a *coro*, from the Spanish for "chorus."

Performance Techniques

Though much of the material is pre-composed, the flute seems to be improvising many of its phrases.

Listen to the first thirty seconds of the recording with these elements in mind.

Listen to the entire recording following this timed listening guide.

LISTENING GUIDE 12.4

TIME	SECTION	DESCRIPTION	LYRICS
0:00	Introduction	A piano and some soft wind instruments begin playing repeating block chords in a two-measure syncopated pattern. The harmony, a minor i chord in the first measure and a IV chord in the second measure, is also outlined in the bass, which plays a slightly different syncopated rhythm. The sound of hand claps and some drum sticks struck together play yet another rhythm.	
0:15		After a brief percussion fill, the *timbales*, *bongos* and *congas* enter with more syncopated rhythms that repeat over the two-measure cycle. A trumpet and some trombones join the piano, playing its same rhythm and harmony.	
0:22		A flute enters playing a mostly stepwise minor melody that repeats over the two-measure cycle.	
0:38	Break	The polyrhythmic texture shifts to a homorhythmic one as the ensemble suddenly begins playing a syncopated rhythm all together for four measures.	
0:46	*Coro*	The polyrhythmic texture begins again (without the brass) and the vocals enter, singing a melody in a minor pentatonic mode. The flute answers each two-measure vocal phrase with a melody that begins with a descending one-octave jump.	Oye como va . . .
1:01	Break	A two-measure version of the homorhythmic break.	
1:05	Instrumental 1	The polyrhythmic texture in the piano, bass, and percussion begins again, this time with a melody in the saxophones that outlines a seventh chord on the first measure and resolves to a pitch in the IV chord. The accents in the melody create a syncopated rhythm.	
1:20		The trombones are added to the texture with yet another syncopated melody.	
1:36		The trumpet and flute are added to the texture with two additional syncopated melodies.	
1:52	Break	The two-measure version of the homorhythmic break.	
1:55	*Coro*	The *coro* returns as a nearly identical repeat of the first verse.	Oye como va . . .
2:12	Instrumental 2	The percussion, bass, and piano play repeating pulsating tones. At first only the lowest saxophone plays along with its own repeating eighth notes, but every two beats, a slightly higher pitch in the chord is added by a new instrument, creating a long crescendo and culminating with the final two beats of the four bars where everyone plays together with the flute playing the highest pitch.	
2:20		A slightly different polyrhythm begins in the rhythm section, and the saxophones introduce a new syncopated melody that moves by leaps downward	

continued

TIME	SECTION	DESCRIPTION	LYRICS
		from the third scale degree of the minor mode. The flute plays what seems to be an improvised melody mostly in the minor mode. The vocalists interject a melody, along with whistling, shouting, and other party-like sounds.	
2:35		The trombones add a repeating figure that creates the effect of a polymeter where a triple meter happens over the existing duple meter.	
2:51		The trumpet adds a repeating figure, playing the ninth (an upper extension) of the i chord over and over in the high register.	
3:07	Break	The four-measure version of the homorhythmic break.	
3:15		The song seems to end, but is followed by many vocal sounds of cheering and shouting, whistling, some striking of the congas, and shouts of "one more time."	
3:27	Instrumental 3	The band seems to respond to the request to play it "one more time" and begins again at the beginning of Instrumental 2, playing it basically the same as the first time, but at a slightly quicker tempo and with different flute improvisations.	
4:29	End		

What Does It Mean?

AESTHETICS

As a dance music, salsa places a particular importance on rhythm. Each subgenre or dance style of salsa has its own distinct rhythm. "Oye Como Va" is a *cha-cha-chá*, a moderate-tempo dance named onomatopoeically for the repeating shuffle sound of three quick steps. At the beginning of the recording, the hand claps clearly outline the *cha-cha-chá* dance rhythm, which dancers start on beat 2 and can be felt as "2–3-cha-cha-cha, 2–3-cha-cha-cha." Over the two-measure repeating cycle, the rhythm would look something like this:

```
1  2  3  4  1  2  3  4  1
x  x  x  xxx  x  x  xxx
```

Concurrent with that hand clap pattern, the piano plays its own syncopated rhythm, a pattern that, as a result of the popularity of "Oye Como Va," has become a *cha-cha-chá* riff synonymous with the song. Its first two chords are on beats 1 and 2 of the first measure, and the last four occur on the offbeats:

```
Beats: 1  2  3  4  1  2  3  4
Piano: x  x     x  x        x  x
```

The third thread in the texture at the beginning of the recording is the bass, which repeats a two-measure ostinato. The basic rhythm of the bass is known as a *tumbao*, in this rhythmic pattern:

```
Beats: 1  2  3  4  1  2  3  4
Bass:  x        x  x     x x  x
```

The *tumbao* in salsa music does not play on the first beat of the second measure, but rather anticipates it, playing the root of the chord of the second measure a half a beat early. (In some *tumbao* patterns, the bass anticipates every measure by up to a full beat, and never plays beat one.) When layered together, the hand claps, piano, and bass patterns form a polyrhythmic structure of interlocking beats:

Beats:	1	2	3	4	1	2	3	4
Claps:	x	x	x	x x x	x	x	x x	
Piano:	x	x		x	x		x	x
Bass:	x			x	x		x x	x

FIGURE 12.22
Salsa dancers
Source: Kumar Sriskandan / Alamy Stock Photo.

In most salsa music, including the *cha-cha-chá*, yet another underlying rhythmic pattern, called *clave*, governs the performance of the entire ensemble. *Clave* is named after an instrument called *claves*, a pair of short, thick, resonant wooden rods that are struck together to produce a short, high-pitched sound. The *claves* often play the *clave* pattern, but sometimes, as in "Oye Como Va," the *clave* pattern is implied rather than heard. *Clave* can take two different rhythmic forms: a "2–3 *clave*" and a "3–2 *clave*." A 2–3 *clave* has two beats in the first half of the ostinato and three in the second half and vice versa for the 3–2 *clave*.

A 2–3 *clave*:

Beats:	1	2	3	4	1	2	3	4
Clave:		x	x		x		x	x

A 3–2 *clave*:

Beats:	1	2	3	4	1	2	3	4
Clave:	x		x		x	x		

"Oye como va" is based on a 2–3 *clave*, though the *clave* is not very pronounced. It most closely corresponds to the piano part, where the first bar is relatively unsyncopated and the second bar is syncopated. If it were added to the texture at the beginning of the recording, a 2–3 *clave* would contribute yet another line to the polyrhythmic structure:

Beats:	1	2	3	4	1	2	3	4
Claps:	x	x	x	x x x	x	x	x x	
Piano:	x	x		x	x		x	x
Bass:	x			x	x		x x	x
Clave:		x	x		x		x	x

As the *timbales* take over, the hand claps and more and more instruments and rhythms are layered on top of this introductory texture, the polythym becomes more and more complex. Salsa musicians must orient their playing around the *clave* ostinato pattern, whether that pattern is heard or implied. When everyone is locked into the feel of the *clave*, it is said to produce just the right groove for the enjoyment of the musicians and for the dancers. When a musician is not locked into the *clave*, or is playing a rhythm that would be better suited to a 3–2 *clave* when the rest of the band is playing rhythms based on a 2–3 *clave*, they are not playing "on *clave*" and other musicians are disappointed that the interlocking polyrhythmic feel cannot be sustained. Tellingly, the word *clave* means "key" or "code." It is the key to organizing and holding together a salsa groove.

 Listen again to "Oye Como Vas" and try clapping along with the various rhythmic patterns of the instruments playing in the introduction. Try to clap the 2–3 *clave* and see if you can stick with it.

> **CULTURAL LINKAGES**

Salsa's polyrhythmic roots may be in African and Afro-Latin musical styles, but it also employs the harmonic sensibilities of jazz, especially the use of upper extensions that build on European-derived triadic harmony by adding desirable dissonances. For example, in the opening piano riff of "Oye Como Va," the piano can be heard switching between the minor i chord (A minor) and the IV chord (D major). On careful listening, the tonic (A) is the highest pitch in both chords, and the only pitch to change from one chord to the next is the lowest pitch (which moves from G to F♯). The pitches in the middle, though hard to hear individually, are G, E, A, C, and D. They stay consistent for each chord and add dissonances (such as the major second between C and D) and upper extensions (E is the ninth of the D major chord) to each one. Later in the song, at the end of the second instrumental (2:51) the trumpet adds the final layer in a polyphonic, polyrhythmic texture by playing a repeating figure on the note B, which is the ninth of the A minor chord and the thirteenth of the D major chord. Adding this upper extension to the harmony means that both chords contain the adjacent pitches A, B, C, D, and E at the same time. This kind of dissonant harmony is something that jazz musicians often value, and, played by an ensemble of horns (saxophones, trombones, trumpet) derived from the jazz big band as part of a multi-layered polyrhythm based on *clave*, it makes sense that Tito Puente considered his music to be Latin jazz.

Listen to "Oye Como Va" one more time, listening this time for how the dissonances and the upper extensions are placed within the polyrhythmic structure, particularly in the trumpet at 2:51 as it creates a dissonance in its repeated pitch. Listen for the sound of the horns as a reflection of the influence of the big band sound.

> **CULTURAL LINKAGES**

Salsa musicians frequently include social commentary in the lyrics of their music. In the early twentieth century, thousands of Cubans and Puerto Ricans had settled in New York City, many in the upper Manhattan neighborhood of East Harlem, which became known as "Spanish Harlem." In the 1960s, a group of Puerto Rican activists called the Young Lords, inspired by the Black Panthers and the Black Power movement, began to take a stand against social inequalities and injustices experienced in this and other Spanish-speaking neighborhoods (*barrios*) in New York and other American cities. Nuyorican and other Puerto Rican and Latin communities around the country, in the spirit of the social upheaval of the 1960s, were mobilized to achieve social and political goals and to resist cultural assimilation. Instead of assimilating they took pride in their Latin roots and in their distinctive communities that had become embedded in the multicultural life of American cities. As musicians began including lyrics that commented on the realities of life in the *barrios*, critiqued American imperialism, and advocated for pan-Latin solidarity, the music that would become known as salsa began to serve as a social resource for individuals and communities. In it they experienced a musical performance of their complex and multifaceted identities in the form of energetic dance music.

> **EMOTIONAL RESONANCE**

Nuyoricans and other Puerto Ricans in the 1960s and 1970s began to view salsa as an icon of their ethnic identity.[72] Its nature as a sophisticated and cosmopolitan urban genre with influences from all over Latin America and elsewhere seemed to connect to their lived experience as Puerto Ricans living a cosmopolitan, urban life in New York City. Instead of a European-style musical nationalism based in rural folk music and cultivated by a state government to showcase a nation's distinctiveness, salsa expressed the national identity of urbanized Puerto Ricans and Nuyoricans as it emerged as a commercial music connecting them with other Latinx nationalities and across boundaries of age and class.

What Is Its History?

This particular *clave* rhythmic pattern (in both 2–3 and 3–2 versions) is called *son clave* because it originates in a genre of music called Cuban *son* (sound, style). A genre of Afro-Cuban music, Cuban *son* (or *son cubano*) developed in the early twentieth century as a synthesis of musical elements with roots in both European and African music. The Spanish began colonizing Cuba in the early sixteenth century, and over they next two and a half centuries more than one million Africans were enslaved and brought to Cuba. The *son clave* of *son cubano* likely has roots in similar five-stroke patterns in much of sub-Saharan Africa, where iron bells play "bell patterns" to keep the beat in drum ensembles. In Cuba these patterns found their way into the Afro-Cuban syncretic religion called *Santería* (Chapter 6, Gateway 26) and eventually into all genres of Afro-Cuban popular music: *mambo*, *son montuno*, *rumba*, *bolero*, *guaguancó*, *guaracha*, and *danzón*, among others.

Salsa as a named music and dance genre emerged in the 1960s and 1970s in New York. But Latin American music was popular in the United States earlier, subsumed under the catch-all category "Latin music." Latin and Afro-Caribbean sounds were consistently featured in 1920s Broadway and Tin Pan Alley music. In the 1930s the Spanish-born Cuban Xavier Cugat (1900–1990), one of the first famous Latin bandleaders in the U.S., appeared in many Hollywood films performing in a variety of Latin styles. In the 1940s Dizzy Gillespie and Cuban drummer Chano Pozo combined Afro-Cuban music with bebop to create Latin jazz, and Cuban band leaders Frank "Machito" Grillo (1912–1984) and Mario Bauzá (1911–1993) mixed Cuban rhythms and big band jazz (Chapter 11, Gateway 46). The Cuban-style dance music *mambo* thrived in New York in the 1940s and 1950s. Puerto Rican band-leaders Machito (*c.* 1908–1984), Pablo "Tito" Rodriguez (1923–1973), and Tito Puente fronted featured acts at New York's Palladium Ballroom, the central hub of New York's Latin music and dance scene. Audiences at the Palladium were diverse: some nights attracted Puerto Ricans, other nights attracted African American audiences, and others attracted mixed audiences. Dancers active in the big band swing scene at the Savoy Ballroom often came to the Palladium, bringing with them their dance steps and contributing to the wide variety of cultural influences in the Latin music and dance scene.

By the 1960s, however, Latin music was experiencing a decline in popularity. Both big bands and large ensembles playing Latin music for dancing had fallen out of favor with the rise of rock music. The *mambo* craze had died out, the end of the era punctuated by the closing of the Palladium Ballroom in 1966. The intense interest in Cuban music that had fueled much of Latin music's development and popularity had also lost its connection to current music in Cuba due to the U.S. embargo against all imports from Cuba in 1962, which was designed to isolate the island nation economically, politically, and culturally in the wake of the Cuban Revolution and the ascendance of Fidel Castro's new government. Because they could no longer innovate alongside musicians arriving from Cuba, Latin musicians in New York in the 1960s began developing their music in their own ways. Instead of big bands, musicians formed smaller ensembles, some based on a small ensemble format called *conjunto*, which in the 1950s had been well established by many Cuban musicians in the New York scene. New York-born Puerto Rican pianist and bandleader Eddie Palmieri (b. 1936) established a *conjunto* that included piano, bass, percussion, flute, trumpets, prominent trombones, and vocals. This kind of *conjunto* ensemble, and others that were basically smaller versions of the large *mambo* orchestras, inspired what became salsa. Palmieri became one of the early stars of salsa on the way to a career that has spanned over five decades and resulted in worldwide fame and countless awards, including a number of Grammys.

Salsa's rise to fame around the world is inseparable from Fania Records. Fania chose the term salsa as a genre label to promote music rooted in Cuban *son*, interconnected with *mambo*, and developed in New York among musicians playing music from a variety of Caribbean and Latin American countries. The origins of salsa as a genre label are not clear. Some argue that Venezuelan radio DJ Phidia Danilo Escalona was the first to use the term in the early 1960s (not unlike the American DJ Alan Freed who created the genre label "rock 'n' roll"). Others claim that a New York publisher named Izzy Sanabría first used the term in the late 1960s. Regardless of its origins, by the

CULTURAL
LINKAGES

FIGURE 12.23
Salsa band and dancers at a club, the Granada, in Los Angeles (2004)
Source: Getty Images / Lawrence K. Ho / Los Angeles Times.

early 1970s salsa was the genre label in common use, due not in a small part to the many albums recorded and promoted by Fania Records. Founded in 1964 by Dominican-born bandleader Johnny Pacheco (b. 1935), Fania launched the careers of many salsa stars, whose recordings topped the charts not only in the *barrios* but also throughout Latin America. The label also put together a legendary supergroup, a gathering of the most successful salsa instrumentalists and singers into one band called the Fania All-Stars. In the 1970s the Fania All-Stars and the many individual salsa artists on the label sold millions of records and performed on tours throughout the Americas. Salsa exploded in popularity in the 1970s, and Fania had played a significant role in transforming it from a music associated with the lower socio-economic classes of the *barrios* to one also celebrated and enjoyed by the middle- and upper-classes throughout the U.S., Latin America, and the Caribbean.

One of Fania's earliest and most successful artists was the Nuyorican trombonist and composer Willie Colon (b. 1950), who signed with the label at age fifteen and two years later in 1967 released his first album, the bestselling *El Malo* (The Bad One). Colon's music is full of examples of lyrics about life in the *barrios*, such as his 1973 "Calle Luna Calle Sol," a cautionary tale that describes the dangers of the streets. It is also a clear example of a two-trombone instrumentation that had become common in salsa. This song, still a staple of salsa bands everywhere, first appeared on an album he recorded with the vocalist Héctor Lavoe (1946–1993) humorously and darkly titled *Lo Mato (Si No Compra Esta LP)*, which loosely means "I'll Kill You (If You Don't Buy This LP)." Colon also emphasized salsa's connection to Puerto Rico and Puerto Rican musicians by featuring the ten-stringed Puerto Rican *cuatro*, among other practices (Chapter 4, Gateway 15). Involved in social activism for most of his life, Colon often deals in his music with the complexities and challenges of life for Puerto Ricans in the United States, in particular on his 1993 album *Hecho en Puerto Rico* (Made in Puerto Rico).

POLITICAL
ACTION

One of Colon's many collaborators was the Panama-born musician and composer Rubén Blades (b. 1948), whose music also emphasizes social activism, including such themes as imperialism, environmentalism, and disarmament, along with critiques of capitalism and the conditions of *barrio* life. Their most successful collaboration was the 1978 album *Siembra* (Planting), arguably the best-selling salsa album of all time. On this album Blades' social commentary is particularly sharp on songs like "Plástico" (Plastic), a critique of capitalist materialism, and the now-classic "Pedro Navaja" (Pedro Knife), a grim story about *barrio* life where, in the end, a small-time criminal (Pedro Navaja) and a prostitute end up killing one another. A favorite son of Panama, Blades has been involved in acting and politics, and even ran for president in Panama in 1994, receiving 17 percent of the vote among seven candidates.

Perhaps the most famous female salsa singer was Celia Cruz (1925–2003), "The Queen of Salsa." Born in Cuba, she was a well-known singer in the 1950s before moving to New York in 1959 in the aftermath of the Cuban Revolution. She worked extensively with Tito Puente before her 1974 album, with Fania co-founder Johnny Pacheco, titled *Celia y Johnny* (1974) launched her into stardom. The song "Quimbará" from the album became one of her classic hits, famously starting out with the line "*rumba* is calling out to me," and featuring Cruz shouting "Azúcar!" (sugar), a signature exclamation of hers that she often shouted during performances to rev up the audience. The most famous song of her later career, "La Vida es un Carnaval" (Life is a Carnival) from the 1998 album *Mi Vida Es Cantar* (My Life is Singing), addressed hardships in life but focused on how celebration, singing, and a positive attitude can help someone survive difficult situations, serve as a powerful antidote to complainers and critics, and even be a force against the evils of war and disease.

Tito Puente, like his close collaborator Celia Cruz, enjoyed wide renown long before salsa was an established genre. He was born to Puerto Rican parents in New York City, spent much of his childhood in Spanish Harlem, and began playing percussion at age ten. After serving in the U.S. Navy during World War II, he studied music formally at the Juilliard School. After that, he built his reputation as a performer and bandleader, becoming known as the King of the Timbales and the King of Mambo in the 1950s as he performed *rumba*, *son*, *cha-cha-chá*, and other genres for audiences who were going crazy for Latin dance music. He enjoyed many successful years as one of the featured acts at the Palladium Ballroom and other venues at the center of the Latin music scene in New York, though his popularity declined along with the popularity of Latin dance music in the 1960s.

FIGURE 12.24
**Celia Cruz
performing in
Mexico City**
Source: Keith
Dannemiller / Alamy
Stock Photo.

He recorded frequently—in the early 1950s he was known to release a recording every week—and 1963's "Oye Como Va" was just one of many of his recordings from the 1960s that, initially, enjoyed only modest success among devotees of his and other Latin music. "Oye Como Va" became a mainstream hit after the Latin rock band Santana released a version of it on their second album, *Abraxas* (1970). Fronted by Mexican American guitarist Carlos Santana, the band became prominent after their performance at the Woodstock festival in 1969. For "Oye Como Va," Santana replaced the piano in the introduction with a Hammond B-3 organ and the flute with the distinctive electric guitar sound of Carlos Santana. He also took over the saxophone and brass lines, turning instrumental sections into guitar solos rooted in rock and the blues. The recording also features an energetic organ solo, soloistic percussion playing, and modified breaks. These elements, combined with Santana's significant popularity in rock, made "Oye Como Va" a hit and reignited Puente's popularity (and his bank account, with royalties paid to him as the songwriter). Santana's massively popular version of the song was a factor in the rise of salsa to popularity throughout the United States and Latin America.

Since Puente had enjoyed great success in the 1950s, before salsa was coined as a genre name, he was reluctant to embrace the term and call himself a salsa musician, though eventually he reconciled himself to the genre label, even working with Fania Records in his later years. By the 1990s Puente, like Cruz, was an icon of Latin music, and the two of them collaborated on hundreds of recordings and performances. Puente himself released over 100 albums and is credited with over 400 compositions. Some regard him as the most important figure of the twentieth century in all of Latin music. "Oye Como Va" had introduced salsa—and Puente—to much of the world, and the last album he recorded, *Mambo Birdland* (1999), featured the song as its final track. After his death in 2000, Latin pop stars that had emerged in the 1980s and 1990s, Gloria Estefan and Ricky Martin, joined Celia Cruz in a tribute performance to Tito Puente and his massive influence at the Latin Grammy Awards. The performance featured a band full of outstanding musicians, and even a video of Puente playing the *timbales*, whose sound was synced up with the band's performance. The performance began with Martin singing "Oye Como Va," a celebration of the enormous contributions of Tito Puente to Latin music, contributions that still resonate today.

WHERE DO I GO FROM HERE?

- Listen to Santana's version of "Oye Como Va" for the way the musical elements of the blues and rock combine with the polyrhythms of Tito Puente's original composition? Can you hear the *clave* in this case?
- Listen to "La Vida es un Carnaval" or "Quimbará" by Celia Cruz. Can you identify some of the musical elements of salsa in these recordings? Can you feel the *clave* pattern based on the way the rhythm fits together even if you can't hear it?

- Find the lyrics to "Plasticó" by Rubén Blades and Willie Colon (and a translation if you need one) and listen to the recording. What other musical influences are obvious from the introduction to the song? What musical elements typical of salsa do you hear? Can you feel the *clave* pattern in this recording? To what extent does the social commentary of the song suit its social function as dance music?

- Are there contemporary Latin pop stars that you listen to? Choose a song by one of them and see if you can connect some of its musical elements to "Oye Como Va" or some of the other music mentioned in this gateway.

CLOSING

Musicians in the period between 1950 and 1975 responded, almost of necessity, to the powerful waves of social change and political unrest sweeping the U.S. and the world during this period. Rock 'n' roll helped a new, young generation of teenagers define themselves in contrast to older generations and express disenchantment with the world they were inheriting. Jazz musicians struggled against the boundaries of their tradition, some by combining it with rock and other popular genres to attract a young audience, some by rejecting the boundaries with avant-garde artistic expressions of ideologies related to the Civil Rights Movement, and some by pushing the limits of older styles such as bebop. Composers of European classical music questioned the nature of music and experimented with new musical ideas at odds with hundreds of years of thinking about music. And salsa music exploded all over the world as Puerto Ricans and Latin Americans everywhere listened and danced to a music that celebrated their multifaceted identities. With the end of the war in Vietnam, a new era of international peace was dawning. Musicians' attention would turn to absorbing and responding to the stylistic changes of this period and to confronting even more directly racial inequality and injustice at home and aboard.

THINGS TO THINK ABOUT

- Music takes a number of forms as protest or resistance music in this chapter. What do the various musical modes of resistance in the gateways to rock, jazz, salsa, and classical music in this chapter share and how are they different from one another? How are the similar to or different from music of protest and resistance today?

- Rock 'n' roll, rock, and rhythm and blues music have long involved the contested crossing of boundaries of race and class, while salsa music exploded into a pan-Latin music that prided itself in crossing boundaries among Latin American communities. Compare these two cases. What are some of the historical and musical factors involved in how these kinds of boundaries are established and negotiated?

NEW TERMS

clave	hard bop	rock 'n' roll
comping	jazz fusion	sound synthesis
concept album	minimalism	*timbales*
cover	modal jazz	tone clusters
feedback	new music ensemble	total serialism
free jazz	prepared piano	urban folk
fuzz box	rhythm and blues	wah-wah pedal

MUSIC AND COMMUNITY (1975–1994)

BETWEEN THE END of the Vietnam War in 1975 and 1994, five hundred years of European colonialism, which began in 1492, came to an end with the dissolution of the last great European empire, the Soviet Union, and the end of white rule over an African majority in South Africa. The Cold War between the United States and the Soviet Union continued during this period (until the fall of the Soviet Union in 1991) and both countries plowed enormous sums of money into their nuclear weaponry and anti-ballistic missile systems. In the United States excessive military spending, along with an oil crisis created by Arab countries angered at American support for Israel, created a long-lasting economic recession with the highest unemployment rates since the Great Depression of the 1930s. The American auto industry, one of the country's most powerful economic engines, faced competition from carmakers in Japan. Unemployment and fear of a nuclear war fueled anger, anxiety, and hopelessness among lower- and middle-class white youth and probably account, in part at least, for the emergence of new aggressive genres of rock.

While the United States survived these economic and political upheavals, the Soviet Union did not. Destabilization in the Middle East, including an Islamic revolution in Iran in 1979, led the Soviet Union to invade and occupy Afghanistan. As it poured more and more money into the military sector of its economy, its citizens, along with those in the other communist countries of eastern Europe, became less and less satisfied with their standard of living compared to what they could see in western Europe. In 1989 communist governments fell across the whole of eastern Europe: in East Germany, Poland, Czechoslovakia, Hungary, Romania, and Bulgaria. In 1990 Yugoslavia dissolved, and war broke out among a number of its former federated republics. In 1991 the Soviet Union collapsed, the Cold War ended, and the communist world was reduced from nineteen countries to five: The People's Republic of China, North Korea, Vietnam, Laos, and Cuba.

In the so-called third world, African decolonization, begun in the 1950s, continued throughout this period. Angola and Mozambique in Southwestern Africa gained independence from Portugal in 1975, ending formal European colonial rule on the continent. However, in southern Africa white rule continued in the independent countries of Rhodesia and South Africa. Black resistance eventually brought democratic rule to Rhodesia, which changed its name to Zimbabwe, in 1980 and to South Africa in 1994, when Nelson Mandela (1918–2013), a political prisoner for more than twenty-five years, was elected president. Many African musicians, by creating new styles and genres of music, joined political leaders, intellectuals, and educators in the creation of national identity and national sentiment.

The political successes in Africa existed in counterpoint with increasing poverty there. The global economy sucked more and more of the world's wealth into the industrialized world, creating economic misery across the globe and pushing many to migrate from rural to urban areas and to leave their countries for the promise of greater prosperity abroad. Rural music traditions in many places were threatened, and new genres of urban music mixed local rural musical styles with

FIGURE 13.1
Paul Simon performing with South African musicians from his *Graceland* album
Source: Getty Images / Rob Verhorst.

elements of urban popular music. Immigrants brought increased ethnic diversity to growing cities, where interethnic musical fusions became commonplace, only partly fueled by the popularity of Paul Simon's best-selling 1986 album *Graceland*, on which he played with South African musicians. In 1987 record company executives in Britain settled on the genre label "**world music**" to describe hybrid musical forms that capitalized on the supposed authenticity of traditional music and the commercial appeal of popular music. This commercial genre label differs from the sense in which the term world music is used in this book. In this book world music refers broadly to all traditional, ethnic, popular, and classical musical traditions beyond the domains of European classical music, American popular music, and jazz.

As the creation of the World Music genre illustrates, not only did people migrate around the world, but their cultures did as well. The United States exported its film, music, and sports cultures to every corner of the globe, and Americans, both long-standing residents and new immigrants, listened to music and

TECHNOLOGY

viewed television shows from all over the world. New technology facilitated the easy passage of these cultural products across political borders and vast expanses of land. Cheap-to-produce and easy-to-pirate audiocassette tapes became available in the 1970s and videocassettes soon followed in the 1980s. Personal computers became a necessity for many in the 1980s, and the internet debuted in the early 1990s, facilitating international communication and making knowledge of cultural and political activity in other cultures as close as a click away.

CULTURAL LINKAGES

Bob Marley, a Jamaican playing a genre called **reggae**, became a hero to working-class, black Caribbean immigrants in Canada and the U.K. and, via recordings, to underprivileged blacks in Brazil, South Africa, and the United States. The poor and oppressed in America and throughout the world learned about a new musical genre of black popular music called **rap** from audiocassettes, radio, videotapes, and MTV, which launched in 1981 and played its first rap video in 1984. Rap music's chronicles of black life in America inspired the poor and disaffected all over the world to adopt the genre for their own need to document their lives and protest the conditions in which they lived. Historians began to write about a distinctive culture they called "the Black Atlantic," which encompasses networks of cultural exchange among black musicians, writers, and other artists from Africa, the Caribbean, the U.S. and the U.K. Music is central to those flows of culture and, in addition to reggae and rap, other vigorous new popular music genres emerged along the Black Atlantic such as Afro-pop in Africa. These and other genres were inspired both by the independence of African countries from European colonial rule in the 1950s and 1960s and by the continued suffering of blacks under repressive, racist political conditions around the world.

Finally, the world was confronted with a new problem: HIV/AIDS, a deadly infectious virus that attacks the immune system. First identified in the U.S. in 1981, it spread around the world, with particularly devastating effects in Africa. It has caused an estimated thirty-six million deaths since then, and today an estimated thirty-five million people are living with HIV/AIDS.

ECONOMIC ACTIVITY

Although a lot of music in this period responded in one way or another to the political and economic crises of the time, not all of it did. The end of the Vietnam War had healed a gaping wound in American culture. Many social and political activists and hippies, having tuned in, turned on, and dropped out in the 1960s, dropped back in, cut their hair, and took mainstream jobs. Musicians felt free to turn inward to the problems of making art and making money from their art. The music industry geared up to take advantage of middle-class disposable income through a proliferation of subgenres of rock and popular music. And local musicians all over the world tried to sell their styles of hybrid World Music in the newly active global marketplace, which had given their efforts a name.

Much of the music we perform and listen to today has its roots in this period. Classical composers returned to and revivified older musical styles. Some jazz musicians continued to seek a larger audience through their fusions with popular music styles, and others did so by honoring "classics" from the past of jazz. In addition to rap and a number of subgenres of rock, other genres of music that suffuse American popular music today got their start in this period, including electronic dance music (EDM), which first emerged as house music in Chicago and techno in Detroit as communities of music lovers experimented with some of the possibilities created by developments in music technology.

GATEWAY 53
RAP AND HIP-HOP

What Is It?

Hip-hop has influenced popular music today arguably more than any other genre. It is enjoyed around the world by audiences of many cultural and class backgrounds, and is a multi-billion dollar industry. Its impact can be heard in all types of popular music and stretches beyond music to film, television, fashion, politics, sports, video games, tourism industries, and many other sectors of society. Long before it was the big business it is today, however, hip-hop culture emerged in the 1970s among communities of African American, Latinx, and Caribbean American youth in economically struggling neighborhoods of the Bronx, located just north of Manhattan in New York City. At its inception **hip-hop culture** was a local phenomenon that included music (made by DJs and MCs), dance (breakdancing), and visual art (graffiti), as well as styles of dress and, later, the practice of producing percussive effects with the voice and mouth called beatboxing.

Hip-hop DJs (an abbreviation for "disc jockey") in the 1970s spun records (discs) for dancing at neighborhood parties, at dance clubs, and in other settings for partying in local communities. They found that dancers were excited by the instrumental "breaks" on funk and salsa recordings, where the vocals dropped out and the rhythm section was featured. Using turntable technology, they figured out ways to insert breaks from one record into the middle of another record and to loop a particular break over and over by playing two copies of the same record on their turntables and alternating from one to the other. First DJs, and later, MCs (an abbreviation for "master of ceremonies") would hype up and control the crowds at these parties not only by speaking on microphones, but also by performing improvised and pre-written rhymes over these so-called "breakbeats," a practice that became known as **rapping**. MCs relied on clever wordplay to boastfully introduce themselves, energize the crowd, describe dance moves, and tell humorous stories with references to local neighborhoods and social groups. Dancers developed an acrobatic style of improvised solo dance on breakbeats known as **breakdancing**, with its young athletic dancers known as "B-boys" and "B-girls." Until the 1979 release of the first commercial hip-hop recording, "Rapper's Delight" by the Sugarhill Gang, rap music was heard mostly in live performance at parties as an element of hip-hop culture. The commercial success of "Rapper's Delight" introduced people across America and around the world to hip-hop and inspired the production of many more rap recordings.

By the late 1980s, rap music had blossomed into a major sector of the popular music industry. Because of this growing commercial success, the rapid innovation of the genre, the wide variety of themes approached, and the influence of recordings released at that time on future developments in hip-hop, the late 1980s and early 1990s are known as the "golden era" of hip-hop, especially with regard to rap on the East Coast. By this time a number of rappers and groups had begun to produce songs that described the social realities of life in poor urban African American communities and related issues of racism, violence, drugs, police brutality, and various forms of discrimination. A group leading the way in this kind of socially engaged hip-hop was Public Enemy from Long Island,

New York. Formed in 1982, Public Enemy included MCs Chuck D (Carlton Ridenhour, b. 1960) and Flavor Flav (William Drayton, b. 1959), DJ Terminator X (Norman Lee Rogers, b. 1966), the "Minister of Information" Professor Griff (Richard Griffin, b. 1960), and a group of men referred to as "The S1W," which stands for "Security of the First World." Our gateway to rap and hip-hop is their hit "Fight the Power" (1989) from their album *Fear of a Black Planet*, produced by their production team called the Bomb Squad (Hank Shocklee, Keith Shocklee, and Eric "Vietnam" Sadler). Like many of their recordings, "Fight the Power" addresses social issues in an aggressive style known as **hardcore rap**, which is typified by expressions of anger and confrontation. "Fight the Power" is regarded as one of the most significant recordings in the history of hip-hop and was written as the theme song for the film *Do the Right Thing* (1989), directed by Spike Lee.

FIGURE 13.2
Public Enemy in 1987. Left to right: Terminator X, Flavor Flav, Professor Griff, and Chuck D
Source: Getty Images / Jack Mitchell.

🔊 **Listen to the first thirty seconds of the recording.**

How Does It Work?

Timbre

Male voices are featured over a plethora of other sounds that mostly come from samples of previous recordings, including guitar, bass, drums, cymbals, turntable scratching, a synthesizer, and additional male and female voices.

Texture

Voices rapping over a thick, multi-layered texture of samples and other recorded sounds.

Rhythm

The track is in four with a steady tempo of around 106 bpm (beats per minute). The samples create dense polyrhythms forming underlying ostinatos for much of the rapping. Chuck D and Flavor Flav rap with a high degree of syncopation. They speed up and slow down, making spaces between words larger and smaller and adding additional layers to the polyrhythm of the samples.

Melody

Rap vocals are spoken, but occupy an area between speech and song. Short melodic fragments that hint at minor pentatonic or major modes appear in a number of the samples.

Harmony

Harmonic aspects of this track are mainly grounded in the sampled bass ostinato that repeats the pitch D throughout. Various other harmonies are suggested by samples throughout the track.

Form

The form alternates between verses of rapping and choruses that feature a repetition of the song's title.

Performance Techniques

TECHNOLOGY

In addition to masterful rapping by Chuck D and Flavor Flav, this recording features two techniques that hip-hop DJs have developed. The first is **scratching**, where DJs spin a break on one turntable and, on the other turntable, move the vinyl record quickly backwards and forwards with one hand to create a rhythmic sound. Since the pitch of the scratching effect is higher when the record moves faster, the DJ can manipulate both rhythm and pitch through scratching, which is usually improvised. Sampling is the second technique. As recording technology developed in the 1980s, hip-hop producers began to create beats in the studio that sounded similar to the live breakbeats of the early DJs through the layering of **samples**, that is, short clips of existing recordings. By 1989 producers were using machines called "samplers" that created samples by converting recorded sound to digital files. Samplers take many different forms: keyboards, boxes with knobs and buttons, or, more common today, software programs that run on computers. Producers manipulate the speed, duration, pitch, and other timbral aspects of samples. They also reverse them and layer them on top of one another. Repeating a short sample is called a "loop." Hip-hop producers layer loops of various lengths on top of one another to create the dense polyrhythmic textures that characterize this music. Public Enemy's production team, the Bomb Squad, used dozens of different samples to construct "Fight the Power."

FIGURE 13.3
A DJ spinning records at a park in East Harlem
Source: Henry Chalfant.

Listen to the entire recording with these elements in mind while following this timed listening guide.

LISTENING GUIDE 13.1

TIME	SECTION	DESCRIPTION	LYRICS
0:00	Introduction	The track opens with an excerpt from a speech by civil rights attorney and activist, Thomas N. Todd. Todd's original speech referred to the many Americans who refused to fight in the Vietnam War.	
0:16	Transition	This three-measure section introduces the tempo by way of a pulsing rhythm produced by a nearly unintelligible vocal that repeats six times. The words are "pump me up," sampled from a 1982 song of the same name by the band Trouble Funk—and played backwards. There is also a line of quickly-moving notes that generally ascends a minor scale with accents every three notes. This line is heavily processed so that the source of the timbre is difficult to distinguish. A snare drum plays eight consecutive accents during the second measure, solidifying the steady tempo. Several other vocal samples are layered together in the third measure.	
0:23	Establishing the groove	These ten bars establish the main groove of the song through a complex layering of at least ten different samples, including the music of soul and funk artist James Brown. In this thick texture at least four vocal lines intertwine: one that repeats the phrase "give it," one that states "come on and get down," some of James Brown's characteristic grunts, and a few other moans and vocal gestures. Other layers include the bass ostinato, a funky repeating guitar riff, a number of different snare drum sounds, a single high pitch on a synthesizer, and various percussion samples.	
0:44	Verse 1	The groove continues as Chuck D raps the first verse and Flavor Flav inserts interjections and joins him on certain phrases. The first verse introduces the song as	1989 . . .

continued

TIME	SECTION	DESCRIPTION	LYRICS
		connected to funk and other African American popular music styles and connects freedom of speech to fighting the power.	
1:12	Chorus	The groove shifts as certain samples are removed and others are added. On the second half of beat four of each measure, the "aah" sound sung in harmony is a sample of the word "I" from the chorus to "I Shot The Sheriff" by Bob Marley and the Wailers. Chuck D and Flavor Flav rap the title of the track, alternating between starting on beat one and starting on beat two.	Fight the power . . .
1:30	Verse 2	The original groove returns and additional samples are layered on top of the groove to respond to and comple-ment the rap at a number of points in the verse. The rap draws on themes such as black pride, vigilance and awareness, and mental strength as necessary traits to fight the power.	As the rhythm . . .
2:07	Chorus	The chorus repeats in a similar fashion to the first chorus.	Fight the power . . .
2:25	Scratching	The main groove returns for an eight-bar break of turn-table scratching. The break turntable scratches eight short phrases, each one beginning with two quick pulses beginning on the second half of beat two.	
2:43	Chorus	The chorus repeats again in similar fashion to first chorus.	Fight the power . . .
3:01	Verse 3	The main groove returns for verse three, again with the addition of samples that interact with the rap. At a number of points, most prominently at around 3:34, there is a highly processed voice singing "yeah," which is a sample from the classic 1982 hip-hop track "Planet Rock" by Afrika Bambaataa & the Soulsonic Force. The rap here deals with the politics of representation (it refers to the lack of any black heroes on postage stamps), challenges the prominence of Elvis Presley, and disparages the 1988 Bobby McFerrin hit "Don't Worry Be Happy."	Elvis . . .
3:41	Chorus	The chorus returns with a much thinner texture than before, this time including the bass line, the drum and percussion samples, the guitar riff, James Brown's grunts, and one other vocal sample.	Fight the power . . .
4:00	Instrumental break	The rap drops out and the texture becomes even thinner for these eight bars. The James Brown and other vocals are replaced by repetitions and syncopations of the "I Shot the Sheriff" sample. The second half of this section brings all of the samples together in a unison syncopated rhythm that repeats four times.	
4:18	Tag	A variation on the main groove begins, which includes the synthesizer sample and various iterations of the "Planet Rock" sample.	What we got to say . . .
4:36	Closing skit	The songs closes with a short skit that sounds like a cut-off radio interview about the future of Public Enemy.	Yo check this out . . .
4:43	End		

What Does It Mean?

In "Fight the Power," many musical elements work together to communicate a political message that addresses racism, the lack of representation of African Americans in the public sphere, and freedom of speech. It advocates for black pride and opposition to the white establishment in "fighting the powers that be." In producing the track, The Bomb Squad used over twenty samples, an unprecedented number in 1989. The ways they put these samples together with the rapping and scratching on "Fight the Power" both draws on the historical meanings of the existing samples and resituates those meanings in a way that makes the political message of the song even more powerful.

The main groove is a two-bar loop made of at least ten samples layered on top of one another, and it repeats as the basis for the majority of the track. Though this kind of layering could only be achieved through the use of sampling technology in the studio, the effect it achieves is quite similar to that of the repeating breaks that hip-hop DJs began creating in the 1970s using turntabling techniques. With sampling and other studio technologies, producers of recorded hip-hop in the studio filled the role of the live DJ at a dance or street party. They maintained the aesthetics of hip-hop breaks ideal for rapping and dance and created new loops with sampling technologies. By including turntable scratching in the section after the second chorus, "Fight the Power" makes the sound of the DJ prominent and aligns the track closely with the sounds of hip-hop culture.

A number of the samples in "Fight the Power" are taken from recordings by James Brown (1933–2006), one of the artists most associated with the innovation of the funk style. **Funk** originated in the mid-1960s and is characterized by complex, multi-layered syncopation and grooves with driving, percussive bass lines, and guitar riffs featuring the wah-wah pedal in combination with percussive effects. James Brown was known for dance-oriented grooves that prioritized rhythm over harmony or melody, as well as for his captivating showmanship, dancing, and percussive shouts and grunts. He also was known for social commentary that encouraged black empowerment, perhaps most notably in his 1968 recording "Say it Loud—I'm Black and I'm Proud."

Brown's vocal performance in "Say it Loud" consists mostly of highly rhythmic speech performed over a repeating groove played by a live band, a forerunner to rapping, which would emerge a decade later. Brown's recordings were among the most commonly sampled by early hip-hop artists. The main groove of "Fight the Power" includes a number of Brown samples, including Brown grunting "uh!" and drums from a number of his recordings. One of the drum samples, performed by drummer Clyde Stubblefield on Brown's 1970 recording "Funky Drummer," is the most sampled drum break in hip-hop and in popular music overall. Public Enemy's indebtedness to Brown is clear in the verses that refer to the sound of the "funky drummer" and include the phrase "I'm black and I'm proud." They draw on Brown's contagious, danceable grooves to build their own new groove, and explicitly connect his political notions of black pride to their own.

Two other samples connect "Fight the Power" to previous recordings by black musicians. In the chorus and the final instrumental break, there is a brief sample from the opening seconds to "I Shot the Sheriff" (1973) by Jamaican reggae group Bob Marley and the Wailers (Chapter 13, Gateway 56). This sample might be difficult to recognize because it is so short, but listeners who know the Bob Marley and the Wailers recording may connect it to the narrative of the song, which is a nuanced comment on justice (and injustice), and to Marley's political views, which address the oppression not only of African Americans, but also of people of African descent the world over. The other sample that repeats several times is an electronically processed voice singing "yeah," taken from the game-changing hip-hop track

> POLITICAL ACTION

> AESTHETICS

FIGURE 13.4
James Brown performing in 1964
Source: Getty Images / Michael Ochs Archive.

"Planet Rock" (1982) by Afrika Bambaataa & the Soulsonic Force. Every time the processed "yeah" is heard, it is as if a voice from hip-hop's past is encouraging Public Enemy. In the tag towards the end of "Fight the Power," Chuck D asks "What we got to say?" but before he and Flavor Flav can answer with "fight the power," there is an interjection of the the electronic "yeah." In this multi-layered call and response, Public Enemy brings one of the most highly regarded hip-hop tracks into a communal affirmation of its political message. Through these and the many other samples used in "Fight the Power," the voices of a great number of black musicians are brought together to create a sense of community and a rich, multi-dimensional message that challenges the powerful and addresses racial injustice.

 Listen again to "Fight the Power" and see whether you can identify a number of layered samples, including James Brown's grunts, the "I" from "I Shot the Sheriff," the "yeah" from "Planet Rock," or any number of others, even if you don't know their source. Also pay attention to the general effect that these multiple layers of samples seem to create.

POLITICAL ACTION

The lyrics in rap are one of the genre's most important sources of meaning. In rap's early years they largely focused on creating an atmosphere for partying, but in the course of the history of hip-hop a wide range of themes have been covered, including the kind of social engagement heard in "Fight the Power." Chuck D's rap and Flavor Flav's responses and interjections evoke ideas of freedom of speech, black pride, revolution, awareness, and mental clarity, as they invite others to fight the power with them. In verse two, Chuck D raps "people, people, we are the same," where "people, people" refers to lyrics from James Brown's 1974 recording "Funky President (People It's Bad)." The contradictory next line, "no we're not the same," suggests that while all humans are inherently equal, the structure of society is unequal. In verse three, Chuck D's rap disparages Elvis Presley, arguably for the way that he, as a white man, popularized and benefitted from the black rhythm and blues styles in the rock 'n' roll of the 1950s. While the lyrics in "Fight the Power" seem to attack Elvis directly, Chuck D in later years asserted that he and his contemporaries have always had great respect for Elvis, but that they have a problem with the way he is viewed as a singular icon at the expense of other black musical heroes they view as important. Also in verse three, Chuck D and Flavor Flav mention Bobby McFerrin's 1988 number one hit "Don't Worry Be Happy." They disagree with the song's message, and Chuck D invites the listener to "slap me right here" if he's caught saying the song's title phrase. Public Enemy's message is clear: this is not a time to live without worries and to be happy. It is a time to fight against oppression.

 Listen to "Fight the Power" again and focus on the lyrics of the rap by Chuck D and Flavor Flav and the way that they interact with one another. Notice the ideas that Flavor Flav adds with his interjections, the differences in timbre and general pitch of the two voices, and any additional cultural, political, or musical references that you hear in the lyrics.

What Is Its History?

TECHNOLOGY

Hip-hop culture in the late 1970s in the Bronx emerged out of a number of existing musical practices. One of these was **disco**, a popular form of dance music in the 1970s enjoyed at nightclubs where audiences danced to continuous music played on records for hours at a time. By using a set of two turntables with adjustable speeds, disco DJs developed techniques of playing uninterrupted music, blending one song into the next without any breaks or abrupt changes in tempo. Early hip-hop DJs like Kool Herc (Clive Campbell, b. 1955, Jamaica), Grandmaster Flash (Joseph Saddler, b. 1958, Barbados), and Afrika Bambaataa (Kevin Donovan, b. 1960, the Bronx) built on disco turntabling techniques and adapted them to hip-hop contexts like neighborhood parties and dance clubs. Kool Herc was the first to adapt these techniques for smooth transitions between records,

Grandmaster Flash refined them, and his protégé Grand Wizard Theodore (Theodore Livingston, b. 1963, the Bronx) invented the scratching technique.

Another precursor to hip-hop is **toasting**, a form of rhythmic storytelling with roots in West Africa and legacies both in American prison culture, where black inmates would brag to one another about their exploits in rhyming poetic form, and in Jamaican popular culture, where, beginning in the 1950s, DJs would improvise "toasts" over the music of mobile sound systems. DJ Kool Herc, born in Kingston, Jamaica, likely heard toasting in his youth and was one of the first to recite rhyming phrases over his breakbeats before that role became the domain of the MC.

After the Sugarhill Gang released their single "Rapper's Delight" in 1979, hip-hop began to shift from existing only as a local phenomenon to becoming well known as a genre with great commercial appeal. In the production of this and other early hip-hop recordings, rather than rapping over breaks put together by a DJ, MCs would rap over tracks that were pre-recorded in the studio by producers and studio musicians. These producers, like Sylvia Robinson (1935–2011), the producer of "Rapper's Delight" and other early hip-hop singles and co-founder of Sugar Hill Records, explored new electronic music technologies such as drum machines and synthesizers in crafting the sounds of their tracks. Afrika Bambaataa's "Planet Rock" (1982) famously uses a Roland TR-808 drum machine and its distinctive sounds, a vocoder, which electronically modifies the human voice (e.g., the "yeah" sampled in "Fight the Power"), and a synthesizer recreation of a melody from "Trans-Europe Express" (1977) by German electronic group Kraftwerk. "Planet Rock," especially its use of timbres of the 808 drum machine, became enormously influential not only in the production of hip-hop music, but also served as an inspiration for innovators of concurrently emerging genres of electronic music like techno and house.

While early hip-hop recordings were generally oriented towards creating an environment for partying, "The Message" (1982) by Grandmaster Flash and the Furious Five and produced by Sylvia Robinson broke new ground as the first hip-hop recording to describe the oppressive conditions of inner-city urban life in the United States. The chorus memorably states "don't push me 'cause I'm close to the edge" and "it's like a jungle sometimes; it makes me wonder how I keep from goin' under." The verses elaborate in detail on the economic struggles, violence, and failing public education that characterized the everyday experience of those living in urban poverty. The track includes mixed-in sounds of the street such as police sirens, and it closes with a skit in which the members of the group are harassed by a police officer and arrested for no apparent reason. "The Message" was a massive hit and paved the way for a whole stream of hip-hop music that was a vehicle for dealing with oppression, marginalization, and struggle related to issues of race, class,

FIGURE 13.5

A DJ named G Man and his crew in the Bronx borough of New York City, 1985

Source: Henry Chalfant.

FIGURE 13.6

Sylvia Robinson in 1983

Source: Getty Images / Michael Ochs Archives.

POLITICAL ACTION

drugs, and politics. During the 1980s, politically oriented hip-hop groups like Public Enemy followed in the footsteps of the social realism of "The Message," many of them in the aggressive style of hardcore rap. Public Enemy's albums *Yo! Bum Rush the Show* (1987), *It Takes a Nation of Millions to Hold Us Back* (1988), and *Fear of a Black Planet* (1990) sample quotes from speeches by Malcolm X, a leading African American activist noted for his fiery critique of white power, and other figures from the 1960s black nationalist and civil rights movements.

On the West Coast, N.W.A (Niggaz with Attitude), Snoop Dogg (Calvin Cordozar Broadus, Jr., b. 1971), and Tupac (2Pac) Shakur (Lesane Crooks, 1971–1996) popularized **gangsta rap**, a hip-hop subgenre that vividly chronicled the so-called gangsta lifestyle of the urban poor of Los Angeles: gang violence, sex, unemployment, and widespread crack cocaine use. N.W.A, with core members Ice Cube (O'Shea Jackson, b. 1969), Dr. Dre (Andre Young, b. 1965), and Eazy-E (Eric Wright, 1973–1995) plus DJ Yella (Antoine Carraby, b. 1967) and MC Ren (Lorenzo Patterson, b. 1969), recorded their first studio album, *Straight Outta Compton*, in 1988. In braggadocious and self-aggrandizing raps, they described in graphic terms life in gang-ridden South Central Los Angeles against a backdrop of the sounds of police sirens and gunshots along with funk (and other) samples, drum machine beats, and synthesizers. Rapping in a laid-back West Coast style, they cataloged police brutality and racial profiling ("Fuck tha Police"), the violence of the streets ("Gangsta Gangsta"), and the constraint radio censorship places on rap artists ("Express Yourself"). *Straight Outta Compton* enjoyed massive success across lines of race and class, appealing to youth in urban black communities and to youth in the white suburbs. Gangsta rap and its profanity-laced and violent lyrics set a new tone for commercial success in hip-hop, and many groups followed in the footsteps of N.W.A to produce their own music celebrating the gangsta lifestyle.

Straight Outta Compton had been released on Ruthless Records, a label co-founded by Eazy-E and manager Jerry Heller (1940–2016), which also released work by artists like Southern California all-women hip-hop group J.J. Fad, the singer Michel'le (Michel'le Toussaint, b. 1970), and, later, Bone Thugs-N-Harmony. After he left N.W.A in 1991, Dr. Dre co-founded Death Row Records, which released a series of multi-platinum selling albums including his first solo album *The Chronic* (1992),

FIGURE 13.7
N.W.A (from left: Dr. Dre, Eazy-E, MC Ren, and DJ Yella)
Source: Getty Images / Lynn Goldsmith.

Snoop Dogg's debut *Doggystyle* (1993), and 2Pac Shakur's *All Eyez on Me* (1996). Dr. Dre's productions departed from the thick, multi-layered sampling on Public Enemy's "Fight the Power." Instead, he often featured only two or three samples, a cleaner, pop-oriented style, slower grooves, and a smooth, laid-back style of rapping. This style was known as G-funk, a subgenre of gangsta rap that became widely popular in the hip-hop of the 1990s.

Other innovators in the golden era of hip-hop included East Coast hardcore group Run-DMC, which combined rock drum beats and guitar riffs with hip-hop conventions and attracted fans of rock. Their 1986 album *Raising Hell* included a new version of "Walk This Way" by the rock group Aerosmith, with vocals by Aerosmith vocalist Steven Tyler and the playing of Aerosmith guitarist Joe Perry. It and *Licensed to Ill* (1986), an album by the first successful white hip-hop group, the Beastie Boys, were the first two multi-platinum rap albums, both of which were produced by Rick Rubin (b. 1963) and released on his label Def Jam Records. In the late 1980s The rapper Rakim (William Michael Griffin Jr., b. 1968) was one of the first to introduce a smooth, laid-back style. His intricate rhyme schemes distinguished him from the more common energetic style of his peers like Chuck D and inspired a new generation of rappers. Rakim's legacy is heard today in the styles of rappers like Nas, Jay-Z, and Common. By the late 1980s female hip-hop groups began to break through to commercial success, with Salt-N-Pepa (Cheryl "Salt" James, Sandra "Pepa" Denton, and Deidra "DJ Spinderella" Roper, who replaced Latoya Hanson) making it first to the charts with their 1987 single "Push It." Queen Latifah (Dana Owens, b. 1970) also achieved commercial success as a hip-hop artist (before going onto a successful career in film and television), releasing the first political commentary by a woman rapper. Her "Ladies First" (1989) responded to male rappers' negative stereotyping of female rappers.

One of the most influential groups of the 1990s was the hardcore group the Wu-Tang Clan, a collective of nine rappers from the projects of Staten Island, New York, whose first album was called *Enter the Wu-Tang (36 Chambers)* (1993). In addition to continuing to innovate within established conventions of hip-hop like sampling and the poetics of rapping about the realities of inner-city life, the Wu-Tang Clan connected their work to the world of Chinese martial arts. They sampled audio from martial arts films and referred to Staten Island as "Shaolin," a reference to the martial art called Shaolin Kung Fu and the Buddhist Shaolin Temple in China's Henan province where it developed. Their recording contract allowed them

FIGURE 13.8
Salt-N-Pepa in 1988. From left, Sandra Denton ("Pepa"), Deidra Roper ("DJ Spinderella"), and Cheryl James ("Salt")
Source: Getty Images / Janette Beckman.

to negotiate their own subsequent deals as solo artists with outside labels, with the caveat that a portion of the earnings from these projects would go back to the group. This new business model enabled the Wu-Tang Clan to pursue other business ventures such as a lucrative clothing line (Wu Wear) and a video game (*Shaolin Style*). The musical and entrepreneurial skills of the group changed the game in the business of hip-hop and set the stage for the further widespread development of the hip-hop industry beyond music.

ECONOMIC ACTIVITY

New York and Los Angeles served as central locations for the development of hip-hop and the hip-hop industry, and in the mid-1990s the two scenes attracted even more attention as they became embroiled in a feud that resulted in the untimely deaths of East Coast rapper The Notorious B.I.G. (Christopher Wallace, aka Biggie Smalls or Biggie, 1972–1997) and West Coast rapper 2Pac Shakur in anonymous drive-by shootings. Since the early 1980s hip-hop scenes have also developed around the United States and the world as rappers have found this now global music useful for commenting on local issues about social marginalization and oppression, for entertainment and partying, and for fame and commercial gain. The best-selling hip-hop artist of all time, widely respected for his rap skills, is Eminem (Marshall Mathers, b. 1972), who was raised by a single mother as one of only a few white families in a predominantly black neighborhood of Detroit. Canadian-born rapper Drake (Aubrey Drake Graham, b. 1986) has released the most hits in the history of the *Billboard* charts for all popular music (by 2018 over 150 songs of his had appeared on the *Billboard* Hot 100 Chart), and has become one of the most celebrated rappers of today.

Since the mid-1990s a host of other extraordinary rappers have entertained audiences, including André 3000 and Big Boi of the group Outkast, Lil' Kim, Nas, Lauryn Hill, 50 Cent, Lil Wayne, Missy Elliot, Nicki Minaj, Kanye West, Jay-Z, and Kendrick Lamar. They have become some of the world's best-known celebrities with business operations across the entertainment industry and beyond. Singer and rapper Lauryn Hill (b. 1975) won the Grammy for Album of the Year for her debut album *The Miseducation of Lauryn Hill* in 1998, the first for a hip-hop album. (The only other has been Outkast's *Speakerboxxx/The Love Below* in 2004.) Jay-Z (Shawn Carter b. 1969) controls a business

ECONOMIC ACTIVITY

FIGURE 13.9
The Wu-Tang Clan in 1997
Source: Getty Images / Bob Berg.

FIGURE 13.10
Kendrick Lamar performing at the 2016 Grammy Awards
Source: Getty Images / Larry Busacca.

empire that extends to fashion, professional sports, beverage companies, and the technology sector. Los Angeles rapper Kendrick Lamar's (b. 1987) "Alright" from his album *To Pimp a Butterfly* (2015) became an anthem for the Black Lives Matter movement, bringing socially conscious hip-hop into the mainstream once again. With contributions from jazz tenor saxophonist Kamasi Washington and jazz keyboardist Robert Glasper, the album connects hip-hop and jazz, exploring some of the two genres' common ground. Through their collaborations, complex use of samples, innovative musical production, entertaining humor, and mind-blowing rapping, hip-hop artists look to the past and interpret the present as they mix and remix old and new sounds together, carrying themselves and their audiences into what they hope is a bright future.

WHERE DO I GO FROM HERE?

- Listen to the version of "Fight the Power" from the film *Do the Right Thing*. What does the saxophone solo by Branford Marsalis (brother of Wynton Marsalis, Chapter 13, Gateway 54) add to the recording?

- Listen to James Brown's "Funky Drummer." Can you find the drum break used in "Fight the Power"?

- In a style called "battle rap" a rapper performs pre-composed or improvised freestyle verses full of insults and bragging, often in a live exchange with another rapper in an attempt to diss the opponent and prove superior skills. What is the earliest video example you can find of a rap battle? Where have you encountered it in popular culture? How many different forms of rap battle can you find? What are their characteristics?

- Listen to "Nuthin' but a 'G' Thang" by Dr. Dre featuring Snoop Doggy Dogg from *The Chronic*. What musical elements define Dr. Dre's G-funk production style? What themes do Dr. Dre and Snoop Dogg deal with in this rap?

- Compare "Fight the Power" with "Fuck tha Police" by N.W.A and "Alright" by Kendrick Lamar. Compare and contrast the ways these songs approach social issues in their lyrics and production.

GATEWAY 54
NEO-TRADITIONAL JAZZ

What Is It?

A number of jazz musicians in the late 1970s and 1980s turned to various styles and sub-genres of jazz that had developed in previous times. This **neo-traditionalism** in jazz focused on celebrating older styles and historical repertoire from earlier in the twentieth century. Probably the most well known of these jazz neo-traditionalists is the New Orleans-born virtuoso trumpet player, composer, and bandleader Wynton Marsalis (b. 1961). Since the 1980s, Marsalis has been involved in many high-profile projects dedicated to preserving, sustaining, and continuing the jazz tradition as a significant aspect of American culture. Though he is interested in retaining tradition, Marsalis often presents music that might seem old in rather new ways. He recorded several albums of new arrangements of jazz standards in the 1980s and 1990s. Our gateway to jazz neo-traditionalism is his recording of the jazz standard "Caravan" originally composed in 1936 by Duke Ellington and Juan Tizol. It is the opening track to the album *Marsalis Standard Time Vol. 1*

FIGURE 13.11
Wynton Marsalis
Source: Getty Images / Stephen J. Cohen.

(1987), which, in addition to Marsalis on trumpet, features Marcus Roberts (b. 1963) on piano, Robert Leslie Hurst III (b. 1964) on upright bass, and Jeff "Tain" Watts (b. 1960) on drums.

 Listen to the first thirty seconds of the recording.

How Does It Work?

Timbre

This recording features the sound of Marsalis' trumpet. During the head he uses a mute, which gives the trumpet a covered timbre, and then plays with an unmuted, clear sound during his solo improvisations. The recording also features piano, upright bass, and drum set.

Texture

The texture is that of a typical jazz quartet. The trumpet plays a melodic line that interacts with the rhythm section of piano, bass, and drums. Sometimes the piano joins the trumpet to harmonize a melody, sometimes the piano plays a solo that interacts with the bass and drums, and sometimes the drums play solo.

Rhythm

The underlying rhythms of the drums, bass, and piano in the opening and some other sections of the recording come together to form a type of groove known generally as a New Orleans groove or feel. This groove features a habanera rhythm in the bass, accents on beats two and four in the drums (beat four gets a stronger accent than beat two), subdivided beats with a slight swing feel, and an active syncopated snare drum. At all other times, the rhythm section plays a straight-ahead swing feel. The bass plays a walking bass line and the drum set plays a heavy swing feel the ride cymbal, accents on two and four on the hi-hat, and occasional lighter fills and hits on the snare and bass drums. The tempo and meter of four are constant throughout this version of "Caravan."

Melody

The melody of the head is mostly in a minor mode, though in some instances it follows a chromatic scale. The melodies of the trumpet and piano improvisations for the most part correspond to the underlying harmonic chord progression outlined in the piano and bass.

Harmony

In the A section, the harmony does not change much, sustaining a V chord before resolving to the minor tonic. The bridge turns the minor tonic into a major chord and cycles briefly through four different major keys that lead back to the minor harmony of the A section.

Form

"Caravan" follows a 64-bar AABA form, with each section lasting 16 bars rather than the more usual 8 bars. This recording, after a short introduction in the drums and piano, follows a head–solos–head form as it repeats the AABA form over and over.

Performance Techniques

The musicians interact with one another constantly as they establish the groove and complement one another's playing during sections fully devoted to improvisation.

Listen to the first thirty seconds of the recording for the interlocking habanera rhythm of the bass and drums.

Listen to the entire recording following this timed listening guide.

LISTENING GUIDE 13.2

TIME	SECTION	FORM	DESCRIPTION
0:00	Introduction		The drums play alone for four bars to set up the New Orleans groove. The bass and piano join for eight more bars, with the piano comping and the bass playing the habanera rhythm.
0:15	Head	A	Marsalis begins playing the head on the trumpet, with the piano playing along with him to create a two-part harmony and adding typical comping between melodic phrases. His version of the A section places many of the melody notes on the upbeat, creating a great deal of syncopation. During the final four bars of the A section, the bass displaces the habanera rhythm so that it begins on beat two instead of beat one, which creates a seemingly off-kilter polyrhythm. The A section is generally the same each time.
0:35		A	The A melody repeats.
0:54		B	In the first two measures of the B section, the groove stops as the rhythm section plays long notes together with the trumpet, though the steady pulse continues to be felt. When the rhythm section begins playing in time again at the start of the third measure, it launches into a swing feel. After the first four notes, instead of playing the melody of "Caravan," Marsalis improvises on the trumpet.
1:14		A	The A melody returns.
1:33	Chorus 1	A	Marsalis begins the first chorus of his improvised solo on some of the lowest pitches on the trumpet, and the rhythm section returns to the New Orleans feel. During the solos, the habanera rhythm continues in the bass throughout each A section without being displaced as it was during the head.
1:53		A	Throughout this A section and his entire solo, Marsalis outlines the underlying harmony and explores the full range of the trumpet, demonstrating his mastery of the instrument.

TIME	SECTION	FORM	DESCRIPTION
2:12		B	The rhythm section switches to the swing feel. At the end of the bridge, Marsalis plays a rhythm that emphasizes several upbeats in a row, referring back to his version of the A section of the head.
2:32		A	The New Orleans feel returns again, and Marsalis plays an ascending line from the lowest range of the trumpet to the instrument's high range in the last few bars of the chorus.
2:51	Chorus 2	A	As Marsalis and the rhythm section reach a high point in pitch and dynamics, a swing feel is played for the first time on an A section, which continues through the end of the bridge of this chorus.
3:11		A	
3:30		B	At the end of the bridge, Marsalis again plays a phrase consisting of all upbeats, referencing earlier moments in the solo as well as his version of the head.
3:50		A	The New Orleans feel returns again for Marsalis' final A section. His return to the low pitches of the trumpet from the beginning of the solo, and his and the rhythm section's gradual decrescendo together signal the end of his solo and sets up the beginning of the piano solo.
4:10	Chorus 3	A	Right from the start of the piano solo, the rhythm section plays the swing feel, which continues throughout the piano solo.
4:29		A	The piano outlines the harmonies of the chords, and also references melodic phrases from the head. For example, starting at 4:41 the piano repeats a three-note fragment of the head twice in a row.
4:49		B	During this bridge, the solo in the right hand of the piano interacts with the comping in the left hand of the piano particularly clearly, which sometimes produces a call and response effect.
5:09		A	The piano creates rhythmic excitement by playing a series of syncopated rhythms, to which the drummer responds with increasing rhythmic variety and activity.
5:28	Chorus 4	A	The piano solo continues with references to the head.
5:48		A	The solo features block chords.
6:07		B	The piano plays a series of full chords to start the bridge, and the drums and bass respond by playing much more loudly and actively.
6:27		A	As the piano descends and starts playing more sparsely in the last four bars, the habanera rhythm returns in the bass and the drums shift back to their part of the New Orleans groove.
6:47	Head	A	The head is restated, sounding mostly the same as the opening head.
7:06		A	The A melody repeats.
7:26		B	After starting the melody on the trumpet, Marsalis gives way to an improvised solo in the piano for the remainder of the bridge.
7:46		A	The final A ends with a tag where the band plays the final phrase of the head three times rather than once.
8:16	End		

What Does It Mean?

This recording of "Caravan" is neo-traditional because it showcases musical elements in jazz that developed between the turn of the twentieth century and 1960. Its use of the traditional head–solos–head form common in jazz stays close to conventions of jazz performance established in the 1940s and 1950s. The AABA form of "Caravan" has roots in the AABA song form of Tin Pan Alley composers in the early twentieth century. By 1987 "Caravan" was a well-established jazz standard. Marsalis' choice of this standard, a composition by Duke Ellington and Ellington band trombonist Juan Tizol, as the opening track on *Marsalis Standard Time Vol. 1* and his decision to maintain its original internal form, harmony, and melody, can be understood as a tribute to Ellington and his significant place in jazz history and a way of Marsalis aligning himself with the tradition that Ellington helped establish.

The improvised solos by Marsalis and pianist Marcus Roberts are based on the underlying harmony and emphasize the dissonances produced by the upper extensions of chords, a bebop tradition. The way the soloists musically communicate with the other musicians and respond to one another's volume, rhythmic patterns, and overall intensity is reminiscent of the innovations of bebop and hard bop musicians in the 1940s and 1950s. In comparison to modal jazz, jazz fusion, and avant-garde and free jazz, this kind of improvisation sounds traditional, as it celebrates and hearkens back to jazz conventions developed in the 1940s and 1950s.

Listen again to "Caravan" for the broader head–solos–head form (another long-standing tradition for the performance of standards) and the AABA form that repeats throughout the recording. Listen to the trumpet solo and the piano solo and compare the ways that they improvise and interact with the other musicians to Charlie Parker's improvisation on "Ko Ko" in the gateway to bebop (Chapter 11, Gateway 46).

Wynton Marsalis' neo-traditionalism, as his recording of "Caravan" illustrates, is richly layered historically. In addition to the Tin Pan Alley song form (AABA) of the 1920s, a jazz standard of the 1930s, and improvisatory and harmonic styles of the 1940s and 1950s, he draws on an even older layer of tradition by including the underlying New Orleans groove as a key part of its rhythm. Established by the drums and the habanera rhythm of the bass for many of the A sections in this recording, the New Orleans groove is most associated today with the music of New Orleans brass bands that perform in street parades, in clubs, and at concerts and festivals (Chapter 10, Gateway 40). This particular New Orleans groove, with its habanera rhythm, is an example of jazz's "Latin tinge," part of a history that stretches back into the nineteenth century. Including this groove on his version of "Caravan" is a way for Marsalis to connect this recording to his and his family's own New Orleans roots and the roots of jazz in that city, and to create another historical layer to this example of neo-traditionalism.

Listen to "Caravan" again, paying close attention to the groove set up mostly by the bass and drums. Notice the shifts between the New Orleans groove and the swing feel in those instruments.

What Is Its History?

By 1975 jazz musicians could choose from a wide range of stylistic options: bebop and hard bop featuring improvisation over repeating cycles of chord changes; modal jazz with improvisation over long stretches of static chords rather than harmonic motion; the "New Thing," which, as free jazz, had challenged many established jazz conventions; and jazz fusion's combinations of jazz with rock, funk, and other popular genres. Many of the musicians who had played on Miles Davis' groundbreaking jazz-rock fusion album *Bitches Brew* (1970) continued their own jazz fusion projects

AESTHETICS

into the 1980s and 1990s, including Herbie Hancock, Wayne Shorter, Joe Zawinul, Chick Corea, and John McLaughlin. But neo-traditionalists rejected this approach. They believed that fusions were abandoning what they considered to be the "jazz tradition." In their view jazz was an art form that had developed historically through the creative work of particular master musicians such as Jelly Roll Morton, Louis Armstrong, and Charlie Parker. They believed that it was important to continue to perform jazz repertoires and styles that had developed among these great masters in the past. Given that jazz was no longer a genre with mass commercial appeal, neo-traditionalists thought it was more important to maintain what they saw as traditional practices in jazz than to adapt the music to the commercial market in search of larger audiences and greater profits.

Wynton Marsalis is the most prominent neo-traditionalist of this period. He was born in New Orleans to a musical family: his father is the jazz pianist and educator Ellis Marsalis (b. 1934), and his most well-known sibling is the tenor saxophonist Branford Marsalis (b. 1960). A trumpet prodigy, Wynton came to national prominence in the 1980s through a number of recording projects, and he is the only artist to win Grammy Awards for both jazz and classical music performance (he did so at age twenty-two in 1983 and again in 1984). In his early career, he was adamant that avant-garde jazz, free jazz, and fusion did not count as jazz, and he focused on the performance and celebration of styles and repertoires developed before 1960. Though he later softened that view, he has devoted much of his energy throughout his career to promoting earlier styles and repertoires of jazz, including tributes to Jelly Roll Morton, Thelonious Monk, Duke Ellington, Charles Mingus, and many others. His oratorio *Blood on the Fields* (1994) features big band instrumentation and includes vocal and instrumental styles from many eras of jazz. In the classical form of an oratorio, it embodies Marsalis' view that jazz is an art music, and connects his expertise as a classical musician to his work promoting jazz in American society. The work received the 1997 Pulitzer Prize for Music, the first awarded to a jazz artist. In effect the Pulitzer jury, without saying so, was supporting the notion of jazz as "America's classical music," a notion that goes hand in hand with the work of Marsalis and other neo-traditionalists.

Marsalis' award also marked a gradual shift in the Pulitzer Prize, which had previously only been awarded to compositions in the classical tradition, and whose board had notoriously rejected a suggestion to award a Special Citation to Duke Ellington for his work in 1965. After Marsalis' 1997 Pulitzer Prize, Ellington was posthumously awarded a Special Citation in 1999. And after the Pulitzer board issued a statement in 2004 that they wanted the annual Music Prize to now honor the "full range of distinguished American musical compositions," free jazz composer and saxophonist Ornette Coleman received the award in 2007 for his album *Sound Grammar*, as did genre-crossing jazz experimenter Henry Threadgill (b. 1944) in 2016 for his album *In for a Penny, In for a Pound*. In 2018 rapper Kendrick Lamar received the Pulitzer for his album *Damn*, the first time a completely non-notated work, and one from popular music, had been recognized by the Pulitzer jury and board. The Pulitzer organization recognized the significance and excellence of the work of these musicians in jazz and hip-hop long after it was already known by their audiences. What these recent awards signify is not that these genres—long considered unworthy of recognition in the classical music world—are achieving greatness for the first time, but rather that institutions like the Pulitzer Prize are changing their understanding of what "great music" means.

FIGURE 13.12
Wynton Marsalis with the Jazz at Lincoln Center Orchestra in 2017
Source: Getty Images / Stephen J. Cohen.

FIGURE 13.13
Herbie Hancock (left) with saxophonist Melissa Aldana, winner of the Thelonious Monk International Jazz Saxophone Competition, and Lee Godown, Global Public Policy staff of General Motors
Source: Getty Images / Paul Morigi.

Regardless of whether their music is receiving awards or recognition, jazz neo-traditionalists, like aficionados of classical music, look to the past to admire what they regard as great masterworks. Even though jazz has always welcomed influence from many parts of the world and musicians outside the United States have been performing music labeled as jazz since even before 1920, neo-traditionalists have focused on celebrating jazz as a uniquely American cultural practice with a rich historical tradition.

Neo-traditionalists recognized (and lamented) that, similar to classical music, jazz by the 1980s did not have broad commercial appeal. But instead of seeking to make the music more commercially accessible, many jazz musicians began to build institutions during this period that could support jazz as an art form, institutions similar to (and sometimes connected with) institutions that support classical music. Wynton Marsalis has been a pillar of one such institution, Jazz at Lincoln Center (JALC), housed at Lincoln Center in New York City alongside the Metropolitan Opera, the New York Philharmonic, the New York City Ballet, and the Juilliard School. JALC began as a concert series in 1987, became an official constituent of Lincoln Center in 1996, and today boasts a facility with three concert venues designed specifically for jazz performance and an annual budget of over $40 million. JALC, with Marsalis as its Managing and Artistic Director, is committed to expanding the audience for jazz through performance (it presents over 500 concerts per year), extensive education programs, and public advocacy.

Another organization that emerged to support jazz in this period is the Thelonious Monk Institute of Jazz, co-founded in 1986 by Monk's son the drummer Thelonious Monk III (b. 1949), the opera singer and philanthropist Maria Fisher (c. 1904–1991), and the jazz trumpet player Clark Terry (1920–2015). The Monk Institute provides tuition-free educational programs, promotes jazz performance and education around the world, and sponsors a renowned annual international competition that focuses on a different instrument each year and has launched successful careers for many of its winners. Winners of the Thelonious Monk Institute of Jazz International Competition such as saxophonist Joshua Redman, trumpet player Ambrose Akinmusire, and vocalists Cécile McLorin Salvant and Gretchen Parlato enjoy successful careers as prominent jazz artists. Herbie Hancock serves as the chairman of the Monk Institute's board of trustees and helps oversee the Monk Institute for Jazz Performance, a tuition-free master of music program at the UCLA Herb Alpert School of Music.

In addition to independent institutions of performance and education like JALC and the Monk Institute, jazz programs at colleges and universities proliferated in the United States and abroad during the period from 1975 to 1994. College-level jazz programs were first offered in the late 1940s, notably at North Texas State College (now the University of North Texas) and the Schillinger House in Boston (now the Berklee College of Music). Since the 1960s university schools of music have become more open to including jazz instruction alongside existing programs in classical performance and composition. By 1989, over 100 colleges and universities in the United States offered degrees in jazz studies, and hundreds of thousands of high school students were performing in school jazz ensembles. As jazz was becoming less commercially viable, it was exploding in popularity in educational institutions, probably not unrelated to the view of jazz as America's classical music. Since the 1980s, classrooms and auditoriums at high schools and universities have emerged as among the main locations for teaching, learning, and performing jazz. Many—but not all—jazz programs developed curricula aligned with the views of jazz neo-traditionalists, and they focused on training students in bebop and hard bop styles of performance, composition, and improvisation. Colleges and universities continue to attract students who are excited to develop their skills in jazz, and most of the active jazz musicians born since 1960 have studied in a university-level jazz program.

WHERE DO I GO FROM HERE?

- Listen to or watch some excerpts of *Blood on the Fields,* the Pulitzer Prize-winning oratorio by Wynton Marsalis. What styles of jazz can you hear in these excerpts? Why is this work called an oratorio?

- Find some recordings of tenor saxophonist Joshua Redman from the early 1990s. To what extent do these recordings sound like neo-traditional jazz? Which musical elements can help us identify neo-traditional aspects of the music?

- The jazz vocalist Jon Hendricks (1921–2017) had a long and prolific career and can be heard on *Blood on the Fields.* His work in the 1980s and early 1990s demonstrates a particularly innovative technique that he helped create called **vocalese**, a process in which instrumental compositions and well-known recorded improvisations are given lyrics and sung instead of played. Listen to his album *Freddie Freeloader* (1990). How do his vocal arrangements of well-known jazz recordings of the past compare with the original recordings on which they are modeled? How does this project compare to Wynton Marsalis' *Standard Time* albums as an example of neo-traditional jazz?

GATEWAY 55
POSTMODERN CLASSICAL MUSIC

What Is It?

One of the significant social issues of the period between 1975 and 1994 was the HIV/AIDS epidemic, which has claimed more than half a million lives in the United States and about thirty-five million worldwide. In addition to responses from the medical, scientific, and political communities, musicians and composers also engaged with this crisis in efforts to raise public awareness, garner support for those suffering from HIV/AIDS, and mourn those who had been lost. Our gateway to classical music of this period is the third movement, "Chaconne: Giulio's Song," of John Corigliano's Symphony No. 1, a composition written out of Corigliano's grief for those whose lives had been taken by AIDS. A *chaconne* is a Baroque triple-meter dance form with a short, repeated ostinato in the bass part over which others play melodic variations. The other movements are "Apologue: Of Rage and Remembrance"; "Tarantella" (an Italian rural dance); and "Epilogue." Composed in 1988, Corigliano wrote about the work, "During the past decade I have lost many friends and colleagues to the AIDS epidemic, and the cumulative effect of those losses has, naturally, deeply affected me. My Symphony No. 1 was generated by feelings of loss, anger, and frustration." The Chicago Symphony commissioned this work and gave its first performance in 1990. Leonard Slatkin conducts the National Symphony Orchestra in this recording.

FIGURE 13.14
John Corigliano with his Oscar for Best Original Score for the 1998 film *The Red Violin*
Source: Getty Images / HECTOR MATA.

 Listen to the quiet, sombre opening of this movement.

How Does It Work?

Timbre

The full orchestra features two solo cellos and solos on woodwinds and horn.

Texture

The texture is varied but the two cellos playing in counterpoint figure prominently, as do instrumental solos over drone-like orchestral accompaniments.

Rhythm

The tempo is slow with long sustained tones. A sense of beat and meter comes and goes.

Melody

The principal melody, Giulio's song, ascends with disjunct leaps.

Harmony

The harmony is dissonant but drone-like.

Form

A single principal melody over a very slow, drone-like ostinato in the low strings is heard throughout.

Performance Techniques

The performance techniques are common to symphonic music.

 Listen for the entrance of Giulio's song and the drone-like texture for the first 1:30 of this performance.

What Does It Mean?

This movement memorializes Corigliano's friends who died of AIDS, including Giulio, an amateur cellist with whom Corigliano used to improvise, and Giulio's cello teacher. Giulio's song is based on a fragment of melody Giulio once improvised. The melodies for Corigliano's other friends, played by the woodwinds and horn, are the composer's settings of one-sentence eulogies he commissioned from a writer friend.

Listen to the entire performance following this timed listening guide.

LISTENING GUIDE 13.3

TIME	DESCRIPTION
0:00	The low strings (the basses, cellos, and violas) enter almost imperceptibly with a series of long sustained tones, which form the chaconne's ostinato.
0:57	The cello enters with Giulio's song, an ascending, disjunct melody of sustained tones over the long, low pitches of the ostinato. A variant of the opening melodic ascent is played a number of times.
4:01	The second cello enters with a two-note stepwise descending motive and joins the first cello in counterpoint, an icon of a conversation (a lesson perhaps) between the two men.
4:39	The first cello replays Giulio's song and the second cello follows in imitative counterpoint, as if listening and understanding his friend's illness.
6:00	A high-pitched held tone announces a new section in which the whole orchestra enters with short melodies in the woodwinds and horn, indexing individual victims of AIDS.
7:05	The solo cello reintroduces Giulio's song, which joins in a chorus with other victims represented by the other instruments and the second cello, replete with the sounding of bell chimes imitating the death knell of church bells at their funerals.

TIME	DESCRIPTION
8:57	The flute and other instruments join the cellos in Giulio's song, creating a new, brighter, perhaps more hopeful timbre, as if rejoicing in his life.
10:23	A crescendo leads to a long sustained tone on the trumpet followed by dramatic low-pitched thuds of a drum, icons of the final nails in the coffin perhaps, and dissonant forte chords in the brass expressing the anguish of those left behind. The steady drum beat, the bells, and the swirling instrumental lines echo the march to the gallows in Hector Berlioz's early-nineteenth-century *Symphonie Fantastique* (Chapter 7, Gateway 28).
13:43	After a violent crescendo, the orchestra subsides to silence, leaving only the faint sound, and memory, of a solo cellist.
13:54	End

The HIV/AIDS epidemic, first reported and named in the early 1980s, devastated the arts community in the United States. Corigliano's Symphony No. 1 memorializes friends who had died or were dying of AIDS by referencing some of their favorite music. The first movement, in memory of a pianist, is called "Of Rage and Remembrance" and alternates an Argentine tango melody to signal nostalgia and remembrance with darker passages iconic of the rage many felt as the disease spread through their community. The second movement, for a music executive, is based on a traditional Italian dance, the *tarantella*. The fourth movement combines themes from the first three movements. The symphony won two Grammy Awards, and Corigliano went on to win the Pulitzer Prize for Music in 2001 for his Symphony No. 2.

Like Corigliano's Symphony No. 1, much of the classical music composed in the period from 1975 to 1994 is relatively accessible. Although it sounds modern rather than traditional, it often features appealing and widely understood tonal harmony, familiar forms and instrumental timbres like the symphony orchestra, and regular, often repetitive, meters and rhythms. Although the music contains plenty of unfamiliar, "modern," dissonant chords and chromatic scales, the composers hoped to attract listeners with iconic references to familiar music from the past of European classical music as well as to contemporary world music, popular music, and jazz. The most important trends in classical composition in this period can be described as **postmodernism** in the general sense that they reacted against the avant-garde modernist musical styles of the 1950s and 1960s.

Postmodernism suffused all the arts in this period. European music, art, and architecture since the 1890s have generally been called "modern" for two reasons. First, modern art was linked to "modern life" based on modern technologies like airplanes, computers, and electronic recordings. Second, modern art broke from nineteenth-century traditions, rejecting tonality in the case of music, figurative painting and sculpture in the case of art, and Baroque decoration and classic colonnaded façades in the case of architecture. In the 1970s some artists in all these disciplines turned their backs on the tenets and styles of modernism. Their art was dubbed postmodernism.

Fundamental to postmodernism is the rejection of the notion of progress in the arts. An earlier modernist ideology argued for continuous progress in the complexity of the arts. Postmodernists rejected this view and reclaimed,

FIGURE 13.15
Mies van der Rohe's modernist IBM tower in Chicago
Source: Teemu008, Wikimedia Commons.

FIGURE 13.16
Frank Lloyd Wright's modernist interior for the Guggenheim Museum in New York
Source: Evan-Amos, Wikimedia Commons.

FIGURE 13.17
The postmodernist Sony Building in New York
Source: David Shankbone, Wikimedia Commons.

reordered, and reindexed the artistic styles of the past to create new art that had not been seen or heard before. Instead of progress, they proposed a kind of circularity or recycling. New postmodern work was at first criticized as vulgar, as it seemed to pander to a popular audience. But in the case of music, postmodernism served to attract the audiences who had been alienated by the modernism of the 1950s and 1960s and its turn away from their expectations and understandings as listeners.

The term postmodernism was first used in the field of architecture, and the change in architectural style in the 1970s and 1980s illustrates visually the difference between modernism and postmodernism. Clean, repeating lines characterized modern architecture, whose archetypal representative is the skyscraper. Ludwig Mies van der Rohe (1886–1959), one of architectural modernisms' founders and most respected figures, built unadorned, rectilinear prisms of steel and class in Chicago in the 1950s and 1960s. Frank Lloyd Wright (1867–1959), another modernist, used a curvier, more sculptural, but nonetheless unadorned approach to the repetition of lines for the interior for the Guggenheim Museum in New York.

Postmodernism responded to the linear, repetitive quality of modern architecture by adding decorative elements borrowed from the architecture of previous eras in a manner commonly called "pastiche." In 1984 Philip Johnson (1906–2005) applied a postmodern sensibility to an otherwise rectilinear modernist skyscraper in New York City, his AT&T (now Sony) Building. The triangular structure at the top is a whimsical reference to similar structures, called pediments, on the top of colonnades in eighteenth-century classical-style architecture and on furniture designed in the so-called Chippendale style. Corigliano's use of the *chaconne* form and his echo of Berlioz's *Symphonie Fantastique* in his Symphony No. 1 are similar postmodern references to music of the past.

What Is Its History?

Postmodernism in music took four forms during the period from 1975 to 1994: postmodernism *per se*, minimalism, the use of familiar forms, and neo-Romanticism. Although much composition in this period is postmodernist in its turn away from modernist complexity and abstraction, the term postmodernism is often applied only to work that, like postmodern architecture, applies familiar styles and forms from the past to a modernist structure. John Corigliano, born to a musical family in New York in 1938 and a professor at the City University of New York (CUNY), was one of the most successful American composers to adopt the pastiche quality of postmodern architecture. In Symphony No. 1 he creates musical collages that paste a panoply of historical styles onto an essentially modernist foundation. Critics and audiences have applauded his compositions for symphony orchestra and wind band, as well as his opera *The Ghosts of Versailles* (1991) and his score for the film *The Red Violin* (1998). Because of their accessibility, they are performed relatively frequently today.

Minimalism was another technique that became respectable in this period. What had begun on the fringes of the classical music scene in the 1960s has, over the last fifty years, entered its mainstream. To give just one example, in 1992 the Metropolitan Opera, one of the most prominent classical music institutions in the United States, commissioned Philip Glass to write an opera called *The Voyage* to commemorate Columbus' sail to the West Indies 500 years earlier.

During this period John Adams (b. 1947) emerged as the most important successor to the minimalist tradition. Born in Massachusetts and educated at Harvard, he taught at the San Francisco Conservatory of Music from 1972 to 1984 and has lived in California since then. Adams extended the limits of minimalism. While still writing music accessible to the general public, he extended the complexity of the minimalist tradition in ways that appealed to professional musicians and sophisticated listeners, some of whom found the repetition in early minimalist work boring. The title of his 1976 *Phrygian Gates* for solo piano refers to his use of a Medieval European church mode (Chapter 2, Gateway 5). "Gates" are a series of changes in texture that appear abruptly throughout the piece. These changes create a sense of progression and anticipation missing from earlier minimalist compositions. Adams joined Philip Glass in the composition of operas with his 1986 *Nixon in China*, premiered at the Houston Grand Opera. Typical of operas from the past, this opera deals with the personal dramas surrounding a major political event, in this case President Richard Nixon's surprising and unexpected diplomatic initiative toward communist China. The music, although rooted in a minimalist sensibility, contains passages that link his work to the other two major trends of this period: references to late-nineteenth-century composers (neo-Romanticism) and an eclectic collage of twentieth-century classical music styles and swing-era jazz (postmodernism).

A number of composers found ways to make their music accessible and understandable to listeners without resorting to the repetitions of minimalism by keeping certain elements, like texture or timbre, constant while varying other elements, by introducing tonality from time to time, or by revivifying traditional forms like sonata form and theme and variations. In the United States Ellen Taaffe Zwilich, born in Florida in 1939 and a professor at Florida State University, used variation technique to such impressive effect in her Symphony No. 1 (1982) that, in 1983, she became the first woman composer to win the Pulitzer Prize for music. The seven-minute-long first movement begins quietly with an ascending third. This motive then reoccurs throughout the movement, reminding listeners of the motivic nature of Beethoven's Fifth Symphony (Chapter 7, Gateway 27) and providing audiences with a level of redundancy typical of virtually all music until the avant-garde of the twentieth century. The rich orchestration, including bell chimes reminiscent of Berlioz's *Symphonie Fantastique*, and some short three- and four-note rhythmic motives, also offer pleasingly familiar anchors within a dissonant, rather static harmonic framework. Her technically sophisticated use of the orchestra in many of her works, including concertos for wind and brass instruments, have gained the favor of major orchestras in the United States.

Neo-Romanticism is a label applied to modern compositions that return in one way or another to nineteenth-century tonality and musical forms. The results are works that tradition-minded concert-goers find comprehensible and enjoyable because they contain so many icons of previous musical experience. George Rochberg (1918–2005), after embracing avant-garde styles early in his career, turned to Romantic-era and early-twentieth-century styles during the 1970s when he found that he could not adequately express, with the compositional techniques he had been using, his grief after the death of his teenage son. Rochberg was born in New Jersey and taught for a number of

> **AESTHETICS**

> **AESTHETICS**

FIGURE 13.18
Ellen Taaffe Zwilich
Source: Getty Images / Mark Kauffman.

years at the University of Pennsylvania. Each movement of his String Quartet No. 5 uses a style associated with a particular composer: some movements reference the tonality of nineteenth-century composers Ludwig van Beethoven, Franz Schubert (1797–1828), and Gustav Mahler (1860–1911). Others employ the challenging harmonies of early-twentieth composers Béla Bartók (1881–1945) and Arnold Schoenberg.

AESTHETICS

Another neo-Romantic composer, David del Tredici, born in California in 1937, worried that his reclamation of older tonal styles would not be well received by his composer colleagues, but he hoped that his appropriation of familiar musical icons would attract concert audiences to modern music. In 1976, after the Chicago Symphony premiered his work *Final Alice* to what one critic described as "the most enthusiastic reception of a new work I have ever heard at a symphony concert," del Tredici captured, in an interview, both the challenge to the avant-garde and the desire to reconnect with audiences through the emotional potential of Romantic-era musical expressiveness:

> I was terrified my colleagues would think I was an idiot . . . For my generation, it is considered vulgar to have an audience really, really like a piece on a first hearing. But why are we writing music except to move people and to be expressive? To have what has moved us move somebody else? Right now, audiences just reject contemporary music. But if they start to like one thing, then they begin to have perspective. That will make a difference.[73]

The work of all the postmodernists of this period reduced and recontextualized the complexities of modernism in ways that invited classical music audiences to listen and take seriously new work situated within the long tradition of European classical music and that responded to events in the world like the HIV/AIDS epidemic. Because of that search for connection to an audience, symphony orchestras and opera companies continue today to program many works of this period.

WHERE DO I GO FROM HERE?

- Listen to Corigliano's Symphony No. 1, Mvt. I, "Apologue: Of Rage and Remembrance." Which musical elements express his grief? What musical icons of emotion do you hear? How does this movement relate to the third movement, "Giulio's Song"?

- Listen to and describe John Adams' *Phrygian Gates* for solo piano. Can you hear the various "gates" that the form passes through? How is the effect similar and different from earlier examples of minimalism such as Terry Riley's *In C*?

- Listen to and describe David del Tredici's *Final Alice*. Do you find yourself responding in a similar manner as the audience at the premier? To what extent does your response, and the sound of the music, resonate with the quote from del Tredici, above?

GATEWAY 56
REGGAE

What Is It?

Reggae is a style of music that emerged in Jamaica in the late 1960s, but became widely popular around the world, especially in Europe, the United States, and Africa, during the period from 1975 to 1994. Our gateway to reggae, "Buffalo Soldier," was recorded in 1978 by Bob Marley and the Wailers. Bob Marley (1945–1981) is arguably one of the world's most famous musicians and singer-songwriters. He co-wrote "Buffalo Soldier" with the Jamaican musician, DJ, and producer Noel "King Sporty" Williams (1943–2015), and the song was first released in 1983, after Marley's death, on the album *Confrontation*.

The term "buffalo soldier" refers to African Americans serving in the segregated regiments of the U.S. Army in the late nineteenth century. The nickname was reportedly given to black soldiers in such regiments by Native American tribes in the 1860s when they faced them in U.S. military campaigns to suppress Native American populations. These deadly battles against Native Americans are known collectively as the "American Indian Wars." In the song's lyrics, Marley transforms the definition of "buffalo soldier," connecting African Americans to the contemporary plight and struggle of descendants of enslaved Africans throughout the African diaspora.

FIGURE 13.19
Bob Marley in 1978
Source: Trinity Mirror / Mirrorpix / Alamy Stock Photo.

 Listen to the recording and focus on the lyrics. How does Marley redefine the "buffalo soldier"?

How Does It Work?

Timbre

Solo male and group vocals, a deep and heavy-sounding bass guitar, drum set, other percussion, electric guitars, a brass and saxophone horn section, organ, piano, and some other keyboards can all be heard in this recording. The timbres of the drum set feature short percussive sounds with rapid decay such as a tightly closed high hat, a punchy bass drum, and a high-pitched snare drum that sounds almost like *timbales*. Unlike most jazz and rock drumming, the resounding cymbals of the drum set are not heard.

Texture

The vocals and brass carry melody lines while a polyrhythmic groove created by the other instruments serves as an accompaniment.

Rhythm

This recording features a typical polyrhythmic reggae groove with a slight swing feel, an emphasis on beats two and four in some guitars and keyboards, bass drum on all four beats of nearly every measure, and the bass and another guitar together playing an ostinato that emphasizes many of the downbeats as well as the swing feel. The tempo, like in most reggae music, is moderate and relaxed.

Melody

The melody is in a major mode and spans a range of about an octave and a half although the opening sung melody uses just five pitches.

Harmony

The harmony is tonal and mostly stays on the I chord, though it occasionally ventures briefly to a related minor chord and a few other chords.

Form

There are three distinct types of strophes (A, B, C) that repeat at various points of the song, sometimes with different words. A bridge section (D) appears once. The form of the song could be outlined like this: Intro – ABABACDACAC

Performance Techniques

The horn section of brass and saxophones frequently interacts with the vocals in a call-and-response manner, echoing the call and response common in music throughout the African diaspora. The female choral responses share some features with African American gospel music.

Listen to the entire song, keeping in mind the musical elements described above and following the timed listening guide.

LISTENING GUIDE 13.4

TIME	SECTION	DESCRIPTION	LYRICS
0:00	Introduction	A brief drum fill on the high-pitched snare drum begins the recording, an opening gesture very common in reggae that signals the tempo and groove. A brief introduction with a melody in the horn section follows.	
0:08	A	The four-measure repeating groove begins, and Marley sings four nearly identical narrow-range melodic phrases that emphasize the third scale degree, each with different lyrics. The harmony predominantly centers on the I chord.	Buffalo soldier . . . Stolen from Africa . . .
0:39	B	In the first B section, the groove continues for two identical four-bar phrases with different harmonies than A. The melody Marley sings in B goes up to a higher range, focusing on the sixth scale degree and introducing a more strained quality in his voice.	When I analyze . . .
0:55	A	The melody and harmony of A return, but the lyrics are slightly modified and the lyrical phrases occur in a new order. The horn section also answers some of the melodic phrases with their own melodies in the mode of call and response.	Taken from Africa . . . Buffalo soldier . . .
1:25	B	B returns with a new set of lyrics and background parts in the horns that alternate between sustained and syncopated notes.	If you know your history . . .
1:41	A	A returns with similar lyrics as previous iterations, but in a new order and with some additions.	Buffalo soldier . . . Fighting on arrival . . .
2:12	C	A new section, C, continues the groove and harmony of A, but has a new, higher melody, sung twice on vocables, that descends stepwise through the major scale and is repeated twice. The horn section again sets up a call and response pattern.	Woe yoy yoy . . .
2:28	D	Another new section, D, shifts the harmony to the key of the relative minor as Marley gestures towards the plight of the buffalo soldier, who is "troddin' through the land."	Buffalo soldier trodding . . .
2:43	A	A returns again with some new lyrics.	Buffalo soldier . . .
3:00			Fighting on arrival . . .
3:14	C	C repeats.	Woe yoy yoy . . .
3:29	A	A repeats one last time, this time with many new lyrics and a call and response pattern between the vocals and the horns on every line.	Troddin' through San Juan . . . Fighting on arrival . . .
4:00	C	C repeats and the recording fades out.	Woe yoy yoy . . .
4:16	End		

What Does It Mean?

Many of reggae's meanings are rooted in the **Rastafari Movement**, which emerged in Jamaica in the first half of the twentieth century. Not all reggae is associated with Rastafari, but the movement's emergence in the context of the colonization of Jamaica sheds some light on the Rastafari-related meaning of "Buffalo Soldier," especially that of its lyrics. Christopher Columbus landed in Jamaica in 1494, and the British captured the island a century and a half later in 1655. Relying on the labor of enslaved Africans, Jamaica became one of the largest sugar producers in the world. By the time Britain outlawed slavery in the 1830s, enslaved Africans outnumbered whites twenty to one in Jamaica. Jamaica achieved its independence from Britain in 1962 at the same time that African countries were becoming independent from Britain and other European countries.

Many blacks in Jamaica turned to African culture and to African intellectuals for inspiration, fueled by frustration among the urban poor and a high murder rate in the capital city, Kingston. One of their heroes was Haile Selassie (1892–1975), the Emperor of Ethiopia from 1930 to 1974 and the first black ruler in twentieth-century Africa. In the 1930s some Jamaicans came to regard him as the second coming of the Biblical Messiah and as God himself, capable of leading black people everywhere into a promised land of freedom, justice, equality, and prosperity. Taking Selassie's given name (Tafari) and princely title (Ras), they called their beliefs and practices, their "way of life" as they put it, the Rastafari Movement. Adherents use marijuana as a spiritual path, wear dreadlocks, and reject mainstream society, which they call Babylon because of its materialism and oppression. They hope to return one day to Zion, the Kingdom of God (whom they call "Jah"), which can refer literally to Ethiopia or Africa, or metaphorically to Africa as a state of mind where being of African descent is a point of pride and self-confidence.

Bob Marley, although raised a Catholic, became the most famous adherent of Rastafari in the 1960s and 1970s. Many of his songs directly reference Jah and Zion and are understood to reference people of African descent suffering in the oppressive world of Babylon. Marley includes black history in the U.S. in this world by calling the buffalo soldiers a "dreadlocked Rasta." In a subtle gesture by Marley, the melody of C comes from an American song called "Mammy's Little Baby Loves Shortnin' Bread" written in 1900 by a white poet in the black dialect of minstrel shows. It quickly entered both black and white folk traditions and suffused popular culture for much of the twentieth century. The Beach Boys recorded a version around the same time Marley recorded "Buffalo Soldier." By substituting African-derived vocables for the song's words, Marley liberates Africans Americans from one form of oppression: white stereotypes of their speech patterns.

In the 1960s and 1970s, a growing sense of shared experience united the African diaspora across what came to be called the Black Atlantic. Descendants of enslaved Africans in the Americas and the Caribbean, black immigrants from Jamaica and Trinidad to Britain, and other populations of African descent were all subject to similar and interrelated conditions of racial injustice. They also participated in networks of cultural exchange throughout this Black Atlantic, including musical ones, that addressed oppression and bias in myriad ways. When Bob Marley sings about how it makes sense to him that the buffalo soldier is a dreadlocked Rasta, he is connecting the struggles of blacks in Jamaica with that of blacks in the United States.

In the song's lyrics Marley both gives a history lesson and re-interprets history. He points out that one oppressed group, African Americans, were fighting for the cause of the United States in the oppression of another group, Native Americans. But he re-defines the buffalo soldier as someone "driven from the mainland [Africa]" to the heart of the Caribbean and the heart of America. After reminding listeners to learn their history, presumably about the African slave trade, Marley calls himself a buffalo soldier, uniting African Americans to himself and to the African diaspora once again. He repeats the phrase "fighting on arrival," to show that enslaved Africans and their descendants have been fighting to survive since they had arrived, even as they were fighting against Native Americans in the United States on behalf of the country that had enslaved them.

> **CULTURAL LINKAGES**

> **POLITICAL ACTION**

CULTURAL
LINKAGES >

One of the characteristics of Rastafari is the way that it conflates and skews linear time, situating the past in the present and history as something that is not long gone but that is continually affecting the present. Historical themes of slavery, displacement from Africa ("the mainland"), black survival, and the celebration of ordinary people, like the buffalo soldier and the dreadlocked rasta, are all brought into the present in this recording and in many other examples of reggae music. In "Buffalo Soldier," for example, Marley presents historical events in seemingly random order, as if they are all happening together at once. For example, the lyrics of each repetition of the A section are in a different order or are replaced by new lyrics referencing some other historical event in non-chronological order. Marley returns cyclically to certain lyrics, such as "buffalo soldier, dreadlocked rasta." Taken together, the lyrics suggest the unity of the Black Atlantic and its complex cyclical dynamics of oppression and hope.

AESTHETICS >

The song's cyclical structure is also present in its repetition of a four-bar chord progression that occurs throughout the A and C sections. The progression begins on an I chord that is emphasized by a repeated note in the bass for two bars, departs briefly to other harmonies in the third bar, and returns, or cycles back, to the I chord for the fourth bar. This four-bar cycle occurs multiple times in each A and C section, for a total of twenty-six times in the course of the song, departing only briefly to the B and D sections, whose four-bar phrases repeat a total of only six times. This is not the first time that music of the African diaspora could be understood as challenged linear time with a cyclical approach. John Coltrane abandoned linear musical logic in *A Love Supreme* (Chapter 12, Gateway 50), and Trinidadian steel pan arrangers interrupt the linear flow of the theme and variations form with their sections called jams that suspend linear time with cyclical repetitions (Chapter 11, Gateway 48).

🔊 **Listen again to "Buffalo Soldier," paying attention to how Marley's lyrics conflate historical time by bringing seemingly disparate events, people, and places together, and to the repeating four-bar cycle of the A and C sections.**

Reggae is also remarkable for its distinctive rhythmic sensibilities. On just about every reggae song, there is a strong emphasis on beats two and four heard prominently in a repetitive, bright "chunk" sound on an electric guitar. In addition to the emphasis on two and four, the upbeats of each beat have an accent of their own. Many instruments play on these beats in the polyrhythmic texture, the most consistent of which is the organ, which can be heard faintly in the background playing every upbeat when the C section is first introduced, and in all of the sections from the A section at 2:43 until the end of the recording. In combination with the strong accents on beats two and four, the upbeats in the organ and other louder instruments give "Buffalo Soldier" reggae's trademark "ga-CHUNK-ga" feel. This feel is related to one of reggae's precursors, ska, a genre that emerged in Jamaica around 1960 and that strongly emphasizes every upbeat, sometimes even leaving downbeats silent.

CULTURAL
LINKAGES >

Because the rhythm is emphasized so strongly in the repeating upbeats and chords on beats two and four played by guitars and keyboard instruments in reggae, the bass is free to take other roles. In "Buffalo Soldier" the notes played in the bass are not particularly sustained, and on other Bob Marley recordings such as "Could You Be Loved" (1980) or "Is This Love" (1978), the bass plays even more freely, joining the melody at times and creating some of its own lines. This freedom in the bass contributes to an even more complex polyrhythm, which, along with call and response patterns, is a shared characteristic of much of the music that has roots in Africa and the African diaspora, including music of salsa, hip-hop, steel pan music, and all varieties of jazz.

🔊 **Listen once more to "Buffalo Soldier" and try to identify some of the individual instruments playing the "ga-CHUNK-ga" rhythmic pattern throughout, along with some other elements of the polyrhythm.**

What Is Its History?

The rise of reggae is part of a complex musical history in Jamaica, and a number of musical genres and styles contributed to its development. One source is religious music with roots in African traditions similar to *Candomblé* in Brazil, *Santería* in Cuba, and *Vodou* in Haiti (Chapter 6, Gateway 26). One of these, *Kumina*, coalesced as a religion in the mid-nineteenth century when, after the abolition of slavery, many Congolese were brought to Jamaica and worked as indentured servants or contract workers. Based in Congolese drumming styles, *kumina* drumming developed out of the religion of the same name and became a style of its own. It inspired drummers like Count Ossie (1926–1976) and other Rastafarians in the 1930s and 1940s. Another reggae precursor is a popular Jamaican folk genre called *mento*, which combined European dance forms with African musical sensibilities and, like Trinidadian calypso (Chapter 11, Gateway 48), was known for its topical songs commenting on social issues of everyday life, often with humor and word play. Though *mento* is popular entertainment, it set a precedent for social commentary in music.

FIGURE 13.20

A group of people setting up a Jamaican-style sound system at Notting Hill Carnival in London, 1983

Source: Getty Images / PYMCA / UIG.

During the 1950s, audiences in Jamaica were interested in hearing the latest music by American rhythm and blues acts blasted by powerful sound systems. But by the time independence was achieved in 1962, a new atmosphere encouraged the cultivation of distinctive forms of music and other arts, and musicians began experimenting with the rhythmic feel of rhythm and blues. In a gradual process, they developed a new type of groove that emphasized every upbeat in a 4/4 meter at a quick tempo, the characteristic sound of what became the genre "ska." The swing shuffle feel of many rhythm and blues recordings includes a harmonic instrument such as a piano or guitar playing every upbeat, but not accented very strongly. In ska these upbeats were transformed into the most heavily accented beats in every measure, as heard in the influential recordings of a band called The Skatalites. Another genre, rocksteady, developed in the mid-1960s. It slowed down the tempo of ska, added an accented hit on beat three in the snare drum, and allowed musicians to experiment with different types of polyrhythms. Groups like the Techniques and the Heptones, influenced by American genres such as soul music, created smooth, sweet-sounding melodies like the melody in the Techniques' recording "Queen Majesty" (1967).

Drawing on rocksteady, ska, *mento*, rhythm and blues, gospel, funk, and even jazz, reggae emerged as a named genre after the term was first used in the title of the song "Do the Reggay," a 1968 recording by a Jamaican band called the Maytals who sang in a close-harmony gospel style. Early reggae stars such as Jimmy Cliff (b. 1948) had been active in either ska or rocksteady (or both) before the naming of the reggae genre, a reminder that the sonic distinctions between music genres can be quite subtle and might say more about how the music is marketed or the make-up of an audience. Even Bob Marley's group, the Wailers, was originally a ska vocal group that he had formed with Peter Tosh (1944–1987) and Bunny Wailer (b. 1947) in 1963. Since the genre's inception, the lyrics of reggae have covered a range of topics from social commentary and Rastafari to the celebration of love and having a good time. Reggae's complex, contagious rhythm makes the body want to move and its often major-key melodies and harmonies are consistent regardless of the subject of the lyrics. The dark political and social critiques of reggae can seem at odds with musical elements that often index a party mood, a juxtaposition not dissimilar to some salsa music

CULTURAL LINKAGES

(Chapter 12, Gateway 52). Perhaps the pleasant-sounding music helps listeners and dancers feel better about the struggles documented in its lyrics. And perhaps its infectious style draws in new listeners unfamiliar with the injustices expressed in the songs.

Bob Marley was born to an Afro-Jamaican mother and a white Jamaican father in central-northern Jamaica. At the age of twelve he moved with his mother to a neighborhood near Kingston called Trenchtown, a place he later referenced in songs such as "No Woman, No Cry" (1974), "Trenchtown Rock" (1971), and others. As a result of his work with the Wailers in the 1960s, he was already popular in Jamaica by the 1970s, and the group had released a number of albums. In 1973 Bob Marley and the Wailers released an album called *Burnin'* on Island Records, a large and influential record label with an international reach. It impressed not only reggae fans but also rock audiences in Britain and the U.S. The first song on *Burnin'* is "Get up, Stand up," whose lyrics urge the oppressed with statements like "stand up for your rights" and "don't give up the fight" in the chorus. The second song evokes "Hallelujah Time," when the crying of children will turn to singing because "but though we bear our burdens now, all afflictions got to end somehow." Another song promises that, because of the poverty and brutality blacks routinely face, "that's why we gonna be burnin' and lootin' tonight." The third song on the album, "I Shot the Sheriff," caught the attention of British rock guitarist Eric Clapton, whose 1974 cover version of the song became a number one hit in the U.S. and brought great attention to Marley and reggae in general in the U.S. and the U.K. (Its sampling in Public Enemy's "Fight the Power" is discussed in Gateway 53).

POLITICAL ACTION

Amid his massive worldwide fame in the 1970s, Marley remained ever passionate about Rastafari and addressing the struggles of Africans and the African diaspora, and about reggae as a vehicle for communicating these passions. In 1978 he performed a number of his hits as the featured artist at a concert with sixteen of reggae's most famous acts called the "One Love Peace Concert." The concert was organized by two imprisoned gangsters from opposing violent political factions who hoped that reggae could bring people together and end the violence between gangs armed by warring political parties, one led by Prime Minister Michael Manley and the other by his rival Edward Seaga. Both politicians were present at the concert. Marley performed "Jammin'," whose lyrics seem to be about musicians and music lovers "jammin'" together and having a good time, but also include references to Zion, Jah, poverty, Elvis (in the same vein as in "Fight the Power"), and other clues that Marley's concept of "jammin'" might be about a social and political sense of harmony as much as it is about a musical one. In the middle of the song, after singing lyrics like "I really wanna jam with you . . . I hope you like jammin' too," Marley began improvising lyrics invoking Emperor Haile Selassie and prayers to God and phrases like "show the people that you gonna unite." He then invited Manley and Seaga to the stage as the band continued to cycle through the groove of the song, joining the hands of these bitter rivals above his head as a hopeful icon for peace and unity and saying "love, prosperity, be with us all, Jah, Rastafari, Selassie." Though the crowd went wild as these political rivals were united physically onstage, the violence in Jamaica did not decrease, and in 1980 during the election year when Seaga unseated Manley as prime minister there were nearly 900 reported murders, more than double that of the previous year. Bob Marley died in 1981 of cancer, undoubtedly convinced that the fighting against oppression and injustice was needed more than ever.

Reggae's rise in global popularity during the 1970s has influenced popular music all around the world. One measure of reggae's continuing importance today is its status as only one of four ethnic or world-music genres recognized with a Grammy Award "field" (the others are Latin, American roots, and World Music). The Best Reggae Album Grammy was first awarded in 1985 and, since then, three of Bob Marley's children—Ziggy Marley (b. 1968), Stephen Marley (b. 1972), and Damien Marley (b. 1978)—have won the category thirteen times among them and another of his sons, Julian Marley (b. 1975), has also been nominated. As early as the late 1960s, adaptations of reggae's rhythmic groove could be heard in recordings like the Beatles' "Ob-La-Di, Ob-La-Da" (1968).

Since reggae's explosion in popularity in the 1970s, musicians in other rock and popular music genres have embraced the style: the chorus of "Hotel California" (1976) by the American rock band the Eagles features a reggae-inflected rhythm; the first two hits of British rock act the Police, "Roxanne" (1978) and "I Can't Stand Losing You" (1978), are based on modified reggae grooves; and the hit Bobby McFerrin song "Don't Worry Be Happy" (1988), whose message Public Enemy rejected in "Fight the Power," recreates a reggae feel through percussive vocal singing and body percussion such as snapping. The infectious rhythmic sensibilities of reggae continue to inspire musicians today from Ariana Grande in her hit 2016 hit single "Side to Side" to Jay-Z (in collaboration with Damien Marley) on the song "Bam" from *4:44* (2017) to country star Carrie Underwood on the song "One Way Ticket" from her 2012 double-platinum-selling album *Blown Away*.

WHERE DO I GO FROM HERE?

- Listen to a few other Bob Marley songs, such as "Get Up, Stand Up," "No Woman, No Cry," or "Three Little Birds." What do these share in common with "Buffalo Soldier" in their lyrical themes, rhythmic grooves, and other musical elements? Where do they differ?

- Find the video of "Jammin'" from the 1978 One Love Peace Concert on YouTube and compare it to another recording of the song. How do the performances differ? What is the effect of Marley bringing the rival politicians on stage for the audience at the concert?

- Listen to Eric Clapton's version of "I Shot the Sheriff." How is it similar to and different from Marley's original version?

- Choose a few examples of popular music that use the sounds of reggae in their music. How are these songs connected to the sound of reggae? To what extent does it matter whether the lyrics to these songs are related to the political and social commentaries of Bob Marley and other reggae musicians?

- Since the late 1970s the style of reggae popularized by Marley has been supplanted in popularity by a genre called "dancehall" in Jamaica, the Jamaican diaspora, and some sectors of mainstream pop. (Dancehall is sometimes loosely categorized as reggae, and Marley's style as "roots reggae.") Listen to some dancehall music from the 1980s or 1990s, and compare it to recent examples of pop music influenced by dancehall, such as "Work" (2016) by Rihanna, "One Dance" (2016) by Drake, or "Sorry" (2015) by Justin Bieber. What musical elements of dancehall do these pop artists exploit? How do these pop examples compare to the music of contemporary dancehall artists like Sean Paul (b. 1971)?

CLOSING

If there is a common theme in music from 1975 to 1994, it has to do with musicians seeking to connect with audiences and communities of listeners. Classical postmodernists and jazz neo-traditionalists sought to create music that would interest and engage larger communities of listeners and those alienated from the avant-garde of the previous period. Rappers began with community dance parties in their neighborhoods in the boroughs of New York and South Central Los Angeles and soon became, according to Chuck D of Public Enemy, "black America's CNN," providing both news and commentary on life and culture in America's cities. Reggae artists understood themselves as speaking to a suffering community that stretched around the Black Atlantic. To engage their communities, musicians in all these genres and styles necessarily evoked the musical histories of their traditions in various ways: neo-traditionalism in jazz, neo-Romanticism in classical music, sampling in rap and hip-hop, and the Ethiopian emperor, R&B, mento, ska, and *kumina* drumming in reggae. No matter the type of music they were making or whether they wanted to make art, make people think, or make them dance, musicians in this period were deeply committed to music as a social practice that brings people together.

THINGS TO THINK ABOUT

- In what ways can each of these gateway examples be considered postmodern? Are there similarities among all of them in this regard?

- What are the similarities and differences between neo-traditionalism in jazz and postmodernism in classical music during the period from 1975 to 1994?

- Compare the ways that rap and reggae dealt with political and social issues facing black communities during the period from 1975 to 1994.

NEW TERMS

breakdancing	neo-traditionalism	scratching
disco	postmodernism	toasting
funk	rap	vocalese
gangsta rap	Rastafari Movement	world music
hardcore rap	reggae	
hip-hop culture	samples	

MUSIC TODAY

MUSIC IN EVERY PERIOD of time and every place in the world is embedded in the cultural, social, economic, political, and intellectual life of the society that makes and supports that music. Musicians, composers, and listeners respond, in one way or another, to the texture of cultural and social life. In some cases they try to influence or change the culture and society through their music making and their musical taste. This claim has been true throughout history and is certainly true of music today.

Among the major currents tugging at American lives today are:

- the wars and ongoing American military presence in Afghanistan and Iraq in the aftermath of the al-Qaeda attack on the U.S. on September 11, 2001;
- a growing awareness of climate change and the specter of environmental disaster;
- a new acceptance of LGBT and other sexualities and gender identities, including the legalization of gay marriage;
- a renewed focus on standing against sexual harassment and advocating for equal rights for all genders in a patriarchal society;
- the concentration of wealth in the hands of the rich and the increasing poverty and lack of opportunity for the poor and the middle class;
- the effect of drugs in many forms on individual lives, on local communities, on the broader social fabric;
- transnational migration and immigration due to poverty and war;
- racial injustice manifested in, among other ways, police shootings;
- the availability of images, news, and music from all over the world through social media like Facebook, internet streaming services like YouTube, and older media such as TV and film.

The gateway recordings in this chapter respond in one way or another to some of these themes in Americans' recent experience.

GATEWAY 57
AMERICAN POPULAR MUSIC TODAY

What Is It?

Popular music today connects with audiences in countless ways, just as it has for decades. It helps people fall in love and deal with heartbreak. It entertains and makes people laugh. It distracts people from their trouble and helps them through it. It engages with social issues and serves as a vehicle for protest. It brings people together, providing ways for them to feel like they belong and take pride

FIGURE 14.1

Lady Gaga standing with a group of sexual-assault survivors at the conclusion of her performance of "Til it Happens to You" at the 2016 Academy Awards

Source:
Getty Images /
MARK RALSTON.

in their identities. Popular music today is popular in part because it connects with audiences in all of these ways and more.

Our gateway to American popular music of the last few years is a song by Lady Gaga (b. 1986), an artist who has amassed a large and loyal following because she engages with fans through her music and persona in so many ways. The song, "Til it Happens to You," was composed by her and songwriter Diane Warren (b. 1956) for *The Hunting Ground*, a 2015 documentary film about sexual assault on college campuses. The song empathizes with survivors of sexual assault and contributes to a growing public awareness about its prevalence. The song's lyrics suggest that standard polite responses to survivors of sexual assault like "I understand" and "This too shall pass" are not adequate. Others cannot understand a person's pain until they have experienced it themselves.

 Listen to the first thirty seconds of the recording.

How Does It Work?

Timbre

The recording features a solo female voice, a string orchestra, piano, drum set, electric guitars, and some background vocals.

Texture

The texture varies somewhat, but at its densest it has three parts: melody, block chords, and a drum part.

Rhythm

The rhythm is in a meter of four beats per measure.

Melody

The melody is mostly in a minor key, but at some points it seems to venture to the relative major of that minor key.

Harmony

The harmony is based on triads and seventh chords, some major and some minor.

Form

The form consists of a verse, a chorus, a section that recurs throughout the song with the same lyrics, and a bridge, a section common in pop music today that usually occurs only once. Most bridges introduce new melodies, harmonies, and lyrics (and sometimes timbres and texture), and forms a **bridge** between two sections, usually two repetitions of the chorus towards the end of a recording. The bridge in "Til It Happens to You" has a new melody, chord progression, and lyrics. The song generally follows a form common in popular music today: Verse 1, Chorus, Verse 2, Chorus, Bridge, Chorus.

Performance Techniques

The loudness gradually increases throughout, building intensity until the end, when the performance suddenly becomes very quiet. Lady Gaga varies the melody from time to time and performs the song in a relatively slow tempo.

Listen to this recording with these elements in mind.

Listen to the entire recording following along with the timed listening guide. Follow the subdivisions (a, a', b, b' and so forth) of the main formal sections (Verses, Chorus, and Bridge) and notice the way Lady Gaga uses loudness and pitch to express the emotions of the lyrics.

LISTENING GUIDE 14.1

TIME	SECTION	DESCRIPTION	LYRICS
0:00	Intro	The string orchestra plays a four-note melody twice establishing a serious mood.	
0:22	Verse 1		
0:22	a	The solo female singer enters singing softly accompanied by chords on piano and the string orchestra. The quietness of the singing may express iconically a sense of sadness and exasperation at receiving trite advice after a painful experience as expressed in the lyrics. A three-pitch melodic phrase, "a," begins the verse.	You tell me . . .
0:30	a'	The same melody repeated with the addition of one new pitch at the end.	You say . . .
0:38	b	A new melody at a slightly higher pitch, subtly expressing the singer's displeasure at unhelpful advice.	Tell me, what . . .
0:45	b'	A varied repeat of the new melody.	Tell me how . . .
0:54	Chorus		
0:54	c	The chorus "Til it happens to you" is introduced with a third melody.	Til it happens . . .
1:06	c'	A repeat of the previous line, with an extended ending that repeats the second half of the phrase. With each repeat Lady Gaga sings more quietly and at lower pitches, as if resigned to her fate.	Til it happens . . .
1:26	Verse 2	The string orchestra, bass, drums, and background electric guitars enter as the singer repeats the melodies of verse 1 with new lyrics.	You tell me . . .
1:58	Chorus	The melody and lyrics to the chorus return. The growing loudness and the entrance of background vocals echoing the singer seems to express a slow transformation on the singer's part from resignation to anger and resistance.	Til it happens . . .
2:30	Bridge	The singer sings the bridge on a new melody based on a repeated and varied short melodic phrase (d). At the end, Lady Gaga goes high in her range to a long-held note on "you don't know," a musical representation of an angry shout and the way she feels about this type of advice.	Til your world . . .
3:06	Chorus	The drums, electric guitars, and bass drop out, and the softer volume and thinner texture of the first verse return as Gaga repeats the chorus text and melody	Til it happens . . .

continued

TIME	SECTION	DESCRIPTION	LYRICS
		(c) as if quietly expressing the pain and loneliness brought on when receiving this kind of advice.	
3:22		The strings, bass, drums, and guitars re-enter loudly and increase in loudness, reaffirming resistance and anger as a more appropriate response.	Til it happens . . .
4:04		All the instruments drop out leaving Gaga to sing alone of her sense of loneliness, with a few scattered notes on the piano.	Til it happens . . .
4:16		End	

What Does It Mean?

Lady Gaga sings the lyrics to "Til it Happens to You" from a first-person perspective, taking on and expressing the perspective of a survivor of sexual assault. Her lyrics address a second person, or a group of people, and they follow a particular pattern. In each verse, the first two lines (a and a') state what the second person or other people are saying or have said, phrases of encouragement that seem trite or hollow. The second two lines of each verse challenge the other person or people with emotionally charged questions, wondering how anyone else could understand or give advice. The chorus follows these lyrics, concluding that others could not possibly understand a painful situation that they have never experienced personally. If a listener knows that this song is associated with a documentary film about sexual assault on university campuses, it will be understood that the lyrics are likely coming from the perspective of a person who has been sexually assaulted. But even if listeners are unaware of the connection of the song to sexual assault, the lyrics are general enough to be able to apply to another trauma or other painful experiences. This is part of what gives popular music its broad appeal: the lyrics have meanings that can be applied to many different situations in ways that listeners find useful and relevant to their lives in one way or another.

"Til it Happens to You" can provide a powerful sense of solidarity, comfort, and empowerment for survivors of sexual assault as well as for individuals who have experienced other sorts of pain or adversity. When pop singers like Lady Gaga sing lyrics from a first-person perspective, they can give voice to individual experiences that listeners may not feel they have had the opportunity to speak about. Hearing Lady Gaga sing the lyrics of "Til it Happens to You" passionately can provide listeners with the sound of another human voice expressing thoughts and feelings similar to their own through poetic and empathetic language.

Those who are familiar with Lady Gaga know that her music frequently includes the electronic sounds of synthesizers and other electronic instruments, as well as relatively fast tempos and beat patterns that are geared towards dancing. By contrast, "Til it Happens to You" has no such electronic sounds, and is a pop song with a relatively slow tempo that uses piano, slightly distorted guitars, bass, and drums in addition to lead vocals and background vocals. This texture and tempo, along with the four-beat meter with accents on the second and fourth beat, place this song in the category of a **pop** or **rock ballad**. The word "ballad" has been used to describe many different types of songs in popular and folk music, but beginning in the 1970s and even more prominently in the 1980s, pop and rock ballads emerged using instrumentation similar to the one in this song, slow tempos, and passionate singing often at the high end of a singer's vocal range. Pop ballads frequently carry themes of romantic love, longing for such love, or a breakup. Famous examples include Whitney Houston's performance of "I Will Always Love You" (1992), Celine Dion's "My Heart Will Go On" (1997), and Bryan Adams' "(Everything I Do) I Do It for You" (1984). When Lady Gaga deals with the complicated feelings after an experience with sexual assault through sounds typical of a pop ballad style, it might set up expectations among listeners of associations with some aspect of a romantic relationship. What "Til it Happens to You" seems to do is put a twist on the conventional themes of a pop ballad. Instead of emphasizing romantic love or a breakup, the song is a pop ballad exploring the psychological and emotional responses linked to the trauma of a sexual assault.

Popular music today is linked to the visual elements of performance more than ever. Concerts with spectacular stage, costume, and lighting design, along with album artwork, music videos, and the visual elements of social media are all significant parts of the popular music industry and experience. With the popularity of YouTube and other video streaming services today, music videos continue to play a crucial role in the consumption and distribution of popular music. The music video for "Til it Happens to You," with scenes from the film *The Hunting Ground*, begins with a warning stating "The following contains graphic content that may be emotionally unsettling but reflects the reality of what is happening daily on college campuses." The song then begins, and the video depicts several instances of sexual assault in what appear to be college dorm rooms and apartments. At the

FIGURE 14.2

From left: film producer/director Amy Ziering, Lady Gaga, music producer/songwriter Diane Warren, and director/writer Kirby Dick at a 2016 screening of *The Hunting Ground*
Source: Getty Images / Rochelle Brodin.

end of the video, each of the survivors of these assaults enters what looks like the hallway of a student residence hall, joining hands or putting their arms around one another and other friends in what appears to be a message of solidarity, support, and hope. The video also notes that a portion of the proceeds from the song will go to organizations supporting sexual assault survivors.

On Twitter, Lady Gaga tweeted to her more than fifty million followers about the song and the video: "Diane Warren and I made 'Til It Happens To You' for people all over the world who suffer from painful life experiences" and "We hope you feel our love and solidarity through the song, and perhaps find some peace in knowing you are not alone through this film." When understanding the meaning of music, especially popular music, it is important to consider the musical elements alongside other elements such as the lyrics, videos, and narratives promoted on social media. Even though people love listening to popular music because its sounds have great meaning to them, it is made even more meaningful by its visual elements and public conversations about it both in the media and on social media.

What Is Its History?

Lady Gaga was born Stefani Joanne Angelina Germanotta in 1986 in New York City. Educated in Catholic schools, she has followed a provocative creative pathway since she adopted her alter ego in 2006, manifested in extraordinary performing costumes, sexually explicit lyrics and music videos, and a number of additional alter egos across a wide spectrum of genders. Although her performances and lyrics may shock some, all these features have their roots in earlier periods of popular music history. Lyrics to popular songs have always been filled with sexual references, mainly in the form of double entendres and metaphors. In the 1970s glam rockers like David Bowie and hard rock musicians like the band Kiss wore flamboyant costumes. Even the Beatles' "mop top" haircuts provoked some ostensibly shocked interviewers' questions when they arrived in New York in 1964. Much of Lady Gaga's music is rooted in a number of electronic dance genres that have emerged since the 1980s, including disco, synthpop, electronica, house, techno, and EDM. Her artistic persona draws in no small part on the way another Italian American singer, Madonna (b. 1958), pushed gender boundaries in the 1980s and 1990s. Lady Gaga has focused greatly on activism in her public

FIGURE 14.3
Lady Gaga and dancers performing at the Super Bowl Halftime Show in 2017
Source: Getty Images / Christopher Polk.

life. Her championing of LGBT issues in her music and as a public figure has been an important element of her career. She is an icon for the gay community, and she credits her gay fans with boosting her career in its early stages.

In 2008 she released her first full-length studio album, *The Fame*, followed by *The Fame Monster* (2009), *Born This Way* (2011), *Artpop* (2013), *Cheek to Cheek* (2014), and *Joanne* (2016). While the first four albums are dominated by electronic sounds such as synthesizers and could be categorized as electropop or synthpop, *Cheek to Cheek* is an album of duets with the jazz singer Tony Bennett, and *Joanne* features few electronic instruments in favor of guitars and pianos and a generally thinner texture. These albums bring more into focus Gaga's vocal abilities, as her voice is competing with fewer other sounds and is heard more clearly and easily. Though it does not appear on any of her studio albums, "Til it Happens to You" would best fit with the stylistic features heard on *Joanne*.

Lady Gaga's music is enjoyed in all sorts of settings, but its most important setting might be dance clubs, where her original recordings or remixed versions of them create an environment for people to connect with their communities, friends, and potential sexual partners as they let loose, dance, and have a good time.

Lady Gaga's recordings have consistently touched themes relevant to contemporary life. For example, *The Fame* and *The Fame Monster* explore the processes and consequences of constructing celebrity as well as the relationship between fans and celebrities. Engaging with fans through social media has been a hallmark of Lady Gaga's career and an integral part of the way that the popular music industry works today. The album *Born This Way* deals with the theme of equality regardless of race, ethnicity, sexuality, or gender; it also deals with themes of individualism, feminism, sex, and religion. All of these themes continue to resonate in the world today as injustice and inequality persist. Lady Gaga's music and the values she promotes draw millions of fans who are seeking these kinds of equality for themselves and others. Her music, whether it is experienced individually while listening or viewing music videos or socially in dance clubs and at spectacular live performances, helps her fans work through the issues of their everyday lives and connects them with others who share their experiences.

WHERE DO I GO FROM HERE?

- Choose one of Lady Gaga's albums and listen to several of the songs. What musical elements do you hear that are shared among the songs? What genre do you associate these elements with? Since genres have a social life, what social traits would the audience for this music share (age group, geographical area, etc.)?

- Watch a music video of one of Lady Gaga's songs, other than "Til it Happens to You." In what ways does the music video enrich the meaning of the song already established by its musical elements? Does it limit the ways that an audience could interpret the song? What does this music video show its audience about the common practices or values of the particular genre of the song?

- Hundreds if not thousands of press articles about Lady Gaga and her music are available online. Choose a song, an album, or a performance, and read several press reviews that address it. How do the reviews address the elements of music, if at all? To what extent do the reviews rely on concepts of genre to explain the meaning of the music or to make decisions about its quality?

- Explore the social media accounts of Lady Gaga and perhaps one or more other pop artists. What are their strategies for engaging with their fans and the public? In what ways are they connecting listeners to their music? In what ways is this different than what might have been possible in, say, 2005, or in 1995? What other social media accounts are associated with each artist (e.g., management companies, record labels, fan pages)? How do these accounts contribute to the ways artists are understood by fans and the public?

GATEWAY 58
JAZZ TODAY

What Is It?

Jazz today is performed and listened to by people from all over the world, young and old, and from every background imaginable, as it has been for most of its history. Jazz musicians, for their part, take pride in the fact that jazz is a musical genre flexible enough to welcome influences from a wide variety of musical styles. Understanding the way they combine the musical elements of jazz with those from other styles is key to understanding what their music means to them and to their audiences.

Bassist, singer, composer, and producer Esperanza Spalding (b. 1984) combines the sounds of jazz with those of other genres in fascinating ways reminiscent of the jazz fusion

FIGURE 14.4
Esperanza Spalding performing in Nice, France, in 2013
Source: Getty Images / Didier Baverel.

of the 1970s. Our gateway to jazz today is "Black Gold," a song from Spalding's 2012 album *Radio Music Society*. She is the composer, arranger, producer, bass player, and lead vocalist on the track. The song features the contemporary R&B singer Algebra Blessett (b. 1976), Benin-born guitarist and vocalist Lionel Loueke (b. 1973), the Savannah Children's Choir, Terri Lyne Carrington (b. 1965) on drums, and Raymond Angry on organ.

 Listen to the first thirty seconds of the recording to get an idea of its sound.

How Does It Work?

Timbre

The timbres feature the clear vocals of Esperanza Spalding and Algebra Blessett along with electric bass, drum set, Hammond B-3 organ, guitar (sometimes in unison with vocables such as by the guitarist), and three horns (tenor saxophone and two trumpets). The organist plays in a way that manipulates the organ's timbre.

Texture

The texture features melodic lines in the vocals and guitar solos, a bass line, and a drum part, and accompanying parts in the organ, guitar, and horns. In "Black Gold" all of these parts interweave with one another in a sometimes dense and complex texture.

Rhythm

The rhythm in this recording is also quite complex with intricate interlocking polyrhythms over a four-beat meter in a steady tempo.

Melody

The vocal and instrumental melodies are mostly in a major key. They also include blue notes and some chromatic movement.

Harmony

Each section of the song is based on a different two-measure repeating harmonic cycle. Sometimes the chords last for four beats each, and sometimes they last for two beats each. The harmony is highly chromatic and full of chords with altered extensions.

Form

The form is organized into two distinct sections: a chorus and a verse that itself has two parts, A and B. After a short nonmetrical introduction on the organ, the form proceeds like this: Chorus–ABAB–Chorus–Guitar Solo (over the Chorus)–B–Chorus–Chorus.

Performance Techniques

The organ's timbre and expressive qualities are notable performance techniques in this performance. In addition to the shifting timbres of the organ made possible by the drawbars of the Hammond B-3 organ (Chapter 8, Gateway 34), the sound at times also seems to shake or waver. This effect is produced on the Hammond B-3 organ by a complex spinning mechanism in a large box called a Leslie speaker that can be attached to the organ. This sound imitates two other sounds in music: **vibrato**, a pulsating slight raising and lowering of the pitch of a tone often heard in operatic singing, and **tremolo**, an electronic effect used on instruments like the electric guitar to quickly and repeatedly raise and lower the volume of the tone. The Leslie speaker combines vibrato and tremolo into a dramatic effect, which is part of the distinctive sound of the Hammond B-3 organ heard in gospel and many genres of popular music and jazz.

Listen to the first minute of this recording, identify the sound of each instrument, and notice the complex texture.

Listen to the entire recording following this timed listening guide.

LISTENING GUIDE 14.2

TIME	SECTION	DESCRIPTION	LYRICS
0:00	Introduction	A high shimmering sound begins the track. It seems to descend briefly, revealing that it is the sound of a Hammond B-3 organ.	
0:08	Chorus	Algebra Blessett sings the first phrase of the chorus, a bluesy descending line, accompanied by only the high frequencies of the organ carrying over from the introduction. Esperanza Spalding sings the second phrase with a similar melody and new lyrics, joined by gentle, pulsatile strikes of the cymbals of the drum set, a counter-melody in the guitar and vocals of Lionel Loueke, and the organ, now playing with a smoother timbre.	Hold your head . . .
0:19		For the second half of the chorus, Blessett and Spalding sing together, and Spalding adds a rhythmic bass line that interlocks with a new syncopated funk-based drum pattern and short accents played by the horn section.	You are . . .

TIME	SECTION	DESCRIPTION	LYRICS
0:32	A	The drums begin playing more sparsely, and Spalding sings the first phrase of A, which is followed by a series of chords with altered extensions played rhythmically by the horns and accented by the drums and bass. Blessett sings the second phrase, followed again by the horns, drums, and bass, along with short improvisations in both the saxophone and Spalding's vocals.	Now maybe . . .
0:56	B	The drums, bass, horns, organ, and guitar all begin playing short, crisp, syncopated rhythms to create another funk groove, with the bass and horns playing the same syncopated rhythm at certain points. Blessett begins the vocal lines and alternates phrases with Spalding. The section ends with a break in the funk groove, over which Raymond Angry plays an improvised bluesy phrase on the organ.	With all the strength . . .
1:12	A	A repeats with new lyrics. It is similar to the first statement of A, but this time the vocal lines, saxophone, guitar, and organ perform in a slightly more improvisatory manner.	They'll be folks . . .
1:36	B	B repeats with the same lyrics and texture, though Spalding and Blessett begin to improvise on the melody and lyrics of the first B section. The end of this B section features a break but with no solo line as in the first B.	Think of all the strength . . .
2:02	Chorus	The funk groove continues in the drums, bass, and horns. The organ plays sustained chords and the guitar plays improvised countermelodies that contribute to the polyrhythmic funk groove.	Hold your head . . .
2:25	guitar solo (Chorus)	Lionel Loueke plays an improvised solo, scat singing in unison with his guitar line. His improvisation outlines the harmonies and their upper extensions in the legacy of bebop musicians and other jazz musicians who have developed this kind of improvisation. The bass, organ, and drums continue the funk groove, with the addition of a on the ride cymbal, which has a long, sustained decay.	
2:48	B	With a smear of the organ and two syncopated hits in the bass, B repeats with its staccato funk groove and more improvisation by the vocalists. The Savannah Children's Choir joins in with gospel style interjections during the second half of this section.	Think of all the strength . . .
3:14	Chorus (extended)	Blessett begins the chorus vocals and Spalding adds improvisatory lines on similar lyrics. After a few repetitions of the line "you are black gold," the children's choir joins in and the key modulates up a half-step. Though the groove doesn't change much, the higher key and thicker texture increases the intensity and energy as the line "you are black gold" repeats eight times.	Hold your head . . .
4:11	Chorus (with tag)	The drums, bass, and horns drop out and the voices sing a version of the chorus accompanied by the organ.	Hold your head . . .

continued

TIME	SECTION	DESCRIPTION	LYRICS
		Blessett and Spalding improvise over the lyrics with the melismas common in gospel and contemporary R&B styles. They are joined by Loueke as he sings and plays on the guitar his own overlapping improvised lines.	
5:14	End		

What Does It Mean?

CULTURAL LINKAGES

In 2012, when Esperanza Spalding released "Black Gold" as the first single from *Radio Music Society*, her press statement emphasized a central aspect of the song's meaning. She wrote:

> This song is singing to our African American heritage before slavery. Over the decades, so much of the strength in the African American community has seeded from resistance and endurance. I wanted to address the part of our heritage spanning back to pre-colonial Africa and the elements of Black pride that draw from our connection to our ancestors in their own land. I particularly wanted to create something that spoke to young boys.[74]

In addition to the expressions of its lyrics, the meaning of "Black Gold" is carried in its combination of musical elements and in the broader context of *Radio Music Society* and Spalding's other work.

AESTHETICS

As a contemporary example of jazz fusion, "Black Gold" includes some musical elements typical of jazz and others from a number of popular styles. Improvisation in the vocals, guitar, and saxophone all point to the long-standing prominence of improvisation in jazz. Lionel Loueke's guitar and vocal solo at 2:25 outlines the underlying harmony with angular phrases, chromaticism, and a reliance on altered extensions, characteristics that are all rooted in bebop. His clean guitar timbre, absent distortion, feedback, and other timbral effects common on the electric guitar in rock and other genres, is common in jazz guitar. Many of his short improvised phrases at the end of the recording also connect to the blues as they emphasize bent pitches and blue notes. His scat singing in unison with his guitar playing suggest that the instrument is intimately connected to the human voice, in a way similar to the ways that musicians playing the blues (and other styles rooted in the blues like rock) have emulated vocal gestures on their instruments.

🔊 **Listen again to Lionel Loueke's guitar solo at 2:25 for the way his improvisation references earlier styles of jazz and blues improvisation.**

The musical elements of "Black Gold" also connect it to other popular genres such as gospel, funk, and soul. These elements position this recording as music that can be enjoyed and appreciated by a broad range of audiences in many different ways and for many different reasons. For example, the organ in "Black Gold," as in much gospel music, is an electric Hammond B-3 organ (Chapter 8, Gateway 34). At the beginning of the recording, the organist Raymond Angry sustains a single chord without changing any of the pitches while, using sliding drawbars on the instrument, he gradually changes the timbre from a shrill, bright sound featuring high frequencies to a more dull sound for a brief moment before returning to the bright sound. Throughout the track, he is manipulating the timbre and the vibrato-tremolo effect of the Leslie speaker as an expressive tool and to contribute to the texture in a variety of ways. Around 4:10, as the drums drop out and in preparation for the final chorus, he changes the timbre of the organ from a bright sound to a cooler or perhaps more mellow timbre. This allows the organ to take a supporting, background role behind the vocal and instrumental improvisations, which are also reminiscent of the kinds of extended, melismatic improvisations gospel soloists might perform with an organist at a church service or gospel concert. The Savannah Children's Choir adds a clear reference to gospel throughout the second half of the recording. All of these elements of gospel music connect "Black Gold" to gospel as a musical genre and are iconic of the music of a supportive church community. With its positive message geared towards children and teens, and the sounds of many people singing and playing music together in the gospel style, "Black Gold" delivers a powerful message of a community coming together to encourage young people to tap into their inner strength, build a sense of self-worth, and take pride in their heritage.

> **SOCIAL BEHAVIOR**

"Black Gold" also references other African American styles. The polyrhythmic danceable drum grooves of Terri Lyne Carrington, Spalding's syncopated bass playing, the tight, percussive hits of the horn section, and the call-and-response improvisatory vocals are reminiscent of the funk and soul style of James Brown in recordings such as his classic song "I Got You (I Feel Good)" (1964). Spalding's melodic and active bass lines often avoid the first beat of the measure and may have roots in the flowing bass lines of Jamaican reggae, which have inspired the bass parts of so many popular songs since the 1960s (Chapter 13, Gateway 56). This confluence of popular genres from black musical traditions in "Black Gold" reinforces Spalding's positioning of the song as a celebration of African heritage.

> **AESTHETICS**

🔊 Listen one more time to "Black Gold," this time listening for the organ, choir, and other gospel influences and for elements that connect this recording to funk, soul, and reggae.

Other tracks on *Radio Music Society* demonstrate Spalding's compelling combination of jazz and popular music genres. One of two covers on the album is "I Can't Help It," originally from *Off the Wall* (1979) by Michael Jackson (1958–2009) and composed by Stevie Wonder (b. 1950), two of the most critically and commercially acclaimed popular musicians of the late twentieth century. To set up a bebop-rooted improvisation by tenor saxophonist Joe Lovano (b. 1952), she begins the song with a Latin groove on the bass referencing Brazilian samba, bringing yet another style from the Black Atlantic into her fusion of jazz with other genres (Chapter 6, Gateway 26). Three other tracks on the album feature a full big band of high school students from the Portland, Oregon-based American Music Program, connecting her and her music to a younger generation of musicians and to the nearly 100-year-old legacy of the big band ensemble in jazz. The title of the album, *Radio Music Society*, hints at Spalding's interest in jazz as a popular music, as she seems to be asserting

> **CULTURAL LINKAGES**

FIGURE 14.5
Esperanza Spalding performing with Joe Lovano (saxophone), Jack DeJohnette (drums), and Leo Genovese (piano) in 2014 at the Barbican Centre in London.
Getty Images / Andy Sheppard

that this broad combination of styles is music for the radio, that is, music that is meant for popular audiences.

In the pattern of a pop music single, Spalding released a music video of "Black Gold" that illustrates the meaning of the lyrics and provides a visual image of Spalding and Blessett trading vocal lines in an improvisatory manner. When the album was released in April 2012, it attracted many more listeners than a typical jazz album and debuted at #10 on the *Billboard* 200, a chart that tracks the popularity of albums of all genres in a given week.

SOCIAL BEHAVIOR

When reflecting on the history of jazz, it is a striking problem that most of the prominent jazz musicians have been men, especially jazz instrumentalists. The various styles of jazz have developed in twentieth-century societies where women have tended to be marginalized, excluded, or stereotyped as inferior. Compounding this problem are histories of jazz that have pushed women out of some of the central roles they have played in the story of jazz. Such histories imply that jazz can only be performed by men, and they offer few (if any) examples for aspiring women musicians that they can belong in jazz settings, other than in the typically female-gendered role of a vocalist. Since the 1990s, however, some of these gender expectations have begun to change in jazz, if ever so slightly. Jazz historians like Sherrie Tucker have undertaken and stimulated research on women jazz musicians throughout the history of jazz, bringing women's contributions into the historical narrative from which they had been excluded. Because of this kind of research, it is more common in histories of jazz today to encounter the work of musicians such as Bessie Smith, Lil Hardin Armstrong, Mary Lou Williams, the pianist and composer who served as a mentor of many of the first bebop musicians, and Melba Liston, the renowned arranger, composer, and trombonist working alongside Dizzy Gillespie and others.

In step with the struggle for equal opportunity, pay, and representation for all genders across many fields in American and other societies, an increasing number of women jazz musicians—both vocalists and instrumentalists—have become prominent in a number of streams of jazz. Diana Krall (b. 1964) and Norah Jones (b. 1979) became well known as jazz vocalists and pianists (in the 1990s and 2000s, respectively), and they have crossed over to popular music styles in a number of ways. More recently, the Chilean tenor saxophonist Melissa Aldana (b. 1988) won the Thelonious Monk International Saxophone Competition in 2013 and has become a well-known player in the New York and international scenes. The Brooklyn-based trumpet player Jaimie Branch (b. 1983) took 2017 by storm, with her energetic and genre-bending album *Fly or Die* topping many critics' year-end lists and bringing jazz into new dialogues with genres like EDM and indie rock. Though adequate gender representation in jazz is still a long ways away, as these and other women musicians are recognized for their mastery, creativity, and excellence in jazz, they offer to audiences and to aspiring musicians a new vision for what gender can look and sound like in jazz.

Sexual harassment where jazz is taught and performed has also contributed to the exclusion of women from jazz. In 2018 "We Have Voice," a collective of musicians involved in jazz, issued a comprehensive Code of Conduct for educational and performance institutions and for people working in the performing arts. It takes an unequivocal stance against gender discrimination and expresses zero tolerance for sexual harassment. In their campaign for "safe(r)" workplaces, the We Have Voice Collective challenges individuals and organizations to transform educational and work environments for all performers. This collective and its growing number of aligned musicians and institutions seek to cultivate spaces for collaborative music making that are safe for people of all genders. They believe that everyone should be able to participate in forms of music making they love without threats to their physical safety or discrimination based on gender.

What Is Its History?

CULTURAL LINKAGES

As a genre rooted in the black community of the United States, jazz has always responded to and dealt with racial injustice. Jazz today is no different. Despite the promise of a "post-racial" age in

America in the wake of Barack Obama's election as the first black president of the United States, police brutality against black men and efforts to suppress the African American vote make the headlines and circulate in social media every day. While civil rights organizations and activist movements have never stopped advocating for equal rights and against racial violence, in this period new movements emerged that added to this ongoing work. The most prominent has been Black Lives Matter, which emerged in 2013 in response to a seeming epidemic of police shootings of black men. Musicians have also added their voices to those of their predecessors in the struggle against these acts of racial violence and other forms of institutional racism in America. For example, rapper Kendrick Lamar's "Alright" from the 2015 album *To Pimp a Butterfly* became an anthem of Black Lives Matter. Some of his live performances of material from that album reenacted and supported acts of protest.

Esperanza Spalding, who released this album a year before Black Lives Matter began, adds her voice to the long history of jazz musicians' engagement with racial oppression, stretching back as least as far as Bessie Smith, Ma Rainey, and other women blues singers who challenged the injustices of their world. Some of Spalding's music on *Radio Music Society* takes an activist stance. "Land of the Free" deals with the case of Cornelius Dupree, a black man exonerated in 2011 after being imprisoned for thirty years for an aggravated robbery he did not commit. "Black Gold," as Spalding asserts in her press release for the song, speaks to injustice from a different angle. She encourages a positive self-image among young black men from a perspective akin to the Black Lives Matter movement and stretching back to James Brown's "Say It Loud." With music grounded in jazz and connected to many styles of black popular music, she joins a long tradition of jazz instrumentalists and singers who have promoted racial equality and celebrated black culture.

FIGURE 14.6
Esperanza Spalding performing the material from *Emily's D+Evolution* in Brooklyn, NY
Source: Getty Images / Al Pereira.

Her biography sheds some light on how she, like many musicians of her generation, came to understand and adopt so many different overlapping stylistic approaches in her music. Born in Portland, Oregon in 1984, she began playing musical instruments at a young age. She performed classical music on the violin in a community chamber orchestra starting when she was five years old. As a teenager, she started playing the bass and soon became active on the local club scene playing blues, funk, and hip-hop, styles that still pervade her music today. After finishing her high school studies at 16, she studied bass at Portland State University before attending the Berklee College of Music in Boston, where she graduated at age twenty and immediately was hired as the youngest faculty member in the school's history. Beyond the college education it provided, the Berklee environment connected Spalding to a community of established musicians, who began to hire her as a collaborator for live performances, tours, and recordings.

AESTHETICS

Spalding's website describes her work as "grounded in jazz traditions but never bound by them." Her studio albums as a solo artist all exemplify this description. In 2006 she released *Junjo*, her first solo album, which draws on jazz and a number of Brazilian and other Latin musical styles. She scat sings on many of the tracks and sings lyrics on others. The album also features her playing the upright bass along with a pianist and a drummer. Her second album, *Esperanza*, released in 2008, features Spalding playing bass, scatting, and singing in English, Spanish, and Portuguese in many styles. The song "I Know You Know" is in a style of jazz-inflected soul; "Love in Time" is a jazz waltz with a swing feel; and "Cuerpo Y Alma" is a Spanish-language version of the jazz standard "Body and Soul." On it she scats in unison with her bass, and the song's original meter of four beats to a measure is transformed to a meter of five beats to a measure. Contributions by vocalist Gretchen Parlato and trumpet player Ambrose Akinmusire, both winners of the Thelonious Monk Institute of Jazz International Competition, align Spalding with some of the other prominent jazz musicians of her generation. Her classical music roots surface on her 2010 album *Chamber Music Society*, where a small string section complements the jazz-based grooves. After *Radio Music Society* (2012), Spalding released *Emily's D+Evolution* in 2016, which leans towards the overlap of jazz and rock. On the album's first track, "Good Lava," a distorted, aggressive guitar sound is heard together with her electric bass and a driving rock beat on the drums.

> **CULTURAL LINKAGES**

Spalding, like many jazz musicians today, has been involved in education initiatives in addition to her teaching at Berklee College of Music. In 2010 she served as the Artist in Residence for the Savannah Children's Choir, who appear on "Black Gold." As part of this program, she taught master classes for young chorus and orchestra students and worked with over 1000 school children. Her decision to record with the big band from the American Music Program for *Radio Music Society* connects her to her Portland roots as she supports the education of young musicians on what turned out to be an award-winning album.

Spalding won the Grammy for Best New Artist in 2011, beating out Justin Bieber, Drake, Florence and the Machine, and Mumford and Sons. She has appeared in performances and on recordings with Prince, Bruno Mars, Alicia Keys, Janelle Monáe, Herbie Hancock, and Wayne Shorter, and has performed at the White House and at the Academy Awards. In 2017 she live-streamed the production of an entire album for seventy-seven hours on social media, a daring project called *Exposure*. People all over the world could open her Facebook fan page and watch her and a studio full of world-class musicians composing, arranging, and recording a full album project, issued as a limited release of 7777 copies.

By working with many styles and musicians from within and beyond the boundaries of jazz and engaging with social media and other technology, Spalding connects with audiences of all ages with a wide diversity of musical tastes. Her music reflects the unprecedented interconnectedness of the world today. She performs musical and social boundary crossing as she celebrates black culture and engages with a plethora of themes and issues. Along with other jazz musicians today, she extends the long tradition of experimenting with new genre combinations in jazz to make music that they find stimulating and that connects with longtime fans of jazz as well as new audiences.

WHERE DO I GO FROM HERE?

- Watch the music video for "Black Gold." How does it enhance (or detract from) the meaning of the song for you? What are some of the narrative and visual elements that complement or enrich the song's meaning?

- Listen to "I Can't Help It" from *Radio Music Society* and compare it to the original version by Michael Jackson and written by Stevie Wonder. What has Spalding added or taken away from the original version? How does her version deploy musical elements of jazz? Which version do you prefer and why?

- Listen to a few tracks from her *Chamber Music Society*. What musical elements typical of classical music is Spalding drawing on for this album? How do they fit together with the other musical styles on the album? Are there other fusions of classical music and jazz that you can find from any time in the 100 years since jazz began to emerge as a musical genre?

- Find some of the other musical projects that vocalist Algebra Blessett, guitarist-vocalist Lionel Loueke, and drummer Terri Lyne Carrington are involved in. Within which styles and genres are they actively performing? Which other artists are they collaborating with?

- Listen to some tracks from the album *Fly or Die* by Jaimie Branch or the album *Back Home* by Melissa Aldana. What styles are they drawing on from jazz and other genres?

GATEWAY 59
CLASSICAL MUSIC TODAY

What Is It?

Composers of classical music today often write new and innovative music within genres that have existed for centuries in classical music: operas, string quartets, symphonies, and concertos. At the same time they engage with new technologies and multimedia, with musical styles from jazz, popular, and world music, and with new challenging techniques on instruments that have long been common in classical music. Our gateway to classical music of the last few years is an example of this kind of innovation within a classical genre: a movement called "Speech" from an oratorio titled *Anthracite Fields* by Julia Wolfe (b. 1958). The text of "Speech" is an excerpt from a speech that John L. Lewis, head of the United Mine Workers Union, gave to the Congressional House Labor Committee in 1947. The choir of the Mendelssohn Club of Philadelphia and an ensemble of musicians called the Bang on a Can All-Stars premiered the work in 2014. In 2015 *Anthracite Fields* was awarded the Pulitzer Prize for composition, and in 2016 Julia Wolfe received a prestigious MacArthur "Genius" Fellowship.

FIGURE 14.7
Julia Wolfe at the Grammy Awards in 2016
Source: Splash News / Alamy Stock Photo.

 Listen to the first thirty seconds of this recording to get a sense of its sound.

How Does It Work?

Timbre

The timbre consists of solo and choral singing by men's voices, a bowed cello and bass played with a scratchy sound, strummed guitar, a clarinet, a drum set, and a synthesizer producing something like the scratchy static on old recordings.

Texture

The texture is varied. Sometimes the soloist and choir sing over a drone-like instrumental accompaniment. Sometimes the soloist's melody interacts with an instrumental melody.

Rhythm

The rhythm alternates between nonmetrical sections that mirror the rhythm of speech and sections with a constant pulse, often in a meter of four.

Melody

The composer uses melody sparingly, instead emphasizing drones and single pitches and chords in isolation.

Harmony

The male chorus often sings in intervals of fifths and seconds.

Form

The form features alternating solo and choral male voices.

Performance Techniques

The singing includes occasional slides between pitches and alternation of loud and soft either abruptly or with crescendos and decrescendos.

Listen to this recording with these elements in mind.

Listen to the entire recording following this timed listening guide.

LISTENING GUIDE 14.3

TIME	DESCRIPTION
0:00	The movement begins with a low-pitched, scratchy-sounding drone. A solo male singer begins the speech singing a melody on just a few pitches in a speech-like, nonmetrical rhythm: "If we must grind up human flesh in this industrial machine that we call modern America." A rhythmic pulse is introduced on the syllables "mo-dern A-mer-i-ca."
0:43	A chorus of men enters singing the same text and melody using harmonies based on the intervals of fifths and seconds. The drone texture thickens somewhat, adding a low-pitched clarinet, an electric guitar, and a drum set. Because they are played softly, these instruments may be difficult to hear.
1:10	The drone-like accompaniment changes character: a drum roll is clearly audible, as is the sound of the cello. The solo singer enters with these words, echoed by a two-part choral response using harmonic seconds: "then before God I assert that those who consume the coal." The electric guitar can be heard accompanying the singer, whose voice quality resembles that of a popular singer more than that of the typical classical choral or solo singer.
1:56	The soloist sings "because we live in comfort" on two very high, straining pitches. The chorus responds in harmony based on seconds: "that those who consume the coal and you and I who benefit from that service."
2:22	The male soloist softly sings an ascending, stepwise melody accompanied by the guitar playing the same melody and a drone tone; in other words, the text becomes quite thin compared to what has come before: "we owe protection to those men and we owe the security to their families if they die." The chorus responds, repeating fragments of the text: "if they die," "those men," and "protection" in a thudding pulse aided by a low-pitched drum beat.
3:55	The soloist and chorus alternate singing the text, "I say it, I voice it, I proclaim it" in a constant pulse at a very loud volume, each phrase of the text on a single pitch.
4:53	The drone texture is abandoned as the soloist sings an ascending, stepwise melody in unison with the synthesizer on the words "And I care not who in heaven or hell opposes it."
5:08	The drone and the chorus return very loudly, singing and playing a drone in harmonic seconds and triple meter on the words, "That is what I believe. That is what I believe, I believe, I believe."
6:06	A brief pause and then the soloist, accompanied by the synthesizer in seconds, quietly concludes with a three-note ascending melody: "And the miners believe that."
6:23	End

What Does It Mean?

AESTHETICS

Part of the meaning of "Speech" derives from its position among the four other movements in *Anthracite Fields*. The composer, Julia Wolfe, chose and created a set of texts that portray life in the anthracite coal-mining communities of Pennsylvania, where she grew up. Their related common themes unify the composition and express various points of view on the experience of coal mining. The first movement text, "Foundations," consists of selected names of coal miners killed in Pennsylvania mine accidents between 1869 and 1916 plus some geological descriptions of the region. The second movement text, "Breaker Boys," is a heart-rending first-person account of the horribly difficult work that children used to perform: picking debris from mined ore. The fourth movement text, "Flowers," is one woman's description of the beauty the women tried to create in their gardens above ground in a mining town while their husbands, sons, and fathers descended into the hell of the mines. The fifth-movement text, "Appliances," simply lists all the activities of daily life that depend on the energy generated by coal and by the hard and dangerous, sometimes fatal, work of coal miners: "bake a cake, go to the gym, blast your guitar, call your girlfriend on the phone." The oratorio's sixty-five-minute length in a concert setting requires a great deal of sustained attention. Within the national debate on the role of coal in our economy, in climate change, and in sustainable sources of clean energy, the composition sheds light on the human cost of mining.

Because of their association with a text, the musical elements in this piece can be interpreted for the way they express and reinforce the meaning of the words. For example, the solo singer is mimicking a speech by a single speaker or orator, an obvious connection to the real-world event on which the movement is based, but nevertheless a choice that the composer needed to make. Throughout the movement the male chorus responds by repeating the soloists' words, their male choral timbres representing the agreement of the miners' community with the speaker's words. The vocal timbre of the soloist does not resemble the timbre of a classically trained singer. It is more like that of a singer of popular music. This aesthetic step away from the style of the classical music, which is supported by wealthy and educated classes, and toward a "common" style, fits a text expressing the words of a working-class coal-mining community.

The nonmetrical quality of the soloist's singing mimics speech, while the pounding, pulsating, constant beat reinforces the miners' insistence on the truth that their leader is speaking.

FIGURE 14.8
Breaker boys from Pittston, Pennsylvania in 1911
Source: Lewis Wickes Hine. Library of Congress. Wikimedia Commons.

FIGURE 14.9
A performance of *Anthracite Fields* with photographic projections in the background
Source: Getty Images / Carolyn Cole.

The harmonies that the chorus sings are typically viewed as dissonant in European classical and American popular musical traditions. The dissonance of the harmony in this movement may disturb some listeners familiar mainly with those traditions. That disturbance, that dissonance, clearly matches the message of the text, which was meant, in 1947 and today, to disrupt the listener's complacency about the treatment of the men whose labor produces the creature comforts people enjoy and take for granted. The harmonic fifths sung by the choir may remind knowledgeable listeners of early polyphonic forms of Christian chant, lending a sacred quality, and a moral urgency, to a modern secular text.

The alternations between softness and loudness express the contrast between a rational, if resigned, presentation of an intractable problem and the anger of the speaker and the miners at their fate and their desire to communicate resolutely their wish for fairer, more humane treatment and working conditions.

The instrumental accompaniment combines instruments and timbres associated with classical music (cello, string bass, clarinet, choral singing) with those from popular music (synthesizer, electric guitar, drum set, and the style of solo singing). The combination of these instruments from different

> CULTURAL
> LINKAGES

categories, genres, and styles in one classical composition represents some of the breadth of contemporary American music. Fans of jazz or classical music or certain genres of popular music may bring to their listening experience specific ideas about what sounds authentic and appropriate in the genres they love. *Anthracite Fields* might be interpreted as a statement about the limits of musical genre in American culture today and the advantages of creative combinations that unify the musical and social divisions associated with categories, genres, and styles.

What Is Its History?

AESTHETICS

When twentieth- and twenty-first-century composers like Julia Wolfe contribute compositions relevant to their times to the repertoire of classical music, they often challenge the conventions of older music and the conventional expectations of their audience. In this piece Wolfe eschews traditional large or small ensembles of European classical instruments in favor of a unique combination of instruments and voices from classical and popular music. Also, for more than a century classical composers like Igor Stravinsky, Dmitri Shostakovich, and Terry Riley have been exploring harmonic dissonance and drones as expressive devices in the context of a music culture that mainly values and experiences consonant harmonies. *Anthracite Fields* is part of this history of harmonic, timbral, and textural innovation in twentieth- and twenty-first-century classical music.

ECONOMIC ACTIVITY

One reason that classical composers today think twice about composing for symphony orchestras is that it is so expensive to do so. Even high-priced tickets are not enough to pay the bills for orchestras and opera companies. These organizations today have to turn to government grants and gifts from wealthy philanthropists to meet their expenses. In the United States, government support of the arts is woefully inadequate. On a per capita basis Germany spends forty times as much on the arts as the United States does. This disparity speaks volumes about the value that these two governments place on the arts.

Government grants are a small part of government support for classical music. Far more comes from public schools, colleges, and universities, which offer music programs whose content consists mainly of exposure to European classical music. Many professional musicians get their starts in such programs, and they are also important patrons of composers in this tradition. Since the ability of arts organizations to pay composers commissions for their works and royalties from music publishing are relatively limited, many composers enjoy full- or part-time employment as university professors. (**Commissions** are promises to pay composers for their work; the sources of funding are government and private granting agencies and wealthy donors.) In this economic context, many classical composers today favor works for small chamber ensembles, which are less expensive to stage and record than compositions for large symphonies and opera companies. *Anthracite Fields* falls into this pattern. Julia Wolfe is a professor of composition at New York University, and a number of private foundations and institutions supported her in the composition, performance, and recording of *Anthracite Fields*.

In addition to its history within the long history of European classical music, the history of *Anthracite Fields* has a history in the work of its composer, Julia Wolfe. Born and raised in Pennsylvania, Julia Wolfe did not begin studying composition formally until after she finished her undergraduate degree at the University of Michigan. She studied piano as a child, but was more interested in playing the music of Broadway musicals than classical music. She picked up the guitar in high school and became interested in folk songs in the vein of singer-songwriter Joni Mitchell. Soon after her undergraduate studies, in the early 1980s, she relocated to New York City and subsequently completed a Master's degree in composition at Yale University in 1986. Like most composers of European-derived classical music today, she was trained as a composer in university settings and she has continued to be involved with various institutions of higher education. (Aside from her position at NYU beginning in 2009, she has long been active in giving master classes and seminars elsewhere.) She also completed a doctorate in composition at Princeton University in 2012, after she was already an established composer. Unlike many composers today, her career is intertwined with an organization that she helped co-found.

This organization, called Bang on a Can, began in 1987 as a one-time event in New York organized by Wolfe and two friends of hers who had also studied composition at Yale in the early 1980s: Michael Gordon (b. 1956) and David Lang (b. 1957). At the time, classical music composition in New York was polarized into two camps. The first camp favored complicated, intellectualized systems for organizing musical sound and was typically performed in formal settings such as concert halls. This music had little appeal to audiences, and composers in this sphere (building on the aesthetics of the by now decades-long tradition of serialism) for the most part privileged rationality, austerity, and complexity of structure over enjoyment by audiences. The second camp rejected this rational, austere, and complicated approach, and instead favored a simpler, more engaging style full of the repetitions associated with minimalism. This music, by Terry Riley, Philip Glass, Steve Reich, and others who got their start in the 1960s, was typically performed in informal settings such as alternative art galleries and loft spaces in New York's Lower East Side and Greenwich Village neighborhoods.

AESTHETICS

As young composers Wolfe, Gordon, and Lang were attracted to some musical elements from each of these polarized scenes. But because of the pretensions of each of the scenes, and because they wanted to engage with popular culture in ways these scenes did not, they didn't feel at home in either one. Their response was to hold a twelve-hour marathon concert at an art gallery in New York's SoHo neighborhood titled "Bang on a Can," where they gathered a group of like-minded musicians to perform their compositions along with the music of composers from both of the polarized camps. Wolfe, Gordon, and Lang were seeking through this marathon to create opportunities for compositions in classical music to cross boundaries of style and genre.

The value of crossing boundaries has remained central to Bang on a Can's activities as it has grown from the 1987 one-day event to an organization today that features an ensemble dedicated to performing new compositions, the "Bang on a Can All-Stars"; an annual summer festival devoted to the development of young composers and performers; a program to commission new compositions from emerging composers; and iterations of the original marathon concert in New York and elsewhere, among other endeavors. Bang on a Can provided a setting where composers of European classical music could incorporate elements of rock, folk, jazz, and pop, ostensibly breaking down the barriers between these different ways of making music. This is one of the features of Julia Wolfe's music, especially the incorporation of elements of rock and folk music into her compositions.

As Bang on a Can developed, Wolfe's co-founders Michael Gordon and David Lang became well known and gained prestige in the world of classical composers earlier than she did. One could argue that this is due to the fact that composition in classical music in the United States and Europe (and elsewhere) is a male-dominated field. Audiences and critics have certain assumptions about composers, one of those being that a composer is typically a man. Other aspects of classical music are also associated with gender, including which genders tend to play certain instruments. Also conductors have typically been men. These associations do not demonstrate "natural" traits of men and women, but rather are constructs based on factors such as associating a human's vocal range with an instrument's range or misguided assumptions about the physical abilities of women versus those of men. Similar to jazz, classical music has emerged from societies that were typically male-dominated, and in which, men typically played instruments and women typically sang. This musical division of labor by gender can even be observed in rural traditions like those in Bulgaria (Chapter 3, Gateway 11). Similar to jazz, efforts have been made in the last few decades to address classical music's gender problem. Blind auditions are now common for most symphony orchestras, preventing those assessing the musicians from making even subconscious judgments based on a person's gender (or race or other elements of their appearance), and resulting in a much greater female representation in the world's orchestras. Granting organizations often have funds dedicated to supporting the work of women; for example, OPERA America, the umbrella service organization for virtually all

SOCIAL BEHAVIOR

professional opera companies in the United States, has an ongoing grant program that financially supports women composers in the development of new operas. Julia Wolfe is an example of how the prominence of an increasing number of women composers today is challenging traditional norms that composers are male, though a large majority of composers of European classical music today are still male.

Anthracite Fields is related to Julia Wolfe's biography in several ways. First, its incorporation of elements of folk music and popular music with those of classical music is a common feature of much of the music Wolfe has composed and is emblematic of the values of Bang on a Can. Second, its focus on the life of coal-mining communities in Pennsylvania connects to Wolfe's roots growing up in Pennsylvania and her geographical proximity to those communities during her early years. Last, the composition is part of a broader, more recent trend in her work: themes related to American history and labor rights. For example, her 2009 composition *Steel Hammer* is a nine-movement work about John Henry, an African American folk hero renowned in the work of steel-driving, the hammering of a steel drill into rock to make holes for explosives, which were blown up to construct railroad tunnels. The most famous legend of John Henry is about a competition between him and a steam-powered steel drill, resulting in his victory and death from exhaustion. *Steel Hammer* explores the various versions of this human-versus-machine legend. Wolfe has also been commissioned by the New York Philharmonic to compose an evening-length piece for orchestra and women's choir about women in the American workforce for the Philharmonic's 2018–2019 season. This piece paints a picture of women working in garment factories in early twentieth-century New York and, like *Anthracite Fields*, involves research into historical documents and interviews. The large-scale composition demonstrates Wolfe's continuing interest in labor rights and American history, with an added consideration of gender and women's rights.

WHERE DO I GO FROM HERE?

- Go to Julia Wolfe's website and listen to another movement, or all the movements, of "Anthracite Fields" or listen to another of her compositions. If you read musical notation, follow along with the score as you listen to Movement 3, "Speech" from *Anthracite Fields*.

- Read about Michael Gordon and David Lang, and listen to one of their compositions created, like *Anthracite Fields*, since 2010. Compare and contrast their work to Wolfe's.

GATEWAY 60
WORLD MUSIC TODAY

What Is It?

World music today is an enormous catch-all of all sorts of musical traditions. Some seem timeless. Some have roots in the Medieval period and the modern era. And many have been created during the long twentieth century as societies modernized, people migrated, and electronic media carried musical styles across vast distances. Today world music includes popular music from Asia (C-pop, J-pop, K-pop) and music mainly known to people in a particular ethnic or minor community. From this grab bag we have chosen a song from the Mexican and Mexican American tradition known as *música norteña* or *norteño* as our gateway to world music today. The name refers to northern Mexico, where it developed. It is popular along the border between Mexico and the United States and with working-class Mexican Americans in California and other border states.

Our gateway recording is a song called "La Bala" (The Bullet) performed by Los Tigres del Norte (The Tigers of the North) from their 2014 album *Realidades* (Realities). A well-known band based in San Jose, California, their roots are in Sinaloa, Mexico. A related border-crossing genre in Texas is called **Tex-Mex**. The song is about gang warfare that results in the death of an innocent child, an all-too-common reality in the U.S. Such storytelling songs about real events are called ***corridos***, possibly deriving from the Spanish word *corer* (to run), describing a running story or commentary. It may also be cognate of the English word courier, a way, like a newspaper, of carrying the news or reinforcing knowledge of familiar events, but in oral rather than written tradition.

FIGURE 14.10
Los Tigres del Norte at the 2011 Latin Grammy Awards
Source: Splash News / Alamy Stock Photo.

 **Listen to the first thirty seconds of the recording.**

How Does It Work?

Timbre

"La Bala" is performed by a male singer to the accompaniment of a small combo called a ***conjunto*** (a group or grouping), in this case a *conjunto norteño*. It consists of a small button accordion, a twelve-string guitar called *bajo sexto* (bass of six strings), bass, and drum set.

Texture

The texture features a solo melody over alternating bass and chords.

Rhythm

This song is performed in a medium tempo duple meter.

Melody

The melody is based on a heptatonic scale with a range of about an octave and a half. The first three verses are sung in a minor mode, and the last four are in a major mode.

Harmony

The harmonies are triadic and frequently repeat in short cycles.

Form

The form is a variant of a strophic song. About halfway through "La Bala," the melody changes so that the form, instead of being AAAA etc. as in a normal strophic song, is AAA (minor mode) BB'BB' (major mode). Within the verses the A strophes are four lines long with the melodic form: abac. The B strophes introduce new melodies: B = defg and B' = defgh.

Performance Techniques

The singer changes the timbre of his voice from relaxed and soft to loud and tense. The accordion player improvises occasional short melodies over the singer's voice and at the end of phrases and whole strophes.

Listen to the first thirty seconds of the recording for the sounds of these instruments and the singer's vocal timbre.

Listen to the entire recording following this timed listening guide.

LISTENING GUIDE 14.4

TIME	SECTION	DESCRIPTION	LYRICS	LYRICS (ENGLISH TRANSLATION)
0:00	Intro	The *conjunto* plays a syncopated introduction.		
0:12	A	The soloist enters in his low register, singing the first verse in a quiet, matter-of-fact way. The melody, in a minor mode, rises in pitch at the end of the strophe.	(a) *Ocho en punto y como siempre, parecía un día normal*	Eight o'clock and as always, it looked like a normal day
			(b) *dos hermanos y un destino, una madre y un papa*	Two brothers and one destiny, a mother and a father
			(a) *siete años tenia el niño, del que les vengo a cantar*	One child was seven years old, about whom I come to sing
			(c) *pero voy a regresarme una semana para atrás*	But I'm going back a week
0:34	A		*Mi hijo el de 18 años, se empezó a descarrilar*	My 18 year old son started derailing
			su promedio era muy bajo, grosero con su mama	His grade average was very low, rude to his mom
			serraba el cuarto con llave, dizque su privacidad	I saw his locked room, signaling his privacy
			pero de armas en mi casa, el ocultaba un arsenal	He hid an arsenal of weapons in my house
0:57	A		*El jueves de esa semana, le conocí un par de amigos*	On Thursday of that week, I met a couple of his friends
			portaban otro semblante, no era gente de su tipo	They acted different, they weren't his type
			cosas raras me callaba, con tal yo de ser su amigo	I shut up about these strange things, I wanted to be his friend
			y por no verlo enojado, le cumplía cualquier capricho	And not to make him angry, I catered to his every whim
1:18	B	The singer changes to a major-mode melody for the next verse and sings in more strained manner than in the first three strophes, ending on the fifth degree of the scale.	(d) *Y ese día fue el final*	And that day was the end
			(e) *que el hijo más pequeñoa la escuela iría a estudiar*	[the last day] That my youngest son would go to study in school
			(f) *los carteles de la mafia cuentas iban a justar*	The accounts of the mafia cartels were going to be settled
			(g) *y con una bala perdida, me destrozaban mi hogar*	And with a stray bullet, they destroyed my home

TIME	SECTION	DESCRIPTION	LYRICS	LYRICS (ENGLISH TRANSLATION)
1:40	B′	The singer repeats the strophe, but adds a short, fifth phrase to end on the tonic.	(d) *La sorpresa es fatal*	The surprise is lethal
			(e) *que el hijo el de 18 muy involucrado esta*	my 18-year-old son is very involved
			(f) *con la muerte, con las drogas, participa en la crueldad*	With death, with drugs, [and he] participates in cruelty
			(g) *y en la muerte de su hermano*	And in the death of his brother
			(h) *fue el autor intelectual*	he was the one who inspired the crime [the instigator]
2:02	B″	Instrumental interlude, a variant of the B melody, ending on the fifth degree of the scale.		
2:21	B		*Soy otro en la suma nada más*	I am nothing more than another in the total
			que es victima del diario en la corrupta sociedad	of victims of the record of this corrupt society
			todo sabemos de alguien que hace daño a los demás	We all know of someone who hurts others
			y sus errores yo solía solapar	But I stayed silent about his misdeeds
2:41	B′		*Y hoy vengo a delatar*	And today I come to turn in
			al matón que anda en la calle, forma parte de mi hogar	The bully who walks in the street and is part of my home
			uno menos que ande suelto al mundo le servirá	One less that will have a place in the world
			si tu conoces un hijo igual al mío,	If you know a son like mine,
			por favor denuncia ya	please report him
3:17	End			

Credit: Song lyrics of "La Bala" courtesy of TN Ediciones Musicales

What Does It Mean?

The meaning of a *corrido* is derived in large part from its lyrics. *Corridos* typically tell stories about themes and individuals (or character types) closely related to the lived experiences of musicians and their audiences. Some *corridos* are dedicated to contemporary or historical heroic figures and tell of their lives and legendary courageous deeds. Others deal with stories about the Mexican Revolution (1910–1917), political corruption, natural disasters, passionate love affairs and deceptions, and various injustices experienced by Mexicans at the hands of Americans, the wealthy, the Mexican government, or those involved in gang and drug-related violence. Today, *corridos* often touch on the injustices faced by poor Mexicans or Mexican Americans such as discrimination and exploitation,

CULTURAL LINKAGES

while celebrating protagonists who exhibit courage, honor, and defiance in the face of these injustices. "La Bala" is a *corrido* that tells the story of the death of a child as a violent consequence of drug-related gang warfare.

Like all *corridos*, "La Bala" is in the form of a strophic song, a song based on repeating strophes, or verses, that contain identical or similar melodies and harmonic chord progressions, but with new lyrics for each repetition of the verse. The story of "La Bala" can be broken into seven parts, each part corresponding to a strophe. The first three strophes are grouped together, and the final four strophes are grouped together in two pairs separated by an instrumental interlude. *Corridos* open with an introductory strophe that presents the characters, time, location, and theme of the story. The following central strophes of a *corrido* tell the events of the story, developing it to its climax and resolution, before the final strophe or strophes present a farewell and a moral lesson provided by the narrator of the story.

In "La Bala" the first strophe introduces the main characters (a family with two sons, a mother, and a father, who is the storyteller) and the timeframe for the story (the important events take place on one particular day, but the story goes back a week to provide background information). It also hints that this particular day will be auspicious with the phrases "it looked like a normal day" and "two brothers and one destiny." The second and third strophes begin the story of the older son becoming involved in a gang and the father's regret in not discouraging his older son from violence and gang activity. The fourth and fifth strophes tell of the death of the younger son as a result of the older son's gang membership. The sixth and seventh strophes present the conclusion and moral lesson: the father-narrator laments his previous silence, decides to turn his older son over to authorities, and urges others to do the same if they know, as he sings, "a son like mine." These formal elements—introduction, body of the story, and farewell/moral lesson—are present in all *corridos* as lyrics tell a story of a protagonist dealing with hardships, adversity, or violence. For "La Bala," the father seems to be the protagonist, and his complex act of courage is turning in his own son.

EMOTIONAL RESONANCE ▷

Some strophic songs, and many *corridos*, employ basically the same harmony and melody for each strophe. The melody of "La Bala," however, makes a shift from a minor mode to a major mode after the third strophe, and introduces a new chord progression. This loosely corresponds to the narrative, where in the first three strophes the narrator is presenting the background to the story the week leading up to the auspicious day, and the final four strophes tell of the death of the younger son and give the moral lesson. In addition to the shift in harmony and melody after the third strophe, the vocalist begins to sing in a higher range and gives his voice a strained timbre. As he sings about the anguish of his younger son's death and his devastation at his older son's role in it, his voice is no longer low and relaxed as it was when he was providing the background for the story. The higher register and the strain and physical energy required seem to be linked with the emotions of the father, emotions that might similarly be communicated through the voice in crying or shouting.

AESTHETICS ▷

The rhythmic structure of *corridos*, including "La Bala," is relatively simple. Historically *corridos* have used a triple meter, though *corridos* like "La Bala" in the *norteño* style (and most of the songs by Los Tigres del Norte) typically use a duple meter. In "La Bala," the bass plays on the main accented beats, the downbeats. The *bajo sexto* and guitar play halfway between the main beats, on the upbeats. The drums play only on the beats and on the upbeats without adding any other accents or syncopation. This sparse rhythm allows the vocal and the text to stand out as the most prominent feature of the song, with the accordion and the fills it plays complementing the melody and the lyrics. The vocal line also avoids rhythmic complexities and embellishments in favor of a clear and understandable presentation of the lyrics.

What Is Its History?

"La Bala" is performed by and (for the most part) for the Mexican American community of the U.S. Its history is connected to the Mexican American community as well as the history of Los Tigres del

Norte. It is also connected to the long history of the *corrido* in Mexico and throughout Latin America, part of which also includes the history of the *norteño* genre. These histories demonstrate the intersections of a number of musical styles with one another in the context of political events and social changes. The *corrido* has its roots in the *romance*, one of many Spanish genres brought to Mexico by Spanish colonists as early as the sixteenth century. The *romance*, like the *corrido*, often told long stories in a form called an *epic ballad*. *Corridos* focused more on contemporary events than the *romance* did. *Corridos* were likely sung as far back as the early nineteenth century in northern Mexico and the area of the border of Mexico and the U.S. Like the *romance* these early *corridos* told long stories in as many as twenty strophes. The basic form of the *corrido* as it exists today became fixed during the Mexican Revolution (1910–1917), when *corridos* dealt with such prominent figures of the Revolution as Pancho Villa and Emiliano Zapata.

During the 1920s, the American recording industry began to recognize, as they did for race records and hillbilly music, the potential for a market among Mexican communities in California and the American southwest. Records featuring *corridos* were produced for, and sold to, a growing Spanish-language audience. By the 1960s recorded *corridos* had become much shorter in duration to fit the standard three-minute song length of records and commercial radio. The 3:10 duration of "La Bala's" seven strophes is evidence of this change in length from long *corridos* of many strophes to shorter ones.

Corridos can be performed in many styles and genres. In "La Bala" we hear the *norteño* genre, with the accordion taking the lead. The accordion most likely arrived in Mexico in the middle of the nineteenth century, introduced in western and northern Mexico and the borderlands by German immigrants. Germans and other Europeans brought a variety of music and dance forms, many of which became associated with the music of *conjuntos*. These influences are still present today not only in the sound of the accordion but also in the two-beat duple meter of one of these dance forms, the polka, which became a widely popular meter for *corridos* and is still the most common meter for *corridos* in the *norteño* style. *Conjuntos* featuring the accordion have spread along with Mexican and Mexican American populations throughout the U.S. and Canada, and *corridos* have continued to tell stories about contemporary life and struggle. *Corridos* and the *norteño conjunto* also appear in other Latin American countries, and their influence is particularly strong in times and places experiencing political and social turmoil.

Los Tigres del Norte (or Los Tigres for short) was formed in the late 1960s by a group of brothers and cousins, all of whom had immigrated from the western Mexican state of Sinaloa to San Jose, California. Their fame spread beyond their local region after they recorded and released the song "Contrabando y Traición" (Smuggling and Betrayal) in 1974. This song is a *narcocorrido*, a type of *corrido* prevalent since the 1970s dealing with drug trafficking as their subject matter. *Narcocorridos* in many cases celebrate drug trafficking and drug traffickers, but Los Tigres have refrained from glorifying the drug trade or glamorizing criminal activity.

As their popularity has grown, Los Tigres del Norte have been one of the leading groups in bringing *norteño* and *corridos* to audiences far beyond the U.S.– Mexico border region. They have sold upwards of thirty million albums, have received seven Grammy awards (including Best Regional Mexican Music Album for *Realidades* in 2015), and maintain a rigorous tour

FIGURE 14.11
Los Tigres del Norte performing in Madrid, Spain in 2009
Source: Getty Images / Eduardo Parra.

CULTURAL
LINKAGES
schedule that includes more than 100 performances per year. Their popularity and critical acclaim are in no small part related to the ways their *corridos* and other songs touch the realities of life for Mexican Americans. For example, the album *Realidades* includes a song called "Era Diferente" (She Was Different) about a lesbian teenager falling in love with a close female friend. The *corrido* provides Los Tigres del Norte and other groups with an effective vehicle for dealing with complex issues facing the community. *Corridos* are, by definition, relevant to contemporary events and will continue to provide audiences with a musical way to navigate oppression, economic strife, violence close to home, and other struggles.

WHERE DO I GO FROM HERE?

- Watch the music video for "La Bala." To what extent does it reinforce the story told and the moral lesson? What position do the musicians hold in the music video? Are they part of the storyline or not? What effect does this have?

- Find other *norteño* bands and compare their music and careers to that of Los Tigres. Do they cover similar material? Are they focused on *corridos* to a similar extent? Is the instrumentation or musical style similar?

- The 1960s featured the rise of the Chicano Movement (or El Movimiento), the Mexican Farmworkers Movement, and civil rights leader Cesar Chavez. Can you find *corridos* related to Chavez and those movements? There are also *corridos* about nearly all important contemporary American political figures and events. What kinds of stories and moral lessons can you find in these kinds of *corridos*?

- *Corridos* and *narcocorridos* occasionally appear in popular culture catering to audiences broader than Latin American communities. One example is the *narcocorrido* that opens episode seven from season two of the American television series *Breaking Bad*. Titled "Negro y Azul" (Black and Blue) by Los Cuates de Sinaloa, the song is dedicated to the fictional character Walter White (a.k.a. Heisenberg). Find this video excerpt. Does this *narcocorrido* exhibit the typical musical and social elements of the *corrido* and *narcocorrido*? Can you find other examples of *corridos* in popular culture for audiences broader than Latin American communities?

CLOSING

Categories and genres, whether large-scale ones like American popular music, European classical music, jazz, and world music or small-scale distinctions between the many kinds of rock music, are useful ways to make sense of the variety in the world of music. But they cannot contain all that variety. Professional musicians have good reason to play within genres because it helps them to develop certain skills to high levels of excellence and to find an audience and sell their performances and recordings to them. But genre boundaries, erected by selective use of particular musical elements, are indefensible against musicians' creativity. Those who cross genre boundaries, like Julia Wolfe and Esperanza Spalding, do so for both creative reasons, because they are excited by the music they hear on the other side of the boundary, and for social reasons, because they want to act ethically and harmoniously with people different from themselves.

CULTURAL
LINKAGES
One of the most exciting aspects of musical life in the long twentieth century, an aspect still going strong today, has been the genre busters, including the long histories of jazz musicians who have embraced European classical music, African music, and American popular music; classical musicians who have connected to jazz and popular music; popular musicians who have used classical music, like string orchestras, to serve their purposes; and traditional musicians from ethnic communities and around the world who understand themselves and their communities within a wide world of connections. They are telling us a lot about the world we live in through their music making. Their sympathy for a wide range of musical expressions articulates metaphorically their

sympathy for a wide range of human linguistic and cultural expression. They are challenging their audiences to listen as attentively as they do to new sounds coming from different people. Whether they explicitly link their music to particular social problems and conflicts facing us today or they simply want us to enjoy their music and have some fun, their music demands of us the same ethical commitment to diversity and difference as they have made in their own creative work.

Some scholars and critics of classical music refer to it as "serious music," implying that other kinds of music are frivolous. The gateways in this chapter clearly show just how serious musicians in all these categories can be. No matter the category they practice and love most, musicians and their audiences, from time to time at least, are using the music they perform and love to make sense of the world in which they live in very serious ways—all the while having some fun and maybe even getting people to dance.

THINGS TO THINK ABOUT

- The gateways in this chapter are all examples of how music engages head-on with challenges facing society today. What are these issues? What other contemporary issues are musicians familiar to you dealing with? In addition to song texts, which elements of music do these musicians use to deal with these issues and how do they do that?

- Can music be both entertaining and fun and comment on serious issues facing musicians and their audiences? Isn't that a contradiction? If not, why not? If so, why?

NEW TERMS

bridge	*corrido*	Tex-Mex
commissions	*música norteña* (*norteño*)	tremolo (electronic)
conjunto	pop or rock ballad	vibrato

WHERE DO WE GO FROM HERE?

ALTHOUGH WE HAVE COME to the end of the book, the opportunity, the need, and the desire to understand music is never ending. For the rest of your life new artists, new genres, new instruments, and new musical ideas will delight, fascinate, inspire, touch, and vex you. As new music enters the horizons of your current understandings, we trust you will seek to understand it by asking these five familiar questions: What is it? How does it work? What does it mean? What is its history? Where do I go to learn more about, and enter into, the artistic, cultural, and social world it opens up?

To start that process and to encourage you to continue your path to richer understandings of music, we conclude this book with a few examples that we think are worth pursuing right now in each of the four large categories of music that are all around us today: popular music, jazz, classical music, and world music. We find each of these examples in some way appealing, intriguing, provoking, or touching. They illustrate the ways that musicians and audiences today are engaging with their social and aesthetic worlds and thinking about their place in the world through the creation and reception of new music. Some of that music is firmly rooted in familiar traditions. Some of it explores new opportunities in technology and media. And some of it crosses stylistic, genre, and social boundaries.

POPULAR MUSIC

During the last ten to fifteen years EDM (electronic dance music) has become one of the most popular genres of popular music. DJs have become stars. With spectacular lighting, multimedia effects, and massive sound systems, their EDM shows fill arenas with fans seeking the thrill of soundwaves pulsing through their bodies, the chance to dance and party, and the experience of an exuberant musical collectivity only possible in that setting. EDM concerts and festivals generate the high spirits we associate with lovers of jazz and swing music during the Roaring Twenties. The top DJs today each regularly take in over twenty million dollars annually, among them Armin van

FIGURE 15.1
Armin van Buuren performing in 2014
Source: Rutger Geerling, Wikimedia Commons.

Buuren (b. 1976) and Tiësto (b. 1969) from the Netherlands, Calvin Harris (b. 1984) from Scotland, and Diplo (b. 1978), Marshmello (b. 1992), Steve Aoki (b. 1977), and The Chain-smokers (Alex Pall, b. 1985, and Andrew Taggart, b. 1989) from the U.S. Many of them churn out hits collaborating with some of the world's biggest popular singers such as Justin Bieber (b. 1994), Demi Lovato (b. 1992), and Frank Ocean (b. 1987). EDM's roots can be traced to the experiments with electronic music by classical composers in the 1950s, Jamaican dub and sound systems of the 1960s, and the music of the black DJs who created Detroit techno and

FIGURE 15.2
Beyoncé performing in 2011 wearing the characteristic yellow of *Oxum*
Source: Asterio Tecson, Adabow, Wikimedia Commons.

Chicago house in the late 1970s and early 1980s. Today EDM encompasses a proliferation of subgenres such as dubstep, ambient, drum and bass, and more.

Popular music artists today continue to engage with social issues related to race and gender, often drawing on African American music and culture. Beyoncé (Beyoncé Knowles-Carter, b. 1981) has built on the gospel-influenced vocal styles of earlier artists like Whitney Houston, along with the sounds of hip-hop and other genres of the African diaspora, to become one of the most celebrated performers in the world. Her 2014 visual album *Lemonade* references hundreds of musical and cultural elements addressing the experience of women in general and black women in particular. In her performance of the song "Hold On" on that album, she dons a yellow dress and emerges from a house full of water to sing a song flavored with rhythmic sensibilities reminiscent of reggae and other music of the Caribbean. Her appearance evokes the *orixá* of water and abundance *Oxum* (Chapter 6, Gateway 26), a deity known not only in *Candomblé* but throughout the African diaspora. She reprised this visual reference at the 2017 Grammys, where she performed visibly pregnant, emphasizing *Oxum*'s association with fertility. In her performance of "Formation" on *Lemonade* and in live performances such as the 2016 Super Bowl halftime show, her all-women backup dancers dressed in military attire reminiscent of the Black Panther Party of the 1960s as she raps "Okay ladies, now let's get in formation." The song celebrates blackness and femininity as gracious and powerful and affirms the necessity of struggle against racial injustice.

A number of popular musicians today are connecting to jazz, classical music, and world music. In 2014 East Coast rapper Nas performed the music of his album *Illmatic* (1994) live with the National Symphony Orchestra at the Kennedy Center in Washington, D.C., a performance broadcast on the PBS special Great Performances. The Swedish extreme metal band Meshuggah has attracted the interest of many jazz and classical musicians and composers. Those from jazz and classical backgrounds might not typically be interested in the sound of screamed vocals, but they are fascinated with the intricate polymeters and quickly shifting rhythms that are part of Meshuggah's signature style. Popular musicians and groups have also collaborated with Hollywood film music composers, including electronic music duo Daft Punk on *Tron* (2010) and the indie-pop group M83 on *Oblivion* (2013). Some, like Jonny Greenwood (b. 1971), the lead guitarist of Radiohead, have even become film composers themselves. He composed the widely celebrated soundtracks for *There Will Be Blood* (2007) and *Phantom Thread* (2017).

JAZZ

Jazz musicians have also continued to break genre boundaries. One of many that are creating exciting new work along these lines is pianist and composer Vijay Iyer (b. 1971). His diverse body of work engages with electronic music technology, Indian classical music traditions, textures common in European classical music, and streams of jazz inspired by John Coltrane and Thelonious Monk. Known for his rhythmic innovations, his work with Indian, West African, and Afro-Cuban musicians, and his engagement with popular culture (such as his cover of Michael Jackson's "Human Nature"), Iyer reflects in his music the cosmopolitan life lived by many musicians and listeners today, whose tastes are not always constrained by genre boundaries but can extend to encompass a wide variety of genres. The pianist Brad Mehldau, who was known in the late 1990s for his jazz trio versions of current pop and rock songs, has recently engaged in duo projects with bluegrass mandolinist Chris Thile (who himself crosses over to jazz and classical music) and with drummer, composer, and electronic musician Mark Giuliana. Mehldau's work has inspired jazz musicians today to perform and improvise over contemporary popular songs, just as musicians during the 1930s and 1940s improvised over songs from Tin Pan Alley and Broadway musicals.

Los Angeles-based tenor saxophonist Kamasi Washington has, on his 2015 album *The Epic* and since then, blurred boundaries between jazz and popular music by performing with his band in such contexts as large outdoor festivals like Coachella in Southern California, Glastonbury in England, and Austin City Limits in Texas. Washington's successful reception by university-aged young people at festivals usually reserved for bands in rock, indie rock, and electronic music genres has challenged preconceptions about what might be considered "jazz." Though he was perhaps first well known outside of jazz for his collaborations with rappers Kendrick Lamar (on *To Pimp a Butterfly*) and Snoop Dogg, his influences are wide-ranging: *The Epic* includes an arrangement of *Clair de Lune* by Claude Debussy, a soul- and R&B-flavored version of "Cherokee" (the jazz standard upon which Charlie Parker's "Ko Ko" is based), and a song called "Malcolm's Theme," which features a text taken from a eulogy for 1950s and 1960s civil rights leader Malcolm X. *The Epic* also has spiritual undertones that suggest it may also be inspired by *A Love Supreme* and other work by John Coltrane.

Other jazz musicians are revisiting long-standing jazz traditions in ways that engage a contemporary audience. The vocalist Cécile McLorin Salvant (b. 1989) has earned praise from audiences and critics alike for fostering the legacy of early black women blues singers, adapting their subversive but ever-so-slightly concealed messages for the issues and listeners of today. She channels a wide range of influences in her recordings and live performances of songs like Bessie Smith's "Wild Women Don't Have the Blues" and "You've Got To Give Me Some," the Beatles' "And I Love Her" (changed to "And I Love Him"), and "Si J'étais Blanche" ("If I Were White") by black American-turned-French singer Joséphine Baker (1906–1975).

The avant-garde in jazz continues to challenge listeners with new musical and social ideas. The flutist Nicole Mitchell

FIGURE 15.3
A Meshuggah concert in 2016
Source: Kinglevel, Edvard Hansson, Wikimedia Commons.

FIGURE 15.4
Vijay Iyer recording his 2017 album "Far from Over"
Source: Lynne Harty.

FIGURE 15.5
Kamasi Washington in 2017
Source: Krists Luhaers, Wikimedia Commons.

FIGURE 15.6
Cécile McLorin Salvant performing at the North Sea Jazz Festival in 2017
Source: Getty Images / Paul Bergen.

FIGURE 15.7
Nicole Mitchell performing in 2005
Source: Getty Images / Jack Vartoogian.

(b. 1967), a former president of the AACM, explores the sounds of the jazz avant-garde with her Black Earth Ensemble. On her website she describes it as "a musical celebration of the African American cultural legacy" by a "woman-led, co-ed, multi-generational group." The group explores a range of styles including swing, blues, avant-garde jazz, and bebop as well as the rhythms of African music, textures and timbres from European classical music, and melodic modes from Indian and Asian musical traditions. Critics perennially include her music and flute playing on their year-end "Best of" lists.

CLASSICAL MUSIC

Symphony orchestras and opera companies have started to break down the walls that literally keep popular audiences from entering their concert venues. During its run at Covent Garden in London, tickets for the opera *Written on Skin* (2012) by British composer George Benjamin and librettist Martin Crimp were available for as little as three British pounds (about four dollars). That meant that audiences of all means, not just opera's typical well-heeled patrons, could afford to attend. And fans of nineteenth-century Italian opera, who might otherwise not be interested in the more experimental aspects of modern opera productions, might be willing to take a chance for such a low price. The opera takes a thirteenth-century tale about a love triangle (remember Tristan and Isolde) and transforms it into a time-bending story for today, with contemporary visuals and costumes by director Katie Mitchell. The lead role is a countertenor, who sings with ornamentation reminiscent of Handel. The music of the five-vocalist cast and 60-piece orchestra features twentieth-century modernist dissonances with hints of Gregorian chant and madrigals as well as instruments such as a glass harmonica (an idiophone that produces sound by the friction of fingers on slowly spinning glass discs), a Renaissance-era bass viol, and Latin percussion like bongos and maracas. The combination of the familiar and modern thrilled enough listeners that the opera has been performed more than eighty times since its premier, a number unheard of for a modern opera.

A number of contemporary opera companies have taken opera productions outside the opera house, with New York companies such as On Site Opera, Heartbeat Opera, and Loft Opera, as well as the touring company Opera on Tap staging mostly traditional operas in non-traditional venues. The Los Angeles experimental opera company The Industry has taken this approach even further in its productions. Its 2015 opera *Hopscotch: A Mobile Opera for 24 Cars* put audience members in twenty-four limousines and drove them to several of twenty-four public locations in downtown Los Angeles. There, singers and instrumentalists performed for the audience and any bystanders on the streets, on nearby rooftops, on the banks of the Los Angeles River, and sometimes in the limousines themselves. The twenty-four concurrently running (and repeating) scenes were live-streamed by handheld cameras to a circle of screens called the "Central Hub," a free-access area in the parking lot of SCI-Arc (the Southern California Institute of Architecture), which funded and collaborated on the project. There, audience members could watch for free any of the scenes they liked while listening on wireless headphones. Conceived by director Yuval Sharon with music by six composers (Veronika Krausas, Marc Lowenstein, Andrew McIntosh, Andrew Norman, Ellen Reid, and David Rosenboom), the opera reached the usual wealthy patrons (who paid around $150 each for tickets), casual, accidental listeners who enjoyed one of its twenty-four parts for free, and those who gathered at the "Central Hub."

FIGURE 15.8
Written on Skin at Opera Philadelphia in 2018
Source: Feast of Music, Wikimedia Commons.

Such performances link modern classical music conceptually to the contemporary art scene and one of its genres, performance art. A number of classical composers combine their music with the visual arts, composing work for performance in art galleries and exploring electronics and multimedia in a range of performance settings. The award-winning Piano Concerto (2014) of Danish composer Simon Steen-Andersen (b. 1976), written for piano, sampler, orchestra, and video, begins with a video of a concert grand piano falling onto a concrete floor from a height of eight meters (about thirty feet). The composition continues with a dialogue between pre-recorded material and live performance expanding on the sound and image of the crashing piano. The ruined piano and its sounds literally destroy one of the central symbols of European classical music while performing the traditional genre of the piano concerto.

FIGURE 15.9
Nico Muhly in 2014
Source: Steven Psano, Wikimedia Commons.

In New York City, Nico Muhly (b. 1981) is perhaps the most prominent member of a composers' scene that brings sounds from indie rock and other pop genres into their work. Muhly's work blends the sounds of contemporary popular music with some of the techniques of his mentor, minimalist composer Philip Glass, to create twenty-first-century post-minimalism. His 2011 opera *Two Boys* tells the story of an online relationship, depicted in internet texting conversations set to minimalist choral singing. It ends in a murder. In addition to his dozens of compositions, he has scored several films and worked with popular groups and musicians such as Grizzly Bear, The National, and Sufjan Stevens, demonstrating a musical fluidity in both classical- and popular-music styles.

WORLD MUSIC

Popular music industries thrive in virtually every country of the world. Artists from musical traditions the world over are celebrating their uniqueness and their connection to the easy global flow of popular music. One of the most famous of these industries produces Korean "K-Pop." It has throngs of fans throughout Asia and wherever Korean and other Asian immigrant populations have settled, particularly in the United States. In Korea a billion-dollar industry has developed around performers who are trained in singing and dancing from a young age. Large entertainment companies bring them together in "boy bands" or "girl groups." The companies cultivate a polished aesthetic and support an efficient system of cranking out hits quickly. In 2017 the boy band BTS (Bangtan Sonyeondan, literally "Bulletproof Boy Scouts") began making waves in the mainstream American market with two songs in the *Billboard* Hot 100, performances at the American Music Awards and

FIGURE 15.10
BTS in 2016
Source: Korean Culture and Information Service, Wikimedia Commons.

FIGURE 15.11
***Bhangra* dancers with *dhol* drums in Punjab**
Source: Onef9day, Wikimedia Commons.

on New Year's Eve at Times Square, and a remix of their hit "Mic Drop" by EDM DJ and producer Steve Aoki. In 2018 they became the first K-pop group to top the *Billboard* albums chart when their album *Love Yourself: Tear* debuted at number one. All born in the mid-1990s, the seven members of BTS sing, rap, and dance while drawing on hip-hop and EDM in their slick pop recordings, music videos, and live performances. Many K-pop bands release versions of their songs with lyrics not only in Korean, but also in Chinese, Japanese, or English. Fans around the world have become obsessive devotees of their favorite groups and individual performers.

In another common move, communities with a distinct local style create modern, cosmopolitan identities by adding sounds from global popular music into the mix. *Bhangra*, a music and dance style with roots in the northwest Indian state of Punjab, has been especially popular among youth in Indian diaspora communities in North America and the United Kingdom. An upbeat music, *bhangra* combines rural traditional music of Punjab and other Indian musical styles with rock, hip-hop, and EDM. The *dhol* (a double-headed Punjabi drum), *sitar*, *tabla*, and other Indian instruments are mixed with electric guitars, synthesizers, and driving hip-hop dance beats. University *bhangra* dance groups prepare elaborate performances and compete against one another at events that honor excellence in performance and strengthen community bonds. Listeners and dancers enjoy a sound that represents and expresses their multiple and overlapping identities as Indians fully participating in an interconnected globalized world.

FIGURE 15.12
Baaba Maal in 2011

Source: Skoll World Forum, Wikimedia Commons.

In a world knit together by the internet and air travel, musicians enjoy innumerable possibilities for collaboration across genres and boundaries, creating music that reinforces existing social identities and builds new ones. Baaba Maal (b. 1953), a vocalist-guitarist from Senegal well known throughout Africa and much of the world, is one such musician. In 2016 he collaborated with banjo-driven British pop act Mumford and Sons, South African pop group Beatenberg, and Malawian-British songwriter-producer team The Very Best on the album *Johannesburg*. It topped the *Billboard* World Music charts in the U.S. A plethora of styles overlap on the album, which includes a subtle nod to the banjo's African roots and its popularity today in pop music and other styles beyond the African diaspora. Maal, along with a number of other well-known African musicians, was also involved as a consultant and musician on the score of the superhero film *Black Panther* (2018). On the soundtrack Maal sings soaring and undulating microtonal melodies during the scene where the fictional high-tech futuristic African nation of Wakanda is first revealed. Prominently heard in the context of a typical Hollywood orchestral score, the sounds of *marimba*s (African xylophones), *mbira*s, African drums, and the rap and hip-hop production of Kendrick Lamar pervade the soundtrack. The music depicts an interconnected African diaspora rich with unity and diversity and helped make the film the third highest grossing movie of all time in the U.S. and the ninth worldwide, at the time of writing. Like all the musicians in this book and musicians in every time and place, Baaba Maal and others collaborating on the soundtrack of *Black Panther* experience and understand the musical traditions around them and create new music that connects them in meaningful ways to the world they live in today.

We invite you to join them in that journey. Where will you go from here?

GLOSSARY

A

'ud a fretless, short-necked, pear-shaped, plucked lute with a vaulted (that is, rounded) back and a peg-box bent back at ninety degrees to the neck *Chapter 3*

a cappella choral singing without instrumental accompaniment 4

accelerando increasing tempo 7

accidental signs used in notation to indicate a pitch higher (sharper) or lower (flatter) than the diatonic pitch with a letter name 2

achieved status a society status or social role based on merit rather than heredity 4

added effect a buzzing or rattling timbral quality added to resonating pitches, a desirable quality heard in some African and African American music 3

additive meters meters that combine beats of two and three pulses that add up to meters of 5 (2+3), 7 (2+2+3), 9 (2+2+2+3), 11 (2+2+3+2+2), and so forth 3

alap in Indian music, a nonmetrical improvisation in a particular melodic mode 4

aleatoric composition a method of composition which leaves the final form of the composition to chance 12

alto a low-pitched female voice or part 4

alto clef (or tenor clef), C clef a five-line staff used for mid-pitched notes 2

antiphons newly composed chanted texts with more elaborate melodies than Biblical chants 2

aria in opera, songs with clear melodies 5

arioso a vocal writing style in opera falling somewhere between the florid, melodic arias and the dry recitatives of Italian opera 8

Ars Nova a new style of rhythmically complex polyphony in fourteenth-century Europe 2

articulation the separation of one note in a melody from another I

ascribed status a social status or social role based on heredity rather than achievement 4

atonality a musical system where there is no determined hierarchy of pitch and no pitch center or key 9

attack the onset of a tone I

authentic cadence a movement at the end of phrases and pieces from a triad built on the fifth degree of the scale (V) to a triad built on the first degree or tonic of the scale (I) 4

B

ballad a short song that tells a story 7

ballad, pop a pop song with a relatively slow tempo 14

banjo a fretted, long-necked plucked lute with five strings running along the neck and a sixth, shorter string running halfway up the neck 7

bar in musical notation a group of beats I

Baroque a word for misshapen pearl used to refer to the elaborate style of art and music from 1600 to 1750 5

bass low-pitched male voice or part 4

bass clef, F clef the five-line staff used for low-pitched notes 2

basso continuo in Baroque music, an instrumental bass line 5

bebop a style of jazz featuring solo improvisation and harmonic complexity, at often very fast tempos 11

bel canto beautiful singing, a style of early nineteenth-century Italian opera 8

bell   an idiophone with a depth greater than its surface diameter   5

big band   a jazz ensemble with a typical instrumentation of five saxophones, four or five trombones, four or five trumpets, and a rhythm section typically including drums, bass, piano, and guitar   10

binary form   AABB melodic form typical of dance music   4

blue notes   pitches on the third and seventh scale degree of the major scale that are lowered to the pitches of a minor mode, common in the blues   9

bluegrass   a genre of rural American music from Appalachia consisting of songs and instrumental tunes played by an ensemble of mandolin, banjo, fiddle, guitar, and bass   7

blues   a strophic song most typically in a repeating AAB form of 12 bars that originated in African American communities of the American South, and deals with the hardships and struggles of daily life   9

bourgeoisie   city dwellers who provided professional services   7

break   a term used in jazz and some popular music for a section of a performance when much of a rhythm section suddenly stops and other ensemble members continue playing (sometimes in solo improvisation) to a silent ongoing pulse   10

breakdancing   acrobatic style of improvised solo dance developed as part of hip-hop culture   13

bridge (1)   a section of a popular music or jazz form that typically departs from yet connects the sections that precede and follow it, such as the B in AABA form   10

bridge (2)   in a song, a section that usually occurs only once connecting two repetitions of the chorus toward the end of the song   14

Broadway musical   a sometimes comic, sometimes serious play with singing and dancing added to the spoken dialogue   10

C

calypso   a style of song that developed in Trinidad in the early twentieth century that provides social commentary on topical issues and events   11

camerata   a room or dormitory and today a name taken by many early music groups   2

Candomblé   an African-derived Brazilian religion   6

canonization   a selection process by which scholars, critics, performers, and audiences at a particular time in history come to regard certain works of art, literature, and music as the most important, the most influential, and possessing the greatest artistic merit   7

cantata   multi-movement religious works for the Lutheran liturgy   5

cantus firmus   a fixed song tune used as the basis for Renaissance sacred vocal polyphony   4

capitalist   owners of enterprises that employ large numbers of workers   7

castrato   a male singer castrated before puberty to prevent his voice from changing from soprano to tenor or bass   5

chamber ensemble   an ensemble that plays in intimate settings such as small rooms (chambers) rather than in large concert halls   6

choral singing   many people, a chorus or choir, together singing a melodic line or set of melodic lines in harmony   4

chord   three or more pitches performed simultaneously   1

chord cluster   a chord that includes many adjacent pitches sounding together   9

chordophones   instruments with vibrating strings   4

chorus (1)   the name given in jazz to one repetition of a form that serves as a basis for improvisation   10

chorus (2)   in a song, a section that repeats throughout the song with the same melody but different lyrics each time   2

chromatic pitches   pitches added to the seven-tone scale, used to add "color"   2

civic nationalism   the notion that began in the eighteenth century that all those defined as "men" living in a nation had "certain inalienable rights," including the right to govern themselves and to be full-fledged citizens, regardless of their ethnic origins or when they or their families arrived in those countries   8

civilization   the culture of cities   2

classic blues   a type of blues more common in cities and towns that typically involved a female singer accompanied typically by a pianist as well as other instrumentalists   9

clave   underlying rhythmic pattern in salsa music   12

clavichord   a Baroque keyboard instrument with metal blades stopping the strings   5

clavier   a generic term for keyboard   5

clawhammer style   playing the banjo by striking strings with the fingernails of a curved hand   7

coda the tail or ending added to the end of a musical composition or performance 3

collective improvisation simultaneous improvisation by two or more players, especially in jazz 10

colotomic structure in Javanese gamelan music, the cycles of low-pitched gongs that "cut" the time into units of varying length 5

commissions promise to pay a composer for a composition 14

comping a term short for "accompanying" used in jazz for the way a guitarist or pianist plays in support of a soloist 12

compound meter a subdivision of beats in duple meter into three pulses per beat 8

concept album an album that is conceived as an integral whole, with interrelated songs arranged in a particular order 12

concerto an instrumental composition for soloist or a small group and orchestra 5

concerto grosso a Baroque instrumental genre that contrasts a small group of soloists with the full orchestra 5

conjunt melodic motion melodies that mainly move through adjacent pitches of a scale 2

conjunto in Latin music, a small group of musicians 14

consort an ensemble of musical instruments, particularly during the Renaissance 4

contrary melodic motion when two lines ascend and descend in opposite directions 2

cornett a piece of wood, often slightly curved and cut in half lengthwise, hollowed out, held together with a leather covering, with six finger holes and a thumb-hole 4

corrido story-telling Mexican song 14

Counter-Reformation a movement to restore the dignity and sanctity of the Roman Catholic Church in the wake of the Protestants' attacks on both 4

counterpoint, contrapuntal texture the simultaneous singing or playing of many melodic lines 2

counterpoint, four-part four voices singing in harmony 2

countertenor falsetto male voice 4

country blues a type of blues that emerged in rural areas that typically involved a male singer accompanying himself on the guitar 9

country music a commercial genre of popular music rooted in early twentieth-century rural music, mostly from white communities of the American South 11

course one string or a set of close-together strings tuned to the same pitch and stopped or pressed onto the fingerboard by one finger 3

cover in popular music, a new version of an existing song 12

crescendo increasing loudness in a musical phrase I

cyclical mass a mass with the same *cantus firmus* (fixed song) for each text in the ordinary of the mass 4

cymbal a metallic idiophone in the shape of a flat plate with no depth 5

D

decay the shape of a tone after the attack until it ends in silence I

decrescendo decreasing loudness in a musical phrase I

development the section in a sonata form where melodies modulate 6

diegetic sound and music sound and music in a film or play that is heard by the characters and in the story world of the film or play 10

disco popular form of dance music in the 1970s enjoyed at nightclubs where audiences danced to continuous music played on records for hours at a time 13

disjunct melodic motion melodies that mainly employ large melodic intervals 2

dominant the fifth degree of a diatonic scale 4

double leading tone chord a chord with two leading tones heard in some Medieval music 2

downbeat the main beats of a measure 6

duple meter a regularly recurring two-beat meter counted 1–2–1–2–1–2 and so on I

dynamics change in the loudness and softness of music I

E

early music European church, court, and concert music composed before 1750 (or by some reckoning before 1650) 2

English horn a low-pitched cousin of the oboe 7

Enlightenment an eighteenth-century political philosophy seeking freedom from autocracy and other forms of authority through the exercise of reason 6, 7

envelope the shape of a tone from attack to decay I

episode in a Baroque fugue, a polyphony section with imitative polyphony based on the subject 5

ethnic nationalism the notion that each nationality (or what are called ethnic groups in the United States today), has a right to its own nation-state 8

European dance form   AABB melodic form in dance music   4

explaining music   statements, descriptions, classifications, labels, analyses, interpretations, and claims about causes and effects that account in words (or diagrams, formulas, and graphs) for particular musical phenomena or set of facts in our musical experience   1

exposition (1)   in a Baroque fugue, the opening section of imitative polyphony   5

exposition (2)   the opening section of sonata form   6

F

falsetto   a "false" voice that allows men, and women, to sing in a register above their normal, speaking vocal range   4

fife   a small side-blown flute   9

feedback   an effect that happens when an audio input, like an electric guitar or a microphone, receives the sound from an audio output, like a speaker, in a loop, which often results in a high-pitched screeching sound   12

figured bass   in Baroque music, numbers below the bass note indicating the number of scale degrees above the bass note that the player should play to create a chord   5

final   the most important pitch of a mode, the pitch it ends on   2

flute   an instrument on which a sound wave in a vibrating column of air is initiated by blowing over an edge   1

folk songs   songs of rural peasants that were idealized as the perfect, ancient, unadulterated expression of the nation, in German *das Folk* (the people)   8

form, musical   the way a performance of music unfolds through time from beginning to end   1

forte   a loud sound   1

fortepiano   literally "loud–soft," a predecessor of the piano with a range of five or six octaves and a lighter, thinner sound than the modern piano   6

free jazz   a style of jazz that emerged in the 1960s seeking to break down conventions of rhythm, pulse, form, texture, and harmony, and departing from the harmonic structures and steady pulse that had long characterized jazz   12

fugue   a tightly organized piece featuring imitative counterpoint   5

fundamental   the slowest vibrating wave in a tone, the one with the longest wave form   1

funk   a musical style that originated in the mid-1960s characterized by complex, multi-layered syncopation and grooves with driving, percussive bass lines, and guitar riffs featuring the wah-wah pedal in combination with percussive effects   13

fuzz box   an electronic effects pedal that distorts timbre   12

G

gaida   Bulgarian bagpipe   3

gamelan   in Java, a large orchestra of around forty instruments made of bronze gongs or metal keys, plus drums and a bowed fiddle   5

gamelan *gong kebyar*   the most popular type of Balinese gamelan orchestra, comprised of mostly bronze percussion instruments and typified by rhythmic complexity and excitement in performance   9

gangsta rap   a hip-hop subgenre that vividly chronicles the so-called gangsta lifestyle of the urban poor of Los Angeles, discussing themes such as gang violence, sex, unemployment, and widespread crack cocaine use   13

gat   the metrical section of a North Indian classical performance   4

gateway   a recording of music and a set of five questions asked of the recording that provide a portal to a world of music   1

genre, musical   a way of labeling and categorizing music that is associated with a community of musicians and listeners   1

Gesamtkuntswerk   Richard Wagner's concept of the "total artwork," where all of the elements of drama (poetry, music, stage design, and acting) were united in one work   8

gharana   a "house" or family of hereditary musicians and their students   4

gong   an idiophone with a surface diameter greater than its depth   5

gospel quartets   four-part singing groups that performed gospel music; black gospel quartets first became popular in the 1930s   8

gospel songs   a genre of Christian religious songs that emerged in the late nineteenth century, characterized by their singability and relative simplicity compared to earlier hymns   8

grand staff   two parallel five-line staffs linked together   2

Gregorian chant a label for monophonic Christian chant preserved in musical notation starting around the ninth century that acknowledges the influence of Pope Gregory I on the liturgy of the Catholic Church 2

groove in jazz and popular music, a short, repeated musical pattern; ostinatos can be rhythmic, melodic, or chordal 11

guitarrón a large guitar-shaped fretted lute 10

guru a music teacher and spiritual guide 4

H

habenera rhythm a Latin rhythm from Cuba characteristic of the tango 9

hard bop a style of jazz that features the rhythms of gospel and rhythm and blues, memorable and simple bluesy melodies, and an aggressive, driving pulse in the drums that often accented beats two and four (known as the "backbeat") in a four-beat measure. It departs from the virtuosic fast-tempo conventions of bebop, favoring instead slower tempos and simpler melodies, though it includes the head–solos–head form and complex harmonies for improvisation that also characterize bebop 12

hardcore rap a style of rap that arose in the East Coast scene in the 1980s that is typified by expressions of anger and confrontation 13

harmonic the sound of an overtone rather than the fundamental 3

harmony a combination of tones sounding simultaneously I

harpsichord a Baroque keyboard instrument with quills plucking the strings 5

head in jazz, a composition that serves as the main melody, usually appearing at the beginning and end of a given performance 10

heterophony, heterophonic texture two or more instruments playing the same melody together, but slightly differently 3

heterorhythm the singers pronounce each syllable of the text at different times 2

hi-hat two cymbals played with a pedal in a drum set 10

hillbilly records a genre created by record companies in the 1920s that targeted a niche market of rural whites. It initially featured musicians playing styles and repertoires, such as ballads and folk songs that had developed in rural areas of Appalachia and the south among immigrants from the British Isles 11

hip-hop culture an initially local phenomenon that arose in New York City among black and Latinx youth and included music (made by DJs and MCs), dance (breakdancing), and visual art (graffiti), as well as styles of dress and, later, the practice of producing percussive effects with the voice and mouth called beatboxing 13

homorhythm the singers pronounce each syllable of the text at the same time 2

honky-tonk music a style of country music performed at "honky-tonk" bars featuring fiddle, acoustic rhythm guitar, bass, electric lead guitar, lap steel guitar, and that absorbed influences from jazz and rhythm and blues. Honky-tonk lyrics focused on personal relationships and heartbreak 11

horn a generic term for buzzed-lip instrument, often with a curved tube 4

horns in jazz, a reference to saxophone, trumpet, trombone, and other wind instruments 10

I

icon, iconic sign a sign type that links two phenomena by similarity or resemblance I

idée fixe an obsession, the recurring theme in all movements of Hector Berlioz's *Symphonie Fantastique* 7

idiophone a class of instrument in which material other than strings, stretched skin, or columns of air vibrates 5

imitation polyphony in which each voice or part enters in succession on the same melody 4

impressionism an artistic movement in late-nineteenth-century France 8

index, indexical sign a sign type that indexes or is associated with or is linked to something else I

Industrial Revolution a period of invention of machines that enabled the more efficient production and transportation of goods and the concentration of wealth in the hands of "industrialists" 7

inherent polyphony the experience of polyphony when a monophonic line is played 1

interval the distance between two different pitches I

J

jazz combo a small jazz ensemble including a rhythm section of drums, bass, and piano or guitar, often along with one or two other instrumental soloists 11

jazz fusion a broad genre label for styles that combine jazz with other styles such as rock and funk 12

jazz standard a song that is frequently used as a vehicle for jazz performance, commonly in a form where a performance of the melody is followed by improvisations over the harmony of the song. Many jazz standards were originally popular songs in the interwar period having been written as Tin Pan Alley songs or having been performed on Broadway 10

K

kettledrum a single-headed, bowl-shaped drum 4

keyboard a generic term used for all types of instruments that employ the layout of long, usually white, keys for the seven-pitch diatonic scale and short, usually black, keys for the five additional chromatic pitches of European music 5

kotekan a technique in Balinese gamelan where melodic and/or rhythmic figurations too fast to be played by one person are divided between two partners in a variety of configurations, sometimes involving a pattern where partners alternate playing every other note 9

L

leading tone (1) a pitch that is a half-step below another pitch that creates a sense of tension until it is resolved on the pitch above 2

leading tone (2) the halfstep relationship between the 7th degree of the scale and the 1st degree of the scale 4

leapwise melodic motion melodies that mainly employ large melodic intervals 2

legato playing the tones of the melody with smooth connections between them 1

Leitmotifs guiding or leading motives, a term coined by Richard Wagner 8

liturgies the ritual rules and practices for sacred services 2

loudness the perception of the amplitude of a tone's wave form 1

lute (1) a generic name for a family of chordophones with a body and a neck 4

lute (2) a Renaissance plucked pear-shaped lute with a vaulted body (that is, a rounded back rather than a flat back) made from a set of thin wooden ribs glued together 4

lyre a stringed instrument with a resonating body and a frame holding five or six strings, which are plucked 2

M

madrigal a genre of polyphonic love songs in Italian and English that first appeared around 1530 4

maqam an Arab melodic mode that specifies intervals between pitches, characteristic melodic gestures, the addition of chromatic pitches, and typical modulations 2

mbira, **Shona** an idiophone with twenty-two tuned plucked metal keys mounted on a soundboard 3

measure in musical notation, a group of beats 1

mehter an Ottoman band of valveless trumpets 9

melisma, melismatic singing each syllable of the text is set to many pitches of the singing 2

melodic motive a short section, usually the first two to five pitches, of a melody 6

melodic shape the form of a melody visible in musical notation: for example, ascending, descending, arc-shaped, undulating, flat 1

melody, melodic line a series of pitches performed over time usually by a single voice or instrument 1

membranophone an instrument made from vibrating skin held to a frame, cylinder, or bowl under extreme tension 4

meter the organization of pulsation or beat 1

metrical music with a beat or pulse 1

microtone, microtonal interval an interval smaller than a half step 2

minimalism a genre label given to compositions that emphasize pulsating repetition of a small number of musical elements, first used in the 1960s 12

minstrel show white entertainers, masked in blackface, imitating and ridiculing both free and enslaved African Americans in ostensibly black styles of speech, dance, and music 7

minuet and trio a middle movement of a Classical-period symphony or work for string quartet named for a slow, courtly dance in triple meter called a minuet; the trio is another minuet, often in a contrasting key 6

modal jazz a style of jazz where musicians improvise over melodic modes that last for long durations rather than over quickly changing harmonies 12

mode a scale with a set of intervals between the pitches and with one or more functions assigned to the pitches in the scale, such as its final or end pitch 2

modernism   the breaking of artistic boundaries, especially at the turn of the twentieth century   8

modes, diatonic   scales based on half steps and whole steps   2

modulate, modulation   the changing of keys in tonal music; any musical change   5

modulation   changes in one or another element of music: a modal modulation, a key modulation, a metric modulation, and so forth   2

monody   a vocal melody accompanied by bass and chords   5

monophony, monophonic texture   a performance with a single line or melody   1

motet   a sacred work composed on a Latin text, either newly created or taken from the Bible, and sung during the Catholic liturgy   4

movement   a named part or section within a long classical composition   2

music drama   the term that Richard Wagner used to describe his works, in place of the term "opera"   8

música norteña **(norteño)**   a musical style from northern Mexico   14

musical, musicality   the capacity of humans to create, perform, organize cognitively, react physically and emotionally to, and interpret the meanings of musical sounds   1

musical nationalism   music composers wrote expressing nationalist sentiments in the hope of inspiring their people   8

N

nationalism   in nineteenth-century Europe, the notion that each ethnic group has the right to its own nation-state   8

neo-traditionalism (in jazz)   a trend in jazz that first emerged in the 1980s that values celebrating older styles and historical repertoire from earlier in the twentieth century   13

neoclassicism   a style of twentieth-century classical music that includes references to elements of Classic period music   11

neumes   a collection of graphic symbols written above the text of Christian chants to indicate the shape and character of a melody   2

new music ensemble   an ensemble dedicated to performing classical music composed mostly since the 1960s and leaning towards the experimental and the avant-garde   12

New Orleans jazz   a style of early jazz where a rhythm section backs up three melodic instruments (usually trumpet or cornet, clarinet, and trombone) that play in polyphony, improvising independent but interrelated melodic lines   10

nondiatonic pitches   pitches other than the seven pitches separated by whole steps and half steps in a heptatonic, diatonic scale   2

nonmetrical   music without a beat or pulse   1

note   a visual representation of a tone in musical notation   1

O

obbligato   in band music, a second melody played simultaneously and in counterpoint with the main melody   9

oblique melodic motion   when one line stays at the same pitch while a second part ascends or descends   2

octave   the interval between two pitches whose ratio of vibration is 2:1; perceived as "the same" pitch   1

opera   a theatrical musical genre that tells stories through recitative, aria, instrumental music, acting, and dancing   5

opus (Op.)   from the Latin for "work," a numerical designation used by Classical-period composers and publishers to identify their compositions in chronological order   6

oratorio   a multi-movement composition that tells a biblical story in the vernacular (local) language rather than in the Latin of the Catholic liturgy   5

orchestration   the art of composing for orchestral instruments singly and in combination   7

ordinary of the Mass   texts included in every celebration of mass   2

organum   polyphonic chanting in parallel fifths and fourths   2

orixás   a pantheon of male and female deities in *Candomblé*   6

ornamentation   the addition of short tones to the main tones of a melody.   1

ostinato   a short, repeated musical pattern; ostinatos can be rhythmic, melodic, or chordal   1

overtone singing   two sounds from one voice, one produced by the vocal cords and the other by resonating the overtones of the throat-produced drone tone in such a way as to create simultaneous high-pitched sounds   1

overtones   waves in a wave form that vibrate faster than the fundamental   1

P

panpipe   a flute that consists of a set of tubes of different lengths, each of which plays one pitch   1

parallel melodic motion   when two lines ascend and descend in parallel   2

pentatonic scale   a scale with five pitches to an octave   3

perfect fifths, perfect fourths   intervals based on frequency ratios of small whole numbers: 3:2 and 4:3   2

perspective   in painting, the illusion, on two dimensions of the canvas, of three-dimensional human experience   4

piano (1)   a soft sound   1

piano (2)   a keyboard instrument on which hammers attached to the keys strike the strings   6

pitch   the perception of the rate of vibration of the fundamental frequency in a tone   1

pizzicato   plucking rather than bowing a violin, viola, cello, or bass   7

plagal cadence, amen cadence   a movement at the end of phrases and pieces from a triad built on the fourth degree of the scale (IV) to a triad built on the first degree or tonic of the scale (I)   4

point of imitation   a particular entrance of imitative polyphony   4

polymeter   the simultaneous presence of two meters in a musical texture   1

polyphony, four-part   four voices singing in harmony   2

polyphony, imitative   each part in the texture sings the same melody, with each part entering one at a time   1

polyphony, polyphonic texture   a performance with many lines or parts   1

polyrhythm   overlapping, interlocking rhythmic patterns   9

polytonality   the simultaneous employment of music in more than one key   9

postmodernism   a general term used in music to refer to arts that reacted to the avant-garde modernist musical styles of the 1950s and 1960s and against linear ideas of progress in the arts. In music, postmodernism between the 1970s and 1990s took four forms: postmodernism *per se*, minimalism, the use of familiar forms, and neo-Romanticism   13

prelude   a piece of music before another piece of music; short, free-form pieces spun out from a single melodic or rhythmic idea   5

prepared piano   a piano into which screws and other objects are inserted between the strings to alter its timbre and emphasize its nature as a percussion instrument   12

program   a narrative expressed in music; in the case of Berlioz's *Symphonie Fantastique*, one describing the internal passions and thoughts that motivated their outward expression in music   7

program music   music composed to express the emotions, moods, and meanings of an unperformed verbal narrative   5

programmatic music, program music   music that expresses sentiments found in a narrative external to the music, such as one in literature or derived from a painting   7

proletariat   wage laborers in factories and industry   7

Proper of the Mass   texts for particular days of the Christian calendar   2

psalms   Biblical poems in praise of God   2

Q

qin   a Chinese zither consisting of a long piece of resonant, lacquered wood over which seven silk strings are stretched   3

R

rag, raag, raga   an Indian melodic mode   4

ragtime   a style often played on the piano featuring a "ragged" or syncopated rhythm accompanied by a steady bassline with regular accents in duple meter   9

range, dynamic   the difference between the loudest and softest tones   1

rap   a genre of music that emerged among black and Latinx youth in New York City in the 1970s and early 1980s featuring spoken rhythmic verses (rapping) over records spun and manipulated by DJs   13

Rastafari Movement   a religious and social movement that arose in Jamaica in the first half of the twentieth century rooted in Abrahamic religious beliefs and centered on Africa as a spiritual homeland and destination. It takes many forms and is often associated with reggae   13

recapitulation   the section in sonata form where the opening themes return   6

recitative   in opera, melodic and rhythmic text recitation   5

recorder   a type of end-blown whistle flute in which air from the player's breath passes through a tube (with a "beak" that goes into the player's mouth) and over the edge of the tube; it has seven fingerholes and a thumbhole 4

reed instrument a vibrating column of air is started either by a two thin pieces of cane or wood beating against one another (a double reed) or one piece of cane beating against a fixed stock (a single reed) 3

reggae a popular music genre from Jamaica 13

Renaissance a period of rebirth of interest in Ancient Greek and Roman culture 4

rhapsody a one-movement composition that has a free-flowing, improvisatory character and that often evokes national sentiment through the use of folk or newly composed folk-like melodies 10

rhythm (1) the temporal dimension of music 1

rhythm (2) the organization of the duration of tones in a performance 1

rhythm and blues a genre label that emerged in the 1940s referring to a wide range of music by African American musicians marketed to African American audiences. In general it featured a strong backbeat (accents on beats 2 and 4), flashy showmanship and choreography, and bands consisting of piano, electric guitar, bass, drums, and saxophone 12

rhythm section in jazz, the portion of a band that includes drums, bass, and piano and/or guitar 11

ritardando, ritard slowing down 1

ritornello returns of an instrumental melody in both instrumental and vocal genres 5

rock 'n' roll a genre label for music that was first used in the 1950s to describe music of rhythm and blues musicians, but marketed to both black and white audiences and inclusive of white singers performing in this style 12

romances twelfth-century Medieval stories written about mythical and legendary figures 8

Romantic Period the term many music historians use to refer to the period of the nineteenth century in European classical music 7

Romanticism expressions in literature, music, and painting of interior experiences of passion, restlessness, longing, and striving; emerged in the nineteenth century 7

rondo form a form that alternates a fixed, returning melody with excursions or episodes to other keys and other melodies (e.g., ABACAD and so on) 6

round a single melody is sung with staggered entrances to create a polyphonic texture 4

rubato ("robbed time" in Italian), an unsteady beat or pulse created by slightly holding one beat and slightly rushing others 7

S

sackbut a buzzed-lip instrument made of metal with a slide to change the length, and thus the pitch, of tones played on it 4

sama'i a composed instrumental form in a meter of ten beats 3

samba song and drumming for the pre-Lenten Carnival 6

samples short clips of existing recordings that are often reproduced in loops and manipulated with any number of effects 13

scale degree the ordinal number of a pitch in ascending order 2

scaled the arrangement of the pitches of a piece of music in ascending order from low to high 1

scat singing a style of improvisation in jazz where singers use vocables, often in ways that imitate the sounds of musical instruments 10

scratching a technique where a DJ moves a vinyl record quickly backwards and forwards with one hand on a turntable to create a rhythmic sound 13

serialism a compositional technique that emerged in the early 1920s where various elements of music were organized into ordered sequences; most notably pitches were often ordered into twelve-tone tone rows 9

shawm a loud, double-reed aerophone 9

Singspiel a musical play in German 6

sitar an Indian long-necked, fretted plucked lute with more than twenty strings 4

snare drum a mid-size cylindrical double-headed drum with a string that buzzes against one drumhead 4

solmization, solfege a pedagogical system of syllables (do-re-mi-fa-sol-la-ti-do) on which singers can sing melodies 2

solo a performance by a single performer 1

sonata an instrumental composition for a soloist or a small group of soloists 5

sonata form the name given by nineteenth-century music theorists to a common Classical-period form, which includes an exposition, a development, and a recapitulation 6

song, strophic   song in which each stanza (or strophe or verse) of the poetry is sung to the same melody   7

soprano   high-pitched female voice or part   4

soul music   a genre of African American popular music that emerged in the 1950s and 1960s and includes elements of gospel, rhythm and blues, and jazz as well as secular lyrics dealing with the oppression of African Americans as well as themes of love, romance, and sex   8

sound synthesis   a process where a waveform created by electronic oscillators can be manipulated to alter the timbre of the sound   12

sousaphone   a version of the tuba invented by John Philip Sousa that marching band players support on their shoulders   9

spirituals   religious songs of African Americans from both during and after the time of slavery   8

staccato   playing the tones of a melody by shortening and leaving spaces between them   1

staff   a set of horizontal lines and spaces on which notes are placed   2

steel pan   a pitched percussion instrument made from steel oil drums by pounding the surface into flat sections that can be tuned   11

steelbands   large ensembles of various sizes of steel pans plus a rhythm section known as the "engine room" consisting of non-pitched percussion instruments including a drum set, congas, large metal scrapers, and irons struck with metal rods   11

stepwise melodic motion   melodies that mainly move through adjacent pitches of a scale   2

stride piano   a style of piano playing that emerged in the first decades of the twentieth century among African American early jazz pianists which featured the left hand "striding" between bass notes and chords, along with heavy syncopation and many other virtuosic techniques   9

string quartet   an ensemble that consists of four players performing on instruments of the violin family: two violins, viola, and cello   6

style, musical   the manner in which musical elements like melody and rhythm are deployed and combined in a large number of pieces or performances   1

subdominant   the fourth degree of a diatonic scale   4

subject   in a Baroque fugue, the opening melody that is then treated to imitative polyphony   5

suite   a set of dance tunes   4

swing feel   a rhythmic feel where a given beat is subdivided in such a way that the first "half" is slightly longer than the second, rather than the subdivisions being of equal length. This feel gives the rhythm a "bounce" and is usually conducive to dancing   9

syllabic singing   each syllable of the text is set to one pitch of the melody   2

symbolist poets   a group of French poets in the late nineteenth century who were known for breaking the formal boundaries of poetic tradition in elusive, free-form, illogical poetry devoid of traditional poetic meters and rhyme schemes   8

symphony   a multi-movement work for string orchestra with the addition of wind instruments and percussion that lacks the contrast between soloist and orchestra of a concerto   6

syncopation   rhythmic accents between strong beats or on weak beats   8

T

tabla   North Indian pair of kettle drums played with the hands   4

tablatures   notations that indicate how an instrument is to be played   3

tal, taal, tala   an Indian rhythmic mode   4

tambourine   a single-headed drum with a narrow frame, somethings with added metal jingles   4

tambura   North Indian plucked lute for playing drone accompaniments   4

taqsim   a nonmetrical improvisation in a particular melodic mode (*maqam* in Arabic, *makam* in Turkish)   3

tempo   the speed of a performance, which may be fast or slow or changing   1

tenor   high-pitched male voice or part   4

territory bands   big bands that performed in a geographic area within a day trip of their home city   10

Tex-Mex   a border-crossing genre in Texas   14

text painting   musical icons for the ideas and sentiments in the text   4

texture, musical   the way musical lines or parts are woven together in a musical performance   1

theka   the basic pattern of strokes on the *tabla* in a given *tala*   4

theme   a melody appearing in sonata form   6

theme and variations   a form based on varied repetitions (in the melody, harmony, or timbre) of a melody   4

theme and variations form   a form that first states a theme and then variations such as changes in melody, meter, key, and/or texture   6

theorbo   a lute with an enormously long neck and fourteen courses of strings capable of playing low-pitched bass tones   5

throat-singing   a single singer produces a drone pitch and, at the same time, uses the mouth to amplify the set of overtones in the drone and produce a high-pitched melody   1

through-composed vocal music   texts sung to melodies that do not repeat or do not repeat in any regular way   2

tihai   a highly syncopated rhythmic pattern played three times at the end of a *sitar* or *tabla* solo   4

timbales   single-headed drums with shallow metal bodies, usually tuned to higher pitches than the tom-toms of a drum set   12

timbre   differences in wave forms that allow us to distinguish one musical instrument or voice from others; tone quality; tone color   1

timpani   single-headed bowl-shaped, kettle drums   5

toasting   a form of rhythmic storytelling with roots in West Africa and legacies both in American prison culture, where black inmates would brag to one another about their exploits in rhyming poetic form, and in Jamaican popular culture, where, beginning in the 1950s, DJs would improvise "toasts" over the music of mobile sound systems   13

tone clusters   chords consisting of many adjacent pitches 12

tone poem   a one-movement symphonic genre involving the "painting" of a scene or the rendering of a narrative   7

tone row   an ordered, non-repeating sequence of the twelve chromatic pitches where none of the pitches is more important than the other   9

tone, musical   sounds that human beings make and interpret as musical consisting of five components: overtone structure, pitch, duration, envelope, and loudness   1

total serialism   the organization of all elements of music, including timbre, texture, rhythm, and dynamics, into "rows" that provide the underlying logic of a composition   12

treble clef, G clef   the five-line staff used for high-pitched notes   2

tremolo   an electronic effect used on instruments like the electric guitar to quickly and repeatedly raise and lower the volume of the tone   14

triads   three-pitch chords built from low to high on the interval of a third: for example, A-C-E and C-E-G   4

triple meter   a regularly recurring three-beat meter counted 1-2-3–1-2-3–1-2-3 and so on   1

tritone   a diminished fifth long known as "the devil's interval"   7

trombone   a buzzed-lip instrument made of metal with a slide to change the length, and thus the pitch, of tones played on it   4

troubador   a Medieval singer of secular songs   4

trumpet   a generic term for a buzzed-lip aerophone, often with a straight tube   4

tune   a short, easily remembered melody for a song or a dance   4

U

underscore   music that is heard accompanying the action in a film   10

understanding music   finding music orderly rather than chaotic; pleasant rather than unpleasant; predictable rather than unpredictable; meaningful rather than meaningless; and familiar rather than unfamiliar   1

unison   a performance with many performers singing the same pitch simultaneously   1

upbeat/offbeat   unaccented beats between downbeats   6

upper extensions   in jazz, chord tones that extend above the octave such as the ninth, the eleventh, or the thirteenth   11

urban folk   a genre that rose to popularity in the 1950s that drew on rural folk songs and Depression-era protest songs, performed by urban intellectuals as social commentary   12

V

verse   in a song, a section that repeats throughout the song with the same melody but different lyrics each time   5

vibrato   a pulsating slight raising and lowering of the pitch of a tone   2

vihuela **(1)**   a flat-backed waisted lute with gut frets tied around the neck and six double courses of gut strings plucked by the fingers   4 *vihuela* **(2)**   a small Mexican guitar-shaped fretted lute   10

viol   one of a family of waisted bowed lutes with frets   4

violin   a high-pitched waisted bowed lute without frets   4

vocables   nonlexical syllables in song lyrics   1

vocalese   a process in which instrumental jazz compositions and well-known recorded improvisations are given lyrics and sung instead of played   13

volte, **sg.** *volta*   a genre of Renaissance dance featuring a dramatic "turn" of the female dancer by the male dancer   4

W

wah-wah pedal   an electronic pedal that modifies the frequencies emphasized in a given tone in a way that, when it is rocked forwards and backwards, it mimics the sound of a human voice saying "wah-wah"   12

walking bass line   a mostly stepwise pulsatile line played by a plucked upright or electric bass in bebop and some other styles of jazz   11

waltz   a ballroom dance for couples in triple meter   7

waveform   a complex set of waves vibrating in air   I

well-tempered   well-tuned and able to play in all keys of the tonal system   5

Western canon   a collection of "great works" in the European traditions of art, literature, and music   7

whole-tone scales   an equidistant six-pitch (hexatonic) scale that eliminates half steps and their directional leading tones   8

world music (1)   a large category of music rooted in communities and outside the mainstream of popular music, classical music, and jazz   1

world music (2)   a genre label created by record company executives in Britain in 1987 to describe hybrid musical forms, capitalizing on the supposed authenticity of traditional music and the commercial appeal of popular music   13

world of music   the music of a composer like Ludwig van Beethoven, a songwriter like Bob Dylan, or a performer like Louis Armstrong; a genre or type of music such as eighteenth-century symphonies or Italian opera, or the blues; or the music of Polish Americans, Arabs, or the Shona people of Zimbabwe   I

Y

yodel, yodeling   alternation between chest-resonated tones and high-pitched, head-resonated tones   1

Z

zither   stringed instrument with a resonator but no added neck   3

SOURCES

Introduction

1. The distinction between icons and indexes as sources of musical emotion is indebted to Thomas Turino, *Music as Social Life: The Politics of Participation* (Chicago: University of Chicago Press, 2008).

Chapter 1

Gateway 1, Music of Foragers

2. This gateway is indebted to Michelle Kisliuk, *Seize the Dance! BaAka Musical Life and the Ethnography of Performance* (New York: Oxford University Press, 1998/2001).

Gateway 2, Music of Nomadic Pastoralists

3. "The river is alive, Rivers sing." Theodore Levin, with Tuvan researcher Valentina Süzükei, *Where Rivers and Mountains Sing: Sound, Music, and Nomadism in Tuva and Beyond* (Bloomington: Indiana University Press, 2006).
4. This gateway is based on Levin, *Where Rivers and Mountains Sing*, p. 29.

Gateway 3, Music of Horticulturalists

5. This gateway is based on the research of French ethnomusicologist Hugo Zemp. See, for example, Hugo Zemp, "Aspects of 'Are'Are Musical Theory," *Ethnomusicology* 23(1) (1978): 5–48.

Chapter 2

Gateway 4, Buddhist Music

6. ". . . according to their good and bad deeds" from Damien Keown, *Buddhism: A Very Short Introduction* (New York: Oxford University Press, 1996).
7. The discussion of the Four Noble Truths is derived from Keown, pp. 46–48.

8. "the ultimate goal of Buddhism is to put an end to suffering and rebirth . . . by fulfilling the human potential for goodness and happiness." Keown, p. 46.
9. "sensually pleasing offering" from Ter Ellingson, "Mandala of Sound: Concepts and Sound Structures in Tibetan Buddhism," Ph.D. dissertation, University of Wisconsin-Madison, 1979.
10. "This music," one Tibetan monk said, "is more beneficial than a hundred years of meditation." Ellingson, p. xiii.
11. The Bon religion acknowledged "nine vocal modulations," including "the dog's voice, barking and growling, . . . the beautiful voiced parrot" and "the fluctuating voice of the lark." Ellingson, p. 101.
12. "body-cavity voice." Ellingson, p. 395.
13. "tone-color chants." Ellingson, p. 467.
14. "voice of the hybrid yak-bull" and the "roaring voice of the [slayer of the] Lord of Death." Ellingson, p. 400.
15. "They will rattle your bones." Mickey Hart in Frankie Wright, "Enchanting Spirit of Buddhism," *Los Angeles Times*, November 16, 1991.
16. To understand melody as an aid to meditative visualization in Tibetan Buddhist ritual liturgies, read Jeffrey W. Cupchik, "Buddhism As Performing Art: Visualizing Music in the Tibetan Sacred Ritual Music Liturgies," *Yale Journal of Music & Religion* 1(1) (2015): 31–62. DOI: https://doi.org/10.17132/2377–231X.1010

Gateway 5, Christian Chant

17. This gateway is based in part on David Hiley, *Gregorian Chant* (Cambridge: Cambridge University Press, 2009).
18. Hildegard's biography is indebted to Sabina Flanagan, *Hildegard of Bingen, 1098–1179: A Visionary Life* (New York: Routledge, 1989).
19. "the heavens were opened to me . . ." and "a low opinion (of myself)" from Hildegard's autobiography, quoted in Flanagan, p. 4.
20. "Who does not bewail . . ." and "helpers . . . can produce . . ." Hiley, p. 174.

Gateway 6, Qur'anic Chant

21. *The Quran*, translated by Maulana Wahiduddin Khan and Prof. Farida Khanam (Chennai, India: Goodread Books, 2009).
22. "divine and inimitable beauty." Kristina Nelson, *The Art of Reciting the Qur'an* (Austin: University of Texas Press, 1985), p. 13.
23. "calms the child and refreshes the camel on the long journey." Nelson, p. 43.
24. "the beautiful melody is a spirit from God which revives burning hearts." Nelson, p. 44.
25. "extract" the meaning of verse "bring the listener closer to the Qur'an." Nelson, p. 64.
26. "If hell is so lovely and pleasant, take me to it." Nelson, p. 65.
27. "Ah, would that I had sent forth [good deeds] for [this] my [future] life" and quoted phrases in the next sentence. Nelson, p. 64.

Gateway 7, Early European Polyphonic Music

28. Machaut's biography is indebted to Elizabeth Eva Leach, *Guillaume de Machaut: Secretary, Poet, Musician* (Ithaca, NY: Cornell University Press, 2011).

Chapter 3

Opening

29. The data on urban populations in 1350 is from Tertius Chandler and Gerald Fox, *Three Thousand Years of Urban Growth* (New York: Academic Press, 1974).

Gateway 8, Music of China

30. Details on the *qin* and *qin* playing are based in part on Bell Yung, "Instruments: Qin," *Garland Encyclopedia of World Music: Volume 7: East Asia: China, Japan, and Korea* (New York: Routledge, 2002), pp. 157–165. This source also contains a transcription of a performance, different from the one in the recordings, of "Three Variations on Yang Pass."
31. The early theory of Chinese music is based in part on Chen Yingshi, "Theory and Notation in China," *Garland Encyclopedia of World Music: Volume 7: East Asia: China, Japan, and Korea* (New York: Routledge, 2002), pp. 115–126.
32. The life of Confucius and the discussion of Confucianism are based on D. Howard Smith, *Confucius* (New York: Charles Scribner's Sons, 1973).

Gateway 9, Music of the Middle East

33. The theory of emotion associated with specific *maqamat* is taken from Habib Hassan Touma, *The Music of the Arabs*, translated by Laurie Schwartz (Portland, Oregon: Amadeus Press, 1996).

34. "a symbol of high Arab culture . . .; it represents both secular musical pleasure and scientific and intellectual thought, and its history is closely connected to the splendors of urban Arab civilization." Scheherazade Qassim Hassan, "Music Instruments of the Arab World," in Virginia Danielson, Scott Marcus, and Dwight Reynolds, eds., *Garland Encyclopedia of World Music, Volume 6: The Middle East* (New York: Routledge, 2002), p. 406.
35. The discussion of emotion and meaning in music is indebted to A. J. Racy, *Making Music in the Arab World: The Culture and Artistry of Tarab* (Cambridge: Cambridge University Press, 2003).

Gateway 10, Music of Africa

36. This gateway, including two short quotes, is based on Paul Berliner, *The Soul of Mbira: Music and Traditions of the Shona People of Zimbabwe* (Chicago: University of Chicago Press, 1993).

Chapter 4

Gateway 16, North Indian Classical Music

37. "could address a god or goddess, laud a king, express feelings of intimate romantic love, describe a season, transmit musicological knowledge, or deal with a metaphysical or religious concept." Bonnie C. Wade, "Hindustani Vocal Music," in Alison Arnold, ed., *The Garland Encyclopedia of World Music, Volume 5: South Asia: The Indian Subcontinent* (New York: Routledge, 2000), p. 164.

Chapter 5

Gateway 18, Baroque orchestral music

38. "about forty girls," from J. Peter Burkholder et al., *A History of Western Music*, 8th ed. (New York: W. W. Norton, 2010), p. 423, quoting from Charles de Brosses, *L'Italie il y a cent ans ou Lettres écrites d'Italie à quelques amis en 1739 et 1740*, ed. M. R. Colomb, vol. 1 (Paris: Alphonse Levavasseur, 1836), pp. 213–214.

Gateway 21, Javanese Court Music

39. This gateway is indebted in part to R. Anderson Sutton, "Java: Central and East Java," in Terry E. Miller and Sean Williams, eds., *The Garland Encyclopedia of World Music: Southeast Asia* (New York: Garland Publishing, 1998), pp. 631–685.
40. "Swept Away . . ." from Sumarsam, *Gamelan: Cultural Interaction and Musical Development in Central Java* (Chicago: University of Chicago Press, 1992, 1995), pp. 27, 60.
41. "Javanese music obeys laws of counterpoint . . ." from Richard Langham Smith, trans., *Debussy on Music* (New York: Knopf, 1977), published in 1913 in *Revue S.I.M.*

Chapter 6

Gateway 22, Classical-period Chamber Music

42. "I barely managed to stay alive . . ." and "Not only did I have the encouragement of constant approval . . ." from Albert Christoph Dies and Georg August Griesinger, "Biographical Accounts of Joseph Haydn," in *Haydn: Two Contemporary Portraits*, translated by Vernon Gotwals (Milwaukee: University of Wisconsin Press, 1963), contains interviews Dies and Griesinger conducted with Haydn and published in 1810.

Gateway 23, Classical-period Symphonies

43. "posterity will not see . . ." H. C. Robbins Landon, *1791: Mozart's Last Year* (London: Flamingo, 1990), p. 171.
44. *Encyclopedia* (Cambridge: Cambridge University Press, 2006), p. 268.

Gateway 26, Music of the Atlantic Slave Trade

45. This gateway is indebted to Larry Crook, *Brazilian Music: Northeastern Traditions and the Heartbeat of a Modern Nation* (Santa Barbara, CA: ABC-Clio, 2005).
46. "the blacks divided by Nations . . ." Lucas Nicolau Parés, *The Formation of Candomblé: Vodun History and Ritual in Brazil* (Chapel Hill: University of North Carolina Press, 2013), p. 67.

Chapter 7

Gateway 27, Beethoven's Symphonies

47. "Joy follows sorrow, sunshine—rain . . ." in Friedrich Kerst and Henry Edward Krehbiel, eds., *Beethoven: The Man and the Artist, as Revealed in His Own Words*, translated by Henry Edward Krehbiel (Boston: IndyPublishing, 2008), p. 15.
48. Goethe quote: "That was a creation . . ." from Will Durant, *The Story of Civilization, Volume 10: Rousseau and Revolution* (New York: Simon & Schuster, 1967), p. 563.
49. Wordsworth quote: "the spontaneous overflow of powerful feelings," cited in Aidan Day, *Romanticism* (New York: Routledge, 1996), p. 2.

Gateway 28, Beethoven's symphonies

50. "I saw the giant form of Beethoven . . ." Hector Berlioz, *The Memoirs of Hector Berlioz*, translated by David Cairns (New York: Random House, 2002), p. 104.

Gateway 29, Romantic-period Piano Music

51. "If the mighty autocrat in the north . . ." Robert Schumann, *Schumann on Music: A Selection from the Writings*, translated and edited by Henry Pleasants (New York: Dover Publications, 1988), p. 14.

52. "Music will perhaps become his [Felix's] profession . . ." Sebastian Hensel, *The Mendelssohn Family 1729–1847*, 4th revised edition, 2 vols (London: Sampson Low, 1884), Vol. I, p. 82.

Gateway 30, Early American Popular Music

53. This gateway is indebted in part to Jacqueline Cogdell DjeDje, "The (Mis)Representation of African American Music: The Role of the Fiddle," *Journal of the Society for American Music* 10 (2016): 1–32.
54. "remarkably well on the violin." Theresa Jenoure, "The Afro-American Fiddler," *Contributions in Black Studies* 5 (2008): 68–81, quote from p. 69.

Chapter 8

Gateway 34, African American Religious Music

55. "There were many times, when we didn't have place to sleep or anything to eat . . ." Andrew Ward, *Dark Midnight When I Rise: The Story of the Jubilee Singers Who Introduced the World to the Music of Black America* (New York: Farrar, Strauss, and Giroux, 2000), p. 132.
56. "People came to despise . . ." Gustavus D. Pike, *The Jubilee Singers of Fisk University and their Campaign for Twenty Thousand Dollars* (Boston: Lee and Shepard, 1873), pp. 107, 99, 77, 92, and 118–119, respectively.
57. "were sacred to our parents." Hollis Robbins and Henry Louis Gates, Jr., eds., *Penguin Portable Nineteenth Century African American Women Writers* (New York: Penguin, 2017), p. 230.
58. "The permanency of the university was assured," Pike, *The Jubilee Singers*, p. 36.

Chapter 9

Gateway 35, The Blues

59. "In addition, relief efforts . . ." is indebted to Angela Davis, *Blues Legacies and Black Feminism: Gertrude "Ma" Rainey, Bessie Smith, and Billie Holiday* (New York: Vintage Books, 1998), pp. 109–110.
60. "She incorporated the blues . . ." is indebted to Michelle R. Scott, *Blues Empress in Black Chattanooga: Bessie Smith and the Emerging Urban South* (Urbana: University of Illinois Press, 2008), p. 120.

Gateway 36, American Band Music

61. "The Union Army is said to have . . ." is indebted to Larry Starr and Christopher Waterman, *American Popular Music: From Minstrelsy to MTV* (Oxford: Oxford University Press, 2003), p. 27.

Gateway 38, Music of Early European Modernists

62. "In the case of *The Rite of Spring* . . ." This paragraph is indebted to Richard Taruskin, *Stravinsky and the Russian Traditions: A Biography of the Works through Mavra* (Berkeley: University of California Press, 1996), pp. 849–966.

63. "Musicologist Richard Taruskin has even speculated . . ." is indebted to Richard Taruskin, "A Myth of the Twentieth Century: The Rite of Spring, the Tradition of the New, and 'The Music Itself,'" *Modernism/Modernity* 2.1 (1995), p. 16.

64. ". . . rhythmic patterns defy all expectations of listeners . . ." is indebted to Matthew McDonald, "*Jeux de Nombres*: Automated Rhythm in *The Rite of Spring*," *Journal of the American Musicological Society* 63(3) (2010): 499–551.

Gateway 39, Balinese Gamelan

65. "On September 14, 1906 . . ." Debbie Guthrie Haer, Juliette Morillot, and Irene Toh, *Bali: A Traveller's Companion* (Paris: Editions Didier Millet, 2001), p. 38.

66. "In the area of culture and music the *puputan*s had three important consequences. First . . ." is indebted to Michael Tenzer, *Balinese Music* (Singapore: Periplus Editions, 1991), p. 23.

67. The paragraph beginning "Gamelan *gong kebyar* emerged between 1910 and 1915, not long after the Dutch colonized Bali . . ." is indebted to Michael Tenzer, *Gamelan Gong Kebyar: The Art of Twentieth-century Balinese Music* (Chicago: University of Chicago Press, 2000), p. 86.

68. On cultural tourism in Bali, we are indebted to Elizabeth Clendinning, "Learning in the 'Global Village': Performing Arts Edutourism in Bali, Indonesia," *MUSICultures* 43(2) (2016).

Chapter 10

Opening

69. "Jazz was a slang word . . ." Lewis Porter, "Where Did 'Jazz,' the Word, Come From? Follow a Trail of Clues," *Deep Dive with Lewis Porter* (blog), WBGO.com, February 26, 2018, http://wbgo.org/post/where-did-jazz-word-come-follow-trail-clues-deep-dive-lewis-porter#stream/0 (accessed April 10, 2018).

Gateway 44, Mexican and Mexican American Mariachi Music

70. This gateway is indebted in part to Lauryn Salazar, "From Fiesta to Festival: Mariachi Music in California and the Southwesternt United States," Ph.D dissertation, University of California, Los Angeles, 2011; and Daniel Sheehy, *Mariachi Music in America: Experiencing Music, Expressing Culture* (New York: Oxford University Press, 2006).

Chapter 12

Gateway 50, Jazz in New Directions

71. "to show how the disadvantaged and the disenfranchised . . ." Muhal Richard Abrams and John Shenoy Jackson, "Association for the Advancement of Creative Musicians," *Black World* 23 (November 1973): 72.

Gateway 52, Salsa

72. Comments on Nuyorican and Puerto Rican national identity are indebted to Peter Manuel, "Puerto Rican Music and Cultural Identity: Creative Appropriation of Cuban Sources from Danza to Salsa," *Ethnomusicology* 38(1994): 249–280.

Chapter 13

Gateway 55, Postmodern in Classical Music

73. The section on neo-Romanticism, including the del Tredici quote, is indebted to Barbara Russano Hanning, *Concise History of Western Music*, 4th ed. (New York: W. W. Norton, 2010), pp. 652–654.

Chapter 14

Gateway 58, Jazz Today

74. "This song is singing to our African American . . ." Patrick Jarenwattananon, "New Esperanza Spalding Song in Time for Black History Month," *National Public Radio*, February 2, 2012, www.npr.org/sections/ablogsupreme/2012/02/02/146287135/new-esperanza-spalding-song-in-time-for-black-history-month (accessed April 25, 2018).

INDEX

12 Years a Slave (film) 258
24 Caprices for Solo Violin, Op. 1
    (Paganini) 220
4:44 (Jay-Z, D. Marley) 437
4'33" (Cage) 395
50 Cent 417

a braccio 112
a cappella 103, 253
A Guest of Honor (Joplin) 283
A Love Supreme (Coltrane) 382–390,
    469
A Survivor from Warsaw (Schoenberg)
    362
A Winter in Majorca (Sand) 221
Abernathy, Ralph 372
Abrams, Muhal Richard 389
Abraxas (Santana) 405
Academy Awards 425, 440, 452
"Acknowledgement" (Coltrane) 382–390
Adams, Bryan 442
Adams, John 429–430
Adderley, Julian "Cannonball" 386
Aeneid (Ovid) 103
Aerosmith 416
aerophone 41, 111
aesthetics 13
Africa, music of 22–28, 80–85
Afrika Bambaataa (Kevin Donovan) 412,
    414–415
agricultural revolution 21
Agrippina (Handel) 148
Akbar the Great 124–125, 127
Akinmusire, Ambrose 424, 452
Alabê, Jorge 197–201
alap 119, 122
Al-'Arayan, Ibrahim 73
Alash 33
Albeniz, Isaac 247
Albinoni, Tomaso 144
Aldana, Melissa 450, 452
Alexander II, Tsar 321

Alexis, Cliff 369
Alighieri, Dante 65
"All Along the Watchtower" (Hendrix)
    373–382
All Eyez on Me (Tupac Shakur) 416
Allegemeine musikalische Zeitung 236
Allen, Thomas 186
alphorn 111
"Alright" (Lamar) 418, 451
altered extensions 352–353
alto part 97
Amadeus (film) 185
Amati, Nicolò 143
American Idol (TV show) 348
American in Paris (Gershwin) 328
American popular music 5–6
Amos 'n' Andy (radio show) 229
Analects (Confucius) 71
An erl, Karel 242
Ancient Period 19, 39–40
And His Mother Called Him Bill
    (Strayhorn) 315–316
"And I Love Her/Him" (Salvant, Beatles)
    469
"And the glory of the Lord" (Handel) 151
Anderson, Marian 258–259
André 3000 417
Andrews Sisters 369
Angry, Raymond 445, 447
Animals, The 380
Anthracite Fields (Wolfe) 453–460
"Anthropology" (Parker) 356
Aoki, Steve 467, 472
Apocalypse Now (film) 242
Appalachian Spring (Copland) 247, 326,
    329
"Appliances" from *Anthracite Fields*
    (Wolfe) 455
Arab music 73–79, 153
Are You Experienced? (Hendrix) 380
'Are'are 33–38, 155
aria 138, 329

armonia 330, 333–334
Armstrong, Lillian (Lil) Hardin 16, 301.
    304, 306, 307, 450.
Armstrong, Louis 4, 16, 83, 16, 271, 299,
    301–308, 348, 351, 423
Arpeggio, definition of 132
Ars Nova 65
Art Ensemble of Chicago 388–389
Articulation, definition of 12
Artpop (Lady Gaga) 444
Ascension (Coltrane) 388
Association for the Advancement of
    Creative Musicians (AACM) 388,
    470
Astaire, Fred 229, 300, 323, 327
Astatke, Mulatu 316
atabaque 197
Atilla the Hun 366
atonality 286, 288, 361–362
au tahana 33–38
Austro–Hungarian Empire 232, 242, 245,
    263–264
authenticity 344–345, 348, 408
Autry, Gene 346
avant–garde, music of the 390–397, 427,
    429, 437
Ayler, Albert 388

BaAka, music of the 22–28, 37
Babbitt, Milton 392–397
BaBenzele, music of the 27–28
Babur 124
Bach, C.P.E. 177, 183–184
Bach, J.C. 184
Bach, Johann Sebastian 16, 130, 145,
    148, 176, 184, 195, 220, 222, 227,
    240, 361; keyboard music of 151–167
Bach, Maria Barbara 158
bachata 201
Back Home (Aldana) 452
"Backwater Blues" (Smith) 265–273,
    376

Baez, Joan 226–227, 379
bagpipes, Bulgarian 85–90; Scottish 90
Bailey, Dixie 355
bajo sexto 117, 459
Baker, Dame Janet 117
Baker, Joséphine 469
Bakersfield sound 347
Bali, music of 265, 289–297
ballad 223, 442; ballad opera 191; epic
    463; pop 442; rock 442
ballade 219
Ballets Russes 252, 284, 287
"Bam" (Jay-Z, D. Marley) 437
"Bamboula: Danse des Negrès"
    (Gottschalk) 229
band music 265, 273–278, 298, 306
Bang on a Can All-Stars 397, 453, 457
banjar 293
banjo 223–330, 271, 281, 301–307,
    309–310, 341, 346–347, 379, 472
"Banjo, The" (Gottschalk) 229–30
bar, definition of 11
barbershop quartet 103
barong 295–296
Baroque; dance 219; keyboard music
    151–158; opera 131–139; orchestral
    music 139–145, 165; sacred music
    145–151
Barry, Chuck 165
Bartered Bride, The (Smetana) 246
Bartók, Béla 179, 430
baryton 178
Basie, Count 314, 323
bass part 97
bass viol 112
basse danse 113
basso buffo 191
basso continuo 137, 138, 145
Battle, Kathleen 186, 258
Baudelaire, Charles 251, 252
Bauza, Mario 403
Bayreuth 251–252
bayyati 73
Beach Boys 380
Beastie Boys 416
Beatenberg 472
Beatles 12, 126, 308, 373, 379–381, 436,
    443, 469
Beaumarchais, Pierre 190
"Beautiful Dreamer" (Foster) 229
bebop 5, 313, 323, 339, 348–356, 370,
    382, 386–387, 389–390, 403, 406,
    422, 424, 447–450, 470
Beethoven, Ludwig van 2, 4, 16, 158,
    165, 169, 176, 180, 185, 202–204,
    212–213, 215–216, 222, 235, 240,
    243, 245–246, 248, 250–251, 361–362,
    429–430; and patronage 171–172;

piano sonatas of 192–196; in pop
    music 378; string quartets of 178;
    symphonies of 204–211
Beggar's Opera, The 149
bel canto 239
Belefonte, Harry 369
"Beleza pura" (Veloso) 201
bell, definition of 164
Bellini, Vincenzo 239, 242
Benedicta: Marian Chants from Norcia
    (Christian chant) 53
Benjamin, George 470
Bennett, Tony 314, 444
Bentley, Dierks 17
Berg, Alban 283, 288
Berkeley, Busby 323
Berklee College of Music 451, 452
Berlin, Irving 300, 316, 321–322,
    326
Berliner, Paul 85
Berlioz, Hector 204, 211–218, 221–222,
    235, 240, 427–429, 245, 250–251
Bernini, Gian Lorenzo 131
Bernstein, Leonard 65, 211, 240, 324
Berry, Chuck 373, 377, 380
Bessie (film) 272–273
Beyoncé (Beyoncé Knowles-Carter)
    468
bhangra 471–472
Bieber, Justin 437, 452, 467
big band 309, 449
Big Boi 417
Big Brother and the Holding Company
    381
Billboard (Magazine) 53, 308, 346, 347,
    377, 417, 450, 471–472
Billy the Kid (Copland) 247, 326
Bingen, Hildegard von *see* Hildegard
    von Bingen
"Bisingo Bwa Bole" (BaAka) 22–28
Bitches Brew (Davis) 387–388, 390,
    422
Bizet, George 281
"Black and Tan Fantasy" (Ellington)
    309–316, 324, 376
"Black Gold" (Spalding) 445–453
Black Panther (film) 472
Black, Brown, and Beige (Ellington) 314,
    316
Blacks Unlimited, The 84
Blackwell, Ed 388
Blades, Rubén 404, 406
Blakey, Art 387, 390
Blanchett, Cate 110
Blessett, Algebra 445, 448, 452
Bley, Paul 388
Bliss, Philip 258
block chord, definition of 35

"Blood Count" (Strayhorn) 316
Blood on the Fields (W. Marsalis) 423,
    425
"Blow My Tears" (Dowland) 117
Blown Away (Underwood) 437
Blue Grass Boys 227
"Blue Moon of Kentucky" (Monroe,
    Presley) 227
blue note 266, 303
Blue Train (Coltrane) 387
bluegrass 227
blues 4, 16, 258, 277, 281, 297, 302,
    305, 307–308, 311, 315–316, 319,
    321, 326, 343, 345–346, 350–351,
    353, 374, 376, 379–382, 385, 387,
    389–390, 405, 414, 451, 446–448,
    451, 469–470; 12-bar 309–312, 323,
    354, 389; classic 226, 228, 265–273;
    country 271–272; electric 376; scale
    of the 324, 376, 378
Blues, The (film) 272
Boccaccio, Giovanni 65
bodhisattva 44–45
"Body and Soul" (Spalding) 451
bolero 403
Bolero (Ravel) 116–117
bolero ranchero 329
Boleyn, Anne 106
Bomb Squad, The 410–411, 413
Bon religion 43
Bone Thugs-N-Harmony 416
bongo 398
Book of Common Prayer 145
Boone, Daniel 226
borbangnadyr 28–33
"Borbangnadyr with Stream Water"
    28–33
Boris Godunov (Mussorgsky) 247
Born This Way (Lady Gaga) 444
Borodin, Alexander 247
bossa nova 201
Bourgeoisie 203
Bowie, David 443
Brahms, Johannes 211, 248, 450
Branch, Jaimie 452
Brandenberg Concerto No. 5 in D Major
    (Bach) 145
branle 113
brass bands 231, 260, 277, 281, 306,
    422
Brazil, music of 197–201
breakbeat 409
breakdancing 409
"Breaker Boys" from *Anthracite Fields*
    (Wolfe) 454
Breaking Bad (TV show) 464
Brightman, Sarah 308
Brooks, Garth 347

Brown, James 259, 412, 413, 418, 449, 451
Brown, Robert 165
Brown, Ruth 377
Brubeck, Dave 387
Bruckner, Anton 211
Bruegel, Pieter 102
Brunelleschi, Filippo 102
BTS (Bangtan Soyeondan) 471
Buddhism 2, 19, 40, 65–66, 122, 159, 163, 394; music of 40–45
"Buffalo Soldier" (Marley) 430–439
"Bukatiende" (Mapfumo) 85
Bulgaria, music of 85–90, 165
Bulgarian Rhapsody "Vardar" (Vladigerov) 328
Bülow, Hans von 241
Burleigh, Henry T. ("Harry") 247, 258
Burnin' (Marley) 436
Burrell, Kenny 10
"But Not for Me" (Burrell) 10
"But who shall abide" (Handel) 151
Buuren, Armin van 467
buzuk 113
buzuq 77, 79, 89
Byrd, Jerry 341, 344

Cabot, John 129
cadence, amen, authentic, and plagal 101
Cage, John 3, 394–397
cakewalk 277
caliph 58
caliphate 77, 83
call-and-response 198, 200, 254–255, 257–258, 310, 431, 449
Calloway, Cab 312–313, 354
calypso 364, 366–367
Cambridge Singers 97
Camerata 59
"Camptown Races" (Foster) 229
cancion ranchera 329
Canciones de mi Padre (Ronstadt) 336
Candomblé 170, 172, 197–201, 223, 257, 259, 435, 468
canon, Western 209
canonization 209
Cano, Natividad (Nati) 336–337
cantata 148
Canterbury Tales, The 65
cantus firmus 100, 101
capitalist 203
"Caravan" (Marsalis) 419–427
Carmen (Bizet) 281
Carmignola, Giuliano 140
Carnaval (Schumann) 222
Carolina Chocolate Drops 226–227
Carousel (Rodgers & Hammerstein) 322

Carrington, Terri Lyne 445, 449, 452
Carson, Fiddlin' John 345–346, 348
Carter Family 346
Carter, A.P. 346
Carter, June 346
Carter, Maybelle 346
Carter, Ron 387
Carter, Sara 346
Cartier, Jacques 129
Casablanca (film) 327
Cash, Johnny 346
Cassanova, Giacomo 191
"Casta diva" from *Norma* (Bellini) 242
castrato 136–137, 191
category, definition of 5
Catherine the Great, Empress 191
Cave, Nick 308
Celia y Johnny (Cruz, Pacheco) 404
ceng-ceng 290, 292
Cervantes, Miguel de 95
cha-cha-chá 400, 405
chaconne 425
"Chaconne: Giulio's Song" (Corigliano) 425–434
chamber ensemble, definition of 173
Chamber Music Society (Spalding) 452
Chamberlin, Jimmy 381
Chambers, Paul 386
Chandler, Chas 380
Chandler, Dee Dee 306
Chanel, Coco 287
chanson 107
"Chant des oyseaux, Le" (Janequin) 107
chant, 19, 40, 65, 118, 285; Ashkenazic 53; Buddhist 40–45; Christian 46–53, 57, 59, 61, 63–64, 66, 96, 99, 141, 455, 470; Qur'anic 54–58, 66–67, 70, 75; Sephardic 53
Charlemagne 50
Charles V, King 116
Charles VI of Austria 144–145
Charles, Ray 259
Charleston 309
Charlie Parker with Strings (LP) 355
Chateaubriand, François–René de 213
Chaucer, Geoffrey 65
Chavez, Cesar 464
Cheek to Cheek (Lady Gaga) 444
"Cherokee" (Parker) 469
Chicago Symphony Orchestra 6, 179, 425, 430
Chieftains, The 32
Children's Corner Suite (Debussy) 252–253
chimurenga 84

China, music of 68–72, 77, 91, 153, 156, 164–165
Chopin, Frédéric 2, 204, 217–222, 228–229, 250, 310, 312
chord, definition of 11
chordophone 112, 114
chorus: group of singers 41, 88, 131, 145–151, 159, 197, 210, 246, 362, 452–455; in jazz performance 116, 301–314, 323, 350–352, 420–422; in song form 253, 369, 410–415, 436–437, 440–442, 446–448
Christian, Charlie 314
Christianity 2, 19, 40, 65–66, 122, 163
Christmas Oratorio (Bach) 157
Christy's Minstrels 228–229
Chronic, The (Dr. Dre) 416, 418
Chuck D (Carleton Ridenhour) 410, 412, 414, 416, 437
"Cinque . . . dieci" (Mozart) 186–192
circle of fifths definition of 70
civilizations, definition of 39
Clair de Lune (Debussy, Washington) 469
"Clair de lune" (Debussy) 252–253
Clapton, Eric 272, 436, 437
Clarinet Concerto (Copland) 326
Clarke, Kenny 339, 353
Clash, The 381
classic country 347
classical music, definition of 6
clave 401
clavichord 151, 156
clavier 152
clawhammer 223, 226
clef, alto, bass, tenor treble 53
Cleveland Show, The (TV show) 229
Cliff, Jimmy 435
Cline, Patsy 347
Cobb, Jimmy 386
col legno 212
Coleman, Ornette 423, 356, 388, 390
collegium musicum 157
Collins, Judy 227
Colon, Willie 404, 406
colonialism 264, 340, 407
colotomic structure 161
Coltrane, John 3, 16, 355, 382–390, 434, 468–469
Columbia Symphony Orchestra 324
Columbus, Christopher 93, 129, 433
combo, jazz 348
"Come Again, Sweet Love Doth Now Invite" (Dowland) 117
Common 417
communism 231, 340
Communist Manifesto 240
concept album 380

Concerti delle donne 106
concerto 139–145, 183; concerto grosso 143–144, 177; organ 149; *ripieno concerto* 143–144, 177
Concerto in F (Gershwin) 328
Concerto Vocale 131
"Confirmation" (Parker) 356
Confrontation (Marley) 430
Confucius 69, 71–72, 106, 220
conga 398
conjunct motion *see* stepwise motion
conjunto norteño 458–472
Conlon, James 339
consort 111
"Contrabando y Traición" (Los Tigres del Norte) 563
contrapuntal *see* counterpoint
Copland, Aaron 247, 326, 329
Coppola, Francis Ford 242
Corea, Chick 423
Corelli, Arcangelo 144, 148
Corgan, Billy 381
Corigliano, John 425–432
cornett 108, 111, 112
corrido 458–464
Cosi fan tutte (Mozart) 192
Cotten, Elizabeth 226
Cotton Club 311, 313
"Could You Be Loved" (Marley) 434
countermelody 319
counterpoint 64; fugal 153–155; species 101
Counter-Reformation 99, 148
countertenor 104
country and western 346
country music 227, 339, 341–348, 379
courante 113
course, string 73
Cowell, Henry 396
Cox, Ida 228
Creation, The (Haydn) 178
crescendo, definition of 12
Cristofori, Bartolomeo 195
Critique of Judgment (Kant) 208–209
Crosby, Bing 229, 300, 327
Crudup, Arthur "Big Boy" 227
Cruz, Celia 404–405
cuatro 117, 404
"Cuerpo Y Alma" (Spalding) 451
Cugat, Xavier 403
cultural linkages 15, 22
cumbia 201
cymbal, definition of 164
Czech Philharmonic 242

da Gama, Vasco 129
da gamba 112
da Ponte, Lorenzo 190–191

Daft Punk 468
Dalai Lama 45
Dameron, Tadd 379
Damn (Lamar) 423
dancehall 437
dance music; Baroque 219; Bulgarian 85–90; Renaissance 107–113
Danton, Georges 190
danzon 403
Daphnis et Chloe (Ravel) 287
Das Jahr: No. 2. February (Mendelssohn, Fanny) 221–222
Das Rheingold (Wagner) 241
"Das Wort sie sollen lassen stahn" (BMV 80) (Bach) 151
Davis, Miles 349, 386–388, 390, 422
de Falla, Manuel 252
de Vere, Edward 106
Death Row Records 416
Deborah (Handel) 149
Debussy, Claude 165–166, 233, 242, 248–253, 283, 287–289, 359, 469
Decameron 65
Deep Forest 37
Def Jam Records 416
DeJohnette, Jack 449
del Tredici, David 430
Dempsey, Jack 300
Denton, Sandra ("Pepa") 417
Depression, Great 299–300, 313, 320, 323, 326, 341, 379, 407
Der fliegende Holländer (Wagner) 240
Descartes, René 170
descrescendo 12
Desperadoes 369
Dett, R. Nathaniel 258
"Deutschland, Dautschland über alles" 175
development, 181
dhalang 163–164
Dharma 43
dhol 472
dhrupad 125
Diaghilev, Sergei 287–288
Diaz, Porfirio 335
Dictionnaire de musique (Rousseau) 170
Diddley, Bo 378
Diderot, Denis 170
Die Entführung aus dem serial (Mozart) 185, 191–192
Die Walküre (Wagner) 241–242
diegetic sound 327
"Dies irae" (Christian chant) 53
Dion, Celine 442
Diplo 467
Dirty Dozen Brass Band 306
disco 414, 443

Divine Comedy 65, 49, 53
Dixie Hummingbirds 258
DJ Yella (Anonie Carraby) 416
djembe 28
"Do the Reggay" (Maytals) 435
Do the Right Thing (film) 410, 418
Dodds, Johnny 301, 307
Doggystyle (Snoop Dogg) 416
dominant, definition of 101
Dominguez, Miguel Martínez 336
Domino, Fats 377
Don Giovanni (Mozart) 190–192, 220
Don Quixote (novel) 95
"Don't Worry Be Happy" (McFerrin) 414, 437
Donizetti, Gaetano 239, 242, 252
Dorsey, Thomas A. 258
Dorsey, Tommy 313, 317
Douglass, Frederic 256
Dowland, John 117
Dr. Dre (Andre Young) 416, 418
Dr. Jekyll and Mr. Hyde (film) 158
Drake (Aubrey Drake Graham) 417, 437, 452
drum and bugle corps 278
drum; bass 113; machine 415–416; set 306; snare 113; tom-tom 306
drut 127
Dudley, Robert 109
Dudley, Shannon 370
duettino 220
Dufay, Guillaume 100–101, 103, 107
Dutrey, Honoré 307
Dvořák, Antonín 179, 233, 246, 247–248, 258, 326
Dylan, Bob 65, 226–227, 371, 373–382
dynamic range, definition of 9
dynamics, definition of 9, 12

Eagles, The 437
early music 59
Early Music Consort of London 107, 110
Eazy-E (Eric Wright) 416
economic activity 16–17
"Ecstasy" (Racy) 79
Edison, Thomas 263
Eight Slavonic Dances, Op. 46, No. 1 (Dvořák) 248
Eighth Blackbird 397
"Ein feste Burg ist unser Gott" (Luther) 148
"Ein feste Burg ist unser Gott" (BMV 80) (Bach) 151
Einstein on the Beach (Glass) 397
Einstein, Albert 264, 287
Eisenhower, Dwight 389
Eisler, Hanns 288

ekonting 225–226
El Malo (Colon) 404
El Rey: Bravo (Puente) 397–406
El Salon Mexico (Copland) 326
Eldridge, Roy 354
Electric Ladyland (Hendrix) 373–382
electronic dance music (EDM) 409, 443, 450, 467, 472
electronica 443
elements of music 9–12
Eliot, Missy 417
Elizabeth (film) 110
Elizabeth I, Queen 106, 109, 116–117, 124, 127
Ellington, Edward Kennedy "Duke" 3, 11, 83, 252, 300–301, 323–324, 328, 351, 376, 309–316, 319, 422–423
Eminem (Marshall Mathers) 417
emotion in music 13–15
Emperor of Atlantis, The (Ullmann) 361
empfindsamer Stil 176
endless melody 241, 251
Engels, Friedrich 240
English Baroque Soloists 145
english horn 212
Enlightenment 169–171
Enter the Wu-Tang (26 Chambers) 417
envelope 9
Epic, The (Washington) 469
episode, fugal 153
"Epistrophy" (Monk) 356
"Era Diferente" (Los Tigres del Norte) 464
erhu 72
Es ist ein Ros entsprungen (Praetorius) 110, 113
Escalona, Phidia Danilo 403
Esperanza (Spalding) 451
Estefan, Gloria 405
Esterházy, Nikolaus 177–178, 183
Esterházy, Paul Anton 177
Esther (Handel) 149
ethnomusicologists, ethnomusicology 22, 165
étude 219
Étude in G–flat Minor, Op. 10, No. 5 (Chopin) 222
Europe, James Reese 277–278, 281
European dance form 108, 116, 140, 143, 212, 218, 274, 279, 298, 310–311, 435
European polyphony, early history of 100–103
"Ev'ry valley shall be exalted" from *Messiah* (Handel) 151
Evans, Bill 386
"(Everything I Do) I Do It for You" (Adams) 442

"Evidence" (Monk) 356
Exorcist, The (film) 53
explaining music 3
exposition, fugal 153
exposition of sonata form 181
"Express Yourself" (N.W.A.) 416
"Exultate, Jubilate" (Mozart) 184

"Fair Phyllis I Saw Sitting All Alone" (Farmer) 103–107
falsetto 104, 330
Falstaff (Verdi) 239
Fame Monster, The (Lady Gaga) 444
Fame, The (Lady Gaga) 444
Fanfare for the Common Man (Copland) 326
Fania Records 403–405
Fantasia (film) 158, 288
Far East Suite (Ellington) 315–316
Farmer, John 103–107, 124
farming, subsistence and music 39
Faust (Goethe) 207
Fauvus, Orval E. 389
Fear of a Black Planet (Public Enemy) 409–418
Fearless (Swift) 348
feedback, audio 380
"Feira de Sete Portas" (Opanije) 201
Feld, Steven 37
festa 199
fiddle 223–224, 226–227, 271, 341–344
field hollers 259, 270
Field, John 220–222
Fiennes, Joseph 110
fife 276
"Fight the Power" (Public Enemy) 409–418, 436–437
figured bass 137
Filhos De Ghandi (Brazil) 201
Filles de Kilimanjaro (Davis) 387
Final Alice (del Tredici) 430
Finlandia (Sibelius) 246
Firebird, The (Stravinsky) 287
Fireworks (Stravinsky) 287
Fisher, Maria 424
Fisk Jubilee Singers 253–259
Fitzgerald, Ella 313, 339, 352
Fitzgerald, F. Scott 299
Five Blind Boys of Alabama 258
flamenco 5, 117
flamenco arabe 117
Flavor Flav (William Drayton) 410, 412, 414
Fleck, Béla 127
Florence and the Machine 452
Florentine camarata 137–138
"Flowers" from *Anthracite Fields* (Wolfe) 455

flûte à bec 111
Fly or Die (Branch) 450, 452
Foo Fighters, The 308
"For unto us a child is born" (Handel) 151
foragers, music of 2, 21, 19, 22–28, 35–36, 304
form, definition of 12
"Formation" (Beyoncé) 468
forte 9
fortepiano 185, 193
Foster, Stephen 228, 256
"Foundations" from *Anthracite Fields* (Wolfe) 454
"Four Seasons" (Vivaldi) 210, 144
Fox Trot 311
Franklin, Aretha 259
Franz II, Emperor 173, 175
Freddie Freeloader (Henricks) 425
Frederick the Great 183
Free Jazz (Coleman) 388
Freed, Alan 377
Freedom Highway (Giddens) 223, 226
"Freight Train" (Cotten) 226
French Revolution 203, 209
"Frere Jacques" 100
Freud, Sigmund 264, 287
frula, Serbian 113
"Fuck tha Police" (N.W.A.) 416, 418
fugue 151–166
fundamental 8
funk 413, 435, 447, 451
"Funky Drummer" (Brown) 418
Fuentes, Rubén 336
Fux, Johann Joseph 101, 177
fuzz box 380

gadulka 86, 88–90, 112
gagaku 91
gaida 86, 88–89, 91
galliarde 110, 113, 117
gamelan 93; Balinese 265, 289–298; definition of 159;
nese 130, 159–166, 252, 394
Ganchev, Nicola 90
Gandera, I Wayan 289, 291
gangsa 290–294
"Gangsta Gangsta" (N.W.A.) 416
Garbarek, Jan 127
Gardiner, John Eliot 145, 151
Garland, Judy 229, 300, 317
Garrison, Jimmy 382, 386
gat 119, 122
gateway, definition of 4
gender and music 15–16, 58, 88, 187, 189–190, 221–222, 235, 378, 439, 443–444, 450, 457–458, 468
genderan 292

genius, musical 5, 208
Genovese, Leo 449
Genuine Negro Jig (Carolina Chocolate Drops) 226
George I, King 149
George III, King 150, 175, 184
Georgia Sea Island Singers 257, 259
Gershwin, George 247, 252, 300, 316–329
Gershwin, Ira 316
Gesamptkunstwerk 240
"Get Up, Stand Up" (Marley) 436–437
G-funk 416
gharana 123
Ghenghis Blues (film) 32
Ghosts of Versailles, The (Corigliano) 429
Giant Steps (Coltrane) 386
Giddens, Rhiannon 223–330
Gilbert, W.S. 322
Gillespie, Dizzy 339, 348–356, 370, 403, 450
Girl Crazy (musical) 316–317, 322
Giuiana, Mark 468
Giulio Cesare in Egitto (Handel) 149
Glasper, Robert 418
Glass, Philip 396–397,429, 457, 471
glee club 103, 253
glissando 212, 324
globalization 129
"Gloria sei dir gesungen" (BMV 80) (Bach) 151
Gnossiennes (Satie) 288
"God Bless America" (Berlin) 300
"God Save the King/Queen" 110, 175
Goethe, Johann Wolfgang von 207, 240
Gone with the Wind (film) 327
gong, definition of 161
gong kebyar 289–298
Gonzales, Rebecca 337
"Good Lava" (Spalding) 452
Good Morning Viet Nam (film) 308
Goodman, Benny 15, 313, 323, 326, 328
Gordon, Dexter 356
Gordon, Michael 457–458
gospel 379, 431, 435, 449
gospel quartet 258
gospel song 258
Gospel Songs: A Choice Collection of Hymns and Tunes (Bliss) 258
"Gott erhalte Franz den Kaiser" 175
Gotterdämmerung (Wagner) 241
Gottschalk, Louis Moreau 229
Graceland (Simon) 408
Gradus ad Parnassum (Fux) 101, 177
Grammy Award 348, 382, 423, 427, 436, 452, 463

Grand Ole Opry 346
Grand Staff 53
Grand traité d'instrumentation et d'orchestration modernes (Berlioz) 216
Grand Wizard Theodore (Theodore Livingston) 415
Grande études de Paganini, S141: No. 3 in G–sharp Minor ("La Campanella") (Liszt) 222
Grande, Ariana 437
Grandmaster Flash (Joseph Saddler) 414–415
Grange, Red 300
Granz, Norman 355
Grateful Dead 32, 45, 381
Great American Songbook 322, 327
Great Awakening 257
Great Masters of Bulgarian Instrumental Folklore, vol. 1 (CD) 90
Greenwood, Jonny 468
Gregorian chant 50, 96
Grieg, Edvard 246
Grillo, Frank "Machito" 403
Grimm, Brothers 246
grito 330, 333–334
Grizzly Bear 471
Grofé, Ferde 328
groove 364, 374, 383–384, 398, 401, 411–414, 416, 419–422, 431–432, 435–437, 447–449, 452
Guadalajara Symphony 336
guaguanco 403
guaracha 403
Guarneri, Giuseppe 143
Guido of Arezzo 52
guitar 113; electric 117; Hawaiian 348; lap steel 342–343; pedal steel 342–343, 347–348
guitarra de golpe 335
guitarrón 117, 329, 330–331, 335
guru 44, 123, 126
Gutenberg, Johannes 101
Guthrie, Woody 379

habanera rhythm 281, 419, 422
Haden, Charlie 388
hafiz 56
Haggard, Merle 347
Haley, Alex 28
"Hallelujah Time" (Marley) 436
"Hallelujah" (Handel) 145–151
Hamilton, Alexander 177
Hamilton, Eliza 177
Hamlet (Shakespeare) 212
Hammerstein, Oscar II 52, 322
Hammond, John 313
Hampton University 258

Hampton, Lionel 314
Hancock, Herbie 27, 387–388, 390, 423–424
Handel, George Frideric 130, 145–151, 153, 156, 167, 176, 185, 191–192
Handy, W.C. 272
hard bop 386–387, 422
Harlem Renaissance 299
harmony, 11; Baroque 137–138, 153; in bebop 352–353; in mariachi 330; Medieval 60–61; Renaissance 101–102; tonal 143–144, 148, 153, 158, 165–166, 173, 236, 242, 249, 265, 274, 283–284, 286–288, 302, 304, 324, 326, 362, 366, 384, 390, 393, 427, 429–430; triadic 98
harpsichord 132, 151, 156
Harris, Calvin 467
Harrison, George 126, 379
Harrison, Lou 396
Hart, Mickey 32, 45
Harvard Glee Club 253
Hawkins, Coleman 271
Haydn, Franz Joseph 2, 116, 169, 171–180, 182–186, 195–196,202, 206, 208, 210, 216, 357
Hayes, Roland 258
Head Hunters (Hancock) 388, 390
head in jazz 302, 419–420
Heartbeat Opera 470
heavy metal 381
Hebrides Overature (Mendelssohn) 216
Hecho en Puerto Rico (Colon) 404
Heller, Jerry 416
Hemmings, Sally 191
Henderson, Fletcher 312–313, 323, 328
Hendricks, Jon 425
Hendrix, Jimmy 3, 10, 272, 373–382, 385, 387
Henry VIII, King 106
Henry, John 458
Henry, Pierre 395
heptatonic 34
Heptones, The 435
Hercules (Handel) 149
Herman, Woody 313
Herrmann, Bernard 289
heterophony 86
Heywood, DuBose 328
High Fidelity (Magazine) 394
High School Musical (film) 240
hi-hat 306
Hildegard von Bingen 16, 46–53, 63, 141
Hill, Lauryn 417
Hill, Teddy 354

hillbilly records 345–346
Hinduism 19, 40, 122, 159, 163, 295, 394
Hines, Earl "Fatha" 354
hip-hop 409–418, 437, 451, 472, 472
Hitchcock, Alfred 289
Hitler, Adolf 175, 242, 300, 339–340, 359, 370
HIV/AIDS and music 425–431
Ho Chi Minh 340
Hodges, Johnny 315
Hodson, Millicent 288
Hoffmann, E.T.A. 208–209
"Hold On" (Beyoncé) 468
Holiday, Billie 7, 313
Holman, Ray 369
Holocaust 341
Holy Roman Empire 50
Homer 327
Honegger, Arthur 252
honky-tonk music 346
Hood, Mantle 165
Hopscotch: A Mobile Opera for 24 Cars 470
horo 88
horticulturalists, music of 2, 19, 21, 33–38
hosho 80, 82
"Hotel California" (Eagles) 437
house music 443, 468, 409
House, Eddie "Son" 272–273
Houston Grand Opera 429
Houston, Whitney 12, 442, 468
Howard, Brittney 16
huapango 329
Hughes, Langston 299
"Human Nature" (Jackson, Iyer) 468
Hungarian Rhapsodies (Liszt) 328
Hungarian Rhapsody No. 2 (Liszt) 246
Hunting Ground, The (film) 440, 443
huro 81–82
Hurst III, Robert Leslie 419
Hurston, Zora Neale 299
Hussain, Zakir 127
Huun-Huur-Tu 32
hydraulis 155
Hymns and Spiritual Songs (Watts) 257

"I Can't Help It" (Jackson, Spalding) 449, 452
"I Can't Stand Losing You" (Police) 437
"I Got Plenty O'Nuttin'" from *Porgy and Bess* (Gershwin) 329
"I Got Rhythm" (Gershwin) 316–323
"I Got You (I Feel Good)" (Brown) 449
"I Know You Know" (Spalding) 451
"I Loves You, Porgy" from *Porgy and Bess* (Gershwin) 329

"I Shot the Sheriff" (Marley, Clapton) 436–437
"I Will Always Love You" (Houston) 12, 442
Ice Cube (O'Shea Jackson) 416
"Ich habe genug" (BMV 146) (Bach) 148, 151
I-Ching (book) 394
icon 14, definition of
idée fixe 212–213
identity; age-group 378; ethnic 84. 329, 402; in mariachi 329, 334–337; national 78, 89–90, 200, 233, 246–247, 288, 326, 328, 407
idiophone 164
Idomeneo, re di Creta (Mozart) 192
Iha, James 381
"Ijexá (Filhos De Ghandi)" (Nunes) 201
Ijexá for Oxum 197–201
Il barbiere di Siviglia (Rossini) 239
Iliad (Homer) 163, 327
"I'm So Lonesome I Could Cry" (Williams) 341–348
Images (Debussy) 252
Imaginary Landscapes No. 4 (Cage) 395
imitation, point of 97
imperialism 264, 340, 402, 404
Impression: Sunrise (Monet) 251
impressionism 248, 251, 264
impromptu 219
improvisation, collective 304
In C (Riley) 390–397, 430
In for a Penny, In for a Pound (Threadgill) 423
In the Steppes of Central Asia (Borodin) 247
indeterminacy 390–397
index, definition of 12
Industrial Revolution 2, 203, 230–231
Infante, Pedro 300
Innis, Louis 341
interlude 183
intervals, perfect fifth, perfect fourth, major second, minor second 63
"Invoking the Spirit of Kindness through Sound" (Tibet) 40–45
iqa'at 76
"Is This Love" (Marley) 434
Islam 2, 19, 40, 54–58, 65–66, 78–79, 123–124, 163
Island Records 436
Isley Brothers 380
Israel in Egypt (Handel) 149
"It Ain't Necessarily So" from *Porgy and Bess* (Gershwin) 329
It Takes a Nation of Millions to Hold Us Back (Public Enemy) 416

Ives, Charles 276, 278
Iyer, Vijay 468

J.J.Fad 416
Jackson, Jesse 372
Jackson, John Shenoy 389
Jackson, Mahalia 258–259, 356, 468
Jackson, Tommy 341
Jacobs, Rene 131
Jamaica, music of 430–439
James, Cheryl ("Salt") 417
James, Elmore 376
"Jammin'" (Marley) 436
Janequin, Clément 107
Jansons, Mariss 357
Japanese court orchestra 7
Java, music of 159–166
Jay–Z 417, 437
Jazz 7; avant–garde 422, 469, 470; bebop 313, 348–356, 422; as classical music 424; cool 387; definition of 299; early 301–308; free 388, 390, 422–423; fusion 422; hard bop 386–387, 422; institutionalization of 422–425; modal 386, 422; neo-traditional 419–425, 437; new directions in 382–390; New Orleans 301–308; swing 309–316; symphonic 328; today 445–454
Jazz at Lincoln Center 424
Jazz Messengers 387, 390
Jazz Singer, The (film) 229, 300, 327
"Jeannie with the Light Brown Hair" (Foster) 229
Jefferson Airplane 381
Jefferson, Blind Lemon 272–273
Jefferson, Thomas 171, 191
Jennens, Charles 145
Jeux (Debussy) 252, 287
Jeux d'eau (Ravel) 253
Jews, in music 240–241, 300, 321, 326, 361–362
Jim Crow 259, 265, 297, 380
Jimi Hendrix Experience 373
Joanne (Lady Gaga) 444
Joffrey Ballet 288
Johannesburg (The Very Best) 472
Johnson, James P. 271, 282–283, 314
Johnson, Philip 428
Johnson, Robert 272, 376, 379
Johnson, William 307
Jolson, Al 229, 322, 327
Jones, Bessie 257, 259
Jones, Elvin 382
Jones, Hank 355
Jones, Norah 450
Jones, Quincy 356
Joplin, Janice 381

Joplin, Scott 279–283, 306, 352
Jordan, Louis 378
Joseph II, Emperor 183–184, 190
Joshi, D.T. 126
Joshua (Handel) 149
Josquin 101, 103, 107
Judaism 19, 40, 122, 158
Judaism in Music (Wagner) 240
Judas Maccabaeus (Handel) 149
Juilliard School 424
"Julie" (Giddens) 223–330
justice, social and racial 312–313, 315,
    353, 370, 373, 377, 389, 414, 433,
    436, 439, 444, 450–451, 461, 468

Kant, Immanuel 208–209
Kapellmeister 110, 149, 177, 184, 195
Karenga, Maulana 28
karma 44
kaval 86, 88–90
kebyar 292–294
kempli 290, 292
kendang 290–293
Kennedy, John F. 371
Kennedy, Robert 371
Kern, Jerome 316, 321–322
"Ketawang Puspawarna" (Java)
    159–166
kettle drum 113
key 139–140
key area 141
keyboard instruments, history of
    155–156
keyboard music, Baroque 151–166
Keys, Alicia 452
Khan, Ali Akbar 126–127
Khan, Allauddin 126
Khan, Genghis 78, 124
Khan, Imdad 126
Khan, Shujaat 126–127
Khan, Ustad Mushtaq Ali 126
Khan, Vilayat 126–127
kick drum 306
kilitan 292
Kind of Blue (Davis) 386
Kinderszenen (R. Schumann) 222
Kinderszenen, Op. 15, VII: Träumerei
    (Daydreaming) (R. Schumann) 222
King and I, The (Rodgers &
    Hammerstein) 322–323
King Kong (film) 327
King, B.B. 272
King, Jr., Dr. Martin Luther 258, 371–372
King's Singers, The 103–104
Kisliuk, Michelle 22
Kiss 443
kithara 396
"Ko Ko" (Parker) 348–356, 422, 469

Kodaly Quartet 173
Konitz, Lee 387
Kool Herc (Clive Campbell) 414–415
kopanitsa 110
"Kopanitsa" (Bulgaria) 85–90
kotekan 292, 294
koto 396
K-pop 471
Kraftwerk 415
Krall, Diana 450
Krausas, Veronika 470
Krauss, Alison 227
kreasi baru 294
Krell, William H. 282
Kronos Quartet 32, 79, 179, 397
Krupa, Gene 314
kudeketera 81–82
Kulthum, Umm 79
Kumina, kumina drumming 435, 437
Kuular, Anatoli 28–33
Kwanzaa 28

"La Bala" (Los Tigres del Norte)
    458–470
La Bohème (Puccini) 239
"Là ci darem la mano" (Mozart) 192, 220
La Clemenza di Tito (Mozart) 185
La Mer (Debussy) 252
La Messe de Nostre Dame (Machaut)
    59–65
"La Negra" (mariachi) 329–338
La resurrezione (Handel) 148
"Ladies First" (Queen Latifah) 417
Lady Gaga 3, 439–445
Lady Macbeth of Mtensk (Shostakovich)
    360
Ladysmith Black Mambazo 10
lama 44
Lamar, Kendrick 417–418, 423,451, 469,
    472
Lancaster, Geoffrey 193
"Land of the Free" (Spalding) 451
Lang, David 457–458
laras 159
"Largo al factotum della città" from *Il
    barbiere di Siviglia* (Rossini) 242
Late Night with David Letterman (TV
    show) 32
Latin American Suite (Ellington)
    315–316
Latin jazz 201, 355, 403
Latin music 201, 403
Latin tinge 281, 352, 422
Lavoe, Hector 404
Le mystère des voix bulgares (CD) 90
Le Nozze di Figaro (Mozart) 186–192,
    203
Led Zeppelin 381

Legato, definition of 12
Leitmotif 240
lelonggoran 293
Lemonade (Beyoncé) 468
Leningrad Symphony 357
Lennon, John 12, 379
Les Demoiselles d'Avignon (Picasso) 264
Lesne, Gerard 117
"Let's Go Crazy" (Prince) 11
Levin, Theodore 33
Levine, James 179
Lewis, Jerry Lee 378
Lewis, John 355, 387
Lewis, John L. 453
Licensed to III (Beastie Boys) 416
Liebestod (Wagner) 234–242
Lieder 106
Lil' Kim 417
Lil' Wayne 417
Lin Youren 68, 72
Lincoln, Abbey 389–390
L'incoronazione di Poppea (Monteverdi)
    131–139
Lindy Hop 309
listening 4
Liston, Melba 16, 355, 450
Liszt, Franz 211, 216, 221–222, 241, 246,
    248, 328
Little Richard 377, 379– 380
Lo Mato (Colon) 404
Loft Opera 470
Lohengrin (Wagner) 240–242
London Symphonies (Haydn) 185
London Symphony Orchestra 284
Long Beach Opera 362
loop 411
Lord Invader (Rupert Grant) 366, 369
Lord Kitchener (Aldwyn Roberts) 363,
    369
Los Angeles Opera 339
Los Angeles Philharmonic 362
Los Cuates de Sinaloa 464
Los Tigres del Norte 458–465
Loudness, definition of 9
Loueke, Lionel 445, 448, 452
Louis XIV, King 130, 143, 165, 170, 190
Lovano, Joe 449
Lovato, Demi 467
"Love in Time" (Spalding) 451
Love Yourself: Tear (BTS) 472
Lowensein, Marc 470
Ludwig II, King 241
Lunceford, Jimmie 312, 323
lute 114–116, 132
Luther, Martin 95, 148, 156
Lutheran chorale 362
Lynn, Loretta 347
lyra, Greek 112–113

M83 468
Má Vlast (Smetana) 242, 246
Ma, Yo–Yo 227
Maal, Baaba 472
mabo 22–28
McCarney, Paul 12, 379
McFerrin, Bobby 412, 414, 437
McGhee, Brownie 228
McGhee, Howard 353
Machaut, Guillaume de 59–65, 67, 96, 100, 103, 106
McIntosh County Shouters, The 257, 259
McIntosh, Andrew 470
McLaughlin, John 127, 423
Macon, Uncle Dave 346, 348
Madonna 6, 443
madrigal 103–107, 138, 139
Magellan, Ferdinand 129
Magic Flute, The (Mozart) 185, 192
Mahabharata 163
Mahler, Gustav 211, 242, 248, 289, 430
mahon'era 81–82
major second 140
Malcolm X 416, 469
"Malcolm's Theme" (K. Washington) 469
Maldonado, Cesar 337
Mallarmé, Stéphane 248–249, 251–252
mambo 403
Mambo Birdland (Puente) 405
"Mammy" (Jolson) 229
"Mammy's Little Baby Loves Shortnin' Bread" 433
mandala 43
Mandela, Nelson 407
Mangkunegara IV, Prince 165
Manley, Michael 436
Mannette, Ellie 369
"Manteca" (Gillespie, Pozo) 356
mantra 43
manyura 159
Mapfumo, Thomas 83–85
"Maple Leaf Rag" (Joplin) 279–283, 352
maqam 57, 73; *bayyati* 75; *hijaz* 75; *rast* 75
Maraire, Dumisani 84
Marche Slave (Tchaikovsky) 247
Marcon, Andrea 140
Maria Theresa, Empress 184
mariachi 3, 100, 300, 329–338
Mariachi Divas de Cindy Shea 337–338
Mariachi Herencia de México 337
Mariachi Las Alteñas 337
Mariachi Los Camperos de Nati Cano 336, 338
Mariachi Los Galleros 337

Mariachi Reyna de Los Angeles 337
Mariachi Sol de México 337
Mariachi Vargas de Tecalitlán 330, 335–336
Marie Antoinette 184
marimba 84. 396, 472
Marley, Bob 4, 408, 412, 430–438
Marley, Damien 436, 437
Marley, Julian 436
Marley, Stephen 436
Marley, Ziggy 436
Mars, Bruno 452
Marsalis Standard Time, Vol. 1 (Marsalis) 419, 422
Marsalis, Branford 418
Marsalis, Ellis 423
Marsalis, Wynton 387, 418, 419–426
Marshmello 467
Martha and the Vandellas 373
Martin, Ricky 405
Marx, Karl 231, 240
Mass in B Minor (Bach) 157
mass, cyclical 100
Matisse, Henri 287
Maytals 435
mazurka 219–220
Mazurka No. 5 in B flat Major, Op. 7, No. 1 (Chopin) 222
mbira 80–85, 91, 154, 304, 385, 472
Mbuti music 165
MC Ren (Lorenzo Patterson) 416
measure 11
Mediatrix Ensemble 46
Medieval Period 19, 39–40
Meditations (Coltrane) 388
Mehldau, Brad 227, 468
Mehta, Zubin 242
mehter 276
maestro di cappella 144
melodia (mariachi) 330
melody, definition of 11
membranophone 113
Mendelssohn Club of Philadelphia 453
Mendelssohn, Fanny 221–222
Mendelssohn, Felix 158, 216, 221–222, 240
mento 435, 437
Menuhin, Yehudi 126
Merchant of Venice, The (Shakespeare) 106
merengue 201
Meshuggah 468
"Message, The" (Grandmaster Flash) 415
Messe de Nostre Dame (Machaut) 59–65, 100, 106
Messiaen, Olivier 339, 360–361, 370

Messiah (Handel) 145–151
Metamorphoses (Ovid) 396
metaphor 15
meter: additive 86; definition of 11
metrical, definition of 11
Metropolitan Opera 179, 424, 429
Mexican American music 329–338, 458–469
Mexico, music of 329–338, 458–469
Meyer, Edgar 127
Mi Vida Es Cantar (Cruz) 404
"Mic Drop" (Aoki) 472
Michelangelo 100
Michel'le (Michel'le Toussaint) 416
Microtone, microtonality 57, 266, 269–270, 310–311, 319, 342, 351, 376, 278
Middle East, music of 54–58, 73–79
Midsummer Night's Dream (Shakespeare) 221
Mighty Sparrow 366–367
Migration, Great 299
Mikado, The (Gilbert & Sullivan) 322
Miles Smiles (Davis) 387
Miley, James "Bubber" 83, 309, 310, 312, 314, 324
Miller, Glenn 313, 340–341
Mingus, Charles 356, 389–390, 423
minimalism 396, 428–429
minstrel show 226–229
Minton's Playhouse 353–354
minuet 177–179, 183, 196, 219
Miranda, Carmen 201
Missa L'homme Armé (Dufay) 100
Missa L'homme Armé Super Voces Musicales (Josquin) 103
Missa Pater Noster (Palestrina) 103
Missa Solemnis (Beethoven) 210
"Mississippi Rag, The" (Krell) 282
Mitchell, Joni 456
Mitchell, Katie 470
Mitchell, Mitch 373
Mitchell, Nicole 469
mode 139–140
Modern Jazz Quartet 387
modernism 248, 264–265, 289, 298
modulation 57, 141
Moldau, The (Smetana) 328, 242–248
Monáe, Janelle 452
Monet, Claude 251
Monk, T.S. (Thelonious III) 356, 424
Monk, Thelonious 323, 353–356, 423, 468
monody 137
monophony 10
Moran, Jason 356
Monroe, Bill 227
Monteverdi Choir 145

Monteverdi, Claudio 107, 130, 131–139, 153, 167, 191–192
"Mooche, The" (Ellington) 11
Morgan, Lee 356
Morehouse College 258
Morley, Thomas 107
Mormon Tabernacle Choir 150–151
Morton, Ferdinand (Jelly Roll) 281–282, 307, 423
Moten, Bennie 314
motet 97
motion, contrary, oblique and parallel 63
movement (section) 59
Mozart, Leopold 184, 195
Mozart, Maria Anna ("Nannerl") 184
Mozart, Wolfgang Amadeus 2, 16, 116–117, 145, 158, 169, 171–172, 178–193, 195–196, 202–203, 206, 208, 215–216, 218, 220–222, 362
Mude, Hakurotwi 80–81
mudra 43
Mugabe, Robert 84
Muhly, Nico 471
Mulligan, Gerry 387
Mumford and Sons 452, 472
music drama 234
Music for the Royal Fireworks (Handel) 150
Music of Changes (Cage) 394
music, cognition of 9; history of 17l; meaning of 13–17; perception 9
música norteña 458–466
música popular brasileira 201
música tropical 201
musical, Broadway 316, 318, 320, 322–323, 338, 468
musicals, movie 327
musique concrète 395
Mussorgsky, Modest 217, 247
Muti, Riccardo 186
My Bondage and My Freedom (Douglass) 256
"My Country Tis of Thee" 110, 175
"My Heart Will Go On" (Dion) 442
My Morning Jacket 308
"My Old Kentucky Home" (Foster) 228
"Mystery Band" (Trinidad) 363–370

N.W.A. (Nigaz with Attitude) 416, 418
Nachtstücke (Schumann) 222
Napoleon 172, 190, 209, 215
narcocorrido 463–464
Narváez, Luys de 113–117, 124
Nas 417
Nashville sound 347
National Guard March (Smetana) 246
National Lampoon's Christmas Vacation (film) 150

National Symphony Orchestra 425
National, The 471
nationalism, civic 232, 247; ethnic 231–233, 241, 247, 259, 402; musical 242–248, 287; musical in America 324–329, 300
nature, sound of 28–33
nay, Arab 76, 79
Nazism 339–340
Neal, Jocelyn 348
Negrete, Jorge 300
"Negro y Azul" (Los Cuates de Sinaloa) 464
Nelson, Kristina 58
Nelson, Willie 32
neoclassicism 289, 359
neolithic revolution 21
neo-Romanticism 428–430, 437
Neue Zeitschrift für musik (magazine) 222
New Age music 252
new music ensemble 397
New Orleans jazz 301–308
New York City Ballet 424
New York Philharmonic 216, 424, 458
Newton, Ernie 341
Newton, Isaac 170
ney, Turkish 79
"Ngoma Yarira" (Mapfumo) 85
Nicholas I, Tsar 220
Nicki Minaj 417
"Night on Bald Mountain" (Mussorgsky) 217
Nijinsky, Vaslav 287
nirvana 43
Nirvana 382
Nixon in China (Adams) 429
Nixon, Richard 429
"No Woman, No Cry" (Marley) 436–437
Noble, Ray 349
nocturne 219, 221
Nocturne No. 1 in E flat Major (Field) 222
Nocturne No. 8 in D flat Major, Op. 27, No. 2 (Chopin) 222
Nocturnes (Debussy) 252
nomadic pastoralists, music of 2, 21, 19, 28–33
Non piu andrai," *Le Nozze di Figaro* (Mozart) 192
nonmetrical 11
Norfolk Rhapsodies (Williams) 328
Norman, Andrew 470
Norman, Jessye 258
norteño 458–467
North India, music of 93, 118–127, 381, 396

"Norwegian Wood" (Lennon & McCartney) 12
notation, musical 51–53, 64, 70, 76, 91
note, definition of 9
Notorious B.I.G., The (Christopher Wallace) 417
Novelletten (Schumann) 222
"Now Is the Month of Maying" (Morley) 107
"Now's the Time" (Parker) 356
Nuestra Herencia (CD) 337
Nunes, Clara 201
"Nuthin' but a 'G' Thang" (Dr. Dre) 418
"Nyamaropa" (Shona) 80–85

O Brother, Where Art Thou? (film) 227
Obama, Barack 451
obbligato 273
Oberlin Conservatory Contemporary Music Ensemble 397
"Ob-La-Di, Ob-La-Da" (Beatles) 436
Oblivion (M83) 468
Ocean, Frank 467
octave 33
Ode for the Birthday of Queen Anne (Handel) 149
"Ode to Joy" (Beethoven) 210
Odyssey (Homer) 327
"Of Rage and Remembrance" from Symphony No. 1 (Corigliano) 427
Off the Wall (Jackson) 449
"Oh, Susanna" (Foster) 228
"Ohimè! Sorge il tremendo fantasma e ne separa," from *Lucia di Lammermoor* (Donizetti) 242
Oklahoma! (Rodgers & Hammerstein) 322
"Old Folks at Home" (Foster) 228
"Old Joe Clark" 230
Oliver, Joe "King" 307
ombak 290
Omolu 201
On Site Opera 470
Ondar, Kongar-ool 32–33
"One Dance" (Drake) 437
"One Way Ticket" (Underwood) 437
Opanije (Brazil) 201
opera 4; Baroque 131–139; history of 186–192; *opera buffa* 191–192; *opera seria* 191; nineteenth-century 234
Opera and Drama (Wagner) 240
Opera on Tap 470
operetta 322
opus, definition of 173
oratorio 145–151, 423
Orbison, Roy 378
Orent, Milt 355

Orfeo (Monteverdi) 138, 192
organ 151–166, 434; Baroque 155–156; Hammond B-3 258–259, 405, 445–449
Organ Concerto, Op. 4, No. 5 (Handel) 145
organum 63, 65
Original Dixieland Jazz Band (ODJB) 305, 308
orixá 197, 199, 468
ornamentation, definition of 12
"Ornithology" (Parker) 356
Ory, Kid 301
ostinato 384, 401, 426; chordal 333
Othello, the Moor of Venice (Shakespeare) 106
Ottoman Empire 78–79, 89, 100–101, 137, 232, 242, 263–264, 276, 298
Outkast 417
Overtone, definition of 9
overtone singing *see* throat-singing
overture 183
Overture to A Midsummer Night's Dream (Mendelssohn) 158
Ovid 395–396
Oxford Camerata 59–65
Oxossi 201
Oxúm 197, 198, 201, 468
"Oye Como Va" (Puente) 397–406

Pacheco, Johnny 404
Paganini, Niccolò 220
Pagodes (Debussy) 165–166, 252–253
Palestrina, Giovanni Pierluigi da 97–103, 165
Palmieri, Eddie 403
panpipe 33
Papazov, Ivo 90
Papillions (Schumann) 222
Parade (Satie) 287
Paris Conservatoire 216
Parker, Charlie 16, 323, 339, 348–356, 370, 387, 422–423, 469
Parks, Rosa 371
Parlato, Gretchen 424, 452
Partch, Harry 396
Partita for 8 Singers (Shaw) 12
Parton, Dolly 12, 347
passamezzo 113
pathet 159
Patti Smith Group 381
Patton, Charley 272
Paul, John 152
Paul, Sean 437
pavane 113
Pavlova, Anna 287
Pearl Jam 382
Peer Gynt Suite No. 1 (Grieg) 246

Pelléas et Mélisande (Debussy) 252
pelog 162
performance techniques, definition of 12
Perkins, Carl 378
Pérotin 65
Perry, Joe 416
perspective, in painting 96, 102
Perugino, Pietro 102
Pet Sounds (Beach Boys) 380
Peter, Paul and Mary 226, 379
Petrushka (Stravinsky) 287
Pettiford, Oscar 353
Phantom Thread (film) 468
Phase II Pan Groove 369
Philip Glass Ensemble 397
Philip II, King 116, 124, 127
Phillips, Sam 378
Philomel (Babbitt) 395, 397
phonograph 17, 231, 263
Phrygian Gates (Adams) 429–430
piano (loudness) 9
Piano Concerto (Steen-Andersen) 471
Piano Concerto, No. 1 (Beethoven) 196
Piano Concerto, No. 24 (Mozart) 196
Piano Sonata in C Minor, No. 8, Op. 13 "Pathetique" (Beethoven) 192–196, 203, 206
Piano Sonata, No. 2, Op. 35 (Chopin) 310, 312
piano, history of 192–196, 203–204; music for 217–222; prepared 394
Picasso, Pablo 264, 287
Pierrot Lunaire (Schoenberg) 288
Pink Floyd 381
pipa 79
Pirates of Penzance, The (Gilbert & Sullivan) 322
"Pisi Ni Tootora" ('Are'are) 33–38
Pissarro, Camille 251
Pitch Perfect (film) 103
pitch: definition of 8; fixed 70–71
"Planet Rock" (Afrika Bambaataa) 415
Plato 106, 220
Please, Please Me (Beatles) 379
Poème electronique (Varèse) 395
pokok 291–293
Police, The 437
political action 16
polka 277, 329
polonaise 219–220
Polonaise No. 3 in A Major, Op. 40, No. 1 ("Military") (Chopin) 222
polymeter 26
polyphony 10; imitative 153–154; inherent 26, 304; stratified 291
polyrhythm 286, 396, 401, 434, 449
polytonality 286–287

"Porgi, Amor" from *Le Nozze di Figaro* (Mozart) 192
Porgy and Bess (Gershwin) 247, 328
Porter, Cole 316
Porter, Lewis 390
Porter, Maggie 256
Portland State University 451
postlude 183
postmodernism in music 425–430
Powell, Bud 339, 353
power chord 15
Pozo, Chano 355–356, 403
Praetorius, Michael 107–113, 124
"Precious Lord, Take My Hand" (T.M. Dorsey, M. Jackson) 259
prelude 183, 219, 151–166
Prélude à l'après-midi d'un faune (Debussy) 248–253
Prelude and Fugue in C Major (Bach) 151–166
Prelude in G Major, Op. 28, No. 3 (Chopin) 222
Presley, Elvis 227, 373, 378–379, 412
Prez, Josquin des *see* Josquin 101, 103
Price, Leontyne 258
prima prattica 138
Prince 11, 452
Professor Griff (Richard Griffin) 410
program (programmatic) music 141, 213, 211–217
proletariat 203
Prophet Muhammad 56, 77
psalm 49
Psycho (film) 289
Public Enemy 3, 409–418, 436–437
Puccini, Giacomo 239, 242
Puente, Tito 397–406
Puerto Rico, music of 397–406
Pulitzer Prize 316, 423, 427, 429, 453
"Pur ti miro, pur ti godo" from *L'Coronazione di Poppea* (Monteverdi) 139
"Push It" (Salt-N-Pepa) 417
Puspawarna (Javanese gamelan) 159
"Putnam's Camp" from *Three Places in New England* (Ives) 276

qanun 76–77
qin 68–72, 91, 156, 165
"Quando me'n vo soletta per la via,'" from *La Bohème* (Puccini) 242
Quartet for the End of Time (Messiaen) 361
Quatro diferencias sobre Guárdame las vacas (Narvaez) 113–117
Queen Latifah (Owens, Dana) 272–273, 417

"Queen Majesty" (Techniques) 435
"Queen of the Night," from *The Magic Flute* (Mozart) 192
"Quia ergo femina" (Bingen) 46–53, 63
Qur'an 54–58, 77

R&B *see* rhythm and blues
rabab, North Indian 125
race records 270, 377
Rachmaninoff, Sergei 289, 328
Racy, A.J. 73–79, 116
Radio Music Society (Spalding) 445–455
Radiohead 381, 468
rag bhairavi 165
raga 118–128
"Raga Bhairvi-Dadra Tal" (North India) 118–128
"Raga Bihag ..." (North India) 127
ragtime 265, 278–283, 306, 326
Ragtime (Novel) 283
Rainey, Gertrude "Ma" 228, 270–271, 273
Raising Hell (Run-DMC) 416
Rakim (William Michael Griffin, Jr.) 416
Ralchev, Petar 90
Ramayana 163
Rameau, Jean-Philippe 144
Ramones, The 381
Rangda 295–296
rap 408–418, 437, 472; gangsta 416
"Rapper's Delight" (Sugarhill Gang) 415
Rapsodie espagnole (Ravel) 328
rasa, in Java 160
Rasmussen, Anne K. 58
Rastafari Movement 430–439
Ravel, Maurice 116–117, 242, 252–253, 287, 328
Redman, Dewey 388
Redman, Joshua 424
Realidades (Los Tigres del Norte) 458–471
rebab 89, 112, 160, 162
rebec 89
Rebirth Brass Band 306
recapitulation 181
recital 6
Reconstruction 2, 233, 297
recorder 108
recordings, musical 261, 263
Red Violin, The (Corigliano) 429
Redding, Noel 373
Redman, Joshua 424–425
Reeves, Jim 347
reggae 3, 408, 430–437
Reich, Steve 396–397, 457
Reid, Ellen 470

"Rejoice greatly, o daughter of Zion" (Handel) 151
Renaissance 133; art of the 95; dance music 107–113; music of 93–117; sacred vocal music of 97–103 secular vocal music of the 103–107
Renegades Steel Orchestra 363
Renoir, Auguste 251
repeat signs 76
Requiem (Mozart) 185, 221–222, 362
requinto jarocho 117
Réveil des oiseaux (Messiaen) 361
Revolver (Beatles) 381
reyong 290–293
Rhapsody in Blue (Gershwin) 247, 300, 324–329
rhapsody, definition of 324
Rhodes, Cecil 84
rhythm and blues 339, 346, 372–373, 377, 379–380, 435, 437
rhythm, definition of 11; in Arab music 76; North Indian 119–121
"Rhythm-a-Ning" (Monk) 356
Rice, Timothy 90
"Ride of the Valkyries, The" from *Die Walküre* (Wagner) 242
Rienzi (Wagner) 240–241
Rifkin, Joshua 283
Rihanna 437
Riley, Terry 390–397, 430, 456–457
Rimbaud, Arthur 251
Rimsky-Korsakov, Nikolai 216, 217, 247, 287
Rinaldo (Handel) 149, 192
Ring of the Nibelung, The (Wagner) 240–241
ring shout 257, 259, 270, 304
riqq 73
ritardando, ritard 34
Ritchie, Jean 227
Rite of Spring, The (Stravinsky) 283–289, 298, 326
ritornello 133, 140, 143, 180
Roach, Max 349, 353, 389
Roberts, Marcus 419, 422
Robeson, Paul 258–259, 323
Robinson, Sylvia 415
Rochberg, George 429
rock 339, 373–382, 407–409
rock, alternative 382; grunge 382; indie 450, 469, 471; punk 381
rock 'n' roll 373, 377–380
Rodeo (Copland) 247, 326
Rodgers, Jimmie 346, 348
Rodgers, Richard 52, 316, 322
Rodriguez, Pablo "Tito" 403
Roerich, Nicholas 288
Rogers, Ginger 300, 323, 327

Rogers, Roy 346
Rolling Stones 373, 381, 380
Rollins, Sonny 323
romances 234, 239–241
romance, Spanish 463
Romanticism 204, 207–209, 211, 215, 219, 230
Romeo and Juliet (Shakespeare) 240, 106, 212
ronde 113
rondo form 144
Ronettes, The 373
Ronstadt, Linda 336
Roots: The Saga of an American Family (book) 28
Roper, Deidra ("DJ Spinderella") 417
Rosen, Max (Maxie Rosenzweig) 321
Rosenboom, David 470
Rossini, Gioacino 234, 239, 242
Rothschild, Jakob Mayer 220
round 100
"Round Midnight" (Monk) 356
Rousseau, Jean-Jacques 170
"Row, row, row your boat" 100
"Roxanne" (Police) 437 (Police)
Royal Academy of Music, The 216
rubato 217–219
Rubin, Rick 416
Rubinstein, Artur 217–219
rumba 403–405
Run-DMC 416
Russell, Curley 348
Russian Easter Festival Overture (Rimsky-Korsakov) 247
Ruth, Babe 300
Ruthless Records 416
Rutter, John 97

sackbut 108, 111–112
Salieri, Antonio 185
salsa 3, 201, 372–373, 397–406, 435
Salt-N-Pepa 417
Salvant, Cécile McLorin 424, 469
sama'i 73, 76
Samaroo, Jit 363, 367, 368
samba 201, 449
sample, sampler 411
Sanabira, Izzy 403
Sand, George 221
Santana, Carlos 405
Santería 170, 200–201, 403, 435
sarangi 126
sarod 125
Satie, Erik 252–253, 287–289
Saul (Handel) 149
Savannah Children's Choir 445, 449, 452
Sawa, George 77

"Say It Loud" (Brown) 451
scale, blues 266, 325
scales, in Javanese music 162
scales, musical 51–53, 57, 63, 70–71, 75, 83; North Indian 119–120; in Shona music 83
Scarlatti, Domenico 156, 158
scat singing 307, 313, 352, 451
Schaeffer, Pierre 395
Schafer, R. Murray 396
"Scheherazade" (Rimsky-Korsakov) 217
scherzo 219
Schiller, Johann Cristoph Friedrich von 210
"Schlummert ein, ihr matten Augen" (BMV 146) (Bach) 151
Schoenberg, Arnold 242, 283, 286, 288–289, 300, 360–362, 394, 396, 430
Schubert, Franz 179, 430
Schumann, Clara 16, 222, 237
Schumann, Robert 220, 222, 246
Scorsese, Martin 272
Scott Joplin: His Complete Works (LP) 283
Scottish Symphony (Mendelssohn) 216
scratching 410, 415
Seaga, Edward 436
Seasons, The (Haydn) 178
seconda prattica 138, 143
Seeger, Anthony 37
Seeger, Mike 226
Seeger, Peggy 226
Seeger, Pete 226, 379
sekaha 293–294, 296
Selassie, Haile 433, 436
Sen, Sharmistha 118–128
sequence, melodic 74
serialism 288–289
serialism, total 392–393
serialism, twelve-tone 362, 392
seventh chord, dominant 154
Sex Pistols 381
Sgt. Pepper's Lonely Hearts Club Band (Beatles) 126, 380
"Shake Sugaree" (Cotton, Giddens) 226
Shakespeare, William 95, 106, 212, 221, 240
Shakkur, Sheikh Hamza 54–58
Shanghai Conservatory of Music 68
Shankar, Ravi 122, 126–127
Shannon, Sharon 12
Sharon, Yuval 470
Shaw, Artie 313
Shaw, Caroline 12
shawm 276
sheet music 316
sheng 72

Sheppard, Ella 256
Shining, The (film) 53
Shirelles, The 373
Shona, music of the 80–85, 91, 154, 385
Shorter, Wayne 387, 388, 423,452
Shostakovich, Dmitri 3, 170, 211, 339, 357–362, 456
Show Boat (Kern & Hammerstein II) 322–323
"Si ch'io vorrei morire" (Monteverdi) 107, 138
"Si J'étais Blanche" (Salvant, J. Baker) 469
Sibelius, Jean 246, 289
Sicut cervus" (Palestrina) 97–103
"Side to Side" (Grande) 437
Siebenbürgen 16
Siegfried (Wagner) 241
Sienbra (Blade, Colon) 404
sign, signal 13; iconic see icon; sign, indexical see index; language 12
Silent Way (Davis) 387
Silk Road 77, 129
Silver, Horace 387
Simon, Paul 408
Simone, Nina 389–390
Sinatra, Frank 314
sinfonia 144–145, 177, 183
Singing Sandra 366
Sing-Off, The (TV) 103
Singspiel 184–185, 191–192, 316
Sirakov, Rumen 90
sitar 118–128, 381, 472
Sixty Horses in My Herd (Huun-Huur-Tu) 32
ska 435, 437
Slatkin, Leonard 425
Slave Songs of the United States (book) 258
Slaves' War, The: The Civil War in the Words of Former Slaves (Ward) 223
Slavonic Dances (Dvořák) 246
slendro 159, 162
Smashing Pumpkins 381–382
Smetana, Bedřich 233, 242–248, 250, 328
Smith, Bessie 228, 265–273, 351, 376, 450, 469
Smith, Mamie 270, 273
Smith, Willie "the Lion" 282–283, 314
Smithson, Harriet 211–213, 215, 240
Snoop Dogg (Calvin Cordozar Broadus, Jr.) 416, 418, 469
"Snowden's Jig (Genuine Negro Jig)" (Carolina Chocolate Drops) 230
social behavior 15–16
solfège (solmization) 52

Solomon (Handel) 149
Solomon Islands, music of the 33–38
Solti, Georg 204, 227
son 405; clave 403 ; cubano 201, 403; jalisciense 330, 333; montuno 403
sonata 141; meaning of 175; sonata, piano 192–196
sonata form 178, 180–181, 187, 357, 359
Sonatas and Interludes (Cage) 394, 397
Song for My Father (Silver) 387
Song of Freedom (Smetana) 246
song, American popular 316–323; definition of 6
Songs without Words, Op. 62, No. 6 ("Spring Song") (Mendelssohn, Felix) 221–222
soprano part 97
Sorrows of Young Werther, The (Goethe) 207–208, 240
"Sorry" (Bieber) 437
soul music 259, 372, 451
Soul Stirrers 258
Sound Grammar (Coleman) 423
Sound of Music, The (Rodgers & Hammerstein) 322
sound quality see timbre
sound synthesis 395
Sousa, John Philip 273–279, 306
South Pacific (Rodgers & Hammerstein) 322–323
Souvenirs de Paganini (Chopin) 220, 222
Soweto Quartet 179
Spalding, Esperanza 16, 445–452, 464
Spanish tinge see Latin tinge
Speakerboxxx/The Love Below (Outkast) 417
"Speech," from Anthracite Fields (Wolfe) 453–459
"Speranza tu mi vai" from L'Coronazione di Poppea (Monteverdi) 139
spirituals 103, 247, 253–259, 270, 277, 304
Springsteen, Bruce 381
St. Cyr, Johnny 301
St. John Passion (Bach) 157
St. Louis Blues (film) 271
St. Matthew Passion (Bach) 157–158
Sts. Ambrose, Augustine, Benedict, and Gregory 49
Staccato, definition of 12
Stalin, Joseph 359–360
Stamitz, Johann 183–184
Staples, Mavis 259
Starr, Ringo 379
"Stars and Stripes Forever, The" (Sousa) 273–279
"Star-spangled Banner" 10, 14

status, achieved and ascribed 123
Steel Hammer (Wolfe) 458
steel pan 339, 363–370, 434
steelband 363–370
Steen-Anderson, Simon 471
Steiner, Max 327
stepwise motion 46
Stevens, Sufjan 471
Stewart, Rod 308
Sting, The (film) 283
Stradivari, Antonio (Stradivarius) 143
Straight Outta Compton (N.W.A.)
    416
Strait, George 347
Strass, Richard 242
Strassburg, Gottfried von 234
Strauss, Richard 217, 248, 289
Stravinsky, Igor 3, 242, 252, 283–289,
    298, 326, 359,456
Strayhorn, Billy 315–316
stretto 154
stride piano 282
string band 227
string quartet, definition of 173
String Quartet No. 5 (Rochberg) 430
String Quartet No. 62 in C Major, Op. 76,
    No. 3, "Emperor"
String Quartet Op. 33 No. 3 ("The Bird")
    (Haydn) 179, 357
String Quartet Op. 18, No. 3 (Beethoven)
    196
strings, sympathetic 118
Strozzi, Barbara 167
"Struttin' with Some Barbecue"
    (Armstrong) 301–308
Stubblefield, Clyde 413
style, 6; Baroque 166, 180, 202, 210;
    Beethoven's 194–195, 206; Classical
    145, 171, 176, 180–183, 186–192
style, galant 176
subdominant 102
subject, fugal 153
Sugarhill Gang 409, 415
Suite Espanola No. 1 (Albeniz) 247
suling 290, 293
Sullivan, Arthur 322
"Sumer is icumen in" (English round)
    100, 103, 141
"Summertime" from *Porgy and Bess*
    (Gershwin) 329
sutra 43–44
Süzükei, Valentina 33
Swami Haridas 124
"Sweet Lullaby" (Deep Forest) 37
Swift, Taylor 347–348
swing jazz 309–316, 470
"Swing Low, Sweet Chariot" 253–259
symbolism 248, 251

symphonic poem *see* tone poem
Symphonie Fantastique (Berlioz)
    211–218, 235, 240, 245, 251,
    427–429
Symphonie pour un seul homme (Henry)
    395
symphonies, Beethoven's 204–211
symphony, definition of 177, 179
Symphony No. 1 (Beethoven) 196
Symphony No. 1 (Corigliano) 425–433
Symphony No. 1 (Shostakovich) 360
Symphony No. 1 (Zwilich) 429
Symphony No. 2 (Beethoven) 209
Symphony No. 3 (Beethoven) 209–210
Symphony No. 4 (Beethoven) 210
Symphony No. 5 in C Minor, Op. 67
    (Beethoven) 204–211
Symphony No. 6 (Beethoven) 210–211,
    245
Symphony No. 7 ("Leningrad")
    (Shostakovich) 357–362
Symphony No. 7 (Beethoven) 210
Symphony No. 8 (Beethoven) 210
Symphony No. 9 (Beethoven) 210–211,
    216, 362
Symphony No. 9 in E Minor "From
    the New World," Op. 95 (Dvořák)
    247–248
Symphony No. 40 in G Minor (Mozart)
    179–186, 206
Symphony No. 100 ("Military") (Haydn)
    186
Symphony No. 101 ("The Clock")
    (Haydn) 186, 210, 357
syncopation 281, 317
synthesizer 395, 415, 416, 455, 472
synthpop 443

tabla 118–119, 381, 472
tablature 70
tabor 108, 113
"Tabuh Sekar Jepun" 289–297
tacet 395
Taj Mahal 272
tajwid 56
tala 118–128, 396
tamboo bamboo 368
tambourine 113
tambura, Bulgarian 86, 88–90; North
    Indian 118
tango 427
Tannhäuser (Wagner) 240
Tansen 118, 124, 125
tantra 43
tapan 86, 90
"Taqasim and Sama'i Bayyati Al–Arayan"
    (Racy) 73–79
taqsim 73

Taruskin, Richard 288
Tatum, Art 7
Taylor, Cecil 388
Tchaikovsky, Pyotr Ilyich 209, 216, 211,
    247, 252
Teagarden, Jack 355
Techniques, The 435
techno 409, 443, 467
technology, definition of 17
teental 127
tempo 12
tenor part 97
Terminator X (Norman Lee Rogers)
    410
Terpsichore (Praetorius) 107–113
Terry, Clark 424
text painting 48, 105, 107, 133, 147, 153,
    208
texture, definition of 10; heterophonic
    see heterophony
"That's All Right" (Presley) 227
The Miseducation of Lauryn Hill (CD)
    417
"The most sacred Queen Elizabeth, her
    galliarde" (Dowland) 117
The Nutcracker and the Mouse King
    (Hoffmann) 209
The Sound of Music (film) 52
theka 119
Thelonious Monk Institute of Jazz 356,
    424, 452
theme 181
theme and variations 173
theorbo 132–133
There Will Be Blood (film) 468
Thile, Chris 227, 468
Thompson, Joe 226
Thompson, Odell 226
Thornton, Argonne "Dense" 348
Thornton, Big Mama 377–378
Threadgill, Henry 423
"Three Little Birds" (Marley) 437
Three Places in New England (Ives) 276,
    278
"Three Variations on Yang Pass" (for *qin*)
    68–72
Threnody (Japanese Children) (Schafer)
    396
tres 117
Thriller (Jackson) 356
throat-singing 28–33
Tibet, music of 40–45
Tiesto 467
tihai 121
"Til It Happens to You" (Lady Gaga)
    439–446
"Till Eulenspiegel's Merry Pranks"
    (Strauss) 217

timbales 397–398, 431
timbre, definition of 9
timpani 143
Timur (Tamerlane) 124
Tin Pan Alley 317, 320–321, 323, 348, 403, 422, 468
tiple 117
Titian 102
Tizol, Juan 419, 422
To Pimp a Butterfly (Lamar) 418, 451, 469
toasting 415
Toccata and Fugue in D Minor 158
Tomorrow Is My Turn (Giddens) 226
tonality *see* harmony, tonal
tone color *see* timbre
tone poem 211, 300
tone quality *see* timbre
tone row 288
tone, musical 8; qualities of 8
Torres Jurado, Antonio de 117
Tosh, Peter 435
tradition, definition of 345
Traité de l'harmonie réduite à ses principes naturels (Rameau) 144
trance, music of 199–200
"Trans-Europe Express" (Kraftwerk) 415
transition in sonata form 181
transmission 7
trap set 306
Treemonisha (Joplin) 283
tremolo 249
"Trenchtown Rock" (Marley) 436
Trendafilov, Dafo 90
triad 98
Trinidad All Stars 369
Trinidad All Steel Pan Orchestra 368
Trinidad, music of 363–370, 434
Tristan und Isolde (Wagner) 234–242, 250–251; Prelude amd *Liebestod* from 234–242
Tristano, Lennie 387
Trois Gymnopédies (Satie) 253
Tron (Daft Punk) 468
troubadour 106
trumpet 111
Tucker, Sherri 450
tumbao 400–401
tune 107
Tupac (2pac Shakur) (Lesane Crooks) 416–417
Turino, Thomas 37, 85
Turner, J.M.W. 207
Turner, Zeke 341
Tuskegee University 258
Tuva, music of 28–33, 37–38, 87; *Back Tuva Future* (Ondar) 32

Twelve Variations on "Ah, vous dirai–je, Maman" (Mozart) 117
Two Boys (Muhly) 471
Two Gentlemen of Verona (Shakespeare) 106
Tyler, Steven 416
Tyner, McCoy 382, 386

U2 381
UCLA Herb Alpert School of Music 424
'ud 73, 91, 113–114, 116–117
Uilleann pipes 89–90
Ullmann, Viktor 360–362. 370
"Und wenn die Welt voll Teufel wär" (BMV 80) (Bach) 151
underscore 327
understanding music 3
Underwood, Carrie 348, 437
University of Michigan Men's Glee Club 253
University of North Texas 424
"Unomathemba" (Ladysmith Black Mambazo) 10
urban folk 379

van der Rohe, Ludwig Mies 428
Varèse, Edgar 395
Vargas, Gaspar 335–336
Vargas, Silvestre 335
Variations on a Theme by Robert Schumann (C. Schumann) 222
Varimezov, Kostadin 90
vaudeville 265
Vaughan, Sarah 314
Vaughan, Stevie Ray 272
Veloso, Caetano 201
Venice Baroque Orchestra 140
Verdi, Giuseppe 239, 242, 252
Verlaine, Paul 251–252
Very Best, The 472
Victoria II, Queen 221
"Viderunt Omnes" (Pérotin) 65
Vienna Conservatory 216
Vienna Philharmonic 16, 186, 204
vihuela 113–117, 329–331
vilambit 127
Villa, Pancho 335, 463
viol 108, 112
Violin Concerto in E Major, RV 269, "Spring" (Vivaldi) 139–145
violin, history of 112, 143
Virgil 103
Vitry, Philippe de 65, 67
Vivaldi, Antonio 130, 139–145, 153, 167, 176, 184, 210
Vladigerov, Pancho 328
Vltava see The Moldau

vocable 307
vocalese
vocoder 415
Vodou 170, 435
"Voi, che sapete che cosa e amor," from *Le Nozze di Figaro* (Mozart) 192 (Mozart)
Voltaire 170
volte 107
"Volte, Suite of" (Praetorius) 107–113
Voyager Golden Record 165–166, 211
Vulchev, Atanas 90

"Wachet auf" (BMV 140) (Bach) 148, 151, 158
Wagner, Cosima 241
Wagner, Richard 2, 216, 233–242, 248, 250–252, 283, 288, 359
wah-wah pedal 376, 413
Wailer, Bunny 435
Wailers, The 412, 435–436
"Walk This Way" (Run–DMC) 416 (Run–DMC)
Walker, T–Bone 376
Waller, Fats 282–283
waltz 217, 219, 277, 451
Waltz in C–sharp Minor, Op. 64, No. 2 (Chopin) 217–222
Ward, Andrew 223
Warren, Dianne 440, 443
Washington, Booker T. 258
Washington, George 177
Washington, Kamasi 356, 418, 469
Wasitodiningrat, K.R.T. 396
"Watermelon Man" (Hancock) 27–28
Waters, Muddy 272, 377, 379
Watkins, Sara and Sean 227
Watson, Doc 227
Watts, Dr. Isaac 257
Watts, Jeff "Tain" 419
waveform 8
wayang kulit 163–164, 166
Weather Report 388
Weavers, The 379
Webb, Chick 313, 323
Webern, Anton 283, 288
Weick, Friedrich 222
Weill, Kurt 361
Well-tempered Clavier, The (Bach) 151–166, 220
Wesendonck, Mathilde 241
West, Kanye 417
West Side Story (Bernstein) 240
Weston, Horace 228
White, George L. 256
Whiteman, Paul 313, 328
Who, The 380

"Why do the nations so furiously rage together" (Handel) 151
Wilcke, Anna Magdelena 158
"Wild Women Don't Have the Blues" (Salvant, B. Smith) 469
Williams, Big Joe 228
Williams, Hank 341–348, 370
Williams, Mary Lou 314, 355–356, 450
Williams, Noel "King Sporty" 430
Williams, Ralph Vaughn 328
Williams, Tony 367, 387
Wilson, Woodrow 300
"Within You, Without You" (Beatles) 126
Wodzi ska, Maria 221
Wolfe, Julia 3. 16, 453–458
Wonder, Stevie 308, 316, 449, 452
Woodstock Festival 380–381, 405
Wordsworth, William 208

work song 259, 270, 304
"Work" (Rihanna) 437
world music 7, 396, 408, 436
world of music 4
Wretzky, D'Arcy 381
Wright, Frank Lloyd 428
writing, invention of 40
Written on Skin (Benjamin) 470
Wu-Tang Clan 417
Wynette, Tammy 347

xiao 72
Xovalyg, Kaigal–ool 32
xun 72

Yale University Glee Club 253
Yo! Bum Rush the Show (Public Enemy) 416
yodeling 24, 341, 346

"You've Got to Give Me Some" (Salvant, B. Smith) 469
Yunakov, Yuri 90

Zachmanov, Stefan 90
Zapata, Emiliano 335, 463
Zappa, Frank 32
Zawinul, Joe 423
"Zefiro torna e di soavi accenti" (Monteverdi) 138–139
Zemp, Hugo 37
Zimmerman, Richard (Dick) 279, 282–283
"Zion hört die Wächter singen" (BMV 80) (Bach) 151
Ziryab 116
zither 68
zouk 201
Zwilich, Ellen Taafe 429